William P. Mackay's Complete Trilogy:

Abundant Grace,
Grace and Truth,
and
The Seeking Saviour

William P. Mackay
Annotated by Anne Fenske

William P. Mackay's Complete Trilogy: Abundant Grace, Grace and Truth, and The Seeking Saviour

© 2024 Exegetica Publishing

Published by Exegetica Publishing, Fort Walton Beach, FL

Annotated by Anne Fenske
Cover design by Karese Arnold

ISBN – 978-1-60265-099-2

All rights reserved. No part of this publication may be reproduced, stored in a retrieval system, or transmitted in any form or by any means – electronic, mechanical, photocopy, recording, or any other – except for brief quotation in printed reviews, without the prior permission of the publisher.

EDITOR'S PREFACE

William Paton Mackay (1839–1885), or W. P. as he liked to be called, may be now known, if known at all, for his tireless work for the gospel of Christ in Scotland during the latter half of the 19th century. Or he could possibly be recognized as the editor of *The British Evangelist: A Monthly Journal Containing Plain Truths of Eternal Importance.* The well-known hymn, "Revive Us Again," was penned by Mackay and it, along with his writings, have blessed an untold number of people over the years.

But Mackay was no "altar boy" in his youth. His life had not a history of attending a church or of Sunday school lessons and learning the tenets of the faith. His Christian mother, however, was steeped in the word of God and prayed for her son. Dearly concerned about the state of his soul as he left for higher education, she sent him off with a Bible she inscribed for him and clearly marked verses of import. Mackay, however, continued a downward drift in his life, no thanks to his selection of friends. His thirst was not for his mother's God, but for drink, particularly whiskey. In fact, the gift of God's word was sold off when money was needed for more drink.

Despite his lifestyle, Mackay did well in school and continued on to medical school, with a thesis in leprosy. As a physician, he eventually became the head of the largest hospital in Edinburgh. His raucous life even included being the president of an atheist society. And then God intervened in a most miraculous way.

Mackay was treating a bricklayer who had fallen off of a ladder. The patient was given no hope but was being kept as comfortable as possible with medications. With much insistence from him, a friend brought him a book from home that proved to be as helpful as the medicine he was receiving. After the patient's death, Mackay's curiosity caused him to look at the book. It was his book – the Bible given to him by his mother many years previously. The book he had pawned for drink. While hiding his shock from his colleagues, his reflection on seeing his name in his mother's handwriting brought a spiritual watershed. Readers of this book would do well to read Mackay's testimony in his own hand as recorded in "The Hospital Patient," *The Tract Magazine and Christian Miscellany*, 1864, p. 71 and reproduced here in Appendix 1.

Readers of all three of these powerful books will find no issues with the minor differences in grammar and punctuation from modern day English. The logical progression of thought entices engagement of the clear explanation of the gospel. *Grace and Truth: Under Twelve Different Aspects* moves from our condemnation all the way to our reward. *Abundant Grace* addresses the seekers questions and provides practical answers for living the Christian life. *The Seeking Saviour* expounds on different aspects of the Lord Jesus Christ. Example after example and story after story bring a fuller understanding of the insurmountable gift of grace.

Throughout all of his writing, Mackay breaks into poetry, whether a couplet or a longer piece, reflecting on the truths just explained. Some of these are already put to music and can be found in various hymn collections over the decades. Other pieces are ripe for an inspired musician to set Mackay's beautiful words to music.

The most well-known, "Revive Us Again," is also the most biblical, reflecting on Psalm 85:6 and Habakkuk 3:2.

> We praise Thee, O God!
> For the Son of Thy love
> For Jesus Who died
> And is now gone above
>
> Hallelujah! Thine the glory
> Hallelujah! Amen
> Hallelujah! Thine the glory
> Revive us again
>
> All glory and praise
> To the Lamb that was slain
> Who has taken our sins
> And has cleansed every stain
>
> Hallelujah! Thine the glory
> Hallelujah! Amen
> Hallelujah! Thine the glory
> Revive us again

The subject of grace is an indefatigable one. The more one reads about grace, the more he is drawn into the bottomless well of its beauty. Could someone fully understand the vast implications of grace, the quest would be closed.

This Mackay collection came about at the urging of Ms. Dottie Connor Bingham who has spent a lifetime studying and teaching grace through New Tribes Missions, Dallas Theological Seminary, and Shepherding Grace. Her encouragement has now made these timeless books available to today's readers.

TRILOGY BOOK NUMBER ONE:

GRACE AND TRUTH

Grace and Truth

Under Twelve Different Aspects.

By
W. P. Mackay, M. A.,
Minister of the Gospel,
HULL.

'Grace and Truth came by JESUS CHRIST.'—*John's Gospel.*

CONTENTS.

		PAGE
'There is no Difference.'	Our Condemnation,	1
Would You Like to be Saved?	Our Justification,	15
'Ye Must be Born Again.'	Our Regeneration,	27
Do You Feel Forgiven?	Our Assurance,	47
Work of the Holy Spirit.	Our Comforter,	57
'Heaven Opened.'	Our Study,	70
Triumph and Conflict	Our State,	80
'Under the Sun.'	Our Walk,	103
'No Confidence in the Flesh.'	Our Sanctification,	126
The Devil.	Our Adversary,	158
'Serving the Lord.'	Our Service,	171
Judgment.	Our Reward,	185

INTRODUCTION.

'The law was given by Moses: grace and truth came by Jesus Christ.' The law showed what man ought to be. Christ showed what man is, and what God is. The law *was given*, but grace and truth *came*. Calvary tells out fully what man's true state is, what God's truth is, and what grace means. The law is what I ought to be to God. Grace tells what God is for me. The first word of law is 'Thou;' the first of grace is 'God,' so loved; but it is grace through truth. God has investigated everything, nothing has been looked over. The greatest sin that any man could possibly commit has been committed, namely, the murder of God's Son. At the same time the greatest grace of God has been manifested.

Man by nature likes neither grace nor truth. He is satisfied neither with perfect justice nor perfect goodness. If John the Baptist comes in righteousness he is hated, and men say he is too harsh, and not human, but hath a devil. If Christ comes in love, He is taunted with being a friend of sinners. So when the righteous requirements of God's law are preached, many people are apt to turn and say, 'Oh yes, but that is too strict; you must allow a little margin for our imperfection.' God says, make no provision for the flesh. Alas! it will take far too much, but allow it nothing. When a sanctified walk, separated from the world and all its belongings, is insisted on, a certain class are sure to call this legal preaching. And on the other hand when the grace of God is preached, man's wisdom makes it out to be toleration of evil and lawless license.

Let us suppose that a convict, who had just finished his term of penal servitude, wished to lead an honest life. He comes to a man who has a large jewellery establishment, and who requires a night-watchman. He is engaged to watch this house through the quiet hours of the night, when he has everything under him, and every opportunity to rob his employer. On the first evening of his watching he meets one of his old companions, who accosts him, 'What are *you* doing here?' 'I'm night-watchman.' 'Over this jeweller's shop?' 'Yes.' 'Does he know what you are?' 'No, no, be silent; if he knew, I should be dismissed.' 'Suppose I let it out that you are a returned convict.' 'Oh, I pray don't, it would be my last day here, and I wish to be honest.' 'Well, you'll require to give me some money to keep quiet.' 'Very well, but don't let any one know.' Thus the poor man would be in sad fear and trembling, lest it should come to the ears of his employer what his previous character had been. He would be in terror lest he should meet any of his old friends, and lest his resources should be exhausted in keeping them quiet.

Let us suppose, however, that instead of the employer engaging the man in ignorance of his character, he went to the convict's cell and said, 'Now I know you, what you are, and what you've done, every robbery you've committed, and that you are worse than you believe yourself to be. I am to give you a chance to become honest. I'll trust you as my night-watchman over my valuable goods.' The man is faithful at his post. He meets old companion after old companion, who threaten to inform upon him. He asks, 'What will you tell about me?' 'That you were the ring-leader of house-breakers.' 'Yes, but my master knows all that better than you do; he knows me better than I know myself.'

Of course this silences them for ever. This latter is *grace and truth*. The man had been treated in grace, but on the ground that all the truth was out, that his character was known. It is thus God deals with us. He deals in grace, but He knows what He is doing, and with whom He is working,—even the chief of sinners. The whole truth is out about us, and God's grace in the face of this saves, gives a new nature, and puts us down before Himself in the highest places of confidence. Man wonders at this. A wicked companion gets converted, his old associates wonder at his boldness in preaching (like Peter who denied

INTRODUCTION.'

Christ, accusing his Jerusalem hearers of having denied him). They think if his audience only knew what they know, they would be suspicious. God know us better than we know ourselves, and this is our joy.

Man does not know GRACE. When unadulterated grace, unmixed grace, the grace of God, God's own love to sinners, is preached, man cannot take it in. 'Oh, this is downright Antinomianism.' This is the cry that was raised against Luther when he preached 'full free justification by grace through faith without the deeds of the law;' the cry that was raised against Paul, that he made void the law, that he told the people they might sin that grace might abound. Now, unless our Christianity provokes this opposition, it is not scriptural Christianity. Unless the gospel we preach, when presented to the natural mind, brings out these thoughts, it is another gospel than Paul's. Every Christian, mark not some of them, has the Antinomian or God-dishonouring 'flesh,' within him to be watched over and mortified; but this is a different matter. People will readily quote 'Faith without works is dead,' 'We must have works,' and so on; and we most certainly coincide. But follow up on the argument by inquiry about the works, and you will too often find that such have very loose ideas of Christian holiness. Such will quite go in for having a Christian name, going religiously to church, being able to criticize a sermon and a preacher, being acquainted with good people, abstaining from all immorality, being honest and respectable; but the moment we cross the boundary line that separates respectable and easy-going make-the-most-of-Christianity, into the rugged, thorny path of identification with a rejected Christ, separation from the world's gaieties, splendours, and 'evil communication,'—dead to it and all that is therein, taking up Christ's yoke, and denying self, —we are met with the expressions, 'too far,' 'pietism,' 'righteous over much,' 'we don't like extremes,' 'legal preaching.'

The *grace of man* would be this, 'Do the best you can by the help of grace, and then wherein you fail grace will step in and make up.' But the first thing the *grace of God* does is to bring '*salvation.*' (Titus ii. 11,) &c.

Or, again, man's grace may take this shape, 'Oh, yes, we believe in the blood, the precious blood of Christ; only faith can save; and now we have found an easy road to heaven—a sort of short cut in which we can live on good terms with the world and worldly men, and also on first-rate terms with religious men, spend our money to make ourselves comfortable, get a name, honour, or riches here, make ourselves as happy as can be in this world, just take of it what we can enjoy, and go on thus so nicely to heaven.' This is another view of the *grace* that *man* knows about; but the *grace of God* teaches that, 'denying ungodliness and worldly lusts, we should live soberly, righteously, and godly in this present world, looking for that blessed hope and the glorious appearing of the great God and our Saviour Jesus Christ' (Titus ii. 12). Thus man knows nothing whatever about the GRACE OF GOD.

Neither does man know TRUTH. He does not know the *truth* about God. He could quite believe that God made the world, and that he is good to a certain extent; but that God looks upon one sin as making a man guilty as really as ten thousand, he cannot understand. Though written as clear as writing can make it in the Book of God, he cannot perceive it. Christ brought out the truth about God, that He could by no means clear the guilty, but that he could impute guilt and impute righteousness. An infidel said, 'Is it justice for an innocent man to die for a guilty—is it consistent with reason, either in justice to the innocent or the guilty?' 'Well, suppose it is not, and we grant it. But what if God became man, and put away sin by the sacrifice of Himself—where is your reasoning now? Our gospel is not an innocent man dying for the guilty merely, but the God-man made sin, and putting it away.' Nor does man know the truth about himself, that he is lost. He thinks that he *may be* lost, not the he *is* lost. He hopes in some vague way, that it will yet be all right with him. Christ brought out the truth about man, that man was hopelessly gone in sin, that he would kill God if he could.

How few there are in *hell* who ever intended to be there! '*Are you to be in heaven?*' Most will answer, '*I hope so.*' 'And what right have you *to hope so?*' I once quickly said to a poor woman who looked as like a good person as any of her neighbours. 'If you have believed in the Lord Jesus Christ, why not say so and thank Him, and then begin to hope (not for pardon, there is no such hope in Scripture) for salvation that is to be revealed at perfected redemption? and if not, what right have you to have such presumption as hoping to get to heaven when you have not believed in the Lord Jesus Christ'? I saw her some time after, radiant with settled joy and peace, and she said, 'Yes, sir, you asked me what right I had to hope, and I was rather astonished, but I did not take your word about it; I went home to my Bible, and there I found that if I was without God, I had to be without hope in this world' (Eph. ii. 12). This led her to discover 'the *sand*' on which she had been building, and by God's Spirit she was led to 'THE ROCK.'

Look at a perfect illustration of grace and truth in the case of the Gentile woman. (Matt. xv. 21-28.)

'*Then* Jesus went thence, and departed into the coasts of Tyre and Sidon.' When? After he had exposed the utter hollowness of man's religion, and the character of the Pharisees' heart. In the beginning of the chapter man brought his religion to Christ, and of course Christ showed that it was the *heart* He dealt with, and not religion.

Verse 8 shows us *where* the heart of man is—with his religions, his traditions of the elders, his observances, his washing of hands, cups, dishes, tables. It is 'far from God.' Verse 19 shows us *what* his heart has in it: 'Evil thoughts, murders, adulteries, fornications, thefts, false witness, blasphemies.' This is what happens when man comes to God with his religion — with what he has. 'Do you want to know where you are, and what you are?' Bring your religion to God. But Jesus now goes away to where there is no religion, but plenty of misery; no professions, but a great deal of need. He had shown what man's heart has in it — He now wishes to show what is in His heart — a heart that is 'full of grace and truth.'

And behold a woman of Canaan came out of the same coasts, and cried unto Him, saying: 'have mercy on me, O Lord, thou Son of David; my daughter is grievously vexed with a devil.' She was a Syrophoenician, a Greek, and Gentile outside of the Jewish territory, a dog in the eyes of every godly Jew. 'Without are dogs.' The dog in the East is not as here domesticated, but is more like a wolf prowling for prey outside the cities — fit emblem of those dwellers by the highways and hedges of Luke xiv., the Gentiles outside the Jewish circle of blessing; and thus we are called 'Gentile dogs.' She had no claim on the 'Son of David.' 'He came to His own.' Her need, her desire, her heart, her faith, were in the right direction; but she must intelligently take the right place in order to be blessed. Her instincts were right; her apprehension of the truth was wrong. This is the reason of that wonderful next word.

'But he answered her not a word.' Many think that this was merely to try her faith — certainly it was; but God accomplishes many ends by one means. He has to manifest not only *grace*, but also *truth*. Had He, as 'Son of David,' blessed her, He would not have kept His true place, for 'He was a minister of the circumcision for the truth of God, to confirm the promises made unto the father' (Rom. xv. 8). And she was 'afar off, an alien from the commonwealth of Israel.' He, as Son of David, 'confirmed the promises;' she was a 'stranger from the covenant of promise;' and when she tried that door, she found it righteously shut, because He is faithful and true. He could have no words with her till He got His own and only place in which He could rise above all dispensational thoughts, and let His grace flow forth. Claims of truth had to be settled first, then the fountain of grace could flow; but her need kept her at the footstool. She asked ignorantly, but was in earnest.

And His disciples came and besought Him, saying, 'Send her away; for she crieth after us.' One or other of two courses they might suggest. Peter might have said, 'She is a Gentile dog; she has no right to you as Son of David; send her away.' This would have been *truth*, but at the expense of *grace*; but Jesus was showing grace as well as truth. John might have said, 'She is a poor, needy woman; just give her what she wants, and send her away.' This would have been *grace*, but at the expense of *truth*. Now Jesus was showing truth as well as grace. This is so like man — he cares for little but his own comfort. 'She crieth after us.' 'Us' always must be consulted. How unlike Him who gave 'Himself for us,' when He came as grace and truth. 'What does it matter about dispensational truths, if sinners are saved?' Such is man's talk — and it matters little to the sinner; but what of God's claims and God's truth? 'We do not study this or that truth because it is not essential.' Essential to you or to God? The disciples could not harmonize grace and truth, and therefore they had to sacrifice the one or the other, but both are to be seen. Man would either repel from God as an angry Judge, and give no good news to any sinner, or He would undermine the pillars of His throne by giving universal salvation; but 'grace and truth came by Jesus Christ.' He now takes occasion from the appeal of the disciples to let out a little of His mind.

But he answered and said, 'I am not sent but unto the lost sheep of the house of Israel.' As 'Son of David,' He keeps by His peculiar mission. She does not belong to the lost sheep of Israel's house; how, therefore can He speak to her or grant her the request she presented? He could not deal as 'Son of David' with a Gentile, because she was not of the house of Israel. Was this not truth, some would even think, to harshness? But this is man's idea of harshness. God's truth is never harsh. Grace without truth is sentimentality. Truth without grace is harshness. All this is only (not to 'send her away,' as was the disciples' easy method, but) to lead her to give Him His true place, and then to take her own true place in which grace could flow to her. Why are we not blessed with God's grace? He is waiting to be gracious. How long will He wait? Till we give Him His true place, and till we take our true place before Him, where He can bless us. When he speaks, she listens, and now takes up her request again.

Then came she and worshipped, saying, 'Lord, help me.' She did not say she was as good as Israel's lost sheep; but she leaves out the title 'Son of David,' and calls Him Lord. 'If He is but sent to Israel's lost sheep, I can't call Him Son of David, and be blessed; but He has another and a higher sovereign name, and that is Lord Jehovah, who can help even me. He won't break down the dispensational wall that keeps the poor Gentile dog away from the promises of the Son of David; but He can rise above it in a power that can reach down to help and succor me.' She gives Him now His true place. This is seen in her not using the title 'Son of David,' but only that one word 'Lord,' His true name to her as a Gentile. 'They that know Thy name will put their trust in Thee.' But she had not quite reached her own true place. She needed something more than help; but Jesus, now addressed as Lord alone, can speak to her and reveal a little more. She listens, believes, and always takes up at each step the thought of the fresh revelation, the words that dropped from His lips, for she was in earnest.

But He answered and said, 'It is not meet to take the children's bread, and to cast it to the dogs.' Here is her name; is she prepared to take it, as well as give Him His? Well might she have said, 'Me a dog, forsooth! I know many so called children of Israel who make a greater profession, and I would not be seen with them.' This would have been natural. When man does not feel his need, he compares himself with others. He vindicates, excuses, palliates himself — 'Many make more profession than I do; yet I would be ashamed to do what they do.' Very possible; that is their business; but what of God's claims on you? She felt that her need was deep, and her answer is according to it. She takes the place the Lord gives her, not what she would choose, but what He indicates.

And she said, 'Truth, Lord. Yet the dogs eat the crumbs which fall from their master's table.' This is the place of power. This is the place of blessing.

INTRODUCTION.'

1st. 'Truth, Lord.' Any name you please — 'a sinner,' 'a dog;' but

2d. If I am a dog, it shall be at your table; and there I'll claim the dog's portion. 'Yet the dogs eat the crumbs.'

> We take the guilty sinner's name,
> The guilty sinner's Saviour claim.

I am a great sinner! 'Truth, Lord;' yet the great sinner claims the great Savior. I am the chief of sinners! 'Truth, Lord;' yet the chief of sinner claims the chief of Saviours. I am ignorant! 'Truth, Lord;' yet my wisdom. I am unrighteous! 'Truth, Lord;' yet Christ is my righteousness. I am unholy! 'Truth, Lord;' yet Christ is my sanctification. I am in bondage! 'Truth, Lord;' yet Christ is my redemption. That 'yet' is the pleading of need from the place that truth has given.

> Mercy and truth are met together;
> Righteousness and peace have kissed each other.

And now what is the answer, and what was the result?

Then Jesus answered and said unto her: 'O woman, great is thy faith; be it unto thee even as thou wilt.' This was the answer, the very resources of Jehovah thrown open for her use. 'And her daughter was made whole from that hour.' And this was the result, 'From that hour.' What hour? The hour in which she said, 'Truth, Lord.' The hour in which she took the dog's place, and claimed the dog's portion. Is this but a crumb from His blessed table? What must the full feast be, when the Church of God, gathered out of Jew and Gentile, shall sit down at the marriage supper as the bride of the Lamb; and every prayer shall have ended, because all have been answered; and the combined glory of grace and truth shall shine out for ever from the brows of all the myriads of sinners, saved by grace, who came in all their degradation and need to the feet of Jesus, giving Him His true place, and taking their true place? Friend, God now waits to be gracious to you; but you must take the dog's place.

In the following papers I have tried to preserve the balance between GRACE AND TRUTH. 'The grace of God' brings salvation, this is the truth of Titus ii. 'The righteousness of God' — God being just and justifying Him that believes in Jesus, is the truth of Rom. iii. I have endeavored to show the grace and truth of God: —

1st. With regard to the justification of a sinner. Grace has to be seen and truth seen, each equal to the other.

2d. With regard to the sanctification or growth in grace of a believer. Grace is seen and truth is seen. 'Being made free from sin and becoming servants to God ye have your fruit unto holiness, and the end everlasting life,' Rom. vi. 22.

I will here give the thread on which the papers in this volume are crystallized: —

1st. '*There is no difference*,' for until a man sees this, he is not in the place where God can bless him. This is fundamental

2nd. *Would you like to be* saved? 'Whosoever will' is pointed to the work of Christ for sinners.

3rd. '*Ye must be born again*' — Wherein are discussed the necessity and nature of regeneration. Regeneration is an act done at the same time as justification — not a work, as many seem to think, confounding it with gradual sanctification. Justification gives a new life, a new nature at the same time perfect in parts but not in development, sanctification being the development of this new life. In this is discussed the question what is the *water*, of which we must be born again?

4th. *Do you feel your sins forgiven?* In this is pointed out that most dangerous error of confounding man's feeling with the testimony of God's word — the confounding of the eighth chapter of Romans with the fifth — the confounding of the Spirit's witness to sonship with 'Being justified by faith we have peace with God' — that we stand *only* on the written word 'Thus saith the Lord' for our 'knowledge of salvation,' as we stand only on the incarnate Word for that salvation itself.

5th. *The work of the Holy Spirit*. The connection and difference between the work of the Spirit in me and Christ's work for me are here considered. Many souls would wish to study the work of the Spirit in them first, but only a saved man can profitably study this; one who has come through the former chapter. 'Do you feel your sins forgiven.' The Holy Ghost is never mentioned in Romans till the fifth chapter. Misplaced truth is the worst error.

6th. '*Heaven opened.*' In which we get a glimpse of the counsels of God in the past, present, and future. Heaven is opened now for us and all that is there is ours. The epistle to the Hebrews discloses our opened heaven.

7th. *Triumph and conflict* come next. The conflict before was between me and God, now it is between me and myself, and this will be a life-long conflict, for every Christian is in the world, has the flesh within and Satan against him. These are typified by Israel in Egypt, which is spiritually the *world* — in the Wilderness, where Amalek (the *flesh*) has to be defeated —and in Canaan, where the Canaanites ('*spiritual wickednesses*') have to be overcome. That 'Satanic trinity' is considered in the three following papers in detail.

8th. '*Under the sun.*' Our great foe 'the world' is here looked at. What is it, and how is it to be overcome?

9th. '*No confidence in the flesh*' — the believer's beacon-fire. Here we consider what true holiness is and what it is not. Not the old nature made better, but the believer as a whole, as an individual, made better by his new nature keeping the old under. In this is shown the all-important truth concerning the existence in the one individual saved man of two distinct natures. The one person has two natures, one that cannot sin because born of God, the other that cannot but sin because born of Satan. Our practical holiness does not consist in assimilation, but in opposition — not in improvement of the old man, but in his mortification. Our responsibility remains in the *individual* person, possessed of these two natures.

10th. *The devil.* The truth so plainly shown in Scripture concerning the real personal existence, and not mere influence of the devil; where he is, what he is doing, and our power over him are stated.

11th. '*Serving the Lord*' now comes in, since we are made free from our foes, since our bands are loosened, we can now serve. 'Let my people go that they may serve me.'

12th. Judgment is looked at as past with regard to the believer's person, present as to the believer's ways, and to come for the believer's works. Many Christians fail to see the perfect balance here between grace and truth — grace putting us for ever beyond judgment, and truth bringing up at the judgment seat of Christ all our deeds done in the body, good or bad.

In issuing a new edition, we would merely record our adoring thanks to Him whose name is Wonderful, for having in any way used these pages as the means of sending light into dark hearts, or of solving difficulties to those who already knew His grace and truth, and leading them more intelligently to walk with Himself.

May the gracious Spirit whose it is to lead into all truth bless what is His own in these pages, to the glory of the ever blessed Lord Jesus Christ, our God and Saviour.

W. P. M.

SPRINGBANK, HULL,
    1st *January*, 1872.

'There is no Difference.'

Our Condemnation.

YOU are always preaching and writing that the vilest and most unworthy are welcome to come to Christ; but what of those that do not feel so very vile?' a sister in the Lord once said to me. This is a most important question, in regard to a class of people very difficult to reach.

She told me that a friend, after having heard a preacher of the gospel describing the awful state of unsaved people, and giving a solemn exhortation to be saved immediately, said, with great surprise, '*But what is it all about? I feel as happy as a bird.*' She really could not understand that anything the man had been saying had any reference to her.

Such people never did anything very bad. They have been trained up under all the influences of a Christianized society. They never knew vice in its open nakedness. They never felt anything at all very evil in their hearts. They have never been face to face with God, nor taken God's idea of sin. In short, they know not the God revealed in Scripture. I do not mean that they are idolaters or infidels in the popular sense of these words. They know a god that is a sort of being for pulpit use, a being that is to be addressed as a matter of course, and religious duty, at times of particular solemnity. They have a few ideas, derived from various sources, of a being called God, but of the God of Holy Scripture they have no conception. The God who judges sinners they do not know; of God's estimate of sin they have never heard.

But let me be distinctly understood as to this most important matter. Let us imagine a man wandering on the top of some high cliffs. A bright warm sun is overhead, and a soft green carpet of grass in beneath his feet. He feels very happy and gay, but he is going nearer to an awful precipice! He is happy, but he is blind. We call, we shout to him to stop. He turns round and says, 'What is it all about? I feel as happy as a bird;' but onward still he goes. Would it not be love on our part to go and take hold of him, and earnestly tell him that a fearful precipice lies a yard before him?

Dear friend, this is where we see you. I have in my mind at this moment an accomplished young lady, amiable, kind, and dutiful, surrounded by all that can make life happy; one who has her neat Bible or Prayer-book, and who is seen most regularly and religiously in her seat in church or chapel every Lord's-day, who takes great interest in deeds of charity, visits the poor, and is very happy. No one ever dared to say to such an one, 'You are on the broad road that leadeth to destruction.' It would be considered highly improper so to do. Perhaps this silent page may be before your eye, and now it would say to you what has been so long unsaid, 'Stop! are you ready to meet God? where shall you spend eternity?' If you were separated this moment from all the dear friends around you, and all those happy scenes, and that comfortable home, and standing before God, what have you to say? I wish to write a little of what He thinks of you. I am not to write about what your parents, your friends, your pastor, or spiritual adviser think of you. They may think most highly of you, and most justly too, as you may be everything that could be desired from a human point of view. But I wish to place before you what God your Maker thinks of you; yes, of you yourself, whoever you may be; the more refined, cultivated, educated, and wealthy, the more would I be in earnest to get your attention. You may be a princess or an empress, but one word expresses God's estimate of you, and that word is — 'SINNER.'

A rich lady one day, when she heard a person speaking of all as sinners, said with great surprise, —

'But ladies are not sinners!'

'Then who are?' she was asked.

'Just young men in their foolish days.'

I have not the slightest doubt but that this is a very common idea, though seldom expressed. A lady who had heard some one preaching this kind of truth called on him and said, —

'Do you mean to say that I must be saved just as my footman?'

'Most certainly.'

'Then I shan't be saved.' Poor lady! that was her business, and this was her fatal decision. My reader, I not only wish to tell you that you are a sinner — you, educated, amiable lady — but that in God's sight you are just the same as the vilest profligate; just the same as the man you heard about who was hanged for murdering his wife. This is most terrible, but it is true. I remember once saying it to a young man who was not like you, but who knew that he was very bad; and said, —

'I believe all are sinners, but I don't believe that all are the same.'

'Well, we have only one authority to refer to and it is within your reach; will you take your Bible, and remember one thing, that it is God who speaks? Turn now to Romans, the 3rd chapter and 22d verse, and at the last clause we read "For there is no difference; for all have sinned, and come short of the glory of God." This is what God has said.'

'Well,' said my friend, 'I never saw that before.'

'But it was there although you never saw it.'

And now, dear reader, you who are happy and amiable, this is the one thing I wish to tell you from God, 'There is no difference.' This is what you never could and never can feel; it is a thing for which you must believe God. As it is God with whom you have to do, I beseech you do not listen one moment to any that would take you from His truth. He says 'there is no difference;' He has proved that the lawless Gentile or heathen and the law-breaking Jew or religious person are equally guilty, and that not one among either the outwardly profane or the outwardly decent is found righteous or good before Him. Of course there are differences in heinousness or degradation of sins. I need not stop to speak of this; we all know it. I wish to tell you what you and I do not by nature know; namely, that there is no difference to where we stand before God. The one question is, guilty or not guilty. There are no degrees as to the fact of guilt. 'He that offends in one point is guilty of all,' and nothing less. He that offends in all points is guilty of all, and nothing more. Therefore, while there are differences among offences, there is no difference as to guilt. Therefore, all men in the world (and you included), have been brought in guilty before God.

Look at the story of the Prodigal Son in the 15th of Luke. The moment he crossed his father's threshold with his pockets full of money and a respectable dress on, he was as really guilty, as really a sinner, as when he was among the swine in his rags. He was more degraded when keeping swine, but not more guilty. In fact, his degradation and husks were his greatest mercies, for these led him to see his guilt. A full pocket and a respectable appearance are the worst things a guilty sinner can have, as these lead him to think that he is rich and increased with goods, and has need of nothing, when in God's sight he is wretched, and miserable, and poor, and blind, and naked. I do not ask you, Are you a sinner in the common use of that word? because you for whom I write are not. You mean by sinner, one who is very wild, profane, disobedient, and lawless. This is as men speak of sinners. God, however, says that there is no difference. The only thing I ask you is this, Have you offended in ONE point — not one point of open sin, but one point in thought or word? You confess to at least one point. God asks no more. If you have offended in one point you are guilty of all. Man would never think this nor say it. But God says it. Suppose that your life were like a book that you have written, and there was only one small blot just like a pin's-point in it, whilst all the other leaves were perfectly clean, and you came and presented it before God; He would put it beside all the blackest lives that ever lived, the blackest histories of the vilest murderers, and thieves, and harlots, and over this collection would be written these words, 'There is no difference.'

You have offended in one point. It is not a question of being a great sinner — it is this question, 'Are you perfect as the Christ of God, the perfect man?' If you had lived for fifty years without committing one sin, or having one wrong wish or thought, and just then you had an evil thought, and afterwards lived another fifty years and died, aged one hundred, with only this one evil thought (not even a word or an action), when you came to stand before God in judgment, He would put you beside all the offscourings of the earth, men who for a hundred years never had a good thought, and He would say, 'There is no difference.'

Of course you think this is very hard, but it is true. God will never ask your opinion whether it ought to be so or not. He has in grace told us already what He will do. You and I, not knowing absolute holiness, cannot understand or appreciate such a judgment. We could never feel that everyone is the same in God's sight as regards guilt. But God says it, and there the matter ends. If you wish to go on risking your chance of escaping hell on the possibility that God has told lies and that these words are not perhaps quite true, that 'there is no difference,' then the judgment-day will declare it to you. I would rather advise you to believe God, against your own ideas and opinions, and simply because He has said it, to proceed as if in His sight, 'there is no difference,' between those we call great and little sinners.

'I cannot believe that all are so bad,' said one, after I had been saying 'there is no difference.'

'But,' I added, 'the Bible says, "there is no difference."'

'But there must be greater sinners than others.'

'Oh, yes. Most certainly. Great offenders are recognized in the Bible; he that owed the fifty and he that owed five hundred pence; but as to guilt, God says, "there is no difference."'

'Well, I cannot see it,' still continued my friend.

'But it is in God's Word, whether you see it or not;' and it is sufficient that God has said it, for His Word is truth. Let me give an illustration. Let us suppose that a bill had been stuck up in this town, saying that recruits were wanted for Her Majesty's Life Guards, and that none would be enlisted but those who were tall and measured not under six feet in height. Let us suppose that many of the young men in the town were anxious to serve in the regiment, and John meets James, and says to him, 'Well, I've more chance than you, for I am taller than you;' and they put back to back and measure themselves with one another, and indeed John is taller than James. And there continues to be much measuring in the town before the day that the recruiting-sergeant comes.

They measure themselves by themselves, and compare themselves among themselves, but they forget one thing — that not only tall men, but men not under six feet are wanted. One man at last says, 'Well, I've measured myself with every man in the town, and I'm the tallest man in it,' and it might be quite true. But will even he be found qualified?

The trial day comes. Each is measured, from the man five feet six inches, to the very tallest. Suppose he is five feet eleven inches and three-quarters. The sergeant cannot let him pass. He is short. He must take his place among the very shortest as to getting into the Life Guards. He is the tallest man in the town, but he is short of this standard, and 'there is no difference' from the very shortest as to his exclusion from the Life Guards. 'There is a difference' in height, but not in qualification.

Thus it is with every sinner. He may be good, or bad, in the sight of men, but 'there is no difference, for all have sinned and come short of the glory of God.' If any man could say, I have come up to God's standard, and this is true, then there would be a difference; but 'come short' is written on every man's brow, therefore there is no difference.

Whether was Adam or Eve the more to blame? This might afford material for a long discussion, and at the end, the heinousness of their crime would be to us a matter of opinion. I have no doubt there might be some shade of degree as to heinousness; but one thing is sure — if their offences were not equally heinous, they were equally driven out. The cherubim that turned every way with the flaming sword, separated both equally from the tree of life; there was no difference.

When the rain began to fall and the waters to rise, after Noah had entered the ark, the people who had their houses high up might have been pitying the poor people who built low down in the valley, as they heard the screams of the drowning. By and by the water sweeps above the little hills, and then those on the high hills, in turn, congratulate themselves upon their high-built villas. But the water still rises; it enters their ground-floors; they rush out of their grand mansions or hovels — for there was no difference — and flee to the tops of the very highest mountains; but only find respite for a few moments, for 'all the high hills, under the whole heaven, were covered; fifteen cubits upward did the waters prevail, and the mountains were covered, and all flesh died that moved upon the earth...and every man; all in whose nostrils was the breath of life, of all that was in the dry land, died, and every living substance was destroyed which was upon the face of the ground.' Under that judgment-flood there was no difference. Look across the wide, level sea, and consider the thousands of caves and stupendous mountain chains that it hides, the plains and valleys, the dens of seaweed and the fortresses of rock; and the level sea rolls equally over all, there is no difference. Drunkard and respectable lady, the hoary-haired sinner and the infant at the mother's breast — all were under that fearful flood, for there was no difference. If you had been there, do you think you would have been made an exception of? You may be able just now to get anything that money can buy. Could money have saved you then? Prince and beggar, strong men and weak, bad and good, were all equally swept away. There was no difference. It has happened already, you see, and it will happen again — not with water, but with fire.

'When Jehovah rained upon Sodom and upon Gomorrah brimstone and fire from Jehovah out of heaven,' there was no difference. All were equally destroyed; very bad and very good shared the same fate. This fearful, unprecedented shower falling out of heaven — brimstone and fire — took everyone by surprise, and destroyed every dweller there. 'He overthrew those cities and all the plain, and all the inhabitants of the cities.' There was no difference.

When Israel was sheltered in the house of bondage from the destroying angel's hand, 'it came to pass that at midnight Jehovah smote all the first-born in the land of Egypt, from the first-born of Pharaoh that sat on his throne, unto the first-born of the captive that was in the dungeon.' Judge and prisoner alike found themselves face to face with death. In the palace and in the hovel the voice of mourning was heard; not one of all the doomed first-born escaped. These first-born might have been beautiful, amiable, educated, and accomplished, or they might have been vile, degraded, ignorant, and hardened; but there was no difference. It is with this God you and I have to do.

When Jericho's walls fell flat before the appointment, the ordinance of God, in righteous judgment 'they (the Israelites) utterly destroyed all that was in the city, both man and woman, young and old.' The strong man and the feeble woman, the active young man and the decrepid old, were equally slain by the edge of the sword. There was no difference.

The flaming sword of the cherubim, the flood of waters, the deluge of fire, the angel of death, and Joshua's sword, all preach to you and me with calm, decided voice, 'There is no difference.' These things were written for us, that we might know what we may expect so that we might not leap in the dark. Nothing will happen which has not been told us.

A brother in the Lord could never get a young lady to think about eternity until he quoted this text, 'The wicked shall be turned into hell, and all the nations that forget God.' That word, 'forget' seemed to haunt her. May it haunt you, dear reader! You do not require to deny God's existence, to mock at Him, to despise Him, to reject Him, to neglect Him; all you have to do is to forget God. Do you know the God who says, 'There is no difference'? Have you forgotten that he identifies you with all descended from Adam? Have you forgotten the God driving our parents out of Eden, and placing a sword crying for blood? Our brother Cain soon forgot; our brother Abel remembered. Have you forgotten the God who swept away all in the days of Noah? Have you forgotten that He is the Judge of quick and dead, and as there was no difference, so there is a day coming when there will be no difference. In the judgment of the quick, 'all the goats are equally on the left hand' — 'there is no difference.' In the judgment of the dead, 'the dead, small and great stand before God' — small and great sinners, young and old, king and serf, peer and peasant — 'and whosoever was not found written in the book of life was cast into the lake of fire,' for 'there is no difference.' Your name may have been written on the communion-roll of any or all the churches, or it may have been written in the sheets of the Newgate[1] conviction-book for murderers, but 'there is no difference.' The lake of fire levels all distinctions. There may be, there are, many and few stripes; there may be, there are, great and small cups full of wrath, but every cup, be it great or small, is full. The lake of fire—fearful thought — rolls its hideous sea of wrath and torment in one surging wave over all that have not been enrolled in the one book of life. In hell, and perhaps only there, for the first time, you will believe that 'there is no difference.' Every one believes it there.

Let me ask you to look at another picture. Three men are hung on three crosses. If you look at them, you will see that 'there is no difference.' If you listen to what they are saying, you will hear one at the one side mocking Him in the centre; and the one on the other side saying, 'Dost not thou fear God, seeing thou art in the same condemnation? And we indeed justly, but this man hath done nothing amiss.' The one in the centre is saying, 'Father, forgive them, for they know not what they do.'

---

[1] Editor's Note: Newgate was Britain's most feared jail for over seven hundred years.

Those suffering 'justly,' and He that did 'nothing amiss,' equally suffer, for 'there is no difference.' Those needing forgiveness, and He praying for their forgiveness, are under the same doom, for 'there is no difference.' Who are they? Those on either hand are two malefactors, or thieves, who die by the condemnation of their law. He in the centre was proved innocent, and He is the Judge of quick and dead. He has taken of his own free-will the load of sin upon Him, and, under sin, He cannot be cleared. Spotless, pure, holy though He was, He cannot escape. God can by no means clear the guilty. 'He hath made Him sin for us, who knew no sin.' He is under our guilt, and 'there is no difference' between Him and the thief —He must suffer. Dear reader, does not this explain all difficulty about an innocent, amiable, virtuous, accomplished lady being on the same level before God as a drunkard and a murderer? Here is God's perfect Son — yea, the very God-man — on the same level with malefactors, and not for Himself, but for us. God became man, and gave Himself for our sins. This satisfaction that the innocent made for the guilty is offered to you, and you may freely have it, for 'there is no difference.'

If the eye of the vilest sinner in this world should perchance rest on this — an outcast from all society, one who has lost all friends and all self-respect, the tottering drunkard coming out of his delirium tremens — I tell you as from God, this Christ is offered to you as God's love-gift. You may reckon Him yours, and proceed upon it as if He were yours as truly as I or any other person in this world do so. You have as much right to claim Him as we, for 'there is no difference' in God's sight —

> 'His blood can make the foulest clean,
> His blood avails for me.'

Thus, my friend, for whom especially I write this, you have to take the lost sinner's place, for God says, 'there is no difference.' As I have said before, I could know this only from God's Word. You have been as happy as a bird all your life, but you forget to find out what God thinks about you. I have tried to show you this from the Bible. I do not ask you if you feel it, for I am sure you never could, neither could any one feel all the catalogue of sins in Romans i. and iii. true against him individually; but God know us better than we know ourselves, and this is His estimate of us.

From the same word, and therefore on the same authority, and on none other, I tell you that God has given you Christ. 'For God so loved the world that He gave His only-begotten Son.' I do not say that you are to feel that Christ is yours, any more than I asked you to feel all the indictment true against you. You are to believe that Christ is yours, as you believe the black accusation against you is yours, only on the authority of God.

I once asked a woman, 'Do you feel that you are condemned?'

'Yes,' she said.

'Now,' I answered, 'that is absurd. You may know and feel you are guilty, but you can only believe you are condemned, because you know you are condemned on the authority of the judge who has pronounced the sentence.'

So on God's authority, and on it alone, I know I am 'condemned already.' And on the same authority alone I know that 'Christ is for ME,' me individually. Just because I accept God's estimate of myself, I have a right to accept God's estimate of His Son for me. I believe the record that God gave of His Son to lost sinners. It looks very humble to say I am too great a sinner, or something similar, thus comparing myself with other sinners; but the humbling bit is that 'there is no difference.'

All are 'condemned already,' but only those who believe it reap the advantage of this. Advantage! What advantage can there be in knowing I am condemned already? Much, because only they who believe themselves condemned can claim a Saviour. And now the 'righteousness of God is by faith of Jesus Christ unto all,' that is to say, it is offered, in the person of Christ, equally unto every person in this world, but is only 'upon all them that believe; for there is no difference, for all have sinned.' 'All,' in Rom. iii. 9, are said to be 'under sin.' So, in ver. 22, all believing ones are under righteousness. It is 'upon all them that believe.' Righteousness is altogether and for ever outside of every man's attainment, for it must be perfect, and all have sinned. Read Rom. iii. 19 to 26. 'Where sin abounded grace did much more abound.' God has proved us all equally by nature and practice 'under sin;' He now has placed all of us who believe 'under grace.'

Thanks be unto God, my dear friend, though you began this paper not knowing yourself as God knows you, you may now, on God's authority, where you are, without moving, claim Christ 'the righteousness of God' as yours, and may rise to tell others like yourself what God think of us and what God has provided for us. It is in love that He will not let you alone. If we are to be 'before Him' for ever, we must be 'holy and without blame in love;' and if so, it is only 'in His Son' that this can be.

Virtuous or vile, decent or indecent, rich or poor, receive and rest upon God's Christ now as He is so freely offered you, and then you may believe (not feel) that your sins are in the depths of the sea, that the shoreless ocean of the love of God flowing through a crucified Saviour has rolled over your millions of sins, and you can triumphantly say, as you look at the ocean covering all that is against you, 'there is no difference.'

If any one is to be kept out of heaven for the believer's sins, that must be Christ, as 'He bore our sins.' God laid on Him our iniquities.

Clad in the skins of God's own making (type of the righteousness of God), Adam and Eve were equally clothed, there was no difference.

Shut in by God's hand into the ark of gopher wood, 'Noah only remained alive, and they that were with him in the ark;' but they all, great and small, man and beast, bird and creeping thing, lion and worm, were equally saved floating nearer and nearer heaven the higher the judgment waters rolled, for there was no difference.

Under shelter of the sprinkled blood every house of Israel was safe even in Egypt, and all equally rejoiced around the roasted lamb, for there was no difference.

Under protection of the scarlet line all found in Rahab's house were equally safe when all in Jericho were destroyed, for there was no difference.

None of all those enrolled in the Lamb's book of life can be cast into the lake of fire. They shall never see the second death, for in that book there is no difference; once there, perfectly safe for ever. God's salvation to lost sinners must always be through judgment. We must accept His ordinance. What was there in skins of beasts, an ark of gopher wood, a few drops of blood, a red cord, or in a certain book? They are God's ordinance, God's perfect way. It will matter little what we think will condemn or save, let us accept God's thoughts for both. God has written out our character. Read Rom. i. 29, 'Being filled with all unrighteousness, fornication, wickedness, covetousness, maliciousness; full of envy murder, debate, deceit, malignity. Whisperers, backbiters, haters of God, despiteful, proud, boasters, inventors of evil things, disobedient to parents, without understanding, covenant-breakers, without natural affection, implacable, unmerciful.' Gal. v. 19, 'Adultery, fornication, uncleanness, lasciviousness, idolatry, witchcraft. Hatred, variance, emulations, wrath, strife, seditions, heresies, envyings, murders, drunkenness, revellings, and such like.'

But I hear some one say, —

'That is the character of a heathen.'

'Yes, friend, it is thine — these are what thy heart is made of. They may be kept under, but they are all there in germ, though not necessarily developed into transgression.'

'Nay, all these are not in my heart.'

'Well, I'm sorry to hear it.'

'Why?'

'Because only this character will be received at Calvary. Only what God has written about us will be accepted by Him: but coming to Calvary with this in our hands, we shall hear his voice saying, "I, even I am He that blotteth out thy transgressions for mine own sake, and will not remember thy sins," and all are gone for ever.'

Why does not every one believe that his heart is desperately wicked? Because it is deceitful above all things, and cannot bear to hear the truth when spoken about itself.

Accept the character God has given to you, and *accept the Saviour He has provided for you.*

>Thou just and holy God,
> Before Thee who can stand?
>Guilty, condemned, all waiting wrath
> In judgment from Thy hand.
>
>One sin deserves a hell,
> A death that ne'er shall die;
>Our sins like sands on ocean's shores
> In million 'gainst us lie.
>
>Thou God of truth and grace,
> We praise Thee for Thy way
>By which the guilty may draw near —
> Their guilt all put away.
>
>Thy Christ who bled and died,
> Up to Thy Throne has gone;
>Himself Thy love-gift we accept,
> We rest on Him alone.
>
>We praise Thee as Thy sons
> Before our Father's face,
>As o'er our every sin now rolls
> The ocean of Thy grace.

Would You Like to be Saved?

Our Justification

'OULD you like to be saved?'
'Indeed I would.'
'And would you like to be saved in God's way?'
'Oh! yes. But I can scarcely see how any poor sinner like me can *know* that here.'

'Well, I wish to place before you a sure road to heaven for the unholiest of us all, and shew you how, by simple believing God, we may know that we are saved.'

'I read my Bible, and I am sure I believe every word in it.'

'I know there are a few who doubt there is a God or the leading doctrines of the Bible. But, by the help of the Spirit of God, I would try to tell you some plain truths which you may not know, or things about which you may have wrong notions — truths about God's relation to you, yourself, personally and individually, and about your seeing, receiving, and taking for yourself God's salvation.'

'Do you know that GOD loves YOU?'

'Ah! yes,' you say, 'He loves us all.'

'Quite true.' But sit down and ask yourself again, 'Do I believe that God loves ME?' To convince you of it, He says in His Bible, and one word is enough from Him — '*God so loved the world*,' and you are part of that world.

But now you say, 'If God so loves me, He will be merciful to me a poor, struggling, failing sinner, if I do the best I can, and

He will overlook my many sins.' Now, this is a point upon which you need to be set right. His name is love; but He is as just as He is merciful, as true as He is gracious, and thus 'can by no means clear the guilty.' He can overlook nothing. You know that Jesus Christ, God Himself manifest in the flesh, came into our position, our place, under our sin, and died a great many years ago. He had no sin of His own, but put away sin by the sacrifice of Himself. Now, God says that He so loved us that he gave us Jesus, and all that we have to do is to believe in Him. Of course you believe that He came and died; but did you ever believe that God gave *Him to you?* 'Ah!' you say, 'I wish I could *feel* that.' But God does not ask you to feel it. He states what He has given to you, and asks you to believe Him. 'God so loved the world that He gave His only begotten Son,' whether you believe it or not. When you accept God's gift you believe in Him.

Jesus Himself told us this when on earth; and surely He did not mean to deceive us. He was speaking about the bitten Israelites in the wilderness. They were all bitten, and a serpent of brass was put upon a pole, and every one that looked lived. This serpent was given to the Israelites whether they looked or not. Supposing that one Israelite had said, I wish I could feel that the serpent is for me, what would you have said? 'Certainly: are you bitten?' That is all you need. Are you a guilty sinner? then you have a right to believe that Jesus is yours. This is the simplicity of the Gospel, which has stumbled many great men, and which seems so foolish to the wise of the world.

People, when they are ill, or begin to think that are to die, try to pray, leave off bad habits, and be good, and do the best they can. Yet, though all these are very proper things to do, they will never save anybody. Supposing these bitten Israelites, instead of looking, had begun to put on poultices, and get ointments, and dressings, and mixtures, to counteract the bites — well, that would have been very sensible, men would say; but God said, LOOK; do as I tell you: — LOOK to that serpent on the pole. So

God's gospel is, 'Believe on the Lord Jesus Christ and thou shalt be saved.'

But you may say, 'I am no worse than my neighbours. If I am lost many will run a bad chance; there are many worse than I am, and I only hope in God's mercy.' Now, this is all a delusion. One sin will damn any man for ever. Sin brought God's Son from heaven to become man and die. It is true many are worse than you, and that they will have a bad chance. That is the very reason I write this for you and for all, because most people are going to hell just now and do not know it. I did not make the calculation. Jesus Christ, who cannot tell a lie, said that there were two roads, a wide and a narrow; that most people go in the wide one, and few go in the narrow one; that the wide one ended in endless misery, and the narrow one in endless happiness. You have only one chance, which is to believe God who says that one sin will send you to hell. You have committed at least one sin. Now accept Christ as your own and only Saviour.

But the great deceiver of the world, that is the devil, who tries to do all he can against God's truth, if he finds that you will not believe yourself to be worse than other people, or that still you have a chance, will take another and opposite course for the devil's statements are like the time of a bad watch, either too fast or too slow. He tells you that either you are too bad, or not bad enough. Now Jesus Christ came to seek and to save the lost. A man who said of himself that he was the chief of sinners is in heaven long ago. The blackest, vilest, most debased, most debauched, polluted, filthy, unclean, hard-hearted, evil-tempered, lying, covetous, thieving, murderous, grey-haired sinner that ever tottered on this side of the grave, is reached by Him who hung between two thieves for sin. God says it: that is all. We cannot understand it. Only this, He chose to do it, and now He tells us. His voice, dear sinner, is still deeper than you, 'Come unto me.' A thief that had reviled Christ after the hand of death was on him is in Paradise, we know. Why not you? And why not be saved now? If not now it may be never.

I once met a poor woman in the south of England. I began to speak to her about heaven and Jesus. She did not understand me. I asked her if she had ever heard of Jesus; she said, NO (most lamentable in this Christian land, so called). I told her that up above those skies Jesus dwelt, and He had so loved us that He had descended from heaven and had become a man. There was a condemned criminal lying waiting execution not far from where we were, and everyone was speaking about him. I said to her, 'You have heard about the man that is to be hanged.'

'Ah yes.'

'Suppose, as he lay in the jail, a knock the night before the execution was heard at the door, and a gentleman walked in, sat down, and said, —

' "You have broken the laws,"

' "Yes, yes," the convict would cry.'

' "You have been condemned."

' "Yes, yes, justly too."

' "You are to be hanged."

' "Yes, to-morrow."

' "I am the Queen's son; I have come from Windsor at Her Majesty's desire, and this is what I am to do: I will take that prison-dress which you have on and sit in your place, and you will take my dress and sit in my place." The convict in astonishment exchanges dresses; he wonders if he is dreaming; the Prince sits down in the convict-dress, and the morning comes; the executioner walks in; he passes the convict; he takes the Prince dressed in the condemned man's dress; he leads him out; he is hanged by the neck till dead; and the man that was condemned walks out free through the opened prison doors.' The poor woman looked in astonishment at this picture of what Christ had done for the sinner — defective in many points, still it impressed on her that great truth of putting the good and innocent one in place of the bad and guilty man.

'Now,' I said, 'this is what the God that created you and me tells us of His Son in this book. Can you read?'

'No,' she said.

'You will believe what I read from God's Word, this book, the Bible, that God has written for us. "Christ hath once suffered for sins, the just for the unjust, that He might bring us to God." (1 Pet. iii. 18.) "When we were yet without strength Christ died for the ungodly." "While we were yet sinners Christ died for us." (Rom. v. 6-8.) She gazed in wonder — she knew she was a sinner. 'Will you believe God,' I continued, 'That He loved you and gave you His Son, the glorious Prince of princes, who once died but is now alive again?' She looked amazed, and trembling said, —

'May I?'

'Not only have I authority to tell you that you may, but God has commanded you to do it, and you will never please God half so much, although you toiled, and wept, and prayed for a million years, as by obeying His voice and taking His gift.'

This is the substance of our conversation, though by the lapse of time I may have forgotten some things and put in others. It seemed to be used by God; for the woman professed at once to believe on Jesus, and to believe God that in Him she had everlasting life. I saw her next evening, and she had a calm joy in her soul; she was longing to hear about that glorious Prince who had been sent to die the convict's death, to preach 'liberty to the captives, and the opening of the prison to the bound.' She resolved to begin to learn to read, so that she might know the truth for herself from the Word of God.

But you may say, I am not so bad as she. I can read. I know all about Jesus. I have always believed.' Yes, you have always believed about Jesus, but have you believed that *He is yours?* You have always believed that He is the Saviour of sinners; but have you believed that *He is yours?* If you have not, you are still condemned, still unsaved, and, in all affection, I would earnestly entreat you, before you read another line, to lay down this book, and take God at His word, never heeding what you feel, nor whatsoever your heart may say (it is a liar); but believe God that he so loved you (put in your name), that He gave Jesus to you (put in your name — that is faith). You see you have not believed always that Jesus is yours, as I have said, but would repeat again, you have not to feel He is yours. If you thus believe Him, then all your sin is for ever gone, as between you and God you are justified from all things, your sins are cast into the depths of the sea, you can never come into condemnation, you are as sure of heaven as if you were there, for God has said it. Certainly your wicked heart within you is not gone. I have often met with poor, distressed souls who were unable to make out how people could know they were saved, thinking that if they were saved they should never have any sin in them. God says, if people (that is, *saved* people) say they have no sin they deceive themselves. All the difference lies in this, having sin IN me, and sin ON me. I once tried to put the way to be saved before a little girl who was wishing to know about it, and I think it shewed her the gospel to the saving of her soul.

'How many people were crucified on Calvary?'

'Three,' she replied. 'Two thieves, and Jesus between.'

'Were both the thieves equally bad?'

'Yes, they suffered justly.'

'Did both die alike?'

'No.'

'What made the difference?'

'One believed on Jesus, the other did not.'

'Now what about sin with regard to these three? The one thief that did not look to Jesus, had he sin IN him?'

'Yes.'

'Had he sin ON him?'

'Yes.'

'And Jesus, had He sin IN Him?'

She thought a little, but she answered rightly, 'No.' (He was holy, harmless, no speck ever defiled Him, He could touch lepers and still be clean.)

'Had He sin ON Him?'

'Yes.'

'His own?'

'No.'

'The thief that looked to Jesus had he sin IN him after he looked?'

'Yes.'

'Had he sin ON him?'

'No.'

This cross still divides the world. We are all sinners, as were both the thieves. On one side are saved sinners, on the other unsaved sinners. On the one side are those who believe God that Jesus is theirs; on the other, those who do not. On the one side are those who have sin IN them, but no sin ON them, because they have left it on the spotless Sin-bearer; on the other, those who have sin both IN them and ON them. And all the people in the world die as those two thieves did. None ever died, or ever will die, without sin IN them. The name of every man when he dies will be *sinner*. The name of each man was *thief* to the very last breath; but one died a saved *thief*, the other died an unsaved *thief*. The one set of men die saved sinners, the other unsaved sinners. The one die with sin ON them, sinking them down to an awful hell; the other die with no sin ON them, and are 'for ever with the Lord.'

'Now, will you not be saved?'

'How *can* I?'

'Simply LOOK.'

'But I have often tried to look, and I have often tried to bring before my mind a picture of Jesus hanging on the cross for me.'

'Now, this is not the way at all: a vision of Christ on the cross, or a dream, or a thought, is not what God gives. Suppose I was laid on my death-bed to-night, and, as I lay, the devil came to me, and told me that I was not saved; suppose I said to him, "Some time ago I had a vision of Christ hanging on the cross for me."

"Ah!" he would say, "that was a delusion I brought before your eyes to deceive you."

"Well, but I dreamt one night that Jesus came close to me, and said, 'Thou are mine.'"

"It was all a delusion."

"I had a thought one day: it just flashed across me all at once, that I was saved."

"Only a delusion." And I could not answer the accusing deceiver. But I will tell you what will put him to flight. I take my Bible and I say, "God *says* that He gave me Jesus."

"How do you know that Jesus is for you?"

"Because God SAYS that He so loved the *world* that He gave His only begotten Son."

"But do you think that so great a sinner as you can be saved by simply believing Jesus is yours?"

"Yes; for God *says*, 'He that believeth on the Son HATH everlasting life.' " And the devil could say nothing; for it is written, "They overcame him by the blood of the Lamb and by the *word* of their testimony." You see I would never dare to bring before him what I felt or what ideas had crossed my mind, but simply and solely *what* God *says*. This is *looking* — this is seeing Jesus in the *Word of God*.'

'Will you not be WASHED in His *blood*, and be made for ever clean?'

'But how can I? What do you mean by His blood? I have often heard about it, and have often tried, while lying on my bed, to bring before my eyes the sight of His blood flowing from His wounded hands and feet, and from His pierced side.'

'Now this is another mistake: blood is a figure for *life taken*. Seeing the blood means believing God about the death of His Son, instead of your death. Being satisfied with Christ's death in the room of yours, this is being washed in the blood. You see no real blood, nor vision, nor picture of blood; but in that blessed Book of God you read, "He was wounded for our (faith says *my*) transgressions, He was bruised for our iniquities, the chastisement of our peace was upon Him, and with His stripes we are healed." Isa. liii. 5. This is seeing the blood.

'Will you not COME to Jesus?'

'But how can I? I have read in the Bible that He said, "Come unto Me, all ye that labour and are heavy laden, and I will give you rest;" and I have often wished I had been on earth when He was here; I wish I had seen Him pass my door, I would have watched Him, and have run to Him and touched His garment. But He is in heaven and how can I come to Him?'

'Now God has most beautifully explained this; for we have not to go up to heaven (Rom. x. 6) to bring Him down, nor to go to the grave to bring Him up; but He is risen and gone to heaven, and He has left His WORD, in which alone He can now be found. This Word may be in your hands and in your memory, that Word which the Holy Ghost has written, and is now urging you to believe, that God so loved you as to give you Jesus. He is asking you in that Word to believe that He is yours. This is "coming to Jesus." Now that He is in heaven, His Spirit and His Word, — His Word from His lips and His Spirit in, through, and with the Word are all that are left; and will these not satisfy? Have you never thought that if you saw your name written in the heavens, or on the sea-shore, and you knew that it had been traced by God's finger, you would then believe that you were saved; but do you think God will make another and special revelation for you? No, no, —you must just take salvation as all the rest of us poor sinners have taken it, by believing the one Book.'

'But have I not to wait God's time?'

'God has only one time — that is, to-day. I read of to-morrow in the Bible. Pharaoh wished the frogs taken from him, but to-morrow. To-morrow is man's time. Now, to-day, is God's. If you came to a stream, would you sit down and say, I will wait till it flows past and when it is dry, then I will cross? Men are not such fools. God is waiting on you. He is calling you. He is beseeching you; and this is his one request, Take my Son whom I have given. He cries to every accountable and rational soul in this world, Will you have Him?'

'Oh, if I could feel a something in me telling me that Christ was mine, I would believe it.'

'Quite wrong again. It is believing something outside of you, trusting Him at God's right hand, and resting on His *sure, eternal Word*.'

You will not throw this aside, will you, and say, I like it, or I do not like it? The poor sinner, saved by the grace of God, who writes to you cannot save you, nor can any man. Tell God what you are to do; tell God that He loves you; tell God that you trust Him; tell God that you believe Him; tell God that He has given you Jesus; tell God that you believe *that* also; tell God that He laid all your sins upon Jesus; tell God that He laid all your sins upon Jesus; tell God that you believe they were on *Him*, and therefore are not on you; tell God you have gone astray, but that you believe Him that your iniquity was laid on Jesus. Thank God for a *finished salvation in Christ*. Tell Him how well-pleased He is with Jesus instead of you; tell Him that you are

> 'A poor sinner and nothing at all,
> But Jesus Christ is your all in all.'

May God Himself shew you, for His name's sake, His simple Gospel of *Christ for you*. A beloved brother said, when coming out of the darkness of self, 'It is the simplicity that stumbles me. It is too good news to be true.' Yes, if man were in it; but it is not too good when we consider with what a God we have to do. You see God can overlook nothing. He can FORGIVE anything. He can by no means clear the guilty. He can take us out of the guilty Adam-standing, and put us into a new, a resurrection Christ-standing. He can save to the uttermost the blackest, vilest sinner that accepts (simply accepts) His gift, Jesus. Will you not receive Him? You may be in poverty, in nakedness, in misery, but God presents you with Jesus. He might have created a world for every one of us; but that would have been nothing compared with what He has given — JESUS. You may have a hard fight here to make ends meet, but having Jesus it will be all the hell you will ever be in. You may have every comfort, and be altogether moral and good as far as man can judge, upright and religious, but without Jesus this will be all the heaven you will ever have. Religiousness, goodness, kindness, beneficence, uprightness, amiability, will not save you. Acceptance of God's gift alone will do so.

Now, what is it to be, ere we part, perhaps, never to converse again for ever — God's simple gospel for the meanest, poorest, weakest capacity, so that even a fool may embrace it; or man's ways, follies, pleasures, religion, world? Jesus is offered to all. Some will accept Him, and some will refuse. You make God a liar if you do not accept. You make yourself a liar, and God true, if you accept Him. Some may know all about Christ the gift of God presented to them, and yet not know Himself. 'Tis eternal life to know Him.' By not receiving Him, they trample under foot the blood of the life-giving Prince. Others receive Him and thank God for Him and are saved.

May the blessed Spirit, the witnesser of Jesus open the eyes of every reader to see Him, incline every fellow-sinner to believe God, and accept His gift.

Call your heart a liar, and believe the record of the only living and true God.

> Nothing, Lord I bring before Thee,
>   Nothing that can meet Thy face;
> But in Jesus I adore Thee,
>   For the riches of Thy Grace,
>   Jesus came in love from heaven,
>   By the Father's love was given,
>   From that death He now has risen,
>   Which He died for me.
>   Jesus died for the sinner,
>   Jesus died for the sinner,
>   Jesus died for the sinner,
>   Jesus died for me.
>
> 'Come to me,' Thy lips have spoken:
>   As I am, O Lord, I come;
> All Thy laws I oft have broken,
>   From Thy side afar did roam.
>
> Boundless love hast Thou been showing,
>   Settling every just demand;
> Jesus as my own I'm knowing,

Thus obey Thy great command.

This the work that stands for ever,
   All my works are useless dross;
Jesus mine! yes, nought can sever
   Me from Him of Calvary's cross.

Precious blood of Him forsaken
   On that cross, in wrath, by God,
Cleanses me; His life was taken,
   When made sin for me He stood.

'Look to me,' He said, who's risen,
   Jesus Christ my Saviour Lord;
Mortal eye can't enter heaven,
   But I see Thee in Thy Word.

Trust Him, claim Him, O believe Him,
   All was done they trust to gain;
On him rest, and now receive Him,
   And with him for ever reign.

'Ye Must be Born Again.'

Our Regeneration.

THOUGH you knew all the duties incumbent upon a royal Prince, this knowledge would not make you a royal Prince. You must be in a position before you can act under the laws of that position. This is the natural order admitted by all men in human things, but quite reversed when they begin to speculate on divine things. God's order is this — I make you sons: walk like sons. Man says, try to walk like sons, and after a shorter or longer time you will be made sons. But we must be brought out of the kingdom of darkness before we can take the first step in the kingdom of light. Before we can enter this kingdom we must have a nature capable of enjoying it. A nature can be implanted only by birth; therefore we must be born again. This subject is gone fully into in John iii.

Nicodemus, a ruler of the Jews, came to Jesus and said to Him, 'WE KNOW,' &c.

Jesus answered him by saying, 'Except a man BE BORN AGAIN,' &c.

There is a great difference between what we *know* and what we *are*; a great difference between our attainments, education, talents, knowledge, and our standing before God, and our relation to God. Nicodemus was an inquiring man, who had been convinced of Christ's claims by external evidences, and whose conscience was now seeking after something deeper and more satisfactory. He comes with this profession of knowledge, 'Rabbi, we know that thou art a teacher come from God: for no man can do these miracles that thou doest, except God be with him.' (John iii. 2.) Jesus, because He knew all men, and all the thoughts of men, answered not the words but the need of Nicodemus, by shewing that all his knowledge would never save him or any other man; for 'Except a man be born again, he cannot see the kingdom of God.' Nicodemus by nature, however well-instructed, could never see God's kingdom.

I. — CHRIST NOT A TEACHER OF THE OLD NATURE.
HE IS FIRST A SAVIOR, THEN A TEACHER.

In the present day, in certain quarters, we hear a good deal about Christ as the perfect man, the perfect example, and the perfect teacher; but here is the answer of Jesus Himself to all such compliments. He came not to teach the old nature — not to teach man as sprung from Adam, but to seek and save the lost, to give the new nature, and to teach saved man. The policy of all who have openly, or in thought, denied the divinity of Christ, is to laud His moral teaching and his Godlike example. They bring well known and fondly cherished truths forward, as if only they believed and preached these great facts; but at the outset they forget this insurmountable barrier to all moral reclamation of the old nature of man, 'Except a man be *born again*, he cannot see the kingdom of God.'

We find others, however, who know Christ, not merely as a teacher, but who also believe in His divinity, that He is God as well as man. In fact, many in our land know every fundamental doctrine in the Bible; but a mere knowledge of doctrine, however true, never introduced a son of Adam into the kingdom of God. Men may have learned what justification, and sanctification, and adoption are; they may be able to distinguish minutely between all the creeds, isms, and heresies, they may be theoretically orthodox, may be able to judge preachers and sermons, may be very ready freely to criticise most men they hear, and graciously pay beautiful compliments to their special favourites, as Nicodemus did to Jesus. They may know, moreover, about the new birth, its necessity and divine origin; but notwithstanding all this, they could not dare to say, as before God, 'Whereas we were blind, now we see.' The greatest amount of theological education never yet saved a man. Creed, or the belief in a certain amount of doctrine, has made Christendom, but never made a Christian. 'Ye must be born again.'

Others again, when their consciences have been reached, try to get this new birth brought about, and begin most zealously to train and trim, to educate and reform their old nature, quite ignorant of what is meant by '*born again.*'

II. — THE OLD NATURE UNCHANGED AND UNCHANGEABLE.

Nicodemus wondered how a man when old could be brought again into this world; but if it were possible, what better would he be? He might have changed his circumstances by this new birth according to the flesh; but would he have changed kingdoms? He would still be in the kingdom of the first Adam; he would still be flesh; for Jesus goes on to say, 'That which is born of the flesh is flesh,' (ver. 6). Water never rose above its level: that which is produced is of the same nature as that which produces. We find people to-day who think that if they were in other circumstances they would have a better chance of getting saved. The rich man thinks that if he were poor, he might have time to think of religion. The poor man, if he could get ends to meet, and had a little more money, would have more leisure to think of God. But the difficulty is not so much in what is *around* us, as in what is *within* us.

Again, the aids of religion are called in, in order that *the flesh* may be *improved*; but after all attempts it is found to be only religious flesh. Man may have all varieties of it; but it never rose to see the kingdom of God. In nature, we speak of the animal kingdom and the vegetable kingdom. If we took a rose from the latter of these kingdoms, and cultivated it and trained it, and by our various arts made it produce all its varieties, we never by these means could bring it into the other kingdom —into the animal kingdom. Or, again, if I take a nettle from the roadside, and bring it into my garden or my hothouse, watch over, dress, water, and warm it, I may produce beautiful nettles, and beautiful varieties of nettle, but I never could get apples from it; that which is produced from the nettle is nettle. We can never gather grapes of thorns, nor figs of thistles.

Man by nature is in the kingdom of the first Adam: no amount of reformation, amelioration, cultivation, civilization, or religiousness, can bring one single man into the kingdom of God. Look through Great Britain and Ireland, — what is the object of the great bulk of the religious machinery? Is it not for cultivating the flesh, in order that, after death, it may see the kingdom of God? This is no guess. It is the sad confession of godly men in all the churches — godly bishops, godly rectors, godly pastors, elders and deacons. All unite in the same complaint, and do their best against it. The majority of respectable religious people, as good as Nicodemus, a master in Israel, do not know the practical power of this truth which stands at the door of God's kingdom. They put salvation at the end of a long series of self-improving processes — God puts the salvation of the soul at the very beginning, and all duties that in their discharge can honor Him, are founded upon this fact. 'Man's chief end is (not to get the soul saved, but) to glorify God and to enjoy Him for ever' — starting with being saved for nothing as the means to this end.

III. — THE ABSOLUTE NECESSITY OF A NEW NATURE.

Before I can enter God's kingdom I must have a new nature, that can appreciate, see, live in, and enjoy that kingdom. Ask a blind man what red is. He has no idea of it because he cannot see, because he has not the capacity. Educate him in the mixing of colours. Tell him that the blue and yellow mixed make green; he may soon remember this, and *know* much more; by that knowledge he never *saw* a colour.

The questions therefore of most importance to you are not, do you know doctrine? do you know Christ's teaching? do you know your Bible? do you know the evidences of Christianity? do you know that Christ is God, that Christ is a Saviour? that He is able and willing to save? You may know all that, and be lost for ever. But, are you born again? Are you a partaker of a new nature, a divine nature? Are you an heir of God? Is your standing now in Christ or in Adam?

Before I can see the kingdom of God, I must have the nature implanted that belongs to that kingdom. This is something more than mere thought of sin forgiven, or righteousness obtained. It is a question of capacity, of fitness to enjoy, of likeness of nature. What an awful thought that so many religiously educated people are lost! What a hell, where the good, decent religious sons of Adam have to be for ever shut up with the profane and the drunkard, and the abominable and the unclean!

Reader, I entreat of you, think. Think for a moment, did Jesus speak truth or tell lies? If He spoke truth, those who have not *been born again*, however intelligent, educated, moral, benevolent, or religious, can never see the kingdom of God, and must, therefore, be swept away for ever with the lost, for there are only two places. What a hell! Frequenters of cathedrals and frequenters of gin-palaces, tract-distributors and pick-pockets, drawing-room-meeting religionists and the off-scourings of the streets! Priests who, with solemn mien[2], pretended to stand between the people and God, and murderers who have been hung for their crimes! Teachers who knew everything in theology, and the profane, the swearer, the blasphemer, the infidel! These things will turn out true, whether you believe them or not. It was seen in the days of Noah. Is it to be your

---

[2] Editor's Note: A somewhat literary term referring to a person's appearance and behavior toward others; **demeanor.**

bitter experience? Hell is real. Eternal punishment is real. Christ's words are true, although they may be doubted, or denied by the majority of men. The awful fact remains. Stop, therefore, high or low, rich or poor, educated or uneducated, intelligent or ignorant, religious man or blasphemer, respectable or profane, think and ask yourself these questions, *Am I born again? Have I a new life?* — a life communicated by the Spirit of God through the truth — born not of flesh, but of water (the word, Eph. v. 26) and the Spirit. *Have I been born twice* —once into this world of Adam, and again into that of God? Friend, if you have not this new birth, it were better that you had never been born; but now as you are, and where you are, whenever you are convinced of the necessity of this new birth, look and live; believe and be saved; take God at His word; He says, 'Ye *must* be born again;' and in the same chapter it is written, 'As Moses lifted up the serpent in the wilderness, even so must the Son of Man be lifted up, that whosoever BELIEVETH on Him should not perish, but have ETERNAL LIFE.' — What God demands, God provides.

IV. — HOW THE NEW NATURE IS IMPLANTED.

This new nature is not implanted by a process, but received by an act of faith. This new nature never sets aside as to actual fact the old, never amalgamates, never becomes incorporated with it, never improves it, but 'lusts' against it in the believer, wars against it, is 'contrary' to it. And how is it implanted? Reader, this is of the greatest importance to you. Are you to look for the new birth in your own frames or feelings, to an ordinance or an act of man. A mistake here is fatal — 'Ye must be born again.' — How?

Jesus answers this, and gives us the three things that are divinely and absolutely essential for the new birth (John iii. 7), seeing the kingdom (ver. 3), entering the kingdom (ver. 5), or having eternal life (ver. 15), all these being but different aspects of the same truth. These three essentials are —

1. Water (ver. 5).

2. The Spirit (ver. 5 and 8).
3. The Son of man lifted up (ver. 14).

Let us consider each shortly: —

I. — WATER.

'Except a man be born of WATER and of the Spirit, he cannot enter the kingdom of God' (ver. 5).

It cannot in any way refer to baptism by water, the application of literal water to a man externally, as that would only wash his body and could not touch his inner man. Some would read the text, 'except a man be born of baptism,' and of course by this doctrine Old Testament saints could not be in the kingdom of God, as they were not baptized. Circumcision could not save a man. 'Neither is that circumcision which is outward in the flesh...Circumcision is that of the heart in the spirit, and not in the letter.' (Rom ii. 28, 29.) No change on a man externally can profit. He may apply much nitre[3] and wash himself with much soap, but his leopard spots of sin still remain. Nor will mere education, reformation, cultivation, training of the old nature, turn flesh into spirit. 'That which is born of the flesh is flesh;' it may be decent or indecent flesh, religious or irreligious, pious or profane, but still flesh.

Some seeing this, and understanding it, have now asked what can the '*water*' mean? This has been answered in several ways. Some say it is the same as the Spirit; others that it is the same as the blood, but 'there are three that bear witness in earth, the Spirit, and the water, and the blood,' so that if water was only another way of expressing either the working of the Spirit or cleansing of the blood, there would be only two bearing testimony — the Spirit and the blood and the water standing for either. We can solve the question by asking what should have come into the mind of Nicodemus when Christ spoke of *water*?

---

[3] Editor's Note: British spelling of the word 'niter.' Potassium nitrate used medicinally.

He, a master in Israel, knew of a laver where every priest had to wash before he could enter into the holy place, for no unwashed foot ever trod that holy place. He, a master in Israel, knew the book of Ezekiel, and the promise to be fulfilled in a coming day to Israel. 'Then will I sprinkle clean water upon you, and ye shall be clean: from all your filthiness and from all your idols will I cleanse you. A new heart also will I give you, and a new spirit will I put within you...And I will put my Spirit within you, and cause you to walk in My *statutes*; and ye shall keep My judgments and do *them*.' (Ezek. xxxvi. 25, 26, 27.)

A teacher in Israel should have been looking for the antitype of temple and laver, and the true water of purification sprinkled to cleanse from defilement. He should have been conversant with the 19th Psalm, which definitely explains what the water is (ver. 9): 'Wherewithal shall a young man *cleanse* his way? By taking heed according to Thy *word*.'

The water here spoken of by Christ and typified in the Old Testament, is the WORD OF GOD, the embodiment, the revelation of God's thoughts.

Let us search the Scriptures as to this: 'Being born again, not of corruptible seed, but of incorruptible, by the *Word of God*, which liveth and abideth for ever. For all flesh is as grass.' (1 Pet. i. 23.) In our text 'flesh' is contrasted with the 'spirit,' here flesh is contrasted with the 'Word.' 'The seed is the *Word of God*' (Luke viii. 11). 'The righteousness which is of faith speaketh on this wise, ...The *Word is nigh* thee' (Rom. x. 6-8). 'Of his own will begat He us with *the Word* of truth' (James i. 18). 'Ye are *clean* through *the Word* which I have spoken unto you' (John xv. 3).

These all show that THE WORD is used by God in the new birth in that place where Christ speaks of water to Nicodemus, but we have more direct evidence in Eph. v. 26, 'That He might sanctify and cleanse it (the Church) with the washing of water by *the Word*.' Thus, from Old Testament type, from New Testament analogy, and from direct scriptural statement in both

Old and New Testaments, the *water* in the new birth is proved to be the '*Word of God.*'

And most important it is to see this. How am I born again by *the word*? Water cleanses by displacement. Uncleanness and water cannot occupy the same space at the same moment: the water displaces the uncleanness, and thus cleanses. The Word of God does not act by teaching 'the flesh,' but by displacing all the thoughts of 'the flesh,' and putting in those of God.

The entrance of God's word gives light (Psalm cxix. 130). Man was lost by hearing Satan; he is saved by hearing God. Man, in his natural Adam-standing, is a chaos — nothing in him can meet or please the eye of God — he is without form and void, darkness brooding over him. When God, therefore, begins to re-create him (for 'we are *His* workmanship, *created* in Christ Jesus unto good works,' Eph. ii. 10), He says 'Let light be,' and light is; and it is by the entrance of His word that this is done.

This word of God judges everything in man; it puts God and His requirements before man. Human opinion is entirely set aside. By nature we are all apt to rest satisfied that there are many worse than we. If I am lost, many will have a bad chance, is sometimes said, and quite true, for God's Word tells us we are all guilty, and as we saw in a former chapter, 'there is no difference,' all condemned already, equally condemned. We compare ourselves with one another, or according as men are estimated, bad, good, or indifferent. God's word comes like water, and washes out all our thoughts and opinions.

'It's my idea,' says one, 'if one tries to live a good life, this is all he can do.' Of course, this is your idea; but all our thoughts are evil, and unless God's Word displaces our ideas we are undone.

'It's my opinion,' says another, 'that we must just do the best we can, and trust in the mercy of God.' Of course this is your opinion—but the action of God's Word is like water to wash out our opinions. The first thing it tells me about myself and about all of us is that we are lost, depraved, guilty, condemned.

But more; the Word of God brings in God's mind about Himself instead of my own; it lets God think for me, God speak for me, God act for me; it makes me passive, because I can be nothing else.

'*Hear*, and your soul shall live' (Isa. lv. 3). Life is on its syllables — man begins to speak, to pray, &c., when he wants to be saved — God says *Hear*! God is praying to us, and should we not answer God's prayer before we begin to pray? He does beseech men by us (2 Cor. v. 20). His prayer is easily answered. He says, 'Will you have my Son?' and the answer is '*Yes*' or '*No*.' By thus hearing the Word of God, and understanding it (Matt. xiii. 23), we receive a new life from God in which God's thoughts reside, and in which they act. Let us now look at the Spirit's work in regeneration.

2. — THE SPIRIT.

We must be born of the SPIRIT — not the Spirit apart from the Word — not the Word apart from the Spirit—not two births — but the one divine new birth. We see Spirit and Word as the *living water* (John vii. 38). 'He that believeth on me, as the Scripture hath said, out of his belly shall flow rivers of living water. But this spake He of the Spirit, which they that believe on Him should receive.' This was seen at Pentecost, when the rivers of living water (read Peter's sermon, a number of Old Testament quotations) flowed out to the salvation of thousands, the words of God carried home by the Spirit — hence *living water*; the Word is the water, but it is stagnant or dead without the Spirit — Spirit and Word make *living water*. Again, Jesus said (John vi. 63), 'the *words* that I speak unto you they are spirit and they are life.' Mere moral suasion as it is called, never yet saved a man. This Word only operates as God's Spirit applies it. The vehicle is the Word, but the power is the Spirit.

If people are famishing in a town, and we tend to send supplies to them, we load the vans and waggons with bread and corn, and make up a large train. The entrance of these waggons will bring life to many a famished family, to many a dying man. Why delay, then? why is the train lying useless at this station where there is plenty? We are waiting for that powerful engine which will speed it along. Screw up the coupling, make all fast; and now not only is the feast ready, but feast and guests are brought together. Christ Himself is the bread, the Word is the waggon, and the Spirit is the engine or power that brings Christ in the Word to us poor perishing sinners.

God made a great feast, and bade many (Luke xiv. 16); none came, and 'none of those men which were bidden shall taste of my supper,' is now what God has said. No merely invited guest ever came. We preach 'Come;' we tell that all things are ready, that the feast is spread, the door open, that 'yet there is room;' but no man by this mere invitation ever came; as one has said, 'God has to fill the chairs, as well as the table.' Five yoke of oxen or a piece of ground are of much more value to a natural man than the richest feast of God. God has to provide the guests as well as the feast. If there were no Christ provided, there would be no feast; if there were no Spirit working, there would be no guests.

Ye must be born of the Spirit. Like produces like. 'That which is born of the flesh' is not merely like 'the flesh,' but is 'flesh,' and 'that which is born of the Spirit' is not like the Spirit, nor is it the Spirit (that would be incarnation), but 'is spirit,' and He dwells in that which He begets.

This is something quite different from 'the flesh' being pardoned, then taught, then toned down, pervaded, and sanctified by the Spirit. We have the man, the I, the existing person the undivided responsibility, '*born again*' by the thoughts of God acting in him in power, and the mind and nature of God communicated to him by the Spirit; and this now is the man's life, as the 'flesh' was his life before. No Christian can have his standing 'in the flesh.' Alas, that ever any of us should walk in the flesh: 'we are not in the flesh;' alas, the flesh is in us still.

A boat has been sailing on the salt ocean; it has come through many a storm, and, half full of the briny water, it is now sailing on the fresh water of the river. It is no longer in the salt water, but the salt water is in it. The Christian has got off the Adam-sea for ever. He is in the Christ-river for ever. Adam is still in him, which he is to mortify and to throw out, but he is not in Adam. He has now a power, and a position, and inclination to judge himself. He knows himself. It was at this point that Paul exclaimed, 'I know that in me — that is, my flesh — dwelleth no good thing.' He is not two persons, but in the one person he has, and will have to his last hour here, two natures diametrically opposite, and actively opposing each other. He now sees that 'the flesh,' lusts against the 'Spirit,' but the Spirit also against the 'flesh,' in order that he may not walk as he used to walk; that these are contrary, and therefore never can be friends, and that he has in him, and will have in him, a foe that is neither to be trifled with nor trusted, but watched, warred with, and mortified.

But his life is in his new nature. He is now a 'partaker of the divine nature,' 'born of God,' 'an heir of God;' and thus it is with every one who is born of the Spirit, Jew or Gentile, for God acts here in sovereignty. Connection with Abraham only gave them a fleshly standing, but a new thing is needed by the Jew as well as the Gentile, and is as free to the Gentile as to the Jew.

The eighth verse of John iii. is a most blessed verse. In it we poor sinners of the Gentiles have got in. Reader, never quarrel with the royal prerogative of God's grace; read Rom. ix., and see that if we do not let God be absolute we have no chance of salvation, for we are all equally 'condemned already.' Praise His grace that hath now appeared to every nation under heaven.

But passing over Christ's testimony of the Father, as given in verses nine to thirteen — (prophets had prophesied, but here is God himself) — let us now look at

3. — THE SON OF MAN LIFTED UP.

This, indeed, is our life. Christ said, 'Ye MUST be born again;' but here is another MUST that He mentions, 'As Moses lifted up the serpent in the wilderness, even so MUST the Son of man be lifted up; that whosoever believeth on Him should not perish but have everlasting life.' God says, Ye *must*, but He also says, I *must*. Your Adam-life is forfeited, and you are under condemnation. The Son of man lifted up is the answer to the forfeit. Satan, who has the power of death, and has every man in his power (for all have sinned), has been destroyed as to his power, his head having been bruised by Christ on the cross. (Heb. ii. 14.) But Christ is now risen, and can communicate His life to any one who believes in Him, He having satisfied every demand of God. The new birth is the communication of a new life. Christ beyond the doom of sin is that life; Christ incarnate before His death cannot be 'our life,' because the judgment against the old life can only be met in *death*.

The 'corn of wheat' must die before the fruit can be produced. The resurrection-life of Christ is therefore the new life preached to the *sinner*, and implanted in him on his *believing* — a life that is perfect, impeccable, indestructible, eternal as the Christ of God is — a life that has already proved victorious over the cross of shame, over death's strongest power—a life that will ere long swallow up mortality.

The Spirit of God applies the Word that speaks about the lifted-up Christ whom we receive and rest upon for salvation, and this is the new birth. Such a life is offered only to a *sinner* — what a comfort! No righteous man, no earth-wise, no rich man ever entered the kingdom of God as such — only as justified sinners. None but *redeemed* sinners sing the song of the kingdom — none but those who, guilty, depraved, lost, have taken their place with roused consciences at the foot of the cross, and there seen the lifted-up Christ. All in that kingdom are '*new creatures*,' clothed in 'the best robe,' with the 'ring,' and the 'shoes,' and 'the fatted calf' slain. What perfection is in the

Word of God! The Word tells me that unless I am born again I cannot enter God's kingdom; but the same word tells me that if I am born again (though only a babe now) I am as sure of spending eternity with my Lord as if I were with Him. No hatred of devils, no enmity of the world, no power of the flesh, shall keep me out. We enter God's kingdom by being born again. We *have* eternal life even now. We have the germs of heaven even here. We do not wait for that life; but 'he that believeth on the son HATH everlasting life' (ver. 36).

We have tried to shew thus briefly what is meant by being 'born of water and of the Spirit.' Read 1 John v. 6 — 'This is He that came by water and blood, not by water only, but by water and blood, and it is the Spirit that beareth witness, because the Spirit is truth. For they that bear witness are three; the *Spirit*, and the *water*, and the *blood*, and the three agree in one.' (Correct translation.)

The *blood* is for expiation; that is, the Son of man lifted up on the cross, and His life taken for ours. 'This is He that came by water and blood' (1 John v. 6).

The *water* is for moral cleansing; that is, the Word of God applied in power to our consciences, Jesus 'came not by water only' (that is to say, not merely a teacher of the word), 'but by water and blood' (He came certainly as the great teacher, but also as the great sacrifice making atonement for sin).

The *Spirit* is the witness from the throne of God to the value of that blood in the presence of God, and the witness to our spirits by applying the word (water), and thus morally cleansing. He is also the source, the framer, and the power of expression of every new feeling, thought, affection, or purpose in the new creation, 'and it is the Spirit that beareth witness, because the Spirit is truth.'

These three agree in one, meet in one point, work out one thing in their testimony, and this is the testimony, that 'God hath given to us eternal life, and this life is in His Son. He that hath the Son, hath life' (1 John v. 11, 12).

What any sinner, therefore, has to do in this new birth is to look to Christ on the cross; and where is he to look to Him now as crucified but in *the Word*. He is to believe what God says about His Son. God says I have given you Christ (John iii. 16). I believe it: therefore I thank God. I do not ask myself do I feel it? but God says it — I appropriate it as mine — I believe His Word by putting in my name where God puts His 'whosoever.' In this Word of God we get the Spirit's witness — that is, God's testimony about His Son. God does the *work*: we believe the *Word*.

Reader, are you *born again*? You are not satisfied with yourself. Nor is God satisfied with you. You are not satisfied with your estimate of the work of Christ. Are you satisfied with God's estimate of it? The Spirit has come to tell out to us the value of that blood. Faith does not consist in my valuing it, but in my accepting God's value of it. God says, 'When I see the blood, I will pass over you.'

If you do not believe God's witness, the Spirit of God in the Word, about his Son, you simply make God a liar. Now you must either make yourself a liar or God. Do you not think that it would be the better way to say, 'Let God be true and *every* man a liar' — myself the first liar? A man does not like to be called a liar, but God says, 'every man.' Until a man calls himself a liar, he makes God one. 'He that believeth not God hath made him a liar, because he believeth not the record that God gave of his Son. And this is the record, that God hath given to us eternal life, and this life is in His Son.' As long as you look within yourself for one idea, one opinion, one thought, you are listening to a liar. Call your heart a liar at once and simply take God at His word, receive His Son as He has given Him to you.

Reader, art *thou* born again? There was a moment that every Israelite had between being bitten and dying; that moment was given him to look and LIVE. That is thy brief moment of life, hast thou looked and lived? God can do no more than He has done to provide life for thee. He spared not His Son!

Do not look to thy wounds, to thy sins, and think thus to get peace. Try no longer earth's prayers, or religions, or works of righteousness. They are but ointments to thy sores, that will never heal, but look away from all to the serpent on the pole. The question is not, whether thou hast great faith or little faith. It did not depend upon the length of the look, nor the earnestness of the look, it was the fact of looking that cured the bitten Israelite. Look and live! thou hast only one brief yet sufficient moment of time.

But how are men spending this little moment? In making money, in indulging the lust of the flesh, the lust of the eye, and the pride of life! In gathering together the dust of their condemned cell into heaps and calling it riches! In gathering the straws that lie in their prison, and making crowns, and, madman-like, playing at kings while death is written as their doom; and the door of escape stands still open!

God is standing over them with this awful word, 'YE MUST BE BORN AGAIN,' and this other wondrous word, 'THE SON OF MAN MUST BE LIFTED UP.' He delivered up His Son to death. What a holy God! What a just, righteous, truthful God. When sin was lying on the sinless Christ, He could not let it pass. Do you think He will let you pass now after that awful day at Calvary? It is there that we read the doom of sin. How shall we escape from him if we neglect His 'so great salvation?' For it is not with God merely as a judge we have to do; for it was His love that planned and wrought the whole redemption work. Double bitter will be your cup of wrath that you have spurned the salvation of such a God who desires to be known by you as LOVE; for in order that *any* poor sinner might be born again, '*God so loved the* WORLD *that He gave His only-begotten Son, that* WHOSOEVER *believeth on Him should not perish, but have everlasting life.*' (John iii. 16.)

Let us suppose that you are convinced of these important realities; that you are lost; that therefore your first need is a *Saviour*, not a *teacher*; that you have not a nature capable of enjoying God; that the new nature is gotten by your being born;

born again of water (the word) and the Spirit, but you cannot understand how this comes about. You cannot understand what is meant by looking to Christ as the bitten Israelites looked to the serpent on the pole. Let me illustrate it by a conversation I had, one day, with a man who had been hearing the gospel preached, and with whom I had to walk some miles.

I began by asking, 'Have you ever thought of the great salvation?'

'Oh, yes,' he replied; 'I have often thought about it.'

'And are you saved?'

'Well, I could not say that — I don't feel as I would like.'

'I quite believe that; but do you think any of us could ever feel perfectly right in this world? But are you at peace with God?'

'I never could say that I am satisfied with myself.'

'But, my friend, I did not ask if you were. It would be a very bad sign if you were satisfied with yourself. But are you at peace with God?'

'Well, I never could feel that I have peace.'

'But I don't ask if you feel at peace with yourself; I hope you never will. Have you peace with God?'

'To tell you the truth, I am not right.'

'How long is it since you began to think of these things?'

'About seven or eight years ago, in the north of Ireland, I was first awakened by a minister preaching on "*Ye must be born again.*" And often since that time I have been trying to feel God's Spirit working in me.'

'And you never have?'

'No; I could not be sure.'

'How could ever any one be sure of what was going on within him, especially as our enemy comes as an angel of light?'

'Well, what am I to do, then?'

'Jesus was the one, you remember, that said, "Ye must be born again." "Except a man be born of water and of the Spirit, he cannot enter the kingdom of God." Now, at the end of all this conversation, Nicodemus did not know how to be saved, but only said, "How can these things be?" even when Jesus Himself was the great Teacher.'

'That's just where I am.'

'Now, what did Jesus do? He took him away to the picture-book for children, and showed him the picture of a dying man looking away from himself to a serpent on a pole, and thus obtaining life; and told him that "as Moses lifted up the serpent in the wilderness, even so must the Son of man be lifted up, that whosoever believeth in Him should not perish, but have eternal life." Now all you have to do is to look and live.'

'But that is just what I've been trying to do, and what I don't know how to do: — what is it to look to Christ?'

'Now I can understand your difficulty; you cannot see Christ with the eyes of your body; you cannot see Him in vision; you say that you cannot feel His presence within you; you cannot feel that you have faith.'

'Exactly; what am I to do?'

'Allow me to give you an illustration.' In some such words I spoke with my friend, and gave him the substance of the following illustration, which seemed to clear away his difficulty; and I trust, by God's blessing, it may enable you to receive God's simple plan, and accept God's salvation for nothing.

You have a rent — say £10 a-year — to pay, having to maintain a large family, and having been recently is distress and out of work, you find it impossible to pay it. Let us suppose that I was able, knew your difficulty, took pity on you, and said to you, —

'John, I hear you have your rent coming on, and having had very hard times, you will never be able to pay it. Now I wish you to use your money for your most pressing wants, to get food and clothing for your wife and family, and *look to me for the rent.*' You, knowing me, and hence believing me, would go away home with a burden off your mind and a happy heart. When you came home next Saturday with your wages, you would tell your wife to spend all the money in getting food and clothing.

'But, John,' she would say, 'are we not to lay aside something for the rent?'

'Oh no,' you would answer; 'I met a man whom I know, and he said, Look to me for the rent, and I believe him.'

And thus weeks would go on, till shortly before the rent-day a neighbor comes in and says, —

'John, I have only got £5 gathered for my rent, and I don't know what I'm to do. How much have you?'

'None at all.'

'What! have you nothing gathered?'

'No, for a friend of mine said, Look to me for the rent.'

'And are you not getting anxious about it?'

'No.'

'Why?'

'Because I trust him.'

'Why?'

'Because I believe him.'

'Why?'

'Because I know him.'

By and by the rent-day comes, and even your wife begins to be suspicious and doubtful, but you have implicit trust in what I said — you have no difficulty in understanding what *look to me for the rent* means; and so, at the appointed hour, I walk in and make my word good, and am happy to find that, against all your neighbour's doubts, against all your wife's fears, and even against all your own tremblings, you have trusted my word and looked to me for the rent.

This is, of course, just an illustration, as I have no doubt you are at the present quite able and willing to pay your own rent; but in the matter of our salvation, though we might be willing, we are totally unable; so the Lord now says, 'Look to Me, and be ye saved.'

Christ on the cross has satisfied God's justice. He paid the debt for the sinner. Men are doing perfectly right things; praying, living moral lives, and giving money for charitable purposes; but all for the wrong end. All these will never save.

God says, '*Look to Me for salvation,*' and then begin to use your time, talents, money, powers, for their legitimate end, to glorify God. Do not try to be holy in order to be saved. That would be like the man laying up for a rent which he could never pay. '*Look to me and be saved*,' says God, and then be holy, because you are sure of salvation on the authority of God. Religion will never save you — even pure religion. God defined pure religion in James i. 27: 'Pure religion, and undefiled, before God and the Father is this, to visit the fatherless and widows in their affliction, and to keep himself unspotted from the world.' By the deeds of the law we cannot be justified; therefore by doing all this we cannot be saved. Religion is the life of a saved man, not the efforts of an unsaved man to get saved. We do not try to do good in order to get a new nature, but we try to do good because we have received a new nature. The work which God will accept from you is not *to* the cross, it is *from* the cross to the crown. Jesus did ALL the *saving-work*. He brought the cross to our level. Get saved by looking to Him and then live to God. Do not look to the feeling of being saved — look away from what is being wrought *in* you to what was wrought *for* you. We are not saved on account of the Spirit working in us, but by means of His work — we are saved on account of Christ dying for us. We are not saved *for* faith, but *through* faith. 'Look to me and be ye saved, all the ends of the earth.'

Lie down as a wounded, helpless, ungodly sinner, and look away from yourself to Jesus crucified for sin.

> *Look unto Me and be ye saved —*
>   Look, men of nations all;
> Look rich and poor, look old and young —
>   Look sinners great and small!
>
> *Look unto Me and be ye saved —*
>   Look now, nor dare delay;
> Look as you are — lost, guilty, dead —
>   Look while "tis called to-day!
> *Look unto Me and be ye saved —*
>   Look from your doubts and fears;

Look from your sins of crimson dye,
   Look from your prayers and tears!

Look unto Me and be ye saved —
   Look to the work all done,
Look to the pierced Son of Man,
   Look to your sin all gone!

Do you feel your Sins Forgiven?

Our Assurance.

O you *feel* that your sins are all forgiven?

'Indeed I do not; but I *know* they are.'

'Now, I cannot understand that. How can any one know it?'

'Most certainly; but how can you say that God ever told you that He forgave you? Did you just feel at a certain time something that you thought was God's voice, inwardly telling you that your sins were pardoned?'

'I certainly did not.'

'Then how can it be? I have tried to get converted as hard as any man could; I have prayed for grace, for strength, for the pardon of my sins, and for the Holy Spirit, and I do not yet feel any difference, and I never could feel as I have heard some men say they have.'

'I quite understand you; I was for years in the same condition.'

'Then how did you get out of it? I know all about the plan of salvation, about the word of Christ, and the necessity of the Spirit; that we must be justified by grace through faith alone without the works of the law; that the promises are all most certainly secure to them that are in Christ; but how am I ever to know whether I am in Him or not?'

'I know that you may have heard some Christians say they *feel* they are pardoned, they *feel* they are saved; but this only tends to mislead. It did mislead me, and I have no doubt it is misleading you. These Christians may mean a right thing, but they state it wrongly. I feel happy because I *know* that my sins are pardoned; and I will shew you how I know that by and by; but I do not *feel* that my sins are pardoned. Let us suppose a case. A poor widow has no money to pay her debts. The creditor comes demanding his righteous due. A friend steps in, and says to the creditor, "I'll pay you the widow's debt;" he puts down the money, and the creditor hands him a slip of paper on which is written, "Received from Widow Blank the sum due, settled," with the creditor's signature affixed. The receipt is handed to the widow, and she feels very happy *because* she knows that her debt is paid. If you were to call that day, and say to the widow, "Do you *feel* that your debt is paid?" what would she say?

'Feel it! What do you mean? There is the receipted account. I don't *feel* that it's paid, but I feel very happy *because it is paid.*'

'Now, do you not see the difference? The feeling is all right, but I do not feel my sin pardoned. I know it, and hence feel happy.'

'But does it not say somewhere in Scripture that the Spirit beareth witness with our spirits?'

'Now, from the very fact that you speak so vaguely about "somewhere in Scripture," I fear that you do not know well what Scripture is. The Bible is not a number of texts strung together at random: it is a perfectly arranged whole. Truth in a wrong connexion is the worst kind of error. You find in Romans viii. 16, this most blessed and wondrous revelation from God, that "The Spirit itself beareth witness with our spirits, that we are the children of God." Mark carefully, this is not given as a ground to know that our sins are forgiven; but comes after the whole revelation of the truth concerning what we have done and what we are, and how our responsibilities are met. It comes after the triumphant assertion of Romans v. I, "Being justified by faith we have peace with God," and that crowning triumph after every question has been settled against us, "There is no condemnation" (Rom. viii. 1). At peace with God, and no condemnation, we now advance into our peculiar place among the creatures of God. Angels are at peace with God and have no condemnation, but they are only servants. Here is something additional, "We are SONS of God," Being taken from the swine-troughs, and getting food and raiment, we would therewith be content, glad that we were in the house at all, even among the servants. But higher than servants are we become, even sons. We may well pause, and say, is this presumption? Dare I say that all things are mine? that I am a child, a son, an heir of God? Yes! indeed you may; the Spirit has been sent to dwell with you and to be in you, as coming from the throne revealing to your spirit (which can now discern spiritual things) that, without presumption, you may lay claim to the title, the relationship, of son of God, heir of God, and joint-heir with Christ. That Spirit is within every believer, and seals only saved ones. He quickens the unsaved. God has sent forth this testimony, and he that is a believer has the "testimony in himself" (1 John v. 10). The important point I wish you to see is this, that the Holy Ghost is never said to bear witness to me, by any internal feeling, that I am at peace with God. It is after a man knows he is saved man that then there is a step further shewn him — namely, that he is a son. He is not only out of prison: he is set at the table of the King, whom he calls "Abba," that is, Father.'

'I quite understand the distinction, but I never saw it before; but if I could know that I was at peace with God I would be quite satisfied.'

'Yes, but God would not; however, this is the first point for you to know — "being justified by *faith* we have peace with God," not by the *feeling* of faith.'

'But don't some people feel it while others do not?'

'Not at all. What I am contending for is, that the forgiveness of sins is a thing that can be felt by no one: and, unless the knowledge of it is founded on the word of God, and that alone, for every one, individually, it will be sinking sand for a deathbed. Scores of anxious people have been deluded into the idea that they knew the gospel when some pleasing emotion passed through their minds. When Satan sees people awakened, and that he cannot keep them quiet, he takes his stand beside the preacher of the gospel, and while he is inviting them to the rock, Satan pushes out planks of feeling. A drowning man will catch at a straw, and the poor troubled one finds a little relief in resting on some plank of quietness of conscience, till storms rage, and then he finds himself with nothing beneath him. I am therefore suspicious when a person tells me he is "a little better." If he does not believe the gospel, he has no right to be any better, and if he has taken the good news to himself, he is entitled to be at perfect peace.'

'Then you don't allow of any feeling?'

'Most certainly I do: but what am I warranted to feel? If I could tell you that you were saved, and you believed it, would you not feel happy?'

'Of course I would.'

'This is what I feel — whenever I say to myself, "I'm saved," don't I feel happy? And the more I realise that my knowledge that I am saved depends only on God's word, the more happy I become.'

'Is there nothing about this "feeling saved" in the Bible?'

'Indeed, there is not. You can easily satisfy yourself by turning to a concordance. Never once is the word put beside "salvation," "forgiveness," or, in fact, anything about a man's peace with God, but we find, in Luke i. 77, that part of John's commission is declared to be "to give KNOWLEDGE of salvation," and in many parts of Scripture we find "knowing our sins forgiven," "knowing in whom we have believed," "knowing we have passed from death to life," "knowing we are born of God." Did Abraham feel he was to have a son when he was so old? No! but he knew it. And how did he know it? Because God said it. He felt glad because he knew it, because he believed what God said. It is really because people do not believe that God means exactly what he says, that we see so many intelligent men who cannot say whether they are saved or not.'

'But I have often thought that I had received Christ and trusted in Him alone; but I find my faith so incapable of producing effects.'

'But did you start saying "I'm saved," before trying to do anything?'

'Oh no! I was always waiting for fruits.'

'Fruits of what? fruits of doubt? Suppose you had got the right fruits, would you then have believed you were saved?'

'Oh yes!'

'That is to say, you would trust the fruits you brought forth rather than God's word — not for your salvation, but for your knowledge of it. But you must be saved, and know you are saved, before one acceptable fruit can be brought forth — else the works are legal. All evangelical obedience is done by a man who is saved, and who does it because he knows that he is saved.'

'Then am I to do nothing?'

'Absolutely and literally nothing. You must take salvation exactly as the thief on the cross did. He could not turn over a new leaf; his last wretched leaf had been turned in reviling his Saviour. He could not do any work for God, for there was a nail through each hand; he could not run in the way of God's commandments, for there was a nail through his feet. And until you stand still and realise that there is a nail through all your self-righting activity, and a nail through all your carnal agility, and accept salvation for nothing, knowing that you are saved simply on the authority of the bare Word of God, you will never be saved. We do not look inward to what we feel, nor outward to what we do — but to the Son of man lifted up, and to God's account of how well He is pleased with Jesus.'

'Well, I think I see what you mean, and it clears up a real difficulty. I am not to examine to see if I *feel* better, *feel* saved, *feel* forgiven, or *feel* happy; but here is the next difficulty —how am I to know it?'

'I will remember that when I began trying to feel converted, I felt myself becoming worse and worse, and my heart getting further and further from peace. Then I began to study this and that theological question. I knew all about what Calvinism and Arminianism were — studied my Bible till I knew its contents pretty well, but at last I found I was not on the right track for salvation at all. I was thinking that salvation came *intellect-wise*, and not *faith-wise*.'

'But a man cannot be saved apart from his understanding?'

'Most certainly not, no more than he can be saved against his will; but the eyes of his understanding must be enlightened, that he may be made willing to receive the gift of salvation in God's way. You see if God had made His salvation dependent upon education or intellect, he would have left the great mass without the chance of salvation until they were tutored up to the requisite point; but as there is *one salvation* for high and low, rich and poor, educated and ignorant, so there is *one method* of receiving it, and of course that must be according to the standard of the most unlearned. Hence the truth of the remark that a friend made to me, "Intellect never helped me to Christ, but it often hindered me."

'I was trying to explain this (which I believe to be of the greatest importance) to some poor people, and I tried to illustrate it in this way. If, in travelling by rail, I had a first-class ticket, I could travel one part of the journey in a first-class carriage, another part in a second, and another in a third, and the railway officials could find no fault; but, if I had only a third-class ticket, I must remain in the third from beginning to end. Thus, in regard to salvation, the educated man can come to the uneducated man's platform; the uneducated cannot rise to his: therefore it is on the common platform on which ALL men can stand that God treats concerning salvation.

'This is the great difficulty; this is why not many great, not many wise, and not many noble can afford to come low enough among the common run of people, to take a guilty sinner's place, receive a lost sinner's Saviour, and rejoice in a condemned sinner's pardon. This is why Christ taught that men had to become like little children before they could get into the kingdom of heaven.'

'I see the justice of your remarks; but tell me, now, how am I to get into the Kingdom?'

'As you said before, you know that it is *of grace* — that is to say, God is waiting to give it to you *all for nothing*, without a feeling in payment, without a prayer as the condition of it, just as the widow's friend dealt with her debt. That it might be of grace, it was made to be by *faith*, not by *attainment* either in intellect or feeling. This is the impression that has been sometimes left upon my mind, after having heard the gospel stated—that faith is the condition which God has demanded from the sinner, in order that he may be saved — that the great Physician will heal the most wretched, sin-burdened soul, but he must receive faith as his *fee*. Now this, as you have no doubt found, would be the most difficult of all fees to procure. Feeling is hard to get up, but faith is harder. Faith is the mere apprehension of grace — thankfully accepting what God has already freely given. Faith puts God in the chief room as the giver, it being more blessed to give than to receive, and lets him do everything, man being the silent and passive receiver of blessing. Faith has to do, not with what I feel toward God, but what God feels toward me, what He has done for me, and what He has told me. Faith does not look into its own formation —it looks out to God's provided substitute for the sinner. Faith does not tell me to *feel* that I am converted, but it fixes me down to the Word of God. Faith tells me to take God at His word. Faith has not to do with what I am thinking of myself, bad or good, but it lets God think for me.

'Two things are to be distinguished, "salvation" and the "knowledge of salvation," First, How am I to get saved? and then, How am I to know it?

'First, then, my *salvation* depends solely and entirely upon the work, the *person*, of Jesus Christ our Lord. (My salvation is supported by His work; His work is supported by His person.)

'Secondly, the *knowledge* that I am saved depends solely on the record, the *word*, the testimony of God. "He that believeth not God, hath made Him a liar, because he believeth not the record (testimony) that God gave of His Son." A man is saved on account of Christ having died in his place, the moment that he accepts Christ; he knows that he is saved whenever he believes the record that God gave of His Son."

'Well now, tell me shortly what "believing in the Lord Jesus Christ is." Of course I believe He is able and willing to save anybody, His atonement is sufficient, and His offer free and full; but how is He to become mine?'

'What is it to believe in a man? What is it to believe in a bank? You do not believe in one who is in the black list — but you can look around and say to yourself, "Well, I believe in so and so," and it is just the same with Christ: I believe in Him — not merely in His historical existence — but I trust Him, I received, I rest upon, Him alone for my salvation.'

'In a word, then, what should I do? I am wishing to take God's way, and willing now to do it. When I begin to go through trains of thought, I feel I get confused, and I should just like to know in a sentence what my path ought to be.'

'*Take the lost sinner's place, and* CLAIM *the lost sinner's Saviour!*'

'"Will the claim be allowed?'

'Yea, God commands thee to claim Him.'

'Can I claim Him?'

'Only a lost sinner can.'

'I am allowed, urged, besought, commanded to take Jesus as mine; surely I have nothing to lose — yea, Lord, I believe Thee, Jesus is mine.'

'I take comfort from the fact that my sins were laid on Christ — I do not *feel* they were there, but God says it — "He was wounded for *our* transgressions; not for those of angels — they had none; not for those of *devils* — they can claim no Saviour; but for those who take the *sinner's* place — "The chastisement of *our* peace was *upon* Him." Therefore it would be unjust to lay it on me believing in Him. He is a real Saviour for real sinners. My only qualification for such a Saviour is that I am such a sinner. And now I believe my sins are not on me — not because I feel them gone, for I do not, but because God says they were laid on Christ.' (Isaiah Iiii. 6).

Robert M'Cheyne[4] says, 'We must not close with Christ because we *feel* Him, but because *God has said it*, and we must take God's word even in the dark.' We do not *feel* we have faith. We accept God's way of dealing with sin.

Man would try to settle God's claims. God Himself has settled the claims, and offers the settled account for nothing. Man would try to make his peace with God. God has come and '*made peace*,' Christ Himself becoming '*our peace*,' and now He '*preached peace*' for the acceptance of all (Eph. ii. 14–17). Most anxious inquirers seem to think that we have to fight against ourselves in order to be saved, whereas we fight against ourselves because we are saved. We have a race to run, but it is not to the cross, it is *from* the cross. Man's way is to believe because we *feel*: God's way is to feel because we believe, and believe because God has said it. Dr. Chalmers[5] says, 'Yet come the enlargement when it will, it must, I admit, come after all through the channel of a simple credence giving to the *sayings of God*, accounted true and faithful sayings. And never does light and peace so fill my heart as when like a little child, I take up the lesson, that God hath laid on His own Son the iniquities of us all.'

Take the lost sinner's place, and claim the lost sinner's Saviour.

---

[4] Editor's Note: Robert Murray M'Cheyne (1813–1843) was a minister in the Church of Scotland from 1835 to 1843 and designed a widely used system for reading through the Bible in one year.

[5] Editor's Note: Thomas Chalmers (1780–1847) was the first Moderator of the Free Church of Scotland after the Disruption, when the preaching of the gospel was the exception in the Church of Scotland. He was at the center of recovery that brought the churches in Scotland from the influence of Modernism to the truth of the gospel.

DO YOU FEEL YOUR SINS FORGIVEN?

No *works of law* have we to boast —
By nature ruined, guilty, lost,
Condemned already; but Thy hand
Provided what Thou didst demand:
We take the guilty sinner's name,
The guilty sinner's Saviour claim.

No *faith* we bring. "Tis Christ alone —
"Tis what He is, what He has done.
He is for us as given by God,
It was for us He shed His blood.
We take the guilty sinner's name,
The guilty sinner's Saviour claim.

We do not *feel* our sins are gone,
But *knew* it from Thy word alone;
We know that Thou our sins didst lay
On Him who has put sin away:
We take the guilty sinner's name,
The guilty sinner's Saviour claim.

Because we *know* our sins forgiven,
We happy feel: our home is Heaven.
O help us now as sons, our God,
To tread the path that Jesus trod:
We take the guilty sinner's name,
The guilty sinner's Saviour claim.

The Work of the Holy Spirit.

Our Comforter.

E are not saved *on account* of the Holy Ghost's work in us; we are saved *by means of* it. We are saved on account of Christ's work for us. The more the Spirit works within us the more shall we desire that work to go on; but the work of Christ on Calvary is finished, and this is our resting-place, our peace, our security. We never can (or never ought) here below to get satisfied with the work of the Spirit wrought within us, but we are satisfied with the work of Christ done for us, and this is eternal rest, this is faith. Many sadly confuse these two divine works. Anxious inquirers are constantly looking within to see what is going on there, instead of looking outward to what was done on Calvary. I wish to draw the reader's attention to three most precious operations of the Spirit of God as seen in the beginning of John's Gospel, —

First, *Born of the Spirit*; chap. iii. 5-8.
Second, *Indwelt by the Spirit*; chap. iv. 14.
Third, *Communicating the Spirit*; chap. vii. 3.

I. BORN OF THE SPIRIT.

Many think that regeneration, or the new birth or quickening, is a process that goes on subsequent to justification. This is a mistake. Regeneration neither goes before nor comes after justification, but is at the same time and is an instantaneous act performed by the Spirit of God, communicating the life of Christ to a man formerly dead in trespasses and sins and having nothing whatever in him that could be transformed into this new creation which He implants. There are two errors against which we must guard:

First, not recognizing or acknowledging the Spirit's special work in regeneration; and

Second, confusing or mixing this with Christ's work done for us.

1st, *It is by a special act of absolute grace that we are born again by the Spirit.* 'The wind bloweth where it listeth,' and so the Jewish Pharisee is compelled to allow God to act as a sovereign. What would be the use of Christ coming, living, dying for sin, rising beyond its doom, and His present intercession, unless the Holy Spirit were here applying to individuals that work, that life by the Word? It is not His influence merely, but Himself, who is now on earth. It is not His Word merely, blessed and essential as it is, but Himself, who applies that Word. Look at the feast in Luke xiv. If Christ had not come and died and risen, there would have been no feast to offer, but if the Holy Spirit were not here, none would come to the feast. So, the parable tells us, 'Compel them to come in;' and the Holy Ghost is the great compeller, making them willing. This is His special work on individuals, not His general work in the world. His work on the world is not in the way of *mercy* but of *conviction*.

In John xvi. 8, we read, when He is come He will *reprove* (ἐλέγξει, literally, *convict by proof* to its confusion) the world —

(1.) '*Of sin*,' because the great sin of which God holds man to be guilty is the crucifixion of His Son; and the presence of the Holy Ghost is the great proof of man's refusing Christ, for the rejected Christ has sent the Spirit, and His presence is continually crying, 'where is thy brother?' hence it is said, 'of sin, because they believe not on Me.'

(2.) '*Of righteousness.*' If man is an ungrateful sinner, God is a righteous God, and if sinful man gave his Saviour a cross of shame, a righteous God gave His Son a throne of glory. This is the great act of righteousness between God and the man Christ. 'Sit thou at My right hand until I make thine enemies thy footstool.' Ps. cx. 1. The presence of the Holy Ghost on the earth is the proof of the righteousness of God. Christ having perfectly glorified God, God glorifies Him as a matter of justice, crowns Him with glory and honour; and we see Him, not by the natural eye, for Christ is not yet manifested on His own throne, but in the interval between rejection and triumph, the Father in righteousness has set Him down on His throne, and sent down the Holy Ghost to testify that He is glorified; therefore it is said, 'of righteousness, because I go to my Father, and ye see me no more.'

(3.) '*Of judgment*,' because, since Satan could not hold Christ in death, a power stronger than Satan's must have appeared, whose power over death must therefore have been set aside and himself judged, for 'through death He destroyed Him that had the power of death, that is, the devil.' The Holy Ghost has come to tell us of this great act of judgment; because the very fact that he has come proves that Christ is risen and is in glory; and the fact that Christ has risen proves that Satan has been judged; and since Satan is 'the prince of this world,' the world has been judged, being set aside in its chosen head; therefore it is said, 'of judgment, because the prince of this world is judged.'

Such is the action of the Holy Ghost *on the world* to its confusion and shame: but His work in quickening is quite a distinct thing. He does not work on 'the old man' in me and make it better, and thus gradually save. He shews me that it cannot be mended. He shews me that I am 'guilty,' 'condemned already,' 'lost,' 'alienated,' 'evil only,' 'continually evil,' 'without God,' 'without hope,' 'without strength,' 'dead.'

I have heard men speak of a remaining spark in the bosom of the unregenerate that required merely to be fanned into a flame by the influences of the Holy Ghost. This is unscriptural (read Gen. vi. 5, &c.). I have heard such speak of a seed of good in every man which the Holy Ghost cultivates, and this they call the new birth. This is utter confusion, and an entire misconception of the figure. Man's co-operation in regeneration is not required, because he has no power to co-operate. He is dead. 'That which is born of the Spirit is spirit.' The work is altogether of God. As it was God who in His own heart before the foundation of the world, planned redemption, and as it was God in His Son who, eighteen hundred years ago, before we were born, secured our redemption, so it is God by His Spirit who now, without our endeavor, apart from our effort, applies this redemption. In fact, the first thing God does is *to make us willing*. How entirely is this work of God! He was alone in eternity; He was alone in creation; He was alone in redemption; He is alone in regeneration which is merely redemption applied. God does not *find* us children; He *makes* us children. But we must look now at another error.

2d. *Confounding the work of the Spirit in us with Christ's work for us*. While the Spirit of God is the sole agent, the truth of God is the sole instrument which he employs. We cannot see the Spirit; we can see the Word. We cannot see His operations: we can read His record about Christ. No doubt it will be merely letters without meaning, until He opens the eyes; but He works only in His appointed channel. He never tells us to look *inward* even to His own operations, for peace, but *outward to Christ*. That is the most Spirit-honouring preaching of the gospel in which you hear most of Christ. Once I heard a very earnest man preaching to anxious inquirers, and he was dwelling continuously and exclusively upon the Spirit's work — its signs and characteristics — with the effect of confusing many of his hearers. For who could obtain scriptural peace with God from what he felt? We get a healthful and heaven-born conflict by marking the Holy Ghost's operations within us, but never peace. This we get by gazing at the Lamb of God on Calvary. I thought, as I heard the preacher, 'I wonder if the holy Ghost would preach in that way if He were standing there,' and I immediately remembered, that 'He shall not speak of (from) Himself,' 'He shall testify of Me;' that is, He will preach Christ. 'He shall take of mine and shall shew it unto you.' 'He shall glorify Me.' This is spiritual preaching, because the preaching of the things of the Spirit, and as He Himself preaches. I believe the more we are depending on the Spirit's working, the more we shall preach what the Spirit wishes us to preach about, and look to Him to apply it. When we begin to point the anxious inquirer to the Spirit's work, this is not how the Spirit Himself would deal with him.

If I began to speak to a working man sitting down to his dinner, and said to him, 'Do you know the muscles employed in mastication?'

'What's that?' he would likely say.

'Well, in eating.'

'Indeed, I do not.'

'And you do not know the nerves that supply them?'

'I'm sure I do not.'

'And the beautiful mechanism and arrangement by which the food is converted into a bolus, and introduced into the stomach?'

'Now you are surely laughing at me.'

'Oh no, I'm not, but all that is most true and interesting; but tell me what do you know?'

'Well, sir, I know that I am hungry, and that this is a good dinner.'

This would be the common-sense and appropriate answer. Even the physiologist, when he is hungry, does not think much of *how* he eats. The two great points are, that he is hungry, and that he has a good dinner. Some are hungry and have not the good food, others have the food and are not hungry. But the qualification for enjoying food is not a knowledge of how to eat, but the being hungry. We do not need to know *how* we are born again in order to be saved. We do not need to know all or anything about the Spirit's work within us in order to get peace (there were people, in Acts xix. 2, who were believers, and who yet said, 'We have not so much as heard whether there be any Holy Ghost'), but we must know about Christ's work *for* us before we can be saved. The greatest physiologist might die of hunger. We might know everything about the Spirit's work, and yet be lost for ever, because we had not received and rested upon Christ offered to us in the gospel.

We are justified by *faith*, but the experience of what goes on within me is sensation, and not *faith*.

Some men seem to have a difficulty with anxious souls (believing them to be dead), to know what to advise them to do. It is the Spirit that quickeneth. Some, therefore, tell sinners at once to pray for the Spirit, thinking thus to simplify matters by reducing it to common-sense — as it seems very plain, since the Spirit quickens, nothing is easier than to cry for that Spirit. But it is not so easy, for a dead man cannot cry. Some, again, tell them to believe the record God gave of His Son — to believe in the Lord Jesus Christ. A dead man cannot speak, and, of course, a dead man cannot believe, so we are in an equal difficulty. Praying and believing are alike impossible with the unregenerate man, without the quickening of the Spirit of God. The great point is to find out what we are commanded to do, what our duty to do. It is to tell every man the good news, and press him instantly to believe it. It is the Spirit that is the agent, but he always uses the truth as the instrument, the truth about a crucified and now risen Christ. Faith does not come by feeling, trying, nor praying, but by *hearing*. The moment I accept Christ as my own individual, personal Saviour who put away my sin, I am warranted to believe that I am born again, and the Spirit in the new man will lust against the flesh in the old man. Peace, indeed, I have with God, that is, Christ, but no peace with myself. There is a faith that is human, and a faith that is Spirit-wrought. The plan is of God; the redemption, the truth, and the faith are all of God. But how can I know whether I have God-wrought faith? Does my faith take hold of what is going on within? That is not of God. Does my faith take hold of, is it taken up with, what was done eighteen hundred years ago on Calvary, and with Him who suffered there? This is God-honouring and saving faith. This is being born of the Spirit. The Spirit introduces by the truth, Christ as the life into my dead soul.

This is quickening, *the renewing* of the Holy Ghost. The Holy Ghost thus gives a *new* nature.

II. INDWELT BY THE SPIRIT.

In John iv. 14 we read of the indwelling of the Spirit 'as a well of water springing up into everlasting life.' This is said only of Christians. The Spirit of God dwells in none but in those whom He has quickened. And He *dwells* in all whom He has quickened (Rom. viii. 9). In some in greater measure than in others; but 'if any man have not the Spirit of Christ he is none of His.' Therefore, all who are Christ's have the Spirit dwelling in them. There is a danger here in *separating* Christ and the Spirit in us, as there is in regeneration of *confounding* Christ's work for me with the Spirit's work in me. It is as linked with Christ, a son as Christ is a son, and heir as Christ is, that the Spirit dwells in the believer, even as He dwelt in Christ, of course in Him without measure. It is thus we have *access*, for through Christ we have access by one Spirit to the Father. It is thus that we can *worship* the Father in spirit and in truth. This lesson he taught the poor confessed sinner at Sychar's well. It is thus that we are practically *sanctified*, more and more separated from evil, for He is the '*Holy*' Ghost, the 'Spirit of holiness.' It is thus we are *comforted and guided*; for Jesus said, If I go away I will send the Comforter (literally *paraclete*, which includes much more than comfort). This same word is used in 1 John ii. 1, for Christ the advocate (literally *paraclete*), one who looks after all our interests. And thus, as Christ looks after all our interests before God, so the other *paraclete* looks after all out interests as we are passing through the wilderness, the divine Servant leading us into all truth; for here again the truth is His channel.

Thus we *live* in the Spirit (all Christians being dead and risen with Christ), and the exhortation is founded on this, 'Let us also *walk* in the Spirit' (Gal. v. 25), principally as being connected with Christ and the members of His body, in every member of which the Spirit dwells. We are to walk in the Spirit, in the practical exercise of brotherly love, and not be *walking as men*. What! are we not *men*? No; we are sons of God indwelt by the Spirit. Men walk in selfishness. The walk in the Spirit is each esteeming another better than himself.

Thus we are '*led* of the Spirit' (Gal. v. 18). All Christian are led. This is not an exhortation, but a privilege. 'For as *many* as are led by the Spirit of God, they are the Sons of God,' and all believers are sons. But though in each Christian the Spirit dwells, the exhortation is given, 'Be filled with the Spirit' as with the air you breathe, so live in the presence of glory, in the light, in fellowship with Father and Son, and thus the atmosphere will be 'the Spirit.' He is spoken of as

1. *A witness*. (1 John v. 6.) He bears true witness, He tells the truth concerning Christ, He is a witness to Jesus Christ having come by water and blood; and every Christian has Him dwelling within him, as we also see in Rom. viii. a witness that we are sons. He is the witness of love and accomplished redemption.

2. *A seal*. As the goods are stamped by the purchaser after they are his own, so, after we believe, we are sealed. Only sons are sealed. The oil was put on the blood of the trespass offering. (Lev. xiv. 25, 28.) In the experience of many these go together; but many, especially in Apostolic days, though they knew their sins were forgiven, did not know they had eternal life. A quickened soul is not necessarily an emancipated soul.

3. *An earnest*. He is the earnest of our inheritance — that is, part of it that we possess now. The Israelites got the grapes from Eshcol while still in the desert. In Rom. viii. 17, we are children (the Spirit bearing witness), and as such sealed; 'but, if children, then heirs; heirs of God and joint-heirs with Christ.' Therefore, since He, as heir, has not taken the inheritance, we do not have it, but suffer now, having the earnest of the inheritance, until the redemption of the purchased possession. 'Ourselves also who have the first fruits of the Spirit, even we ourselves groan within

ourselves, waiting for the adoption, to wit the redemption of the body.' (Rom. viii. 23.)

III. COMMUNICATING THE SPIRIT.

In John vii. 38, we read, 'He that believeth on Me, out of his belly shall flow rivers of living water.' Thus those who have been quickened, and who are indwelt by the Spirit, are not the channels through which He is ministered to others. The waters once flowed from a smitten rock. The water flowed from Christ's wounded side, and it is only as we are smitten, exercised, subdued, that these rivers will flow from us. Only as we come thus to Christ, and drink, shall living waters flow from us. Alas! how little of the Spirit we see flowing from those professing to be quickened by the Spirit. Is it not because we are drawing little from the great fountainhead? 'Let him come unto Me and drink.' It is truly through saved sinners that God is now to send forth His river of life. 'The love of God is shed abroad in our hearts by the Holy Ghost.' And this love of God we are to point out in rivers in this arid desert as witnesses of God; first, by carrying the gospel to our fellow-sinners, and telling of that Christ whom we know, and who is offered to them; and, second, by ministering love to all the saints of God in building up and comforting them. And it is only as our own affections and thoughts, that is, all our inner man, is filled with the pure water from the fountain, that the rivers can flow.

In connection with the three operations of the Spirit of God which we have been considering, namely, *quickened, indwelt,* and *communicating,* we may look — 1st. At Christ himself; 2d. At the Church corporately; 3d. At each individual believer, —

1st. As quickened by the Spirit.

Christ was born of the Spirit. This was His incarnation as we read in the angel's answer to Mary in Luke i. 35. 'That holy thing which shall be born of thee shall be called the Son of God.' (Luke i. 35.) The meat-offering had to be mingled with oil. (Lev. ii. 4.)

The Church corporately in the *resurrection* of Christ. (Rom. i. 4; 1 Pet. i. 3.) He was quickened by the Spirit, as the head of the body. (1 Pet. iii. 18.)

The *individual* believer; when the Spirit applies the truth to his conscience. (James i. 18.) 'Of His own will begat He us with the word of truth.

2d. Indwelt by the Spirit.

Christ we see sealed with the Spirit when at His baptism, the Spirit, as a dove, rested on Him. The meat-offering had to be anointed with oil. (Lev. ii. 4.) 'Him hath God the father sealed.' (John vi. 27.)

The Church, we see at Pentecost, not merely quickened, but formed into a temple for God on the earth: the true temple, filled with the true glory. And we see this accomplished in fulfilment of Acts i. 8. 'Ye shall receive power after that the Holy Ghost is come upon you, and ye shall be witnesses *unto me* (1.) both in Jerusalem and in all Judea, (2.) and in Samaria, (3.) and unto the uttermost part of the earth. The Holy Ghost thus fell on,

1. The Jews, when they were *waiting in prayer* (Acts ii. 4), in obedience to Jesus' resurrection command, 'wait for the promise of the Father which ye have heard of Me.' (Acts i. 4.) They had heard of Him in John xiv. to xvi.

2. In Samaria, by the *laying on of the apostles' hands* (Acts viii. 17).

3. The Gentiles, in the *preaching of the Word* (Acts x. 44). And thus is the Spirit now given. In this latter method was the proper Gentile pentecost our pentecost. Thus it is in the preaching of the Word that we are to expect the blessing of the Spirit.

The individual is seen in his sealing: when by believing the record of the witness he receives his emancipation, his conscious liberty and peace with God, taking his place as a son, with the Holy Ghost as the testifier, and waiting with Him as the earnest of the inheritance.

3d. Communicating the Spirit.

Christ in His ministry and prophetic work communicated the Spirit.

The Church is seen communicating the Spirit, in the preaching of the apostles, at and subsequent to, Pentecost, in the Scriptures they have left, and all collective testimony from their day to this, that has been in accordance with the Word of God.

Individuals, in the outflow of love in our place, in the wilderness, as evangelists, teachers, pastors, or in any service to God.

[Each of these words, BORN, INDWELT, and COMMUNICATING, has its opposite severally in the three words spoken about the Spirit, RESIST, GRIEVE, and QUENCH.]

I. The Spirit may be *resisted*.

Acts vii. 51: 'Ye stiff-necked and uncircumcised in heart and ears, ye do always resist the Holy Ghost.' This is addressed to the unconverted who resist Him as a *quickener*.

II. The Spirit may be *grieved*.

Eph. iv. 30: 'Grieve not the Holy Spirit of God, whereby ye are sealed unto the day of redemption.' This is addressed only to saved people who can grieve Him as an *indwelling* Spirit. This shews what a friend He is to us. If you had committed some great sin, your mother would be grieved, your enemy would be rejoiced. You can grieve only a friend. What a touching appeal, fellow-believer! What will the consequence be? In love He will reprove. He will rebuke our consciences, until we are consciously cleansed, and He can again dwell in us ungrieved.

III. The Spirit may be *quenched*.

1 Thess. v. 19: 'Quench not the Spirit.' Many have been perplexed with this text, thinking that it had reference to the *indwelling* of the Spirit. You may grieve Him thus, but no believer can quench Him thus; 'For they shall never perish;' but the next verse, 'Despise not prophesyings,' explains it. A Christian cannot quench the Spirit in himself, but by refusing to allow Him to work from a fellow-Christian, he thus may quench Him. It is thus the Spirit in His communications who may be quenched.

As He can be resisted in His testimony which is His instrument in *quickening*, and grieved in His person as *indwelling*, so he can be quenched in His gifts as *communicating* life. If I despise the humblest channel that God has formed and filled to dispense His streams of life, and put a sluice upon their flow, I stop His testimony, I quench the Spirit. It has nothing whatever to do with the indwelling of the Spirit. That can never be quenched; for the foundation of God standeth sure. But what a solemn warning in this day of self-seeking and pretensions! *Resist* is the word applied to the unconverted. *Grieve* is that applied to the individual Christian. *Quench* is that which has reference to the saints when gathered together, waiting on the Spirit.

The sin against the Holy Ghost has often been spoken about. All sin is against the Holy Ghost. What Christ spoke about in such solemn and awful words in Matt. xii., was '*blasphemy* against the Holy Ghost,' and if the context is looked at it will be seen that this blasphemy consisted in giving Satan the credit of doing what was known to be God's work.

Bring your ignorance to the holy Spirit, the great teacher, who by his precious truth will lead you into all truth.

> No, not the love without the blood;
>   That were to me no love at all;
> It could not reach my sinful soul,
>   Nor hush the fears which me appal.
>
> I need the love, I need the blood,
>   I need the grace, the cross, the grave,
> I need the resurrection-power,
>   A soul like mine to purge and save.
>
> Love that condemns the sinner's sin,
>   Yet, in condemning, pardon seals;
> That saves from righteous wrath, and yet,
>   In saving, righteousness reveals.
>
> Love boundless as Jehovah's self,
>   Love holy as His righteous law,

Love unsolicited, unbought,
   The love proclaimed on Golgotha.

This is the love that calms my heart,
   That soothes each conscience-pang within,
That pacifies my guilty dread,
   And frees me from the power of sin.

The love that blotteth out each stain,
   That plucketh hence each deadly sting,
That fills me with the peace of God,
   Unseals my lips and bids me sing.

The love that liberates and saves,
   That this poor straitened soul expands,
That lifts me to the heaven of heavens,
   The shrine above not made with hands.

The love that quickens into zeal,
   That makes me self-denied and true,
That leads me out of what is old,
   And brings me into what is new;

That purifies and cheers and calms,
   That knows no change and no decay,
The love that loves for evermore,
   Celestial sunshine, endless day.

'Heaven Opened.'

Our Study.

'So He drove out the man.' — GEN. iii. 24.

HE gates have closed that guard the way to the tree of life. The flaming sword turns every way, so that no flesh can approach and live. Man has sinned. God is righteous. Well might angels weep as they beheld such a sight. HEAVEN IS SHUT. God dwells in His secret place. Thunders and lightnings are round about Him. Clouds of thickest darkness hides Him from man. The blood of Abel's Lamb, the rejection of Cain's first-fruits, attest the fact. Heaven is shut. The blood-sprinkled door-posts, the thousands of altars, the myriads of bleeding victims, the smoke ever ascending from the fires of judgment, the unceasing priestly work, all proclaim heaven's doors are shut.

But *promise* shone through the dark cloud of *judgment*, and the glory of One coming to deliver was revealed; and while the captive Israelite sat in his desolation beside the ruins of Chebar he wrote, "The heavens were opened, and I saw visions of God." (Ezek. i. 1.) Thus we see heaven opened concerning,

1. CHRIST IN PROPHECY.

And it is God who opens, it is God who shews the visions. The visions were about the glory of God and His relation to Israel, the cloud, the chariot of His glory then departing as with winds and wheels from His dwelling on earth. His ancient people are seen scattered and broken, but the heavens do not close (in vision) until again the glory of God fills the temple, and besides the whole earth is filled with His glory, and heaven and earth are finally united under the righteous sway of the Prince of Peace, the coming deliverer. May He hasten that glorious day!

2. CHRIST IN OBEDIENCE.

But turn now to another scene, — Matt. iii. 16. In Jordan's waters stands a spotless, perfect Man, in the place where the godly Jews confessed sin in the baptism of repentance. Grace (not sin) has brought Him hither, that He might fulfil all righteousness, and when He came as the perfect servant in the sinner's place, 'LO, THE HEAVENS WERE OPENED unto Him, and He saw the Spirit of God descending like a dove, and lighting upon Him; and lo, a voice from heaven, saying, This is My beloved Son, in whom I am well pleased.' This is heaven opening on Christ in obedience.

Jesus Christ was the only perfectly obedient man that earth has seen. Never had earth beheld such a sight, the glorious sun had never before risen on such a day. God is looking down from an opened heaven upon a Man, and on that Man His eye can rest with perfect satisfaction, perfect complacency. .God declares Him to be His Son. As Man, He is anointed for His work with the seal of the Father. The Holy Ghost descends on the meek, the lowly, the obedient One. He Himself is the Person on whom the *heavens open*. The Father testifies of Him; the Holy Ghost testifies of Him; the eyes of the believing ones are turned towards Him. On no other object in the God-hating, God-rejecting world, could God's eye have rested. The Spirit, like the dove of Noah, looked over all the waste of waters, and found no rest but on the ark. He was the solitary witness for God in this world which He had made: so if the scene is an opened heaven and God looking down upon the earth, the sole attraction there is Jesus, the Son of God, the Son of man.

> 'It is the Father's voice that cries,
> 'Mid the deep silence of the skies,
> This, this is my beloved Son,
> In Him I joy, in Him alone.'

Again, we read of heaven being opened (John i. 51) in connection with

3. CHRIST IN GOVERNMENT.

Here we have an intimation of the future righteous and peaceful government of earth united with heaven under the Son of man — where Jesus Himself says, 'Verily, verily I say unto you, hereafter ye shall see HEAVEN OPEN, and the angels of God ascending and descending upon the Son of man.' Nathanael, the representative of the godly Jews, had confessed Him to be the Son of God and king of Israel; and Jesus now told him that those who received Him, when He was on earth, should see yet greater things than those which had convinced him; and further, they should see *heaven open*, and He who had come down to be the *Son of Man*, the Man of sorrows, should, in that name, be the object of the ministry of God's highest creatures. This will be true in all its fulness to those of Israel whom Nathanael represented, in a coming day. Meantime, we see heaven open, and all the ministry between heaven and earth carried on through Him. Our thoughts are taken back to Jacob at his 'Bethel' (Gen. xxviii. 12), where, from his pillow of stone, a ladder reached to heaven, on which angels ascended and descended, and we see Jesus uniting earth to heaven, for He has been raised up and set at His father's right hand; and in Him we are raised from the grave of earth to the seats in heaven, quickened together with Christ, raised up together and made to sit in heavenly places in Him. The scene is changed, but the object to which all eyes are turned is the same. An opened heaven no longer looks upon the Son of God in humiliation, but upon that same Son of man uniting heaven and earth, God and His creature, and on Him as the object of the ministry of the angelic hosts. Blessed time for this poor groaning, misgoverned earth! Then will be known the full power of the Lord of hosts, who has said that He will 'open unto you the windows of heaven, and pour out a blessing, that there shall not be room enough to receive it' (Mal. iii. 10). Meantime, we gladly take rejection with Him, until He sits on His own throne, for if we suffer with Him, we shall also reign. Our next spectacle of an open heaven is the sample of what an open heaven sees now on earth, and our place here under the kings of the earth who are plotting against the Lord and His anointed. Heaven is opened on

4. CHRIST IN THE GLORY OF GOD.

To the rejected disciple (Acts vii. 55). 'Stephen being full of the Holy Ghost, looked up steadfastly unto heaven, and saw the glory of God, and Jesus standing on the right hand of God, and said, behold, I see the HEAVENS OPENED, and the Son of man standing on the right hand of God.' Man had rejected Christ; God had taken Him to His own right hand. Man, in his most inveterate hatred of God, had sent out of the world the only Person in it on whom God's eye could gaze with complacency. Heaven can open now upon nothing on this earth. When it opens it is itself the scene; but the object to the mind of God, and to the believer full of the Holy Ghost, is still the same Jesus. Stephen was being sent after his Master. The Third Person of the Trinity in him was being rejected as the Second Person had been at the cross. The Son of man would still *stand* to return, until His testimony had been rejected; He is now set down waiting till His enemies are made His footstool. What a glorious sight to the believer in testimony, in rejection, in martyrdom! He sees not the stones, he hears not the derisive shout, he beholds not the fiendish gesture, "he sees *heaven opened.*" (Heaven opened *on* Jesus; it opens *to* us.) So it is with us now: whatever enmity of men or devils may be around us, faith now sees heaven opened and Jesus at the right hand of God for us. It is no longer the eye of God delighting to look through an opened heaven upon His Son on earth, it is the Christian himself looking from earth into an opened heaven, and seeing all the glory of God, and better than all the glory, and above the highest of even God's heavenly glories, 'the Son of man,' there for him.

Never before had such a sight been seen, a glorified MAN at God's right hand. Prophets had spoken of it — but here is the fact. Glory was native to heaven — but now we see the *Son of man* in the glory of God. What a gospel for every sinner, for every son of man, did Stephen preach, when, filled with the Spirit, he told out that heaven was opened, and the Son of man there! Is my reader a weak and trembling one, and can hardly dare to think that he is saved, and quite conscious that he has never been filled with the Holy Ghost? Listen to the glorious good news that God Himself has commanded to be told to every one: *heaven is opened* — the veil is rent — God's hand has done it; not open now for God to look on us merely, but open for us to look upon God. The gates of Eden have been opened —Christ is the Door — and further, the *Son of man* is there. As Son of God He never required to leave, and go back to, that glory; but as Son of man He never would have been there unless God had been vindicated — God had been glorified in the putting away of sin — sin that lay upon man — the sin of the world. "It is finished." This is God's good news; a quickened sinner, and open heaven, and an exalted Substitute! This is the ground of my peace. Not what I *feel* — not the suppression of God-dishonouring thoughts — not success in the conflict—not growth in grace — not the feeling of an indwelling Spirit—not a growing more like God — but the sure testimony of God to an open heaven and the Son of man before Him. What more do we need than what God has done? The tombs are rent as if to show that the sinner is to meet God now in life, in resurrection, therefore Stephen, a poor sinner, stands filled with the Holy Ghost. The veil is rent to show that the way into the holiest of all is now made manifest, therefore, heaven is open to the believing sinner. The Lord is risen, and is at the right hand of God, and He is there the Son of man for me. An unveiled God, an opened tomb, a glorified Son of man — what more, dear trembling soul, do you want? The natural eye has never seen this; faith alone, by the Holy Ghost, beholds such a glory. Light from earth has never pierced the midnight darkness in which God is enveloped. The flaming sword still turns every way to guard "the tree of life," but where it fell; there is no entrance into Paradise but by the Door. There is no mercy to sinners but in Christ. The world knew not the darkness in which God wrapped His Son, when on the cross He was dealing with sin. The last hour of light the world had was spent in wagging their heads at, and spitting upon the Light of Life. No unquickened man saw Jesus in resurrection (Acts x. 41). Faith alone can see Jesus thus; the self-emptied sinner alone can rest, where God has found rest, in the glorified Son of man.

Again we see heaven opened. In Acts x. 11, Peter 'saw *heaven opened*, and a certain vessel descending unto him as it had been a great sheet, knit at the four corners, and let down to the earth.' Heaven is opened to explain the mystery of

5. THE CHURCH FORMED.

The Church of God had been hid in God. It is not according to earthly and Jewish distinctions of clean and unclean. It is not according to the thought that the Moabite and Ammonite should not come into the Israelitish congregation of God. This was true (Neh. xiii. 1) — is true, and ever shall be true. But, here is something new. The middle wall of partition is broken down, and there is neither Jew nor Gentile. This was never revealed nor prophesied about before. The Gentile was to be blessed, but immediately through the Jew, and that will yet take place. Peter saw clean and unclean on an equality, not the unclean benefited by the clean. Those that were far off, and those that were nigh, that is, the Jews, nationally separated to God, and the Gentiles outside of God's calling, all now stand equally guilty, and equally to be blessed by God. To Peter had been given the Keys of the Kingdom (not of the Church), and he opened the door first to the Jews in his sermon in Acts ii. at Pentecost; and then, after this heaven-given vision, to the Gentiles, in the person of the centurion (Acts x. 44), and since the door has thus been opened, equally to both, no national distinction recognized, this key is no longer necessary. We now have the Holy Ghost sent down from heaven. This is the vision of the true dwelling place of God on the earth — the body of Christ. The middle wall of partition between Jew and Gentile was broken down, and his servants were sent to gather out of every nation, kindred, and tongue, His Church, which is to consist of all kinds of saved sinners, that in the ages to come 'He might show the exceeding riches of His grace.' May we be thus living on Christ, and thus doing His will — partners in His work of ingathering now, soon to be with Him in the glory above! For again do we see heaven opened on

6. THE CHURCH SEATED.

'After, this, I looked, and behold a door was opened in heaven. And the first voice which I heard...said, Come up hither, and I will show thee things which must be hereafter (Rev. iv. 1, &c.).' In the apocalyptic vision, John had seen the Son of man in glory, as the first of the three great divisions of the vision (Rev. i. 19). He had also seen God's Church history—'the things that are' — the second great division, in the history of the seven Churches (Rev. ii. iii.). And he is now to behold 'the things which must be hereafter' as the third division. But the Church represented in the throned elders has been caught up (1 Thess. iv.), and is now seen seated with Christ on thrones (Rev. iv.) before all the judgment is poured out. They shall judge the world. They are like Abraham, the friend of God, apart from

Sodom, hearing all that is to fall on Sodom. This is what we are waiting for, to be caught up to meet the Lord in the air, and to be set with Him on His throne (Rev. iii. 21). What a contrast to the martyred Stephen! This is the Church triumphant, that was the Church militant. Well may we praise the Lord for this little glimpse into an opened heaven, for He would have our hearts to rest on the blessed thought that we shall be enthroned around the crowned Jesus, before He comes to execute His wrath. For this is not all: — Again heaven will be opened, not in the vision of prophecy, not on the meek, lowly Jesus, not on His suffering people, nor to show His calmly seated Church, but to show

7. CHRIST AND HIS SAINTS IN JUDGMENT.

He comes with myriads of His saints. Christ with the Church is now seen rising up in the exercise of judgment, as John says in Rev. xix. 11 — 'I saw HEAVEN OPENED, and behold a white horse; and He that sat upon him was called Faithful and True, and in righteousness He doth judge and make war. His eyes were as a flame of fire, and on His head were many crowns; and He had a name written, that no man knew but He Himself. And He was clothed with a vesture dipped in blood: and His name is called the WORD OF GOD (John i. 1). And the armies in heaven followed Him upon white horses, clothed in fine linen, white and clean. And out of His mouth goeth a sharp sword, that with it He should smite the nations: and he shall rule them with a rod of iron; and He treadeth the winepress of the fierceness and wrath of Almighty God. And He hath on His vesture and on His thigh a name written KING OF KINGS, AND LORD OF LORDS.' Such is the awful opening of Heaven upon a God-dishonouring earth, when the rejected, crucified Son of man shall disperse the midnight darkness in which this earth is wrapped, by the flash of his judgment-sword. That funeral pall of blackest dye which has hung over this doomed world from the sixth hour of that most awful crucifixion day, shall be torn asunder by His hand when He executes judgment. Then will be seen, not the deluge of water, as when, in Gen. vii. 11. the window of heaven were opened, but wrath from heaven, the wrath of the Lamb. What a day! what a reality! The book of mercy closed! Christ risen up! the door shut! The sword unsheathed! How the scene is changed! No longer humiliation — no longer angelic ministry — no longer His martyred followers; but His fierce vengeance — His own right hand — His own sword girt on His thigh — His now triumphant co-heirs riding forth in victory, and breaking to pieces all before Him. Still the object is Jesus the WORD of God. For it is Christ Himself who is our study, let Him be on earth, in heaven, or joining earth to heaven, rejected or reigning, suffering or subduing. That same pierced brow which wore the thorny crown is now to be decked with many crowns, for,

> 'The crowns that are now round the false one's brow
> Shall be worn by earth's rightful Lord.'

That same pierced hand shall draw the sword from its scabbard; those same wounded feet shall press the snowy clouds, and 'every eye shall see Him, and they also that pierced Him: and all kindreds of the earth shall wail because of Him.' God Himself breaks the silence; everything is now felt by every one to be REAL. The oft-rejected Christ is seen to be real; the scorned judgment is seen to be real; an open heaven is seen to be real; an eternal hell is seen to be real; the winepress of the fierceness and wrath of Almighty God is seen to be real; the wrath of the Lamb is seen to be real.

Flee from the wrath to come, and study Jesus who has opened heaven, and who is all the glory within an open heaven.

> Heaven was opened — Jesus came;
> He revealed the Father's name.
>   Took our place to bear our load,
> God has owned Him from above,
> Sent the Spirit, like a dove,
>   Sealed Him and with Him abode. — MATT. iii. 10.

Heaven is opened — Lo! we see
Christ who died upon the tree
    Joining earth to heaven above — JOHN i. 51.
Angels, servants from the throne,
Blessings bring through Him alone;
    Richest token of His love.
Heaven is opened — glorious day
Jesus hath put sin away;
    Men of every tongue and race,
Jew and Gentile, bond and free,
All are welcome equally, — ACTS x. 11.
    All may share God's matchless grace.

Heaven is opened — Christ has gone
Into heaven, His work is done;
    Him we follow, Him alone.
He whom men have crucified,
Son of man now glorified, — ACTS vii. 55.
    Sits upon His Father's throne.

Heaven is opened — on the throne
See the One whom men disown — REV. iv. xi.
    Now the judge of quick and dead.
Lo! the temple, Christ the light,
He who by His wondrous might
    Bruised forever Satan's head.

Heaven will open yet again — REV xix. 11.
We with Him shall judge and reign.
    Every eye shall see His face;
Proud rebellious men shall quail,
Nations, kindreds, all shall wail,
    All who scorned His truth and grace.

Triumph and Conflict.

Our State.

'S sorrowful, yet always rejoicing.' — Such was Paul's experience (2 Cor. vi. 10). The saved man is a great mystery to the unsaved; happy yet sad; triumphing, yet troubled; having no sin on him, and yet having sin in him; having no condemnation, and still having fearful conflict. Saved now, yet working out his salvation, and waiting for salvation. Even among saved man themselves there is great misunderstanding. Some are engaged more with the triumph side, others with the conflict side of a Christian's experience. We find both most fully brought out in Scripture, each having its own place and importance. The Christian's conflict takes rise and character from his triumph. We get much instruction by looking at the illustrations of a believer's triumph, walk, and conflict, as contained in the figures of the Old Testament; for we know that 'Whatsoever things were written aforetime were written for our learning, that we through patience and comfort of the Scriptures might have hope' (ROM. xv. 4). Let us look at Israel's history. We find the Israelites

I. Sheltered by blood from God's hand in judgment in Egypt, and testifying for God in the midst of godlessness.

2. Redeemed by power. Taken through the Red Sea by the power of God's might, and living by faith in the wilderness.

3. Entered into their possessions, and in Canaan fighting the battles of the Lord. Let us look at these in detail.

I. — SHELTERED BY BLOOD.

THE ISRAELITE IN EGYPT.

The Lord spake unto Moses and Aaron in the land of Egypt, saying, 'This month shall be unto you the beginning of months: it shall be the first month of the year to you. Speak ye unto all the congregation of Israel, saying, In the tenth day of this month they shall take to them every man a lamb…Your lamb shall be without blemish, a male of the first year…And they shall take of the blood and strike it on the two side posts and on the upper door post of the houses wherein they shall eat it…For I will pass through the land of Egypt this night, and will smite all the first born in the land of Egypt, both man and beast, and against all the gods of Egypt I will execute judgment: I am Jehovah. And the blood shall be to you for a token upon the houses where you are, and *when I see the blood I will pass over you*, and the plague shall not be upon you, to destroy you, when I smite the land of Egypt.' (Exodus xii.) In Egypt the Israelite had thus a triumph and had also a conflict.

1. *Triumph.* — He rejoiced because he trusted to the blood on the lintel, and to the word of his Jehovah God, who had said, 'when I see the blood I will pass over you.' So the Christian in this world rejoices, not in the thought that he is pure and sinless, but in the fact that Christ died for his sins. We see this fully explained in the Epistle to the Romans, iii. 21 to v. 11.

God could pass over because the blood was on the lintel.
The Israelite could rejoice because he believed God.
Thus God can now justify the ungodly.

'When I see the blood I will pass over you' (Exod. xii. 13).
'Being now justified by His blood' (Rom. v. 9).

The believer can rejoice being at peace with God.

'The blood shall be to you for a token' (Exod. xii. 13).
'Being justified by faith we have peace with God' (Rom. v. 1).

Sheltered by blood, we feast upon the roasted Lamb with bitter herbs, unleavened bread, and in the pilgrim garb — at perfect peace, for 'it is Christ that died.'

>   Heirs of Salvation,
>   Chosen of God;
>   Past condemnation,
>   Sheltered by blood.
> Even in Egypt feed we on the Lamb,
> Keeping the Statutes of God the I AM.
>   In the world around 'tis night
>   Where the feast is spread 'tis bright,
>   Israel's Lord is Israel's light.
> 'Tis Jesus, 'tis Jesus, our Saviour from above,
> 'Tis Jesus, 'tis Jesus, 'tis Jesus whom we love.

2. *Conflict.* — There would have been *an unscriptural conflict* in Egypt, if an Israelite had tried by any and every means to put off the hand that was crying for blood, except by God's own ordained means, the blood on the lintel; the acceptance of God's estimate of the value of the blood that he himself had appointed. This unscriptural conflict we find in modern times, in man's efforts by prayers and religiousness, and penances, and sorrows, to live a good *life,* when God is demanding the *death* of the sinner for his sins. And how often do we see the sad spectacle of a man in a condemned world trying to get up religion or devotion, or anything else to meet the wrath of God against his sins, when he is condemned already! This is the state of man as depicted in Rom. i. 18, to iii. 20.

But there is a *scriptural conflict* — namely, the conflict against

THE WORLD.

The Christian presents a strange anomaly that cannot be seen perfectly in the figure of an Israelite sheltered by blood in Egypt. He has been taken entirely out of Egypt, and yet he is sent back to Egypt, as Jesus said to His Father in John xvii. 18, concerning His followers, 'As thou hast sent Me into the world, even so have I also sent them into the world.' According to the illustration, every Christian in one aspect, and a very practical aspect, is still in Egypt, that is the world 'which spiritually is called Egypt where also our Lord was crucified' (Rev. xi. 8). So Jesus prayed: — 'I pray not that thou shouldest take them out of the world, but that thou shouldest keep them from the evil' (John xvii. 15). Being thus in the world and not of it, with souls saved, but with bodies still liable to disease and death, and all creation under the curse, 'We that are in this tabernacle do groan being burdened, not for that we would be unclothed but clothed upon that mortality might be swallowed up in life' (2 Cor. v. 4). And 'we know that the whole creation groaneth and travaileth in pain together until now. And not only they, but ourselves also which have the first fruits of the Spirit, even we ourselves groan within ourselves waiting for the adoption, to wit the redemption of our body' (Rom. viii. 23). These are groans which should not be stifled, but encouraged. The more that we are in harmony with the mind of God the more will these groanings be heard; not the groaning of an anxious soul to get peace, which God has already provided and presented, but the groanings of the saint who is waiting for his body to be fashioned like unto Christ's body of glory. This is evidently quite different from fighting against indwelling corruption. We are like the Israelites waiting till all the chosen of the Lord shall have actually had the blood on the lintel, which will be completed only when the Lord comes. We have been sent into this world to persuade men to come under the protecting power of the blood of Jesus, and thus be sheltered from wrath. Meanwhile our place is described in the 17th chapter of John, where we find that the Christian is

Given to Christ out of the world (ver. 6).
Left in the world (vers. 11 and 15).
Not of the world (ver. 14).
Hated by the world (ver. 14).
Kept from the evil of the world (ver. 15).

Sent into the world (ver. 18).

Preaching the word to the world (ver. 20).

'God forbid that I should glory save in the cross of our Lord Jesus Christ, by whom the world is crucified unto me and I unto the world.' (Gal. vi. 44).

II. — REDEEMED BY POWER.

THE ISRAELITES IN THE WILDERNESS.

1. *Triumph*. — A quickened soul is first exercised about what *he has done*, — that he has sinned; and then, as we have seen, he gets peace, because forgiven through the blood of Christ who died for him. But he very soon finds out a further distress, not arising from what he has done, but from what *he is* — *a sinner*. This is described in Rom. v. 12, 'As by one man sin entered into the world,' He has been sheltered from God's hand in judgment, but he finds he requires a new life in which to serve God. The Israelites found themselves, after having been delivered from the death of their first-born, with *rocks* at either side, *foes* behind, and *the sea* before. So the Christian was *born* a sinner; his own sinful *nature* is unchanged and unchangeable; and the *law* of God is against him — three obstacles much more terrible than those of the Israelites. Many a quickened soul in such a case is ready to cry, 'Hast thou taken us away to die in the wilderness?' (Exod. xiv. 11.) 'Who shall deliver me?' (Rom. vii. 24.)

But God does not say, 'I have taken you away to die,' but He says, "*go forward*" (Exod. xiv. 15). God is for us, and His power is exercised through death, through the territory, the last domain of law. Man's extremity is God's opportunity. A way is made in the sea. 'The Lord saved Israel that day out of the hands of the Egyptians: and Israel saw the Egyptians dead upon the sea-shore' (Exod. xiv. 30). This deliverance points not so much to Christ dying, as to Christ 'raised again for our justification;' not to justification by blood, but 'to justification of life,' Rom. v. 18 (in Christ as risen from the dead): 'For if when we were enemies we were reconciled to God by the *death* of His Son, much more being reconciled we shall be saved by *His life*,' that is His life in resurrection. Not only are we out of the *house* of bondage, but we are out of the *land* of Egypt. Every Christian has a right to say — 'Not only has God sheltered me by blood, but He has saved my soul by His power; not only have I peace with God, but God is for me; not only has God's hand been stayed from visiting me for my sins in wrath, but God's hand has been manifested in destroying all my enemies; not only am I not condemned, but there is no condemnation; not only did Christ die for me, but my standing is in Christ risen from the dead' (Rom. viii. 1). 'It is Christ that died, yea, rather, that is risen again.' (Rom viii. 34.)

> Pilgrims and strangers,
> Captives no more:
> Wilderness rangers,
> Sing we on shore.
> God in His power parted hath the sea,
> Foes all have perished, His people are free.
> By the pillar safely led,
> By the manna daily fed,
> Now the homeward way we tread.
> 'Tis Jesus, 'tis Jesus, our Shepherd here below:
> 'Tis Jesus, 'tis Jesus, 'tis Jesus whom we know.

2. *Conflict.* — There is an *unscriptural conflict* here also: — How am I a sinner in the world, under law, to get out of my old standing in Adam and to get into the wilderness with God?

If the Israelites had tried to scale the rocky precipices on either hand, the barriers of nature, instead of taking God's way by a new and supernatural path altogether, this would have been an illustration of a quickened sinner trying to climb this mighty obstacle 'born in sin,' this mountain of his nature, instead of taking God's way out of it, as seen in Romans v. 19, 'As by one man's disobedience many were made sinners, so by the obedience *of one* shall many be made righteous.'

If the Israelites had turned on the foes behind, and had tried to fight their way through, instead of standing still to see the salvation of God, this would have been an illustration of a quickened sinner trying to fight against and extirpate his evil nature, or make it better, and thus try to get delivered from the wages of sin, instead of taking God's way in Romans vi. 23, 'eternal life through *Jesus Christ* our Lord.'

If a quickened sinner were attempting to get deliverance from the power of the law of God and its righteous demands, by trying to make that which cannot be subject to the law of God a willing servant, he should be as the Egyptians, trying to get through where faith alone could walk, 'Which the Egyptians assaying to do were *drowned*.' That is the doom of man's efforts; but in Christ Jesus we have died, we have risen. RECKON therefore yourself dead indeed unto sin. It is not that we feel dead to it, or are dead to its motions; but as Christ died to it, so we reckon ourselves dead. Instead of crying therefore when I find such a holy law inoperative in bringing my God-hating nature into subjection, 'Who shall deliver me?' (Rom. vii. 24) and stopping there, I look back on all my foes dead on the shore. Christ's grave is empty now, and God looks at me as in Christ Jesus. And every question of sins and sin is settled for ever. Christ, my sins, and myself, were all nailed to Calvary's cross. I believe this fact, that Christ is risen. I accept God's meaning which He has attached to this fact, that I am now not in my sins. I can now sing, in spirit, the triumph song of Moses on the wilderness shore of the Red Sea, and truly say, in the language of Romans viii., 'There is therefore now no condemnation to me in Christ Jesus, for the law of the Spirit of life in Christ Jesus hath made me free from the law of sin and death.'

But also a *scriptural* conflict now begins — namely, the conflict against

THE FLESH.

This is not a conflict to obtain peace; not a conflict to get deliverance from condemnation, not even that sympathetic and

God-honouring groaning of Romans viii. 18-28, but conflict against myself. It is not the conflict against the world. If we look at Israel as the illustration, we find that there were no Egyptians in the wilderness, only Jehovah's congregation is there. We are now shut in with God: God's enemies are our enemies; we are on His side, even against ourselves. We have been crucified and raised; we have sung the song of victory; we triumph in Christ Jesus, and now we have conflict in earnest with our own evil natures. The man who realizes that he has got once and for ever into the standing described in Rom. viii. 1, 'There is therefore now no condemnation to them that are in Christ Jesus,' with all his triumph, realizes tremendous deadly conflict, not around him, but within him, not struggling to get acceptance with God but keeping his body under, looking at his own unchanged and unchangeable evil nature within him with something of the abhorrence of God — every day confessing his sin, every day requiring the Advocate. After the Israelites had sung the triumph song on the wilderness shore of the Red Sea, after they had received the pillar cloud to guide them, bread from heaven to feed them, and the water from the rock to refresh them, '*then* came Amalek and fought with Israel in Rephidim.' Does this not give us an illustration of the lusting between the flesh and the Spirit as seen in Galatians v. 17, 'The flesh lusteth against the Spirit, and the Spirit against the flesh, and these are contrary the one to the other?' This 'lusting' or warfare goes on, not that we may cry, 'O wretched man, who shall deliver,' but 'that ye may not do the things that ye would' (*lit.*). This is a tremendous personal reality in every saved man. At the same moment that he is rejoicing in Christ Jesus, he has no confidence in the flesh which is still actually within him, and thus he has a warfare every day against himself.

Read Exodus xvii. 8-16, where we get the account of the conflict: Joshua, the captain of the Lord, fights with Amalek (son of Eliphaz, eldest son of Esau); Moses is on the hill-top with the rod, holding up his hands in intercession to God, supported by Aaron and Hur, one holding up each arm, for as long as his arms were held up Israel prevailed. And Joshua discomfited Amalek with the edge of the sword. An altar is raised, called Jehovah my banner for the Lord will have war with Amalek, not once for all, but *from generation to generation*. This is all after the Red Sea has been crossed.

This gives us an illustration of how the Spirit of Jesus fights against the flesh. The Advocate is with the Father on high, and He is Jesus Christ the righteous, the spotless high Priest, making continual intercession for us. The Spirit overcomes the flesh by the Word of God. This is all after we have joyfully sung the victory-anthem recorded in Romans viii. 'There is no condemnation to them that are in Christ Jesus.' And indeed we have a specimen of the mighty sword we are now to wield by the Spirit in us in the practical exhortations laid down in the last chapters of the epistle to the Romans, commencing with chapter xii.

As the Israelites found that the sword of Joshua and the prayers of Moses routed the heathen Amalek, so the Christian finds that there is nothing like the truth of God, the authority of God, the sword of the Spirit, accompanied by the intercession of Jesus on high for the unsubject flesh within him. All the wilderness conflict has this character: 'Thou shalt remember all the way which the Lord thy God led thee these forty years in the wilderness, to *humble* thee and *prove* thee, to *know* what was in thine heart, whether thou wouldst *keep* His commandments or not.' (Deut. viii. 2.)

Beloved brethren, 'seeing then that ye are risen with Christ, mortify therefore your members which are upon the earth.'

We have triumph because we are forgiven. We have conflict because we sin.

We have triumph for we are saved. We have conflict because we are sinners, although saved.

We have triumph over our Adam-nature, for we are not in Adam, but in Christ. We have conflict within us, for, alas! we often 'walk as men.'

We 'are not in the flesh,' therefore we have triumph. The flesh is in us, therefore we have conflict.

We are 'not under law,' therefore we have triumph. Jesus said, 'If ye love me, keep my commandments,' therefore we have conflict. We are not (υπο νομον) *under law*, neither are we (ανομοι) *lawless*, but we are (εννομοι) *inlawed* — that is, *under authority*, or duly subject to Christ.

Christ has taken charge, not only of our salvation, but of our conflict and our walk. Grace saves, but Grace also teaches. Neither is it by an internal power only that we are guided, but by external authority or commandment. We do not walk in the paths of righteousness, merely because *we see* them to be righteous, but because God has *ordered* them. The former would be self-pleasing, the latter is God-pleasing, and if ever the question should arise between what I feel and see to be right, and what God says is right, then I must obey God rather than my own feelings. Abraham did not understand how it was right to sacrifice his son, but he believed God, and offered his son because God told him.

As long as the Israelites were in the wilderness, they were seen in themselves, as needy and sinful, while God was proving Himself bountiful and gracious. We find a wonderful illustration of God's provision for the Christian's need very near the end of the Israelites' march. In Numbers xxi, we have a sad picture of their murmurings, and at verse 6 we read, 'The Lord sent fiery serpents among the people, and they bit the people; and much people of Israel died. Therefore the people came to Moses, and said, we have sinned, for we have spoken against the Lord, and against thee; pray unto the Lord, that He take away the serpents from us. And Moses prayed for the people. And the Lord said unto Moses, make thee a fiery serpent, and set it upon a pole; and it shall come to pass, that every one that is bitten, when he looketh upon it, shall live. And Moses made a serpent of brass, and put it upon a pole, and it came to pass, that if a serpent had bitten any man, when he beheld the serpent of brass, he lived.'

As long as the Christian is in this world, he will have sin in him, and his power against it is Jesus crucified. The Son of Man lifted up on the cross is what withers up practically and daily our rebellion, waywardness and perversity, and in Him God sees no iniquity in Jacob and no perverseness in Israel. And if we say we have no sin, we deceive ourselves, and the truth is not in us.

III. — SEATED IN HEAVENLY PLACES IN CHRIST JESUS.

THE ISRAELITES IN CANAAN.

1. *Triumph.* — Israel under Joshua got through the Jordan, as Israel under Moses got through the Red Sea. All Canaan was theirs, 'From the wilderness and this Lebanon even unto the great river, the river Euphrates, all the land of the Hittites, and unto the great sea, toward the going down of the sun, shall be your coast.' (Joshua i. 4.) This was the land flowing with milk and honey; the land in which they were to have long life and prosperity; the land wherein they were to swell and be fed. The Israelites were blessed with all temporal blessings in earthly places in Canaan. Of us, as Christians, now it is said: God '*hath* blessed us with *all* spiritual blessings in heavenly places in Christ.' Certainly, we have many blessings which we never think of, and never have thought of, but we can think of none which we do not have in Christ. Every Christian has Christ — nothing less. He may not know all: who does? We strive that we may know Him, that we may grow in grace, and in 'the knowledge of our Lord and Saviour.' In Christ every Christian is blessed with every spiritual blessing in heavenly places.

He is quickened, raised, seated already in heavenly places in Christ. Therefore, according to the illustration, he is in Canaan as to his triumph; for as Christ is, so are we in this world. He is dead, risen, seated, so are we in Him. (Eph. i., ii., iii.)

>   Canaan possessors,
>   Safe in the land.
>   Victors, confessors;
>   Banner in hand.
> Jordan's deep river evermore behind,
> Cares of the desert no longer in mind.
>   Egypt's stigma rolled away,
>   Canaan's corn our strength and stay,
>   Triumph we the live-long day.
> 'Tis Jesus, 'tis Jesus, the Christ of God alone;
> 'Tis Jesus, 'tis Jesus, 'tis Jesus whom we own.

2. *Conflict.* — There is an *unscriptural conflict* here, as we have seen in Egypt and the wilderness. This conflict is said to be (Ephesians vi. 12) 'not against flesh and blood.' There is more in this simple statement than might at first appear. We are in the world, we are not of it. Our work is not to fight to put the world right. This is the mistake of all who have taken, or may take, the sword to fight the Lord's battles in this dispensation. We are here to act in grace as children of the Father, and to save men from the world. Our enemies are spiritual, not men in the flesh. We are not sanctified Jews, praying the 109th Psalm, and slaying men, women, and children. That was the right thing in Canaan; it is the wrong thing in the places in which we stand. Not only as far as bloodshed, but the principle goes down to every wrestling with the weapons of this world. Have I been cheated? what is my remedy? Go to law? Nay. But then I shall suffer loss. Very well, suffer (1 Cor. vi. 7; 1 Pet. ii. 20). The believer is done with all "flesh and blood" conflict. He may be called a fool, a madman — one that has no interest as a citizen, as a politician, a person of Utopian ideas and transcendental schemes. He is content so to be styled, and moreover is not to retort. His life is hid with Christ in God. All contact with the world's ways can but defile him. 'Flesh and blood' is not the platform on which he wars. World philanthropists he may admire; world reformers he may be thankful for; but he hears his Master say, 'Let the dead bury their dead' (if decently buried, so

much the more agreeable for us, 'follow thou Me.' But there is a *scriptural conflict*, namely, the conflict against

THE DEVIL.

All Canaan was given to Joshua; but we read that they had to enter in and take possession of it personally — 'every place that the *sole of your foot shall tread upon*, that have I given unto you' (Joshua i. 3). They had to fight for every inch of the land. First Jericho fell, then Ai, until Joshua routed his thirty-one kings. Read Joshua xii. And after we are told that we are already raised and seated in Christ, that we already have been blessed with all spiritual blessings in heavenly places in Christ, the conflict is put before us in the very heavenly places where we are blessed, as Joshua's fighting with Canaan's kings was in Canaan.

This conflict is not against the world nor the flesh — we have considered these already — but it is against Satan the accuser, wicked spirits ruling the darkness, demons that hate the light (Eph. vi. 12).

1st. What are they? 'Principalities and powers.' They possess strength of evil, strong wills, more powerful than ours. They originally derived strength from God, and their apostate will rises from themselves.

2d. What do they do? They have *power* over the world as governing it, for it is in darkness and they are 'the rulers of the darkness of this world.'

3d. Where do they dwell? They *dwell* 'in heavenly places,' and thus ever endeavor to obtain a religious and delusive ascendency over us, for they are 'spiritual wickednesses.' And what do we require for these forces who dispute our possessions? This is not Pharaoh keeping us in bondage; not Amalek fighting with us, but the Canaanites disputing our own possessions. The former two we were saved from; the latter we have to meet in their true attitude, as keeping us from our rightful places as the redeemed of God. We fight, clad in the armour of God. 'Be strong in the Lord and in the power of His might. Put on the whole armour of God, that ye may be able to stand against the wiles of *the devil*. For we wrestle not against flesh and blood, but against principalities, against powers, against the rulers of the darkness of this world, against spiritual wickedness in heavenly places. Wherefore take unto you the whole armour of God, that ye may be able to withstand in the evil day, and having done all to stand. Stand, therefore, having your loins girt about with truth, and having on the breastplate of righteousness; and your feet shod with the preparation of the gospel of peace; above all, taking the shield of faith, wherewith ye shall be able to quench all of the fiery darts of the wicked. And take the helmet of salvation, and the sword of the Spirit, which is the word of God: praying always with all prayer and supplication in the Spirit, and watching thereunto with all perseverance and supplication for all saints' (Eph. vi. 10-18). This is neither to 'get peace,' nor to avoid condemnation, nor to get into 'heavenly places.' It is not with the judgment of God, nor the law of God, nor sin within me. This conflict is against the wiles of the adversary, who, day and night, tries to deprive me of all that God has given, and all that faith enjoys.

Let us see how all this bears upon us. Some look upon a Christian as our of Egypt, now in the Wilderness, and waiting to reach Canaan. This may have some truth in it, but it does not convey the whole truth as to our position.

Others look upon it thus: — We are in Canaan by faith: we are in the Wilderness in fact; and we may be in Egypt, Wilderness, or Canaan as to experience. Again, there is truth here, but I do not think it is exactly put as subsequent Scripture warrants. Let us shortly sum up all the above: —

HEB. XI. 28-30.

I. — 'Through faith he (Moses) kept the Passover, and the sprinkling of blood, lest he that destroyed the first-born should touch them.'

Exod. xii. — Rom. v. 1-11. Triumph by blood.

John xvii. — Rom. viii. 22-28. Conflict with the WORLD.

II. — 'By faith they passed through the Red Sea as by dry land, which the Egyptians assaying to do were drowned.'

Exod. xiv. 15; xv. — Rom. viii. Triumph in power.
Exod. xvii. 8-16. — Gal. v. 17. Conflict with the FLESH.
III. — 'By faith the walls of Jericho fell down after they were compassed about seven days.'
Josh. i. — Eph. i. — Triumph in our inheritance.
Josh. xii. — Eph. v. — Conflict with the DEVIL.

'All these things happened unto them for types, and they are written for our admonition' (1 Cor. x. 11). By *faith*, therefore, according to the above parallel, we are *in Christ*, who is far above all Egyptian judgment, all Wilderness weariness, or even all Canaan conflicts. In actual *fact* we are still in the world; and in individual *experience* we have still clouds and sunshine, joy and sorrow, storm and calm. Thus there are three things the Christian has to distinguish: 1st, his Standing; 2nd, his State; 3rd, his Experience, — His standing before God, his state in this world, and his own experience as he passes through this world.

1. THE CHRISTIAN'S STANDING.

All Christians are by faith in the eternal calm of God having everything that the work of Christ has secured. We are far above all principalities and powers in Him who is alive for evermore, who is the Living One, and was once dead. We are as near to God as Christ is, for we are made nigh by His blood; and we are as dear to God as Christ is, for Jesus, speaking to His Father, says, 'Thou hast loved them as Thou hast loved me' (John xvii. 23). In Him we possess all the fulness of God. But as to fact, we find another side of the truth, which is, —

2. THE CHRISTIAN'S STATE.

According as we look at it, all Christians are still in *Egypt*. Not an enemy is really destroyed. The *world* is around us and against us. We are sheltered by blood, and still we are in a condemned world. We are eternally justified, and by grace we are saved persons; still, in plain English, in Scripture language, we are just where we were as to our surroundings.

Again we are, as to fact, still in the *Wilderness*, requiring guidance by the eye of our Father every day. As the Israelites of old had no sign-posts nor highways in the trackless dessert, and were guided by the pillar-cloud, so human wisdom and human advice can never direct the Christian in his heavenward journey. God's word is His light. As the Israelites had to get their bread daily from heaven, marching through a barren wilderness, so the Christian gets no food for his new nature in that which his fellow-men all around him enjoy. He says, 'The life which I now live in the flesh, I live by the faith of the Son of God. who loved me and gave Himself for me' (Gal. ii. 20), Every day the Israelites required the water from the Rock in the dry and parched land, so the Christian daily drinks the truth of God. Christ is his daily refreshment. These are for our *weariness*. The Israelites likewise had Joshua to fight, and Moses to pray, against their foe Amalek; so we have the Spirit to war against the flesh, and our advocate with the Father. Jesus presents the blood for us on high, and daily we require our feet to be washed from all earthly defilement. These are God's provisions for our *sin*.

Again, as to fact, we are in the *Canaan* conflict, following our Joshua through all his wars, which are our wars. Every Christian is really, as to fact, in Egypt, in the Wilderness, and in Canaan, at one and the same time. Different aspects may be more prominently ours at one time than at another, and this constitutes experience. The experience of Christians is not always Christian experience.

3. THE CHRISTIAN'S EXPERIENCE.

What do we find the every-day experience of Christians to be? According as a Christian understands what his standing is and what his state is, so will be his experience. But every Christian's experience must be 'a walking with God.' He may be, as to experience, sheltered by blood, and hardly knowing it, like an Israelite in Egypt not realizing the safety that there was under the blood-sprinkled lintel. He may be consciously at peace with God by the blood, but still trembling under the fear of coming into condemnation, like an Israelite not seeing the path through the sea, and trembling lest Pharaoh's host destroy him; but he will be walking with God up to the light that he has. He may be rejoicing on the solid ground of Christ risen, having for ever done with all against him, and having God now for him consciously, and he thus wa'ks with God, like an Israelite passed through the Red Sea, and entered upon the wilderness journey. And, finally, he may be walking as in heavenly places, like an Israelite through the Jordan and settled in Canaan. He is God's workmanship, and is now getting into the mystery of His will (Eph. i. 9), having lost sight of the thought of his own salvation, and being absorbed in God — as the aged pilgrims have told us, that for years they had never had a thought about their own salvation — as the aged Bengel[6] said, 'The same old terms.' And it is only when in conscious experience we have been taken thus far, that we can study God for His own sake and for what He is. This is the furthest we can reach here.

The *standing* of every believer before God in Christ Jesus, known only by faith here, is the same, and is independent of his realizing it or enjoying it.

The actual *state* of every Christian upon the earth is likewise the same. What an anomaly any Christian is in the world! A son of God walking through a God-hating world, with a God-hating devil its head, and having within him a God-hating nature; the fact being that every Christian, as to conflict down here, is in Egypt, in the Wilderness, and in Canaan.

The *experience* of every Christian is not the same, but varies in different people, and in the same person at different times, according as he knows his standing before God, knows his state

---

[6] Johann Albrecht Bengel (1687–1752), was a Lutheran pietist clergyman and Greek language scholar known for his edition of the Greek New Testament and his commentaries on it.

and walks in the Spirit. Thus we find the reason of so much seeming contradiction in Scripture, and in the writings of God-taught men. I am sometimes confronted with a passage in a man's writings, and asked, 'Do you believe that?'

'Yes,' I answer; 'and do you believe that?' — a directly opposite statement (seemingly), and again I say, —

'Yes,' because I find the same expressions in God's word.

They all reconcile themselves in our own consciousness, if we are submissive enough to wait and learn God's mind. I wish that you, my Christian reader, may distinctly see the difference between what the Christian is in God's sight, and what he is in this world, and also why there is so much difference in different Christians. There is one path, and but one path, in which our God and Father would have us walk; that is the path of His own Son here in conscious sonship, witnessing for Him as if we were in Egypt, the Wilderness, and Canaan, taking sides with Him against the world, against ourselves, and against the devil. This is Christian experience; but, alas! this is not always the experience of Christians. This may depend upon their not rightly dividing the word of truth, or their not seeing the truth in its many aspects. If we draw up a few seeming contradictions from God's word concerning the Christian in parallel columns, if we read down one of them we shall find the experience of some Christians; if again we read down the other, we shall find the experience of another class of Christians — but Christian experience is the harmonious and scriptural blending of both. (I wonder what angels think as they see such sons of God here!) Did not Paul know this strange contradiction? I saw an infidel tract the other day meant to prove the Bible to be false, by drawing up in parallel columns about a dozen contradictions found in Scripture, such as 'Whosoever is born of God sinneth not,' and 'If we say we have no sin, we deceive ourselves,' &c.; and I thought, 'Are the infidels really so far back?' so I commend the following four dozen instead of one, to their notice, and promise more when these are understood. The poor infidel never heard of a new creation and an old in the same man. He knows only the old, and patches it.

Well-known.	Yet unknown.
Behold we live.	Dying.
Always rejoicing.	Yet sorrowful.
Making many rich.	Yet poor.
Possessing all things.	Having nothing.
Ye have put off the old man.	Put off all these.
Ye have put on the new man.	Put on therefore.
Who can be against us?	World, devil and flesh.
Who shall lay anything to our charge?	The Accuser accuses the brethren day and night.
Who is he that condemneth?	We judge ourselves.
He that is born of God sinneth not.	If we say that we have no sin we deceive ourselves.
We are not in the flesh.	As long as we are in the flesh.
Not under law.	Keep my commandments.
He that believeth in the Son hath everlasting life.	We live if ye stand fast in the Lord.
The Lord's freemen.	Christ's slaves.
Being made free from sin.	Blood cleanseth (not has cleansed) us from all sin.
Accepted in the Beloved.	We labour to be accepted (in service).
We are not in the flesh, but in the Spirit.	The flesh lusts against the spirit, and the spirit against the flesh.
God who always causeth us to triumph.	What great conflict I have for you.
We are already saved.	We are working out our salvation.
	We are waiting for salvation.
Let us therefore as many as be *perfect*.	Not as though I were already *perfect*.
Ye are *complete* in Him.	We pray that we may stand *complete* in all the will of God.
Seeing ye have *purified* your souls.	Let every one that hath this hope in Him *purify* himself.
Ye are *unleavened*.	Purge out the old *leaven*.

Father who hath made us *meet* to be partakers of the inheritance of the saints in light.	When He shall appear we shall be *like* Him.
Always confident.	With fear and trembling.
Through death He destroyed Him that had the power of death.	The last enemy that shall be destroyed is death.
Everywhere and in all things —	
To be full, and	To be hungry.
To abound, and	To suffer need (Phil. iv. I2).
Dead to sin.	Let not sin therefore reign.
Risen with Christ.	Mortify therefore your members which are upon the earth.
I am strong.	When I am weak.
We have an anchor sure and steadfast.	Make your calling and election sure.
They shall never perish.	Lest I should be a castaway.
Why as though living in the world.	The life which we now live in the flesh.
I am dead.	Nevertheless I live.
We are sanctified, justified; Christ our sanctification.	We pray that we may be sanctified wholly.
Seated in heavenly places in Christ.	We are in the world.
Bear ye one another's burdens.	Everyman shall bear his own burden.
Your bodies are the temples of the Holy Ghost.	I know that in me (that is, in my flesh) dwelleth no good thing.
Saved from sin.	Chief of sinners.
Justified by faith.	Justified by works.
Sanctified by blood and will of God.	Sanctified by the word and Spirit.
Saints by call.	Purified by progress.
We (Christians) shall not come into judgment.	We (Christians) must all appear before the judgment seat of Christ.

All these seeming contradictions are thoroughly explained when one sees the difference between our standing and our state. If I reckon my standing according to my state, I am in a low and God-dishonouring experience. If I bring the power and character of my standing to mould my state, then I shall have a happy and God-honouring experience.

The Lamb on the cross has purchased all.	The Lamb from the throne, when He returns in power, shall claim all, and actually take all.
In Egypt it is the blood of the Lamb.	Romans and Galatians shew us the power that brought us out and keeps us in Egypt.
In Amalek's fight it is the blood of the Lamb who is the advocate on high, that is presented.	Hebrews look at the Christian as always in the Wilderness.
It is by the blood of the Lamb that the accuser of the brethren is overcome. Clad in God's armour we fight.	Ephesians is the book of our Canaan.

Soon faith will be fact. May our blessed Lord grant it. Not at death will this be true of the whole Church of God, but when He returns. Our experience will then be both what faith and fact are; our state shall then be as our standing; our standing shall be our state. We shall then be 'like Him,' soul and body. Do you not long for the time when the last of the bride shall be under the shelter of the blood-sprinkled lintel, and we shall be caught up together from a doomed *world*, — when the last conflict with Amalek shall have been fought, and his remembrance blotted out for ever; the *flesh* for ever left; 'sins and iniquities remembered no more for ever;' when the accuser of the brethren shall have been cast out of the heavenly place, and every opposing *spiritual wickedness* shall have been routed; when our Joshua, by His judgment warfare (Rev. iv to xxii.), shall have cleared the inheritance: Then, in the splendour of the Lamb on the throne, we shall be manifested as the sons of God, the body of Christ, the bride of the Lamb.

Fellow Christian, are you making your experience the standard for your walk? This is wrong.

Are you making your state your standard? This also in wrong.

But God would have us make our standing our standard. This honours Him. This gives conquering power.

Our attitude now is to wait calmly for the hour when all will be ours, in fact and also in experience which is now ours in faith only; when our standing shall be our state. Even the Apostle Paul has not yet all; he is waiting with the Lord for what he was waiting for while here, — 'not to be unclothed, but clothed upon, that mortality might be swallowed up of life.' (2 Cor. v.) This is why resurrection, not death, is our hope — why we wait for the Lord's coming for us, and not for our going to Him. We do not wait for happiness merely, we wait for what will bring to a close this great paradox between *standing* and *state*, and also terminate that unseen state of disembodied souls with the Lord in Paradise. 'Even so, come, Lord Jesus.' 'Beloved, now are we the sons of God; and it doth not yet appear what we shall be: but we know that when He shall appear we shall be like Him; for we shall see Him as He is. And every one that hath this hope in Him purifieth himself, even as He is pure.' (1 John iii. 2.)

The world, the devil, and the flesh give you conflict. The Father, the Son, and the Holy Ghost give you triumph.

> Praise the Lord with hearts and voices,
>   Gathered in His holy name;
> Every quicken'd soul rejoices,
>   Hearing of the Saviour's fame.
>
> Praise the living God who gave us,
>   Lost and ruin'd as we lay,
> His beloved Son to save us,
>   Bearing all our sin away.
>
> Praise the Lord for all His guiding,
>   Snares so thickly round us lie;
> We in His own light abiding,
>   Are directed by His eye.
>
> Praise Him for His long forbearance;

How our sin His heart must pain;
Righteous is His loving-kindness,
   Cleansing us from every stain.

Praise Him, enemies assail us,
   As we through the desert go;
But His sword can never fail, us,
   It shall silence very foe.

Praise Him for the manna given,
   Falling freshly every day;
Jesus Christ, our Lord from heaven,
   Is our food through all the way.

Praise Him for the water flowing,
   Freely in its boundless tide;
Christ the smitten Rock we're knowing,
   Pierced for us His wounded side.

Praise Him through the desert marching,
   Onward to the golden shore;
For our Saviour we are watching,
   And we'll praise Him evermore.

'Under the Sun.'

Our Walk.

ECCLESIATES.

N reading the book of Ecclesiastes I have been struck with the frequent occurrence of this expression '*Under the sun.*' It occurs twenty-nine times in this book of ten chapters, and is nowhere else in the Bible. 'Under the heavens' is thrice mentioned, and 'upon the earth' four times.

I have met Christians who have been sadly perplexed by several expressions in this book which seem so contradictory to other parts of the Scripture. Infidels have also exultingly brought some of its detached sentences as sanctioning their blasphemies. Legalists and Unitarians have quoted some of its precepts as proving their man-exalting and God-dishonouring doctrines. Worldly professors use its verses as a warrant for their worldliness, and an excuse for their practices.

That expression, '*under the sun*,' is the thread on which the whole book is crystallized. If we remember this, we shall have not the slightest difficulty in meeting infidel opposition or world-hearted profession. Solomon was the wisest as he was the richest king, trying all that was 'under the sun.' The Holy Spirit has, in these few chapters, with divine accuracy, given us his experience, and 'what can the man do that cometh after the king?' He had plenty of money, and all the resources where men think pleasure is to be found 'under the sun' — wine, music, works, vineyards, gardens, orchards, fruit trees, waterpools, servants, possessions of cattle, silver, gold, peculiar treasures, men-singers, women-singers, musical instruments of all sorts — in short, whatever his eyes desired he kept not from them (chap. ii). A better collection could not be brought together for any man 'under the sun.'

And with all his enjoyment he still kept his wisdom, as he says, 'yet acquainting mine heart with wisdom.' But in such multiplied sources of pleasure did he not tarry too long at the enjoyment of one side of his nature, and leave some other corner untried? Nay; he found a season for everything. For loving, for hating, for laughing, for weeping, for dancing, for mourning, for all he had a time. He saw that after all he had tried *under the sun* he was no better than a beast; for as we look at a man and a beast *'under the sun,'* a common grace shuts out the light of the sun equally from the horse and his rider.

It is *'under the sun'* that the outward eye sees, and if the things seen are all that we are to have, there is nothing better than what Solomon says — 'Behold that which I have *seen*: it is good and comely to eat and to drink, and to enjoy the good of all his labour that he taketh under the sun all the days of his life, which God giveth Him; for it is his *portion*.' The *things seen* give eating, drinking, and enjoyment of labour as the only portion. This is the highest good, according to what was seen by the greatest philosopher, as looking at things *'under the sun.'* He was also a great student. Read 1 Kings iv. 33.

As to the higher part of man, we find a wonderful text in Eccl. ix. 1: 'No man knoweth either love or hatred by all that is before him.' No; we have to look *above* us for love and hatred, not *before* us, that is to say, in this world. By what is before us we are asked to remember our Creator, but are never turned to our Redeemer. Hence, *'under the sun,'* we find men scarcely dare rise above the names Creator, Providence. And when we do remember this great Creator, as creatures under His sun, we find that the conclusion of all, the ultimate limit we can reach is to know His demands upon us; as His demands in their own place and nature on a tree or an animal; His demand on us as creatures — the whole duty of man, which no man ever did or can do, is to 'fear God and keep His commandments.'

This wisest and richest man found *under the sun* no profit in all his labour; nothing new; wicked man in judgment; oppression of the right; folly and wisdom going to the same end; chance seeming to regulate all; many sore evils consequent, notwithstanding what he says in 1 Kings v. 4: 'The Lord my God hath given me rest on every side, so that there is neither adversary nor evil occurrent.' In short, he found the beginning vanity, the middle vanity, the end vanity. The sum of all *under the sun*, — vanity of vanities.

How complete is the change when we turn to contemplate Him who comes from far above the sun, who created the sun and the earth, and descended to the earth from His rainbow-circled throne. When Christ came, He did not reveal the name 'Creator;' it was the name 'Father.' Christ was the last test of all *under the sun*. The whole world has now been brought in guilty before God. Man's duty was to receive Christ instead of which he gave Him a cross.

God is love, and God was manifest in the flesh; perfect love, perfect light. Eternal life has been here from above the sun. Hatred against sin has been seen, as nowhere else it can be seen, when, made sin for us, the sinless One drained the cup of the wrath of God. Love for the sinner has been seen, as nowhere else it can be seen, in that 'God so loved the world that he gave His only begotten Son, that whosoever believeth in Him should not perish, but have everlasting life.'

A sister who had realized her position as witnessing for Jesus, and had come to understand what is meant by Solomon's time for everything 'under the sun,' wrote about a marriage party at which she had to be present. After describing what happened, she said, 'We then left very early, leaving the gay party to practise Solomon.'

We that have believed in the Son have got a most strange and anomalous position *under the sun*. 'As He is, so are we in this world.' As the Son of man dead, risen, and now in heaven in the fulness of His Father's love, so are we in this world. We have nothing whatever to do with what is '*under the sun,*' beyond getting through this world as simply as possible. 'If ye then be risen with Christ, seek those things which are *above*, where Christ sitteth on the right hand of God. Set your affection (it is literally *mind*, as in the passage 'who *mind* earthly things') on things *above* — *not* on things on the earth, for ye are dead, and your life is hid with Christ in God.' All this is intended to draw us away from what is under the sun to what is *above*, even to Jesus Himself. What is the occasion of all the worldly walk of so many professing Christians? We are not asking what the originating cause is. There is a difference between the originating cause and the occasion, sometimes called the predisposing and exciting causes. The originating or predisposing cause is found in this, that all Christians have in them the old Adam nature, unchanged and unchangeable, which lusts against the new, which abhors the things unseen and the walk by faith, which feeds upon the things seen, feasts on and revels in this present world. But there are several occasions or exciting causes which stir this old nature into conformity with the world. Let us look at three of the chief occasions of worldliness:

1st, Ignorance of self.

2d, Ignorance of what the world is.

3d, Ignorance of what God says about that world.

I. IGNORANCE OF SELF.

Christians not being aware of the worldly-minded foe within is a very common occasion of worldliness. They come nearer and nearer to the world, thinking themselves safe, and still doing nothing wrong, not knowing that it is like bringing gunpowder near the fire. If Christians would realize that they have a nature within them that feeds upon God's dishonor, they would be more watchful and prayerful. Every Christian has within him a traitor which loves the world, its ways and its principles, in some shape or other; a traitor which, but for the power of an ever present Spirit, would surrender the keys of the citadel at once to the world outside; a traitor which is not subject to the law of God, nor indeed can be; a traitor which is not to be trifled with, far less trusted; a traitor which is ever planning and scheming for its own gratification, and which is capable of anything evil. Christian! watch and pray against this foe within, as well as against foes without. Every Christian has the flesh still within him, which is a traitor against God.

II. IGNORANCE OF WHAT THE WORLD IS.

When we do not know what 'the world' is, we are very prone to slip into worldliness before we are aware. Some profess not to be clear upon what is worldly. They know, however, the meaning well enough of getting on in 'the world.' Some look at '*the world*' as that which is glaringly wicked, or God-dishonouring in other people. The poor man speaks of the rich man in his grand house as being in the world, or the great man who never thinks of God. While all this may be true, every man has his '*world*' into which he is tempted to go: the meanest as well as the greatest, the most secluded as those in the centre of a great city. A pretty ribbon or a new dress, a good dinner or a nice party, may be as much '*the world*' as the gayest and most fashionable assembly.

Often the question is asked, Is it right to go here or there? to do this or that? Is this of '*the world*' or not? God has given us a perfect criterion: 'All that is in the world...is not of the Father, but is of the world.' This makes all plain to a child with the Father. Is this of the Father? If not, it is of the world. How well every Christian understands this in some measure! Does the size of your world not increase just in proportion as you know the Father? Things are now classed under the title '*world*,' that were not thought to be worldly when we started the race. The road gets narrower as this thing and the other thing are seen to be of '*the world*,' till we are walking in the lonely path with the lonely Man.

Fellow-Christian, do you not see something this year to be of '*the world*' that you did not see last year? Have you been thus learning the Father? Is it a sign that the Father is being known more when we hear of professing Christians, yes, even deacons, elders, pastors, countenancing the worldly meeting, the gay assembly, or the dancing party? And where is the harm? is asked by many a voice. Ask at the entrance of many a fashionable gathering, '*Is this of the Father?*' and you will get the contempt that your presence there deserves. For the world loves and knows it won: your presence asking such a question would be an intrusion.

This spirit of the world is paralyzing the whole of Christian energy, as it is leavening the whole of Christendom. No wonder that there is a slumber as of death over our land, an unaccountable nightmare resting on the spirits of many Christian men, a feeling that we are just at the awful pause before some fearful explosion. Christians take the world's ways and party strifes in its politics and rule, blunting the edge of their spiritual nature, harming their conscience, condescending to mingle in the world's battles. Let the potsherds of earth strive with the potsherds thereof. Where are the garments unspotted by the world? Christians also are mixed up with the world's company, sitting at the world's table, happy with the world's joys and jokes, singing the world's songs , and their bleeding Lord hanging at their side, each world thought or action doing dishonour to Him.

Young disciples are especially liable to be carried away with the cultivated, respectable, educated, quiet, polite, agreeable, pleasant, worldly companion. Young disciples, in the name of Him who hung on Calvary for you, keep no company with any unconverted person. You may have to meet them at school or in business, but never keep company with them. 'Come out from among them and be ye separate.' A young disciple was once asked concerning a companion, —

'Well, was she a friend or an enemy?'

'In what way?'

'A friend or an enemy to Jesus?'

'I really could not say.'

'But you know that all are either friends or foes; there is not a third company. Is she converted?'

'I don't think so.'

'Then, of course, we know to whom she belongs. Let us be friends to all Jesus' friends, and enemies to all Jesus' enemies — loving them, praying for them, and trying to get them converted, but coming out from among them, and being separate.'

My brother, will that cross, will that bleeding One, not draw thy thoughts, thy words, thyself, away from this cruel world? Let them quaff their wine, let them chorus the revel song. Let them have their time to dance. They are *'under the sun.'* *'Under the sun'* He died for thee. That sun was darkened when He was thinking of thee. He loved thee. Thy name as an individual, was in His omniscient mind, when in darkness and agony He was forsaken of His God. Nails and a cross never kept Him there. He Himself made that iron and that wood, but love kept Him on the cross. Thou hast said, 'He loved me, and gave Himself for me.' His cross, His grave, separate thee from *'the world,'* as they separate thee from thy sins. Dost thou realise that every unconverted man is reckoned by thy Lord as a murderer? that this world is under the charge of murdering the Lamb of God?

In this land, at this moment, it is difficult to know the *church* from the *world*. The world, 'of the earth earthy,' has said to the Church, the bride of the Lamb, of the heavens, 'heavenly,' 'Come a little down to us, and we will rise a little up to you, and we can shake hands and agree.' This in the present day is called *liberality, charity, large-heartedness,* and he who dares to dissent is called a bigot, one of peculiar views, a man of extremes.

'The world' makes its social gathering and invites the Christian. A compromise is effected. The Christian leaves at home his peculiar testimony for his rejected Lord. 'The world' lays aside a little of its open worldliness, and they thus agree. 'The world' has been raised somewhat. Its tone has been elevated. The Christian has come down from his high standing ground, and has lost his place as the separated one — His Lord is dishonoured, and this is modern liberality! The world and the Christian agree, and God's name, God's glory, the offence of the cross, are given up as the price of the agreement!

Yea, some have shown their ignorance and heartlessness so much as to bring in Christ's example, and make His conduct a cloak for their worldliness, and the Holy Jesus a minister of sin. True, no one was ever such a friend to the sinner as Jesus, and no one was so separate from sinners. Did He contract any defilement by sitting and eating with sinners? It would be blasphemy to think it. Can you perfectly manifest Jesus wherever you go? But the rule here, as everywhere, is perfect and simple, 'Whether, therefore, ye eat or drink, or whatsoever ye do, do all to the glory of God' (1 Cor. x. 31). Do you keep company with that friend because it is for the glory of God? Do you accept that invitation to dinner because it is for the glory of God? or not rather because you will enjoy it, and perhaps meet some one you like, or something else for you, and is this following Jesus? Not a word did He speak, not a thought did He think, not a step did He take, but was for God's glory. Not a company He entered, but this was His *only* reason for going. Is it yours? Let conscience answer. And if you can go on with worldly people and in worldly ways, either you will reap daily and bitter sorrow, and have to come in broken and contrite spirit to the footstool of grace, or you have no heart for the crucified one. You know not the Christ whom the world crucified. You are not Christ's one. You are not a Christian!

At this present day there is nothing that is leavening Christendom more evidently than this worldliness — worldly policy, worldly ways of advancing the cause of Christ, worldly principles, worldly maxims, worldly motives, worldly vindications of conduct, worldly schemes and artifices, all are employed, and worldly arguments are finally adduced, shewing that all such are quite in proper place.

The spirit of competition, which is 'the life of trade,' has been adopted in those unchrist-like divisions in the Church of the living God. Artifice and trickery with world-shows, bazaars, and such-like, are used to extract money from the pockets of willing and unwilling victims to advance God's kingdom! the Lord all the time loving the cheerful giver. But cheerful or not cheerful, the worldly church principle is, the money must be obtained! [Read *Babylon's great bazaar*, Revelations xviii. 12 and 13 — *gold* at the head of the list, *souls of men* at the foot — not very unlike what may be seen in Christianised Britain!]

In the mixture of world and church of this nineteenth century in Britain, who could discern the Bride of the Crucified One? Everything goes on comfortably. There is little of the taking up of 'the cross;' many excuses for conformity to this world.

I heard not very long ago of one who, standing very high in 'the Church' as a leading and devoted Christian, at a marriage party publicly announced that such a season was for enjoyment, and that such enjoyment should take the form of singing songs, &c.; holy hymns and such-like were not appropriate. Certainly it was the time for enjoyment. And if 'any man is merry, *let him sing psalms.*' But this does not suit modern mixtures of 'Church' and 'world,' fashionable Christianity!

Religion, with its psalms and hymns and spiritual songs, may do well very well for Sunday; for solemn times; for deaths or for funerals; for prayers, morning and night, at family worship; but for enjoyment, for merry-making, let us have a worldly son, or some foolish love-sonnet, before all the means that God has ordained as the channels for our joy!

This is what is called *intelligent* Christianity. 'Rejoice' is the motto of such men, but they forget '*in the Lord.*' Man's songs, man's dancing, are their channels of joy — 'psalms, hymns, and spiritual songs,' God's channel. The judgment-day will try all. Beloved fellow-Christian, rejoice *now*, as you would look back from your death-bed with satisfaction and say, '''Twas not of the world.'

In travelling by rail, take out your Bible and quietly begin to read for your own instruction, in the presence of your fellow-passengers, and you will quickly observe that eyes are upon you in strange wonder — the eyes of those, too, who wish to be called *Christians*, but who cannot understand any man reading the Bible for *enjoyment*. The Bible, they think, should be read as a duty; but a piece of trash, in the shape of some yellow-boarded novel, or some new article of man's folly, is much more palatable and enjoyable. Dear reader, are you getting much enjoyment from the reading of the bare Word of your Father? This will fill you with His ideas, and displace your own. This will show you that there is much more '*of the world*' than perhaps you dreamt of; that all '*under the sun*' is equally vain for instruction or for enjoyment. This leads us to the consideration of the third occasion of this most deplorable and painful, though too common spectacle, of worldliness in a Christian.

III. IGNORANCE OF WHAT GOD SAYS ABOUT THE WORLD.

God alone knows the world thoroughly. There are three words in Scripture translated world; 1st, Kosmos (κοσμος), which literally means the world in its perfect order and arrangement, as opposed to chaos; 2nd, Aion (αιων), which literally mans a period of time, an age; and 3rd, Oikoumenè (οικουμενη), literally meaning the inhabited world.

Especially with the two first have we at present to do. What could be more beautiful than the arrangement of this perfectly ordered world — the cosmos that God brought out of chaos: The world, in this sense, in itself is not evil; but its rightful Lord has been crucified, and therefore in this age, or dispensation, or period of the world, all must be away from God. By and by all things in heaven and in earth shall be gloriously under the one head, Christ, when the cosmos, the beautiful world, will appear in purer glory than it its pristine beauty, when it shall be not the present age, but the day of the Son of man, 'the age to come' (Heb. ii. 5). Meanwhile the trail of the serpent defiles all. Its beautiful dells, and mountains, and plains, are polluted by the presence of men in rebellion against a holy God, and the unavenged blood of its martyred Lord is lying on it calling aloud for vengeance.

When the Spirit of God begins the practical exhortation to the Romans, in the 12th chapter, the first command of detail, after presenting our bodies living sacrifices, is, 'Be not conformed to this world;' that is, 'be not conformed *to this age.*' Until a man knows this foundation-principle he cannot go on to the other related duties. Be done with the spirit of the age. Why? Because the age is under Satan, who is the god of this age (2 Cor. iv. 4). Its rulers are the rulers of the darkness of this age (Eph. vi. 12). And Christ 'gave Himself for our sins, that He might deliver us from this present evil age, according to the will of God and our Father' (Gal. i. 4). The cause of Demas forsaking Paul was that he 'loved this present age' (2 Tim. iv. 10); and earth's wisdom is not the study of the Christian, for we do not speak 'the wisdom of this age, nor of the princes of this age' (1 Cor. ii. 6).

Christ our Lord and Saviour alone we own to be King of kings, but in this age the devil is prince of this world (John xvi. 11); and he declared this to Christ, the only true KING in Matt. iv. 8, when he said he would give Him all the kingdoms of the world. The Creator was in the world made by Him, and the world did not know Him, but hated and crucified Him. The wisdom of this world is foolishness with God, and its power weakness. 'We have received not the spirit of the world, but the spirit which is of God' (1 Cor. ii.). And God has chosen the foolish things, the weak things, the base things of this world as His own vessels.

My reader, listen to God's own word — 'Know ye not that the friendship of the world is enmity with God? whosoever, therefore, will be a friend of the world is the enemy of God' (James iv. 4). Would you not rather be on terms of friendship with that noble lord, or great man *in this world*; on speaking terms with those that the world loved to honour? And have you made up your mind for the guaranteed consequence? Thou art an enemy of God. 'Love not the world, neither the things that are in the world. If any man love the world, the love of the Father is not Him' (1 John ii. 15).

A man is known by the company he keeps, by the books he enjoys. Do you not enjoy a nice worldly dinner-party, where there is nothing very evil done, but all the events of the world discussed, much better than attending two or three prayer or worship meetings in a week? Have you made choice of the alternative? The love of the Father is not in you. 'They are of the world, therefore speak they of the world, and the world heareth them: (1 John iv. 5). 'We know that we are of God, and the whole world lieth in the wicked one' (1 John v. 19).

My reader, pause and think. Are you deceiving yourself? Do you love *the world*? If, as before God, you cannot deny it, then the love of the Father is not in you. You go to church; you are very respectable on Sundays and week-days; you are honest, and charitable, and kind; but you love the world. Your feasts and solemnities are an abomination unto God. You cannot force yourself to hate the world. It is natural to love it. By your love you prove that you have not the nature in you that abhors the world; that, therefore, you have not been born again, but have been deceiving yourself. I would solemnly advise you, before God, to begin from the beginning by getting converted. Cain was the first to try to make the world comfortable apart from God. God made him a vagabond. He built a city. He was the father of all the great world-improvers, with their harps and organs. No doubt they had made themselves very happy; no doubt they had their music and dancing; perhaps oratorios on the dying words of Abel, or the taking up of Enoch, as the 'Messiah' and 'Elijah' now-a-days. Having considered these occasions of worldliness, let us consider —

IV. THE PLACE OF A CHRISTIAN UNDER THE SUN.

Read John xvii., and there we find, —

First. At verse 9, Christ says, 'I pray not for the world, but for them which Thou hast *given me.*' As given by the Father to Christ, we Christians are separated from this world by the eternal gift of the Father, and by the intercessory prayer of the Son. Mingling with the world, we break through that wondrous chain that Jesus became a man to form; we do despite to the Father's purpose, we trample on the prayers of the Son.

Second. In verses 11 and 15 we are spoken of as *left* in the world: 'I am no more in the world, but these are in the world,' And as He is, so are we. Are we living His life, reproducing Christ here as those that are left to do so? He was the light while here; we are the light of the world during His absence. Brother, did you ever feel lonely because Jesus was not here, because you have been left? Are you mingling with the world? You do dishonour to that heart which reckoned on your love while left here.

Third. *Hated* by the world: 'The world hath hated them,' because the world hated Him. Many Christians are persecuted for their own sake, and not for righteousness' sake. Christians may be hated for their own disagreeable ways; but are you hated for your likeness to Christ? He said, 'they hated Me without a cause.' Do they hate you because you manifest His holy name? Are you mingling with the world? If so, you are trying to escape the hatred, yea, you are silently consenting that the world did right in hating your gracious Redeemer.

Fourth. '*Not of* the world,' verses 14 and 16. This is the cause of the former. The world loves its own. We are citizens of heaven. Heaven is our Fatherland. Heaven is our home. Heaven is our metropolis. We are foreigners here. We are like the Abyssinian captives, while they were in the chains of the king of that country. A few moments more, and, beloved fellow-captive, the chains shall fall, and we shall neither be in nor of the world. We are not of it, just as Jesus was not of it. A homeless, lonely stranger, the great Sojourner had 'not where to lay His head.'

We are here under protest. We protest against the awful power that the world-rulers have used in former days, and not one of whom has publicly protested against, namely, Pilate's boast, 'I have power to crucify Thee.' We glory in this, that we are identified with the murdered Man. Are you mingling with the world? By so doing you are denying your fatherland, you are ashamed of your citizenship.

Fifth. Ver. 15. While left in this world we are *kept* from the evil in it. Are we to rush near the evil from which our blessed Lord prayed His Father we might be *kept*? Are we to break through a Father's love, a Father's watchful care, and join the ranks of the aliens? Do we search at the broken cisterns, and thirst again for more and more of the music and dancing '*under the sun*,' while we are those that are *kept*? Tremendous evil! All the more tremendous because, unseen and unrealized, it is around us and from it we have to be kept. Nothing but Jesus' constant prayer, and the Father's constant, untiring love, could keep us.

Sixth. Ver. 18. We are sent into the world. As Christ was sent, so are we. We must be out of a place before we can be sent into it. The cross took us out of the world. We were crucified to it. In resurrection-life we are sent back to it, to be here as specimens of saved sinners, resurrection-men, stranger-witnesses, men that cannot be understood, men whose life is hid with Christ in God. Are you mingling with what is '*under the sun*?' If so, you deny the resurrection of Christ, and your resurrection with Him, and that you are sent into the world, and have to maintain your character as one who has been thus sent.

Seventh. Ver. 20. We are to *preach* to the world. All that are to be saved will be so by the instrumentality of saved man, sinners like themselves carrying the word of life to the dead. There is a strange infatuation in some men's minds, that because we are in the world to do the Lord's work, that therefore we must become somewhat assimilated to the world in order to get to its level! But the Christian is 'a light.' Light does not do its work by assimilation with darkness, but by opposition to it. The Christian's power in carrying the Word to a dead world is not in becoming like the dead, but in manifesting his new life, going to dead sinners with the omnipotence of God, and preaching His resurrection gospel, and not schemes of reformation, nor anything else except this gospel, knowing that the 'gospel is the power of God.' The Christian's wisdom is not that which schemes and plots for success according to worldly tactics, but in direct opposition to all; seeming to be downright foolishness. Saul's armour looks very strong; David's sling and stone seem quite contemptible.

We do our duty to the world only as we keep our Nazarite separated character. We shine brightly only as we oppose the darkness. We benefit mankind only as we glorify God and testify for the Crucified One. We are despised by man and chastened of God if we mingle with the world and 'blow hot and bold.' Christ spues out of His mouth the lukewarm.

'I am not a man of extremes,' says the *beau-ideal* of modern fashionable Christianity. 'I wish you were either cold or hot,' says God. 'Let God be true, and every man a liar.'

Let us 'make the best of both worlds,' says man. 'If any man love the world, the love of the Father is not in him,' says God.

'Secure friends here, and still keep a hope of heaven hereafter,' says man. 'The friendship of the world is enmity with God,' says God.

'Let us take our time for everything here "*under the sun*," — dancing, laughter, amusements, comfort, position,' is man's creed. 'If any man will come after Me, let him deny himself, and take up his cross and follow Me,' is what God says. As you sow you shall reap.

'Truly the light is sweet, and a pleasant thing it is for the eyes to behold the sun; but if a man live many years, and rejoice in them all, yet let him remember the days of darkness, for they shall be many. All that cometh is vanity. Rejoice, O young man, in thy youth; and let thy heart cheer thee in the days of thy youth, and walk in the ways of thine heart, and in the sight of thine eyes; but know thou, that for all these things God will bring thee into judgment' (Eccles. xi. 7-9). — Man, who shall live for ever, giving up his eternity for present pleasure, giving up Christ for the world, is like one who is colour-blind, that is, like a person who can see well enough his way through the world, but cannot distinguish between red and green, or any other of the beautiful hues that are seen in the rainbow. They that see colour in all its beauty and diversity, as God has made it, cannot but think it a great misfortune for those who cannot distinguish one colour from another. They see the crocus and the snowdrop the same as the green grass, and it again as the stone wall. Everything to them is either black or white, and the glorious rainbow is not distinguished from the black cloud that it spans. Everything is to them like an engraving, and the lilies of the field, that we are asked to consider, have no more beauty than is derived from their shape and position. It is a misfortune, but the unfortunate one does not know his loss. How true is that saying of Sir John Herschel,[7] referring to this colour-blindness: '*What we never knew we never miss*!' How true in the great realities of our existence! How many people go about this world and have never seen the most glorious sight that ever burst upon it — the perfect love of God to sinners, and the perfect hatred of God against sin; or rather, have never seen the most glorious Person that ever trod this earth as the sacrifice for their sin, as their propitiation, as the object to fill their hearts now and for ever!

They never knew Him, and they never miss Him. If you were saying 'Christ is not in the world, do you miss Him?' the idea would startle many. Others would feel that they would not at all like Him to be always where they were; they would not feel free if He were always sitting at their table, or went with them wherever they went. Have you never heard people say, when a godly man had left their company, 'Well, I'm glad he's gone;

---

[7] Editor's Note: Sir John Frederick William Herschel, 1st Baronet (1792–1871) was an English mathematician, astronomer, chemist, inventor, and experimental photographer who investigated color blindness.

we couldn't do anything before him?' How would you like Christ to be always beside you? Far from missing Him, you are really very glad He is not here. Thank God there are those who have known Him, that do miss Him, and are waiting for Him. Why does the lady of the world so enjoy company, while the pierced Christ is never missed? Because she never knew Him. Why do the men of the world enjoy their learning, their riches, or their pleasure, and do not miss Christ, God's greatest gift? Because they never knew Him. They wonder that people can enjoy prayer-meeting, gospel preachings, or Bible-readings, and always enjoy them — ready for them in the morning, at noon, or evening. They pity such. Is it not like the man who is colour-blind, pitying us as we stand in rapt enjoyment admiring the glorious rainbow? He feels the rain falling, but can see and admire no rainbow. We see the magnificent colouring of the rainbow, and forget the rain. They never knew the joy of the being the Lord's, therefore they never miss it. And what is left in the world after Christ is taken away? He once was here, and God looked on Him well-pleased; but man in his blindness crucified this only worthy object on earth, and what is left? God has told us 'All that is in the world' —

1st. 'The Lust of the Flesh.'

2d. 'The Lust of the Eye,' and, —

3d. 'The Pride of Life.' There are no other motive powers I the world but these. This trinity is reigning in power to-day as in the days of John the apostle.

1st. '*The lust of the flesh.*' — This has to do with the things by which the senses, taste and touch, and all merely animal gratifications, are nourished. This is the lowest and most universal. Rich and poor equally are under its power. What shall we eat, what shall we drink? Such do not eat to live, they live to eat, to enjoy themselves, to satisfy all the fleshly lusts that war against the soul. Thus we read of those that 'walk after the flesh, in the lust of uncleanness,' who serve 'divers lusts,' lewdness, wantonness. This is why tipplers[8] and drunkards enjoy the world, till they forget name, business, wife and family, body and soul, for drink, which is the front door admitting to every other lust of the flesh. A man may be under the lust of the flesh who is not a drunkard, but who wishes to enjoy himself on this side of his nature.

2d. '*The lust of the eye.*' — This has to do with the senses of seeing, hearing, and so on. Here the man has not only desires, but means to gratify them. What shall we see? Some new thing, some new Vanity Fair. The Athenians would listen to anything new, quite kindred to this lust of the eye. This is the second motive power in the world. What will please the eye and tickle the ear? This is what finds its craving satisfied in theatres, pantomimes, operas, concerts, sentimental and comic songs. They are all of one class: something that will satisfy their powers of *investigation* as the lust of the flesh has to do with the senses of *enjoyment*. This is even carried into the worship of the church; for what is ritualism but the lust of the eye? The lust of the eye is here gratified with gorgeous dresses, childish paraphernalia, sacred imitations of a pantomime, all accompanied by the solemn notes of worship performed on a splendid and solemn machine for making sound, worship done by proxy, to which the worshipper listens and worships by another, and for which he pays. And then people conclusively to prove it, say, 'But we *so* enjoy it.' Of course. The lust of the eye is just the eye gratified. 'But wasn't the theatre very entertaining and grand?' Of course, and whenever Satan fails to make such things attractive, he must try something else for the lust of the eye. 'Turn away mine eyes from beholding vanity' (Ps. cxix. 37).

3d. '*The pride of life.*' — This is not what shall we eat? nor what shall we drink? nor what shall we see? But how shall we be seen? Wherewithal shall we be clothed? What is the modern evening-party, and even a good deal of modern church-going? Either the lust of the eye or pride of life — either the lust to *see*

---

[8] Editor's Note: A person who makes a habit of getting drunk.

or *to be* seen. How can I be thought to be great? How can I make a noise in the world? — How grand can my parties by, and excel all others? This requires, seeks, and obtains the opportunities for display. How can I reach the pinnacle of earth's fame? How can I be a great scholar? How can I be a great preacher? How can I be anything great? I know such and such great men. I know Lord so-and-so, and am intimate with Lady so-and-so. These are some of the sentences of 'the pride of life.' Bengel says this pride of life 'is that which leads forth lust abroad, and diffuses it more largely into the world, so that a man *wishes to be as great as possible*, in goods, in dress, in plate, in furniture, in buildings, in estates, in servants, in his retinue, in his equipage, in his offices.'

Is not one or other of these the key-note to the heart of every man in the world? Are these not what all your friends, relatives, and yourself, by nature have pleasure in? Perhaps they do not like one, but they will have another. How am I to get out of it? As long as I am 'of the world,' I cannot but get what is in the world. God says there is nothing in the world but these. You say you have Christ. Is He enough? If you ask such a question, you never knew Him, you do not miss Him. Suppose the lust of the flesh, the lust of the eye, the pride of life, were out of the world. I guarantee that its millions would miss them. Suppose good dinners, good parties, good theatres, thrilling novels, good worldly amusements, and greatness in something of the world were gone, many would miss them and be miserable without them. But they are all doomed, and all that enjoy them. 'The world passeth away, and the lust thereof, but he that doeth the will of God abideth forever.'

Let us see how man got this threefold rope bound round him, and how he is to get it broken. He got it in the first Adam. It is broken when he gets into the second, then he is not of the world nor of what is in it.

THE FIRST ADAM'S FAILURE.
(*Introducing the Principles of the World.*)

1st. 'The tree was good for food.' This was the *lust of the flesh.*

2d. 'Pleasant to the eyes.' This was the *lust of the eye.*

3d. 'A tree to be desired to make one wise.' This was the *pride of life.*

THE SECOND ADAM'S VICTORY.
(*Overcoming the god of this World.*)

1st, 'Command that these stones be made bread.' This was the *lust of the flesh*, overcome by the Word, 'Man shall not live by bread alone, but by every word that proceedeth out of the mouth of God.'

2d, 'The Devil *sheweth* Him all the kingdoms of the world and the glory of them, and saith unto Him, all these things will I give thee if thou wilt fall down and worship me.' This was the *lust of the eye*, overcome by the Word, 'Thou shalt worship the Lord thy God, and Him only shalt thou serve.'

3d, Being set on a pinnacle of the temple. 'Cast thyself down: for it is written He shall give His angels charge concerning thee.' This was the *pride of life*, overcome by that Word, 'Thou shalt not tempt the Lord thy God.'

'This is the victory that overcometh the world, even our faith.' We live upon what is unseen. It is your time, we say to the worldling. Go on in the world with all it has, the lust of the flesh, the lust of the eye, and the pride of life. It is all the heaven you will ever see. We can well bide out time, for this is all the hell we shall see. Especially to young disciples is the exhortation needed, 'Love not the world.' Their tendency is to the world; the warmth of nature, and the vigour of youth drag the young Christian downward. His only safety is in total separation from the world.

He is not called to retire to a monastery. Jesus prayed not that we should be taken out of the world, but kept from the evil of the world. It is as really a sin to become a nun or a hermit as it is to mingle with the world. The Christian is to be like the fishes that were clean: they must have scales and fins, the scales to keep out the water, and fins to steer through it. He is not to be taken out of the world, but to go through it, and keep from all that is in it, 'enduring as seeing Him who is invisible.' The world sees no beauty in Him; they do not miss Him, because they never knew Him. They are totally blind to what He is. Not so the Christian. His Saviour is Christ. His life is Christ. His object is Christ. This world is a wilderness, because all that is in it has nothing of Christ. Dear fellow-sinner, tremble at your enjoyment of earth's stores. Shall you ever know the only One worth knowing? You do not know Him now: 'What we never knew we never miss.'

Know Him above the sun, and you will *soon understand what is meant by 'under the sun.'*

> Away from communion and walking with God,
> Man entered his own way and earth's path he trod;
> 'The world' in its course to destruction rolls on,
> With vanity stamped on all *'under the sun.'*
>
> In Eden, at Sinai, at Calvary's cross,
> The world has been tried; all its glory is dross;
> Man's failure at each step since time was begun
> Has brought in as guilty, all *'under the sun.'*
>
> Condemned by our God even now in this world,
> The stroke of His wrath soon 'gainst men shall be hurled;
> Yet still with his dancing, to wrath he will run,
> And try to find rest in all *'under the sun.'*
>
> But God has determined lost sinners to save,
> To bear all our burdens His own Son He gave;
> He bled for our sin, and the word is all done,
> God offer Him now, to all *'under the sun.'*

As one with Him now we are seen on His Cross.
The fame and the fortune of earth are but loss;
We died in the death of the crucified One,
His grave severs us from all *'under the sun.'*

The mad world may revel in mirth o'er Him slain,
For this is their heaven, their god is their gain;
The sun clad in darkness, He died all alone,
And bore all our hell, when thus *'under the sun.'*

On Christ throned above, our affection is set,
From whence He shall come in His glory so great,
The last battle fought and the victory won,
His saints are caught up, from all *'under the sun.'*

'No Confidence in the Flesh.'

Our Sanctification.

'O you know what in a Government would deserve a vote of *want of confidence*?'

'Indeed, I have little to say in politics on one side or the other, but there is a government against which I would with all my heart give a vote of *no confidence*.'

'What is that?'

'The government of an evil heart within, which is ever striving for the reins of power.'

'I agree with you; this is first: self-government is man's first duty.'

'I find that the evil heart, or "the flesh," as it is called in Scripture, is branded by the Holy Ghost with this mark, "No confidence." Look at Phil. iii. 3. Three steps may be seen in that wonderful passage —

1st, Worship God in the Spirit;

2d, Rejoice in Christ Jesus;

3d, Have no confidence in the flesh.

God is seeking worshippers — those who can worship Him in spirit and in truth. This is no legal drudgery, nor the vain attempts of men to get into favour with God. You hear people converted and unconverted, speaking of going to worship God. How could an unconverted man worship in spirit and in truth, when he neither has the Spirit in him nor has come to the Truth? and this alone is true worship. It is no mere routine of Christian duties — singing, praying, preaching, or hearing; but it is the outflow of heartfelt adoration to God — it may be in silence, or in song or thanksgiving, but it is giving God back something, giving back His own gift, thinking God's thoughts about Christ.'

'And how can this high step be reached?'

'The Spirit's method is by making us "rejoice in Christ Jesus." No man can worship acceptably unless his joy is in Christ Jesus. In fact, worship is the overflow back to God of the full cup of joy. Why is there so little true worship? Because there is so little rejoicing in Christ Jesus. I know some are considered great authorities who would hardly dare to say they are saved, and have often wondered what such think of this text, "Rejoice in Christ Jesus." A brother truly remarked that many Christians' Bibles should be printed, "Mourn in the Lord always; and again I say, mourn." "Rejoice in the Lord alway" is as really a command as "Thou shalt not steal;" and our blessed Lord said, "If ye love Me, keep My commandments." Hence we are not merely allowed to rejoice, but authoritatively commanded, and if we do not, we are guilty of disobedience.'

'But do you always rejoice?'

'Now this is a very common way of getting away from the authority of God, by comparing ourselves with one another instead of bowing to God's demands. Alas! no, I do not rejoice always; but when I do not, I have to confess it as my sin, just as I have to confess every hour that I do not love God and my neighbor perfectly.'

'Many earnest men disobey this commandment of the Holy Ghost, I am sure, because they feel the evil of their own hearts so strongly.'

'Now this is most absurd from a scriptural point of view. In fact, the very step on which a Christian plants his foot, and thence rises to true joy and true worship, is the total setting aside of his own evil nature, as so utterly worthless, unimprovable, and corrupt, that he determines, by God's help, he will have no confidence in it. If a man gets thoroughly into this scriptural truth about "the flesh," or rather, if it enters into him by the power of the Holy Ghost, he will soon rise into the higher experience of rejoicing in Christ Jesus, and then worshipping God in the Spirit.

'We shall try briefly to note the Scriptures that give us the history, character, and relations of this terrible foe, and from Scripture we shall find that man as man is no better and no worse that when he was driven out of Eden. Science and art have done much. Printing, railways, telegraphs, and many other inventions have appeared. Time and space, as to this little planet, have been almost annihilated. But what about real progress God-ward? With all man's so-called improvements, are there fewer thieves? Has honesty risen much above the level of policy? Are servants more obedient to their masters? Are children more obedient to their parents? Development has been going on; but, alas! what a development! The elements of all that has been developed were in Adam after the fall. Before the fall, Adam in innocence had body, soul, and spirit, with a will subject to God's will. By the fall he got the fatal acquisition, "the flesh,"—a self-will—a will independent of God's.'

Astronomers tell us that planets are kept in their courses by two forces acting in different directions, the resultant of which is the curve they describe round the sun. The one of these forces would draw the planet *from* the sun, the other would draw the planet *to* the sun. The one force is centrifugal,[9] the other is centripetal.[10] Man, revolving around God in the communion of innocence, having received the breath of life from God, making him immortal, and having been made in the image of God, acted as the representative of God on earth below. By the fall he severed his centripetal connection, or that when he heard God's voice was to hide himself. He has now acquired this fatal self-will. He has got the power to disobey God. The fatal freedom is his that some planet let loose from its circular path would have; and now, in his mad, desolating, destructive, rebellious,

---

[9] Editor's Note: The apparent force that is felt by an object moving in a curved path that acts outwardly away from the center of rotation.

[10] Editor's Note: The force that is necessary to keep an object moving in a curved path and that is directed inward toward the center of rotation.

God-dishonouring freedom, as man, is rushing on to everlasting chaos, confusion, and night, 'the blackness of darkness for ever.' The least thing could sever the link that joined man in probation to God. Disobedience to one test-act did it. Man died (became separated from God) the moment he ate the forbidden fruit. What has been the history of the world ever since?

Our modern sages tell us that it has been the education of the world, that at Babel men were divided into classes, that under law man's education began in earnest, that Christ came as one of this great series of teachers, and now the Spirit in our day is going on to complete the education. This sounds very well, but it is only man's thought. Scripture shows us that the history of the world is the history of sin; that man is away from God and must be (not educated, but) saved, or perish for ever. The ritualist tells us that man is to be *Religionized*; God tells us that he is to be *born again*. The rationalist tells us he has been going on with his *education*; God tells us he is '*condemned* already,' and is incapable of being educated until His grace save him (Tit. ii.).

We have seen whence 'the flesh' was acquired: let us look at it —

I. AS TRIED AND DESCRIBED BY GOD.

There are two distinct though connected questions:
First, What is the history of 'the flesh?'
Second, How is 'the flesh' described in Scripture?

I may state here, that there is often confusion in men's minds concerning what 'the flesh' is. This partly arises from the word 'flesh' being used in two quite different senses in Scripture. In the majority of cases in the New Testament the words rightly translated 'flesh' and 'fleshly,' have to do with the flesh of the body, such as 'flesh and blood,' 'Jesus Christ came in the flesh,' which of course is not the evil nature which is spoken of in the other use of the word. There was an old heresy which made sin resident in the flesh of the body, and this led men to practice tortures and penance; but very few ever have such a thought now. There are about a hundred passages in which 'flesh' has this first meaning. In the fifty others in which the word is used it refers to the evil nature, the alienated affections, the self-will of man as away from God.

First, *What is the history of the flesh?*

A solution of arsenic in a glass full of water is very like the water, and cannot be detected by the eye. The chemist, in order to prove to the satisfaction of all that it is the deadly poison, takes one portion and to it adds something else, which, whenever it comes in contact with the arsenic in the water, makes it assume a well-known colour, showing at once what it is. He then takes another quantity and adds something else to it to confirm this, until by various tests he has shown us exactly what it is, and proved beyond a doubt that it is that poison. God has been doing this with man; not, as the rationalist would persuade us, trying to improve the arsenic, and make it a harmless drink — arsenic remains arsenic. A farmer, having a hundred acres of land, when trying certain manures and crops, does not require to put all the land under one trial, but may have a hundred distinct trials on his hundred acres. God did not try man twice in innocence. He did not put two nations under law. Man is man, all as to nature being of the same material. Let us look at some of these tests that God has been employing from age to age.

1st, As an innocent man, God gave him one test — a thing which in itself had no moral value. He was allowed all the fruit in the garden except that upon one tree. The simplicity of the test made it all the more important. Man chose his own way; showed his independence, that is to say, sin as to his will. God knew what was in man. It was not for Himself He tried man. He knew the end from the beginning; but that all might know it, and every mouth be stopped, man was tested.

2d, After the fall, man was tried as having a will opposed to God, and a conscience that told of God's demands. Man had the knowledge now of good and evil. His conscience told him what he *ought* to do; he had no external laws to obey. 'Leave a man to his conscience,' we hear it said. We answer, 'He has been left,' and what do we see? That as the one test acting on innocent man brought out his independence or sin as to the will, so man, with the flesh in him left to conscience, manifested his corruption or depravity of heart in lust, or sin as to the affections; for we read, 'God *saw* that the wickedness of man was great in the earth, and that *every* imagination (purposes and desires) of the thoughts of his heart was only evil continually.' Look at these three words, '*every*,' that is without exception, not one good, rotten to the core; '*only*' unadulterated evil, unmixed sinfulness; '*continually*' at every moment, in so-called good moments as well as bad. What a picture, man when he was left to his conscience, thus presented! God alone saw man's heart in its innate hideousness; and so, after man had been thus tested for nearly two thousand years, till sin reached its height, God destroyed all the teeming millions, in His wrath emptied out into destruction the earth odious in His presence, as a chemist hastens to throw out some noxious compound made between a poison and a test. We find God covenanting with Noah, and giving His promise to Abraham, and His *law* to Moses. This brings us to the third test.

3d, The law — the perfect rule of human righteousness, given to one nation, as the test was before given to one man, and conscience had tried all the world (the whole Gentile world being proved guilty by conscience and the light of nature, as seen in Rom. i.). What did the law do? Did it bring the nation to God? Here is what the Holy Ghost says, 'Wherefore then serveth the law? It was added *for the sake of (lit.)* transgression' (Gal. iii. 19). What was independence, that is, sin of the will or corruption — that is, sin of lust before — was now seen to be transgression — that is to say, sin in relation to law. 'Where no law is, there is no transgression.' We know, very well, there was sin — so much that the whole world had to be drowned; but law showed sin to be transgression. A test, before it is of any use, must be perfect. If the test is imperfect, the results will prove nothing; but 'God's law is perfect,' it is 'holy, and just, and good;' and the moment it came in contact with 'the flesh' —with sinful man — it brought out his character as radically disobedient. Making the golden calf, and thus, breaking the first words of the law, was man's reception of the law. The law was weak to make sinful men holy, not in itself, but weak through the flesh. Fouler and fouler the filthy water of the flesh is shown to be. Can anything be worse than independence (away from God), corruption, and transgression? Yes, one thing more was needed before the trial of the flesh could be completed. Passing over man's declension under kings subject to God, and Gentile wickedness in unlimited monarchy over the whole world, we come to Christ as the last test at the 'end of the world' under trial.

4th, Christ is seen as a test of men. A servant might be very independent, or very corrupt, or break his master's commands, but he might never, with all this, have thought of taking his master's life. If the testing process had stopped short of Christ as a test, the nature of the flesh would not have been fully seen; but He has proved what man is. We are so much accustomed to think of Christ as a Saviour, that we seldom think of Him as coming to bring out 'what was in man.' Read Mark xii. 1-10. After showing man in his treatment of subordinate servants, the Lord says, ver. 6, 'Having yet, therefore, one Son, His well-beloved, He sent Him also *last* unto them saying, "They will reverence My Son." ' We know well what they did: they slew the King's Son, showing thus their enmity to the King. Enmity against God Himself is the highest point rebellion can reach. This was never seen till Christ came; and this is the education of the world! Let us recapitulate what we have seen to be the character of man from his history. God tested him, and the very first thing recorded under each test is evil.

1st, As tried in innocence, his *independence* was seen — that is, sin as to the will.

2nd, As tried by conscience, his *corruption* was seen — that is, sin as to the heart.

3rd, As tried by law, his *transgression* was seen — that is, sin as to commandment.

4th, As tried by Christ, his *enmity* was seen — that is, sin as to a person.

The complete character of the poison is now seen — 'the flesh' would kill God if it could. Man in the 'flesh' slaughtered the God-man. Friend, you have that nature in your bosom.

Second, *How is the flesh described?*

How does God describe it in the doctrinal statements of His word? It is remarkable that it is not until the full proof had been given of what the flesh can do — namely, crucify Christ — that we get it spoken of and fully exposed by God, and from God get its true character. The flesh is not borne with now on account of the hardness of men's hearts, for the darkness is past, and the true light now shineth. In Rom. vii. 18, Paul says, 'I know that in me (that is, in my *flesh*) dwelleth no good thing.' This proves the existence of two natures in the Christian as well as the fearfully depraved character of the flesh. The Holy Ghost dwelt in the new nature in Paul as He dwells in every Christian. But besides his new nature there was still the old, unchanged and unchangeable. None but a saved man can know that there is *nothing good* whatever in the 'flesh.' Many moral unconverted men believe that there are many bad things in it, but none of them believe that there is nothing good. 'Even the worst have their good points' is man's estimate (and quite true as to human morality); but God's estimate is 'nothing good.' Read Gen. vi. 5. All confess they are sinners, but few that they (as sprung from Adam) are nothing but sinners. The extent of the ruin, the nature of the depravity, and the steps by which it was reached, are of comparatively little importance, since in every unconverted man (as God sees him) there is no good thing.

A friend who had been led to see this, thus wrote to me, 'I have labelled all *my* feelings with God's label, "No good thing."' When very bad characters get converted, their friends often say, 'But you see he was a thoughtless young man, and he was led away, but he was not so bad as some;' and so on with a great deal of palliation and whining sentimentalism, instead of affixing to him God's estimate of every unconverted man, 'No good thing.'

Some people think because they understand a great deal of theological truth, that this is good. Unless the man has been born again, all his knowledge however good in itself is reckoned 'no good thing' to him.

Some think that because they feel devotional amid solemn sights and plaintive pealing pipes of praising machinery, there must be some soft corner for divine things in their hearts after all, but God all the while says, '*No good thing.*' Hearing the 'Dead March in Saul'[11] played by a military band at a soldier's funeral has often moved many to tears, and I do not wonder at the most stolid being moved in their feelings; but what does mere feeling or emotion amount to? — '*No good thing.*'

Some again suppose because their consciences get disturbed at certain sins, that this is so much good. Man has nothing to boast of in having a conscience, not even if he followed its right leadings. It never gave him a new nature. Every man has a conscience, that is to say — the knowledge of good and evil. A man cannot make a warm day because he has a thermometer which shows when it is warm. Neither has a man anything good, because he has within him that which tells him what is good, and what is evil. Let us look at other Scriptures to find out a little more what the flesh is.

Gal. v. 19, 'The works of *the flesh* are manifest, which are, adultery, fornication, uncleanness, lasciviousness, idolatry, witchcraft, hatred, variance, emulations, wrath, strife, seditions, heresies, envyings, murders, drunkenness, revellings, and such like.' What a fountain of all uncleanness! In 2 Peter ii. 18 we find what feeds the flesh: 'For when they speak great swelling words of vanity, they allure through the lusts of *the flesh.*' The

---

[11] Editor's Note: The work, *Saul*, which Handel composed in 1738, includes the famous "Dead March," a funeral anthem for Saul and his son Jonathan following their deaths in the Battle of Mount Gilboa at the hands of the Philistines.

flesh loves pompousness, it hates humility. 2 Pet. ii. 10 speaks of 'them that walk after *the flesh* in the lust of uncleanness, and despise government—presumptuous, self-willed.' 'Self-will' (that is, liking and choosing one's own way rather than God's), 'is, in fact, the very essence of the flesh.' Man must have what he wills, and desires, whatever the consequences be, whatever God says; Satan, of course, at the same time blinding us as to what God's will is. The world is also in close alliance with its lusts: 1 John ii. 16, 'all that is in the world, the lust of *the flesh*, and the lust of the eyes, and the pride of life, is not of the Father, but is of the world.'

Rom. viii. 3-7 gives us the nature of the flesh as opposed to *law*, to *life*, and to *God*, just as we saw it in its progressive history. Ver. 3. 'What the law could not do in that it was weak through the flesh;' ver. 7, 'The carnal mind (literally the mind of *the flesh*) is not subject to the *law* of God, neither indeed can be.' It opposed the law, broke it, was stirred up to more evil by it. Again, as to life: ver. 6, 'To be carnally minded (literally the mind of *the flesh*) is *death;*' and as to God, 'The *carnal* mind is *enmity* against God;' ver. 8, 'So then they that are in *the flesh* cannot please God.' Friend, pause a minute. Are you in the flesh? Do what you may, you 'cannot please God.' Give all your time and money to the Lord, yet you 'cannot please God.' Let us now look at 'the flesh' —

II. — AS TO THE SINNER'S SALVATION.

We need not dwell long on this, as we have seen what God's character of it is. 'The flesh' is never sanctified nor improved. It can only be condemned.

Christ came in the likeness of sinful flesh, and for sin condemned 'sin in *the flesh*.' 'The flesh' is never forgiven. It is judged, set aside, condemned. Though my sins were like scarlet, the precious blood has cleansed them, and I am forgiven, but the flesh never is. God never improves it, and God never forgives it, neither should we. We are saved from this awful depravity and corruption in which we were born, not by any process or work, any more than we are justified from our sins by a work.

We get out of *the flesh* just as we got into it. We got into it by our birth; we get out of it by a new birth. We got into it in a representative head, Adam; we get out of it in the representative head, Christ. Christ on the cross not only had our iniquities laid upon Him, but also condemned 'sin in *the flesh*;' that is to say, not the guilt of sin, but sin in the nature; not the branches, but the root; not the streams, but the fountain.

Many are trying to improve 'the flesh,' and would take much comfort if they could only feel themselves getting a little better; whereas God wishes us to have no confidence in it whatever, and to 'reckon ourselves dead indeed *unto sin*.' How could any one by any effort of will, without a new nature, subdue his flesh when it is just self-will? It would only be will against will, which is an absurdity.

But if I receive God's Christ as the One dead and now risen, reckoning myself dead to sin, I bring in God's will done in Christ's work about sin, and I thus 'thank God through Jesus Christ our Lord,' and begin to walk in newness of life. And though there is still conflict, I know that 'with the mind I myself (what God reckons as me in Christ) serve the law of God, but with the flesh the law of sin;' but that 'there is no condemnation to them in Christ Jesus.' Whether are you in Christ Jesus or in the flesh? You cannot be in both.

Your standing is either in Christ risen or in Adam fallen. There is no third man. Adam was the first man, and all the trial was only of the first man. Christ is the second man, and there is no third. He is the last. He is the second man, but he is the last Adam (1 Cor. xv. 45, 49).

III. — AS TO THE CHRISTIAN'S LIFE.

New Testament Scripture is very plain on two points:

1st. The Christian is not in *the flesh*. Paul could speak of himself and of all Christians thus, 'When we *were* in the flesh' (Rom. vii. 5), of course thus implying that they are not in it now.

2d. '*The flesh*' is still in the Christian. Paul said, 'In me, that is in my flesh, dwelleth no good thing.' (Rom. vii. 18.) If we mistake or forget one or other of these facts, we shall get into great confusion, and shall have lessened power in dealing with this enemy.

1st. THE CHRISTIAN IS NOT IN THE FLESH.

'Ye *are not* in the flesh but in the Spirit, if so be that the Spirit of God dwell in you.' (Rom. viii. 9.) The Spirit of God dwells in all Christians, therefore this is true of all. 'They that are Christ's *have crucified* the flesh with the affections and lusts.' (Gal. v. 24.) Not, 'are to crucify,' or 'ought to,' but '*have crucified.*' 'In whom also ye are circumcised with the circumcision made without hands, in putting off the body of the sins of *the flesh* by the circumcision of Christ.' (Col. ii. 11.) Every Christian is out of Adam and in Christ. He is sailing now in the river of life; whereas, by nature, his boat is tossing on the river of death. It is said of the children of Israel in the wilderness, so wicked and so perverse, God 'hath not beheld iniquity in Jacob neither hath He seen perverseness in Israel.' (Num. xxiii. 21.) So when God looks at a sinner in Christ He sees the sinner dressed in all the beauty of Christ, and sees none of the sinner's iniquity nor perverseness.

The Holy Spirit, by the pen of the Apostle Paul, brings out this very clearly in the second chapter of Galatians, where a line of argument is pursued similar to that contained in the sixth of Romans. In Romans, after Paul brings in 'all the world,' Jew and Gentile, 'guilty before God,' and demonstrates the victory of grace over sin, he goes on in the sixth chapter to show Christ, in resurrection, as the immediate and effective power of personal holiness.

In the second of Galatians he takes occasion, from Peter refusing to take a meal with certain persons, to show the true position and standing of all believers in the Lord Jesus Christ. A straw shows the direction of the current. If Peter could not have intercourse with Gentiles who had been cleansed in the blood of Jesus and placed in a position of righteousness that no legal observances could effect or help him to keep and walk in, the whole 'gospel of the grace of God' would be undermined. (Read Gal. ii.)

Paul shows that both Peter and himself, Jews as they were, children of the promise, and not 'sinners of the Gentiles,' had to fall into the sinner's place, and accept Christ the gift of God.

Peter, in Acts xv. 11, stands up for the very same doctrine: — 'We believe that, through the grace of the Lord Jesus Christ, we (Jews) shall be saved, even as they (sinners of the Gentiles).'

Paul says, in effect, if the law could justify them, they had been doing wrong in preaching Christ. Does Christ need the law to help Him to present the believer to God? We consider it blasphemous to think that Christ would be a minister of sin. But having been judged, condemned, and slain by the law, do we now go back to be saved or helped by it? If so, we prove by this very act that we are 'transgressors;' for in that case we should never have left it at all. Grace and law cannot help each other in our salvation — the adoption of grace is the giving up of law for salvation.

The Apostle, in the 18th and following verses (Gal. ii.) places himself as representing all believers, and goes on to show that men can serve God, and live acceptably to Him — only through death and resurrection. 'For I through the law am dead.' This, of course, cannot mean that I am morally dead to the knowledge of its demands; nor that I am dead in the sense of seeking my justification by the old dispensation under law; but *through* the law have died,' or have judicially met my doom. God said, 'In the day that thou eatest thereof thou shalt surely die.' The flaming sword that guarded Paradise has demanded my blood. 'I have died.' 'The soul that sinneth it shall die.' 'I have died.'

The law has exacted its demands. 'The wages of sin is death.' These wages have been paid. 'I have died.'

But, since I through the law have died, in perfect righteousness and justice I have now died *to* its every claim, and the sword cannot be bathed in blood twice for the same offence. The wages of my sin cannot be demanded twice. The murderer hanging dead at the jibbet[12] of justice, is dead to every demand they can bring against him.

Daniel, by serving his God, had brought himself under the penalty of the laws of the Medes and Persians, which said, 'He shall be cast into the den of lions.' But, sitting at the bottom of that den, with the lions' mouths graciously stopped, he could say — 'I am dead *to* the law of the Medes and Persians.' And when Darius raised him on the morrow, he did so in perfect righteousness, as far as the demands of the law of the Medes and Persians were concerned, and no enemy of Daniel, no adviser of Darius, could punish the prophet for law-breaking, nor point a suspicious finger at him as he sat with Darius — he could now live to Darius. 'I through the law am dead to the law,' only, however, 'that I might live unto God.' — 'He that has died is justified from sin' (Rom. vi. 7). This death and resurrection scheme is no figure of speech, but an awful reality as seen at Calvary, and a reality (judicially and experimentally) to the sinner on believing in Jesus. We have life out of death.

The 19th verse is a counterpart of the 18th. The 18th, as it were, expresses the truth abstractly. The 19th meets this question — 'What! is Saul the Pharisee, Saul, the persecutor, Saul the professor, Saul the legalist, dead?' He is; but this is where I find an end of myself — on the cross of Christ: 'I am crucified with Christ.' This is sometimes explained, 'as Christ was crucified, and suffered at the hands of the world, so I'll bear the cross along with Him.' It is indeed a blessed truth that we have fellowship with Him in His sufferings for righteousness, and that as followers of Jesus, we are to take up *our* cross and follow

---

[12] Editor's Note: Gallows.

Him: but the truth in this passage answers to the statement in the former verse, 'I through the law have died;' and to that in Romans vi. 6, 'Knowing that our old man is (has been) crucified.' 'I have been crucified with Christ.' (The verb is in the perfect passive.) The stroke of justice against me fell on Him. My cup was drained by Him; my wages of sin were paid out to Him; my separation from God was in His cry, 'My God, my God, why hast thou forsaken me?' My hell was borne by Him — the perfectly righteous One fulfilling all law, and then bearing its penalty for me the unrighteous, condemned, dead one. 'He suffered, the Just for the unjust, that He might bring us to God.' And, looking back on His cross, and identifying myself with Him, I can say, —

> '*I through the law am dead*,'
> '*I am crucified with Christ*.'

No demand can be made against Christ; for, after justice had been appeased, God raised Him up from the dead by the Holy Spirit; and as there could never come one single question concerning sin against Him who had become the sin-bearer (after having borne sin, He had been raised in righteousness), so I, quickened into this 'newness of life,' go free. I was not justified when Christ rose, but He was raised again for my justification; and on believing I reckon myself dead, and can say,

—

> '*I am dead to the law*,'
> '*Crucified; nevertheless I live*,'

live in this resurrection-life, live in this life that Jesus has beyond His grave, beyond the demands of law, beyond the doom of sin, for it is 'yet not (literally *no longer*) I, but Christ liveth in me'– –no longer Saul the Pharisee—Saul the pretender to—and striver after righteousness by law' but one who has submitted himself to God's righteousness—one who has submitted himself to be put out of existence judicially—that is to say, in God's reckoning—and is now known only as one who is living in Christ, living unto God,—

> *'That I might live unto God;'*
> *'Yet not I, but Christ liveth in me.'*

A man is thus made fit for living unto God, not by amendment and reformation, but through *death* and *resurrection*; the flesh might and does attempt the former, in the latter God alone can work. This 'sanctification of the spirit' is *all* of God.

'The *life* which I now live,' is in a foreign, uncongenial clime —where I have no friends—no food—no rest; it lives by faith,' on what will be its life for ever, 'the Son of God.' This life feeds on love: for its object is Jesus, 'who loved me and gave Himself for me.'

Thus I have not only forgiveness of sins in Christ, but righteousness also; for I could no more get righteousness by law than I could forgiveness. But now are we 'the righteousness of God in Him.' 'For is righteousness come by law, Christ is dead in vain;' but we are in Him 'who of God is made unto us wisdom, and righteousness, and sanctification, and redemption' (1 Cor. i. 30).

> *'With Christ we died to sin —*
> *Lay buried in His tomb;*
> *But quickened now with Him our life,*
> *We stand beyond our doom.'*

Thus the apostle Paul places the believer in perfect acceptance before God — Christ his title — Christ his righteousness — Christ his meetness — Christ his all and in all. Made a 'partaker of the divine nature,' the believer has now that which can enjoy God, and commune with Him.

But what has all this truth to do with the Christian's every-day life, one may ask? Much, very much indeed; for there can be no real progress made by us in the Christian course until the ground of our standing before God be righteously and conclusively settled.

Being born of Adam, 'of the will of the flesh,' we are heirs of Adam's nature, its guilt, its actings, and its doom, 'by nature the children of wrath.' So having received Christ, 'being born of God,' we are reckoned as one with Christ, we were crucified with Christ, and thus met the doom of sin in Christ: and now we live to God in the life of Christ, a life in resurrection, as truly getting a new nature at the second birth, as we got the Adam-nature at the first. God reckons us as being thus in His sight; and we believing, and thus getting into God's reckoning, have 'peace with God, through our Lord Jesus Christ.'

2d. THE FLESH IS IN THE CHRISTIAN.

No Christian ever lived, or ever will live, on earth without sin in him. Indeed it is after I know Christ that I really know the utter worthlessness of the flesh, that 'in me (that is in my flesh) dwelleth no good thing' (Rom. vii. 18). Now the opposition will be felt between this perfectly holy nature, begotten in me in connexion with Christ risen and gone to the Father, and this perfectly sinful nature. Now it is that I know the meaning of 'sin that *dwelleth* in me,' which can never be uprooted here, for it *dwelleth* in me; not sins coming from me, or felt by me, but sin the innate principle, no accident nor habit, 'sin *dwelleth* in me.' Formerly I might have assumed that the doctrine of *in-dwelling sin* was true, but now 'Í know' (Rom. vii. 18), that is, the truth applied to my conscience, by the Holy Ghost. Now I know, 'That the disposition of the flesh (*lit.*) is enmity against God, for it is not subject to the law of God, *neither indeed can be*' (Rom. viii. 7).

From the above it will be seen that salvation is something more than a mere payment of debt, a covering over of iniquity, the gift of a white robe of righteousness, a setting right of the faculties of the soul, for which out of gratitude to God, and aided by His Spirit, the Christian is now to live a holy life. There is also a new birth, the implantation of a nature which not only makes a man live to serve God out of gratitude, but which in its very essence is *from* God. The spring of all true Christian holiness is the presence and operative power of the indwelling Spirit, working indeed through a man's natural faculties, but on objects above and beyond what the Adam-life can see, apprehend, live on, or enjoy. Three very important and practical propositions arise out of the foregoing truths.

1*st*, The Christian has two natures in one person.

2*d*, How does the Christian grow in grace?

3*d*, The Christian daily confesses his sins and is daily forgiven.

I. *The Christian has two* distinct *natures in one responsible person.*

The Christian is not two persons, the one perfectly sinful, and the other perfectly sinless, shut up together in one chamber; but he has two natures, the 'old' and the 'new man' in the one responsible person; he has that born of the flesh, which is not merely flesh-like but *flesh*, and that born of the Spirit, which is not merely spiritual but *spirit*.

The sinner living 'in the flesh,' 'dead in trespasses and sins,' was pardoned, accepted, and made a saint — Christ having died and risen for him, by being born again, which was accomplished by getting this life of Christ, begotten in him by the Holy Ghost in reality and not in figure. As a saint, he is now 'not in the flesh,' though the flesh is in him, but he is in the Spirit, and is responsible for the uprisings and sins of the old man. He is henceforth pardoned as a son according to the value of the blood presented before God *for him*, the person, the individual now become a Christian, the man possessed of these two natures, who should be walking 'in the spirit,' though ever and anon he is made to stumble through the power of 'the flesh.' Thus the saint does not advance in sanctifications by a change being effected in the character of either nature, but in the gradual development of 'the new man' by means of the inworking of the Holy Ghost, and in the daily mortification of the members which are upon the earth. The man is thus gradually sanctified and made more like Jesus. This is growth 'in grace.' How blessed! We are saved 'by *grace*;' we stand 'in *grace*' — we grow 'in *grace*.' The life of the child is perfectly human; we have to grow to be men. The smallest leaflet on the furthest branch of the vine has the same vine-life as the largest branch, the trunk or the root. God's seed implanted is a perfect life; we have to grow up to the stature of men. We would again sum up, in brief, regarding this new life which we have already discoursed on at length in the chapter on the work of the Spirit.

In John iii. we get the origin and communication of this life, 'Ye must be born again' (ver. 7): something external, all of God, must be implanted; not something already in me wrought on and purified. 'Of water and of the Spirit:' the word of God applied by the Spirit purifies us as to our thoughts, feelings, and affections.

In John iv. we get the indwelling of the Spirit — the gift of Christ — as the one energizing power in the new man, represented as 'a well of water springing up into everlasting life' (iv. 14).

In chap. vii. we get the outflow of this Spirit, in the activities of the new man on all around him, through no new channels, no new faculties of mind, but 'out of his belly shall flow rivers of living water' (ver. 38).

2. *How does the Christian* grow *in grace?*
Does his heart get better?

The Spirit of God in John teaches that in a converted man there is a new fountain.

Many Christians seem to think that all we get at conversion is a divinely given *filter* to the old fountain, which will gradually increase in its power until it renders the filthy waters of the old fountain clean. In Galatians v. 15-26, the whole point is stated.

Two *fountains* are spoken of in the converted man, sending out their natural streams. The streams from the old fountain, the flesh, are given at the 19th verse, 'Adultery, fornication, uncleanness, lasciviousness, idolatry, witchcraft, hatred, variance, emulations, wrath, strife, seditions, heresies, envyings, murders, drunkenness, revellings. Are we anywhere taught in Scripture that this evil nature is refined, is purified? Certainly, indeed, the man, the individual, is purified, is cleansed, made more holy, is morally sanctified; but it is in altogether another way than by trying to cure what is 'incurably wicked.' The streams from the new fountain — the Spirit —are given at the 22nd verse, 'love, joy, peace, long-suffering, gentleness, goodness, faith, meekness, temperance;' and we are told that the Christian's holy life is walking in the Spirit, mortifying the 'members which are upon the earth' (Col. iii. 5), keeping them in their place of death, 'not fulfilling the lusts of the flesh.' This is God's way; He asks for a holy walk, and moreover has not left us powerless, as helpless slaves under the flesh, but has placed us in a position above it, as masters over it — for 'the flesh lusteth against the Spirit,' also the 'Spirit against the flesh, and these are contrary the one to the other' (therefore they can never be merged the one into the other, nor come to peaceable terms) '*in order that* (literally) ye may not do the things that ye would.' Not, as generally understood, that I should wish to do good things but cannot (we get that aspect of truth in the case of a quickened man under law in Rom. vii. 19, but it is another thought here); on the contrary, by the flesh-nature I wish to do evil things, but now I have the Spirit indwelling and acting, who will not let me do those evil things I otherwise would.

Many Christians do not know that we get a new creation put into us at the new birth: hence they do not realise the existence in the believer of two diametrically opposite and actively opposing natures. Ignorance of these things is at the root of many soul-confounding errors in doctrine and practice.

If salvation consisted merely in having forgiveness, the powers of the mind being set right, and the will wrought on and sanctified, we might be saved to-day and lost to-morrow; in Christ to-day and out of Him to-morrow. But if I get a divine life — the child's life 'quickened together with Christ,' united to Christ by the Holy Ghost sent down from heaven — I am as eternally saved as Christ is safe, being a 'member of His body, of His flesh, and of His bones' (Eph. v. 30).

Again, if my sinful propensities have merely to be toned down, so that they gradually die out, one by one, until all of them are out of existence; if I were to live long enough, and were sufficiently zealous, watchful, and prayerful, I might obtain perfection as to holiness, in this moral sense, — might live without having sin at all. This we know is opposed to all Scripture teaching, for (it is written of Christians) 'If we say that we have no sin, we deceive ourselves, and the truth is not in us.' It is equally opposed to all conscientious Christian experience, for while we *ought* at all times to walk 'in the Spirit' without sinning, we know that the unchanged and unchangeable root of sin remains till we go hence. That kind of teaching which speaks of the attainment of perfection in the walk of a Christian — that is to say, the possibility of sinless perfection, perfect sanctification in the flesh, tends miserable to tone down sin, and make it a slight matter, and sacrilegiously brings down God's standard of holiness to human attainment, instead of having all in Christ; Christ *for me* — my Substitute: Christ *in me* — my life.

In 1 John iii. 9, we read, 'Whosoever is born of God doth not commit sin; for His seed remaineth in him, and he cannot sin, because he is born of God.' Mark very carefully that this is not written concerning a few advanced Christians who had reached a high state of perfection. It is written concerning the youngest disciple: 'Whosoever is born of God.' And would it not be strange to think that anything born of God could sin? The difficulty in the passage vanishes when I understand that the Christian has two natures, one born of God, perfect and sinless (God's seed is in him), the other born of Adam, imperfect and sinful. Whenever a Christian commits a sin, he is shewing that he is born of Adam. It is not as born of God he sins, but as born of

Adam. Should we not watch over ourselves, and pray for much grace, to enable us always to live as sons of God and not as sons of Adam?

It is Christians who are told, in Phil. iii. 3, to have no 'confidence in the flesh.' Those who are the true circumcision of God have no confidence in any religious culture, advantages, or natural privileges. Paul could boast more than any man of natural trainings for the flesh. Born under and brought up in all God's ordinances, he yet had to renounce all. God's ordinance can never implant life. All our many privileges could never implant the new life. They can, and do develop the life, as the heat, sunshine, rain, and culture do a seed; but an act of God's Spirit is required to implant the seed. These same privileges may only the more surely seal the ruin of a man who has not been converted, and it may be impossible to renew him to repentance. The sun hardens clay as it softens wax. Paul thought all his natural advantages but loss. He had no confidence in the flesh. Two are striving for the mastery in every Christian, the flesh and the spirit — 'for the flesh lusts against the Spirit, and the Spirit against the flesh.' But we have now the upper hand, and sin shall not have dominion over us. It is by opposition and warfare, not by assimilation and agreement, that we grow in the Christian life. We are not daily sanctified by the 'flesh' getting better or less, but by the new nature in us growing and being strengthened by the indwelling Spirit of God, and thus successfully opposing the first risings of the flesh. We cannot expel the flesh — we reckon it dead, put it off, and keep it under. We mortify our members which are upon the earth. We cannot root out the vile weeds — we keep the scythe going cutting them down.

All Christians would wish to be led by the Spirit: but they forget the first step, to start with a vote of *'no confidence'* in the flesh. At every subsequent step there will then be watchfulness as well as looking to Jesus, who is our strength. The Christian has not so much to fear 'the flesh' in its outwardly gross forms, as in its thoughts and desires. It is comparatively easy not to steal, not to tell lies, not to swear, not to be a drunkard.

Many moral, unconverted men are specimens of the highest external right-doing, but it is in its secret workings, workings that are natural to us, that we have the flesh most to dread.

Our path is that of obedience and love in the footsteps of our Lord, where the righteous requirements of the law are 'fulfilled in us, who walk not after *the flesh*, but after the Spirit' (Rom. viii. 4), for the flesh gave us nothing in the past, and can profit us nothing for the future: thus 'We are debtors not to the flesh, to live after the flesh.' For 'If ye live after the flesh, ye shall die; but if ye through the Spirit do mortify the deeds of the body, ye shall live' (Rom viii. 12, 13). Our sonship cannot be taken from us, but we can have no living fellowship with God if we thus walk. 'Living after the flesh' and communion are impossible, and cannot go together. Death is separation from God — not 'ceasing to exist;' for we know that not even the lost thus perish. Death is ceasing to exist in one state or condition, and existing in another state separated from God.

Take care, fellow-disciple, of getting into a deadened state of soul. We have the flesh in us, yet we have no authority, but the reverse, for living after it, 'as if we walked according to the flesh' (2 Cor. x. 2). Stamp upon it 'No confidence' — 'Put ye on the Lord Jesus Christ, and make not provision for the flesh, to fulfil the lusts thereof' (Rom. xiii. 14). Alas! how often we make provision for it! How the flesh feasts upon praise and flattery! It likes to be flattered, and when it is not flattered, it begins to flatter. It understands nothing about being of 'no reputation.' It likes to be something, or to do something. 'Though I be nothing' is not in its vocabulary. Have I done something for the Lord? Have I been the poor, humble channel to convey water to a soul? The flesh likes to know it. 'Let not thy left hand know what thy right hand doeth' — is God's way. 'Let not only your left hand, but let every person know' — is man's way. 'I did so and so. I was used in so and so.' Oh, this fearful self! This awful I! And then it, of course, vindicates itself. 'Oh, but it is for God's glory that I tell it!' Yes, this may be the worst part of the whole — taking a little to self under semblance of giving all to God. 'No provision,' 'no confidence' in your own evil nature, or any other person's. Take care of being 'vainly puffed up' by the mind of the flesh (Cor. ii. 18). Do not be unkind to a fellow-believer by bringing near him that which the flesh enjoys. Do not bring sparks near gunpowder. 'Oh, you did well to-day!' said one to another who had preached the gospel. 'Yes,' he replied, 'Satan told me that before I left the pulpit.' Let us not serve Satan after this sort.

None are in greater danger than those who are used to gather in souls. I knew one who was constantly used of God in doing all kinds of good, and when he did speak, it was always about what other people had been doing. To tell faults to a friend himself, is faithfulness. All that is good of him tell to others. God tells us of our faults. He stands up for us against every accuser. Another I knew who could speak of what self had been used in doing, but could not bear to hear of others being used. What a God-dishonouring, flesh-gratifying as well as foolish course! Are we not members one of another? I heard it said of a dear Christian one day, 'Yes, such a one lives upon praise.' Do you live upon the rejected Lord, who made Himself of no reputation, or on praise? Husks that the swine live upon! Make no provision for the flesh.

'Having, therefore, these promises (the Lord Almighty to be our Father), dearly beloved, let us cleanse ourselves from all filthiness of *the flesh* and spirit, perfecting holiness in the fear of God.' (2 Cor. vii. 1.) You cannot be growing in grace, advancing in holiness, in these providings for the flesh. While the grace of God is not to be dimmed for a moment, let us remember that we are under the righteous government of our Father, and 'he that soweth to his flesh shall of the flesh reap corruption.' Christians suffer, and suffer sadly, by sowing to or making provision for the flesh. Our only safeguard is Christ. With our eye steadfastly and constantly fixed on Him —following Him, copying Him, filled with Him — we shall be led into holiness of life, and neither into licentiousness nor into legalism. For while at the one extreme we may be led into licentiousness or carelessness of walk by our subtle foes, we may meet another danger, which is asceticism and penance, a dishonor to the body by coming under worldly ordinances (such as touch not, taste not, handle not), which look very like holiness and consecration to God in neglecting our bodies, but the only effect is that they tend 'to the satisfying of the flesh.' (Col. ii. 20.) For it feasts on whatever is against Christ, and is satisfied with whatever takes the eye from Him.

'But will not the Holy Spirit keep His own from all this?' I have been asked. 'Yes; but the way He does keep us from the power of the flesh is by satisfaction.' Whatever feeds the spirit starves the flesh. So the apostle Peter by the Holy Ghost says, 'Dearly beloved, I beseech you, as strangers and pilgrims, abstain from fleshly lusts, which war against the soul.' (1 Pet. ii. 11.) The ways of men around are strange ways to us. They think these advices far above human reach (and so they are) but we are living the life of Christ; and as such, we are to hate, 'even the garment spotted by the flesh.' (Jude 23.) Alas! how little watching and praying there is among Christians — how little we live on Christ! If we lived with Him ever before us, ever filling us, our only satisfaction, our joy for ever, what power should we gain over 'the flesh!'

Christians learn what the 'flesh' is —

1st, By experience of its unmingled vileness before conversion; or of its horrid lusts and sad sins after conversion; or

2d, By taking God's character of it from His Word.

When God gives us His 'Memoirs of olden times,' He does not leave out the actings of the flesh. When the 'chronicles of the spirits of just men made perfect' pass before us in Heb. xi., their sins and iniquities are remembered no more, I have been much struck with the unreal life people are led into by reading memoirs of good people, where the good in their lives is told but not the evil; where the triumph is seen but not the conflict. It is just the 'novel literature,' that gives such unreal ideas to young people, and unfits them for everyday life. So most memoirs, by not bringing prominently forward the everyday conflicts, the evil foe within, often do more real harm than permanent good. Read God's own histories. Many human ones would do for angels or seraphs to read, but they are not for militant saints. 'Follow me,' says the Perfect One, and 'Jesus only,' is enough.

Dear worker-for-God, 'let no man take thy crown.' Take care of this foe. A brother in the Lord used to say often to himself, before going to do anything for God, as preaching, &c., 'Now soul, honour bright, is this for the glory of God?' We need a great deal more of bright, sterling honour between God and our souls, and also between one another. We fear the flesh most from its gradual uprisings. It has begun to work often before we are aware, and not till some text meets us straight in the face do we discover that the flesh has been working. Again, our religionized and pious flesh is often a great snare; that is to say, we sometimes begin to think that a Christian's 'flesh' is better than an unconverted man's 'flesh;' but, if we do, we proceed on false grounds, and will reap nothing but failure. First look to Jesus, away from your vile, unimproveable heart, live in the Spirit and keep looking to Jesus until you see Him as He is, and then you shall be like Him, done with this evil heart, this corrupt nature, this self-willed flesh. Meantime we have to be daily, hourly confessing sin, and in this having the most blessed communion with God — 'in light' that makes everything manifest, and overlooks nothing.

3. *The Christian daily confesses his sins and is daily forgiven.*

A perfect statement of the whole position, walk, and restoration of a Christian is found in 1 John i. If we are to have fellowship with the Father and the Son, we must have that life implanted in us by the Holy Ghost, that eternal, indestructible, perfect life, which is capable of having fellowship with God — that nature which throbs in harmony with God's nature, for we are 'partakers of the Divine nature.' (2 Pet. i. 4.)

'We are *now* sons.' Our place is now in the light and in the Spirit, and thus in communion; if we were walking in darkness, in unloving ways, it would be merely *saying* we have fellowship, and not the truth. God is now revealed as without a veil, and, wondrous truth! we saved sinners walk 'IN THE LIGHT as God is in the light' — in the exercise of that pure and perfect love (His perfect commandment) that this whole epistle is inculcating (1 John ii. 9), following in the steps of Him who could say to the vilest confessed sinner, when accused by Pharisees, 'Neither do I condemn thee, go and sin no more.' He was *'the light of the world,'* and becomes to all such as this sinner at His feet the *'light of life'* (John viii. 12). Thus 'we have fellowship with one another,' because having communion and fellowship each with God. Here shall we be able to judge our own sins; in this very place, not when we get out of 'the light,' but 'in the light,' 'the blood of Jesus Christ His Son cleanseth *us* (believers, sons, those who have been born again) from all sin.' The blood is once applied and is of continued efficacy — not has cleansed or did cleanse but '*cleanseth* us from all sin.' The effect of light is not to make us believe or feel that we have no sin in us. Sin will be in every man, saint or sinner, till he goes hence; for 'If we say that we have no sin, we deceive ourselves and the truth is not in us.' And how am I to do with these sins that are still uprising and which the light makes manifest, for the more light there is in a room the more the dust is seen? Listen to God's simple plan!

'If we confess our sins, He is faithful and just to forgive us our sins, and to cleanse us from all unrighteousness.' Confess our *sins*, not our *sin*, not merely say, 'We are all sinners: God be merciful to me a sinner;' but judging the uprisings of the evil spring, according to God's standard of perfect holiness, which is Christ, confess all known sins, deeds, looks, thoughts. What heart-searching this implies! 'If we *confess* our sins,' not merely in words, we shall have a real individual dealing with our Father, not certainly as condemned sinners before an angry judge, but all the more close and real, because we are accepted sons dealing with such a holy, gracious Father.

'He is faithful and just.' It is no longer a matter of love and mercy, — *these* have indeed provided the way: but He is 'faithful,' for He hath said it, He is 'just,' on account of the blood presented there, 'to forgive,' and it is inexcusable unbelief not to 'confess,' confide, and believe that we are forgiven on the spot, and thus be ever walking in the light with a calm, holy joy.

The first two verses of the second chapter give the apostle's practical interpretation of these doctrines. 'My little children, these things write I unto you, that ye *sin not.*' 'Be ye holy, for I am holy' (1 Pet. i. 16). Walk 'in the Spirit,' in the energy of the new life, and in the light; mortifying the deeds of the old man. This is certainly our aim, but in this we fail, aiming yet not attaining.

But 'if any man sin, we have an advocate' (a paraclete, literally), 'with the Father, Jesus Christ *the Righteous*, and He is the propitiation for our sins; and not for ours only but also for the whole world.' That is to say, if any of us Christians commit any sin as He sees sin, in His character of advocate He cleanses us from it. This is very blessed, for while we have to confess all known sin, and thus get it off our consciences, there are many sins which we do not see; but He has made Himself responsible to cleanse us from all sin which His holy eye sees. Our advocate does not say that we, His clients, are guilty and then plead for mercy. And He is a righteous advocate, therefore He can by no means clear the guilty, but, wondrous wisdom! wondrous truth! wondrous grace! He took our guilt upon Him, and now points to His own death as that which cleanses us from all sin. He sees the sin — He satisfies the Father — He is the advocate. He meets the accuser — He is the propitiation. What a perfect paraclete with the Father, ever keeping us clean by His blood before Him, as the paraclete, the Holy ghost, whom He sent, is ever keeping us clean down here by the Word, washing the feet of those who are 'clean every whit' (John xiii.), removing from our consciences every thing that *He sees* would interrupt our fellowship and communion, by the word which He whispers to us (Eph. v. 26)!

BELIEVING BROTHER, — You have died and 'risen with Christ.' Is your affection set on those 'things which are above?' Do you think you have got into God's mind concerning your standing and acceptance? Blessed, most blessed, if you have! But does this lead you to be more holy, more Christlike, more heavenly-minded, more anxious to walk in the way of God? If I, as a Christian, am 'not under the law' (Rom. vi. 14), I am certainly under my Lord's commandments. 'If ye love Me keep My commandments' (John xiv. 15). 'For this is the love of God, that we should believe on the name of His Son Jesus Christ, and' (having believed — having the new life) 'love one another, as He gave us commandment' (1 John iii. 23). If we read all the practical directions at the end of Romans, Ephesians, Colossians, &c., we shall find that Christians had to be again and again reminded whose they were, and how they ought to walk.

Two truths have to be kept in mind — the Christian is not under the law-principle — so much being exacted for so much — the task-master's whip held over his head, with its 'do-this-and-live' demands — but is quickened into the life from God, in subjection to his *Lord*, 'en-lawed to Christ' (1 Cor. ix. 21): and walking in this wilderness, he is only too glad, amid confusion here, to know in what direction his Father's finger points, so that with all his soul he may judge his own sinful flesh, and walk whither his Father directs. Thus, in a very blessed way, the son delights in the law (the *torah*, literally 'fingerpoint') of his Father; he makes it his study day and night. Are you loving to be guided by the eye of God along the platform of His eternal love, which is based on His infinite justice? Watch against a mere doctrinal or intellectual grasp of truth. Without the living power 'knowledge puffeth up.' Beware of the pestilential swamps of a hateful antinomianism, that spirit of the flesh, so common all around in this day, and so apt to lurk in every heart. To whom much is given of him shall much be required. God has made you a son of such a Father-God, in that blessed, holy, separated walk, linked in eternal union with His own beloved Son. Shall we not walk like sons?

This reckoning of myself as crucified with Christ, put out of existence, as it were, in the crucifixion of Christ, and now identified with the living, risen Jesus, is not mysticism, but one of God's most important realities — foolishness, indeed, to the worldly-wise — a mystery, revealed by the Holy Ghost only to those who, self-emptied and helpless, listen as little children. When you believed in the Lord Jesus Christ did you not leave all your sins in the grave of Jesus (in God's reckoning)? Are they not sunk into the depths of the sea, to be remembered no more? Were you crucified with Christ? Then you have left the world also at Jesus' grave: the cross as truly stands between the Christian and 'the world,' as between the Christian and his sins. 'One with Christ,' in acceptance with the Father, makes you one with Him in His rejection by the world. The former you have by faith, the latter as a necessary consequence from the exhibited life of this faith.

Do you see yourself at the cross, forgiven all your trespasses? That blessed voice that acquitted you, says, 'Go and sin no more.' Do you see yourself at the cross, 'justified from all things,' and set down in perfect righteousness before God? Know, dear brother, that you have to justify your own profession of faith before men, by the good works of faith which they can understand and appreciate; and also you have to justify, before men, that God who you say has acquitted you and set you down before Himself, in His own righteousness, which is Christ.

Do you see yourself as one set apart by that blood which has been taken from the altar into 'the holiest of all,' and reckoned by God as one whose 'life is hid with Christ in God'? Know, dear brother, that you are to be purifying yourself, even as He is pure. Having His place of life and righteousness inside the veil, we feel it a high privilege to take His place of testimony and rejection outside the camp. In the language of faith, and regarding myself as God reckons me — once crucified, but now alive in Christ Jesus, I can say —

> 'So nigh, so very nigh to God,
>   I cannot nearer be;
> For in the person of His Son,
>   I am as near as He.'

And the necessary consequence of knowing this, and living in the power of it, will be a closer, holier walk with God; and my prayer and cry, the longing of my flesh-clogged soul, as I pant after conscious nearness, will ever be —

> 'Nearer still nearer, Lord, my God,
>   I long to walk with Thee;
> To know more fully Him I know,
>   My prayer, my joy shall be;
> To live more like a ransomed child,
>   Till Christ Himself I see.'

Shall we not then, knowing that our 'citizenship is in heaven' (Phil. iii. 20), with the risen Christ as our rule, and His walk here as our example, soar upward, onward, and homeward —living above the world, the devil, and the flesh — 'strong in the grace that is in Christ Jesus,' having the 'joy of the Lord as our strength?'

STRIVING ONE, — Are you trying to perfect in the flesh that whish has been begun in the Spirit? Do you count it a small matter that Christ has died for you, and that you are now in Him? What more can you have? You are conscientiously striving after holiness; but still you are constantly thinking and talking much more about the old man in you, than Christ for you and in you. Why is this? You are not reckoning as God as reckoned, and hence this useless warfare. There is a fight — the fight of faith, the fight I have as a saint against God's foes and mine, the world, the devil, and the flesh. This is 'a good fight.' There is also a most ignoble and Christ-dishonouring fight, a fight by which I try to make the flesh better; to purify the filthy fountain; to wash the rags of the prodigal instead of accepting the best robe — a living perfect, entire Christ. 'The just shall LIVE by faith,' as well as be begotten by faith. Remember that there can be no holy walk with God unless I know that He has made me a son.

God is well pleased with Christ, why are you not pleased with Him?

'Ah!' you say, 'I am satisfied with Christ; but not with myself.'

Will you ever be pleased with yourself? Would it be well for you if you were so? Well, then, at once, by faith, adopt Paul's language, 'No longer I, but Christ' — Christ for me! Whether it were Paul or Peter, he had just to fall into the poor Gentile sinner's place, and plead, 'I am a sinner; therefore, Christ for me.'

'But I am not a great sinner,' you say.

He died for all kinds of sinners.

'But I am too great a sinner,' do you say?

Do you deserve to be nailed to a cross as an accursed thing? How far did Jesus descend to reach your case? Are there any steps needed to lead from your position to His? He was made a curse for us; He lay in the tomb, and you — 'dead in trespasses and sins' — are lying in the tomb. Has He not come down to the very spot where you are? Are there any stepping stones needed between two, when both are lying side by side in the place of death? Ah, no; the gospel of Christ is — The Saviour for the sinner! Christ for me! God's way of life for my way of death!

He came down even to the grave, and became the dead One for me. I believe in Him, and, as one with Him, I leap at one bound straight out of my grave up to His throne. 'I am crucified with Christ, nevertheless I live; yet not I, but Christ liveth in me.' This is not a matter of feeling, but all a matter of faith, merely apprehending the grace of God, 'I live by the faith of the Son of God, who loved me and gave Himself for me' (Gal. ii. 20).

The moment you lose faith in your creed — 'I for myself,' and have faith in God's — 'Christ for me,' you are 'born again,' you are 'crucified with Christ,' and are now living in His risen life.

'*Have no confidence in the* flesh,' *and then you will rejoice in Christ Jesus and worship God in the Spirit.*

With Christ we *died* to sin,	Rom. vi. 8.
Lay *buried* in His tomb;	Rom. vi. 4.
But *quicken'd* now with Him, our Life,	Eph. ii. 5.
We stand beyond our doom!	Rom. vi. 7.
Our God in wondrous love,	Eph. ii. 4.
Hath *raised* us who were dead;	Eph. ii. 6.
And in the heavenlies, *made us sit*	Eph. ii. 6.
In Christ our living Head.	Eph. i. 22.
For us He now appears	Heb. ix. 24.
Within the veil above;	Heb. vi. 19.
Accepted, and complete in Him,	Eph. i. 6.
We triumph in His love.	Rom. viii. 39.
In Christ we now are made	1 Co. i. 30.
The righteousness of God;	2 Co. v. 21.
As sons of God, and *heirs* with Christ,	1 Jo. v. 1.
We follow where He trod.	Col. iii. 1.
Rejected and despised,	Is. liii. 3.
He bore the open shame;	Heb. xii. 2.
As *fellow-sufferers*, journeying home,	Rom. viii. 17.
We glory in His name.	Acts v. 41.
Soon will the Bridegroom come,	Rev. xxii. 20.
His Bride from earth to call!	1 Thes. iv. 16.
We, *glorified* with Him, shall reign,	Rev. xx. 4.
Till God be all in all.	1 Co. xv. 28.

The Devil.

Our Adversary.

'DO not believe in eternal punishment,' said a man one day to a friend of mine. 'But that does not alter the fact,' replied my friend. This remark led to the man's conversion. Is it wise to shut the eye to danger? We know best how to deal with a foe when we know all about himself, his plans, his tactics.

Wellington[13] became the greatest conqueror by knowing his enemies, their strength, and their stratagems. He is the skilled surgeon who has thought over all the possible dangers that may arise, and is prepared to meet them. When the builder of the Menai Bridge[14] was suggesting various cautions, his coadjutors sometimes said to him that he was raising difficulties. 'No,' he answered, 'I'm solving them.' And so for every accident he was prepared.

In our spiritual conflict it is folly to despise the strength of our foes, it is wisdom to reckon on a power infinitely stronger. Many in the present day do not believe that there is a devil. They do not feel or realise any workings on their consciousness as of

---

[13] Editor's Note: Arthur Wellesley was the Duke of Wellington, 1st Marquess of Wellington (1769–1852), the Anglo-Irish military commander best known for leading the decisive victory over Napoleon's forces at Waterloo.

[14] Editor's Note: The Menai Bridge, built in 1826, was a triumph of civil engineering and was the biggest suspension bridge in the world at the time, reducing the danger to travelers crossing the Straits.

an external power. They think, therefore, that the devil is merely a word of the theologian, an expression that may be used to deceive and frighten children, but that intelligent men in this nineteenth century are not to be so deceived. With their friends of old they 'say that there is neither angel nor spirit' (Acts xxiii. 8). But this does not alter the fact that there is a devil. Men may conscientiously, and therefore strongly, believe a lie. In fact we find, in 2 Thess. ii. 10, that because men 'received not the love of the truth that they might be saved, for this cause God shall send them strong delusions that they should believe a lie, that they all might be damned who believed not the truth but had pleasure in unrighteousness.'

Others who believe, from the teaching of Scripture, that there is a devil, have little knowledge of his personality. They do not seem to realise that he is as truly a person, though invisible, as the Son of God, his great opponent. They think of Satan as a mere influence or power. They tell us that they have devil enough when they have their own evil heart. And true enough, it is 'deceitful above all things, and incurably wicked.' But that Satan is a present, scheming, watchful, cunning being, going about seeking our destruction, is realized by few; and by those few very imperfectly.

REV. XII.

In the twelfth chapter of Revelation we have depicted a remarkable series of his workings. May the Lord open up to our minds from this passage the reality of his existence as a person, the subtlety and determination of his plans, and the power that has been provided to meet him at every step.

I do not now enter into the interpretation of this graphic scene, however blessed it may be to the soul that reads and understands it; but I would rather try to glean a few practical lessons from the moral truths revealed to us in this picture, which, in all its details, has yet to be fulfilled. Before adducing these, I would merely glance at the characters that figure in the scene, that in gathering these lessons we may not confuse the mind of the intelligent reader who is looking for a deeper and closer rendering of it.

In chap. xi. 19, the temple of God is open in heaven (for Jesus and His elders are now seen as there since chap. iv.), and *the ark* of His covenant is shown as taken of His grace, and the *lightning*, as token of His judgment, before we are introduced to the great scene of chap. xii. We are told who the dragon is, verse 9, 'That old serpent, called the devil and Satan, who deceiveth the whole world' — like the *aliases* of a habit-and-repute criminal. The man-child, from Ps. ii., Isa. ix. 6, &c., is evidently Jesus, ver. 5, 'a man-child who was to rule all nations with a rod of iron.' His mother, in symbolic language, of course being Israel, from whom, according to the flesh, Christ was born, seen as the faithful remnant persecuted and preserved through the tribulation of the short 1,260 days after Satan has been cast out of heaven — where the saints have been seen seated (chap. iv.) — to the earth where he is in great wrath, for his time is short ere he be chained in the pit.

I. THE DEVOURER.

Read the 4th verse of this twelfth chapter: 'And the Dragon stood before the woman which was ready to be delivered, for to *devour* her child as soon as it was born.'

Jesus is said to be born King of the Jews in Matt. i. Look at chap. ii.: there we find the devil's first attempt to devour Him as soon as He was born. Herod, his tool, slew 'all the children that were in Bethlehem and in all the coasts thereof from two years old and under,' and the weeping of Rachel is the sad witness to the devil's awful power, but through the almighty wisdom of God the young child's life is spared. Thwarted in this murderous plan, he comes with plausible temptation, trying to make Him leave the place of the Sent One and the Servant; but the Word of God made him flee for a season. In Gethsemane we again find Satan; but last and most awful of all, we see this great dragon, the serpent, at Calvary, bruising His heel, trying to hold Him in his death-hold, wounding Him with his venomed sting. The devourer feels now sure of his prey. Jesus is in the jaws of death. Chains of hell are around Him. 'Shall the prey be taken from the mighty, shall the lawful captive be delivered?' Yes: there is a greater power than the mighty one here, there is the Almighty. There is a power higher than even that seen in Creation or Providence; there is the power of coming out from under death — laying down the life and taking it up again. 'Through death He destroyed him that had the power of death, that is the devil.' Not only has Satan failed to devour the Prince of Life, but he has got his head bruised. This is the venomous serpent on the pole, whose power has thus been destroyed by the Son of man lifted up (John iii.) The sting has been wrenched from the serpent's jaws. The keys of death and the grave are now hung at the girdle of the glorious Conqueror, who has fought the fight alone, by weakness showing Himself to be Almighty.

> 'By weakness and defeat
>   He won the meed and crown;
> Trod all our foes beneath His feet,
>   By being trodden down.
>
> 'He hell in hell laid low;
>   Made sin, He sin o'erthrew;
> Bow'd to the grave, destroy'd it so,
>   And death by dying slew.'

'For this purpose the Son of God was manifested, that He might destroy the words of the devil.' (1 John iii. 8.) The Lord is risen, yea, He is ascended as a man, a glorified man, beyond the power of Satan. He is seated as the subject One. The servant who undertook for man has been 'caught up unto God and to His throne,' and we find that this is the deliverance that is mentioned in Rev. xii. 5. It is a question now to be settled between Satan and the God who has raised Jesus up, between the power of Satan and the throne-power of the Almighty God. Justice and power have vindicated Christ's title to bruise the serpent's head, and take His position as man, the highest in heaven on God's own throne.

The serpent in Eden tempted the woman and ruined mankind. God said, 'I will put enmity between thee and the woman, between they seed and her seed.' Blessed by God, He has put the enmity, and it cannot be taken away. What a fearful friendship it would have been if God had left man in the friendship that Adam began with Satan! All along the stream of time Satan has been at his devouring work. To-day, he is 'going about as a roaring lion, seeking whom he may *devour*.' Do we realise this? It surely means something. I believe it means far more than we suppose. By how many different ways does he accomplish this! If he can keep people in their natural state of death, he is as sure of his prey as if he had them with him in everlasting burning. If he can lull them, soothe them, deceive them, blind them, he has them sure, and they will be an easy prey.

He knows that life is communicated by the Spirit applying the *word* of the living God — that word that tells of a victorious Conqueror, a risen Christ, of Him who liveth and was dead, and is alive again for evermore. That word links the believer to Him who was caught up to God's throne, and tells him that he is identified with the victorious conqueror of death, that he is united to death's master. Wherefore, Satan is very busy when the gospel of God is preached, so we read that there is a class of people that hear the word: 'then cometh the devil, and taketh away *the word* out of their hearts, *lest* they should believe and be saved.' (Luke viii. 12.) What a devil-like intention! Does every preacher of the gospel realise this, that such an enemy is among his audience? Does every hearer realise it, that such a seemingly simple thing may leave him in the jaws of Satan for ever? If men do not believe that they must be born again, in order to enter the Kingdom of God, Satan does. If men do not believe that the 'entrance of the word gives light,' Satan does. He takes this word away *lest* it save them. Satan is a clever theologian. He knows the Bible: he believes it, he can quote it, he can use it for his own fiendish ends. After the gospel is preached, he is ever ready to snatch away the word. 'What did you think of that preacher?' is the common introduction, after the gospel is preached, to a series of criticisms on his merits and demerits, and a pretty sure token that in the discussion concerning the messenger the message is to be forgotten. '*Lest they should believe and be saved!*' If Satan can keep out that seed, he will let the man cultivate the field, be very attentive to it, water it, spend much time on it: in plain words, he will let men be moral and philanthropic, be religious, and make profession, contend stoutly for sound orthodoxy, and clever theology, if he can keep out the seed of life.

Satan knows that there is life in a *look* at the crucified One, therefore he will let the wounded sinner apply ointments and plasters, and all sorts of palliatives to his sin-bitten soul; but will use all his power to keep him from beholding the Lamb of God. A look at the brazen serpent cured those bitten by fiery serpents — a look at Him who destroyed the great serpent's power, immediately and for ever saves those who are ready to be devoured by the mighty dragon, for 'as Moses lifted up the serpent in the wilderness, even so must the Son of man be lifted up, that whosoever believeth in Him, should not perish, but have eternal life.' By many devices the great deceiver succeeds in hiding this life-giving cross; for 'If our gospel be hid to them that are lost; in whom the *god of this world* hath blinded the minds of them which believe not, lest the light of the glorious gospel of Christ who is the image of God, should shine unto them.' Truly, O Appollyon, Abaddon, thou art the deceiver of the whole world. What fools men are! Reader, are you led captive at his will; are you in his meshes, within the teeth of his jaws, ready to be devoured? Are you not only led captive of your lusts, but bound hand and foot by Satan?

Believing reader, in Jesus thou art safe. He is at God's throne; thou art there in Him; this is thy safety. God's throne is safe, he cannot devour it, therefore he cannot devour thee. He has done his utmost as to devouring thee; he is eternally foiled. His power is broken. The poison, the cruelty of the great dragon, that old serpent, have been met and overcome by the 'Lamb in the midst of the throne.'

Is 'the evil one,' 'the wicked one' thy destroyer? — 'The Holy One' is thy preserver.

Is 'the angel of the bottomless pit' at thy back with his belching flame? — 'The King of Glory' is the Captain of thy salvation.

Is the knife of him that is 'a murderer from the beginning' whetted to be plunged into thy bosom? — 'The Prince of Life' is thy life.

Is 'the prince of darkness' trying to enwrap thy soul? — 'The Light of Life' surrounds thy goings.

Does Satan come as an angel of light? — We have received the blessed Spirit, by whom we can detect his wiles; we are not ignorant of his devices. Let us be sober and vigilant against such a foe. We have to pick our steps. Being now in Christ soon we shall be 'caught up' in reality, body and soul, entirely and for ever beyond his power, wiles, devices, and snares. Yes, we shall be caught up together with all the saints of Jesus, to meet our Conqueror in the air, and be ever with Him; and 'the God of peace shall bruise Satan under your feet shortly.' (Rom. xvi. 20.)

After he is thus foiled, and cannot *devour* us, does he leave us? Nay! But we find Satan in this same twelfth chapter (ver. 10), as

II. THE ACCUSER.

'He ACCUSES the brethren before God day and night.' Michael and his angels are to cast him down to the earth at the beginning of the times of great trial, but meantime he is there, not certainly in the 'light,' God's dwelling-place, in the third, the highest, heaven, but as the Prince of the Power of the Air, having power to stand before God and accuse the brethren. That Satan has access into God's presence may startle some who have not thought about it; but it is the teaching of Scripture. 1 Kings xxii. 21, shows that a lying spirit appeared before God, to put lies into the mouths of Ahab's advisers.

Again, in Job i. 6, we read — 'Now there was a day when the sons of God came to present themselves before the Lord, and Satan came also among them,' to accuse Job. In Zech. iii. it is written — 'He shewed me Joshua the high priest standing before the angel of the Lord, and Satan standing at his right hand to resist him.' In Eph. vi. 12 — 'We wrestle not against flesh and blood, but against...spiritual wickedness in heavenly places.' Day and night, dear fellow-Christians, he has access to God, and accuses us before Him; sometimes truly, alas! How often does he first tempt and then accuse! How much failure of ours can he put his hand upon! and besides he is a slanderer, a false accuser. He is not the accuser of the world, but only of 'the brethren,' but he 'deceiveth the whole world.'

What is our strength? 'If any man sin, we have an advocate with the Father,' one who never slumbers nor sleeps. We speak much, and we cannot dwell too much, upon the finished work of Jesus; but how precious is the unfinished, untiring, unremittent work of our blessed Lord! If the accuser speaks of sin, He points to the blood, that with which, for us, He has entered into the heavens.

'He is Jesus Christ the righteous, and He is the propitiation for our sins.' The accuser has to find fault with Him, for we are in Him. Nothing short of this appeal to the presented blood will silence his insinuations and overcome his accusations. So it is said (ver. 11), 'They overcame him by the *blood* of the Lamb.' Saints do not cast him out of heaven; angels do that, but the brethren overcome him while he is there, and is accusing them. This is before God.

In my own experience of all his accusations I bring the sword of the Spirit, the Word of God, apart from all my feelings and states, and say to all his accusings, as to his temptations, 'It is written.' Thus Jesus overcame him when he was on earth, therefore it is said that not only 'they overcame him by the blood of the Lamb,' but also by 'the *word* of their testimony.' 'Resist the devil and he will flee from you' — for he is a coward at heart; 'neither give place to the devil.' The blood and the word shut his mouth for ever and are the answer to his gravest accusations, be they true or false. Though our sins are as scarlet, Jesus points to the blood, and they become 'white as snow;' 'red like crimson,' He says they become as wool. 'If we confess our sins, He is faithful' — why? because His *word* has said it — 'and just' — why? because of the *blood* presented — 'to forgive us our sins, and to cleanse us from all unrighteousness.' The blood of Jesus Christ *cleanseth* us from ALL sin.

Is the father of lies against us? — the living truth is for us. Is he desiring to sift us as wheat? — Jesus is constantly praying that our faith may never fail us, for by that shield we can quench all Satan's fiery darts, meet all his accusations, and, in the calm consciousness of eternal peace with God, wait upon Him, do His commandments, and receive the power that will make us love not our lives unto death. (Rev. xii. 11.)

He cannot *devour* us: we are in Christ.

He is overcome when he *accuses* us; Christ's blood is for us. Does he leave us? No. He exercises his power against us now, as

III. THE PERSECUTOR.

Read Rev. xii. 13. 'When the dragon saw that he was cast unto the earth he *persecuted* the woman.' And here his cunning is taxed to its utmost; varying with times and peoples, tastes and civilization. His manner changes, but the rank venom of his sting is always the same — the deluge from his mouth always poured upon us. He brings into his service all kinds of tools; the stake, the inquisition, the scaffold in one age more refined but as real persecution in another; the ill-will and planning of the world, and what is worse than all, the evil-speaking and slandering of fellow-Christians. Individually, beloved friends, let us ask, are we washing one another's feet, or advancing Satan's work, being used as his tools in speaking evil of those things that we know not? You may know what it is to be misunderstood, misrepresented, maligned, looked at with suspicion by a fellow-Christian, and may have felt it to be the direst persecution, more painful than thumbscrews; — watch and pray lest you in turn be thus used against others. We do not feel the reality of the common adversary, else we should be all more united and of one accord, continuing in brotherly love. Soldiers may have their disputes, quarrels, and even duels, when in the barracks and on home service, but on the battle-field the bitterest are shoulder to shoulder against one common foe.

Against all his persecutions, what is the provision? ver. 14. power for flight to the wilderness, and being fed there by God. He has given us of His Spirit the spirit of truth and sonship, He has shut us into the wilderness, and there we have found Himself our provision. A quaint old divine used to say, 'the devil acts like a bull-dog to bark at us, and drive us closer to Christ.' The Psalms are the experience of David in the place of the poor man in the wilderness finding his all in God. What a blessed thing that Satan's persecutions but drive us nearer to our only good! The wilderness is the happiest place, when we get there from the hand of our living, loving Father, His own manna, His own drink, and the guidance of His pillar cloud. Christ is all.

> 'In the desert, God will teach thee
>   What the God that thou hast found,
> Patient, gracious, powerful, holy,
>   All His grace shall there abound.
>
> 'Though thy way be long and dreary,
>   Eagle strength He'll still renew;
> Garments fresh, and feet unweary,
>   Tell how God hath brought thee through.

To be alone with God — to be in the wilderness with God — to be fed by God. Is this not life? Is this not joy? It was better to be with David on the lonely hill-side, than with Saul in his costly palaces. Manna, water and guidance are all I need; what more could I take, for this is Jesus, God's own joy, God's own delight, God's own rest, day by day, new every day, it cannot be kept for to-morrow; yesterday's will not do for to-day. How the hatred of the devil brings glory to God!

His *devourings* bring us to the 'caught up' Christ, and are thus met by *life in victory*.

His *accusations* bring us to the 'blood of the Lamb,' and are met by *life taken for us*.

His *persecutions* bring us to the wilderness provisions, and are met by *life nourished*.

After all this we have nothing more to fear, we can fear no evil, God is with us, as above and independent of all circumstance we find God for us, a table spread in the wilderness in presence of our enemies. He may still show his venom after he is thoroughly defeated, for we next find him as

IV. THE BLASPHEMER.

This is seen in Rev. xiii. 5, 6, in the person of the beast to whom Satan gives power. 'He opened his mouth in blasphemy against God to blaspheme His name and His tabernacle, and them that dwell in heaven.' But blasphemies can do us little harm. We need no fortification against them. At school we have seen the big boy that used to lord it over all the little ones subdued, conquered, and on the ground. In his defeat he could only call bad names, which he knew could do no harm. Even though Satan slay the body, this touches not our life — it is hid with Christ in God. Can he devour that? It is because of the name we bear that the blasphemies of hell are poured upon us. There are the 'synagogues of Satan,' in which the blasphemous doctrines of devils are taught. We fear not the servants of Satan, though homage on all sides be paid to him by all classes, in their business and pleasure, and the crowns of earth be laid at his feet.

Those whose names are written from the foundation of the world in the book of the Lamb slain, can listen to his blasphemies, can rejoice in the Lord, though he should slay their bodies, and they can afford to wait for their inheritance.

What can I now say, unsaved sinner, to you? You are in the *jaws of the devil*. He is your father: is he to be your tormentor day and night for ever in that awful hell which was never prepared for you, but 'prepared for the devil and his angels?' Look at the judgment of the living nations, the contrast between the blessing and cursing — 'blessed of my Father,' but not cursed of my Father — 'Kingdom prepared for you,' but 'fire prepared for the devil and his angels.' One look outward to Jesus and you are saved; not a look inward to a feeling that can give nothing but despair to the conscientious soul. God has given you Jesus, and in Him is all. Are you not satisfied with Jesus for you? God is.

Fellow believer, rejoice in the Lord: the greatest enemy's power is broken: soon he will really and as to fact, as he is already judicially and to faith, be bruised beneath thy feet. Jesus is thine, and all His power and dominion, and might, and glory, and inheritance, are thine, and, above all, His heart, His love, Himself, is thine.

In Him we conquer the devourer;

In Him we overcome the accuser;

In Him we defy the persecutor;

In Him we are beyond the blasphemer. 'More than conquerors through Him that loved us.'

Come with your weakness and find shelter in the all-powerful Jesus.

EPH. vi. 11-18.

Be strong in Jehovah, though hard be the fight,
We'll conquer, we know, in the power of His might;
Put on the whole armour of God every one,
For it alone shelters till victory's won.

Thus we sing while we march through the midst of our foes,
Who stand all determined our way to oppose;
We shall conquer their legion, our battle song raise;

THE DEVIL.

The Lord is our Captain; His name ever praise.

Thus armed we shall stand and shall meet Satan's wiles;
We know his devices, the world he beguiles;
It is not against flesh and blood that we fight,
But powers that would force us from heavenly light.

With loins girt with truth may we stand in the fight,
And righteousness placed as our breastplate so bright;
Our feet shod with sandals prepared for the war,
The gospel of peace which our foes shall not mar.

Above all Faith's shield we must grasp 'gainst our foes.
By it we shall quench every dart Satan throws;
Salvation our helmet, bestowed by our Lord,
The sword of the Spirit His conquering word.

The trumpet is sounding, the trumpet of war,
Not peace while we wait for our bright morning Star;
We watch where the foe would surprise or alarm,
By prayer we shall nerve for the fight every arm.

Lord, give us more faith thus to meet every foe,
Thus Satan is conquered and shall be laid low;
This, this is the triumph o'er earth and its gain
O'er sin still within, but which never shall reign.

'Serving the Lord.'

Our Work.

I WAS very much interested lately, in reading the life of Dr. Chalmers, to see how many years he preached the gospel to others, and, by his own confession, was still unconverted. I thought of that text, 'lest *preaching* to others I myself should be a castaway.' Paul does not say, 'lest after being *born again* I should be a castaway;' we know that this is impossible. But a man may preach with the most powerful eloquence to others, and still be unsaved. Many in this Christian land begin very early to engage in some good work. At a certain time they become members of the church, as it is said; alas! how often not knowing whether they are saved or not. They then may take a young class in the *Sabbath* school, have a district to visit, look after the affairs of the church, or the necessities of the poor, become, perhaps a deacon and then an elder, or it may be a preacher, and all this time they may have never had this matter definitely, finally, conclusively settled, 'Am I saved?' They trust they are on the right road to be saved, which of course is the leading idea in all legalism, ritualism, and popery, and an entire ignoring of the Bible method.

Some do the best they can, and strive, it may be, with prayers and tears and resolutions and determinations, *in order* to get into God's favour, and thereby in the long run to receive eternal life, with the pardon of all their sins.

Others work and do the best they can, and strive as the former, *because* they know they *are* accepted already — *because* they know they *have* the pardon of all their sins —*because* they know they *hav*e eternal life. The former is false service, the latter is true.

I. FALSE SERVICE.

There are those who believe in justification by faith, and other doctrines of grace, and who yet think that if they do their duty, and try to serve God as sincerely and faithfully as they can, He will, at the last, overlook their many failures, in some vague way or other, for Christ's sake, and reward them for the good deeds which they have done, and give them at the judgment day everlasting life.

Now, this is quite a mistake, and arises from a total misapprehension of God's character and man's condition. God's character is perfect, and before I can be engaged in acceptable service I must be in harmony with this character. In order to be a proper servant of God, I *must start with being perfectly accepted* by God.

Man's position is not that of one who is only a little out of God's mind, and who by a few sincere and vigorous efforts may be put right; but of one who is really dead, so far as connection with God is concerned. He is separated from God, and therefore from truth, from goodness, from life. In God is all truth, all goodness, all life; outside of Him there is none. Man, by nature, is born out of fellowship with God, and therefore he has not the slightest power to serve God acceptably, for he has not the life that can move in the direction of God, and in which he can serve Him. The movements in Christian service of an unconverted man are the galvanic movements of a corpse, which may seem very energetic; yet, alas, it is but a corpse that moves! All Scripture and experience tell us these two truths concerning God's character and man's condition.

Wherefore, dear friend, unless thou hast been born again, quickened into a new life from death, thou canst not serve God acceptably. Thou mayest strive day and night in all sincerity, but thou art dead; thou mayest visit the sick and minister to the dying (the holiest privileges of the saved one); all is vain; thou mayest comfort and assist the widow and the fatherless, and have the prayers of many an orphan for thy reward, and yet be no better as to thy standing before God than the profligate and the profane; thou mayest give of thy bread to the poor; thou mayest support the cause of Christ in all its missions and churches at home and abroad; thou mayest give half of thy income to the advancement of the Lord's work and not one penny stand to thy credit before God. Cain's sacrifice, beautiful, fair, and lovely as it was, and presented by a man who was at that time a professor of religion, and a sincere worshipper, was rejected by God. And so it is still. God will reject you and your sacrifice unless you come as one at peace with Him through *His* sacrifice, and not as one coming to make friends with God by your sacrifice. If you are out of Christ, your *good* deeds as well as your *bad* deeds are an abomination to God. All your 'righteousnesses are as *filthy rags*' (Isa. lxiv. 6), not only failing to cover you, but *defiling* you. '*Whatsoever* is not of faith is sin' Rom. xiv. 23). You may be true to your friends; you may do your duty as parents, and provide for your own; but it is all sin: for, as saith the Scripture, 'the ploughing of the wicked is sin' (Prov. xxi. 4). Every action, however commendable in the Christian, and however much binding upon you as a moral duty, is reckoned by God, if done by you, to be a sin, because it is the action of one not at peace with Him through His own peace. 'Without faith it is impossible to please God' (Heb. xi. 6). This is God's theology, however hard it may seem, and however much opposed to your ideas, and to the prevailing ideas of the world concerning good works and their reward. '*Dead works*' is stamped on all your deeds. Until you serve God as one who is saved, all your service will but intensify your anguish in the pit of woe, whither the Christless, the seemingly good and fair, beautiful and noble, are all swept together with the vile, the loathsome, the idolater, the profane. There are not two hells. Where will you spend eternity?

II. TRUE SERVICE.

Half an hour ago you may have been serving in the dark, as an unforgiven one, and, during the next half hour, you may pass from death unto life, and thus stand on the ground of the accepted servant. God is perfect: to meet God I must meet Him in perfection. There is no perfection in me; but He has provided the means by which each of us may at once become acceptable *servants*, by first becoming accepted *sons*. Jesus, His only-begotten and well-beloved Son, eternally in the Father's bosom, took upon Him our nature, descended to our place of responsibility and service, and approved Himself to be the perfect Servant in that very place in which we had failed; became sin for us, was obedient unto death, having gone through all the billows of God's wrath, has been raised from the dead, and is now at the Father's right hand. If, therefore, we become by faith identified with Him, we can see in Him all our responsibilities under the law met; we can look into His empty grave, and reckon our sins buried there; and now, as those who are beyond the doom of sin, and beyond its judgment, we can serve in 'newness of life,' a resurrection-life. This, and nothing else, is the foundation of true service, the service of love, the service of sons; for we now stand in Christ's place of sonship as He once, in grace, occupied our place of death.

We ask you, is this not a real vantage ground for service? What a wretched menial service it is to be working hard for life, and doubting whether it can ever be obtained! The true service is working *from* the Cross, not *to* the Cross. The corpse does not bestir itself to get life, but it is the living man who works because he has life. Be not deceived. This is God's plan; *life*, then *service*. Ask yourselves now the question, 'Am I serving because I have life? Because I am saved?' Then it is evident that you *know* you are saved — you 'know that you are of God.' (1 John v. 19.)

But perhaps some one may be thinking, 'Well, I've been doing this little and that little, but I have never been conscious of being born again.' Stop, then, dear friend, at once, and make it sure. Turn on the spot from thy service, and get rid of thy sin. By believing in Him who, as the perfect servant, bare our sins in His own body on the tree. (1 Peter ii. 24.) Get into Christ —in His perfection thou canst meet and serve the living God.

'But,' you may ask, 'how am I to get into Him?' Simply by knowing Him (John xvii. 3); by believing on Him (John iii. 36); by trusting in Him (2 Tim. i. 12). God has given Him to you already. (John iii. 16.) You do not require to go to heaven to beseech God to send you Jesus to die for sin. (Rom. x. 6.) No; 'For God so loved the world that He gave His only-begotten Son.' And Christ dieth no more. In the love-gift of God, Jesus is yours. If you go to hell, it must be over *a given Christ*.

When the poor men in the cotton manufacturing districts were starving, moved with pity you sent your money to the committee for distributing bread to them. Now, suppose some poor man, with his wife and children sitting in their empty room, the last of their furniture having been sold for bread — a few stones for seats, and a bunch of straw their bed; no fire on the hearth; no crust of bread in the cupboard, the last having been consumed a couple of days before; children crying for bread; the mother's eyes refusing to weep; the father's skeleton hands clasped in anguish; no bread, and no work; starvation, dire starvation staring them in the face! A knock is heard at the door, a man comes in with a loaf and lays it on the table, and says, '*That is yours*, for the people of Britain have so pitied you that they have sent this bread. Rise, eat, rejoice, and starve no more.' Suppose that poor man would neither touch the loaf himself, nor let his wife nor children taste it, but said, 'How can it be mine? I never got a pennyworth of bread but by the sweat of my brow; there must be some mistake. I cannot take this; not having wrought for it, it cannot be mine.' Everybody would have shouted, '*Eat, man! eat*, and ask no questions, for you are starving, and the messenger's word is enough. He said the loaf was yours.'

Fellow-sinner, this is but a faint picture of *your condition* and *God's provision*. JESUS, His perfect provision for the soul's need, *has been* sent, *has* suffered for sin, and has gone back in righteousness to the Father. Are you not on the edge of eternal damnation, and do you begin to ask questions about your warrant to take Christ? He is yours in the gift of God. Yea, more, God *commands* you to use Him (1 John iii. 23). Dare you disobey God by continuing unsaved?

How can I serve the Lord until I can say, 'He is *my* Lord?'

A gentleman had paid his money for the ransom of a slave, and had given her her freedom. She had been born a slave, and knew not what freedom meant. Her tears fell fast on the signed parchment which her deliverer brought to prove it to her; she only looked at him with fear. At last he got ready to go his way, and as he told her what she must do when he was gone, it did dawn on her what freedom was. With the first breath, 'I will follow him,' she said: 'I will follow him; I will serve him all my days;' and to every reason against it she only cried, 'He redeemed me! He redeemed me! He redeemed me!'

When strangers used to visit that master's house, and noticed, as all did, the loving constant service of the glad-hearted girl, and asked her why she was so eager with unbidden service, night by night, and day by day, she had but one answer, and she loved to give it, —

'HE REDEEMED ME! HE REDEEMED ME! HE REDEEMED ME!'

Is this *your* motive-power for serving God — 'He redeemed me?' — or is it only, 'Well, I hope I may yet be found among the redeemed, and meanwhile I do the best I can?' Wretched slavery, with the chain of death or doubt hanging on the limbs! Rather take God at His word now, and joyfully exclaim, 'O Lord, truly I am Thy servant.... Thou hast loosed my bonds' (Psalm cxvi. 16).

III. A WORD TO FELLOW-SERVANTS.

I would now speak a word to you who are fellow-workers for, and fellow-sufferers with, Jesus. It is only now that we can have fellowship with Him in His service as the rejected of earth. Let us then be 'instant in season, out of season.'

'*He redeemed me!*' Let it be written as with letters of gold on every page of your diary. While in your mission of love you visit the poor, the sick, and the dying, may it ever be your first work to point them to JESUS. While in every way striving to alleviate misery, even if it were by giving but a cup of cold water, let the main thing be to speak of JESUS. Be careful ever to have the single eye, and do nothing to be seen of men. Do nothing to men; do all to God; and have no master but your Redeemer. Be bound to serve by no chain but that of love. If a great sphere be denied you, occupy the small one. If it is not yours to preach to hundreds or thousands, be like Him who spent a sultry noon under a scorching sun by the well side, that He might impart the water of life to a worthless woman. 'Whatsoever thy hand findeth to do, do it with thy might;' do not wait for to-morrow and for some great opportunity, but do the little service, whatever it may be, do it *now*. Draw all your strength from God, depending on Him alone.

The great work is that which is done on individual responsibility — 'My own work.' Jesus says, 'Whatsoever ye shall ask the Father in my name, He will give you.' (John xvi. 23.) '*Whatsoever*,' without limit, without restraint, without bound, so that you may ask anything you please. Dear fellow-worker, do you feel as if this were too much, and say, 'I cannot have God's arm so under my will?' It is, nevertheless, true. What! can a creature thus prevail with the Creator? Yes, indeed, and the reason is, that we have been made 'partakers of the divine nature' (2 Pet. i. 4), because before God we are as Jesus is — as near, as dear. We are *in* Him, and being in Him, every request, proceeding from this new nature, is in perfect harmony with the Divine Mind.

We may well say with such a petition, What grace, Lord! what condescension! what love! Thou hast not spared Thy Son! Thou hast made me one with Him. Thou hast said, whatsoever I will I shall receive; and therefore, Lord, my will is *whatsoever Thou wilt*. I give Thee back Thy behest. It is too much for me to bear, and now, from the very depths of my soul, I pray, 'Father, "Thy will be done!" Lead me in Thy will; may everything I do be in Thy mind;' and then, *asking* will but be the promptings of that divine life in me, and *receiving* but the natural issue from the hand of Him who is the fountain of that life. What a service of joy! Such a life has no outward bustle and noise, no running hither and thither, but, like the light, it cannot be hid. Quietly it beams wherever it exists. It is calm as the gentle heat of the summer sun noiselessly warming all around. Thus energized by the life from above, meet parent and child, friend and neighbor, rich and poor, and the brighter will be your 'crown of righteousness.' Servants faithful to their earthly masters shall receive the reward of the inheritance at the judgment-seat of Christ. (Col. iii. 24.) It will then appear that it was better to have spoken 'five words' (1 Cor. xiv. 19) for God, than to have spoken 'ten thousand words' to make 'a fair shew in the flesh' (Gal. vi. 12), and please men; better to have been eloquent for God in the calm silence of a life pointing to Jesus, than to have made earth ring with high-sounding words and world-patching schemes.

'It was not any word that was ever spoken to me,' said an old and oft-approved servant of God to a brother in the Lord, from whom I heard the narrative; 'it was no word that wakened me up from my death of sin, but the moving of a dying man's finger. My mother had often prayed for me, and tried to lead me to Jesus; but I hated God, and when I escaped from her control grew to be a wild sinner and such a bold infidel that all her godly friends were afraid to see me; but, in the providence of God, I was left to watch alone by the bedside of a tailor, a poor deformed fellow, when he lay a-dying. He had often spoken to me of Jesus but I had never heeded him more than my mother, or any of the others. When I was nursing him there that day, he plead with me many times to mind my soul, but I was perfectly hard; all he could say had no effect. But at last, when the death-rattle was in his throat, and I saw that he could speak no longer, he just raised his hand and pointed with his finger to the sky. *That* stirred me, and I had no rest till Jesus gave me rest."

The judgment-seat is coming. Fellow-Christian, no question will be raised there about thy standing, about thy salvation. As to safety thou art already passed from death unto life, and wilt not come into judgment; but as to service, thy works will be judged. The judgment is by fire. Whatsoever stands that trial stands to thy credit — if nothing stands, then thy works will all be lost though thou thyself art saved as by fire.

There are two kinds of works — one class symbolized in scripture under the heading of wood, hay, stubble; the other gold, silver, precious stones. Every work is on one side or the other. You will observe that wood, hay, and stubble are greatest in quantity. But it is not quantity that the fire regards; a ton of hay is as easily and as surely burned as a pound. Many in our day have the greatest regard for quantity — great works, much activity. How little the striving after the pure gold, the silver, and the precious stones! How mixed is the life-work of the best man! A layer of wood, a grain of gold, then a large quantity of hay, then a little silver, plenty of stubble, how few precious stones: but the fire sifts all! At that awful catastrophe at Abergele,[15] where railway carriages and living men and women were burned to ashes, diamonds, gold watches, and silver ornaments were found afterwards among the rubbish. The peer could not be distinguished from the servant; wood could not be separated from bone; but the diamond was still bright, and the gold and silver still precious. What a happy day is coming to every Christian! He will be so glad to see in one blaze, as upon one funeral pile, all that in his life ever dishonoured his Lord, or

---

[15] Editor's Note: The Abergele rail disaster took place near Abergele, North, in August 1868 and was the worst railway crash in Great Britain up till then.

was not done with the single eye: only that will reappear in glory, which was to God's glory here, and he, already glorified, can at that tribunal appreciate nothing but what is in harmony with glory.

When at school our great ambition was to be first in the class. Who will be first then of all the class of Christians? Very different will be God's order then from our order now! The great of earth and preachers (even those who were of greatest eminence) perhaps giving place to some poor old starving widow, or some little child. I am convinced that many of those who are called great and well known and honoured Christians, will in that day, as to reward for the single eye, be far behind some poor, weak, despised ones of earth, whose power was in the secret place with God. God judges with righteous judgment.

Rich Christian, what of thy gold then? will it be accounted stubble in the glory? or art thou exchanging it now into the currency of heaven? Were I to travel in a foreign land, I could not get on very well with my British money. Even in England those coming from Scotland find it difficult to exchange Scotch notes. Before we go abroad we change as much money as we may require into the coin of that realm. Friend, this is for what thy life here is still given: 'Make to yourselves friends of the mammon of unrighteousness, that when ye fail they may receive you into everlasting habitations.' So said the Master, and many disciples have wondered and not understood the passage. It is simply 'Exchange your money into the currency of heaven.'

'The mammon of unrighteousness;' that is to say, in the Jewish economy it was a sign of a righteous man that his basket and store were full, that he had plenty of cattle, that he was rich. Now since Christ's rejection it is not so. The unrighteous have God's money in this age. The normal lot of the Christian is poverty; nowhere to lay the head, since there was 'no room in the inn' for the Master. But suppose a man with a large fortune gets converted; what is he to do with this mammon of unrighteousness? Is he to hoard it up and add to it, and die a rich man? Nay. Is he at once and heedlessly to throw it away? Nay.

He is to make it his friend. Exchange it into the coin of heaven. If he waits till he dies, none can be put into his coffin that will arise with him. But there is a method of sending it on before: the Lord has taught it. How many cups of cold water can it buy? These count, if given with the single eye. How many Bibles and missionaries to the heathen? Ten thousand channels are easily found when wanted. Whatever you do, make your money not your enemy, as it will be if you use it for self, but your friend, so that when you are done with money it may not be done with you, but will be standing to meet you in a new dress, in the gold and silver and precious stones at the throne, in the 'Well done' of the Master. Poor brother, thy poverty is no bar. One talent well used is more than ten abused, and money is but a poor talent.

It is not an occasional or periodic earnestness that God desires, but a calm, constant, life-long work. A man moving about this world with the Holy Ghost within him, prepared for anything, at every step, by every look and word, testifying for his Lord, conscious of no effort, but living in calm peace with his Saviour God, in the unhindered power of an inner life, in the patient hope of a glory soon to dawn, is the type of God's true servant. His service does not depend on his rank, his circumstances, his position: these are all subservient to what the man is. He may be the wealthiest in the world, or have to sweep a street, but his joy in the service is the same. Such will have a natural entrance into the courts above, where the servants serve their Lord day and night.

> O send me forth, my Saviour,
>   O send me for Thy glory,
> Regarding not the praise of man,
> And trampling on the fear of man,
>   And fighting for Thy glory, Thy glory.
>
> There is a man who often stands
>   Between me and Thy glory,
>   His name is self,
>   My carnal self,
>   Self-seeking self,

> Stands 'twixt me and Thy glory.
>
> O mortify him, mortify him,
>   Put him down, my Saviour,
> Exalt Thyself alone: lift high
>   The banner of the cross,
>   And in its folds
> Conceal the standard-bearer.

Dear fellow-servant, get so accustomed to serve your LORD JESUS CHRIST and Him alone, that your entrance into glory will not be unnatural, and thus an abundant entrance will be yours.

Every child of God, great and small, has a work; his or her own work. A brother in the Lord greatly surprised an old bed-ridden follower of the Lord by coming in with a smile to her one day, and saying, —

'I've got some work for you to do.'

'Me! what work! what can I do?'

'Oh, there's a little district meeting to be started, and you are to have special charge of it in praying about it.'

She got deeply interested in the people attending the little meeting, and this work did her and them much good. I saw a young boy confined to bed one day, and I told him he had a work to do. He had found Jesus, but he looked a little surprised. 'You have to pray and preach,' I said. — He smiled in surprise. — 'Yes, you have to pray for those that carry forth the gospel, and you have to lie there and preach sermons to all that come in, sermons on faith, patience, meekness, gentleness, adorning on your back, as we on our feet ought to do the doctrine of God our Saviour.' The same thought came also from the lips of another young disciple, now in the presence of the Lord, waiting the resurrection beauty in which he will be clothed with all those who have been faithful unto death — who have endured to the end. He said, 'We *all* must speak for Jesus,' when it was suggested that some might be too young to bear testimony to Jesus.

Listen to what God says He has done for you, and then begin to speak and act for God.

We all must speak for Jesus,
   Who hath redemption wrought,
Who gave us peace and pardon,
   Which by His blood He bought.
We all must speak for Jesus,
   To show how much we owe
To Him who died to save us
   From death and endless woe.

We all must speak for Jesus,
   The aged and the young,
With manhood's fearless accents —
   With childhood's lisping tongue.
We all must speak for Jesus,
   His people far and near —
The rich and poor on land or wave;
   The peasant and the peer.

We all must speak for Jesus,
       Where'er our lot may fall,
To brothers, sisters, neighbours,
       In cottage and in hall.
We all must speak for Jesus,
       The world in darkness lies.
With Him against the mighty
       Together we must rise.

We all must speak for Jesus,
   'Twill ofttimes try us sore,
But streams of grace, to aid us,
   Into our hearts He'll pour.
We all must speak for Jesus,
   Till He shall come again,
Proclaim His glorious gospel,
   His crown and endless reign.

Judgment.

Our Reward.

I DON'T think we can know we are saved till the judgment day.'

'But it matters very little what we think, for God says that His Bible was written, that we may *know* that we have eternal life' (1 John v. 13).

This is the answer to such a false and absurd statement; God's word was written that we might antedate the judgment day and know its issues now. Do you think that the Apostle Paul, after having been 1800 years with the Lord, is to stand at the judgment day to know whether he is saved or not? This is most evidently absurd. In John v. 20-30 we get the whole point settled by infinite wisdom. If you have not 'passed from death unto life' down here below, and are thus standing in the rank of those who 'shall not come into judgment,' you will be damned to all eternity. As the tree falls it lies. The godly man cries, 'Enter not into judgment with Thy servant, for in Thy sight shall no man living be justified' (Psalm cxliii. 2). Through death and resurrection in Christ, as those who have been judged and justified, we are prepared for eternity. From the above mistake, however, some are often inclined to flee to another.

'How can I be judged after I am saved?'

'But God says *we* must *all* appear before the judgment-seat of Christ that *every one* may receive the things done in his body, according to that he hath done, whether it be good or bad' (2 Cor. v. 10), and this is the answer to such a statement. Perfectly reconcilable are these two. We shall never by judged as to whether we are saved or lost, but every deed we have done shall be judged, deeds we have forgotten, deeds we did not know we had done. Those who are in Christ shall rejoice to see all their rubbish burned. Only then shall they know what grace has done for them; then they shall receive their rewards. Those not in Christ shall be destroyed with their works. 'If the righteous scarcely be saved where shall the ungodly and the sinner appear?' We are justified by faith; we are judged according to our works. Many, even Christians, forget this, and think that because, as to justification, judicially our sins are blotted out, that therefore there will be no judgment. This is most unscriptural. We are saved as to our persons, but we must all appear before the judgment seat of Christ. Our every motive shall then receive its exact value. 'What manner of persons ought we to be?' Is it not practical infidelity on this point that leads Christians often to be careless? Beware! God is not mocked: whatsoever a man sows that shall he also reap.

I. THE SON OF GOD HEALING.

In the beginning of John v. we see the contrast between the quickening power of Jesus and the weakness of legal ordinance, in the history of the infirm man at the pool of Bethesda, who had the desire for health, but not the power to profit by the occasional means — the angel's visit. To will was present with him, but to perform he could not. How like a man under law: 'But what the law could not do, in that it was weak through the flesh,' God did in Jesus. Jesus came to the powerless one, and by His word cured him: 'Arise, take up thy bed and walk.' Strength came on the spot. Here is the life manifested now: God manifest in the flesh: *the Son of God.*

II. THE SON OF MAN REJECTED.

The Jews, thinking themselves far better than Jesus, sought to kill Him because He wrought on the Sabbath. He showed that God could not rest amid sin and misery, and that He and the Father were one. The Jews sought to kill Him. What a marvel!

God manifest in the flesh could become the victim of man's hatred! The Creator submitted to be killed by the creature! Yes; for He was *the Son of Man*.

Jesus now shows them the whole truth concerning the matter. He was not another God, but in full union with the Father; did 'nothing of Himself' (there cannot be two independent supreme Beings), 'but what He seeth the Father do;' and there is nothing that the Father does which He does not show the Son. Christ speaks of Himself as God. He also speaks of Himself as in a position to do the Father's will, as the perfect servant who can be seen of men.

III. JESUS, THE QUICKENER AND JUDGE.

To show His glory in so doing, He speaks of two things (verses 21, 22): — 'He *quickeneth* whom He will;' and the Father hath 'committed all *judgment* unto the Son.' As Son of God He gives *life*; but as Son of Man he may be 'rejected,' 'disallowed,' 'disowned,' 'despised,' 'dishonoured;' therefore, 'the Father judgeth no man, but hath committed *all judgment* unto the Son, that all (even His rejecters) should honour the Son, even as they honour the Father.' If we do not receive Him in grace, we must honour Him by being judged by Him; and all are divided into these two classes. Men have many distinctions in society — high and low, rich and poor, old and young, good, bad, indifferent, very good, very bad; but the great division of mankind before God is into those who have been *quickened* by Jesus, the Son of God, or who shall come into *judgment*, under Jesus, the Son of Man. To which class do *you* belong? There must be no mistake on this point, for a slip here is fatal for ever. God has left no doubt about the means of knowing it. He has given us a perfect test by which we may know infallibly, emphasized by a double '*verily*' from the mouth of Incarnate Truth.

IV. EVERY BELIEVER HATH EVERLASTING LIFE.

'Verily, verily, I say unto you, he that heareth My word, and believeth Him who sent Me, *hath* everlasting life.' '*He* that heareth My word.' This is the word that brought order out of chaos, light out of darkness. This is the word that made myriads of stars revolve around their centres. This is the word that forms man and beast, and tree and rock, that formed 'the sea' and the 'dry land.' This is the word that Jairus' daughter heard as she lay on her couch in the sleep of death. This is the word that the son of the weeping widow heard at Nain's gate, as he was being carried out on his bier. This is the word that Lazarus heard as he lay rotting in his tomb, and hearing, came forth a living man. Whosoever now hears that word, and trusts that Father who sent Jesus, by believing this life-giving word, '*hath* everlasting life.' Anxious soul, you have often said, Would that I could see Him with these eyes, I would draw from Him one word that would give me life. Would that I could see Him walking past my door, I would rush out and grasp His robe and be healed, as the poor woman was who touched His garment. Yes, but is His word not the same now, and far more important to us? — that blessed Word which His Spirit of truth has written about Him, and whispers into your soul concerning Him? For say not in thine heart who shall ascend up into heaven to bring Christ down? He *has* come down, or who shall descend to the grave to bring Him up? He *is* risen. He is gone above. But His *word* is in thy mouth and in thy heart, and will it not satisfy you — His word, which is nigh to you, close to you, 'the word of salvation which we preach?' 'Hear, and your soul shall live.' What a contradiction! Can metaphysics explain it? Can man's reason fathom it? Yet we believe it. Man's line is too short for man's need, but he that believeth '*hath everlasting life.*' It is not a life on probation (as Adam's, which could be lost), but *everlasting* life, Jesus' own life; for it is 'no longer I, but *Christ that liveth in me.*' It is not that he *shall have*, but 'hath.' It is not the promise of a future blessing after the last day, but the gift and present possession of *life now*! *Heareth, believeth, hath*: what a gospel for poor dead sinners! We need no longer wait at 'pools,' for Jesus has come down; no longer do we seek and are unable to find, for He has come 'to seek and to save' the lost. He has come to undertake for those that are 'without strength.' What dishonor then, can there be like doubting His 'WORD!' The devil says, *Dare you believe* such good news? The Holy Ghost says, *Dare you doubt it?* The devil says, It would be presumption to hear His word, as if it were for *you*. The Holy Ghost says that it is just for *you*, and it would be the highest presumption, and a resisting of Him, to stop your ears.

V. – BEYOND DEATH AND JUDGMENT NOW.

Besides having *life*, he that 'heareth and believeth' has something more. 'He shall not come into *judgment*.' (It is the same word in the Greek as at verse 22, and should be so translated.) Why? Because '*He is passed from death unto life.*' The everlasting life that we in believing get, is a life in resurrection: life in a risen Christ. What a wonderful truth from Jesus' own lips! 'Shall not come into judgment,' as touching my guilt, my sins, my standing as a living man descended from the first Adam, but reckoned as condemned, judged, dead, buried, and now *alive* '*unto* God,' Already in Christ, on resurrection ground. This in no way interferes with our appearance as Christians before the tribunal of Christ (1 Cor. v.), for judgment concerning our actions as believers; where we shall get reward, according to the just judgment of our Lord and Master — a most blessed, solemn, and sanctifying thought; but it places the believer, as to his standing, on new ground, beyond the judgment of sin, beyond its doom, beyond his death, in a new life, in which he can now serve God, in which he can stand with joy at that tribunal. How different is God's religion from man's notions of it! Man thinks that God's religion is at best a mere preparation for death and judgment; whereas our blessed Teacher shews us, in this 'word' of His, that it is a *life beyond death and beyond judgment*! Christian, stand up alive unto God. Start up from thy sleep a living man. Thou shalt not come into judgment, but are passed *from death unto life*. All hearers of *His* word, who trust in Him, have this immunity, whether they *realise* it or not. Jesus' word has settled all, and it is blasphemy to doubt it. Have you heard Him speak? You may have heard men preach the gospel. Have you really heard good news for yourself from God Himself?

VI. THE TWO HOURS.

Jesus in the fifth chapter of John points to TWO PERIODS in which His power would be manifested, and speaks of the two classes of people on whom that power would be displayed. 'The *hour* is coming, and now is, when the dead shall hear the voice of the *Son of God*, and they that hear shall live.' Man was dead spiritually by sin, he is dead in sin, and Jesus came and quickened him. The hour was *then*, and is going on still, in which He is causing the dead to hear His voice and live. Thousands have been saved in this hour by hearing the voice of the *Son of God*. For the Father hath given Jesus as the *Son of God* manifested here in the flesh 'to have life in Himself;' 'for,' said John, 'the life was manifested, and we have seen it, and bear witness, and shew unto you that eternal life which was with the Father, and was manifested unto us.' But all do not wish to receive Him, all will not hear Him; the most part reject, disown, cast Him out. To meet this state of things, the Father 'hath given Him authority to execute judgment, because He is the *Son of Man*.'

As 'Son of Man,' He was despised and dishonoured; as 'Son of Man,' He shall claim His kingdom; as 'Son of Man,' He shall 'execute judgment upon His rejectors;' as 'Son of Man,' all nations shall be gathered before Him for judgment; as 'Son of Man,' He shall break His foes with a rod of iron; as 'Son of Man,' He shall 'reign in righteousness;' as 'Son of Man,' He shall sit on the 'great white throne,' and before Him shall stand 'the dead, small and great.' Grace, love, mercy, pity, pardon, life, having all been rejected, what now is left but wrath, destruction, vengeance, judgment, death? 'The Son of Man' — Jesus of Nazareth — the King of the Jews, shall then be on the THRONE, not on the CROSS; and not in Hebrew and Greek and Latin only will this be known, but all men of every tongue shall honour Him as they honour the Father, and shall own as King of kings and Lord of lords this 'Son of Man.'

'Marvel not at this: for the HOUR is coming, in the which all that are in the graves shall hear His voice and shall come forth; they that have done good unto the resurrection of life, and they that have done evil unto the resurrection of judgment.' In the first HOUR, which has already lasted upwards of 1800 years, the dead in trespasses and sins have been getting life; the other HOUR is not yet come, but in it two things will happen. Those that have done good shall be quickened to a resurrection of LIFE — the quickening work of the Son of God being then, and not till then, perfectly completed — He being 'the Omega,' as well as 'the Alpha.' Those that have done evil shall also be raised, but to a resurrection of judgment — which, in their case shall certainly be eternal damnation. The whole line of thought is judgment (it is the same words as in verses 22 and 24), a judgment not of two Gods but of the one God, who has but one mind, one will, one judgment, though acting in different persons. All men, saved or lost, shall rise, because Christ is risen.

Reader, in which resurrection wilt thou share, that of life or of judgment? Wilt thou listen to the 'Son of God,' or dost thou await the judgment of the 'Son of Man?' Now is the time of passing from off the judgment ground through thy death into His life. There will be no change after thy spirit has left thy body. *Now*, this moment, as thou readest this line, pause and ask, *Have I passed from death unto life*? If not, hear His voice at this moment; believe His Father's love-message, whilst thou hearest 'His word,' 'God so loved the *world*' ('a term co-extensive with its rational and accountable generations') 'that He gave his only begotten Son, that whosoever' (of all the dead, ruined, God-hating sinners in it) 'believeth in Him should not perish, but have everlasting life.' 'This man receiveth *sinners*,' 'a designation that misses no one individual of the species.' That thou are not already in hell is due only to the tolerance of that God against whom thou daily sinnest. This is the HOUR of grace, of life, of pardon: the next HOUR must be the HOUR of vengeance, of judgment, of wrath. Sooner or later thou wilt know these *realities*. If you get into heaven at all, it must be by hearing His word and believing Him. Then, why not now? Are you afraid of making sure of being in heaven soon? It is heaven on earth, if you knew it, to be *alive in a living Christ*. Why not antedate your heaven by beginning it now, even if you knew your hour would lengthen out ever so long? 'In Christ all are made alive.' But what a difference in the doom of the two classes who are made alive by Him! One is made alive because His Spirit dwells in them, the other because He is the powerful judge that condemns them to the lake of fire for ever.

VII. THE BOOK CLOSED AND OPENED.

In Isa, lxi. I, we read, 'The Spirit of the Lord God is upon me, because the Lord hath anointed me to preach good tidings unto the meek, He hath sent me to bind up the broken-hearted, to proclaim liberty to the captives, and the opening of the prison to the bound. To proclaim THE ACCEPTABLE YEAR OF THE LORD, and the *day of vengeance of our God*. And in Luke iv, 18 when Jesus in the synagogue applied this to Himself, He finishes with 'the acceptable year of the Lord.' He does not go on to say, 'the day of vengeance of our God;' but it is written, 'He closed the book, and He gave it again to the minister, and sat down.' What a gospel is in that omission! On it has been hung the forbearance of these eighteen centuries. What love, what long-suffering is in that word, '*He closed the book*,' that book which spoke of vengeance. The proclamation in this hour is, 'the acceptable year of the Lord' — grace, life from the Son of God; but what a day that will be when the book is opened, 'the day of vengeance of our God,' the execution of the judgement of the Son of Man!

In Rev. v. we see the acceptable year has revolved, the redeemed, worshipping, praising elders are gathered around Himself, and now the book is brought forward, and one of the elders says, 'Behold the lion of the tribe of Juda, the root of David, hath prevailed to *open the book*, and to loose the seven seals thereof.' This is the book of terrible wrath, the opening of the seals of which inaugurates fearful judgment upon a Christ-rejecting world. Wilt thou be under the vials of wrath, or wilt thou hear of life? 'The book' is closed as yet. He has handed it to His servants; He has left them to proclaim His grace, His gospel, and He has *sat down* waiting till His enemies are made His footstool. What a gospel! A closed book of vengeance, an open heaven, a preached gospel, a seated Christ, life from the Son of God! What a day is coming! An open book of wrath, the door of mercy shut, no more room, a risen Christ, judgment executed by the Son of Man!

Let me, in conclusion, place before you the teaching of Scripture concerning judgment as to a believer. There is,

1st, THE JUDGMENT OF SIN.

This was at Calvary when Christ stood in the place of the sinner, putting away sin by the sacrifice of Himself. He was made sin for us, bare our sins in His own body on the tree, was wounded for our transgressions, was bruised for our iniquities, when God laid our iniquities on Him. This was when He cried, 'My God, My God, why hast thou forsaken Me?' That was for us. When we believe in Him this judgment can never alight on us. If we reject Him this will be our doom in an eternal hell. It is this judgment spoken of in the passage above that the believer is beyond. He is no longer a convict. He is a son. He has not to meet the sentence of a judge. He is under the authority and discipline of his Father, and as such he will be judged; but how great the difference! He will not be judged to see whether he is a convict or a son; he will be judged as a son, for there is,

2d, THE JUDGMENT-SEAT OF CHRIST.

'We must all appear before the judgment-seat of Christ.' Every Christian will render his account of everything he has done, every vain and idle word, every idle action, every deceit he has practiced. Christian merchant, every trick of trade will then appear. Christian lady, every little polite lie will appear then. When that lady came to see you yesterday, you remarked when you saw her coming, 'Oh! here is that disagreeable person, I wonder she comes here;' and when you went into your drawing-room, with a smile you said to her, 'Oh! I'm so glad to see you.' — And you were not. — It was a lie.

Every one will suffer loss in as far as he has acted against his Lord's mind. Be ye holy for I am holy. Nothing will stand then but that which has proceeded from the new nature, which is holy. Our wisdom, in prospect of that day of rewards, is to starve the old man and feed the new; to mortify the members which are upon the earth; to reproduce Christ in our daily life, since we have received Christ our everlasting life; to walk in the exhibition of that grace and truth which we have received; to *adorn* (we cannot make it true or false, but we can adorn) the doctrine of God our Saviour in all things.

Take care that you do not suffer loss in that day. In 1 Thess. iv. we find it will be when we are caught up out of this world to meet the Lord in the air. But the saint will be *glorified* when he reaches that tribunal, and one of his highest joys will be to see all his selfish words burned up, and all that was for God placed on his crown of righteousness. The crown of *gold* belongs to all the saints, for that is what Christ is, but the crown of *righteousness* is the righteous reward given to each according to his individual faithfulness. May we be using this world so as to gain this crown. May we now, as those not of the world, be packing up our goods and sending them on before. *Grace* has saved us and placed us beyond judgment; *truth* will give exact rewards to us as sons when we shall be openly acknowledged and acquitted in that day of judgment, and made perfectly blessed in the full enjoying of God to all eternity. And then, in the endless ages, the eternal day of God, when God is all and all, we shall be the brightest specimens of the righteousness and truth of God, and we shall also show in these ages to come 'the exceeding riches of His grace.'

Grace and truth came by Jesus Christ.

Grace and truth are now preached and exhibited in the conversion and walk of the Christian.

Grace and truth shall be fully manifested, and their power fully known to us as the glorified of the Lord, only at the glorious tribunal of Christ, and then for evermore.

Stand up from among the dead, and patiently work as one waiting for the judgment seat of Christ.

> 'Tis first the true and then the beautiful,
>   Not first the beautiful and then the true;
> First the wild moor with rock, and reed, and pool,
>   Then the gay garden rich in scent and hue.
>
> 'Tis first the good and then the beautiful,
>   Not first the beautiful and then the good;
> First the rough seed sown in the rougher soil,
>   Then the flower blossom or the branching wood.
>
> Not first the glad and then the sorrowful,
>   But first the sorrowful and then the glad;
> Tears for a day: for earth of tears if full,
>   Then we forget that we were ever sad.
>
> Not first the bright, and after that the dark,
>   But first the dark, and after that the bright;
> First the thick cloud, and then the rainbow's arc,
>   First the dark grave, then resurrection light.
>
> 'Tis first the night — stern night of storm and war,
>   Long night of heavy clouds, and veiled skies;
> Then the far sparkle of the Morning Star,
>   That bids the saints awake, and dawn arise.

TRILOGY BOOK NUMBER TWO:

THE SEEKING SAVIOUR

THE SEEKING SAVIOUR,

AND OTHER BIBLE THEMES.

by the late
Dr. W. P. Mackay M.A.,
of Hull.
Author of *Grace and Truth*, etc.

PREFACE.

In making the following collection of articles on various Scripture subjects we are only carrying out the design of the author. He had commenced the work and spoken of it several times. Methinks, if he had got a glimpse into the future at the dawn of this year, the book would have been in the hands of friends and lovers of the truth some months ago. We believe the great enemy and deceiver tried in various ways to prevent the departed one using his pen; he knew well how his ranks had been thinned through the pages of "Grace and Truth," and therefore his wisdom was to try by all means to prevent anything of a similar aim being produced. The composition in many parts is blunt and homely. One literary friend wrote regarding it: "It is difficult to prune without hurting the vigour;" so as we prefer having it in its native vigour, we rather give it to you unpruned.

The title we have chosen is one which perhaps the Son of man, Who so often gave Himself this name, rejoices in more than any other. God commenced the seeking; as soon as there was a wandering sinner to be sought, we hear, "Adam, where art thou?" and it has never ceased since then. And now through these pages our desire and prayer is that many lost ones may be found and safely sheltered in the fold of the Good Shepherd.

"The Great Shepherd" of the twenty-third Psalm, we believe, was more frequently preached upon than any other subject in England, Scotland, Ireland, and America; it was always fresh and beautiful, suited to all classes and kinds of people, the aged and the young.

"The Claims of the Man Jesus" was a subject that was studied and preached upon ten years ago; there was manifest power and blessing on the evening on which it was first delivered. As the congregation were asked, "Who believes in this rejected Man?" hundreds rose to their feet in testimony of their faith in Him.

The study of "The Writing on the Cross" was done in student days twenty years ago; may the Hoy Ghost bless it to the strengthening of the faith of some in the precious Word which is our unerring chart!

The thoughts given on "The Name of God" and "His Name's Sake" comprise many years' study; "His Name's Sake" was written about two years ago. We remember well, the triumph with which the writer held it up in manuscript, because he always felt he had gained a victory when he got his fast-flowing thoughts written on paper.

"The Glory of God" was the subject of his last sermon on earth; the one Lord's Day he reveled in preaching on "The Glory," and the next he had entered the pearly gates and was beholding His glory. There was no theme that he more rejoiced in than God's exaltation. Man was nothing in his view, nowhere—a failure in every position; but he had intense apprehension and appreciation of God. A friend said after enjoying his preaching for some months, "I have learned one thing since I came here,—I have learned to know God." As the voice is heard no more, may the printed pages have a similar result, and to His Name will be all the praise.

M. L. MACKAY.

10, MORNINGSIDE DRIVE
    EDINBURGH, *Nov.* 1885.

CONTENTS.

PREFACE . . . . . .

THE SEEKING SAVIOUR. . . . 1

THE GREAT SHEPHERD 10

"UNTIL" 17

SERVING AND FOLLOWING . . . 20

THE SACRIFICE, THE PRIEST, AND THE SAVIOUR 27

THE POWER THAT THE WORLD KNOWS NOTHING 38
    ABOUT

CHRIST THE POWER OF GOD . . . 47

"SAY NOT IN THINE HEART" . . . 54

RIGHTEOUSNESS, HUMAN AND DIVINE . 59

JOB'S QUESTION AND PAUL'S ANSWER . 65

THE CLAIMS OF THE MAN JESUS . . 72

THE WRITING ON THE CROSS . . 90

THE NAME OF GOD	98
EMMANUEL-JESUS	111
HIS NAME	114
MY NAME'S SAKE	121
THE GLORY OF GOD	128
THE TWO ANTHEMS	145
"FOR EVER"	152

THE SEEKING SAVIOUR.

"For the Son of Man is come to seek and to save that which was lost."—LUKE xix. 10.

ALL Christians rejoice in the reality of the divinity of our Lord and Saviour Jesus Christ; but is it not of great importance to keep in our hearts the reality of His humanity, especially when Holy Scripture tells us that "Every spirit that confesseth that Jesus Christ is come in the flesh is of God"? Among all the accounts of our Lord's life on earth, Luke presents Him most fully as a Man. Matthew traces His genealogy only up to Abraham, and presents Him as a real Jew; Mark gives us no genealogy, but begins with His Gospel-ministry; and John gives what might be called His Divine genealogy—"The Word was God;" Luke traces His genealogy up to Adam, thus showing Him to be the Son of Man.

Our theme is the Son of Man, and His work as told to us in Luke xix. 10: "For the Son of Man is come to seek and to save that which was lost." There is a beautiful because Divine fitness in Luke communicating to us this statement in its connection. Luke was not an apostle. Very little is known of him besides his being "the beloved physician," who certainly obeyed the second part of the evangelical commission—"to heal the sick," although we do not hear much of his preaching "the kingdom of God." It is a precious thought that the Saviour Himself, in sending out the twelve, thought of man both with regard to his spiritual and bodily needs. A Christian physician above all men is able to look at men as men. Has he to cure disease? He sees man as made in the image of God, and knows nothing of difference between the best and the worst. He is as careful in setting the fractured limb of the burglar as in ministering to the lameness of an empress. And where he sees an opportunity he can most deftly place a word that may be of spiritual power to his patient. Thus Luke the recorder has been chosen with Divine wisdom to give us many characteristic accounts of God's love of men. Only Luke tells us of the Good Samaritan; the Shepherd going after the lost sheep; the woman seeking for the coin that was lost; the Father receiving the prodigal; the Pharisee and the publican; Christ's interview with Zacchæus; the penitent thief, and many other wonders of grace.

In the nineteenth chapter of Luke we find that Zacchæus, the chief among the tax-gatherers, was very anxious to see this wonderful Man of whom he had heard, namely Jesus. There was a crowd, and he was little; but neither his own inability nor the presence of the crowd conquered him. He found a point of vantage on a sycamore tree, and our Lord, fully understanding the wish of Zacchæus and the small grain of faith that was working in him, told him He was to become his Guest. All murmured, not knowing the grace of the Saviour, and to the murmurings Zacchæus answered by a vindication of himself. Fifty per cent. of what he had he gave to the poor, not a mere legal ten per cent.; and had he taken anything wrongfully from any one, he gave him four times its value—a most conscientious, upright man. This we hold to have been the practice of his life before he met Jesus, and his vindication of his moral uprightness when they all murmured at Jesus going to him.

Jesus, however, makes very short work of all this self-vindication, as He did with Nicodemus, that very good natural man who came and paid Him the highest compliments, and who received this answer: "Ye must be born again."

The conduct of Zacchæus was very proper and commendable, but our Lord says, "This day is *salvation* come to this house, forasmuch as he also is a son of Abraham. For the Son of Man is come to seek and to save that which was *lost*." Let us now look at this Divine reason for salvation coming to a self-righteous sinner's house:

First, the *Person*—"*The Son of Man.*"

Second, His *work*—"*is come to seek and to save.*"

Third, the *objects* of His work—"*that which was lost.*"

I. The PERSON.—The Son of Man. This is a wonderful name, and a name that our Lord seems always desirous of being used.

Does it not tell us of at least three things? 1. Humiliation; 2. Perfection; 3. Heirship.

1. *Humiliation.*—He reached His crown by the cross. Before His honour was humility. He, "being in the form of God, thought is not robbery to be equal with God: but made Himself of no reputation, and took upon Him the form of a servant, and was made in the likeness of men: and being found in fashion as a man, He humbled Himself, and became obedient unto death, even the death of the cross." He passed by angels, for He never became an angel; passed by all the principalities and powers in heavenly places, all the peers of glory, and came in the strength of His own strong love to be the Son of Man, to be one of us, in order that He might be one with us. He laid aside the crown and the scepter of the universe to enter into the circumstances, sorrows, and responsibilities of man; to handle the saw and the axe, and to be the working man in the midst of His own great work:

> "The foxes found rest, and the birds had their nest
>   In the shade of the cedar tree,
> But Thy couch was the sod, O Thou Son of God!
>   In the deserts of Galilee."

2. His *Perfection.*—Can one man live to the glory of God, and without sin? Behold the perfect, sinless Son of Man, "holy, harmless, undefiled, separate from sinners." Adam failed, by the temptation to become as a god. The Son of Man prevailed, by taking the subject part of a man. He answered the devil's temptation by no appeal to His divinity, but to the Scripture given for man's use. The first man, through her who was to have been a help-meet for him, fell by indulging in the lust of the flesh ("the tree was good for food"), the lust of the eyes ("it was pleasant to the eyes"), and the pride of life ("a tree to be desired to make one wise").

The Son of Man showed His perfection when tempted by the devil, manifesting Himself as THE promised Seed. The Son, in resisting by the Word of God the temptations of the devil, rested upon the written Word: "By the word of Thy lips I have kept me from the paths of the destroyer." When the lust of the flesh was suggested, He answered: "It is written, Man shall not live by bread alone." When the lust of the eye was before Him: "It is written, Thou shalt worship the Lord thy God, and Him only shalt thou serve." And when the pride of life was temptingly exposed: "It is written, Thou shalt not tempt the Lord the God."

Have we seen His humiliation as Son of Man? We also see His perfection in exaltation as claimed by Him in this title; for He claimed in it that which had been written by the prophet Daniel: "I saw in the night visions, and, behold, one like the Son of Man came with the clouds of heaven, and came to the Ancient of Days, and they brought Him near before Him. And there was given Him dominion, and glory, and a kingdom, that all people, nations, and languages should serve Him. His dominion is an everlasting dominion which shall not pass away, and His kingdom that which shall not be destroyed."

3. *Heirship.*—The Son of Man is Heir of man. We have great exactness in 1 Cor. xv. 45-47, where Christ is spoken of as "the *last* Adam," and "the *second* man;" that is to say, there are two men, the first one a total failure, the second his Son and Heir, "the Lord from heaven," in "Whom is all perfection." And there never will be another representative head (Adam), for "the last Adam" had come, and has been known as "a quickening Spirit." Cain is not spoken of as the son of man, neither is Abel nor Seth; the Seed of the woman alone secures this title and with it serves Himself Heir to all man's possessions. And what are these? "The cattle upon a thousand hills" are the Lord's. The gold in all the mines and the pearls in all the oceans belong to their Maker. What, then, is man's possession, and what can he leave as peculiarly his own to his son and heir? Only one thing, and that is his sin. Behold the Son of Man in anguish under it! Behold Him bearing "our sins in His own body on the tree!" "Behold the Lamb of God, Who taketh away the sin of the world!" If there had been no sin to bear, there would have been no Son of Man; if there had been no Son of Man, there would have been no sin put away.

II. His WORK.—When He has become Son of Man, we find Him doing a work commensurate with this wonderful title.

1. He has come. 2. He has come to seek. 3. He has come to save.

1. He has *come*.—How precious is the word "come" as found in Scripture: "Come now and let us reason together," says the condescending and loving Jehovah. "Come unto Me, all ye that labour and are heavy-laden," is the word of the Son of Man. "Come, ye blessed of My Father, inherit, the kingdom prepared for you," will be the glad summons of the Judge of all the earth. But however precious "Come" may be, "*is* come" is much more so, and can alone make the invitation possible. That is to say, the Son of Man did not say to man, "Come," till He Himself had come.

No sooner had the tempter ruined Creation work, than the Redeemer-God began His work, and came to seek the wondering Adam in these words of pathetic tenderness: "Adam, where art thou?" And through type and symbols God has been coming to man, and at last "the Son of Man is come." Glorious event in the annals of eternity! Glorious climax of the history of time! Glorious manifestation of the God of heaven! Glorious provision for the sons of men! He has spanned all the distance between heaven and earth. He has bridged all the chasm between an angry God and a guilty sinner. He has in His own person shown the true Jacob's ladder stretching from the throne of God to the rock-bound cover of the sinner's tomb. The lifeboat's noble crew do not invite the ship-wrecked sailors to come to the life-boat until the life-boat has gone to them; so Christ does not say, "Come," until He Himself "is come." He has annihilated the distance. He can say, "I came down from heaven." "The Son of Man came not to be ministered unto, but to minister, and to give His life a ransom for many." He came not "to call the righteous, but sinners to repentance." "This is a faithful saying, and worthy of all acceptation, that Christ Jesus came into the world to save sinners." Christ Jesus came from His Father and His eternal love, His crown, His throne, "into the world," this distant, fallen, groaning, sin-doomed, God-hating world.

2. He came to *seek*.—"Seek ye the Lord." is a Divine injunction, and as a duty is binding on all creatures whom God has made. The law given to Israel discovered how loth man was to seek God, so that we find in Romans iii. 11, among the various accusations brought against man, this one is prominent, "There is none that seeketh after God." But now grace has revealed to us this

wonderful fact, that God in the person of the Son is seeking the sinner. Adam ran from God when he fell, but God went after him, seeking him, as much as to say, If ye flee from Me, and if ye prefer the devil's lie to My truth, and prefer to do without Me, I come to seek you. I wish you back. I do not wish to do without you, — "Adam, where art thou?" He sought out the fishermen and their friends at Galilee's sea. He sought for little Zacchæus in the midst of a crowd as he was on the sycamore-tree. Reader, He is seeking for you now, as you may be seated in the tree of your own self-righteousness or self-importance or self-greatness. But it is only as one descending from all such morality trees or self-sufficiency trees that you can be found by the seeking Saviour.

3. He has come to *save* as well as to seek.—"The grace of God that bringeth salvation hath appeared to all men." His mission is very specific; His work is very exact: He came not to instruct men in science or art, to teach them how to use the geologist's hammer, the astronomer's telescope, or the student's microscope. All these could be discovered and employed by the reason of man. He came not to solve or settle the questions arising between science and religion. He came not to teach politics, or to decide whether unlimited monarchy or constitutional government or democracy is the best method. He came to *save*—to save us from the *penalty* of sin by His atonement. "For by grace are ye saved through faith; and that not of yourselves;" "receiving the end of your faith, even the salvation of your souls;" to save us from the *power* of sin by His Holy Spirit by Whom we work out our "own salvation with fear and trembling," knowing the "it is God Who worketh in us, both to will and to do of His good pleasure;" to save us from the *presence* of sin by the completed top-stone put upon His work. For "to them that look for Him shall He appear the second time without sin unto salvation."

Salvation-work has been His great work since creation-work was marred. Salvation-work is the work revealed from Genesis to Revelation. Salvation was the work of the Father till the Son appeared (for "My Father worketh hitherto"). In type and sacrifice, in blood and fire, in history and prophecy, salvation was the work. When the Son came it was still to work at salvation, by precept, and example, by lessons and parables, by suffering, and finally at the

Cross to say, "It is finished." The Son of Man is come to save; and since His day the Third Person of the blessed Trinity, the Holy Ghost, has come to unfold to us this salvation, to carry on this divine work among men, this heavenly work on earth, this eternal work in time, and by letter and instruction and unseen and unheard influence to convey to us conviction, repentance, conversion, regeneration, salvation; and to the Father, Son, and Holy Ghost we bow as to the God of our salvation.

III. Those interested in this work, THE LOST.

Lost has bound up in its letters (1) the idea *guilty*; (2) the idea *corrupt*; (3) the idea *valued*.

1. The lost is *guilty*.—"All we like sheep have gone astray," etc. We have left the fountain of living waters, and hewed out for ourselves "broken cisterns, that can hold no water." We have offended; and he who offendeth "in one point is guilty of all." The holy law as an impartial jury has brought in the verdict "Guilty." And thus we are lost to Him Who created us. We have brought ourselves under the curse of His holy law. Yea, we are guilty, as bound up in the same humanity of the apostolic accusation, "Ye have killed the Prince of Life."

2. The lost is *corrupt*.—Intended for the Creator's use, we are now by nature and practice of no use to Him, utterly "unprofitable:" the fine gold has become dim. Intended to show His power and Godhead in this world, we have sunk beneath the level of beasts; so that humanity has even worshipped birds, four-footed beasts, and creeping things." We have not only been guilty of specific breakings of God's holy law, by which we are seen to be trangressors, but our natures are fallen, we are depraved and corrupt, the imagination of the thoughts of the heart only evil continually. And the work of a seeking Saviour is required not only to pardon our transgressions, but to cover our sin. Self-will, self-seeking, and self-pleasing have taken the place of God's will, God-seeking, and God-pleasing; and thus while self is gratified we are lost to God.

3. The lost is *valued*.—While passing through the street, if a straw dropped from my hand I should think nothing and say nothing about it. But should I lose a five-pound note, I should at once think of and speak of my loss. And why? Because I knew its

value and could do very badly with its loss. "I have lost the sheep," says the shepherd, because to him it was valuable. "I have lost my piece of silver," says the woman, because she could ill afford to lose it. "I have lost my boy," says the father, because he loved the boy. The lost is valued, the lost is loved. Oh, what love is in that little word of one syllable, "lost!" You even may not feel that you have lost God; but the grace and value and appreciation all begin on His side. You have chosen the world, the devil, and the flesh; but God says: I love you, I do not wish to do without you. I feel I have lost something. Suns and stars, planets and comets, day and night, summer and winter, are all under My control. The reins of ten thousand stars and systems are held in My uncreated hands. Angels that excel in strength rejoice to do My will, and obey My commandments. The sea hears My voice and calms its waves. "The floods clap their hand" to My glory. The forests shake at My presence. Flowers bloom to reflect the beauty of the Eternal. Yea, even "fire, hail, snow, and vapours" fulfil My words; "fruitful trees, and all cedars; beasts and all cattle," join in allegiance. Oh, thou vicegerent[1] of God, made in His image, placed at the head of creation! I have Lost thee. Still I love thee, have so loved thee that I have said, Thou are lost to Me; so loved thee that I have sent My only-begotten Son to seek thee. And only the lost sinner lies in the pathway of the seeking Saviour.

What is the answer, my fellow lost one, that you and I have to make? Let us do it together; for "there is no difference: for all have sinned and come short of the glory of God." Yes, Lord, we are guilty; we are corrupt; we are lost. We would write "Lost" on the palms of our hands, on the soles of our feet; in all we do and wherever we go we are lost. "Lost" we engrave on our intellects, our wills, our affections; at all times, under all circumstances, and in all our faculties, we but say "Lost." We wait not for the judgment-bar to hear the doom. We accept Thy judgment, "Lost." But we joyfully hear through that word the echo from the eternal realities, "Loved." We hear it from the incarnate Word, "It is finished." And as we are and where we are we joyfully believe the

---

[1] Editor's Note: An administrative deputy of a king or magistrate.

message that Thou, O Father, hast sent by the Spirit to us, that "the Son of Man is come to seek and to save that which was lost."

And on our part we take the lost sinner's place, and claim the lost sinner's Saviour.

THE GREAT SHEPHERD.

PSALM xxiii.

 HIS subject is an old theme, one which most of us have been acquainted with from the time we sat on our mother's knee. The twenty-third Psalm is one of the most perfect lyrical gems that the world has ever seen. We have read it many a time, but it is always fresh.

"The Lord is my Shepherd!" It is a wonderful thing that He should condescend to make Himself our Shepherd. Three times in the New Testament is the Lord spoken of as a Shepherd: once in the Gospel of John, once in the First Epistle of Peter, and once in that wonderful letter to the Hebrews. In John x. 11 you read, "I am the Good Shepherd;" in Hebrews xiii. 20, "Now the God of peace, that brought again from the dead our Lord Jesus, that Great Shepherd of the sheep, through the blood of the everlasting covenant, made you perfect in every good work to do His will;" and lastly, if you look at the First Epistle of Peter v. 4, you will find this written, "And when the Chief Shepherd shall appear, ye shall receive a crown of glory that fadeth not away." Each mention of the word has a distinct adjective, one the "Good Shepherd," one the "Great Shepherd," and the third the "Chief Shepherd."

Now we shall look first at the twenty-third Psalm in its glorious setting. It is a perfect gem. Most gems look well or not just as the setting they are in sets them off properly or not. But this gem, which would be beautiful in any setting, shines out all the more here on account of the inimitable lustre of its setting. With the twenty-second Psalm on the one hand and the twenty-fourth on the other, it could not fail to be beautiful. The Twenty-second, you know, is the psalm of that wonderful hour of Calvary. It was the psalm used by our Lord during His crucifixion; and it is thus the expression of our Saviour's feelings at that dreadful hour. Then we come into the twenty-third Psalm, the psalm of Christian experience, the psalm of the journey, the psalm of the desert, the psalm of the wilderness. And then there is the glorious twenty-fourth Psalm. It is not the dying psalm! Nor the weariness and the weeping of the desert; but desert cares are over, and weeping gone; and we have the magnificent psalm of the glory of the King.

We have the Good Shepherd in the twenty-second Psalm, the Great Shepherd in the twenty-third Psalm, and the Chief Shepherd in the twenty-fourth Psalm. We have

Cross, desert, and crown.

The cross, that is the twenty-second Psalm; the wilderness, that is the twenty-third; the crown, that is the twenty-fourth. First, then, we have the Good Shepherd laying down His life with the cry, "Why hast Thou forsaken Me?" Then we have the Great Shepherd. For He must needs be a Great Shepherd, with such a great flock of sheep, and very stupid ones, too, sometimes, to look after. We are going through this great wilderness, wandering about, and the Lord is the Great Shepherd looking after His flock. And then in the twenty-fourth Psalm we have the Chief Shepherd, who rewards all the under-shepherds. Looking then at its setting, the Good Shepherd on the one hand and the Chief Shepherd on the other, we look at the guidance of the Great Shepherd. And in passing let me say a word on one point. We hear a great deal at the present time of the goodness of God. They have made out that God is so good that He will never punish any one. And this belief is gaining ground daily, even among Christians, I am sorry to say; they try to explain away Christ's doctrine of everlasting punishment. Some go so far as to say that no one will be eternally punished; that all will be let off. But Christ says, "I am the Good Shepherd, and I lay down My life for the sheep." There is no letting off there. There is the punishment of sin in the crucifixion of the Son of God for His sheep.

Now in the psalm of the wilderness we have a wonderful perfection. The first verse is the theme of it all, and the challenge of faith. The Psalmist puts the Lord between him and circumstances, and boldly challenges any one or anything to come between him and God. It is the challenge of faith. "Come what may," the believer can say, "I shall not want." I have not in the past wanted anything, or do not at the present want anything, but "I shall not want," because the Lord is my Shepherd. Of course our human nature will perhaps want many things; it may want the very necessaries of life; but those are not real wants. God says that they who trust in Him shall never want any good thing.

The last verse is the summation of the whole matter, as the first is the challenge. The second verse makes provision for our *Weakness*, and speaks about the pastures where the Great Shepherd leads His sheep. The great thing in a shepherd is to know all the best pastures, and where the greenest grass grows, so that his sheep may get the best possible food. Now Christ leads us into the greenest pastures, and by the still waters. The thoughtfulness of knowledge with the preparedness of power makes the guidance perfect. There is not a difficulty that has arisen, is arising, or will arise, but the Lord has anticipated it, and met it, and provided for it. His wisdom anticipated it; His power provided for it. But the believer may say, "I am weak, I am going through the desert, and I can get nothing from the earth," for there is nothing that springs form the earth that will feed your faith. In other words, there are no waving cornfields in the desert. What will He send you? Manna down from heaven. He will send you better than angels' food. "He maketh me to lie down in green pastures; He leadeth me beside the still waters. "The pillar-cloud of His own eye leads me.

"He maketh me to lie down." This is the quietness of perfect confidence. The hungry sheep does not lie down in green pastures; only the satisfied one does so. This is conscious communion with God, not the activity of service. We cannot always fight; we must have communion. In warfare you must not put on the sleeping dress, but the fighting dress. Our loins girt about with truth, having on the breastplate of righteousness, and our feet shod with the preparation *of* the gospel of peace, and above all the shield of faith, and the helmet of salvation, and lastly the sword of the Spirit,— that is the armour we are to wear when we go forth to the battle. That is the activity of battle. But if you are always battling, you will find that you cannot always stand. The more we are in the quietness of perfect communion, the more shall we be able to stand the hardships of war.

You often hear of believers, especially young disciples, who get up into the heights of bliss, and want to stay there. They mount up with wings as eagles; and you may let them stay there, for they will be brought down to the daily fight of life soon enough. And after the mounting what is there? "They shall run and not be weary." And then shall they mount again? No, "they shall walk and not faint." That is a patient continuance in well-doing. And it is sometimes harder to do that than to mount with eagles' wings; to keep amid the storms, and troubles, and sunshine of life a steady Christian walk and conversation. God's ways are various. It is not always sowing and reaping. He sometimes, after a time of refreshing and revival, sends a winnowing time; and none but those who are firmly resting on the Rock of Ages will stand through it all.

But after this you would think that was enough; but no, having done all, we are to "stand"—stand! Yes, it needs grace to stand. Sometimes when the battle is pressing against us hard, we cannot do more than keep our ground, and it requires almighty grace to enable us to do even that. And after the mounting, and after the running, and after the walking, and after the standing, you might think that was surely enough. But there is a lower step yet. "He maketh me to lie down" in the quietness of confidence and communion.

The third verse points us to the question of

Sin still present in the believer, and requiring daily cleansing. Here it is no question of quickening, but of cleansing. But this He, the Great Shepherd, had also anticipated and met, so "He restoreth my soul. He leadeth me in the paths of righteousness for His name's sake." There is my weakness; He gives me food. He thought I would be sinful,— "He restoreth my soul."

Then in the fourth verse, when the Psalmist comes to speak about this awful thing,

Death, there is a transition in the form of speech. At first, you notice he spoke about God; now he changes and speaks to God. "Yea, though I walk through the valley of the shadow of death, I will fear no evil; for *Thou* art with me; Thy rod and Thy staff, they comfort me." Does he not say, "For He will be with me"? No. "For Thou art with me." "He" sounds as though He were high up in the heavens,—"Thou," that He is close beside me, down on our earth. "Thou art with me." A Friend, more intimate than any friend on earth—a Friend, more dear than any friend on earth, a Friend to dry every tear, a Friend who will stand by the grave and will weep with you and with me. He has a human heart, and He will not only stand by you, but He will weep with you, for He is a Man of sorrows and acquainted with grief.

It is not "I am going to tread the valley of death after awhile." I do not believe the deathbed is the valley of the shadow of death. I believe we enter it from our cradle. The Hebrew word could be rendered quite as correctly, "I am now treading the valley of death." John Bunyan, in the *Pilgrim's Progress*, makes Christian go through a river of death, which he finds deep and rapid and difficult to get through. Now according to the illustration of Joshua's crossing of Jordan, the Christian goes through dry-shod, and he can triumphantly sing—

"Where are thy waves, O Jordan?
   Thy emptied bed lies dry,
And all thy power is broken,
   Thy waters stand on high.
I fear not Jordan's river;
   Its flood is pass'd for me;
And, hasting dry-shod over,
   I soon at rest shall be.

"I do not dread death's valley,
   To me a pasture green;
For there, beside still waters,
   Is laid its peaceful scene.
I do not fear death's shadow,
   A shadow ne'er can harm;
I must rejoice in Jesus,
   When resting on His arm."

"I will fear no evil, for Thou art with me; Thy rod and Thy staff, they comfort me." We need both the rod and the staff, the rod to correct and the staff to support, and they both comfort.

In the fifth verse we come to *our enemies*—principalities and powers in heavenly places. These He has thought of and met as my Great Shepherd. Both lion and bear are known to Him and met by Him, and there is nothing left for me but to sit at His table under His banner of love. "Thou preparest a table before me in the presence of mine enemies." He gives me the place of a royal priest beside Him. "Thou anointest my head with oil." Surely we have now reached the running over of our blessings, "My cup runneth over." The Lord hath filled it to overflowing. There is water from the overflowing cup to refresh the earth, and there is incense from the adoring heart to ascend to God in worship. And let me say, in passing, to all Christian workers, Sunday-school teachers, and others, you will do very little good except with the overflow. We must ourselves be so filled with Divine truth, that we cannot contain it all, so that it will overflow, and the overflow will bless others. Unless you are filled to overflowing yourselves, never try to fill others, because you will need all you have got, and have none to spare.

This is the finishing of it all—myself not wanting, but running over to bless others. What more do we want? We have seen everything met: weakness, sins, death, and foes. What more can we want? Yes, there is still something more. We have to look at our footprints left in the sands of the desert. He thought of this; therefore "surely goodness and mercy shall follow me all the days of my life; and I will dwell in the house of the Lord for ever." Before us we have Himself: "Thou leadest me." Then "Thou art with me," the Lord protecting either flank. We are guarded, you see, in the front, and on either side, but there is still the unprotected rear. "Surely goodness and mercy shall follow me all the days of my life." These great twin-brothers, goodness and mercy, follow us from behind. And it does not say they have followed us merely in the past, but they shall follow us all the days of our life. The Psalm opened with the bold challenge, "I shall not want." "Find out anything, if you can, that I want." Now it closes with another challenge, which no one can gainsay, "Goodness and mercy shall follow me all the days of my life." We are protected on every side; and then there is nothing before us but the bright city of God, "the house of the Lord for ever."

"City of the pearl-bright portal,
   City of the jasper wall,
City of the golden pavement,
   Seat of endless festival,
City of Jehovah, Salem,
   City of eternity,
To thy bridal hall of gladness
   From this prison would I flee;
Heir of glory,
   That shall be for thee and me."

"UNTIL."

HE shepherd seeks the lost sheep "UNTIL he find it" (Luke xv. 4). And it is only the lost sheep that lies in the pathway of the seeking shepherd. If I take the place of a lost sinner, and nothing else, it is not so much my part to seek Christ as His to seek me. This is grace. He seeks until He finds; He does not stop in His search until He and we meet. Alas! our part is only straying.

The word of LAW would be, "They that seek Me early shall find Me" (Prov. viii. 17). And the consequence of man being put on this ground is stated by God Himself: *"There is none that seeketh after God"* (Rom. iii. 11).

The holy, just, and good law of God came demanding of us love to God, and proved that what God justly demands from man He has not got, and cannot get, so that, without exception, it may be said of all men who ought to have sought after God, *"There is none that seeketh after God."*

GRACE comes in now, and says, "I will seek you, and I will seek until I find." Thank God, it is He who breaks in, upon us, and not we upon Him. We would willingly remain among those who "forget" God. Our wills are free only to wander, and get further from Him. In fact, the first thing God does in breaking in upon our enmity is "to make us willing."

Our part is to take the place of a sinner and nothing else. Most people believe they are sinners, but comparatively few believe that they are sinners and nothing else but *sinners*.

As truly as He hath shown us that we are lost, and nothing but lost, so surely can we gladly claim that seeking Shepherd, for He seeks *until* he finds.

Nothing stops Him in His search; not all the hatred of man or devils; not all the malice and spite and envy of the chief priests; not all the murmurings of the Pharisees and scribes; not all the waywardness of the wandering sheep; nor the indifference and degradation of those for whom He is searching. He will have His joy, the joy that rejoices not UNTIL it finds.

2. But there is another and an awful "UNTIL" in Luke xvii. 27: "They did eat, they drank, they married wives, they were given in marriage, UNTIL the day that Noah entered into the ark, and the flood came and destroyed them all; and as it was in the days of Noah, so shall it be in the days of the Son of Man."

That little word "UNTIL" tells out the sad story of what man is. Men will please themselves, let God's claims or God's grace be where they may. And thus will they go on "UNTIL!"

But every history has its UNTIL. The course of the vilest infidel is brought to a close by an UNTIL. The world's race to destruction will be consummated in that UNTIL. Vain are the thoughts of those who think of the gradual conversion of the world. They go on as JESUS CHRIST said they would—careless, and wholly engrossed with their own affairs, *until* the Lord comes.

This is not each man knowing the Lord from the least to the greatest. The world goes on in rebellion and self-pleasing *until* the Lord comes and sweeps them away as with the besom[2] of destruction. May we be now as men that believe this, and tell out the virtues of a Christ for sinners until that day!

Few of us, I fear, realise that there is a way of *keeping* out of hell, but no way of *getting* out of it.

That vain imagination, that the punishment of the wicked will not be eternal, is sapping the very foundations of Christian action. What is the use of Christian effort? let us take things quietly if, after suffering for a while in a purgatorial hell, all are to be restored!

May God have mercy on us for our lukewarmness, and stir us all up to believe His simple word, that *until* Jesus comes men will go on in their mad career, but that this is the limit to their proud waves; for we again read that

3. The heavens will receive Jesus Christ "UNTIL the times of restitution of all things which God hath spoken," etc. And this *until*, while bringing glorious and final salvation to the Christ-

---

[2] Editor's Note: A broom made of twigs.

receiver, restoration to God's ancient people, and emancipation to a groaning creation, is the time of destruction of all Christ's rejecters. For God says (Acts iii. 21, 23), that in the time of the restitution of all things "it shall come to pass that *every* soul which will not hear that Prophet (JESUS) shall be DESTROYED from among the people."

"Let God be true, and every man a liar." Christ will remain away UNTIL this time of mingled salvation and destruction: *salvation* to all who were sought out and found by Him; *destruction* to all who rejected Him, it being one of God's impossibilities to renew such to repentance. Solemn words! May we make our calling and election sure!

"He came not to call the righteous, but *sinners*." Thus called and thus saved, we can patiently wait, leaning on the precious word, while even some that profess Christ's name are leaning to their own understandings, and taking their own ideas as their light, or, while a godless, reckless world is posting on to destruction, taking no warning, dancing madly, blindly on, UNTIL (and what an *until* it will be!)—*until* He shall gird His sword on His thigh, to slay, and not to heal; and, in the midst of their calamity and dreadful fear, His word is:—"*I will laugh at your calamity; I will mock when your fear cometh*" (Prov. i. 26).

SERVING AND FOLLOWING.

"If any man serve Me, let him follow Me."—JOHN xii. 26.

E are quite prepared to hear this, "If any man follow Me, he ought to serve Me," but it is the converse of this we have in this text. Is there not much Christless energy, restlessness, and activity among workers simply because there is so little following of Christ? Who are Christian workers? should every child of God not be a Christian worker? The mothers and daughters at home work for the Lord as well as the evangelist and preacher.

Every member of the body should work, and if from not working some joint has become stiff, it has to be brought into working trim by gradually giving it a little to do day by day. Christ says to the sinner, Come to Me, and I will give you rest; He says to the worker, Take My yoke and learn of Me, and you will find rest.

As the former part of this gracious passage shows how the sinner is to *get* rest, so this shows how the worker is to *find* his rest. This, therefore, could never refer to an unsaved man, and should never be applied to any except to those who are consciously converted. A dead horse could never be harnessed to draw the plough. You would not put a yoke on a cold corpse: and an unsaved man is dead (Eph. ii. 1); therefore you cannot apply the yoke to him.

But to such as have life, these words must be very potential, very solemn, very encouraging, *"Take My yoke upon you."* What a fellowship! What grace to give us to be sharers in His yoke! And what was His yoke? I think we obtain some indication of its meaning if we do not dislocate the passage from its preceding context, but view it in the connection in which it stands. In the former verses He was upbraiding the cities wherein most of His mighty works had been done; where He had been working good works, and had been called a devil; relieving men, and blamed for so doing, as one who had fellowship with Satan. Scornfully "despised and rejected of men, a Man of sorrows and acquainted with grief." This was His "yoke," rejection, when acting in pure grace! And this is the yoke we are to take. Do good to men, and be blamed for it. Do many good things, get many reproaches; lavish your love on this world, and be content to be misunderstood; lavish your goods as to God, and get no return but side-looks from men. "Take *My* yoke," says our Lord and Master. The road may be thorny, but it has been trodden before by Him. Do you know "the fellowship of His sufferings"? He says, "If any man will come after Me, let him deny himself, and take up his cross, and follow Me." Are you under His yoke, and no other yoke? Not the yoke of a God dishonouring legalism; not the yoke of conformity to the world in its fashions, its smiles, its sneers, its gentilities, its ways of acting, its manner of judging; and its opinions of this and that. "My yoke" is all the Christian needs, and all the Christian wants.

"*Learn of Me.*" Here again we have this beautiful, comprehensive ME. Reader, do you know its power? It is *Me*. Not My servants, not My angels, not My prophets, but ME. How many sit and learn of some great saint, genernally taking his distinctive faults, like cracks in reflecting mirrors, rather than his graces. A dear brother said one day, he believed the memoir of a distinguished saint "had done much harm." "How can the be?" I asked. "Because," said he, "men wish to get into his experience, and then think they will get his feelings. If they could only pray as often, read so much of the Bible, get up at such an hour, conform to all the rules he laid down for his conduct, it would be all right with them, instead of going directly to the Lord Himself." There is real truth in this.

"*Learn of Me,*" says Jesus. Do it by praying, by communing, by singing, by reading, by meditating, by watching His wondrous hand, —it matters little in what way it is done, but, at all costs, get to the only worthy pattern "*Me*," and "learn of ME."

"*For I am meek and lowly in heart.*" How unlike the maxims and practice of men—every man for himself! Stand up for your rights! Let no man trample upon you! Do not be reckoned a fool!

Get a character for being sharp, shrewd, and that no one is able to overreach you! How different this from the simplicity of the child with the single eye, learning of Jesus to be "meek and lowly;" following Him who, "when He was reviled, reviled not again," but was dumb before His accusers.

The true Christian walk is to learn of Jesus to be least of all and servant of all, without being proud of the service. "Bearing all things, believing all things, hoping all things, enduring all things;" content to be nothing, or to do anything, for Christ; to stand still, to advance, or to go whither that lustrous guiding Eye directs. Thus, and only thus, "ye shall *find* rest unto your souls."

How calmly and joyously did Jesus, who had said, "Lo, I come to do *Thy* will," turn from earth's rejections, earth's scorn and hardness, after he had done many mighty works, to His Father, saying, "I thank Thee, O Father!"

In the parallel passage in Luke we are informed that "Jesus *rejoiced in spirit*, and said, I thank Thee, O Father, Lord of heaven and earth, that Thou hast hid these things from the wise and prudent, and hast revealed them unto babes. Even so, Father; for so it seemed good in Thy sight" (Matt. xi. 25; Luke x. 21).

Cast out by men, He found His rest in God; and this yoke of His He asks *you* to bear, and this is the rest He asks you to *find*. Our rest is not in service, not in much doing, not in a restless unbelief, not in an uneasy annoyance at not having a great crowd to speak to, and thus have an opportunity of doing a greater amount of good, but in *His Father*.

How many of the true saints of God are in bondage to their little bit of service, in their own little corner of the mighty vineyard!

Our particular ways of doing things are often a yoke. Alas! is it not the common sin of all the workers for God, that they get under yokes to their work, and when the character or sphere of their work changes, they are fretted and disconcerted, instead of resting in calm, childlike, simple faith on the unchanging Father?

Are we first following, then serving? Are we serving Him in the following? We fear that there are more who serve but do not follow than those who follow and do not serve. How much Christless work there is! How much this following Jesus, this learning of Him, this bearing His yoke, strips us of all that is of self! Live only for others—live as Christ lived—walk behind Him, and be of no reputation—cheerfully spend for Him—cheerfully want with Him—need nothing else but Him.

My fellow Christian, only in thus following Jesus can you find rest. You have tried many other things. Long ago you found none in the world; since then you have been seeking rest in this and that. Have you perfect rest in the yoke-bearing of Jesus? Only thus will you find that His yoke is *easy* and His burden *light*. Nothing else will suit that Divine life which God has implanted but His yoke. And this is a *rest* not to be got once for all, but is a rest we are to be ever seeking, and ever finding.

There is a rest that is obtained at first, and it is *for ever*; that is the rest in the atonement and person of Jesus,—rest from the consciousness of all guilt imputed and condemnation to be incurred. For there neither is, nor can be, any condemnation to us, who are "in Christ Jesus;" for He has eternally settled that question for us eighteen hundred years ago, and He "dieth no more."

But there is this day-by-day *finding* of rest to our souls in bearing His yoke. The more yoke-bearing the more rest-finding. In these days of restless activity in every department of the Church and world, activity in business, politics, science, art, and religion, in the desire for the novelty, and the consequent unrest, there is much need of standing still and listening to the voice of God's aged prophet, as with freshness he echoes the words of our blessed Lord through these many centuries. "Thus saith the Lord, Stand ye in the ways, and see, and ask for the old paths, where is the good way, and *walk therein, and ye shall find rest for your souls*" (Jer. vi. 16).

These paths Jesus trod—in these paths His followers, those who have come and got rest as humility sinners, love to walk. In Philippians ii. We get Christ's humiliation, the worker's example; in Philippians iii., Christ in exaltation, the worker's aim. Philippians is the letter of Christian experience, and twenty-eight times "joy" or "rejoice," or some such word is used; and Paul wrote it from a Romish prison chained to a soldier. He had already sung himself and Silas out of the prison at Philippi, and no doubt the jailer would appreciate this call to universal joy. How could Paul thus joy in his chains? Simply because he put God between him and all circumstances. Sense and unbelief put circumstances between us and God. Faith, that thus brings real joy, puts God between me and my riches, me and my poverty, me and my adversity, me and my prosperity—perhaps a more difficult thing—and, whatever comes, faith puts God first.

"Let nothing be done through strife or vain-glory; but in lowliness of mind let each esteem other better than themselves." Paul understood the frailties and jealousies of Christian workers—amongst their equals, not among either their superiors or inferiors. In the same letter he says, "I beseech Euodias, and beseech Syntyche, that they be of the same mind in the Lord." Possibly both had been energetic in sending contributions to Paul, but perhaps had been at variance as to their district, or some other disputed point. In Luke ix. the apostles with all authority and power, could not cast out a devil; and the reason was, they were contending who should be greatest. God often cannot own, or show that He does own, Christian workers, because it would minister to their pride.

"Let this mind be in you, which was also in Christ Jesus." This is the true spirit of a Christian worker following in service, imitating the perfect Worker.

The Perfect Worker.

"Who, being in the form of God, thought it not robbery to be equal with God." Here we have His highest glory. He is contrasted with Adam, who desired to be on an equality with God by an act of robbery; but Christ Jesus had it by right, and not by grasping robbery; and in the path of perfect service the first thing He did was—

"He made Himself of no reputation;" and this is the very thing that most servants of Christ aim at making—a reputation. This is what the great mass of Christians encourage the servants to make—a reputation; and this is where we find the root of the total failure of Christian workers, the desire to make a reputation. He has great reputation as a teacher, evangelist, preacher, visitor, or anything else. Then let him beware, and study Philippians ii.

He is but a poor Sunday-school teacher! then, praise God, he may be in the place to be used without his ambition or self-conceit being added to. A little taper may kindle a big fire. He is but a poor preacher, weak minister, or only an insignificant layman; then let him read for his joy Phil. ii. "But I have a reputation to make," says one; "I have a name to get as a popular preacher, an intellectual preacher, a logical preacher, an oratorical preacher, a profound preacher, an attractive preacher;" then look out, my friend, and read Phil. ii., and let this mind be in you which was in Christ Jesus, who "made Himself of no reputation." Until we find that we have to please God *alone*, independent of self and self's ambition, we shall have little of Christ's mind. He stepped from the throne which He had by right to the servant's place, which He entered by choice, to show what obedience was, obedience in life, obedience in death, and obedience even in glory, when He takes the crown from the Father. But when He "took upon Him the form of a servant," He did not become an angel, but came down to the lower service.

"Was made in the likeness of men," and was there seen, not as man in his strength and glory, but being found in fashion as a man, "He humbled Himself, and became obedient unto death;" and when death came did not choose the death of peace or honour, but the felon's death, the death of shame, "even the death of the cross." Wherefore God also hath highly exalted Him.

Fellow-worker, this is the path to the Well done! This is the following Him in which true serving is found. Let this mind be in you.

May we day by day be seeking to trace every footstep, bear His light and easy yoke along the path of His perfect obedience—that only good, comfortable, safe path for His disciples—and sing each day with calm confidence and joyful lips:—

> "I love to kiss each print where Christ
>   Did set His pilgrim feet;
> Nor can I fear that blessed path
>   Whose traces are so sweet.
>
> "Lead on, lead on triumphantly,
>   O blessed Lord! lead on;
> Faith's pilgrims' sons behind Thee seek

The road that Thou hast gone.

"He always wins who sides with God,
    To him no chance is lost;
God's will is sweetest to him when
    It triumphs at his cost.

"Ill that God blesses is our good,
    And unblest good is ill;
And all is right that seems most wrong,
    If it be His sweet will."

THE SACRIFICE, THE PRIEST, AND THE SAVIOUR.

E see these three—Sacrifice, Priest, and Saviour—connected in that wondrous chain of doctrine in the end of Heb. ix. 24-28, where we find the word *appear* three times repeated—

1. He appeared to put away sin as the Sacrifice.
2. He appears before God for us as the Priest.
3. He shall appear the second time for final salvation.

Each of these has a different word in the Greek, used, as we might expect, with a Divine propriety, in each case serving only to elucidate the different aspects under which the Lord Jesus is here seen.

1. He appeared, that is, *became manifest* as the One who ever existed, but now came to be visible.

2. He appears, that is, *officially*; for He always appeared before God, but now it is "*for us*." Compare Exod. xxxiii. 13, where this word is used in the Septuagint.

3. He shall *appear*, that is, *shall be seen* face to face, as a man with his friend. This is the word used in connection with Christ risen (1 Cor. xv. 5), etc.

1. THE SACRIFICE.

"Now once, in the end of the world, *hath He appeared* to put away sin by the sacrifice of Himself." He who was the invisible God took to Himself a true body, and became manifest to this world, NOT merely a manifestation of God, but God Himself manifest in the flesh. Wondrous thought! God has appeared; God has been manifested; God has been seen; God has been treading this earth, and has been seen by mortals' eyes. When was He here? On what errand did He come? How did He perform His work?

1. *The time when* He appeared—"Now, once, at the end of the world." What? Has the world come to its end? Yes, Christ gathered up the lines of all the past ages. He appeared at the end of the world, as under the period of man's trial. Man was proved utterly bad by Christ's coming, and His cross is the end of man's probation.

"In these last days God hath spoken to us by His Son." He sent His Son "*last.*" He is the "last Adam." The last and worst thing against man is now out. He would kill God if he could. He killed God manifest in the flesh. This has brought the world to its end. The world is "condemned already." God is only delaying the execution of the sentence to manifest His grace. After a man is condemned, his history is done. What of all the vaunted histories and progress of the race? God looks at the period since the Cross as a blank—as a timeless gap, in which there is no earth-history, but a wondrous unearthly, heavenly calling going on, gathering people out of the world to share the throne with His Son.

Now. Yes, during these eighteen centuries the relative position of parties has remained fixed, the world doomed, and God, saving, out of it. "Now is the day of salvation." It has been one great long-suffering *now* since Calvary. If we belong to the world, we are doomed—we are at our end already. If we are only in the world, but not of it, our sin is gone—we are safe.

2. THE WORK DONE. "He appeared, to put away sin." What? Was sin put away eighteen hundred years ago? If it was not, Chris's mission failed, for He came to put away sin. He died in vain if sin be not put away. Friend, do you not realise this fact, that sin was put away by Christ before you were born? Are not all your efforts to try to get sin away? Is all your unrest not occasioned by the feeling that sin is not put away? If you are trying to put away your sin, or to get your sin put away, you know nothing about the gospel. Let us look at a few things that this does not mean.

(1) It does not mean that, as to its *presence in this world*, sin has been put away. Alas! no one can look to our streets, our jails, our asylums, our infirmaries, our newspapers, and dream of such a thought. It has been left to the too-wise Neologist[3] to shut his eyes,

---

[3] Editor's Note: A proponent of a new doctrine.

and call evil good. I have just been wondering why they don't deny the existence of death. They deny the resurrection; they deny the existence of sin, why not of death? Is death not a mere idea? Is death a reality? No philosopher ever felt death and told us what it is. The fact that I see it could be as easily got over as the fact of hundreds having seen a man risen from the dead is got over. Reason, so called, gets over anything. When they have got rid of the servant, *sin*, it should be very easy to get rid of the wages, *death*. Is it not wonderful that they still let God speak, though they do try to tell us about the debt of nature? They still must know that death is the wages of sin, the Divine appointment. "It is *appointed* to men once to die." Sin exists all around as really as its wages, death; therefore that its existence is done away with in the world is not meant by the expression here. And moreover, God has settled the matter, for after Christ died and put away sin, He says, "If we say we have not sinned, we make Him a liar."

(2) It does not mean that, as to its *presence in the heart* of any man, sin is put away. We appeal to every man who knows what sin is, and, though he is the oldest saint in the world, he, if conscientious, must confess that in him, that is, in his flesh, there dwells no good thing. One of the greatest signs of growth in grace is the judgment of sin within.

It is as walking in the light that we detect our sin, and, above all, the God of truth has said, "If we say we have not sin, we deceive ourselves, and the truth is not in us" (1 John i. 8). Therefore all your ideas of trying to get rid of the feeling of sin are absurd, and all your efforts in that direction are worse than useless. If you did not feel any sin in you, it would be the worst thing possible. Don't try to get rid of the feeling of sin. Look to God's Christ, who has put it away.

What does this mean? Mark, it is not that He put away *sins*— "Behold the Lamb of God, that taketh away" (not the *sins*, but) "the *sin* of the world." Look at it from God's point of view, and you will be able to get a more scriptural grasp of the thought. Take away your mind from yourself, or any other sinner—your ruin or your salvation. Look at the existence of sin in the moral government of God. God is not the Author of it. God's name has been dishonoured; God's glory has been assailed; God's character has been compromised. The foul blot, sin, has been put on the fair creation of God. Christ comes, saying, I will put it away; I will erase the dark blot; I will vindicate Thy name; I will manifest Thy character. And, in prospect of it completed, He exclaimed, "I have *glorified* Thee upon the earth." Mark, this is altogether independent of any single man's salvation.

Had every soul from Adam down to the last man rejected God's offered mercy, Christ would, by His death, have glorified God by the putting away of sin. Man is always taken up with himself; but the first note from the choirs in harmony with the chorus of heaven is, "Glory to God in the highest;" then, bless His name! "Peace on earth."

And is it not of far more consequence that God should be glorified than that sinners should be saved? Thanks be to God, both are accomplished by CHRIST; but the latter has its value only as the former is its foundation.

Since God has been glorified as to the existence of sin, and in the person of His Son it has been put away, He can send forth His heralds, proclaiming a righteous way, by which the vilest sinner, born in sin, steeped in sin, may approach to Himself. He can now tell the messengers to go into all the world and tell the good news, that there is a way in which God is just, and can not only pardon, but justify sinners. He is now held forth as the meeting-place between God and any sinner in the whole world.

"How did you see the truth?" I once asked a man.

"From an expression you once used in preaching."

"What was that?"

"That God was dealing with us now in the gospel, not on the sin-question, but the Son-question."

Blessed be God, this is His good news. Of course, if we refuse to accept of His Son, we remain in our condemned state under all our sins, with the superadded one of rejecting God's offed salvation.

Suppose a harbour of refuge has been made, everything is ready to let in the ships that are riding out in the stormy ocean, the ponderous gates that are swung across its entrances being opened. Any ship, now, in all the ocean may get into the harbour through these gates, but the actual state of each is in no way changed if it remains outside—only this, they know of safety, and won't take it. Thus has out Lord Jesus Christ taken away the barrier—the legal just barrier—sin between man and God, glorifying God. Any poor, heavy-laden, tempest-tossed soul may come to Him, and through Him to eternal rest.

Nothing will all this avail for them but only as they are in Him. He Himself is offered for the acceptance of all, and how shall we escape if we neglect so great salvation? Without money and without price are His conditions. He will in no wise cast out whoever comes. Though sins be like scarlet, He can make them white as snow; though red like crimson, they shall be as wool. The chief of sinners is in heaven; therefore God cannot be dealing with us individually on the sin-question. The platform is entirely changed. God's law has been magnified; God Himself has been glorified. Sin has been put away as the barrier between God and the sinner. Sin has been put away as the platform on which God now transacts business with man.

His one question now is—What have you to do with My Son? Do you accept Him? Do you accept My way of putting away sin? Do you accept of His putting away of sin as the putting away of your sins? Then you are justified, accepted, complete, in Him. Do you neglect Him? Then how great must be your condemnation. "This is the condemnation that light is come into the world, and men loved darkness rather than light." Better would it have been for you never to have heard of such a Saviour, than, having heard of Him, to refuse to receive Him. "He that believeth on Him is not condemned; but he that believeth not is condemned already, because he hath not believed in the name of the only begotten Son of God." How shall we escape if we neglect so great salvation?

3. *The Person sacrificed.*—"Himself." Wonderful truth! Had millions of angels, and tens of millions of the highest created intelligences, been sacrificed, they never could have put sin away. It required Himself, and Himself did it. It did not require our agency, for our agency was useless; but Himself did it. Poor ignorant man tries by his own sacrifice to please God. Mans' efforts are always to try, like Adam, to make a covering for himself; God's way is to cover us first, and then ask us to work. Not all the offerings of Old Testament days could put away a single sin; but

no sooner did sin and the great Sin-bearer meet, than He burned it up by His own intrinsic essential merit.

Man, when he touched a leper, was defiled; Christ, when He touched a leper, was not only not defiled, but cured the leper. When we touch sin, we are contaminated; when Christ touched sin, He consumed it. Himself is the central word of all the revelation and the counsels of God. Himself is the alone sacrifice. Himself is the sum of every believer's creed—the Alpha, the Omega, the beginning, the ending, the first, and the last, of all his theology. We think much of His work, because it is that which is more close to us. It is that on which we stand; but what is the work without the Person? We stand on the work, but the work stands on the Person. God has given us first Himself, and in Himself the work.

The first note of all true scriptural preaching is *Himself*. The power with the anxious is giving them *Himself*, and in *Himself*, His work. The power to raise the struggling believer is knowing Jesus *Himself*, the One who was dead and is now alive for evermore. And the centre of all worship, the subject of all praise, the object to fill every eye in the coming glory, will be *Himself* seen as the Man of Calvary, who now once in the end of the world appeared to put away sin by the sacrifice of *Himself*.

II. THE PRIEST.

In these days of apostacy, it is well to consider Jesus Christ as our great High Priest, who hath entered for us within the veil. Are there any priests, then, on earth? Yes. All true believers are priests; and no minister, no pastor, no teacher can be called a priest in any other sense than that in which all Christians are. All Christians are not pastors, are not teachers, but all Christians are priests (Rev. i. 6, and xx. 6); and any Christian who assumes a special priesthood over other Christians is denying the High-priesthood of Christ. He hath made us unto our God a kingdom of priests made nigh, with the power and in the place where we can worship and serve as the royal priesthood. Wondrous truth!

But we are to consider not the priesthood of Christians, but the priesthood of Christ as *now* exercised for us, and as keeping us right all the way through our journey. And we see this in the second use of the word "*appear*" in Heb. ix.

"For Christ is not entered into the holy places made with hands, the figures of the true, but into heaven itself, not to APPEAR in the presence of God for us." And is not this what we need when we come to understand that sin has been put away, that our sins have been borne by the great Sacrifice? We have been brought in to the presence of God by faith, but that very presence reveals to us that we are ever prone to sin and get defiled. God knows this, and God provided, and His provision is, that Jesus as our Priest now "appears" in the presence of God for us.

Sin has been put away by Him as the victim. Wrath has been poured out upon Him. The wrath, the condemnation, the judgment that were prepared against the sinner who believes, are gone now in Christ. There is no cup of wrath for the believer now. There is now no condemnation—he shall not come into judgment; for Christ *has appeared* and put away sin. The Victim's blood has been shed, and is accepted for us. We need Him now as our Priest appearing in the true holy place, and who offers there His own blood; and peace, pardon, and reconciliation are the only notes that are heard from the throne of God, coming to every believer over that offered blood. Let us consider—

1st, *Where* He appears. He "appears in the presence of God." He was always in the bosom of His Father; now He has taken our place, and representatively, according, not to the value of what He had as God, but of what He has acquired as the God-man who put away sin by the sacrifice of Himself. He is in the presence of perfect holiness, perfect light; and this is our place maintained, as procured, by the value of the precious Blood. Do we really believe that the sanctuary is our place? In the resplendent light of this Holiest of the holies, we learn the meaning of two words. These words are *sin* and *holiness*.

We begin to get into God's thoughts about sin. We begin to realise that "whatsoever is not of faith is sin." Solemn words! It was because Jesus prayed for Peter that he was convinced of his sin. Christ's advocacy shows me what I am, leads me to judge my ways, my sins, myself, in the light of God. Everything inconsistent with the light of the "Holiest" is set aside when we understand what the "Holiest" is, and realise that our walk is there.

We begin to understand what holiness is—that holiness without which no man shall see the Lord. As to our standing, we know that Christ is our sanctification, perfect and unchangeable; but in our walk with God in the light, we cannot see God unless we are walking in practical holiness. Place the smallest coin over the eye of the best-seeing man, and in the midst of the all-pervading light around, he will be in darkness. Place the slightest unconfessed sin on the spiritual eye of the strongest believer as he walks in the light, and we can realise that without holiness no man shall *see* the Lord. Blessed be His name, all is done that we may be partakers of His holiness, and his advocacy will not cease in the Holiest till that is accomplished.

2nd, *When* He appears. "Christ is entered...into heaven itself NOW, to appear"—now in the midst of all our wilderness experience; now, just when we require Him most; now, when we are sinners. It was when Satan desired to sift Peter that Jesus prayed. In the coming glory, when we shall be with, and perfectly like our Lord, while we stand upon His merit, we shall require no more His advocacy, His precious blood to wash out stains; but it is *now* that we require Him, and it is now that He appears in the presence of God for us. Not only did He once appear on earth and put away sin, but He *now* appears, at this present hour, before God on our behalf.

He has not come out of heaven at each suing of His believing one, and die over again; but He has with Him where He is the merit of His death, which has the continued efficacy before God. It is not that Christ has washed my sins all away, and now tells me to make my way to heaven, which I'll reach if I hold on, but *now* He appears, now, after I have believed; now I see Him by faith ever presenting to the eye of God His own precious blood, which cleanseth me from all sin. *Now* in the midst of the opposition of the world, the temptation of Satan, and the un-subject evil nature still within, Jesus is for us before God. *Now* as we rise each morning, afresh to the battle and the death, to the triumph and the conflict, we can go forward with the certainty that God is for us.

3rd, *For whom* He appears. "For us." He never required to leave heaven to die, and to return to His native home for Himself. It was for us He came, for us He died, for us He has again entered heaven. It is not for angels He appears; they stand on their own creature merit. He appears for us. We put in no claim but as He presents it. He looks after all our interests, for it is for us He appears.

He does not appear for the unsaved. He died for the unsaved, but He has entered into haven for us, the saved. We claim Christ at Calvary as unsaved. We claim Christ in the Holiest as saved sinners. We must be justified before we can claim the merits of what is now being carried on before God. In other words, we must first be sons before we can lay claim to Christ's advocacy, which is God's provision for the walk of His own children.

Neither is it "for us" as pure and spotless and perfectly holy. We shall not be like Him till we see Him as He is. But it is for us as journeying through the wilderness, in which we are apt to contract sin, and if any of us (saved ones) sin, we have Him as our Advocate with the Father, Jesus Christ the righteous.

III. THE SAVIOUR.

"As it is appointed unto men once to die:
"And after this the judgment:
"So Christ was once offered to bear the sins of many:
"And to them that look for Him shall He appear the second time without sin unto salvation."

This is the Divine Proportion, or Rule of Three, the great parallel God has drawn between the TWO MEN, the only two men that were seen by Him, the first Adam and the last Adam. The first two factors tell us what we have in Adam, death and judgment: death as the end of this state, judgment as the beginning of another and an eternal state. The second two factors tell us what we have in Christ—our sins borne and salvation given; our sins borne as the end of our Adam state, salvation, complete and final, as the beginning of our glorified state, and

As (in the case of *men*, all sprung from Adam)

Death is to *judgment*,

So (in the case of *saints*, all sprung from the Second Adam, all born of God)

Christ *bearing sin* is to

Christ appearing the second time *for salvation*.

In the day thou eatest thou shalt die. Adam ate; therefore it is appointed unto men once to die, and after death the judgment, which must be eternal wrath. David trembled at the thought, and said, "Enter not into judgment with Thy servant, for in Thy sight shall no man living be justified" (Psalm cxliii. 2). If God judges me I am condemned. Blessed by God for ever! This is not our place. We do not stand in the first Adam. The first factors of the proportion are not ours in Christ; death and judgment are past for us in Him; we are "dead" (Col. iii. 3); "we shall not come into judgment" (John v. 24).

Instead of death, we have "Christ was once offered," and He not only put sin away, but He bore our sins. All our sins, believing in Him, were on Him when He bore the wrath due to sin. They are gone for ever; therefore, since the sin is gone, the death is gone for the believer. He may be put asleep by Jesus, but we (Christians) shall not all sleep (1 Cor. xv. 51). There is no necessity for any Christian dying. There is a Divine appointment for men as men dying. We know that some saved men have not died, and many saved men will not die. But this fearful doom hangs over all men out of Christ—death, and they cannot get rid of it. Gnash at it, groan at it, philosophise about it, as they may, there it stands calmly as the appointment of God.

Instead of judgment we have "Christ appearing the second time without sin unto salvation." As truly as the enemy Death, which men know well about, stands across the path, so surely will the sword of judgement fall on every Christless soul; but in Christ we look not for judgment, but for salvation. There is no question of sin now. He put it away. He bore our sins. Sin and sins have been dismissed. He had to do with them the first time He appeared, but the last time He appears He will have no sin on Him. He will enter into no question of sin, death, or judgment with His own, but *salvation*, final and perfect, will be His great work then. We shall then be perfectly saved as to our bodies, as we are now as to our souls.

As He appeared and put away sin, so only as sinners "without strength," "ungodly," "lost," "condemned," "dead," could we claim Him. As He now appears for us only as the ransomed of the Lord, the redeemed from men, the royal priesthood, so He will appear the second time only to them that look for Him.

Of that day or hour no man knows; but He that shall come will come and will not tarry. His first appearing to put away sin was death to all men, merely men, and to us who are the sons of God, now believing in His name, it is the bearing of our sins. His appearing the second time is judgment to all men, merely men, and is salvation to us who look for Him. *Knowing* that He is coming and *looking* for Him, are two things quite different. The head may tell us the former; the heart must be exercised for the latter. He shall come as the great Saviour, saving us by power out of the enemy's hand. This is salvation is our hope; this salvation is nearer than when be believed. Instead of judgment we are to be saved out of the midst of the whole doomed scene. Is this not a blessed hope—His glorious appearing? At death our bodies are still left in the hands of the enemy, but His appearing is our hope.

Friend, are you a *man*? Then your end is death. "It is appointed unto men once to die, and after death the judgment." Your only chance is to accept Christ, and then you will look for Him and His salvation which He shall bring, every trace of sin being gone.

Look back to Him as the Sacrifice, who appeared once and put away your sin.

Look up to Him now as the Priest appearing in the presence of God, keeping us ever clean there.

Look forward for Him who will appear the second time without sin unto salvation.

THE POWER THAT THE WORLD KNOWS NOTHING ABOUT.

"For I am not ashamed of the gospel of Christ: for it is the power of God unto salvation to every one that believeth."—ROM. i. 16.

HIS was the reason Paul gave for his readiness to preach the gospel at Rome, the centre of the world's wisdom, to Greeks or to barbarians, to wise or unwise. For, let man be cultivated or uncultivated, wise or ignorant, he is lost; let him be rich or poor, he is lost, and needs nothing less than salvation. But the gospel is sufficient, however contemptible in the eyes of the great men at Rome, however foolish to human wisdom. It is the sufficient and sole power God now uses. Let us look.

1st. The power God is using. His gospel.
2nd. The purpose God is working out. Salvation.
3rd. The people God is blessing. Every one that believes.

I. THE POWER GOD IS USING.

His gospel. This is the only moral engine God is using to reclaim lost man. Man has his hundreds of schemes, his philanthropic societies, his improvement of man as he is, his reformation or alleviation of the first Adam, his many levers or helps to the gospel. God has but one power, which requires no help, and that is "His gospel." The words, "of Christ," are not in the best manuscripts, though certainly it is the gospel of Christ (2 Cor. x. 4), but the thought in Rom. i. is, that it is God's own good news, "The gospel of God" (i. 1). Good news to bad men is the wonderful and solitary lever God is using. The reception of a testimony outside of us is the only way by which we can deal with God. Therefore, since it is news to us, we have nothing whatever in it but hearing it. It is not that in itself the good news has any intrinsic power, but the message that this good news brings is "concerning Jesus Christ our Lord" (v. 3). The good news tells of God's justice perfectly satisfied, God's law magnified, God's demands all met, and God glorified, while sin has been put away, for God's Son is risen. Had He but died, there would have been no good news: the good news is "Christ has died; yea rather, is risen." God is now proclaimed as just, while justifying sinners. It is because the gospel tells of God's demands being met that it is of use to the sinner's conscience.

For God's demands are first. The need of the sinner, the good of man, the elevation of the race, the progress of mankind, are not the first questions, but the glory of God, the vindication of His name, the equipoise[4] of all His attributes preserved, an all-perfect, all-equal, because all-infinite God.

The gospel proclaims His perfect love and His perfect hate: His perfect love to the sinner, His perfect hatred against sin. Man could be satisfied with the exhibition of love, but tries to get out of the reach of the demands of justice against sin. In our day there is a great deal of talk about the love of God, though what is meant is not love at all, but the overlooking and winking at sin, the toleration of evil.

There is the cause of the deep-seated hatred to "the blood theology." We hear a great deal concerning following in the footsteps of the great Example, Christ, following Him in His devotion to God; but where in all this is there rest to the conscience of a man who instinctively feels that God is just, and, come what may, that that justice must be upheld, though it should entail the eternal perdition of every creature? God can by no means clear the guilty. There is a great deal of whining sentimentality about God being so good, and so loving, and so merciful, forgetting that His justice is equal to His love, His righteousness to His grace, because each is infinite.

There is no such thing as God having a darling attribute. It is a human invention, measuring God by man. He is certainly showing His grace, a love all His own, in seeking out the vilest, and putting

---

[4] Editor's Note: A state of equilibrium; counterbalance.

them on the throne of His Son, and taking them to His own heart; but it is a grace that flows through righteousness, through the settling of His every righteous demand, and the gospel comes revealing this. The law came demanding man's perfect obedience to God; the gospel comes revealing God's perfect provision for man.

All the grounds of the gospel have been laid; therefore it can be preached. Everything on God's part has been done; therefore it has only to be proclaimed. Nothing can be added to make the work more God-glorifying, for God would not order His terms to be preached till they were perfectly adjusted. He is the offended party. He has made the conditions; He has satisfied the conditions; and now He proclaims that all has been adjusted for our acceptance. Ours is the place of simple acquiescence.

Hence the good news is God's power. If it fail to reclaim the vilest, then nothing will succeed. It has saved the vilest, and it is waste of time in a Christian to be at anything except this gospel.

Let the world reform itself; all very well; we are thankful for it. Let the dead bury their dead, and if they do it decently we are very glad; but the voice to us from Jesus is, "Follow Me." How many dear Christians waste their energies at all sorts of worldly mixed plans, instead of using the one lever—God's own one power—His Gospel.

In reading this text, we seem to see the apostle, as it were, standing on the quarterdeck of a small contemptible ship, built on a new principle from all other ships of war, with his flag, "the Gospel," nailed up, and boldly saying, "Laugh on, ye wise, ye powerful; this is in your eyes foolishness and weakness; but wait a little. I'm not ashamed of it, and am prepared to bring it to Rome, and lay it alongside all the heaviest gunboats or men-of-war. For it is the power of God, and will blow to pieces all that is of man."

Or, says, Paul, "I have got the true philosopher's stone, that will not certainly change everything it touches into gold, but will do far more: it will change even the vilest sinner whom it touches into an heir of God, will raise him from the dunghill to the throne, will make the beggar a prince." What a talisman Paul and every believer carries with him, the very power of God unto salvation! Fellow-Christian, are we using this wondrous "power of God," believing it is what it is? Why is there so little power? Because there is so little gospel. In the gospel is the power of God. Are we ashamed to stand up at all times with it, and *with it alone*?

And is it not hard, over and over again, dear brother, to go out with this same message, of glad tidings, and repeat the old story, and believe that it is the power of God? Human wisdom would suggest something else, something additional, but the gospel is all. We do not go out to make experiments to see whether the gospel is the power of God—that is unbelief, and will not be blessed; but, starting on the ground that we have in our hand, the only power God will use, in the simplicity of confidence we proclaim His good news to all. We can't save a man; let us tell the story that God can use. We can't give the blow, but we can hold the instrument straight, on which the hammer descends which will rend the rock. How often is preached what God could not bless, except by making the hearers disbelieve it!

II. THE PURPOSE GOD IS WORKING OUT.

It is the power of God *unto salvation*. God is not come to help them who help themselves, nor to give pity or good advice, reformation or amelioration, but to give *salvation*. The force of the original word is "extrication."

Many people seem to think that preaching the gospel gives people a nice easy pillow to lie down on and enjoy themselves—that it gives them an easy short cut to heaven, and now they can take their ease. In other words, people look at salvation as equivalent to toleration to continue in the world, and of the world, with a good prospect for eternity, rather than an extrication out of the world and its ways. Unless we are extricated from the world, our religion is useless. "If any man love the world, the love of the Father is not in him."

Salvation is a deep and wide word. It is deep, and goes to the root of every principle that is away from God. It lays the axe at the root of every tree. It is wide and all-embracing. It is often confounded with justification, but is much wider. Hence, the confusion in some minds. Salvation, which from first to last is of God, begins with a man as he is, and never leaves him till he is set on the throne of Christ. There are three aspects in salvation to every

Christian. 1st. *A past salvation.* 2nd. *A present salvation.* 3rd. *A future salvation.*

1st. *A past salvation.*—Every Christian can say, "By grace I am a saved person." "I have received the end of my faith, even the salvation of my soul." This salvation is equivalent to justification. It has extricated us for ever out of the state of condemnation, and for ever out of the state of condemnation, and saved our souls from the grasp of him in whose arms lies the whole world. This can never be added to, and, blessed be God, can never be taken from. So the apostle could say, "Unto us who *are saved*" (1 Cor. i. 18). Thank God, it is not merely pardon of sin, but a taking of our souls out of the prison of condemnation, where we were legally held, and placing us in the place of sons, in His own beloved Son Jesus Christ.

This is the foundation of salvation, our perfect justification, unto which the gospel is the power of God—a justification in a new life out of death; our souls made alive, quickened together with Christ, for it is a resurrection salvation, from first to last; now of our souls, by-and-bye of our bodies.

The moment a man believes, he is perfectly saved as to his soul, as safe as those in heaven, for Jesus has Himself taken upon Him the responsibility of presenting us at His Father's house.

2nd. There is a *present salvation.*—I mean by that a salvation which is going on in the believer from day to day. The former was an act, this is a work; so that it can be said, "Work out *your own salvation.*" Not certainly work *for it*, but work *out* what God has wrought in, and be sure it is "your own" first. This is the gradual extrication of ourselves from all that is around and within opposed to our Father-God.

The first was the salvation of the soul of a condemned sinner; this is the extrication of an accepted son from all that is against the place into which he has been brought. Before a man has received the first, the enmity is between him and God; afterwards, and during this second process, the enmity is between him and himself. This is his progressive sanctification of growth in grace, and the good news from God is still God's power to extricate him thus day by day in his walk. It is a mere idle fable of self-deceived ones who dream or suppose that even any child of God in this world can live without having sin in him.

We have been asked if we did not believe that a Christian could reach sinlessness (entire sanctification, it is called, which, in this sense is unscriptural and very dangerous teaching), that is to say, living perfectly in love, without having any sin in him, and if it was to be believed, because a man said so; but no, all such statements are to be judged by the Word, and if the greatest saint on earth came to us, and said that he had reached a point of perfect sanctification, that is, that he did not now sin we would simply and conclusively quote, *"If we say we have no sin, we deceive ourselves, and the truth is not is us."*

In the one aspect of sanctification—separation to God by blood—all believers are perfectly sanctified the moment they believe in the Lord Jesus Christ.

There is a sickly and unscriptural notion of perfect sanctification by attainment, spreading among some who talk of reaching to and attaining this so-called sanctification; suffice it to say that it is not in Scripture, and is merely the competitive spirit of the flesh brought into the things of God, by which we would wish to be before our fellow-Christians, and profess to have attained an undefined something, unlike the apostle, "not as though I had already attained."

Against such we must give no uncertain sound. No Christian ever reaches perfect sanctification. The perfect sanctification which he has in Christ is common to all believers, and is by faith the moment he is converted. There is not other except his gradual and progressive daily mortification of his earthly members, his gradual extrication out of all around that is inconsistent with the Divine nature implanted at regeneration. And in this aspect the righteous scarcely are saved (1 Peter iv. 18), but our God of salvation is able to save to the uttermost of time (Heb. vii. 25). And at every stage, to every saint, it will be always necessary to say, "Be ye holy, as God is holy," which proves he is not yet and will not be in the body; therefore "work out your own salvation with fear and trembling, for it is God" (not Paul or yourself) "that worketh in you, both to will and to do of His good pleasure."

3rd. *A future salvation*. This is accomplished, not even at death; though then the soul of the believer, being perfect in holiness, is absent from the body and present with the Lord, yet his body rests in the grace till the resurrection—the final extrication at the last of the man from the last power that holds—for the last enemy that will be put under is death. This is our hope. We are saved by hope, not as to our souls, but as to our bodies, our all. The salvation which is at the end of our faith is that of our *souls*; the salvation which is at the end of our hope is that of our *bodies*. This is the salvation unto which we are "kept by the power of God" (1 Peter i. 5). And it is this salvation that is "nearer than when we believed." Death is not our hope. Death does not end our scene here. There is the claiming, the redemption by power of the purchased possession. This is our hope, "When He shall appear, we shall be like Him," and not till then. So "to them that look for Him shall He appear the second time without sin *unto salvation*."

There is no question of sin whatever, then, but final perfect salvation of the whole body of Christ by power, as well as by purchase and practice.

Thus we are saved, we are being saved, and we are to be saved; saved by faith, saved by working, saved by hoping. May we rightly divide the word of truth! (2 Tim. ii. 15). We can never be justified by hoping. That is by faith; we have for a helmet the hope of salvation, and God's great purpose with us is to extricate, to deliver us from this present evil world, and to deliver us from condemnation and wrath, from the power and presence of our evil hearts, and the power and dominion of Satan—from death and him that had the power of death.

Blessed, glorious Divine purpose! He will have us before Him, but as holy and without blame, in love, according to the necessities of His own nature. He will have us to Himself as dear children, according to the purpose of His grace.

May He give us plainly to see our perfect salvation in Christ, to diligently press forward working out our own salvation, and to patiently wait for the salvation that will be revealed!

And His own good news is His own power unto this, His own Divine salvation. Is salvation not of God? Is our God not the God of salvation? And this leads us to our third point, Who are the happy recipients of this salvation?

III. THE PEOPLE GOD IS BLESSING.

"To every one that believeth." It has no limit, and yet it has a limit. It has no limit in its offer; it is to every one. It has a limit in its application; it is to every one that believeth. It is "unto all" in its offer; but it is only "upon all that believe" in its application. There is no question about anterior fitness, or felt want or position in respect to wealth or righteousness.

The offer is to all, high or low, rich or poor. It is on the principle of faith alone this salvation is secured; but all who do believe have. This is what humbles man. This is what makes it to be of grace, for it is of faith that it might be of grace.

"Are you saved?"

"No."

"Then you never heard the gospel?"

"Oh yes, I sit under an evangelical minister."

"I don't doubt it, neither do I doubt but that he has preached the gospel, very likely, every Lord's-day in your ears, but you never heard it."

"How do you make that out?"

"Because God says, *Hear*, and your soul shall live."

"*What* am I to hear?"

"*News*; that is, something you never knew before—you could not have known before or guessed at before. News from God to you; not news for sinners merely, but news *for you*. Not only news, but good news. Good news, not concerning you; for if you or I were in it, there would be no news, far less good news; but 'good news concerning his Son Jesus Christ our Lord' (Rom. i. 3). That Christ is for you, simply because you are a sinner."

"What, Christ for me individually, as if there were not another sinner in the world?"

"Exactly, and when you receive and rest on Him, by believing the good news for yourself, you will say, Well, I never thought that was all—it is so simple—I am content no longer to strive to acquire, but quietly to acquiesce in the God-made plan. God laid my sin on Christ. God did all the work. God said, 'It is finished.' God comes with His own gospel, His own power, His own salvation; and better news you never heard and never will hear; believe, then, where you are, and as you are, as news, as good news. Believe and live, for 'the gospel is the power of God unto salvation to every one that believeth; to the Jew first and also to the Greek. For therein is the righteousness of God revealed from faith to faith.'"

CHRIST THE POWER OF GOD.

IN considering this subject, the power of God, one would at first think that we should look to the manifestation of His power as seen in the rolling river, the majestic Niagara, roaring, rushing over with its millions and millions of tons of water, eclipsing all the steam-power that man could put together; or we may take our stand by the ocean and see it tossing the ships that man has built, and dashing them to pieces as children's toys, or the thunderstorm and the lightning flash, and say, Look what a God we have! Or we might take the telescope, and direct your eye away from this little speck called earth, to look at the stars at night, and see there millions and millions beyond what the naked eye can see revolving, the nebulæ that we observe in the galaxy of the heavens, and to know that He upholds all these by the Word of His power, and that He keeps the reins of the government of millions of stars, of many times larger dimensions than this little speck of creation, in His grasp.

When we think of all this, well may we exclaim, "When I consider Thy heavens, the work of Thy fingers, the moon and the stars which Thou hast ordained, what is man?" We are lost in silent wonder. Let us also take the microscope and rub off the dust from the butterfly's wing, and we shall find that each speck of dust is a gorgeously chiselled feather, and the living God who has chiselled these feathers in the most perfect and beauteous form has counted the hairs of your head and mine, and has named every sparrow. His power is seen in what He can condescend to, as well as in what He upholds, in the majesty of His might.

But we are not to contemplate the power of the God of creation, to study His grandeur, though it is profitable for us to do so. Man has drifted from God, and so our little planet is bounded by death. Death goes round about it; death envelops it physically. Seven miles up there is death. No man can live there. A band of death is round our globe; but in a more real sense our fallen creation is bounded by the grave. Man's power can do much. He can almost annihilate time and space. He can tie the globe with a string, and take the lightning and send it as his message. He can bring creation under his feet, and do mighty things, but he is limited by the grave; the tomb he has never been able to pass through; the grave he has never been able to span; but the peculiar manifestation of the power of our King begins where man's power ends.

I. *The Power of the Cross.*—In 1 Cor. i. 18: "For the preaching of the cross is to them that perish foolishness; but unto us which are saved it is the power of God." The cross was not only death, but the most shameful death—the death of the felon—and this death, suffered by Jesus, becomes the power of God; for the moment that creation work was marred, the Lord God came in with the promise of the bruising of the serpent's head, setting forth that it was through death the new creation was to be begun—showing that it was by death His new power was to be set forth, and that as soon as creation work was marred redemption work was begun.

When the Lord was here and was found fault with, and challenged on the creation Sabbath for working, those men who found fault with Him, as the destroyer of disease and of death, did not see that while God never can go against His commands, He can rise up in His power above all; and that He who has seen His creation marred has begun in another sphere, in another work, and in another country, the country beyond the grave, through death and resurrection. So He tells us: "My Father worketh hitherto, and I work"—working in the activity of His redeeming love; and then He goes on to say, because He is the Son of God, that now we may meet Him as Quickener through the grave, or we must meet Him as the Judge, the Son of Man, and then we shall have to meet the doom that is ours. Thus we approach the cross as the power of God, to guilty men. "For after that, in the wisdom of God, the world by wisdom knew not God, it please God by the foolishness of preaching to save them that believe. For the Jews require a sign, and the Greeks seek after wisdom; but we preach Christ crucified, unto the Jews a stumbling-block, and unto the Greeks foolishness; but unto them which are called, both Jews and Greeks, Christ the power of God." Christ the power of God has come into the domain of death, and met the demand of death, and this is why Christ is the power of God unto salvation. The blood has paid the debt, the blood that runs in a scarlet line from the gates of Eden to the great white throne, and which then is the theme of the redeemed to all eternity. "Thou hast redeemed us with Thy blood"—the blood which tells of a life taken for a life forfeited. That is what satisfies God, although it is a stumbling-block to the Jew and foolishness to the Greek, both ancient and modern. To the one who requires a sign in these days, the blood will still be a scandal. To the man who wants wisdom, the blood puts all his wisdom in the dust. Why? Because it tells that Christ has entered into the domain where neither man's wisdom nor power is available. In the grave man has no knowledge and no power—the cross is the power of God. But—

II. *The Power of the Resurrection.*—"And declared to be the Son of God with power, according to the Spirit of holiness, by the resurrection from the dead" (Rom. i. 4). This is abstract—not His own resurrection, but by resurrection from the dead. He has authority over the grave, the resurrection of good and bad—the resurrection that He has in His own right and in His own power, in which God raised Him from the dead—the resurrection that quickens us to go with Him, and the resurrection that He has of the ungodly to quicken them, and to bring them to the bar of judgment, whether they will or not, —all resurrection declares Him to be the Son of God, and thus in the resurrection we have the Lord Jesus Christ shown to be the powerful One.

If He went into the grave, He has been raised on the other side of the doom of sin; if He went into the domain of death, He is declared not to be the Son of God in power by resurrection. He went into the monster's jaws and plucked out the sting. He was there in the power of the eternal God, and He is raised again from the dead, beyond all the powers of Satan and the grave, and is now raised to the throne of God, as we read in Eph. i. 18: "That ye may know what is the hope of His calling, and what the riches of the glory of His inheritance in the saints, and what *is* the exceeding greatness of His power to us-ward who believe, according to the working of His mighty power, which He wrought in Christ, when He raised Him from the dead." He was crucified in weakness but was raised by power. We have seen Him thus in the power of the cross, also in the power of the empty tomb, the power of the resurrection, but we again see—

III. *The Power of His Quickening.*—For we are quickened together with Him. He is revealed not only as the risen One, but as the quickening One. He that was dead *for* sin, and we that are dead *in* sin, were quickened together by the Spirit of power. The power of God is thus given to men who were dead. God would have been for ever incommunicable to dead sinners unless Jesus Christ, who was the life, had come into the place of death, and had been raised by the glory of the Father; but now are we kings together with Him. One other thought in Heb. vii. the 14th to the 25th verse inclusive.

IV. *The Power of His Intercession.*—Christ intercedes for His own, whom He has justified and quickened. On high He is the Great High-priest, entering in with His own blood to appear in the presence of God for us, now to keep us clean, and He is there making intercession, according to the unsullied holiness of the presence of God. There He is, "ever living to make intercession. It is He who has begun it at the cross, with whom we are quickened together from the tomb. He goes on to the end of our experiences, difficulties, and dangers. He is up yonder on the Throne to save to the uttermost, that is to say, of time. He is our Advocate with the Father. He is our High-priest before God. "It is Christ that died, yea rather, that is risen again, who is ever at the right hand of God, who also maketh intercession for us. Who shall separate us from the love of Christ?"

V. *His Indwelling Power.*—Romans viii. 26: "Likewise the spirit also helpeth our infirmities: for we know not what we should pray for as we ought: but the Spirit Himself maketh intercession for us with groanings which cannot be uttered." If we have an Intercessor yonder, we have in Intercessor here; and as the Intercessor yonder is *for* His people. The Spirit does not dwell in an unconverted man. He quickens the unconverted. He seals, and dwells in, the believer. There is a Christ for every sinner, and a Spirit ready to quicken him in connection with that Christ, but the Spirit only makes intercession within those who are the Lord's. So we have Christ in His power dwelling in us here by His Spirit, and we have Christ in His power appealing for us yonder; and in His power we go onward and pray that we may know the power of His resurrection and the fellowship of His suffering—to know that we are thus identified with the risen One. This is our standing and state here on earth; now on account of that power within us—the holy God—we boldly affirm that sin shall not have dominion over us. Reckon yourselves dead indeed unto sin. Of course it does not say sin shall not have it presence; but it is a question of its dominion. Why? Because the Spirit of God is within us. "Reckon" yourselves—it is not "feel" yourselves dead. If I were really dead, and felt dead, it would be absurd to tell me to reckon myself dead to sin. Suppose I go to a registrar and say—

"There is a man in this parish who wants a vote."

"What is his name?"

"James Blank."

"Why, he is dead more than a year ago, and he can't have a vote."

That is what you and I have to say to our old nature.

"You have no vote; you have nothing to do with the government of me now. We are dead to sin, and the obsolete man is off the register"—the old man has gone, so far as voting is concerned. It is only the new man in Christ Jesus who has a right to my service. Let me take a familiar illustration. When the man with the palsy was healed, he did not merely get healing but power. "Rise, take up thy bed, and walk," and so he carried his bed. Before this the bed carried him. He was dependent upon his bed, and upon those who each took a corner; but now, as soon as we have got into Christ, it is, Rise, take up thy bed, and walk. Take the case of the reformed drunkard. Why, when he used to pass public-houses, the cursed desire for drink was paramount over his conscience and the interests of wife and family; but now, being dead to sin, he says to this craving, "You have no vote." He carries the obsolete man to the prayer or conference meeting, instead of the old man carrying him into the public-house. So it is with us, "Rise, take up thy bed." We have power now, and sin shall not have dominion over us.

VI. *The Power of His Gospel.*—"For I am not ashamed of the Gospel of Christ: for it is the power of God unto salvation to every one that believeth; to the Jew first, and also to the Greek." Christ speaks through us, and now we can use the power He has given us.

In order to have this power we let God speak as much as possible, and ourselves to speak as little as possible. In the days of His humiliation He gave all power and authority to His apostles—power and authority to cast out devils and one came to Him and said, "Your apostles could not do it." Why? Because there arose a reasoning among them as to which should be greatest. I believe that we often lose our power by thinking we are something. There are Peter and Andrew; the man comes to be healed, but neither of them can do it. Peter could not be trusted with seeing that devil under him. Peter might say, "I am sorry for my dear brother, Andrew, but if he had been like me he would have been successful." Brethren, in the holy work of God, the "holy self" often comes in. Whatsoever there is of self, let us cast it from us, and lean wholly and solely upon the Lord, and trust in the power of His might. Self-seeking is all the fouler when it enters the domain of God. By nature we all wish to be above and beyond our fellows; may we have the desire to lift high the banner of the cross, and in its fold conceal the standard-bearer. May the standard-bearers be all hid and Christ alone seen. Then, indeed, should we feel that we had in our hands the Gospel of God, which is the power of God unto salvation. We pray much for the Holy Ghost—the working power, and always ought to do so, but I would say, "Go to your knees and ask God to show you what the Gospel is," for God has said that the Gospel is the power. None of us can save a soul, but we can hold the instrument by which God can do it. We need nothing to add to that old Gospel, and nothing to be taken from it. When Paul was about to bring it to the walls of Rome, he said, "I am not ashamed to take it to Rome also, for it is the power of God," and we have it thus still.

VII. *The Power of His Return.*—Lastly, the revelation which is to come is the manifested power of our King. It is hidden just now, and why? Christ has been rejected. "And I heard a loud voice saying in heaven, Now is come salvation, and strength, and the kingdom of our God, and the power of His Christ: for the accuser of our brethren is cast down, which accused them before our God day and night" (Rev. xii. 10). His power shall be from the river to the ends of the earth, when all nations shall be blessed in Him and call Him blessed, when He shall have broken His enemies to pieces, when His power shall be manifested in all its majesty.

And now we are waiting for Him in the midst of His foes—waiting for the power of our King to be seen in all its glory, when He shall reign, and we with Him, and when He shall put down all rule, and all authority and power; for He must reign till He hath put all enemies under His feet, and delivered up the kingdom to God, even the Father, and then shall be seen to all His adoring saints, His loyal subjects, the principalities and powers of heaven, the wonderful power of our King in its majestic reach from Cross to Crown.

What a glorious hope is ours, reserved for an everlasting inheritance! while we know that this sin-stricken earth is reserved for fire. In Jude we have the judgment at the beginning of the day of the Lord, when the Lord cometh with the myriads of His saints. We who have been caught up previously, according to 1 Thess. iv.,—our blessed hope—come with Him to execute judgment on all. 2 Peter iii. 10 gives us the judgment at the end of the same day. The day of grace has already lasted nearly two millenniums. The day of the Lord's reign is, according to Scripture, a thousand years. In the evening of this day "the heavens shall pass away with a great noise, and the elements shall melt with fervent heat; the earth also and the works that are therein shall be burned up. Seeing that all these things shall be dissolved, what manner of persons ought we to be in all holy conversation and godliness, looking for and hasting unto the coming of the day of God, wherein the heavens, being on fire, shall be dissolved, and the elements shall melt with fervent heat? Nevertheless, we according to His promise, look for new heavens and a new earth, wherein dwelleth righteousness."

"SAY NOT IN THINE HEART."

ROMANS x. 6.

AN always begins to suggest the remedy for himself; God has expected that man will say something in his heart so He advises him not to do it.

"Say not in thine heart,"—for this is the one thing man begins to do, to guess, to say "peradventure," "perhaps," and "I hope so." "Say not in thine heart." You and I have to meet God whether we wish it or like it or not, how long soever we may put it off (for we have the fatal freedom to put it off), it is coming, we must meet the God with whom we have to do; there is a hereafter, and you and I have to be in it; and our condition in that hereafter is to be fixed now, and you and I have something to do with the conditions which fix that state; therefore "say not in thine heart."

This is what the righteousness of faith speaketh with authority. As an oracle from God it comes, asking you and me to hear because it speaks.

I. It speaks to us negatively; it tells us what *not* to do.

II. It speaks to us positively; it tells us what to do.

The former verse tells us that "Moses describeth the righteousness which is of the law. That the man which doeth these things shall live by them." No man ever did them, so no man ever lived by them, and Moses does not describe the *man*, but the "righteousness of the law which saith," an idea which has never had a tangible reality; the word which the Divine writer has chosen is "describeth," painteth the righteousness of the law, but the righteousness of faith comes speaking and asking us to believe. No man ever kept the law, so no man ever lived by it, but the righteousness of faith comes speaking on this wise, "Say not in thine heart." Most people anxious about their salvation are communing with their own hearts, and not listening to the conditions which God lays down.

A young man during the last week entered my room, and paused some time before he spoke. At last he said he had applied to several people, but all had passed him on to some one else, saying it was not their business. He said, "I have read several religious books, yours among the rest, and I want to know how to get my soul saved."

I replied, "I will not pass you on, for it is my business to heal you if I can. What is your disease?" He hesitated, so I said, "You cannot feel as you would like to do; is that it?" "Yes, that is it; I cannot feel right." I said, "You have to do with the just and holy God, who will never change His laws for us, a God of infinite majesty, and you begin to talk of your *feelings*; would it not be better to find out the conditions He has laid down?

"If you owed £100, would it not be better to try and work with your hands to pay it off than to talk of how you *feel* about your debt? Or suppose I appoint you by letter to come to my house at twelve to-morrow; you come, and are told that I have been out half-an-hour and shall not return for two hours. When I see you, I say, 'Oh, I felt you would not come.' You show me my own letter, and say, 'You appointed me to come at twelve.' We have nothing to do with feelings; we have to do with the Book and what God says in it. It is not my feelings or yours. What is the use of that when there are conditions laid down?"

Submission is the point, not the details so much, not the clearness of reception, as the submission to the dictates of another, so the longing soul will be satisfied. I believe no one went to hell who longed for Christ. The devil would say, "Go away; we have no room for Christ here." I said to the young man, "Will you submit? It is all laid down here; you have only to endorse the cheque; we have it here payable to sinner or bearer, a blank cheque signed and sealed in blood, and any man can lift it up out of this verse, 'That if thou shalt confess with thy mouth the Lord Jesus, and believe in thine heart that God hath raised Him from the dead, thou shalt be saved;' he can endorse it on the back, and it is payable on demand." He saw he had to look away from himself to what had been done by another, that God was pleased to say He was satisfied with the work done on Calvary's Cross, and if He is pleased I may be thankful to accept it. I think the young man went away rejoicing in Christ's finished work.

If I could have a trumpet tongue which would sound from one end of Britain to the other, there is one thing I would like to say to one class of people: not to Christians, for they have got to the root of the matter, and they will, "some on boards and some on broken pieces of the ship," all get safe to land; not to the godless, for they do not care, and I may not have the capacity to reach them; but to a large class, a middle class, not careless nor doubting, not running to excess of rioting, but not standing on the rock; and the text I would preach from to them would be, "Say not in thine heart;" go not by what thy heart says. To turn men in to what they feel, instead of *out to* what God has done and said, is the crying heresy of the present day, and this is our mission—to come with the oracles of God as contrasted with feelings. "Say not in thine heart," because all men are ready to go by what they feel, and three-quarters of evangelic preaching is founded upon this sensational religion, "Do you feel God's Spirit working within you? Do you feel getting better?—then go on and get to heaven." Many good men have said it, but it is not in my Bible from Genesis to Revelation. I have searched from board to board, and the word feeling in connection with salvation is not to be found in it. I believe it has been got from the devil. The adversary of souls goes with the preacher, night after night, and does all he can to thwart the Word; he comes as an angel of light, not as the serpent, for then you would not listen to him; he comes neither outwardly immoral, nor outwardly out-and-out for Christ. If he came as a liar, you would say, "Get thee behind me, Satan;" if he came and said the Bible was not true, and there was no hell and no heaven, you would say, "Get thee behind me, Satan;" all these are lies, and you would find them out soon; so he will not do this with you who are better taught, but he will come as an angel of light; or if he sees you inclined to one line of things, he will give you what will please you, lest you should hear and be saved.

Our whole powers are devoted week after week to get people saved; his whole work is to blind people, for "if our gospel be hid, it is hid to them that are lost, in whom the god of this world hath blinded the minds of them which believe not, lest the light of the glorious gospel of Christ, who is the image of God, should shine unto them." What a diabolical work, to keep people unsaved! Like those wreckers that rear the beacon-light on the iron-bound shore, that the sailor may be dashed to pieces, even so he rears a beacon-light, but it leads to death, ruin, and desolation.

Satan has substituted two things for the gospel which is the power of God. To those who have a traditional Christianity he finds he must do other things than contradict the Bible; so he comes and substitutes one truth for another, and there are two great lines of truth which he has taken and put in the place of one and the same truth. The one is the *life* of Christ; this was one great thing I was taught in early life, and my idea was that in order to be saved I must live a life like His; children are taught this still, for the devil has taken that grand truth that we should *imitate* the life of Christ, and he has put it in the place of Calvary and Golgotha, and the dying Lamb of God. We need not begin with Christ at Bethlehem; He began with us there; we begin with His death, and having secured His death, we go back and retrace the steps of His life; I believe Satan has invented no greater error than that of substituting the life of Christ for His death. The Apostle Paul says, "God forbid that I should glory save in the *cross* of our Lord Jesus Christ," not the manger.

The next truth he has put in a false position is the *work* of the Holy Ghost *in* me, in place of Christ's work *for* me. I believe that the work of God the Spirit, in every regenerated man, in bearing witness that he is a child of God, is quite a step in advance of being saved. Israel was saved, but the people were never called the children of God; Abraham and Moses never had the spirit of sonship whereby we cry, "Abba, Father;" but we must never put the work of the Spirit of God in the place of the work of the Son of God; we must never think that what the Spirit works *in* us is to be taken as the ground of peace. I know the fearful Slough of Despond, the fearful darkness and despair a man gets into by looking into his own heart: the more conscientious a man is who looks into himself, the more despairing he gets if he is taught to look into his own heart, and into the work of God the Holy Ghost there, as the foundation on which to rest his hope of eternal life. The less the conscience speaks, the more peace the man gets; the keener the conscience is, the more despair the man is plunged into. I have seen conscientious people almost driven to madness, because they were never satisfied with God's work going on in their heart, and I have heard others glibly talk of being satisfied with themselves, and this because their consciences had never placed before them an eternal hell; "Say not in thine heart," for the righteousness of faith speaks, and you are to listen to it.

Do not try to rear a ladder from earth to heaven because God has fixed a ladder from heaven to earth. I am never, and should never be, satisfied with the work of the Holy Ghost *in* me, but I am, and should be, satisfied with the work of Christ *for* me on the cross. The work of Christ on the cross is the ground of our salvation, and we may be satisfied with that alone; the more the Holy Ghost works in a man the more will he be dissatisfied; the more faith a man has the more loudly will he cry, "Increase my faith;" it is too good to get only a little of; the more hope, the more love he has wrought in him by the Holy Ghost, the more he is dissatisfied with them and longs for their increase. Of faith, hope, and love we may desire more, but we can never say this of the work on Calvary's Cross— the more we see of it the more we are satisfied with it.

"The cross still stands unchanged,
   Though heaven is now His home;
The might stone is rolled away,
   But yonder is His tomb.

And yonder is my peace,
The grave of all my woes!
I know the Son of God has come,
I know He died and rose.

I change, He changes not,
The Christ can never die,
His love, not mine, the resting-place,
   His truth, not mine, the tie."

RIGHTEOUSNESS, HUMAN AND DIVINE.

"The righteousness which is of faith."—ROMANS x. 6.

THIS is a remarkable expression; the righteousness which is of the law can be well understood; it is the right doing between man and man, and between God and man. If you buy a good article from a man and pay him his just demands for it, you are neither obliged to, not obliging, him; in other words, you are equally righteous according to the righteousness which is of the law—it is a straightforward business transaction, you doing your part rightly, and he doing his; it is paying twenty shillings in the pound.

But what is the righteousness which is of faith? We shall see it—

1. As contrasted with the righteousness which is of the law: "He that *doeth* these things shall live by them." The righteousness of faith is not on the same line of rails at all; it is in contrast.

2. This righteousness which is of faith, when it speaks on this wise, tells us what has to be done that it may be exhibited, nothing less than the incarnation and resurrection of Christ.

3. We see the utter uselessness and needlessness of all man's efforts to do this work which the righteousness which is of faith demands: "Say not in thine heart, Who shall ascend into heaven? (that is, to bring Christ down); or, Who shall descend into the deep? (that is, to bring up Christ again from the dead)."

4. We shall find the part which man plays in securing the righteousness which is of faith. "If thou shalt confess with thy mouth the Lord Jesus, and shalt believe in thine heart that God hath raised Him from the dead, thou shalt be saved."

5. We shall see not only the past which man plays, but the medium which unites him to this righteousness of faith: "The *word is nigh thee, even in thy mouth and thy heart*," that is, the word of faith.

6. We shall see why this righteousness of faith thus benefits men: "For with the heart man believeth unto righteousness, and with the mouth confession is made unto salvation."

7. We shall see, lastly, the ground of it all: "For there is no difference between the Jew and the Greek, for the same Lord over all is rich unto all that call upon Him."

(1) The righteousness which is of faith is contrasted with the righteousness which is of the law. It is utterly useless for any one of us to attempt to secure righteousness on the ground of law-keeping, for if from this moment until we were a hundred years old we never committed one sin, it would be all up with us; we have sinned in the past, the line of continuity is broken, and we must get upon another line altogether; the righteousness which is of faith comes in when the righteousness which is of the law is broken. The doing and the living go together, for the law does not say, *Do, and be saved*, it does not imply that the man is lost, but "he that doeth those things shall live by them," and the moment the doing is not perfected according to the law the man is lost.

Men study the laws of God in nature, and think how exact He is, and yet they think His moral laws can be broken with impunity. He never puts summer in the place of winter; the sun always rises and sets to a minute, so that men can predict its course for a thousand years at any part of the earth's surface, for it has never been known to be a second before or behind time. The stars come to their meridian to the one-thousandth part of a second, and their exactitude is so great that the difference of a hair's breadth in their place in the heavens would be far too large a divergence,—so exact is God. Are His moral laws likely to be less exact?

(2) Now we want to look into the work that has to be done,— Christ has to come out of heaven to go to the grave, to come out of the grave and to go into heaven before this righteousness which is of faith can be accomplished. Hence in the

3rd place, we see the uselessness and needlessness of men trying to accomplish it. Can you go up to heaven to bring Christ down?

Righteousness, Human and Divine. 61

can you descend into the deep to bring up Christ again from the dead? It is needless, inasmuch as the work is done; it is hopeless, inasmuch as man has no power to do it. Therefore we see, in the

4th place, that the part which man plays in securing this righteousness is very simple. "If thou shalt confess with thy mouth the Lord Jesus," made Lord by incarnation and resurrection," and shalt believe in thine heart that God hath raised Him from the dead, thou shalt be saved." We see the medium,

5th. The word, the simple act of faith which links him to Jesus Christ, because

6th, "With the heart man believeth unto righteousness, and with the mouth confession is made unto salvation," and the ground

7th, Is, that there is no difference. This truth is at the root of all revelation from God to sinful men. There is no difference. St. Paul uses this expression twice; the first time in the third chapter of Romans, "There is no difference, for all have sinned and come short of the glory of God." Man does not like this truth when it is preached; it is often denounced as absurd and heretical, but it has stood since Paul's day. Cultivated men do not like to be brought down to the level of the murderer and drunkard; and without doubt there is a difference in the *degree*, but not in the guilt of moral delinquency There is a difference as to the depth in which men are down in the mud, but all are together in the horrible pit and miry clay.

People waste their time in mud-measuring. One says, "My foot is only covered with the mud, but look at that fellow, he is ankle-deep in it;" the one who is ankle-deep in the mud says, "Look at that man, he is up to the knees in mud;" while he, in his turn, says, "I am not so bad as that man, he is up to the neck in mud." It is of no use to talk like that: here is a rope-ladder to help you all up from the pit. "Oh," says one, "I am as good as my neighbour, and better than many." Very true, perhaps, but that is only the difference between being up to the knees in mud or up to the neck; if you are in the pit, you need a rope-ladder that you may get out and place your feet on a rock, for there is no difference. One man with decent boots on, and only one foot a little muddy, says, "I do not believe there is no difference. Do you mean to say I am no better than that fellow there up to his neck in mud?" No, my friend; and very likely the man up to his neck will get hold of the ladder first, for he is so shocked at the mud that he is glad to get out of it; while the respectable man spends his time in arguing about the depth of mud he is in. It is not mud-measuring, but salvation, we have to do with, for "there is no difference, for all have sinned and come short of the glory of God."

Here in the 10th chapter we have the other "no difference," and it is about God's grace. There is no difference this time, for the same free God has the same free grace for every sinner out of hell: this is the foundation for the righteousness of faith being given to us.

The work that has to be done is no other and no less than the incarnation and resurrection of the Lord Jesus Christ. Incarnation alone is useless, death alone is useless; resurrection is what makes the righteousness of faith applicable to us. It is significant that while man has invented, and annually celebrates, what he calls the day of Christ's nativity or Christmas, and another day which he calls Good Friday, or the day of Christ's death, God has appointed no such days, but *one* day to be celebrated, not yearly, but weekly, to keep in memory, not the birth of Christ, which would condemn us, nor the death of Christ, which would bring us in guilty of murder, but the resurrection of Christ, which shows what God is for the sinner—the Lord's day, which tells us of resurrection, and assures us that we have not to ascend into heaven to bring down Christ, nor descend into the deep, to bring Him up from the dead, but that the Lord became incarnate in order that He might rise. It does not say anything of death, because it is implied in resurrection.

If you and I accept the righteousness which is of faith, we gain it by the incarnation and resurrection of the Lord Jesus Christ. Many people think they will reach heaven by a sort of guess-road; you ask a man, "If you were to drop down dead in an hour's time, where would your soul be?"

"What is the use of frightening me like that? what do you mean by it?"

"If God were to withdraw His hand for one moment, and your heart were to stop beating, you would be a corpse; then where should you be?"

"Oh, I hope—" he would most likely say, but "I *hope*" is nothing; it is a miserable wriggle out of the difficulty. "Have you gone up to heaven or down to the deep? for the righteousness which is of faith says that work has to be done."

"I trust God will be merciful."

You never read of mercy at the day of judgment. "Inasmuch as ye did it…inasmuch as ye did it not."… "Come, ye blessed,…depart, ye cursed;" not one word of mercy, for there is no mercy at the judgment-seat of God. We know the whole of the elements which enter into the judgment. We do not know who are saved or who are lost; all we can say of the best man on earth is that he professes to be converted, and we do not see anything in his conduct which is contrary to that profession. Human beings have to judge others by their actions, not by their faith. God only sees the heart; and we are not to get a verdict from human judges, or from our own feelings, but to await the sentence of the unerring Judge.

How may I get a favourable one? God has instituted the Lord's say to this end, that those who are saved may come and worship, and that those who are not saved may hear what they are to do. Just as the business of the week-days must be done, so the business of this day must be done. This business is not to hear a sermon and criticize it. If I were a salesman, I should not like a person to come into my shop, and spend an hour and a half in looking over all my goods, and then go away without buying anything—that is not business. I want to do business for eternity. I want not to write nor preach what people like, but to get hold of a man's conscience, and to ask him, Have you the righteousness which is of faith? Are you resting on the incarnation and resurrection of the Lord Jesus Christ?

Think of the day and the ordeal of judgment. Will you plead guilty or not guilty? Guilty, not of living a wretchedly bad life as a thief or a murderer, but of breaking God's law in *one* point? You say, "I must acknowledge breaking it at one point." Then you are guilty. Have you any excuse to make? "Yes, much." Have you prayed? "Yes, all my life." Then pray on. Have you been charitable? "Oh yes, I give to the Hull Infirmary[5] and to the Indian

---

[5] Editor's Note: A teaching hospital in the city of Hull started in 1782.

Famine Fund."[6] Then sell all you have and give to the poor. You say, "That is very hard." Yes, but I cannot help it: such is the way you have chosen with your excuses, prayers, and good works. Another man pleads "Guilty" at once. Have you any excuses, any prayers, any good deeds, any endeavours to do right to plead in your behalf? "No." Have you nothing good to say for yourself? Are you only fit to be cast away from God? "I have not a single excuse or palliation[7] to present." Then God says, "I have nothing but a Saviour for one so bad as you are." If you come as a sinner alone, not sinner and company, God will give you Christ, for it is grace now, as it will be judgment then. The righteousness which is of faith is for any man who will take the place where righteousness can flow—the place of the lost sinner now; for "Behold, now is the accepted time; behold, now is the day of salvation."

---

[6] Editor's Note: A government fund to help the Indians during the famine of 1896–1897. Over one million people died during the famine.

[7] Editor's Note: Apologetic covering.

JOB'S QUESTION AND PAUL'S ANSWER.

OB, in his distress, raised this question, "*How should man be just with God?*" (ix. 2). The divinely-appointed sacrifices in Israel, the ancient idolatries and sacrifices of Greece and Rome, the modern abominations to false gods in heathenism, all tell out that conscience as well as law ever keeps before fallen man this fundamental question. Man has never, even to his own satisfaction, answered this question so that, where he is conscientious, his whole life is taken up in seeking for an answer in his own efforts, and finding none.

Paul has answered it, or rather God the Holy Ghost, by the pen of Paul, in the letter to the Romans (iii. 26), where he tells us that Christ came, and shows how God Himself can be "just, and the Justifier of him who believeth in Jesus." Under several aspects do we find justification in the Scripture: —

1st, Justification by God.
2nd, Justification by grace.
3rd, Justification by blood.
4th, Justification by resurrection.
5th, Justification of life.
6th, Justification by faith.
7th, Justification by works.

1*st, Justification by God.*—What a wondrous truth! God steps in Himself and justifies the sinner. The process by which this is accomplished, and the vindication and manifestation of all His attributes in this justification, we shall shortly consider; but *the fact* is the first thing to take hold of, that God has come in for our justification. "Even as David also describeth the blessedness of the man unto whom *God* imputeth righteousness without works"

(Rom. iv. 6). So also Isaiah (liii. 6), "*The Lord* hath laid on Him the iniquity of us all." *God* is "the Justifier of him who believeth in Jesus" (Rom. iii. 26). "Who shall lay anything to the charge of God's elect? Shall *God* that justifieth?" (Rom. viii. 33). And He only has the right to lay to our charge—but He justifies us. He is spoken of as "*Him* that justifieth the ungodly" (Rom. iv. 5). Man is going about trying to secure his justification; he will not stand still and let God justify him. Jesus told the religious people of His day (Luke xvi. 15), "Ye are they which justify yourselves;" and as long as we are attempting to justify ourselves, we cannot submit to let God justify us. We excuse, palliate, cover over our sin, until we understand this fact, that it is *God* that justifies.

2nd, Justification by grace.—God could point to unfallen angels, and say against all accusers, "These stand in creature righteousness," but He could not justify them by grace, for they never required it. In order to see the meaning of this expression, we must understand what and where man is when God steps in to justify him. In the Epistle to the Romans, it is not until *all men in the world*—good, bad, and indifferent—have been brought in guilty before God, that God opens up His secret. It is not until man at his extremity cries, How then shall men be just with God? in the sight of His inflexible justice and stern, unbending judgment, that God steps in and answers his question by opening up the treasures of His grace. The criminal has been found guilty at the bar, the judge has pronounced the sentence, the convict now awaits execution; his prayers, his tears cannot save him; he is condemned. It is in vain that he loudly calls for mercy, and promises amendment for the future; the sentence has been passed; the law is inflexible, and his blood is demanded: now is the time for grace. That Judge who has condemned has planned the way by which the condemned criminal may become a loyal subject. He wishes to show the exceeding riches of His grace in His kindness to that condemned man. The thought arises in the Judge's heart; for it is for His own name's sake that He does it; and thus we are justified freely by His *grace*" (Rom. iii. 24; Titus iii. 7). But what of the justice of the Judge? Is it to be sacrificed? What of the inflexible character of His law? Is it to be tampered with? Nay, verily. This leads us to consider—

3rd, *Justification by blood.*—He spared not His Son, but gave Him up to the death for us (blood being the emblem for "life taken"). So we are spoken of as "being now justified by His *blood*" (Rom. v. 9). Death has been demanded. Christ has died; the penalty has been paid. So if we are justified freely by His grace, it is "through the redemption that is in Christ Jesus, whom God hath set forth a propitiation through faith in His *blood*" (Rom iii. 24, 25). Man could tolerate a certain kind of grace, or an interest in Christ's holy life, but he cannot bear the "blood" theology. But the keynote of God's justification is blood. Blood is the procuring cause, as this passage proves to a demonstration. The Judge was gracious; therefore He gave His Son for the criminal. The Judge was just; therefore He could not spare the life of His Son. God's justice is now displayed to the universe in the blood of His Son, as nowhere else it could be seen. It is according to the positive value of this precious blood that we are now justified. God's justice demanded death; God's grace provided blood. So the obedient One, under all the load, says, "But Thou art holy, O Thou that inhabitest the praises of Israel!" (Psalm xxii). He vindicates God while He feels the judgment-stroke pouring out His precious blood, and thus puts away the sin that He bore; and thus His precious "*blood* cleanseth us from *all* sin," sins of omission as well as sins of commission. Some seem to think that something less or something else than His blood can cleanse from the sin of failing to come up to obey His precepts, while the blood is required only for the sin of actual commission; but sins of omission are as really sin as sins of commission; and blessed be God, "His blood cleanseth us from ALL sin." And we are justified by His blood as the alone procuring, efficacious, meritorious cause. To nothing else in Scripture is justification attributed as a meritorious cause. "By Him all who believe are justified *from all things*" (Acts xiii. 39).

4*th, Justification by resurrection.*—"Jesus our Lord was delivered for our offences, was raised again for our justification" (Rom. iv. 25). Christ was made sin for us, went into our very place of condemnation under the wrath of God; but God in justice to Him has raised Him out of that place, thus justifying Him, and thus openly preaching to every clime,[8] where the fact of His resurrection is known, that the legal barrier between Him and any sinner accepting Christ has been removed. It is not that there is merit or value in the putting away of sin in Christ's resurrection—the precious blood alone does that—but there is the exhibition of the satisfaction of God's justice in the finished work of Christ. Christ, on Calvary, reckoned up the penalty demanded, gave Himself as an equivalent, paid thus in equivalent the amount demanded; but God, in raising Christ from the dead, has as it were with His own hand receipted the account, so that not only have we it *paid* by our Surety, but *settled* by Him Who made the just demand. It was for our offences that He was delivered. It was for our justification He was raised. How vague and imperfect are the ideas of justification entertained by many Christians, may be seen in the infrequent use of the resurrection of Christ, which is here so intimately linked with justification. "If Christ be not raised, ye are yet in your sins" (1 Cor. xv. 17); and conversely, "If Christ is raised, ye are not in your sins."

His resurrection tells us that God is for us, and that God is for us in consistency, yea, in exhibition of His own majestic justice; so in Rom. x. 9 the righteousness of faith speaks thus, "Say not in thine heart, Who shall ascend into heaven? (that is, to bring Christ down from above); or, Who shall descend into the deep? (that is, to bring up Christ again from the dead)," for the WORD tells us, that "If thou shalt confess with thy mouth the Lord Jesus, and shalt believe in thine heart that God *hath raised Him from the dead*, thou shalt be saved." "Who is he that condemneth?" (Christ most certainly should). "Shall Christ that died, *yea, rather* that is risen again?" (Rom. viii. 34). "If when we were enemies we were reconciled to God by the death of His Son, *much more*, being reconciled we shall be saved by His life" (His *resurrection* life) (Rom. v. 10). Thus there is the most intimate and necessary connection between justification and resurrection. The Judge's Son, Who, according to the Judge's grace, took the place of the condemned criminal, has shed His blood, but has been raised from the dead, and now stands beyond the forfeit of His life, and the *living* One is the assurance to

---

[8] Editor's Note: Climate.

the condemned one that there is no condemnation. "He was raised *for*" (not on account of, but *for*) "our justification."

5*th, Justification of life* (Rom. v. 18).—(Lit.) "As by one offence judgment came upon all men to condemnation, even so by one righteousness the free gift came upon" (rather to or towards) "all men, unto justification of *life*." This carries us a step further in the perfect exhibition of the justification of the believer. Not only did Christ come to save, not only did He shed His precious blood, not only did He stand my Surety, not only was He raised from the dead as my Head and Representative, but I am quickened together with Him in this risen life. We are reckoned as having died, and now been raised together with Christ (Eph. ii.). Says the Psalmist, "Enter not into judgement with Thy servant: for in Thy sight shall *no* man *living* be justified" (Psalm cxliii. 2). I am justified, not as living in the first Adam life, but as having died out of the Adam state, and now being raised and quickened with Christ. Romans vi. is the full exhibition of this.

We do not get justification and acceptance now before God by a simple restoration to us of that which was lost in Adam. After the penalty has been paid by our Surety, and He has been raised, we are, as in Christ, taken out of the old condemnation-place, and set down in a new, a resurrection (therefore justified) life, and in the very place that Christ occupies, in virtue of what He has done. In other words, the old things are blotted out as by the cold hand of the grave. We make an entirely new start, as men that have been dead and are now alive again, living the life of Christ. This is "justification of life." This is the "*newness* of life"—not freshness, or a merely sanctified walk, but life in entirely new circumstances, Christ's resurrection-life, in which we are now to walk, as those who have died to sin. So we are called on to "reckon ourselves *dead* indeed to sin, but alive unto God, through Jesus Christ our Lord" (Rom. vi. 11); and (ver. 7) "he that is *dead* is justified from sin." It is only as those who have died (in Christ), and who are alive in a life that knows no condemnation (Christ's risen life), that we can say we are justified from sin. Such is the bearing of Christ's death and resurrection on our justification *of life*.

Eph. i. 6 tells us that we are "accepted in the Beloved, in whom we have redemption through His blood, the forgiveness of sins."

Here we have three things—forgiveness, redemption, acceptance. We are not yet redeemed by power; but, so far as our sins and their forgiveness are concerned, we do have redemption. And is there One in whom God delights, whom God loves, in all His universe? We are accepted in that beloved One—not in the Adamic state perfected, not in the angelic state communicated; but accepted in Him Who is the beloved Son, in His resurrection state—quickened with Him after all the responsibilities of the Adamic state had been justly met—children in Jesus Christ to God Himself. And as Christ is (not was), so are we in this world. If we continue our illustration, it will be only to show how far surpassing man's power is God's justification. Not only has the Judge in His grace given his Son, Whose blood was shed, and Who was raised from the dead, but through that risen Son He communicates life to the condemned criminal, who therefore takes his place as a son—not by some gratuitous assumption or temporary adoption, but by an innate right, having now a son's life, and hence a son's position. This is "justification of life."

6th, Justification by faith.—"Being justified by faith, we have peace with God" (Rom. v. 1). Faith is the acceptance of God's method of justification; faith appropriates what grace provides; faith apprehends what grace presents. It is not faith that justifies; but by grace are ye saved through faith. All has been finished centuries ago. Faith now gives credence and credit to the record, and accepts the scheme for the individual sinner—accepts God's condition of death and resurrection in the Surety, and is thus counted for righteousness, as apprehending all that God's justice has demanded and grace has provided. The moment we accept Christ we are justified from all things; we can never be more justified (we then only begin to grow in grace). But it must be *by faith*, not by feeling. Many anxious ones are looking for that to be faith: the experience of what goes on within me is sense, it is not faith. Faith believes not what we feel, but what God says—"He that believeth not God hath made Him a liar; because he believeth not the record that God gave of His Son. And this is the record, that God hath given to us eternal life, and this life is in His Son" (1 John v. 11). It is of faith that it might be of grace. To make it absolutely free and open to any kind of sinner, no condition was imposed. God comes with a free gift, and only asks us to accept it. The moment we do, we have peace (not with ourselves) with God, for Christ is our peace.

7th, Justified by works (James ii. 24).—Certainly these are not deeds of the law—"By the deeds of the law there shall no flesh be justified in His sight" (Rom. iii. 20). They are works of *faith*. (Look at the instance in James' Epistle,—Abraham's seemed to be against the law of the sixth commandment.) The works of faith show to men that there is faith, just as the figs on a tree show that the root is a fig root. If a man *say* he has faith—I say to him, *Show me* your works. (It is not, Show *God*. He can see faith—I can't.) My works justify my faith before men, as my faith justifies myself before God. A Christian is in a low state when he is searching for this faith among his works. He is in a doubtful state when he has to persuade other men that he has faith, who fail to see it in his works. My faith rests on Jesus Christ alone for salvation, and the words concerning Him for the knowledge of salvation. My exhibition to men of faith stands on my works of faith alone. The condemned criminal has accepted the terms, the provision of the Judge,—that is, justification by faith. He now lives as the Judge's son, honours the Judge's will, obeys the Judge's commandments, walks, acts, speaks, as becomes the son's place, so that men at once see that he is living in the Judge's home as the Judge's son.

God justifies us as the Author and Executor.
Grace justifies us as the reason in God.
Blood justifies us as the meritorious cause.
Resurrection justifies us as God's own assurance.
Life (in resurrection) justifies us as our position before God.
Faith justifies us as the instrument.
Works justify us as the evidence to others.

THE CLAIMS OF THE MAN JESUS.

"The Jews answered Him, saying, For a good work we stone Thee not, but for blasphemy; and because that Thou, being a man, makest Thyself God."—JOHN x. 33.

HIS is a very solemn statement—"Thou being a man, makest Thyself God." That was the opinion, at any rate, that the Jews had of Christ's own claims when He came into the world.

They had no difficulty in knowing what He professed to be; but they had great difficulty in believing that it was true. They had no difficulty in knowing what His claims were, but they had great difficulty in granting them.

They were not like modern Unitarians, who would make out that God had not said in His Bible that the Messiah would come as "God manifest in the flesh;" they allowed that, but said that it was blasphemy in Him to say that of Himself. That was what Judaism said, and what it says still. They should have been aware that there was a text in Zechariah which says, "Awake, O sword, against my Shepherd, and against the man that is *my Fellow*, saith the Lord of Hosts"—that there Jehovah's fellow was a man. Over and over again did the Jews attempt to kill Him because He called Himself God, or the Son of God in a way in which no human created being is so—the Uncreated, Eternal Son—the Son of God. This is what these rulers impeached Him for saying of Himself. Here it is strongly put, "Because that Thou, being a man, makest Thyself God." In the 5th of John we read at the 18th verse, "Therefore the Jews sought the more to kill Him, because He not only had broken the Sabbath, but said also that God was His Father, making Himself equal with God." The claim was fellowship with God. "He made Himself equal with God."

Then, if we pass on to His crucifixion, we shall find that this was the head and front of His accusation. John xix. 7, "The Jews answered Him, We have a law, and by our law He ought to die, because He made Himself the Son of God." This was His death-warrant—what they put upon His indictment as the greatest of all His crimes. In the Gospel by Matthew, xxvi. 63-66, He is indicted and condemned for the same thing,—"But Jesus held His peace. And the high-priest answered and said unto Him, I adjure Thee, by the living God, that Thou tell us whether Thou be the Christ, the Son of God. Jesus saith unto him, Thou hast said: nevertheless I say unto you, Hereafter shall ye see the Son of man sitting on the right hand of power, and coming in the clouds of heaven. Then the high-priest rent his clothes, saying, He hath spoken blasphemy; what further need have we of witnesses? behold, now ye have heard His blasphemy. What think ye? They answered and said, He is guilty of death." In the high-priest's estimation it seemed a greater sin than claiming to be the Son of God, that He pictured Himself coming in the clouds of heaven, and sitting on the right hand of power as Son of man; that He, as the Son of man, would be raised up to be Head over every created thing; and that He would sit, and reign, and govern with God as man. This was great blasphemy to their minds.

Then we come to the title and accusation put upon the cross. "The superscription of His accusation was written over, *The King of the Jews*." Mark does not give us any other part—not even "Jesus of Nazareth." The chief part of the accusation was that He was the *King of the Jews*—the Messiah promised to the fathers, to fulfil all the promises made to Abraham and David. As such He was to sit on the throne of Israel—King of the Jews—God's own chosen people.

Thus we find a three-fold claim made by Christ; and all the three claims were disallowed by the Jews:—

First, "that He, being a man, made Himself God," as John tells us, the Son of God, equal with God, very God Himself.

Second, that He was the Son of man, Who would yet put everything on earth that opposed Him under His feet, and govern the whole creation.

Third, that He was the King of the Jews, Who should establish the throne of Israel, and at last sit thereon.

These are the three great names which are the centres of all His powers and greatest claims on this earth:—

The Son of God, by which He has wrought out redemption for His people.

The King of the Jews, to establish them in their own land in the latter day. He will restore Israel, and reign over His own people in His title of King of the Jews.

The Son of man, under which title He is to be Lord of all creation. All shall then know Him, even from the least to the greatest, and give Him obedience.

We read in the 8th Psalm, "Thou hast put all things under His feet; all sheep and oxen, yea, and the beasts of the field; the fowl of the air, and the fish of the sea." These are representative of the different classes of creatures—the oxen and sheep, or domesticated animals; the beasts of the field, or wild animals; the feathered tribe, and the fish of the sea; and all are to be under Him. Though we see not yet all things put under Him still in counsel they are put under Him. This was so far seen while He was on earth. When He was tempted of the devil it was among the wild beasts of the desert, but they did not touch Him. When baptized, a dove was used by the Hoy Ghost. When asked to pay the unjust tax, He said, Go and open that fish's mouth, and there was the money. When He required a quadruped to ride into Jerusalem, there was the colt of an ass just at hand. And when He wanted to rebuke Peter in the midst of his blasphemy, the cock was ready to crow. Whether birds of the air, fish of the sea, or animals, wild or tame, all were subject to Him as the Son of man.

The Son of God.

Such claims as He advanced have never been advanced by any man before nor since. We are so accustomed by traditional upbringing to a sort of hereditary belief of truth that we are apt to take it second-hand, and lose its power. We are in danger of having this blessed book more in our heads than in our hearts, from being brought up in the nurture and admonition of the Lord. It is good to be so brought up, but what we have by custom we generally have not so firm a grasp of. So that when infidelity assails us we have to fall back again on the pure Revelation of God—what saith the Lord? We have a sort of traditional belief that the Bible is all right and that Christ is the only Saviour, and that the way by which evangelical preachers tell us to go to heaven is the correct one. Indeed we take for granted that to believe on the Lord Jesus Christ is the way to be saved.

But to believe all that about Christ is not the same as believing in Him. To believe in Him is the saving thing. No matter what I have been: if I believe on the Lord Jesus Christ, I shall be saved; and if I don't and do everything else, I shall be damned. If you do everything else, you are damned if you don't do that. He has made this the crucial, testing point, "Believe on the Lord Jesus Christ, and thou shalt be saved." If that had been all, it would not have been so testing, but the opposite is equally true, for it is written, "He that believeth not shall be damned." The stately king that believes not shall be damned. The poor peasant that believes not shall be damned. The rich man and the poor alike that believe not shall be damned. The learned and unlearned shall be equally damned that do not believe in Christ. Be he the least sinner that ever lived, or the greatest sinner that ever lived; I cannot help it; he shall be damned if he believes not on the Lord Jesus Christ. If I had been judge, I would have said the good moral man will get to heaven and the gross offender only go to hell; but I am here not to make the rule of life, but to declare it. He that believeth not shall be damned, and I cannot alter it. It will not make it true if I preach something else. So upon faith in Christ turns the whole question between God and man? The blackest sinner that believes on Christ and claims Him as his own Saviour is saved for ever, and the best man on earth that comes to God without Christ must be damned. Thus you see Christ is made the turning point. The question to us, therefore, is, Do you believe on the Lord Jesus Christ? We have no new gospel to bring before you, though we trust we shall be enabled to give you some fresh aspect of it.

I have been revolving this text very much in my mind—"Believe on the Lord Jesus Christ, and thou shalt be saved."

I don't know another in all creation that I believe in. We cannot believe in our dearest friends. I will tell you why,—it is because we do not believe in ourselves. After that it is not likely we will believe in them. But I do believe in the Lord Jesus Christ. I can believe in you so far, and you can believe in me so far. If I say, I will come and preach to you, I will come as far as lies in my power. Nothing short of some catastrophe will prevent me coming; and you believe me thus far. But to believe wholly in any man or woman out of heaven we cannot, we dare not, because we do not believe in ourselves. Let me bring an instance before you. You remember the claimant that was so notoriously before the public not long ago. He advanced great claims, and put people to a great deal of trouble, and perplexed the minds of many people as to whether or not he was what he professed to be. I thought he was the genuine article for a time. During the first trial, and up to a certain stage in it, I believed in him. I thought he was the real Sir Roger Tichborne. The trial went on, and fair play fifty times told was given him, but it would not do; his roguery came out bit by bit, till it became more and more evident that he was an impostor. All that could be got in his favour was hunted up and brought forward. Every witness that could be trusted was heard on his side. Still his case would not hold water. It was patent that he was not the true heir of the estates. Moreover, those who had most to do with it, and heard and knew all the outs and ins of the case, formed independent judgments solemnly, unanimously, and heartily against him. The impartiality of the judge and jury was patent to all; and they, as well as the great voice of the English people, pronounced that no such blackguard has appeared for many years. Who believes in him now that he is proved guilty? In fact, nobody, unless very peculiarly constituted can any longer have faith in him. I do not believe in him. He came forward claiming these estates, and has put their rightful possessors to extraordinary trouble and expense, as well as the country at large; but it has now been proved that he is no more Sir Roger Tichborne than I am.

THE GREATNESS OF HIS CLAIMS.

But the One whom I ask you to believe in makes far greater claims than those of that impostor. His claims were nothing to the claims of the Lord Jesus Christ. The throne of the Jewish nation is His Who was born King of the Jews. And more than that, the throne of the whole earth is His as the Son of man. And not only that, but the throne of the universe is His as the Son of God. Did you ever hear of such claims? He claimed by birth the throne of His father David, King of the Jews, and was crucified as such. He claimed also that, as Son of man, He would sit on the right hand of the power of God, and put all His enemies under His feet; that as the Second Man—the last Adam—He would restore all that the first Adam lost; that all on earth, both small and great, should yet bow down to Him as rightful King of nations. And not only that, but that He was the Son of God—equal with the Father—God Himself, the Creator of all things; that He is Lord of all that ever was or will be encircled round the throne of God, and Possessor of everything in the universe as Heir of God. Did you ever hear of such claims as these? The question is, Who believes in Him as such? The Jews did not.

He came to His own nation that He professed to be King of, and they would not have Him. They cried, "Away with Him; crucify Him, crucify Him." They preferred Barabbas to Him. What is Barabbas? He was a robber. Did you ever look at the history of the Jewish nation from that day to this? If you do, and look also at their Bible history as a nation, you will find it to be one of robbery from beginning to end. I can never read accounts of them anywhere, and especially in their own serials, without repeating the word "robbery." Their robber king, ever since they chose him, has ruled them with a dreadful consistency—robbery, robbery, robbery, has been the one history of the nation. Thus the Jews, His own nation and people to whom He came, would not have Him. They clung to a Gentile monarch, crying, "We have no king but Cæsar."

Then, again, the world was made by Him as the Son of man, and the world did not know Him, and hence did not believe in Him. The Jews would not have the Son of David; nor would the Gentiles have the Son of man; for once, both Jew and Gentile were united to cast Him out. All refused to have Him. This introduces the weak side of our Client's case. A good counsel always labours to get evidence to support the weak side of his client's case. Now I am pleading the cause of the Lord Jesus Christ. I shall bring strong evidence to prove what is supposed to be the weak side of His claims; and I am to put the case before you as jurymen, and ask you to give a candid decision as before the living God. I care not if the enemy, Satan, himself be called; I am quite prepared to meet him with unchallengeable evidence. Though the devil comes with all these six thousand years' experiences against us, I shall put the case as fairly as I can, and I fear not the issue.

When He came to this earth He was born in the worst of all circumstances. Although really the King of the Jews, the Son of man, and the Son of God, He was born among the beasts in a despised part of the land called Bethlehem. He spent the greater part of His life on earth in great seclusion. He was a carpenter working at the planes and saws; and for thirty years He did not publicly advance His claims. Then when He entered on His ministry, and came forward as the King of the Jews, they would not recognize Him. I cannot put it very much stronger against Him than that. He came to His own estates, and His own servants would not receive Him. He came to His own house and possessions, and His people kept Him out of both. So much for His claim as King of the Jews.

The Jews to a man rejected Him, except a few broken-down fishermen and others. Just a few of these ignorant, poor people stood up for Him. Just a few of those sentimental, weeping people, who had not much head, such alone dared to cry Hosanna in His presence. He never drew any great people round about Him. He went about despised and rejected of men, a Man of sorrows, and acquainted with grief. He was in the world, and the world was made by Him, and yet it knew nothing about Him. And when He came to His departure out of this world, the Jews forsook Him, and the Gentiles, too, mocked and scourged Him. His friends even, who, we would have thought, would have stood up for Him,—even His friends left him. His disciples forsook Him and fled. One betrayed Him; another swore that he never knew Him; not one of them stood by him. And every man on earth left Him. We can see nothing around Him but a mob of infuriated Jews, and Gentile soldiers with their spears at His breast.

All on earth left Him, and all hell was let loose upon Him. He has come now to the crisis. Now is the crucial point, for He is to be given into the hands of God to be tested. Now we shall see if He is an impostor. He has been given in to the hands of men, and they nailed Him to a tree; now He is in the hands of God; and hearken to His cry, "My God, my God, why hast Thou forsaken me?" He is not only forsaken by all on earth, and all in hell, by Jews and Gentiles, by foes and friends, but He is forsaken by God Himself. Does this not prove against Him? I am pleading the opposite side just now, because I am determined to give you all that can be said against Him first. Now it is perfectly sure that His claim has been disallowed. Therefore "we did esteem Him *stricken, smitten* of God, and *afflicted.*" That is what the Jews said. You see, say they, that He is an impostor, for God has smitten Him for His imposition, and for saying that He was the Christ, the Son of God. His history now seems to prove Him an impostor. Jews and Gentiles all say He is an impostor. In fact, heaven, earth, and hell seem now against His claims.

His Claims Disallowed.

Have you anything else to say against Him? Not one of His claims has been allowed. All has been against Him as the one who claims to be the King of the Jews, the Son of man and equal with God. What have we now to say on His behalf? Well, we have just one short question to ask, and upon it we hang all our case. As to what you have said against Him, we admit it all; it is all true. We shall see what you, the jury, say when we bring forward our evidence. Remember, my readers, you will all give a verdict as you read. It must be one way or other before God. We are now to put our case before you, and speak for our Client. We have not a long speech to make. Nor are we to try to convince you by any outburst of eloquence. Oratorical machinery never yet convinced a sinner of his sins, any more than it convinced a conscientious jury that a man was guilty against clear evidence to the contrary. If I were a juryman I should want nothing but the facts of the case. Well, I have only one short question to ask my opponents, and one question is all we need to ask. On that we hang all our case, and demand a verdict in favour of our Client. What is this question? We quite allow all that has been said—that He was rejected, crucified, slain, and buried; but we now ask, Where is He? *Where is He now*? In vain do you go to the sepulcher, and search the tomb for Him. Where is He?

"Well," says my opponent, "I thought you would ask that; but my answer is, The disciples carried away His body during the night."

"Would you kindly give evidence for that, because I have some rebutting evidence?"

"Well, I have a strong military leader, with his band of soldiers, who were set as a watch over His sealed grave."

"Roman soldiers, I know you are true men; what do you know of this matter? Is it true that you were set there as a watch?"

"Yes, we were, and that on pain of death to every one of us should He be removed."

"And is it true that there was a stone rolled to the mouth of His grave?"

"Yes, a huge stone, in order that no ordinary force should break into it."

"And more than that, this stone was sealed with the governor's seal, that none should dare to touch it. Well, you did everything that you possibly could to make it secure?"

"Yes, we did."

By the way, my friends, you see how the wriggling of the serpent always discovers itself. A straightforward, conscientious man can never be deceived by the devil, because he goes in a straight line. The line of downright, genuine honesty and the line of Satan's procedure can never go together—they are the opposite of parallel. The reason is, because Satan always uses crooked, round-about arguments; and if you meet him, with clear and correct statements of truth, he will flee from you. So if the world had not taken such precautions against all possibility of Christ's body being stolen—setting a great stone, the governor's seal, and a strong guard to watch it—it would not have been so easy now to prove that He was raised from the dead.

"Well, then, soldier No. 1, do you mean to say, after all that, that the disciples stole the body of Christ out of the tomb?"

"Yes, they took it away when we were sleeping."

"Indeed! And in what way did they do it?"

"Well, we cannot exactly say."

"Worse, and worse! And how do you know that they did it at all?" No answer. You see, when a man is guilty, he makes himself ridiculous all round. I ask you, jurymen, what is the strength of such evidence as that? "You step down, sir; your evidence is worse than useless.

"Soldier No. 2, come up! How do you account for the removal of Jesus of Nazareth out of the tomb? Is He risen?"

"Oh, no; He is not risen."

"Where is He, then?"

"Well, we happened to fall asleep a bit, and His disciples came and stole the body away."

"Did you see them through your sleep?"

"No, but we are all agreed that it was they who took it away."

I need not waste your time, jurymen, because if we bring them all forward, they have all the same story to tell. Having heard one, you have heard them all. It is evident there has been some bribery behind the scene. Their theory is that His disciples took it away, and buried it somewhere else. If you ask each of them he is sure of it; and he is sure of it because he was sound asleep when it was done. Satan, have you any other theory for the defence of your position? Have you any other way of accounting for this body being removed, in spite of this stone, and the royal seal, and the guard of Roman soldiers? No, he has not. His case rests on the evidence of a few sleeping soldiers! Do you maintain, on such evidence as that, that His disciples took His body out of that sepulcher, and embalmed it, and stowed it away in some secluded place out of everybody's reach and den? In vain shall ye search for it there. Jews and Gentiles, men and devils, in vain shall ye search for it; for His is not there at all. He is risen; and I shall now prove it by unimpeachable evidence.

Proof that He is risen from the Dead.

Bring in Mary to the witness-box.

"Now, Mary, what have you to say? Who was it that you saw on that first day of the week, who said, 'Touch me not, but go and tell my brethren'?"

"That was my Lord and Master. I saw Him with my own eyes risen from the dead, and no man will convince me that it was not so. And He also showed Himself to Peter and John, and the rest of the disciples, as was said."

"That will do, Mary, from you. That is very good evidence, but we want better still." Some may say that she was a poor sentimental woman, and her evidence cannot be trusted.

Bring forward the Old Testament witnesses next. I do not found so much on it, though it is strong, circumstantial, corroborative evidence. You will observe all my witnesses say He rose on the third day. Well, all Old Testament witnesses say He would do so. Whence this corroboration? How does it happen that all Christendom from that day to this sets aside the first day of the week to worship God instead of the Sabbath or seventh day? There is a strong coincidence, unaccountable on any ground but that Christ rose on that day.

Here come now His disciples and apostles.

"What have you to say on this question?"

"Well, we were all assembled together on the first day of the week, and our Lord appeared right in the midst of us, and said, 'Peace be unto you.' He showed Himself unto us, risen from the dead on that Lord's day. We are all eye-witnesses of that fact. There is, and can be, no doubt about it whatever."

"Well, that will do for you; that is good sound evidence." We are simply letting you hear the evidence, without comment, because we have many more good witnesses.

Here is another one; let us question him.

"What is your name, sir?"

"My name is Thomas."

"What are you?"

"I was born a sceptic. I am the greatest doubter of all the apostles. They used to call me sceptical Thomas." (You see, God made use of the skepticism of Thomas to prove His resurrection. The testimony of a sceptic is the very best evidence."

"Well then, Thomas, are you convinced that this Jesus of Nazareth is alive from the dead?"

"Well, I was a great doubter as to that. I did not believe every story about it that I heard; nor would I take it from the testimony of two, three, or four witnesses; but my doubts are all clean gone now, because I know for certain that He is risen from the dead."

"How do you know that so well now?"

"Because I saw Him with mine own eyes, and thrust my own fingers into the prints of the nails in His body."

"So you are perfectly sure it was the Lord?"

"Yes, perfectly sure; and there is no man will ever convince me that it was not. As long as life lasts my skepticism as to that is gone."

Well then, readers, we hope you will give that testimony its due weight in forming your verdict. We have now a large multitude of five hundred brethren that saw Him at once. You can question any of them for their evidence. So we may dismiss these five hundred brethren without further examination.

PAUL'S EVIDENCE.

Here is a noble-looking man, with a determined look, closed lips, and silvered hair.

"Who art thou?"

"I am Paul, the apostle of the Gentiles. I was once Saul the persecutor, a blasphemous and injurious person. I haled to judgment and death all who believed in this crucified Man, and was exceeding mad against them."

"Why, I thought you would have been called as a witness for the opposition, since you did everything within your reach to destroy the hated and despised sect who believed in this Man. How is it that you have come over to be a witness on His side?"

"Well, as I was going on in my career of persecuting His followers, a light brighter than a midday sun struck me to the ground, and there I saw this Man of Calvary in the brightest effulgence of the glory of God. *He is on the throne of God.* Ah! ye poor soldiers of Rome, how did He get up there? Did His disciples make a ladder up to that throne, in order to place Him there? There He is now. How got He there, if He be an impostor?"

"Tell us, Paul the aged, did He say anything to you?"

"He said, 'I am Jesus, whom thou persecutest.' And from that day to this He has made me another and a new man; and I am now going onward to that crown."

Is he not a noble witness—Paul? I think he is the first man in heaven I should like to see after our blessed Lord. What a clean cut he made with the devil, and what a bold stand for Christ! He counted all his gain, position, and prospects but dung, and went broad everywhere preaching the faith he once destroyed; working even with his own hands to make the gospel preaching free of charge. One time he had preached some eighteen months and had got nothing, and they took him outside the city to give him his wages, and gave him thirty-nine lashes with a whip. "Forty stripes save one" he gloried in when standing up for this rejected Man. And when he got them he sang hallelujah. "Our light affliction, which is but for a moment, worketh for us a far more exceeding and eternal weight of glory." There is a witness who believes in our Client! Having suffered the loss of all, and the torture of thirty-nine lashes with the whip thrice told, and then sung hallelujah over it all.

"You may now go, Paul; your evidence will carry its own weight with it."

STEPHEN'S EVIDENCE.

Here is another true witness. He is a great preacher. But he is not an apostle, nor is he an elder, but just a deacon, and withal a sensible, peaceful-looking man.

"What is your name?"

He looks down very humbly and replies, "I am deacon Stephen."

"What were you?"

"I happen to be the first martyr of this dispensation among those who believe and preach that this Jesus of Nazareth is the Christ, the Son of God. And for this they dragged me out and stoned me."

"Were you not very much afraid when you saw the great crowds gathered, and the huge stones coming upon you?"

"Not I. I never saw one of them."

"What so filled your gaze that you did not see them?"

"I saw heaven opened."

"That is something wonderful! And it was that, that did not let you see the stones when they were flying on you, breaking your bones and taking your life? You had heard the angel choirs singing, and saw the blood-washed throng, with palms in their hands and crowns of gold? It is a grand place, heaven, with its gates of pearls and streets of gold. Were you not very much impressed with the sight?"

"I did not see one of them. I saw the Son of man standing on the right hand of God."

"Well, I am just taking evidence for that very purpose now; are you sure you saw Him?"

"Yes; I saw neither angel nor saint, but I did see the Son of man—the crucified Man of Calvary—with the prints of the nails in His hands, standing on the right hand of God. I saw nothing of the sorrows of earth, nor of the glory of heaven, but the Man of Calvary standing on God's right hand."

Jurymen, are you now ready to give your verdict? You have heard numerous competent witnesses declare that they have seen Him in heaven itself, standing at God's right hand. Shall I now ask your verdict? Are you satisfied with the evidence? No, I shall not ask it yet, because I have my best Witness to call still. I shall bring my best Witness last.

I have brought a woman, a sceptic, five hundred brethren, a converted persecutor, and a martyred deacon, but I cannot bring a single unconverted man who saw Christ after His resurrection. Paul saw Him when unconverted, but the sight converted him. Not one of my witnesses is from that regiment which is going on the broad way to destruction. Satan dare not put some of his witnesses into the box. They have such bad characters; but you can examine the characters of all mine, and you will find them true to the core— they are kings and priests unto God.

The Witness of the Spirit.

Well, I have my best Witness last, and that is not Peter, nor John, nor Paul, but the Third Person of the Trinity, the Holy Spirit. He came down when Christ was glorified. Now with deepest reverence and worshipping awe we ask Him who He is? and He replies,—

"I am the Spirit of Truth, come to take of the things of Christ, and publish them."

"Why art Thou here on earth?"

"I have come out from the throne of God, because the man, Christ Jesus, was glorified there."

"Is He glorified?"

"I could not have come down here unless He, as glorified Man, had taken His place on the throne of God; but now He has sent Me to gather together in one what He has purchased with His own blood, and to form a habitation of God on the earth."

"So it is settled, then, that the Man of Calvary is on the throne of His Father, God, in heaven?"

"Yes. 'Being found in fashion as a man, He humbled Himself, and became obedient unto death, even the death of the cross. Wherefore God also hath highly exalted Him, and given Him a name which is above every name; that at the name of Jesus every knee should bow, of things in heaven, and things in earth, and things under the earth; and that every tongue should confess that Jesus Christ is Lord, to the glory of God the Father."

"Thou hast come from heaven to tell this?"

"Yes. 'This is He that came by water and blood, even Jesus Christ; not by water only, but by water and blood. And it is the Spirit that *beareth witness*' " (1 John v. 6).

What can we have after such evidence? This is the true witness of the Third Person of the Trinity—concerning an exalted Christ. "He shall not speak of Himself." That is plain. And why was that? In order that we should not build upon His work in our hearts, but upon Christ's work , of which He testifies. I used to make a gross mistake in thinking that the witness of the Spirit was what I felt within me. What is the witness of the Spirit? Is it what you feel your heart saying? No, that is the evidence of a liar. My friend, I cannot tell you all that His witness takes in, but I can tell you that what your heart says is not the witness of the Spirit. And in case there should be any mistake about His witness, it is written—it is all printed. I have not time to read over all that He has said of this risen Christ, but you can read it for yourselves. You will see it from the 2nd chapter of the Acts of the Apostles to the 22nd chapter of the Revelation. There is His evidence. That is the witness of the Spirit, which He indited after His descent at Pentecost.

Christ ascended, and the Spirit has come to bear witness to the fact, and all that He says is laid before you to be received as evidence. Now, are you to believe the evidence of your own erring heart? or the evidence of this Spirit? I don't believe my own heart as to any Divine truth. Whenever my heart contradicts the testimony of the Spirit I say to it, You are a liar, and there the controversy ends.

WHO BELIEVES IN HIM NOW?

Well, friends, who believes in this rejected Man now? Who believes in the Lord Jesus Christ? Does every one of my readers believe in Him? I ask you at least to believe in Him *now*, if you never did before, and in your inmost soul say so to the living God. In spite of all the infidels on earth and devils in hell, I believe in Him that He is the Christ, the Son of God. If never before, I say, Christ for me. Friend, do you say that? We may indeed by reckoned as fools for believing in Him—greater fools than those who still believe in a false claimant. After our Hero's own people would have nothing to do with Him, after He has been forsaken by man and God, condemned and persecuted, no wonder if we are counted fools for believing in Him. Think how few do believe in Him. Surely we are credulous. The whole world is against Him, and lieth in the wicked one. Well, now, do you believe in my Client? I have said what I can for Him, and am determined to live, and if need be die believing in Him. Christ for me!

My friends, the devil has great skill and mighty power in deceiving souls, but we do not fear him more than our own hearts. If you meet him always with God's firm testimony, that will silence him.

If we are identified with this rejected Man, we must be rejected by the world, the devil, and the flesh; and we have no sword where with to fight them but the sword of the Spirit, which is the Word of God. Though you should be the most ignorant man living—not able to put two lines together, or spell your own name—if you use that Word of God you will gain the battle.

Look at the poor Jewish nation. "We did esteem Him stricken, smitten of God, and afflicted." They went wrong by not receiving and using both sides of the truth. They took the black side, and left the bright. "We did esteem Him stricken, smitten of God, and afflicted, *but*." I like the little "*buts*" of the Bible. A "but" shunts the train off one line of rails on to the other—off from the line of danger to the line of safety. The "buts" of the Bible are the shunting-points of the Bible. "But"—another line of rails altogether—"He was wounded for our transgressions, He was bruised for our iniquities, the chastisement of our peace was upon Him, and with His stripes we are healed." "For He was delivered for our offences, and raised again for our justification." Ah, there is the gospel. It is not as if we had nothing to believe in. How many of us are prepared to stand up and say, I believe in this murdered Man—Jesus of Nazareth? Everything is against us. If the world were consistent it would stand and laugh at us. That is the offence of the cross. And if you are not getting insults thrown at you, and getting reviled and laughed at, you are not accepting the Christ of Calvary; for the world is not one whit changed from what it was when it cried out, "Away with Him, away with Him; crucify Him, crucify Him." It is the same at heart.

Jurymen, will you give your verdict now? Do you believe in Christ? Will you give your vote for Him? He that believeth is saved. Believe now! Give your verdict for Him, and you are saved for ever. Now, are you to answer this appeal with, Christ for me? Or are you to believe the devil's lie? He is the father of lies, and all the evidences for his case are a few sleeping soldiers. Think of all the evidences the Spirit has advanced to prove that He is risen from the dead. And remember all rests on the question of His resurrection. If Christ be not raised, we are still in our sins, and our faith is vain. But if Christ be raised from the dead, we are not in our sins. Are you, my friend, identifying yourself with this outcast

Man of Calvary; then, since He is raised from under your sins, your standing is not in your sins, but in Him.

Well, I think you surely can have no hesitation in giving your verdict in His favour now. Do you believe in Christ or no? Every man of earth believes in somebody—either in Christ, or in some other person, or in himself.

Look at the Papist; he believes in the Pope. He believes everything the Pope says. Not what the Bible says, but what Mother Church says, and that interpreted by the Pope, whom, of course, he believes to be infallible!

Then look at the Rationalist; you cannot fix him down to believe in anything, or any one but himself. The Secularist, Unitarian, and so-called Rationalist, believe in none but themselves. They croak and cry out about the self-evident absurdities of the Gospel; yet scarcely two of them believe the same thing, and nothing is sure but that they believe in themselves.

Well, now, you may not believe in the Pope, but take care lest you believe in your own heart. Beware of Romanism on the one hand, trusting in another besides Christ, and skepticism on the other, which is trusting in yourself; but "believe on the Lord Jesus Christ, and thou shalt be saved." Yes, believe in Him against your own heart. Men of the world, will you have Him? It is not that you are a great sinner or a little one. We don't ask anything about what you are. It is not, Do you believe in this or that church, or creed, or religion? No; and that is why Christ is made the test for every man. You see, it is belief in a Person; just giving your verdict for Christ. "Believe on the Lord Jesus Christ, and thou shalt be saved." Friend, do you say, Christ for me? Yes, I do, with all my heart; Christ for me. Well, thank God, you are saved for ever; for God says, "He that heareth My word, and *believeth on* Him Who sent Me, *hath* everlasting life, and *shall not* come into condemnation; but *is passed* from death unto life."

And if your own heart, after that, says to you, or any man or devil or angel says to you, You may not be saved after all, just reply, "The Lord hath laid on Him the iniquity of us all;" and He who bore my sins on the cross in now on the throne of God. Christ is risen; therefore I am not in my sins.

THE WRITING ON THE CROSS.

HAT God has given us by inspired men a perfect revelation of His mind, to be communicated to us by the Holy Ghost, is not believed by many who profess the name of Christ.

A very good Christian brother rather startled me (he is now with his Lord) some years ago by pointing out the discrepancies of the four Evangelists with regard to the writing on the cross, and after careful study I wrote the following to a perplexed enquirer.

"I have been thinking over the conversation that we had about the word of God, and am more and more convinced that our only sure standing ground is on the fact that we have a Divine and certain communication of God's mind, expressed in words that we can understand. You may remember that we were not meeting the arguments of those who deny the truths of the Scripture altogether—the avowed and open infidel—but considering the position of those who believe in some way or other that we have God's ideas, but with no Divine certainty as to language in which it is told to us.

"To the former class, the out-and-out unbeliever, the only thing we can say is what a brother wrote to one of them, 'Do you know that your only chance of escaping hell is, that the Bible is a parcel of lies?' Many of the class are ignorant because they wish so to be, or at least have not taken the trouble to investigate the facts, and for this neglect they will be judged. If a man is not responsible for his *beliefs*, he is responsible for the *attention* he has given to investigate the whole question. But the will is concerned. They hear or read what have been the stock objections of infidels in every age, and bring these forward with great pretensions to originality, as if they had got something new and fresh. They have all been answered centuries ago, but it would not suit their one-sided enlightenment to take the trouble to investigate the *pro* and the *con*. The light having been thus rejected, darkness, as just judgment, must follow. The after-sincerity of the man may be the surest sign and seal of his darkness. God pronounces a solemn word over such as are thus willingly ignorant, a word to which all of us ought to take heed, because true for every rejected light (1 Cor. xiv. 36, 37). In speaking of the reception of Paul's writings as from God, the Holy Ghost thus finishes, 'If any man be ignorant, let him be ignorant.'

"But very many Christians, while shuddering at such audacity, and believing that without a Divine communication there can be no faith, have still very unfixed notions, very vague ideas concerning the fact that we have the very WORD of God now in our hands. They believe God has in some sort of way communicated His mind to man; that we have the substance, the ideas from God. Well, if even this be allowed, if these ideas are searched, we shall find in Scripture its idea of its own inspiration as to its nature and extent. Scripture is its own interpreter, its own proof. I shall tell you what made me receive the Bible as the Word of God. In the first place, it alone gave me a photograph of myself as I knew myself. It told me that every imagination of my heart was only evil continually, and no system of philosophy ever did so. It then showed me the only remedy consistent with God's love, justice, and holiness-substitution and the implantation of a new life; all this was Divine. The Bible alone met my case; I received it. It has evidences, external and internal, I believe, that cannot be answered. I have investigated them for myself. I have found them more than satisfactory, but the great evidence is that which comes to my conscience. The sun needs no rushlight to show that it shines. You can never define *red* to a blind man.

"Scripture is God's Word to man; in it, therefore, we see a perfect union of the Divine and human, as in the incarnate *logos*, very God, very man. Every word is Divine; every word is human. It is not man's word, and it is no mechanical inspiration. It is God using man's faculties to write His Word. What a rest for our weary souls, as they have fluttered for years, like the dove above the waste of waters, with the mournful cry, *What is truth?* to be able to settle on the ark, with conscience at rest, the reason satisfied, and the heart filled, on such a ground. 'All Scripture is given by the inspiration of God [theopneust], and is profitable for doctrine,' etc.

"Could the idea of the certain revelation of God be put in a form of words more absolute than this, spoken by the apostle Paul, 'Which things also we speak, not in the WORDS which man's wisdom teacheth, but which the Holy Ghost teacheth'?

"A great German scholar was discussing some point with an English divine. The Englishman, to support his point, appealed to something Paul had written. The German, in deep thought, said: 'Paul-Paul! oh, yes, I have read some of his letters, but I do not agree with him.'

"The poor wise man, I suppose, had not heard of a Holy Ghost who spoke the WORDS, not Paul. And this is the school of advanced thought, this is the school from which we are to get our theology!

" 'Prophecy came not in old time by the will of man; but holy men of God spake moved by the Holy Ghost' (2 Peter i. 21).

" 'Paul also, according to the wisdom given unto him, hath written unto you, ... which they that are unlearned and unstable wrest, as they do also *the other scriptures*'—which are God-breathed—which are a unity—scriptures which 'cannot be broken.'

" 'God ... *spake* in time past unto the fathers by the prophets' (Heb. i. 1).

"Jesus said to His disciples, 'It is not ye that speak, but the Spirit of your Father which speaketh in you' (Matt. x. 20). And Paul could appeal to the same truth: 'Since ye seek a proof of Christ speaking in me' (2 Cor. xiii. 3).

"John says, 'He that knoweth God heareth us; he that is not of God heareth not us' (1 John iv. 6). It was not Peter, it was not Paul, it was not John, it was God through and by each of these.

" 'He that despiseth, despiseth not man, but God, who hath also given unto us His Holy Spirit' (1 Thess. iv. 8).

" 'For this cause also thank we God without ceasing, because when ye received the Word of God which ye heard of us, ye received it not as the word of men, but as it is in truth, the WORD OF GOD.'

"We have got the Scriptures, the *words* of God. May God teach us to search them more, and know His mind! There are difficulties—difficulties on every hand. How could it be otherwise? Can the finite so easily deal with the Infinite, and comprehend His thoughts? But let us, as beings in the infancy of our existence, conscious of ignorance, patiently sit at the feet of the great Teacher, and many, if not all, will disappear. But let us cling to this great broad principle—that God has spoken, that He has spoken in human language, distinctly, definitely, certainly, unmistakably; that the Scriptures are the words of God. This is the great sheet-anchor to our souls. We may be tossed up and down on the billows, but the anchor holds, and it alone will keep us from drifting without compass, without chart, without pilot, among the rocks, shoals, and quicksands of this dark tempestuous night of doubt, lawlessness, and infidelity. These days of trial need tried material. 'Nothing will stand the fire but asbestos.' That asbestos is the Word of God; for empires will totter, kingdoms crumble, heaven be rolled back as an old garment, earth melt with fire, but the only asbestos, the Word of God, will endure for ever. We are therefore jealous over every sentence, every word, for not an iota of it shall perish. Therefore it is that I said to you, that I had been so happy to see the beautiful harmony, of the writing of the cross, which has been a pet theme in the hands of loose interpreters, to show the fallacy of the position we have indicated above.

"One night, while looking at the passage with some brethren in the Lord, one theory after another was advanced, which did not satisfy some of us. One writer on the Gospel was brought forward, who said, that by this one simple illustration he could show the absurdity of holding that 'every word and phrase of the Scripture is absolutely true.' Others, while going in for the doctrine of 'the WORDS of God,' say, with a strange inconsistency, 'Well, the difference is so slight; but the sense is here.' I cannot understand the logic of such a statement, which says, 'The substance (!) of the story is told in four distinct sets of terms, though not giving the words'—I think this gives up the whole point. All allow the substance is there; but we hold there is more. It is not a story; it is an exact writing. I need hardly notice another theory which twists out the four from the three different languages in which the words were written. Let us now look at the Word itself. You are aware that the harmony of the Gospels is a moral harmony, showing the character of our Lord Jesus Christ under four aspects, not merely supplementary, but divinely, giving the story of the Son of David—the King (Matthew); the Song of God, the servant of man (Mark); the Son of man for this world (Luke); and God manifest in the flesh, very God of very God (John).

"It was asked, while we were looking at the words over the cross, 'If the four daily papers of a city had given as different an account of a certain writing, we should have said, "The substance is in all, but the exact words are not given." ' Now this looks specious; but let us look at it. The four Evangelists are not as four daily papers, to give curious particulars to mankind; nor is there one mind breathing through these four papers, making their diversity a unity, as in the Evangelists. But you could suppose four writers giving a correct history of the life of a man; one describing him as a poet, another as a military tactician, another as a kind benefactor, another his connection with a noble genealogy.

"Now suppose there was written on his tomb this epitaph—'Here lies A— B—, son of C— D—, and father of E— F—. He was a pure and simple poet, a wise and skillful officer, a kind and thoughtful benefactor.' The first historian describing him as a poet, might write, 'On his tombstone were written these words, "He was a pure and simple poet;" ' the second describing the military man, 'On his tombstone were these words—"He was a wise and skillful officer;" ' the third telling his story to the poor he had benefited—'He was a kind and thoughtful benefactor;' and the fourth proving his position from the genealogical tree, would say, 'On his tombstone is written—"He was son of C— D—, and father of E— F—." ' Would any of these by wrong? would they not all give the *words*? There is not this discrepancy among the four accounts we have before us. Of course we must keep in mind that the differences between the four Evangelists on this matter are of the minutest character. If each of them had said that they gave the whole writing on the cross, there would then have been some difficulty; but if you will notice the formulas with which each introduces the writing, you will find the *they are all different*; not one says exactly that he gives just what the other gives. It will not do to turn and say, 'But these *mean* all the same thing—they are just the same.'

"If I were adjusting a microscope, and on looking thought it you saw nothing but a confused haze, and if I then gave the slightest turn to the adjusting-screw, and you were to say, 'You have scarcely touched it,'—look at the object now, and it is in perfect focus. If the difference is very small, the disturbing cause must be very small also. All confess the smallness of the difference between the Evangelists' account; all that we show is that they do not say exactly in words that they give just the same thing. The weight and import of the particular formula remain with the philologist and exegete to discuss; we merely point out the fact. We get the true WORDS, and nothing but the true WORDS, from each; we get ALL the WORDS (at least as many as God wishes us to get) from their united testimony.

"Matthew says it was 'His *accusation* written—
THIS IS JESUS, ... THE KING OF THE JEWS.'

"Mark says, 'The *superscription of His accusation* was written over,
.... THE KING OF THE JEWS.
(the important part of the accusation).

"Luke says, '*A superscription* also was written,
THIS IS ... THE KING OF THE JEWS.'

"John says, 'Pilate wrote a *title*' (he alone puts in Nazareth),
'.. JESUS OF NAZARETH, THE KING OF THE JEWS.'

"Thus the accusation, the superscription, the title, is, 'THIS IS JESUS OF NAZARETH, THE KING OF THE JEWS.' There is the most perfect harmony in seeming diversity. The Spirit alone can show us the beauty. These things are spiritually discerned. We have got greater confidence in the *words* of our blessed Father-God since we saw the perfect unity of mind in all the book."

Matthew, who tells us that the Old Testament Emmanuel (God with us) is now translated into the name Jesus (Jehovah our Saviour)—for none but God could save, and if God condescends to be with us it must be as a Saviour—informs us that the Crucified One is Jesus, and that this accusation written was set up over His head, "THIS IS JESUS THE KING OF THE JEWS." Note carefully that each reports Him as "The King of the Jews."

Mark, who relates to us the servant work of our Lord, says nothing about "Jesus" as the Messiah promised to the fathers, but gives us the "head and front of His offending" to the Jews, not His accusation, but the superscription of His accusation. Gentiles had nothing to do with that, but he tells us that "a superscription was written over Him in letters of Greek, and Latin, and Hebrew, THIS IS THE KING OF THE JEWS."

John, whose writing was about God manifest in the flesh coming to His own kingdom, and His own Jews receiving Him not, and being in the world of which He was Creator, and the men of the world not knowing Him, tells us of the *title* that Pilate wrote.

In no other Evangelist do we read of the despised name, the Nazarene. "Can any good thing come out of Nazareth?" Very God of very God. John's great message was to be branded on His cross of shame with the despised of all despised titles, not as the grand titles of earth which men covet. Thus we have it in full, with the exception of "This is," but in perfect accord with the scope of the Gospel, "Jesus of Nazareth, the King of the Jews." The chief priests of the Jews are reported in this Gospel to have objected to this; but what Pilate wrote, God kept for all time. I would not have dwelt on this matter so fully, had it not been that so honest and faithful a commentator as Dean Alford,[9] has given the power and influence of this great and good name to those who deny plenary inspiration, and takes this theme as a test point. I quote from the sixth edition of his full Commentary (1868), page 20, "*The title over the cross* was written in Greek. According, then, to the verbal inspiration theory, each Evangelist has recorded the *exact words* of the inscription, not the *general sense*, but the *inscription* itself—not a letter less or more." It is very strange that a teacher of such ability should have lost sight of the fact that not one Evangelist says he gave the inscription itself in the general sense.

Surely, apart from inspiration, we must give a man credit for saying what he means, and meaning what he says. If I say to a friend, I went to the top of Ben Nevis,[10] and he was interested only in the locality, I would be perfectly correct. If I said to a

---

[9] Editor's Note: Henry Alford (1810–1871) was an English churchman, theologian, textual critic, scholar, poet, hymnodist, and writer.

[10] Editor's Note: Ben Nevis is the highest mountain in Scotland, the United Kingdom, and the British Isles.

meteorological friend, I went to the top of Ben Nevis and examined the instruments, I am still verbally and absolutely correct. If I said to another doctor friend, I went to the top of Ben Nevis to examine one of the observers who was not in health, I would be still correct. If I told a preacher friend that I went to the top of Ben Nevis to give away some copies of the *British Evangelist*, would not this be correct? and all contained in the one visit. And thus our faith is all the more strengthened when we find false witness against the Scriptures. Not one of the Evangelists says that he gives the whole inscription. What they do profess to give, they give in Divine perfectness.

HIS ACCUSATION.
THE SUPERSCRIPTION OF HIS ACCUSATION.
A SUPERSCRIPTION.
A TITLE.

We are not affirming that we understand all that is meant in these distinctions. We merely state them for study.

THE NAME OF GOD.

"The name of the Lord is a strong tower: the righteous runneth into it, and are safe."—PROVERBS xviii. 10.

THAT name which was written, that He could by no means clear the guilty, is the strong tower to us, into which we run and are safe.

A rock commands the city of Edinburgh, and on the top is a castle, and if you look at that castle from the streets around,—you will see the frowning guns pointing down and commanding every street. If an enemy entered that city, and attempted to attack the garrison, those inside could sweep every street, and woe to the men outside. But walk up the esplanade,[11] cross the drawbridge, climb the steps up to the castle, and then you will find yourself standing by the side of the flag-staff, *inside the guns*; that is where the righteous are in Christ. By nature we see God against us;' we see mount Sinai and hear the Lord's imperative words, "Thou shalt," and "Thou shalt not," and "He that offends in one point is guilty of all," and "He can by no means clear the guilty." Where can the poor sinner stand? But look to Him who came from the Father—the Way, the Truth, and the Life came from the centre of God down to the sinner's place, and in Him we go back to the very centre of God, and find ourselves *inside the guns*. For the very attributes of God that were against us—His righteousness, holiness, justice, truth—are now the very things that are for us, and we are made the very righteousness of God in Christ. God is just; that is the pillow on which the believer lies every night. Not that God is merely loving and merciful; but that God is so

---

[11] Editor's Note: A level open stretch of paved or grassy ground.

righteous, so just, so truthful, so holy, that He will not visit us with the doom He visited on His Son.

> "Payment God will not twice demand—
> First from my bleeding Surety's hand,
> And then again from me."

You may be aware that through Scripture there are different names given to the great God, the Creator of Heaven and Earth, and our Saviour. His *name* is that by which God reveals His personal presence in certain relations to man, His self-manifestations in certain characters, that side of His nature which He is pleased to turn to man.

GOD.

The first, and most comprehensive, is the name *God*. You generally find out a man's theology by the name he uses for God. The name that the mere philosopher uses is *Nature*; he speaks of the laws of nature. We know only of the laws of our God, and "nature" is an idea that these philosophers have introduced to get rid of the great Creator and God. And then you will find others, who do not look so much at nature, who have another name for God: they call Him *Providence*. Go to the unconverted farmer, and ask him why in the spring-time he throws away his grain? It is because he believes in Providence, a providential God, who will look after foods for man and beast. It is the name of God *he* believes in, and he trusts it accordingly. "They that know Thy name will put their trust in Thee;" and it is according as we know the name of God we trust in Him. The philosopher knows that the tides ebb and flow, the sun and moon rise and set; he knows the name *Nature*, and he trusts accordingly. The man that knows *Providence*, and knows no other, trusts accordingly.

But the name we first get revealed to us in Scripture, and the most comprehensive of all names, is the name GOD. If you look into the first chapter of Genesis, you will find this first name, and you find no other name in that chapter. We there see God, the great originating cause of all things—God, the great and glorious One, fashioning and furnishing all things, perfecting all things by the word of His power. You find Him making light spring out of darkness, form out of chaos, and repletion out of the void. Adam was put under responsibility to walk manifesting that power, made in the image of God, with dominion over the creatures; at the fall he lost the *likeness* of God, but the *image* of God he still has. An image has not necessarily likeness; and man stands at the head of all creation, and separated from all creation. Let the philosophers try to bring this to the smallest limit they can, man is still the image of God, with dominion over the creation.

ALMIGHTY.

Secondly, we come to another name, which you will find in the 17th chapter of Genesis. "The Lord appeared to Abraham and said unto him, I am the ALMIGHTY GOD." This is the second circle within the first, telling out a little more of what God is. He is *almighty*. Abraham was to come out before that God, and to walk before Him perfect. He says, "Walk before me, and be thou perfect." As Adam walked in the image of God manifesting God's name, we find that Abraham was to walk manifesting in perfection the attributes in which he was related to God, and especially glorifying the almightiness of God; against hope he believed in hope. One might have said to Abraham, "You play a foolish part." "Nay," he might have replied; "I am manifesting what the Almighty God is." That name was the tower into which Abraham went. In all the difficulties of his path afterwards, we see the almightiness of God manifested through him, the human instrument that God had chosen.

JEHOVAH.

Thirdly, we come to another name brought out more fully, which we find in the 6th chapter of Exodus. "Then the Lord said unto Moses, Now shalt thou see what I will do to Pharaoh: for with a strong hand shall he let them go, and with a strong hand shall he drive them out of his land. And God spake unto Moses, and said, I am JEHOVAH: and I appeared unto Abraham, unto Isaac, and unto

Jacob, by the name of God almighty, but by my name JEHOVAH was I not known to them." This is a new name. He is dealing on the ground of redemption. The word that composed the name Jehovah was known before, but God adopted it as His new relationship name with the children of Israel, whom He was to redeem. He did not assume it until the era of redemption came. We find two explanations of this name in the book of Exodus: this name that is a strong tower, into which the righteous run and are safe. You will find the first explanation of this name that Israel knew in Exod. vi. 6, with these seven "I wills":—

"Wherefore say unto the children of Israel, I am Jehovah.

"And I will *bring you out* from under the burdens of the Egyptians,

"And I will *rid you* out of their bondage,

"And I will *redeem you* with a stretched-out arm, and with great judgments,

"And I will *take you to me* for a people,

"And I will *be to you* a God" [not merely a redemption *from* something, but *to* an object—to God Himself]. "And ye shall know that I am the Lord your God, which bringeth you from under the burdens of the Egyptians.

"And I will *bring you in* unto the land, concerning the which I did swear to give it to Abraham, to Isaac, and to Jacob;

"And I will *give it you* for a heritage. I am Jehovah."

This is the strong name of Jehovah, and it was into this name Moses ran and was safe. By it he brought all the judgments upon Pharaoh; he opened the sea, and he went through all the desert under the shadow of this name Jehovah. So, now, we find that Israel was to walk in the perfect manifestation of that Jehovah-name, for we read in Deuteronomy xviii. 13, "Thou shalt be *perfect* with Jehovah thy God." They were not only to know Jehovah, but they were to manifest His name before the nations and amongst the nations: "Thou shalt be perfect with Jehovah thy God." Thus it was they fought against Amalek, and thus it was they not only prayed for the destruction of the nations, but with the sword accomplished it; and it would have been their sin to have spared one of them, because they were manifesting His name Jehovah.

Let us look at the other aspect of this name, the other half of that name Jehovah. In the sixth chapter of Exodus, we have the part that tells us of His redeeming power; but in the thirty-third chapter we read, "And he (Moses) said, I beseech Thee, show me Thy glory. And He said, I will make all my *goodness* pass before thee, and I will proclaim the name of Jehovah before thee; and will be gracious to whom I will be gracious, and will show mercy on whom I will show mercy"—not merely of redeeming power, but goodness or pardoning love. We find it revealed in the fifth verse of the thirty-fourth chapter. "And Jehovah descended in a cloud, and stood with him there, and proclaimed the *name of Jehovah*. And Jehovah passed by before him"—we shall use that word Jehovah, because there is another word in the Hebrew which means *Lord*, and which might confuse some—"and proclaimed, Jehovah, Jehovah-God, merciful and gracious, long-suffering and abundant in goodness and truth, keeping mercy for thousands, forgiving iniquity, and transgression, and sin, and that will by no means clear the guilty; visiting the iniquity of the fathers upon the children, unto the third and to the fourth generation." You see, the gracious character of Jehovah here manifested is not that of one looking over sin. God can look over nothing; blessed by His name, He can *forgive* anything. All must be brought to the light on the ground of that precious blood of the Crucified but now Risen One, that blood which cleanseth us from all sin. Jehovah is the name all through the wanderings of the children of Israel, and if we search in the Old Testament history, we find that this is the name used all along until Christ came. We find He is

Jehovah Jireh—Jehovah will provide (Gen. xxii. 14);

Jehovah Rophecha—Jehovah that healeth thee (Exod. xv. 26);

Jehovah Nissi—Jehovah my banner, when Israel was fighting with Amalek, for the flesh lusts against the Spirit, and the Spirit against the flesh (Exod. xvii. 15);

Jehovah Shalom—Jehovah send peace (Judges vi. 24);

Jehovah Shammah—Jehovah is there. When Ezekiel was looking at the departing glory, and onward to the coming glory, he saw the city having Jehovah as its light (Ezek. xlviii. 35).

Jehovah Tsidkenu—Jehovah our righteousness (Jer. Xxiii. 6).

Thus we see God bringing out of the secrets of His own heart further and further manifestations of what He is Himself. Is He not a strong tower into which the righteous run and are safe—safe for ever!

THE NAMES ELOHIM AND JEHOVAH, GOD AND LORD.

Many critics, not seeing the wonderfully Divine purpose in the use of "God" and "Lord" in the book of Genesis, have *fancied* and *guessed* that there were two documents, and that "the way in which the two names are used can *only* be due to difference of authorship!" The man who believes he has God's words and Christ's Bible cares little whether there were two documents or two hundred, for to him they are words "Which the Holy Ghost teacheth;" but to say that the use of two names "can only be due to difference of authorship" is the presumption of ignorance. If we have the Word of God, who can say positively to what it can be due unless God the Author informs us? Let us suppose the following as an illustration. A gentleman enters his office and says to a clerk, "sit down. I wish a history of this business to be written out, and write as follows:—'The *master*, finding his business rapidly increasing, gathered his men, and said, We must have a new warehouse, and the *master* drew plans, and the *master* superintended the erection, and when the building was finished the *master* gave a great supper to the men (among whom was his son). And he said to his son, I intend to depart for a foreign land, and you, having had practical experience, are to be manager till I come back; and the *father* gave instructions to the son, and the *father* in the presence of the men gave all authority to the son, and the *father* departed, and the son took his place, and every month the *father* wrote to the son, and the son to the *father*, and the men were very much interested in the travels of their master," and so on with the history.

We have two names used here, "master" and "father." How much would we think of the common sense of the man who said, "The way in which the two names are used can *only* be due to two clerks having been used"?

In Genesis i, we have the name "God," because it is the Creator in the widest display of His wisdom and power. In Genesis ii. we have "Lord God," due to the fact that here we have God in moral relation to His creature and creation. Just as in the above illustration we had "master" with the men and "father" with the son, se we have here "Creator" (God) with the creation, and "Creator Master" (Lord God) with His created servant.

Turn up a few passages where the names are together. Genesis vii. 16, "They that went in, went in male and female of all flesh, as *God* had commanded him: and *the Lord* shut him in." What can be more mechanical and contemptible than the double document idea here? What can be more appropriate and instructive than to see Divine design in the change? The *God* of creation commanded lion and lamb to come to the ark when Noah's voice would have been powerless, but the *Lord*, to whom Noah was responsible, for whom Noah wrought, and to whom Noah was especially related as contrasted with creation, this *Lord* looked after him and shut him in.

1 Sam. xvii. 47: David was to slay Goliath "that all the earth may know that there is *a God* in Israel" (the Creator of all the earth alone could be known by the heathen in His power, but Israel had to learn more), "and all this assembly shall know that *the Lord* saveth not with sword and spear."

2 Chron. xviii. 31: "Jehoshaphat cried out, and the *Lord* helped *him*, and *God* moved *them* to depart." The Creator was only *God* to the heathen, He was in addition to this, *Lord* in Israel (we retain the English names, as we write for those who have no pretensions to Hebrew), so the *Lord* helped Jehoshaphat and *God* moved the enemy. The boy spoke to his father, and his father, the master, gave commandment to the servants. Can we use such language, and may God not be allowed to do it without the necessity of employing two documents?

We quite grant that there *may have been* any number of traditions, documents, and direct statements from God. The first chapter necessarily is a pure and simple revelation from God without any man's aid, documentary or traditional. But to say there *must have been* two documents we consider to manifest a mere superficial acquaintance with the words of the book, and a lamentable exhibition of ignorance as to what is in it.

Psalm vi. 9 says, "They that know Thy name will put their trust in Thee," and a scriptural apprehension of what is in the *name* will give the only key to the propriety and purpose of its use.

"He that dwelleth in the secret place of *the Most High* shall abide under the shadow of *the Almighty*. I will say of *Jehovah*, He is my refuge and my fortress: my *God*, in Him will I trust."

But as we have been coming into circle after circle of this great name, God, the Creator—God, the Almighty—Jehovah, the I Am, we have still another name; but it was not revealed by Adam, it was not revealed by Abraham, nor by Moses. He kept it for Himself to reveal; so He says in the 22nd Psalm, "I will declare *Thy name* unto my brethren." He is promising us something more than God. He is promising us something more than Almighty. He is promising us something more than Jehovah. "I have another name to reveal, and I will do it myself." This is the promise; and the fulfilment of it you find in John xx. 17: "Jesus saith unto her, Touch me not; for I am not yet ascended to my

FATHER.

But go to my brethren, and say unto them, I ascend unto my Father, and *your Father*; and to my God, and your God." "I ascend unto my Father," that is the eternal relationship; but think of this, "and *your* Father." That is a name we have no right to claim by nature. We can all call Him *God*, and ought to, as His creatures, but Father is only known in resurrection. The great opposition to the glorious truth of God now is, that men are taught that they have a universal Father, ready to forgive and pardon all their sin, and so merciful and loving, that He can never think of damning any one. Look at Calvary's cross, see Him who hangs there, hear His cry, "My God, my God, why hast Thou forsaken me?" It is at Calvary we get the truth of that great name, at Calvary we know what it cost God. It is there that we get the awful truth of condemnation. The God-man had to cry, "If it be possible let this cup pass from me." Can God spare any when HE was not spared? If it were possible, would not God have let Him go free who had no sin of His own?

"How shall we escape if we neglect so great salvation?" Calvary settles all arguments. Let us keep close to Calvary.

After Calvary He says, "My Father"—the eternal relationship—and "your Father." And He gives us the secret of how we get into this relationship. Until He had come to the furthest limit of creation, yea, until He was made sin for us, and was on the cross, forsaken by God, cast out from heaven and earth, He never had called His Father, God; but now in that hour of darkness, in agony He cries, "My God, my God, why hast Thou forsaken me?" "My God" was the word He took in that suffering, and substitution, and atonement. "My *God*," *we* should have cried for ever in an eternal hell. He took our creature relation, and said, "My God," that *we* might be able to say, "*Our Father*." "I ascend unto my Father, and your Father; and to my God, and your God." Has He not revealed the name? Yes. He it was who was with the Father from all eternity. In this circle of names we have go to the inner circle now, not the most *comprehensive* but the most *intensive*; the most comprehensive is God, the most intensive is *Father*. Circle after circle He passes in His outward journey to seek us the lost ones, for He came form the Father, but not only from the Father, but the innermost circle of that circle, for He came from "the bosom of the Father;" and He has come down with all His love to the sinner's place, that He might call this Father God, that He might never rest until He had set us down in His retracing journey, with a thief as His first trophy, into the very bosom of the Father.

> "The love wherewith He loves the Son,
> Such is His love to me."

That is our place for ever. We can go no more out; we are in the bosom of the Father for ever.

Is it not remarkable that two of the greatest revelations that ever came from heaven to earth were entrusted not to great scholars, or even great theologians, but to two humble women? At Sychar's well[12]—"I that speak unto thee am He"—was told to a poor

---

[12] Editor's Note: Jacob's Well, also known as Jacob's Fountain or the Well of Sychar, is a **Christian holy site** located in the West Bank.

weeping penitent the great fact of the advent of the Messias and with it, to her ear alone, that remarkable revelation of the sweeping away of Judaism, that "God is a Spirit, and they that worship Him must worship Him in spirit and in truth." The other was in resurrection to Mary. Even Peter and John had rushed off, and were thus deprived of being the bearers of the tidings of an opened heaven, and 'I ascend to My Father and your Father, to My God and your God," was again given to a weeping woman. The moral condition of these helpless vessels which He chose shows the line that we must go on if we are to get into the mind of God concerning His truth. Leave God out, and then we have nothing but a human compilation; bring Him in, and we have a Divine book, perfect in every part, to be interpreted on Divine principles, as containing Divine facts, and manifesting Divine purposes.

As the God of Adam, He is the God of Creation; as the God of Abraham, He is the Almighty; as the God of Israel, He is Jehovah; but as the God and Father of our Lord Jesus Christ, He is our God and Father in Him.

To each of these names there is a *perfection* corresponding. Matt. v. 43 is left for us who were to be His believing ones, when He went away: "Ye have heard that it hath been said, Thou shalt love thy neighbor, and hate thine enemy. But I say unto you, Love your enemies, bless them that curse you, do good to them that hate you, and pray for them that despitefully use you and persecute you: that ye *may be* the children of your Father which is in heaven; for He maketh His sun to rise on the evil and on the good, and sendeth rain on the just and on the unjust. Be ye therefore *perfect*, even as your *Father* which is in heaven is perfect." This is not acquirement; it is manifestation. You never could reach up to be sons; but now that you are sons, you are called to manifest what the Son was manifesting when He was here in a world that rejected Him. And we are to manifest Him, and so "ye shall be the children of your Father which is in heaven." For "if ye love them which love you, what reward have ye? do not even the publicans the same? And if ye salute your brethren only, what do ye more than others? do not even the publicans so? Be ye therefore perfect, even as your Father which is in heaven is perfect."

Look at that beautiful word, "perfect." Some people dream of reaching a state of sinless perfection here—speak of reaching *it* by prayer, or faith, or some other road. This undefined *it* is nowhere in Scripture. Such only show their ignorance of how *perfect* is used in Scripture. God has definitely fixed His word against such a dangerous doctrine in these words: "If we (who are walking in the light, and, in the former verse, have been cleansed from all sin) say that we have no sin, we deceive ourselves" (1 John i. 9), thus most conclusively proving that being cleansed from sin is not cleansed from the existence of sin within, as many would attempt to teach. Perfection is manifesting on earth what God has revealed to us from heaven, according to the relationship into which God has called us, and which He wishes men to know through us. Thus we see each is called to manifest according to what is revealed.

Adam perfect before God (Gen. ii. 19).

Abraham perfect before the Almighty (Gen. xvii. 1).

Israel perfect before Jehovah (Deut. xviii. 13).

Saints now perfect before the Father (Matt. v. 48).

Job is called perfect by God; and what do we find? The man that God calls perfect abhors himself. What a glorious lesson for us, that as Christ is, so are we! yet we abhor ourselves. We know little of perfection in Christ if we are not more and more, day by day, abhorring ourselves. "Be ye therefore perfect," not as the Almighty, not as Jehovah, but, "Be ye therefore perfect, even as your *Father* which is in heaven is perfect." We are to be manifesting perfect grace coming out of the Father's heart to a world of sinners, telling out the love He has to a poor lost world—doing good to them that hate us, walking in His steps, and not bearing the character of loving our friends and hating our enemies; but "love your enemies, bless them that curse you, do good to them that hate you, and pray for them which despitefully use you and persecute you."

Thus we find that the character even of the little babes in Christ is, "they have known the Father," and are manifesting the perfect grace of the Father down here. But we find in 2 Corinthians, chap. vi., that we have lost nothing in comprehensiveness while gaining in intensity; we have reached the very bosom of the Father; and all that is His is ours. "What agreement hath the temple of God with idols? For ye are the temple of the living God; as God hath said, I will dwell in them and walk in them; and I will be their *God*, and they shall be my people. Wherefore, come out from among them, and be ye separate, saith the Lord, and touch not the unclean thing; and I will receive you, and will be a *Father* unto you, and ye shall be my sons and daughters, saith *Jehovah the Almighty*." We have God, Jehovah, and the Almighty, and here is our Father; for He is the God and Father of our Lord Jesus Christ. "They that know Thy name will put their trust in Thee." It is as the God and Father of our Lord Jesus Christ we now trust Him, and He is our God and Father in Him; and let us never dissociate these two names, God and Father, which he bears to us.

Because He is the *God* of our Lord Jesus Christ, we stand as it were at the top of the highest height of all His glory, far above all principalities and powers. We look down and say, What has God wrought! He has brought poor sinners from the dunghill to the throne. Some seem inclined to quarrel with God because they are born sinners. Friend, it is no misfortune to be born a sinner, for if we had not been born sinners we could never have had the hope of being seated on the throne, even as He is on His Father's throne. The misfortune is, that "light is come into the world, and men loved darkness rather than light, because their deeds were evil." There is a Saviour for *every* sinner, but He had to say, when amongst sinners, "Ye *will* not come to Me that ye might have life." We who have come to Him are beyond angels and beyond all creation, because we are identified with the lost sinner's Saviour, and in Him stand at the very height of the glory of God.

Because He is the *Father* of our Lord Jesus Christ, we look upward into an infinity and eternity of love—a love that is all for us—a love that is fed by itself—a love that ever in its activities is being exercised for our needs, pouring out its rivers on the most arid hearts, taking the greatest pains and care with the unworthy—a love all Divine, all unearthly—a love that is before and above all the glory—a love that planned the glory for us, and prepared us for the glory—a love that was manifested by the glory; as Jesus says—"The glory thou gavest me I have given them"—for what purpose?—"that the world may believe that Thou hast loved them, as Thou hast loved Me"—a love that has saved us, borne with us, cleanses us, and will present us spotless in that glory—a love that will be our study for ever—a love that passeth knowledge, an ocean without a bottom and without a shore.

EMMANUEL-JESUS.

"THE angel of the Lord appeared unto him in a dream, saying, Joseph...thou shalt call His name Jesus, for He shall save His people from their sins. Now all this was done that it might be fulfilled which was spoken of the Lord by the prophet, saying, ...They shall call His name Emmanuel, which being interpreted is, God with us" (Matt. i. 20-23).

If we look at this prophecy and this fulfilment, we find two most important truths.

1st. If we are to have a Saviour, that Saviour must be God.

2nd. If God is to be with us, it must be as our Saviour.

1st. If we are to have a Saviour, He must be God. Jesus came to His own—He came to save His own. This refers primarily to the Jews, who are said to be Jehovah's own, and to belong to none others; this shows that Jesus is Jehovah. But further, this calling of the Son of Mary Jesus, Saviour, is the fulfilling of the text, "God with us." If heaven had been searched from end to end, no angel could have saved a lost sinner. If heaven had been emptied, and every intelligent being that God had created had been offered up as a sacrifice to God no sinner could have been saved.

If, added to this, all the human race and all the lost angels, every creature existing, as created by God in heaven, earth, and hell, had been offered up on one tremendous sacrificial altar, no sin would have been blotted out. The most holy and perfect creature, or the greatest number of creatures, could never satisfy Divine justice as to the atonement of one sin, simply because when in the service of God any creature is called upon by God to give up his life, he merely does his duty, merely gives God back what he received. He has nothing over to atone for sin.

None but "God with us" could become "Jesus our Saviour." The uncreated all-creating One, in whom is life, could become sin, could lay down His life, could give Himself for our sins, could be the Saviour of sinners.

2nd. If God is to be with us, He must be with us as a Saviour. He is with angels, as they do His will in angelic purity, as their Creator and Master. He walked with Adam in innocence in the intimacy of the garden, but all this is lost. He cannot come now to train and teach us. Cain made this fatal mistake. He thought he was on the Eden terms with God. Nicodemus made this mistake, leaving out of count the Son of man lifted up; he would have God with him as a Teacher. Not so. He must be a Saviour, or He cannot be "with men."

As that word "God with us" comes out from the throne of God, and penetrates through the thick vapour of sin that surrounds this earth, it becomes changed into Jesus. As the prophecy rolls onward to its accomplishment, the angel of Jehovah gives the necessary translation of "God with us." Its translation, not into Hebrew, or Greek, or Latin, or English, or any other Babel tongue, but into the language of the sinner's need, let that sinner be barbarian, Scythian, bond or free, black or white, "God with us," when translated into the language of need, becomes "Jesus—Saviour from sins."

And how truly we find Him coming to the sinner's place, in order that He might be the sinner's Saviour! Infidelity may stumble at the genealogy of Matthew i. The needy sinner reads it with joyful heart, as there he reads that God became one of us that He might become one with us, and so might become Jesus our Saviour. When man writes his genealogy, he tries to bring in the great names and leave out the unworthy. If he could only get some of the blood-royal, or the blood of the nobles, to appear in his genealogical tree, he would be exceedingly pleased. The needy sinner watches with wondrous interest what God has left out and what God has added to that list of names.

God has intentionally left out the names of three kings—Ahaziah, Joash, and Amaziah—from the list. He has added three that did not require to appear—Tamar, Rahab, and the wife of Urias. Read their histories in the Old Testament, and then adore His sovereign grace. To say no more about them, though much might be said, they were all Canaanites, belonging to the cursed son of Ham, who were commanded to be extirpated[13] root and branch. Ruth is another who is added. She was a Moabitess, and the Ammonite and Moabite were not to come into the congregation of God for ever.

> "Sovereign grace o'er sin abounding,
> Who its length or depth can tell?
> 'Tis a deep that knows no sounding."

Thus our Saviour is God, and God is with us as Saviour—really a Man, really the seed of the woman—really one with the sinner—He who knew no sin made sin for us. Because He is one with us He can come under sin, can be made sin, can bear the penalty of sin, can die for sin; because He is God He can bear our sins, He can put away sin, He can bear its doom, He can destroy him that had the power of death. He has risen; and this is Emmanuel-Jesus, God with us—our Saviour. Reader, none can save you but God. God can treat with you on no ground until you have accepted Him as your Saviour. Modern rationalism easily gets away from this by passing over the terrible factor "sin." Modern ritualism brings religion to God, while God is waiting to be "with us" as Jesus the Saviour.

---

[13] Editor's Note: To destroy completely, to pull up by the root.

HIS NAME.

TO continue the subject of the different names of our Lord, we here give a careful investigation of Scripture in as few words as possible. It is of great importance to study all Scripture in such a way as to derive our doctrines from Scripture, and not make Scripture fit into our doctrines.

In our following study we have examined fifteen names, titles, and combinations used concerning our LORD JESUS CHRIST. There are many others, such as Son of Man, Son of God, King of kings, etc., which open up quite a different line of things.

On pages 105 and 106 we give a table which, in itself, is very instructive. We give the number of occurrences of each name before and after Pentecost, as found in the New Testament.

What strikes us at the first glance is the frequency of the simple name "JESUS" before Pentecost, and its rare occurrence after Pentecost, and that *"The Lord Jesus Christ"* is *never* mentioned before Pentecost, and in one form or another is used 99 times after Pentecost. Take in connection with this one of the first Pentecostal utterances (Acts ii. 36), "God hath made that same Jesus whom ye have crucified both Lord and Christ."

Book.	Jesus.	Christ.	Lord.	Jesus Christ.	Christ Jesus.
MATTHEW	169	14	51	2	...
MARK	92	6	17	1	...
LUKE	97	12	85	...	...
JOHN	252	19	43	2	...
(After Pentecost)					
THE ACTS	30	14	92	10	1
ROMANS	2	36	26	13	6
1 CORINTHIANS	2	47	53	6	3
2 CORINTHIANS	5	38	21	6	...
GALATIANS	...	23	2	8	5
EPHESIANS	1	27	17	5	6
PHILIPPIANS	1	18	10	9	8
COLOSSIANS	...	19	8	1	2
1 THESSALONIANS	3	3	13	...	2
2 THESSALONIANS	...	2	10	...	...
1 TIMOTHY	...	2	3	3	5
2 TIMOTHY	...	1	14	3	7
TITUS	...	...	...	3	...
PHILEMON	...	1	3	2	2
HEBREWS	8	9	16	3	1
JAMES	...	...	12	...	...
1 PETER	...	10	5	9	2
2 PETER	...	...	10	2	...
1 JOHN	4	2	...	8	...
2 JOHN	...	2	...	1	...
3 JOHN	...	...	...	...	...
JUDE	...	...	3	2	...
REVELATION	6	4	8	6	...
AFTER PENTECOST	62	260	326	102	50
BEFORE ,,	614	51	196	5	0
IN ALL	676	311	522	107	50

Lord Jesus.	Lord Christ.	Jesus Our Lord.	Christ The Lord.	Lord Jesus Christ.	Christ Jesus Our Lord.	Jesus Christ Our Lord.	Christ Jesus The Lord.	Christ Jesus My Lord.	Lord And Saviour Jesus Christ.
1			1						
15				5					
2		1		9		4			
3				10	1	2			
3				5			1		
1				3					
1				7	1				
1				2				1	
1	1			2			1		
3				9					
1				11					
				4	1	1			
				2	1				
				1					
1				2					
1									
				2					
		1		3					3
				1					
				3					
1.				1					
34	1	2	0	82	4	7	2	1	3
1	0	0	1	0	0	0	0	0	0
35	1	2	1	82	4	7	2	1	3

It will be beyond our power to go over every passage. We shall therefore confine ourselves to the exceptional cases.

1. Jesus occurs 614 times as the name of the Babe from Bethlehem, the Man from Nazareth, the Sufferer of Golgotha. The 62 times after Pentecost—the proclamation of his Lordship—are thus derived:—

In the Acts of the Apostles it is used 30 times after Pentecost, which we might have expected, thus nearly taking up half the number, as showing to the Jew that Jesus was the Messias promised to the fathers.

"Jesus of Nazareth...ye have taken, and by wicked hands have crucified and slain" (Acts ii. 22).

"This Jesus hath God raised up" (ii. 32).

"God hath made that same Jesus whom ye have crucified both Lord and Christ" (ii. 36).

"The God of Abraham hath glorified His Son Jesus" (iii. 13).

"God having raised up His Son Jesus, sent Him to bless you" (iii. 26).

"The Sadducees being grieved that they taught the people, and preached through Jesus the resurrection from the dead" (iv. 2).

"They took knowledge of them that they had been with Jesus" (iv. 13).

"Commanded them not to speak at all, nor teach in the name of Jesus" (iv. 18).

"Against Thy holy Child Jesus, whom Thou hast anointed" (iv. 27).

"The God of our fathers raised up Jesus, whom ye slew and hanged on a tree" (v. 30).

"They commanded that they should not speak in the name of Jesus" (v. 40).

"We have heard him say that this Jesus of Nazareth shall destroy this place" (vi. 14).

"Stephen saw the glory of God, and Jesus standing on the right hand of God" (vii. 55).

"Philip preached unto him (the eunuch) Jesus" (viii. 35).

"The Lord said (to Saul), I am Jesus, whom thou persecutest" (ix. 5).

"He (Paul) had preached boldly at Damascus in the name of Jesus" (ix. 27).

"Peter said, God anointed Jesus of Nazareth with the Holy ghost" (x. 38).

"Paul said, Of this man's (David) seed hath God, according to promise, raised unto Israel a Saviour, Jesus" (xiii. 23).

"He hath raised up Jesus again" (xiii. 33).

"This Jesus, whom I (Paul) preach unto you, is Christ" (xvii. 3).

"There is another King, one Jesus" (xvii. 7).

"He preached unto them Jesus and the resurrection" (xvii. 18).

"Silas and Timotheus testified to the Jews that Jesus was Christ" (xviii. 5).

"Certain of the vagabond Jews, exorcists took upon them to call over them which had evil spirits the name of the Lord Jesus, saying, We adjure you by Jesus, whom Paul preacheth" (xix. 13).

"The evil spirit answered and said, Jesus I know, and Paul I know, but who are ye?" (xix. 15).

"He said unto me, I am Jesus of Nazareth, whom thou persecutest" (xxii. 18).

"One Jesus, who was dead, whom Paul affirmed to be alive" (xxv. 19).

"Contrary to the name of Jesus of Nazareth" (xxvi. 9).

"He said, I am Jesus, whom thou persecutest" (xxvi. 15).

"Persuading them concerning Jesus" (xxviii. 23).

In Romans it is used twice—

"That He might be just, and the Justifier of him who believeth in Jesus" (iii. 26).

"The Spirit of Him who raised up Jesus from the dead" (viii. 11).

In 1 Corinthians twice in the verse xii. 3—

"No man speaking by the Spirit of God calleth Jesus accursed, and that no man can say that Jesus is Lord but by the Holy Ghost."

In 2 Corinthians five times: —

"Ourselves your servants for Jesus' sake" (iv. 5).

"That the life also of Jesus might be made manifest in our body. For we which live are always delivered unto death for Jesus' sake, that the life also of Jesus might be made manifest in our mortal body" (iv. 10, 11).

"He who raised up the Lord Jesus shall raise up us also by Jesus" (iv. 14).

In Ephesians once, "As the truth is in Jesus" (iv. 21).

In Philippians once, "At the name of Jesus every knee should bow" (ii. 10).

In 1 Thessalonians it appears three times—

"Jesus, who delivered us from the wrath to come" (i. 10).

"If we believe that Jesus died and rose again, even so them also who sleep in Jesus will God bring with Him" (iv. 14).

In Hebrews it appears eight times—

"We see not yet all things put under him, but we see Jesus, who was made a little lower than the angels" (ii. 9).

"Seeing then that we have a great High-priest that is passed unto the heavens, Jesus the Son of God, let us hold fast our profession" (iv. 14).

"Whither the Forerunner is for us entered, even Jesus" (vi. 20).

"By so much was Jesus made a Surety of a better testament" (vii. 22).

"Having boldness to enter into the holiest by the blood of Jesus" (x. 19)

"Looking unto Jesus, the Author and Finisher of faith" (xii. 2).

"Ye are come…to Jesus, the Mediator of the new covenant" (xii. 24).

"Jesus, that He might sanctify the people with His own blood, suffered without the gate" (xiii. 12).

In 1 John we find four mentions of "Jesus"—

"Who is a liar—but he that denieth that Jesus is the Christ?" (ii. 22).

"Whosoever shall confess that Jesus is the Son of God, God dwelleth in Him" (iv. 15).

"Whosoever believeth that Jesus is the Christ is born of God" (v. 1).

"Who is he that overcometh the world but he that believeth that Jesus is the Son of God?" (v. 5).

In Revelation it is used six times—

"Here are they that keep the commandments of God and the faith of Jesus" (xiv. 12).

"The blood of the martyrs of Jesus" (xvii. 6).

"I am thy fellow-servant and of thy brethren that have the testimony of Jesus: worship God: for the testimony of Jesus is the spirit of prophecy" (xix. 10).

"The souls of them that were beheaded for the witness of Jesus" (xx. 4).

"I Jesus have sent mine angel to testify unto you these things in the churches" (xxii. 16).

In Galatians, Colossians, 2 Thessalonians, 1 Timothy, 2 Timothy, Titus, Philemon, James, 1 Peter, 2 Peter, 2 John, 3 John, Jude, the name "Jesus" never appears alone.

From the consideration of these names, and the time at which they were used, we may gather that the names most in accordance with Scripture, most commonly used after Pentecost, and therefore most suitable for us who live in these days, are either— "Christ," "the Lord," "Jesus Christ," or "the Lord Jesus Christ."

"MY NAME'S SAKE."

IMMEDIATELY after our Lord, in teaching His disciples how to pray, revealed to them their position as children, though still far from home, and thus warranted to address His Father as their Father, and say, "Our Father who art in Heaven," He instructed them to add, "Hallowed by Thy name." We thus join in worship with all the loyal universe of God, animate and inanimate.

"Praise ye Him all His ANGELS. Praise ye Him, all His hosts. Praise ye Him, sun and moon: praise Him, all ye stars of light.

"Praise ye Him, ye HEAVEN of heavens, and ye waters that be above the heavens. Let them praise the name of the Lord.

"Praise the Lord from the EARTH, ye dragons, and all deeps: fire and hail, snow and vapours; stormy winds, fulfilling His word; mountains and all hills; fruitful trees and all cedars; beasts and all cattle; creeping things and flying fowl: kings of the earth, and all people; princes, and all judges of the earth: both young men and maidens; old men and children: let them praise the name of the Lord; for His name alone is excellent; His glory is above the earth and heaven…Let everything that hath breath praise the Lord. Praise ye the Lord."

While we are loving sons, we are devout worshippers, and take our stand beside the adoring living ones, who rest not day and night, saying, "Holy, holy, holy, Lord God Almighty, who was, and is, and is to come;" and falling down before Him that sits on the throne, we worship Him that liveth for ever and ever, and cast our crowns before the throne, saying, "Thou art worthy, O Lord, to receive glory and honour, and power; for Thou hast created all things, and for Thy pleasure they are and were created." And deeper still does our worship reach as we enter into the hall of redemption, for we can sing a new song, saying, "Thou art worthy to take the book, and to open the seals thereof; for Thou wast slain, and hast redeemed us to God by Thy blood, out of every kindred, and tongue, and people, and nation, and hast made us unto our God kings and priests; and we shall reign on the earth." And every creature which is in heaven, and on the earth, and under the earth, and such as are in the sea, in millennial glory will sing, "Blessing, and honour, and glory, and power, be unto Him that sitteth upon the throne for ever and ever."

"Hallowed be Thy name!" The name of the Lord is a strong tower. The righteous run into it, and are safe. What is in a name? The revelation of the unrevealed to darkened man; the photograph of the Eternal sent into time; earth's miniature of heaven's glory. While the Uncreated One has revealed Himself under many names, He has "in these last days spoken unto us by His Son, whom He hath appointed Heir of all things; by whom also He made the worlds, being the brightness of His glory, and the express image of His person." Only in Christ can we read the true name of God. We purpose to draw the attention of our readers to a few leading lines of study connected with "His name," and its bearing on us.

1. *Forgiveness.*—1 John ii. 12, "I write unto you, little children, because your sins are forgiven you for *His name's sake*." The door of admission now for every child of Adam into the place of childhood with the Father is the door of forgiveness. Education, moral culture, reformation, sanctification are all taught inside, but the only door is forgiveness. That door has not been opened by our prayers, our tears, our groans, our works, or our feeling, but by His own hand, and for His name's sake. We did not draw to Him till He came to us. The debt was paid on Calvary's Cross; the Resurrection is the divinely-signed receipt for the abolished debt. "His name's sake" is the blank cheque handed down from and signed by God Himself to every sin-burdened soul, in which he can insert his own iniquity, transgression, and sin. What is the value of a cheque on a bank? In itself only the value of the paper and the penny stamp upon it. But let a name be attached to it, and it then has all the value of the full resources of the one who has signed it. All heaven's resources are opened to the sinner accepting this Divine cheque.

Are the sins like scarlet? Is heaven not now the resting-place of Him whose blood can make the foulest clean, and for whose name's sake they shall be white as snow? Are they red like crimson, the damning colour of the hands of the murderer, red with the blood of a spotless victim? They shall be as wool, for forgiveness was preached first to Jerusalem murderers of the Prince of Life. Does the black indictment of Isaiah xliii. 23, 24, culminate in "Thou hast made me to serve with thy sins; thou hast wearied me with thine iniquities"? Are the resources of heaven available for this? Listen to the words of the God of truth as He proclaims free pardon to the most ungrateful of sinners: "I, even I, am He that blotteth out thy transgressions, for *Mine own sake*, and will not remember thy sins."

Mark, it is not merely out of pity for us, far less on account of any external activity, self-righteous agility, or internal emotion on our part, but for *His own sake*. Glorious foundation; adamantine,[14] everlasting, immovable rock on which we build. In Him "we have redemption through His blood, the forgiveness of sins, according to the riches of His grace."

2. *Guidance.*—Psalm xxiii. 3, "He restoreth my soul: He leadeth me in the paths of righteousness for *His name's sake*." The justified man needs daily forgiveness. The quickened soul needs to be restored. The restored soul needs to be led. All this has been anticipated, and all has been met, because all is linked with His name, and "His name shall endure for ever: His name shall be continued as long as the sun." All within and around us is in constant change. Frames, feelings, fancies, tears, prayers, resolution, faith, hope, love, all have their ebbs and flows, but His name is the same yesterday, to-day, and for ever.

Has His blood been once presented at the throne for us, and accepted by us for justification before that throne? It is of continued and unceasing efficacy, and thus the blood of Jesus Christ is cleansing us (at every breath we breathe) from all sin. Am I prone to wander, prone to make mistakes, prone to follow the fleshly desires, prone to trip and fall into the mire? He restoreth my soul.

---

[14] Editor's Note: Made of or having the quality of being unshakeable. Adamant was a stone (such as a diamond) formerly believed to be of impenetrable hardness.

Would it be a disgrace for me to dishonor my Saviour Redeemer, and cast a blot on that name I bear? He leadeth me in the paths of righteousness for His name's sake. His honour is compromised, and He is my Guardian Redeemer. He upholdeth my steps, because His name is in them. On my eagle's wings He has committed to me His name. In my unwearied running He has given me His name to carry. In mine unfainting walk His name supports me. In the day of opposition, in my single-handed combat, when, having done all, I am now to stand, His name is shield, sword, and helmet unto me; and in lying down in His green pastures, it is His name which is my food. No turn of the way but is known to Him. Let him that nameth the name of Christ depart from all iniquity. He leadeth me for His name's sake.

3. *Communion.*—Matt. xviii. 20, "Where two or three are gathered together *in My name*, there am I in the midst of them." The forgiven and restored sinner is not condemned to tread a solitary path, even though it lies through the wilderness. The heaven-blessed soul is not called to partake of his joys alone. He has even in the desert a fellowship of God with fellow-sinners, saved by the same sovereign grace. He is to get sympathy from, and to have sympathy with others. Their numbers may be very small—only two or three—but the communion is very real. He requires no elaborate system of regulations or code of rules to claim this Divine communion on earth. "His name" is enough. The most elaborate and costly building that an ordinary man may have built is only the grand mansion or castle of Mr. Greatpurse; but a lowly cottage in which Her Majesty resides becomes a palace. The most gorgeously architectured building without God is a mere mass of building material. But His name with His first disciples at Jerusalem turned an upper ordinary family room into a heavenly temple, a Divine palace.

The most eloquent preaching is but pleasing talk springing from human brains if "His name" is not its burden. The poorest elocutionist brimful of his name brings all heaven before the eyes of those who have the spiritual faculty of seeing. The most elaborate prayers may be but words of fancy, feeling, or education; but "His name," breathed with stammering tongue and from groaning heart, will open the windows of heaven, sending down blessings, that we have not room enough to receive. Magnificent music, splendid instruments, thoroughly trained singers, without "His name" as the centre of all their praise, may command the applause of the ear and reach the rafters of the building, but they have nothing pleasing to the ear of God; but in His name we offer the sacrifice of praise continually, that is, the fruit of our lips, giving thanks to His name. Let us exalt *His name* TOGETHER.

4. *Activity.*—3 John 7, "For His name's sake they went forth, taking nothing of the Gentiles." Accepted according to the Victim's blood inside the veil, we are rejected with the Victim's flesh outside the camp. Our happy communion leads us to our living activity, dependent entirely on His name, independent of all the nations on the earth, their favours or frowns, their support or spite, their patronage or persecution. There is a fellowship through His name in this Divine activity on the earth. There is a giving and receiving. There is the Joshua wielding the sword, and the Moses on the hill-top with arms uplifted and arms upheld by Aaron and Hur.

"Beloved, thou doest faithfully whatsoever thou doest to the brethren, and to strangers, who have borne witness of thy love before the Church; whom, if thou bring forward on their journey after a godly sort, thou shalt do well; because that for His name's sake they went forth, taking nothing of the Gentiles. We, therefore, ought to receive such, that we might be fellow-helpers to the truth." This was written by an Apostle who knew much of His name, who in his younger days had lain on His bosom, and knew what it was to be independent of men, nature, or the world, and now in his old age puts himself alongside of the younger Gaius of the well-beloved, encouraging him that "we might be fellow helpers to the truth." The older and more experienced saint wrote this cheering word to the younger.

Flattery is abominable, but cheering words to solitary labourers in the activity of their mission for His name are as water on the dry desert. In works of faith, labours of love and patience of hope, we are all prone to get disheartened. "His name" of good cheer warms us up again. So many mistakes, difficulties, worries, and disappointments lie in the path of the man who is endeavouring to live for His name alone, that there is not a Christian but occasionally needs a word of God-cheer to support him and throw him on His name. Suspicious, insinuations, cold-shouldering, want of sympathy, malicious words, silent ignoring, are common enough. Let us imitate the more excellent way of John the aged, drawing close to his hundredth year, that we may be fellow-helpers to the truth.

5. *Testimony.*—Acts ii. 21, "Whosoever shall call on *the name* of the Lord shall be saved." "The Lord said unto him (Ananias), Go thy way, for he (Paul) is a chosen vessel unto Me to bear *My name* before the Gentiles, and kings, and the children of Israel" (Acts ix. 15).

Peter was the Apostle to the circumcision, and he had to begin his testimony at Jerusalem, to be extended to Judæa, Samaria, and thence unto the uttermost part of the earth. Paul, on the other hand, was the Apostle to the Gentiles, and he was to testify inwards towards the children of Israel. But the subject of each was the same. They were not left to choose their text. "The name of the Lord" was the salvation preached by Peter, the keynote of his testimony. "My name" was what Paul was to bear before Gentiles, kings, and Israel's children. Arts and sciences, politics and philosophy, earth's enactments or human cultus, were all secondary. "His name" was emblazoned on their banner, and under that flag they had the royal authority of Heaven to bear the testimony to every creature.

We can sue for sufferance when we wish men to listen to our opinions, ideas, or thoughts, but with all the calm majesty and full Divine authority of our message, we can carry the standard that He gives us from palace to hovel, from frozen iceberg to coral strand, to barbarian, Scythian, black or white, bond or free, Jew or Gentile, and looking every responsible fellow-being steadfastly in the face, can say on Heaven's authority, "If *thou* shalt confess with *thy* mouth the Lord Jesus, and shalt believe in *thine* heart that God hath raised Him from the dead, *thou* shalt be saved.

6. *Shame.*—Acts v. 41, "And they departed from the presence of the council, rejoicing that they were counted worthy to suffer shame for *His name's sake.*" This is the only crown that an unsympathetic world can give to those who bear His name in testimony. It is the crown of thorns in miniature—His suffering for

righteousness at the hands of men. We can never touch His suffering at the hands of God for sin. And this shame carries with it a special blessing, because it is for His name it is obtained. Peter, who was foremost in bearing this shame for His name, writes more fully of it in his first letter, in the first chapter of which he tells us of the Old Testament Scriptures foretelling "the sufferings of Christ and the glory that should follow." In the second chapter, "This is thankworthy (or the character of grace), if a man for conscience toward God endure grief, suffering wrongfully. For what glory is it if, when ye be buffeted for your faults, ye shall take it patiently? But if when ye do well and suffer for it, ye take it patiently, this is acceptable with God," suffering as Christ suffered. When He suffered He threatened not, but committed Himself to Him that judgeth righteously. In the third chapter, "If ye suffer for righteousness' sake, happy are ye; and be not afraid of their terror, neither be troubled." In the fourth chapter, "Rejoice, inasmuch as ye are partakers of Christ's sufferings. If ye be reproached for *the name* of Christ, happy are ye. If any man suffer as a Christian, let him not be ashamed, but let him glorify God on this behalf."

7. *Glory.*—Rev. xxii. 4, "They shall see His face, and *His name* shall be in their foreheads." Soon the cross will give place to the crown, the curse from the earth will be removed, the glory will take the place of the shame, the forgiving and forgiveness having done their work for ever, the leading through the desert finished, the isolated gatherings now consolidated into one grand multitude—all nations now blessed in Him, and calling Him blessed, but still His name shall endure for ever. The outstanding feature of saint-ship will carry the impress of His name for ever. Angels may excel in strength and in wisdom, and may love to do His will; but the God and Father of our Lord Jesus Christ, revealed to us in Him who is the Lamb of God, taking away the world's sin , will be the name by which saints are known through the millennial age, and to the ages of ages, in that light which eclipses all human lights of candle or all natural light of the sun, for we shine in the light of God, and His name shall stamp each brow.

"They that know THY NAME will put their trust in Thee."
"HALLOWED BE THY NAME."

THE GLORY OF GOD.

"Glory to God in the highest."—LUKE ii. 14.
"But God, who commanded the light to shine out of darkness, hath shined in our hearts, to give the light of the knowledge of the glory of God in the face of Jesus Christ."—2 COR. iv. 16.

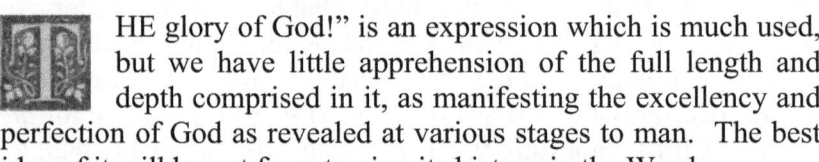HE glory of God!" is an expression which is much used, but we have little apprehension of the full length and depth comprised in it, as manifesting the excellency and perfection of God as revealed at various stages to man. The best idea of it will be got from tracing its history in the Word.

When man had been placed before God in Eden, and he had failed, we find that God came down, and in righteous execution of His sentence, He drove him out of Paradise, and placed the cherubim, and the sword, and the flame, and the gate to keep him out; and no man dare now come to God but with the recognition that He is a "consuming fire." He dare not come but recognizing the claims of God on him as a sinner; for the Shekinah flame was between God and the sinner.

THE GLORY WITH ISRAEL.

We now see a glorious change in the relative position of the sinner, his God, and the glory. Typical redemption put man typically with God at the right side of the glory. This we see in Israel redeemed from the earth.

1. *In the wilderness.*—The first time we read of the sinner's position with regard to this glory being changed is in Exod. xiii. 17, "And it came to pass, when Pharaoh had let the people go, that God led them not through the way of the land of the Philistines, although that was near" (God often does not take the nearest way. It would have been a great pity if Christ had said to Peter, "I have prayed the

Father that you should not be tempted." Peter would have lost a great deal); "for God said, Lest peradventure the people repent when they see war, and they return to Egypt." We are not converted to peace with *ourselves*, but to peace with *God*; we are not converted to *sleep*, but to wear the helmet, and not to lie down, but to go through the desert; but if we have to go through a desert, we have a constant untiring leader. And this is the attitude in which we now meet the pillar-cloud of the glory of Jehovah.

A constant leader.—"And they took their journey from Succoth, and encamped in Etham, in the edge of the wilderness. And Jehovah went before them by day in a *pillar of a cloud*, to lead them the way; and by night in a pillar *of fire*, to give them light; to go by day and night. He took not away the pillar of the cloud by day, nor the pillar of fire by night, from before the people."

Protecting.—"And the angel of God, which went before the camp of Israel, removed, and went behind them; and the *pillar of the cloud* went from before their face, and stood behind them. And it came between the camp of the Egyptians and the camp of Israel; and it was a cloud and darkness to them, but it gave light by night to see; so that the one came not near the other all night" (Exod. xiv. 19, 20). The redeemed people, those that had been redeemed by the blood sprinkled, are thus put at the Godward side of the flame, and it is now placed between them and their foes; the flame that manifested the might of God has now been transferred to the rear of the camp of Israel, and God is visibly *for* His people, on the ground of redemption seen in the shed blood. This refers to an earthly redeemed people, yet it gives a glorious illustration of where the heavenly people redeemed by the precious blood of Jesus stand. God had put up the flame now, and His people are seen at the Godward side of the flame, and the enemy at the far side. It guides the children of God day and night, for by night and day, storm and calm, He is always the same, independent of circumstances. Peter saw the *waves*, and began to sink. And really the waves had nothing to do with it, for it is as easy to walk on the top of the waves as on a sea of glass, each impossible by nature. By day and by night the pillar of the glory of Jehovah led the Israelites, but it was darkness to the Egyptians. Yes, many an unconverted man would try to do what the Christian, the saved one, does. It is a solemn text, "Which the Egyptians assaying to do were drowned." What is light to a Christian, to the unconverted one is darkness; what is the pathway to faith is destruction to unbelief. "If our gospel be hid, it is hid to them that are lost."

Avenging.—"And it came to pass, that in the morning-watch, Jehovah" (this is His relation-name to Israel—this is preferable to "the Lord") "looked unto the host of the Egyptians through the *pillar of fire and of the cloud*, and troubled the host of the Egyptians." Not only darkness, but trouble to that Egyptian host.

Providing food.—"And it came to pass, as Aaron spake unto the whole congregation of the children of Israel, that they looked toward the wilderness, and, behold, *the glory of Jehovah* appeared in the cloud. And the Lord spake unto Moses saying, I have heard the murmurings of the children of Israel; speak unto them, saying, At even ye shall eat flesh, and in the morning ye shall be filled with bread" (Exod. xvi. 10-12). Manna and quails were given from Jehovah, their God.

In law, a devouring flame.—Look at chap. xxiv. vers. 15, 16, "And Moses went up into the mount, and a cloud covered the mount. And the *glory of Jehovah* abode upon Mount Sinai, and the cloud covered it six days: and the seventh day He called unto Moses out of the cloud. And the sight of the glory of Jehovah was like devouring fire on the top of the mount in the eyes of the children of Israel."

His name—in pardoning mercy.—Again we read, in chap. xxxiii. ver. 18, "And he (Moses) said, I beseech Thee, show me *Thy glory*." Then in chap xxxiv. ver. 4-7, "And Jehovah descended in *the cloud*, and stood with him there, and proclaimed the name of Jehovah," etc. This cloud went with Israel all the way through; it was their token from Jehovah telling them when they were to move and when to stop. They had no power over that cloud; it had the power over them; and we find that at the giving of the name of Jehovah, Jehovah Himself descended to the place where He was manifested—where His name was known.

Filling the finished tabernacle.—Turn to chap. xi. ver. 33, "So Moses finished the work. Then a cloud covered the tent of the congregation, and *the glory of Jehovah* filled the tabernacle. And Moses was not able to enter into the tent of the congregation, because the cloud abode thereon, and the glory of Jehovah filled the tabernacle." It was the cloud that abode thereon. The cloud was above the tabernacle and as the cloud moved on, the glory moved on, keeping its place; for when the cloud was taken up, the children of Israel went on; but if the cloud were not taken up, then they went not on, "for the cloud of Jehovah was upon the tabernacle by day, and fire was on it by night, in the sight of all the house of Israel, throughout all their journey." Thus we see the book of Exodus has ended in a contrast with what the book of Genesis begins. In Genesis, God was making a home for man; in Exodus, man was making a home for God: God in Genesis preparing a beautiful dwelling on earth for man to manifest Him, but sin had come in, and the consequence of sin has been seen; but now a most glorious thing has been brought in, for God has come to dwell with man, and the glory of God fills the place that man had made, on the ground of redemption—redemption by blood—redemption by the power of God, through the Red Sea, bringing them on through all their journeys, and the glory of Jehovah is now under the roof that man has made.

Consecration.—Turn now to Lev. ix. 22: "And Aaron lifted up his hand toward the people, and blessed them, and came down from offering of the sin-offering, and the burnt-offering, and the peace-offerings. And Moses and Aaron went into the tabernacle of the congregation, and came out, and blessed the people; and the *glory of Jehovah* appeared unto all the people. And there came a fire out from before Jehovah, and consumed upon the altar the burnt-offering and the fat; which when all the people saw, they shouted, and fell on their faces." Our God is always a consuming fire. We see here a manifested acceptance, showing that the offering was well-pleasing to Jehovah.

Over the mercy-seat.—"And Jehovah said unto Moses, Speak unto Aaron thy brother, that he come not at all times into the holy place within the veil before the mercy-seat, which is upon the ark, that he die not; for I will appear *in the cloud* upon the mercy-seat" (Lev. xvi. 2). God appears now in His great apostolic capacity, in the very holiest of all, whither the blood was carried. Turn to Numbers, where we get the arranging of the host of Jehovah.

The responsible adviser.—"And when the *cloud* tarried long upon the tabernacle many days, then the children of Israel kept the charge of Jehovah, and journeyed not" (Numb. ix. 19). Look at the repetition of that word, the *cloud*, the *cloud*, the *cloud,* the *cloud*; it is, the glory of God, the glory of God, the glory of God, the glory of God, ringing through our ears at every stage and step of our pilgrimage.

In needed discipline.—Alas that this manifestation of the glory should be required! It comes in very solemnly here; we have discipline to exercise; it is the same appearance, the same glory of Jehovah. "And the Lord came down in the *pillar of the cloud*, and stood in the door of the tabernacle, and called Aaron and Miriam: and they both came forth;" and what was it for now? "Our God is a consuming fire." And He said, "Hear now my words: If there be a prophet among you, I, Jehovah, will make myself known unto him in a vision, and will speak unto him in a dream: (Numb. xii. 5, 6). And Miriam was smitten with leprosy.

In just vindication.—The majority went against the faithful two. Majorities are not always right. Joshua and Caleb were the only two of the faithful *minority*, cast out by the great majority, who met to stone them. The congregation turned on them, and bade them stone them with stones. What happened? "And the *glory of Jehovah* appeared in the tabernacle of the congregation before all the children of Israel" (Numb. xiv. 10), and vindicated these two. And still another more solemn appearance.

In righteous judgment.—"And Korah gathered all the congregation against them unto the door of the tabernacle of the congregation; and *the glory of Jehovah* appeared unto all the congregation"(Numb. xvi. 19). "And there came out a fire from Jehovah, and consumed the two hundred and fifty men that offered incense" (ver. 35). And so now, as we see, the judgment was manifested upon them by the glory of Jehovah. The glory of Jehovah is very silent. I have often been asked, "Is there any work of God going on at such and such a place?" My answer is, "I never yet found God ceasing to work." I have seen God working in power, when He was coming with His breath, and sweeping hundreds down, and converting people by scores at a time. I have seen Him come with the wind, winnowing the wheat from the chaff, sifting, and seeing who will stand. That is the work of God; it is as really the work of God to find out who are on the Lord's side, as to justify the sinner believing in Jesus. Thank God for sifting times, for winnowing work. Then God may be working in His strange, but necessary, work of discipline, vindication, or judgment. But still He is the same God of all grace.

Providing water.—"And Moses and Aaron went from the presence of the assembly unto the door of the tabernacle of the congregation, and they fell upon their faces; and the glory of Jehovah appeared unto them. And the Lord spake unto Moses, saying, Take the rod, and gather thou the assembly together, thou and Aaron thy brother, and speak ye unto the rock before their eyes; and it shall give forth his water, and thou shalt bring forth to them water out of the rock; so thou shalt give the congregation and their beasts drink" (Numb. xx. 6-8).

Unwearied to the end.—Leaders and human guides may *die*, *pass away*, or *change*, but the leading glory of Jehovah continues ever the same to the journey's end—He saves to the uttermost of time. Read Deut. xxxi. 14, 15, "And the Lord said unto Moses, Behold, thy days approach that thou must die; call Joshua, and present yourselves in the tabernacle of the congregation, that I may give him a charge. And Moses and Joshua went and presented themselves in the tabernacle of the congregation, and the Lord appeared in the tabernacle in a *pillar of cloud*, and the pillar of the cloud stood over the door of the tabernacle." Thus ends the wilderness march of the redeemed host, in which we have seen the pillar of cloud, the glory of Jehovah, appearing at all times for doctrine, for reproof, for correction, for instruction in righteousness; whether as looking to the enemy, as for God's claims, or the congregation's need, all was under and connected with that glory—their leader, their responsible leader, their continuous leader, their avenging leader, their leader to the end, their provider of bread and water, their centre of worship and acceptance, their meeting-place with Jehovah, in holiness and grace, smiting Miriam with leprosy, devouring the apostates, or forgiving iniquity, transgression, and sin. As we have thus traced the path of the glory through the wilderness, let us look at it still as connected with Israel.

2. *In the land.*—The tabernacle of the wilderness changes, but the glory changes not, for the glory of the tabernacle is the glory of the temple, the glory of the wilderness is the glory of the land, and the glory of the desert is the glory of the kingdom. The moving glory has become the permanent glory, but that which let Israel through the pathless waste was the same glory as in the days of David and Solomon. "It came even to pass, as the trumpeters and singers were as one, to make one sound to be heard in praising and thanking Jehovah; and when they lifted up their voice with the trumpets, and cymbals, and instruments of music, and praised Jehovah, saying, For He is good; for His mercy endureth for ever: that then the house was filled with *a cloud*, even the house of Jehovah: so that the priests could not stand to minister by reason of the cloud; for *the glory of Jehovah* had filled the house of God" (2 Chron. v. 13). I think we have often too little worship, adoration, praise; we are very earnest in *prayer*—and I don't think we can be too earnest in prayer—but let us not forget or neglect praise to God. Let us know the meaning of worship. What is worship? Worship is not telling God what we are, or asking God to give us anything, nor teaching saints, nor telling out God's love to sinners; it is giving God back His own,—giving God back! Yes; and is it not wonderful? What was their worship? Praising and thanking Jehovah: "And when they lifted up their voices,...and praised Jehovah, saying, For He is good, and His mercy endureth for ever." This is the refrain, the chorus through all their goings, "He is good, for His mercy endureth for ever." It was thus giving Him back His own, telling him concerning His all-forbearing mercy, in spite of all their sin and failure.

And what have we to give Him back? I have often thought it was as when Jehovah revealed His name. If you had heard those dead rocks when each part was proclaimed, the rocks echoed it back—"Jehovah, Jehovah," the rocks echo; "Jehovah," "merciful and gracious," "merciful and gracious," "long-suffering," "long-suffering." The echo of those cold stones was worship to God. Look at sleeping Saint Dorcas; she is lying dead; here stand some of the benefited ones. Here is a mother with her little daughter. "Ah! that saint was my best friend." Oh! is it not pure religion "to *visit* the fatherless and the widows in their affliction"? Jesus never sent a servant with His gifts; He came Himself, "and grace and truth came by Jesus Christ." Do not hand down your gifts, or send them by a servant—visit. The weeping ones may have been coming one by one to the house of Dorcas; and a mother takes up a little dress: "Look, she made this, and that, and this other for my dear little daughter." This was worship, telling out what she made, what she did, what she was; and we come to our Father God, and say, This is what He is, what He was, what He did, for "He is good, and His mercy endureth for ever." That is worship,—that is the overflow of the full heart.

As the priests of old were telling out what He was and did, praising and thanking the Lord when the *singers* were as one, "then the house was filled with a cloud, even the house of Jehovah. So that the priests could not stand to minister by reason of the cloud; for the glory of Jehovah had filled the house of God." There is nothing like the glory of Jehovah for putting all the priests of God on their faces. We must get the glory of Jehovah not in the cloud of the Popish of Ritualistic incense; if we attempt it we are crucifying Christ again, for if we use the type we mean the Antitype has not come, but has yet to come and be crucified again; but as with one heart we know something about "the glory," and take our place under "the glory," there is then no room for the flesh; the glory of Jehovah fills the house. But I must take you to solemn but very real scenes at which we must look. We have been tracing the glory of Jehovah as telling out what Jehovah was to Israel in the desert and in the land; but Israel is drifting into apostasy, and carried into captivity and righteous judgement. Israel is to be cut off as the vessel to contain "The glory" on the earth, and so the glory must depart; so we look now at this sad scene.

3. *The glory departing.*—Read at Ezek. i. 4, "And I looked, and, behold, a whirlwind came out of the north, a *great cloud*, and a *fire unfolding itself*, and a brightness was about it, and out of the midst thereof as the colour of amber, out of the midst of the fire." "And above the firmament that was over their heads was the likeness of a throne, as the appearance of a sapphire-stone; and upon the likeness of the throne was the likeness as the appearance of a man above upon it. And I saw as the colour of amber, as the appearance of fire round about within it; from the appearance of his loins even

upward, and from the appearance of his loins even downward, I saw as it were the appearance of fire, and it had brightness round about. As the appearance of the bow that is in the cloud in the day of rain, so was the appearance of the brightness round about. This was the appearance of the likeness of the glory of Jehovah" (vers. 26-28).

"Then I arose, and went forth into the plain: and, behold, the *glory of Jehovah* stood there, as the glory which I saw by the river of Chebar; and I fell on my face" (iii. 23). "And, behold, the *glory of the God of Israel* was there, according to the vision that I saw in the plain" (viii. 4).

"And *the glory* of the God *of Israel* was gone up from the cherub, whereupon He was, to the threshold of the house" (Ezek. ix. 3). Such is the departing glory; and we find Ezekiel seeing it symbolized under revolving wheels and fluttering wings, going away from the house it had filled with so much beauty and glory. All has failed in man's hands. Whatever event of God rests to any extent upon man is a failure; what is of God solely stands. Thus Israel under law was man under trial—not to find out if he were a sinner, but to see if he were a reclaimable sinner. Where, then, was the law? It was added for the sake of transgressions, until "the seed" came to whom the promise was made, ordained through angels in the hand of a Mediator; but the Mediator implies two parties, for the Mediator is not of one. If I have a bridge remarkable for strength, however strong one pier of the bridge may be, if the other pier be weak, the whole bridge gives way. But "God is *one*," and there is one Mediator between God and man, the Man Christ Jesus. *God is one.* It is not one pier sound, and the other feeble. God is one, and we are in God, for the God-man, Christ Jesus, spans the distance.

But I will take you to another scene of this glory, no longer in the midst of the beloved nation Israel, nor in faint shadow-symbol, but in real manifestation.

THE GLORY IN THE MAN CHRIST JESUS.

Turn to Luke ii. ver. 9, "And, lo! the angel of Jehovah came upon them, and the *glory of Jehovah* shone round about them."

(They were *shepherds*, not princes.) Ah! we have not lost sight of it yet; the glory is back again. "The glory of Jehovah shone round about them, and they were sore afraid." The blessed One is come. God is manifest in the flesh. This is the true likeness of God, the express image of His person. Well may the anthems rise louder than at the temple's dedication: "Glory to God in the highest, on the earth (not merely Israel) peace," etc.

But in another passage (Luke ix. vers 28-32) we get a little heaven, a glimpse, a specimen of the glory, as the high-priest's breastplate was the glory in miniature. "And it came to pass about an eight days after these sayings, He took Peter, and James, and John, and went up into a mountain to pray. And as He prayed, the fashion of His countenance was altered, and His raiment was white and glistening. And, behold, there talked with Him two men, which were Moses and Elias, who appeared *in glory*, and spake of His decease which He should accomplish at Jerusalem. But Peter and they that were with him were heavy with sleep; and when they were awake they saw *His glory*." They had then the specimen of the coming glory. He had told them that there were some standing there who would not taste of death till they saw the kingdom of God. He now fulfils His promise in the case of Peter, James, and John, and gives them here the representation of it. They saw Him in His glory.

Read another text—John i. 14 (which of course is the key to all the rest): "And the Word was made flesh, and dwelt among us. And we beheld His glory, *the glory as of the only-begotten of the Father*, full of grace and truth." This is the glory we now see, not the glory of Jehovah merely—He was this—but "the glory of the Father, full of grace and truth." "The law was given by Moses; but grace and truth were given by Jesus Christ"? no; but "*came* by Jesus Christ," for He was not the manifestation of God, as the Rationalist would have us to believe, just as good men are manifestations of God; no, no; *He was the manifest in the flesh.* "He was the glory as of the only-begotten of the Father, full of grace and truth." God has come in the glory of His grace. And what has man done with Him: The only One on whom God could look with unmixed complacency— the only One on whom God could open heaven, man casts out, disowns, rejects, cries concerning Him, "Away with Him!" we will have nothing to do with Him; we cannot have on earth the glory of heaven. When He came up from Jordan, heaven opened upon Him; it had never opened on anyone else. He is the glory of heaven; He is as the glory for earth.

"The Lamb is all the glory of Emmanuel's land."

He is the centre of heaven and earth. When on the earth, as He stood there in the place of confessed sin, God was looking, and all were asked to look at Him; heaven opened upon Him, and man would have nothing to do with such glory, for it burns up man. And in man's deepest hate, He would say, "I have glorified Thee upon the earth; glorify Thou Me with Thine own self, with the glory I had with Thee before the world was." But if man cast Him out, God said, "Sit Thou at my right hand until I make Thine enemies Thy footstool." The glory of Jehovah, the glory of the Father, the fulness of grace and truth, has been rejected by men, and is now in heaven. If we are to see the glory of God to live under the glory of God, to work for the glory of God, it must be as seeing the unseen, living by faith, entering through the veil into an opened heaven.

THE GLORY OF GOD FOR US NOW AS SEEN IN THE FACE OF JESUS CHRIST.

In Acts vii., Stephen begins to speak about the God of glory; and they could not hear of that. He begins with *the God of glory*, and ends with *the glory of God*. "When they heard these things, they were cut to the heart, and they gnashed on him with their teeth. But he, being full of the Holy Ghost, looked up steadfastly into heaven, and saw *the glory of God*, and Jesus standing on the right hand of God" (vers. 54, 55). If you and I are to see the glory of God, it must be through an open heaven. You will search in vain for it on the earth—no glory of God there. The conditions to see the glory of God now are an open heaven, men full of the Holy Ghost, prepared for the martyr's doom. Remember there is no other place where you can see Him. He is dead, and he is buried, and He is alive again. Oh! what a glorious gospel we have to the glory of God! "The Lord laid upon Him" my iniquity; for if I had had to lay my sins, I might have left some of them out; but the Lord knew me better than I knew myself—the Lord laid them on Him. I remember the case of a young friend to whom I was talking. I could not get him to see the doctrine of the substitution of the just for the unjust; at last I quoted that text to him. He saw it all.

"Oh!" said he, "I like that text the best."

"Why?"

"Because there is nothing about *believing* in it."

If you and I have to get up faith, it is the worst work we have to do. Some may say, "I wish I had the right kind of faith." Suppose you had, you would then come to God and say, "Oh, look what nice faith I have got!" Faith is the fee they wish to give God for saving them. "It is by grace ye are saved through faith, and that not of yourselves; it is the gift of God."

Wondrous truth! if any one has to be condemned for my sin, it is the Lord Jesus Christ; but blessed by God, He has been condemned, He has been laid low, *He* was bruised for my iniquities, and the chastisement of my peace was upon *Him*. Where is He now? Heaven is opened, and He is the Man yonder on the throne of God; and I lose sight of the glory of God, because I see the glorious Man, I see Jesus.

> "I will not gaze on glory,
>   But on my Saviour's face;
> Not on the crown He giveth,
>   But on His pierced hand;
> The Lamb is all the glory
>   Of Emmanuel's land."

"And he said, Behold, I see the heavens opened, and the Son of Man standing on the right hand of God" (vers. 55, 56). Was He waiting for his own Jews yet to come back before He finally sat down, until His enemies were made His footstool?

Now we get that wonderful word with which we started. When we see the glory it is in the *face of Jesus Christ*, and it is the manifestation of a *Man*, the whole fulness of grace and truth; gazing on a seated Christ, with judgment gone and sin gone, and heaven opened to the needy sinner down here; it is glory for ever, glory now in the face of Jesus Christ. We are the temple of God on the earth now (Eph. ii. 21). From us alone do the rays of glory shine to a dead world; hence we read, "But we all with open face, beholding as in a glass the *glory of the Lord*, are changed into the same image from glory to glory" (2 Cor. iii. 18). We gaze through an opened heaven on Him; the glory of His face is reflected from our faces to this poor world. We were, in chap. iii. 2, "a letter;" now we are "a mirror," and thus manifest glory after glory of Him to the world. Just as we remain by faith unveiled before Him we represent Him here. Alas! how poorly we have served this needy world! how little we remain before Him! and how little do we therefore reflect Him! Some think that, in order to gain the world, we must assimilate to their darkness. This would be like a mirror being placed out of the light into the midst of a dark room. The more we oppose the world, the more we work for its good. The more we sit before the glory, the more perfectly we shall shine it out on others. The Lord give us to go on from glory to glory, and to do all as under that glory! And better days are coming: it is not to be always rejection; it is not to be always the stones and the martyrdom; we can wait for our possessions; our time is coming.

The Glory that is yet to come.

You will find, as early as in Numbers xiv. 21, this word or promise, "As truly as I live, all the earth shall be filled with *the glory of Jehovah*;" not merely shall we see it outside the earth, through an open heaven, on the throne of God, but the earth itself filled with the glory of God. We know it has not as yet been filled. It has been going on from bad to worse; but all the earth is to be filled with this same glory. We work for that glory; and if we work in any other way, or for any other motive, we are not in the mind of God. And now we are looking for the time when the whole earth shall be filled with *the glory of Jehovah*. But that time cannot come till the glory comes back; and there is no glory but in the face of Jesus Christ; and until the face of Jesus Christ is seen, the glory of Jehovah cannot fill this earth.

You find in Isaiah iv. 5 and 6, "And Jehovah will create upon every dwelling-place of Mount Zion, and upon her assemblies, a cloud and smoke by day, and the shining of a *flaming fire* by night; for upon all the *glory* shall be a defence."

The Glory of God.

As we saw it departing in Ezekiel, se we see it returning in Ezekiel xliii. 1: "Afterwards he brought me to the gate, even the gate that looketh toward the east; and, behold, the *glory of the God of Israel* came from the way of the east; and His voice was like a noise of many waters; and the earth shined with His glory."

And still another in the prophet Haggai ii. 7-9, "And I will shake all nations, and the desire of all nations shall come: and I will fill this house *with glory*, saith the Lord of hosts... The *glory* of this latter house shall be greater than of the former, saith the Lord of hosts."

And then, lastly, in the book of Revelation xxi. 10, "And he carried me away in the spirit to a great and high mountain, and showed me that great city, the holy Jerusalem, descending out of heaven from God, having *the glory of God*; and her light was like unto a stone, most precious, even like a jasper stone." "And I saw no temple therein; for the Lord God Almighty and the *Lamb* are the (Glory that is Yet to Come)—temple of it." The *Lord God Almighty* and the *Lamb*. We are back to where we started. The lamb in Egypt and the Lamb in glory; the lamb at the beginning and the Lamb in the end. The Lamb brings in the thought of blood,—life forfeited, life taken, redemption accomplished, and that is the ground of all the glory. Do you know what the enemy is at now? They are taunting us about our blood-theology. That is the point we shall have to stand up for in this day.

I remember when at school we used to have to work out long problems; and I have often worked out some problem in algebra, and at the end come to a most absurd result. What was the reason? Merely one line left out. Our great Rationalistic thinkers have brought out a wondrously stupid result with all their thinking, a very unscriptural result; and why? They forget one factor, and that factor is SIN. The Bible is the history of *sin*, and the doctrine of that Bible is the doctrine of *sin* put away, from Genesis to Revelation. "Without shedding of blood" (*blood, blood and sin* go together) "there is no remission of sin." They tell us that we preach the theology of the shambles. Let us stand by the blood-theology. Sound it in every ear. God first shed *blood* in providing a covering for the sinner Adam; God last shed *blood* in sheathing His sword in the Man His fellow. He is the Alpha and Omega, the beginning and ending, the First and the Last, the Author and Finisher, of the "blood-theology." It is blood from Eden down to the great white throne, and beyond it. In that coming glory, it is Jehovah, God, and the Lamb. "The Lamb Himself is the glory thereof, and the city hath no need of the sun, neither of the moon, for *the glory of God*" (have we not seen it?) "doth light it, and the Lamb is the light thereof."

WHO SHALL BE ABLE TO STAND?

Unconverted man! have you come up to the standard of the glory of God? "I am better than my neighbor." Measure yourself by the glory of God. If you are equal to Christ, you are fit for heaven; and if you are one inch short of it, you are unfit for heaven. Good, moral people think there is some difference between what we call great sinners and little sinners. God says there is no difference in His sight. If a man comes and says, "I cannot *feel* all this, that there is no difference (who could?), but I *believe* it, for God has said it," that man believes God and not his own feelings.

I was speaking to a lady some time ago. She said, "There *must* be a difference." I said, "*God* says there is none, as in Romans we have, 'For *all* have sinned, and come short of *the glory of God*,' " and I tried to illustrate it thus:—

Suppose there are some men wishing to get into the Queen's body-guard, and the qualification is that each must be six feet high. They are measuring themselves by themselves, and comparing themselves with themselves, which is not wise. One man says, "I am the tallest man in the village; *I* shall be admitted." Here is a man five feet six, eight, ten, eleven,—they forgot one thing, they forgot to put themselves along a six-foot rail and measure themselves with it. So here is a sinner; he measures himself with his neighbours. Have you measured yourselves with the *glory of God* and said, "I am as He is"? The day of trial comes. The man of five feet six is measured and rejected, likewise the next, till the measurer comes to the five feet eleven man; he takes him and puts him beside the six-foot measure. He is short, and *he* is rejected too, *just as really as the five feet six man*. What Scripture tells us is this, there is no difference, "for all have sinned and come *short* of the

The Glory of God.

glory of God." And if you have come short *one inch*, it is the same as if you came short six feet.

And I ask you also this question, dear brother in Christ—In the light of that glory, *who shall be able to stand?*

All the greatest of earth's history have been prostrated before it. If we look at chap. xx. ver. 18 of Exodus, the redeemed people were unable to stand; and in Hebrews xii. 21, when Moses speaks of this, he says, "I exceedingly fear and quake." Then, again, in Exod. xxxiii. 23, "And I will take away mine hand, and thou shalt see my back parts, but my face shall not be seen."

So that *Moses* was unable to stand.

Then, if we go on, as we read, in 1 Chron. xxi. 16 we find another passage, "And David lifted up his eyes, and saw the angel of the Lord stand between the earth and the heaven, having a drawn sword in his hand stretched out over Jerusalem. Then David and the elders of Israel, who were clothed in sackcloth, fell upon their faces."

So that *David* was unable to stand.

And again, we find in 2 Chron. v. 14, "So that the priests could not stand to minister by reason of the cloud; for the glory of the Lord had filled the house of God."

So that the *priests* were unable to stand.

When Job *saw* the glorious One, he had to exclaim (xlii. 6), "Wherefore I abhor myself, and repent in dust and ashes."

So *Job* was unable to stand.

And, if we go on to Isaiah, vi. 5, we find "Then said I, Woe is me! For I am undone; because I am a man of unclean lips, and I dwell in the midst of a people of unclean lips; for mine eyes have seen the King, the Lord of hosts."

Isaiah was unable to stand.

And in Ezekiel i. 28, we find, "And when I saw it, I fell upon my face."

Ezekiel was unable to stand.

And if we come to Daniel, that precious man who loved "the book," we find (chap. x. 8), "Therefore I was left alone, and saw this great vision, and there remained no strength in me."

Daniel was unable to stand.

Then we find, in Matt. xvii. 6, "When the disciples heard it, they fell on their faces, and were sore afraid."

The *disciples* were unable to stand.

And then, in Acts ix. 3, when the Apostle Paul saw the glory, suddenly there shined round about him a light from heaven; and he fell to the earth.

Thus *Paul* was unable to stand.

And, last of all, in Rev. i. 17, "And when I saw Him, I fell at His feet as dead."

John, who lay in His bosom, was unable to stand seeing Him is glory. And then He came with the touch of His almighty resurrection, glorious power, and put it on him, and identified Himself with that power; and now not only was John able to stand, but to see Him and all the judgments and torments, and give the hallelujah to His God, as thus being able to stand by His resurrection touch in the glory of God; and that is the place in which we stand. John was then as much at home in the midst of thundering and wrath as on the tender breast of his loving Lord, because he had been made able to stand. Do you know the meaning, the power of the glory of God? Have you beheld that glory by faith in the face of Jesus Christ? Are you reflecting that glory? Are you working under the power of that glory, and that glory alone? Then, when that glory unclouded dawns, you shall be able to stand.

THE TWO ANTHEMS.

Luke ii. 13, 14.	Luke xix. 38, 39.
"Glory to God in the highest,	"Blessed be the King that cometh in the name of the Lord.
And on earth peace Goodwill toward men"	Peace in heaven, And glory in the highest."
(good pleasure in men).	

HE Lord Jesus had now finished His public ministry, and was about entering on the most momentous work the world ever heard of; the question of sin was to be settled. His disciples, energized by the Spirit of God, give the Omega Song, as angels had sung the Alpha Song—the angles sang the Song of Annunciation; men, the Song of Departure, and fitly so. In the former we see Christ a Divine Stranger coming upon a mission to earth. In the latter we find the Rejected One accomplishing His Father's will, yet sent to a death of doom by wicked hands. Let us put the two alongside and see—

I. The different choristers employed.
II. The change in the order of the words in the two anthems.
III. The change in their substance.
IV. What is common to both.

I. The choir that sang the first anthem were angels. These heralded the coming of Christ as a body-guard—the advent of Him who had not where to lay His head. These told out God's purposes of glory in the highest; peace, best of blessings, on earth; God's good pleasure in man—first in His Son, then in the myriads saved by Him, who shall do His will in heaven, when God shall see his good pleasure fulfilled in men. In the Anthem of Departure, the singers are men, those who had clung to their Master through good and evil report; who had acknowledged His Kingship, and received Him as sent from God. Here we find redeemed hearts singing Him back to heaven, as angels had sung Him down from heaven.

II. We find a reversal in the order of the words. The Anthem of Departure ends with "glory in the highest." The Anthem of the Annunciation commences with it. There is a Divine propriety in this. Angels from heaven begin with that which lies nearest them—God's eternal purpose. Man begins with that which is nearest to him—"Blessed be the King." It is like the rainbow, but inverted. One limb of the bow begins at the throne; the apex is on earth. Angels descend down one limb; redeemed sinners ascend by the other. Peace, the apex, is on earth. We, inverting the bow, commence with what is on earth, and end with that which is in heaven, and so we get the rainbow from heaven to earth.

III. We find a change in the substance of the two anthems: peace in heaven in Luke xix., peace on earth in Luke ii. Glory in the highest in the former, glory *to God* omitted. In the Anthem of Departure, God's good pleasure in man omitted, and its place taken by "Blessed be the King." This looks at the representative character of the King who comes to reign and accomplish God's good pleasure in men. One clause of each anthem is nearly alike; another clause of each has a different application; while the third we find opposed in each.

Men have not listened to the words of the Departure Anthem, and so have got wrong thoughts concerning peace. There never has been peace on earth since Christ left, nor will be till He returns. We cannot get peace while the Prince of Peace is rejected, since the world has said, "We will not have this Man to reign over us." The peace of the Christian now is in heaven. This is our centre. Peace now is only to be got by faith in a rejected Christ—He is our peace. The saints of God have got their headquarters in heaven, heavenly men sent back to earth, taken out of the world by faith in Christ's death, sent back to it with a new life by faith in His resurrection. We get from above—

(*a*) Our birth.

(*b*) Our calling.
(*c*) Our testimony.
(*d*) Our blessings.
(*e*) Our worship.
(*f*) Our hope.
(*g*) Our home.

All these are heavenly witnesses for God down here. We are to get our information from the heavenly book, and so to bear testimony for God among rebels who reject Him.

The Crimean War,[15] the Franco-Germanic War,[16] the Turko-Russian War,[17] are all fresh in the memories of this generation. Has there ever been universal peace in this world since the days of Christ? The anthem of the angelic host is perfect.

Nothing could be more perfect, comprehensive, and intensive, than that beautiful *Gloria in Excelsis*.

(1) "Glory to God in the highest." The whole universe must re-echo this note. Not a sun, nor planet, nor comet, nor system, but sounds back this strain. Mountain, rock, river, and ocean, peal forth its music. Forest and field, and everything that hath breath, add Amen. And first, above, and beyond all things for which Christ came, was the showing glory to God in the highest, infinitely beyond man's interests or thought, hopes or fears. But we descend from the generic song of all the universe to the specific note for earth.

(2) "On earth peace." We know the desolation of war, the absurdity of war, the unreasonableness of war, the inhumanity of war. We have yet to learn the supreme, God-like blessings of peace on earth. The path of the Prince of Peace was correctly notified by the angelic anthem. But men by wicked hands took Him, imprisoned Him, and murdered Him, finding no fault in Him. A sense of the most common justice would tell us that "Peace on earth" must be postponed till this murder of the Just One be

---

[15] Editor's Note: October 1853 to February 1856.

[16] Editor's Note: July19, 1870 to January 28, 1871.

[17] Editor's Note: A series of twelve wars fought between the Russian Empire and the Ottoman Empire between the 16th and 20th centuries making it one of the longest series of military conflicts in European history.

investigated and avenged, and He shall return in His glory to establish His kingdom in peace. So He taught us, "When ye shall hear of wars and commotions, be not terrified, for these things must first come to pass....And when these things begin to come to pass, then look up and lift up your head, for your redemption draweth nigh." "Our God shall come and shall not keep silence." Men have to beat their "ploughshares into swords" (Joel iii. 10) before they beat their "swords into ploughshares" (Isa. ii. 4). Science can tell us much of human steps rising up to heaven; it can tell us nothing of that ladder let down from heaven to earth on which angels ascend and descend. Nothing but "a sword" can be for the earth till the Prince of Peace is accepted as Lord,

> "When the crowns that are now
> Round the false one's brow
> Shall be worn by earth's rightful Lord."

Not only have we the widest circle, "the highest," giving glory to God by the mission of Christ, and the more limited one, "earth," gaining peace, but we have the condition of the individuals on earth detailed.

(3) "Good pleasure in men." For this, we believe, is by far the most correct and satisfactory explanation of the original. "Goodwill to men" is in every way unsatisfactory, weak, and untenable. We believe "God's good pleasure in men" solves all the difficulties. The universe, the earth, and men, are thus thought of in the three parts of this "*Gloria*." It is the same thought as "This is My beloved Son, in whom I am *well pleased*" (see *eudokia*, in Matt. xi. 26; Luke x. 21; Rom x. 1; Eph. i. 5-9; Phil. i. 15, ii. 13; 2 Thess. i. 11, besides the very frequent use of the verb). God was now for the first time well pleased with a Man; saw His good pleasure in a Man, and the divinely-given guarantee that not only in this Man, but on the many men to be saved by, identified with, and sanctified through, this Man, His good pleasure should rest with complacency. His delight shall be in the sons of men, in individuals now, but in the whole earth as such by-and-bye, when men shall be blessed in Him, and call Him blessed; when none shall say to his neighbor, Know the Lord, because all shall know Him,

and universal peace shall be on the earth, and this little planet shall choir forth without discord among the other orbs of God, its true note of praise blending with all others in glory to God in the highest.

Our hope is Christ. The Jew rightly looked for an earthly hope. Christ's feet shall again stand on the Mount of Olives (Zech. xiv. 4). We look for Him in the air (1 Thess. iv. 17). Then we shall come with Him to share His glory (Zech. xiv. 5). Then will peace be brought to this poor earth. Then shall all nations be blessed in Him. The Gospel is to be preached as a witness to all nations, to gather out a people for the Lord (Acts xv. 14). Popular remedies are tried to effect that which will only be effected when God brings in His Only-begotten into the world again, and sets up a kingdom, the Bride, the Church, reigning with her Lord (Rev. xx. 6). Peace has been transferred to heaven, and will be there so long as its Representative is there. Then, when He returns, shall be the consummation of that of which the Annunciation Anthem was the announcement; then from every part of God's creation—save from the banished lost ones—shall the cry echo, "Glory to God in the highest!" Then shall the earthly and heavenly choirs join in the universal song of praise—

> "Thou art coming! We are waiting
> With a hope that cannot fail,
> Asking not the day nor hour;
> Resting on Thy word of power,
> Anchored safe within the veil
> Time appointed may be long,
> But the vision must be sure;
> Certainty shall make us strong,
> Joyful patience can endure!"

"LORD JESUS, COME."

"Surely I come quickly. Amen. Even so, come, Lord Jesus."— REV. xxii. 20.

LORD JESUS, come!

Thy spirit taught Thy bride
To long to be beside (Rom. viii. 2, 3.)
Her Lord, who bought her with His blood,
Who in her place of doom once stood:
    Lord Jesus, come!

    Lord Jesus, come!
From idols turned, in grace,
We seek our Father's face; (1 Thess. i. 9.)
We serve Him by His Spirit given;
We wait for Thee, our Lord from Heaven:
    Lord Jesus, come!

    Lord Jesus, come!
Our hope, our joy, our crown,
Our glory and renown; (1 Thess. iii. 13.)
Our hearts unblameable, do Thou
In holiness establish now:
    Lord Jesus, come!

    Lord Jesus, come!
The comfort of Thine own,
To claim Thy rightful throne, (1 Thess. iv. 16.)
Thy sleeping saints to raise; then we,
Who live, from earth caught up shall be:
    Lord Jesus, come!

    Lord Jesus, come!
Thy scattered nation lies
An outcast in our eyes, (Rom. xi.)
But shall be gathered—this Thy word—
By Thee, as David's Son and Lord:
    Lord Jesus, come!

    Lord Jesus, come!
The whole creation's groan
Shall cease by Thee alone (Rom. viii. 23.)
Appearing on this earth again,

As Son of Man o'er earth to reign:
    Lord Jesus, come!

    Lord Jesus, come!
Though many scoff and say,
Where is His coming day?   (2 Peter iii. 4.)
And even virgins wise now sleep,
And for their Lord no vigil keep:
    Lord Jesus, come!

    Lord Jesus, come!
May none of us e'er say,
That Thou dost long delay,   (Luke xii. 45.)
And live as those afar that roam;
Thy Spirit and Thy bride say, Come:
    Lord Jesus, come!

"FOR EVER."

HO in every-day life, in the things of men, falls into any mistake about the words 'for ever,' or supposes that 'for ever' always means the same duration? No; the context always decides the sense.

"A father gave to a child a plaything. The child (but five years old) asked, 'How long is this to be mine?' The father replied, 'For ever.' And the child said, 'Then it is my own, my very own; and I may burn it if I like, or give it to my sister.'...If I say, God is 'for ever,' how long does this 'for ever' last?

" ''Tis an endless for ever, the life of God.'

And if, when the earth and time are past, God, in God's *endless for ever*, declares something is to be 'for ever,' 'tis an *endless* for ever which God so pronounces, and will make good too. The bliss and blessedness of those who love the Lord Jesus Christ is as endless as is He who has loved them, and whom they love; and the woe of those brought up for judgment after man's for evers have ceased, and sent into torment, is to an endless for ever, where their worm dieth not, and where their fire is not quenched (Mark ix. 44). God's Word does use the words 'for ever' in the same way as do men for durations which have an end; but there it is said of something in *man's* day, and not when man's day, with all its subdivisions of time, is past (*e.g.*, the passover—a feast for an ordinance for ever (Exod. xii. 14-17)—done away in Christ). The 'for ever' of the Mosaic economy, with its mediatorships, priesthood, sanctuary, nation, etc., seeing that it all pointed on to Another, the Lord Jesus Christ, was necessarily limited to the duration of that economy. Just as the 'for ever' of a man's service to another was limited to his life (*e.g.*, 2 Kings v. 27, 'Leprosy cleave to thee and to thy seed for ever'). How different is the 'for ever' in the above cases from its sense where it is used either of

"(1) God Himself,

"(2) Of the truth of His Word,

"(3) Of the blessedness which awaits His own people. That of which, when time is done, and it is in God's eternity, the weal[18] or the woe is 'for ever,' is surely an endless position, whether of the good bound up in one bundle of life with the Christ of God, or

"(4) Of those wicked, raised up in the day of God, still haters of Him and of His Son.

"My statement is plain, and, I trust, distinct. The words 'for ever,' 'ever,' etc., if they are applied to any thing or person, in man's day, may be a duration limited by the context, short or long.

"But, if presented to us as being said of God, or of anything found in His presence when man's day is past, then they are as much for perpetuity as is the God who announces them; then for ever is as long as He endures."

ROM. i. 25

For ever, the lifetime of God,
   The Maker and Monarch of all,
An endless for ever with Him,
   We Him as the blessed shall call.

ROM. ix. 5.

For ever, our Lord Jesus Christ
   Over all God blessed shall be;
The Man who was slain, now as crown'd
   With glory and honour, we see.

HEB. xiii. 8.

For ever, Christ Jesus the same
   To-day as He was yesterday,
On the cross or the great white throne,
   Or now in our wilderness way.

1 PETER i. 23-25.

For ever, the word of our God

---

[18] Editor's Note: A sound, healthy, or prosperous state.

Doth live holy, perfect, and sure;
What Jehovah in judgment or grace
    Has spoken shall ever endure.

GAL. i. 5; REV. iv. 9.

For ever and ever to God
    The glory and honour shall be,
To him who is set on the throne,
    The Lamb who was slain on the tree.

REV. xx. 10.

For ever and ever shall all,
    Who neglected or scorn'd at the light,
Be under the wrath of their God,
    Tormented by day and by night.

1 THESS. iv. 17; REV. xxii. 5.

For ever and ever shall all,
    Who accepted the Christ that was slain,
Be like Him in whitest array,
    And with Him eternally reign.

TRILOGY BOOK NUMBER THREE:

ABUNDANT GRACE

ABUNDANT GRACE.

ADDRESSES ON SALVATION
WARFARE, LIFE, AND HOPE

BY

Dr. W. P. Mackay

PREFATORY NOTE.

BY REV. JAS. H. BROOKES, D.D.[1]

THE following addresses will be found to possess a sevenfold charm for believers. They exhibit a rare knowledge of the Gospel, they are thoroughly scriptural, they are so simple that a child can understand them, they are very instructive, they are fragrant with the name of Jesus, they are warm with the breath of the Holy Spirit, and they are most comforting. The pilgrim journey of the beloved and lamented author was soon over, but if the value and duration of mortal existence can be estimated by true testimony faithfully borne, by earnest work nobly done, he lived much longer than most men who have reached their threescore years and ten; for in his powerful book, *Grace and Truth*, and in these precious memorials, "He being dead yet speaketh," and will continue to speak until Jesus comes.

All who heard him must have been profoundly impressed by his intense zeal for the honour of Christ, and by his tender yearning for the souls of men. Nor was his anxiety confined to those who have never made a "profession of religion," as it is called, but his concern reached out to the vast multitude that gave no evidence of an experience beyond such a poor and paltry profession. Indeed the latter need to be pitied and prayed for, no less than the former. They are certainly in no less danger, nay, they are in greater danger, because their dread of judgment has been lulled to sleep by an empty "form of godliness," from which it is to be feared they will not awake, until startled by the thunder crash of the last day. Many—not few, but many—in that day will plead that they have preached and done wonderful works in the name of Jesus, who will meet their plea with the words of doom, "I never knew you." The most appalling sentence in the Bible is, "I know thy words, that thou hast a name, that thou livest, and art dead."

---

[1] Editor's Note: James Hall Brookes (1830–1897) was an American Presbyterian pastor, Christian leader, and author.

The modern Elijah, some of whose utterances are here preserved, was bold as a lion in seeking to arouse slumbering "members of the church." He was altogether indifferent to human applause or censure; and it was obviously his aim to finish his course with joy, and the ministry which he had received of the Lord Jesus, to testify the gospel of the grace of God. Every sermon he preached, every page he wrote, glowed with the spirit of entire consecration that led the Apostle to exclaim, "To me to live is Christ, and to die is gain;" and the subject of his last discourse on earth, "The glory of God," towered before him like a pillar of cloud by day, and a pillar of fire by night.

Many will recall with sad interest now the stirring appeals he made in Chicago during his last service in America. In one of them he said, "If ever I utter the words 'I think,' when speaking to the people, I hope they will go to sleep, and remain asleep, until I have done with thinking. We are not to give men our thoughts, but God's words." At another time he was describing the splendid cathedral of Cologne, which he had recently visited with a friend. "What are those letters just beneath the topmost stone of the lofty tower?" asked Dr. Mackay. "I see nothing," replied his companion. "Then I will tell you what they are: 'RESERVED FOR FIRE,'" shouted the ardent preacher. These two statements explain the meaning of the book now offered to the public. It does not give man's thoughts, but God's words. It is also the final testimony of one on whose heart and lips eternity was burned with a live coal from off the altar, shriveling up everything earthly into utter insignificance. With him the hope of our Lord's return was a vivid reality; and though he was not permitted to remain until that promised advent, he is still waiting for it in sure and blessed expectation. In the light of this bright hope, growing brighter every moment, we may well say—

> "Oh, false, ungrateful words, to call the grave
>   Man's long, last home!
> 'Tis but a lodging held from week to week
>   Till Christ shall come."

St. Louis, Mo., U.S.A.

MEMORABILIA.

BY MISS ANNIE MACPHERSON.

MY dear friend,—Your pressing letter, requesting me to recall brief memories of our beloved brother, the late Dr. Mackay of Hull, I cannot refuse, though in the very heat of departure for the thirty-fourth voyage across the deep waters.

I open my Bagster pocket Bible,[2] and on the first blank page there is the following text, placed there by Dr. Mackay, when it was given to me in '75 by the pence of 200 of our poor east end widows. He said, "It was the verse he much loved, and that it was greatly needed by all Christians in these days of so much talking about the higher life; what we required was more of the lower life—lying down in the green pastures, feeding upon his own words, drawing our strength therefrom." "WITH ALL LOWLINESS AND MEEKNESS, WITH LONG SUFFERING, FORBEARING ONE ANOTHER IN LOVE." Eph. iv. 2.

Again, the last letter received is from a fellow-worker travelling in Scotland, and who was privileged to hear Dr. Mackay's last sermon. She writes: "We remained in Oban over another Sunday on purpose to hear him again, when on Saturday the sad news of his death arrived. He had preached to the Oban Volunteers on the previous Sunday morning, and though pouring wet, as also in the evening, the place was crowded out on both occasions. His text was, in the morning, 'Fight the good fight of faith;' and in the evening it was 'Glory to God in the highest, and on earth peace,

---

[2] Editor's Note: Samuel Bagster the elder (1772–1851) was the founder of the publishing firm of Bagster & Sons. In 1816, Bagster brought out the English version of the polyglot Bible, a pocket-sized Bible (16 printed pages on a sheet vs. the typical 4 or 8).

good will toward men.' On the first his points were these: 1. The Enrollment. 2. The Drill. 3. The Armour. 4. The Battle. In the evening he seemed as though he could not leave off, and then left his discourse to be *finished* the next Sunday evening. As it was, he gave us ten sermons in one, soaring into flights of eloquence, as he tried to tell us of the glory of God, and closing with such a simple gospel as he said, '*I speak as a dying man to dying men.*' He then told how God could not be merciful at the expense of justice, and illustrating by Daniel going down to the den how law had been kept, &c., &c. I seem to hear his voice ringing out, 'I through the law am dead to the law;' and now he said the poor sinner had not to come and steal a pardon while justice slept, but mercy handed a pardon on the point of the sword of justice."

His theme ever was one of "mercy and judgment," holy apostolic boldness, which spared no pains or strength to win opportunities to proclaim the Gospel.

During the first six months of '75 he had travelled 6000 miles by rail, preaching the Gospel in the British Isles, returning very frequently in the middle of the night, to be back to his own church on the Sabbath.

All other themes and efforts he considered were not to be compared with the spread of the Gospel. On one occasion I was laboring in Hull for a week of services in connection with the Ladies' Gospel Temperance Work,[3] and finding that Dr. Mackay's was the only church that had no Band of Hope[4] gatherings for the young, I pleaded earnestly with our late dear brother; but he ever met all my arguments with, "That is not the Gospel, that is not the Gospel"—to the great regret of his fellow-Christians, who longed for his influence. Once, returning from the Believers' Meetings in Dublin, accompanied by my brother-in-law, Mr. Merry, we travelled from Holyhead to Chester with Dr. and Mrs. Mackay, and for two hours we compared life-notes upon our first lessons in *trusting* our God for *temporal* as well as spiritual answers to prayer.

---

[3] Editor's Note: Temperance societies began to be formed in the 1830s to campaign against alcohol.

[4] Editor's Note: A UK Christian charity begun in 1847 which educates children and young people about drug and alcohol abuse.

In turn we told each other of the wondrous faithfulness of our God making good that promise, "I WILL NOT FAIL THEE NOR FORSAKE THEE." Seldom do those who are but stewards of His silver and gold know the trials of those who live many lives in one for the salvation of the souls of others.

When a student, and not long converted, Dr. Mackay's soul longed to tell others the story that had melted his own proud heart. He had heard of Duncan Matheson,[5] the evangelist, being at a fair preaching to crowds. He determined to go and join him, and offer his best. Reaching the railway station, he found that he had five shillings in his pocket, the exact amount required, leaving him not another fraction. But he had a simple trust that his heavenly Father knew all about it, and all would be well. All day long he preached, and at eve an old weaver accosted him, and offered him hospitality, and half of a bed in an old garret, in the name of the Lord. The next morning he was crying to the Lord to guide his way, and if he was worthy to preach the blessed Gospel, would He open His gracious hand and supply His child's present wants? Bidding the kind weaver farewell, he went down the street where he was, when a young man who had heard him preach the previous day met him, and said, the Lord has told me to give you that,—laying a golden sovereign in his hand, and thanking him heartily for the words of eternal life.

With his wants thus supplied, the young convert proceeded to the next place where Duncan Matheson was holding outdoor services. The Lord had accepted his desire to spread the glorious news of salvation. All "lowliness and meekness" was the glowing charm of this bold and valiant servant of God. He had a fascination for the tender and reserved spirits whom he had probed out of their shells by using the sharp sword of the Spirit with dexterous might. The "fearful and unbelieving" I have known would write and ask (to them) the most puzzling questions, and have their reply most speedily.

To our poor struggling east London widows, two hundred of them was not too small a crowd to draw forth the whole heart and

---

[5] Editor's Note: Matheson (1824–1869) is described as Scotland's forgotten evangelist.

strength, and for a whole evening, of our beloved brother. Although they were poor and old, he suited his Gospel message, and made them all so happy, and the hearts of the workers burned within them as he talked of his blessed Lord.

On one occasion, asking Dr. Mackay if he could at all account for the great blessing that had accompanied his writing the book, "Grace and Truth." He replied, "I cannot explain it; only this I know, that I was ten long years writing it. When I found myself in the company of good and well-instructed men, I would introduce the subject of one of its chapters for conversation, and any fresh light gained, home I went and rewrote the chapter once more, accompanying this by much prayer and proving by the Word."

We mourn the mysterious providence that has removed this "instructed scribe," and able preacher and writer, from our midst, especially when the truth as it is in Jesus is being assailed upon all sides, iniquity abounding, and the love of many waxing cold. May the addresses now being published strengthen thousands to "arise and shine, for their Light has come"—waiting, watching, and working as those who may be ushered the next moment into the great eternity.

> "Be brave, and dare to stand alone
>   Against the foe,
> Thy Saviour stood alone for thee,
>   Long long ago.
> Be not a coward in the fight
>   Look up! be strong!
> The morn of victory is near,
>   The Day of Song!"

BOY'S HOME, STRATFORD, ONT,
    Sept. 30th, 1885.

BIOGRAPHICAL.

THE late Dr. Mackay was born at Montrose, and was educated for the medical profession, but his tastes led him rather in the direction of the ministry than the practice of medicine, and when about 30 years of age he gave up the latter for the former, though at the time he accepted the call to the Church at Hull he was qualifying at Edinburgh for his M.D. diploma, the examination to obtain which he passed after he had gone to Hull, and was ordained a minister. His aptitude for evangelical mission work was first noticed by Prof. J. Y. Simpson, the inventor of chloroform, who encouraged him to exercise his power in that direction. He subsequently, while passing through college, became associated with the celebrated Scotch evangelist, Duncan Matheson, in whose mission through Scotland and Ireland he took an active part, working with much earnestness and success. He afterwards wrote his little book, "Grace and Truth," which obtained a very wide circulation, and created considerable stir in a certain section of the religious world. It had, we believe, a powerful effect upon the mind of Mr. D. L. Moody,[6] evangelist, exercising an important influence in regard to many of his views, and giving him an impetus in the prosecution of the mission work he had already commenced. The circumstances attending Dr. Mackay's settlement in Hull were characteristic of the man. The founders of the Presbyterian Church at present worshipping in the elegant edifice in Prospect Street were at the time—now about sixteen years ago—occupying the Royal Institute. They were comparatively few in number, but earnest and vigorous; and Dr.

---

[6] Editor's Note: Dwight L. Moody (1837–1899), was an American evangelist and publisher who founded the Moody Church, Northfield School, Mount Hermon School, Moody Bible Institute, and Moody Publishers.

Mackay having paid them a visit for the purpose of occupying their pulpit for three Sundays, they were so impressed by his manner, that he was just the man to build up a new cause, they decided upon giving him "a call." This invitation was signed by twenty-four persons. Dr. Mackay had then determined to devote his life to the ministry, and was already so popular in the Presbyterian denomination that he had received similar calls from other churches, some signed by hundreds of persons; but he decided to accept that from Hull, because, he said, the congregation at that place was the weakest that had called him. Having been ordained a minister, he took up his abode in Hull, where he resided up to the time of his death, his pastorate of the church there being his first and only one. Shortly after he went to Hull the church at the corner of Baker Street and Prospect Street was for sale, and being offered to the newly-established Presbyterian congregation it was purchased by them. Upon the new building being occupied, Dr. Mackay, quickly gathered around him a large congregation, amongst whom he labored with much success. He was greatly beloved by his church, which comprised some of the most earnest and energetic Christian workers in the town.

Dr. Mackay was a man of strongly marked individuality of character, of a naturally buoyant and hopeful disposition, of great energy and capacity for work, and great robustness and penetration of intellect. He had the gift of mastering any subject to which he devoted his attention, and had the wonderful faculty of making an abstruse and difficult subject clear and intelligible by the ordinary mind. Any persons who have read his book "Grace and Truth" will be able to form a pretty correct idea of his style of preaching.

For fourteen years he took no fixed income from his church. He took what friends chose to give towards ministerial support through means of a box placed in the lobby of his church. This arose largely from his unselfish, self-denying spirit, and from a desire that his congregation might be able to give more liberally to the extension of the Saviour's kingdom at home and abroad.

Not only amongst his own people was he popular, but there was not a congregation in Hull where he was not well known and always heartily welcomed, his face being perhaps more familiar on the public platforms of the town in connection with religious enterprises than that of any other minister in Hull. His services were sought for all over the country, and he was always a prominent figure in the Perth, Dublin, and Mildmay conferences. On two occasions he visited America for the purpose of attending similar conferences. On the occasion of Messrs. Moody and Sankey's first visit to Great Britain he took part in their mission both in London and Edinburgh, this being work in which he delighted, and in which he excelled; his labours in connection therewith being often carried on beyond what should be the ordinary limits of physical endurance, his capacity for work appearing almost inexhaustible. His style of exposition and address was unique, and his matter bristled with illustration and anecdote, draws from his long and varied experience and capacious memory. He was often abrupt, sometimes startling his hearers by the oddity of his expressions, and frequently humorous. His fervid rugged eloquence at all times compelled the attention of his audience, whether he was speaking from the platform or the pulpit; and his congregation never left without having learned some fresh truth or gained further insight into an old one. In private life he was exceedingly genial, and could converse with ease and accuracy on topics of all kinds, his fund of anecdote rendering him a pleasant companion.

Dr. Mackay was an earnest student of the Scriptures, and while he ever maintained that the Bible is its own best interpreter, he had no sympathy with those who claimed that they needed not the help afforded by the labours of others in connection with its study. He availed himself of every possible help, and all gained by him, he at once turned into current coin, and passed it into circulation among others.

Men eminent in Christian work—Mr. D. L. Moody with others—have acknowledged their obligations to Dr. Mackay as a teacher of the English Bible, and have preached the Word with greater fulness and certainty for having been closeted with him over the pages which present it to people's view.

His copy of the Scriptures became quite a curiosity. He called it "Enhakkore," after the water-yielding jawbone wherewith Samson slew a thousand men. It was indeed the "well of him that cried." Bound at first in limp, he had it bound in boards, in view of work in the closet and in large meetings. The pages were blackened with constant thumbing, and ink lines under pregnant passages or across the page from one of these to another.

His constant study of Scripture in private was not the sole secret of his power as a teacher and preacher of Jesus Christ; but undoubtedly it accounts for a considerable portion of that power, and great success in doing good, which followed and attended its exercise.

It may not be generally known that to Dr. Mackay we are indebted for the soul-stirring hymn—

"We praise Thee, O God, for the Son of Thy love,
For Jesus who died, and is now gone above."

He was leading in prayer at a public meeting. With a soul filled with gratitude to God, he, unconscious of any effort at poetical effect, made use of these words, and he was afterwards led to adopt them as the first verse of this now popular hymn.

Dr. Mackay was best known to the churches generally as the author of that well-known book, "Grace and Truth." It contains the substance of addresses given by him in the earlier years of his evangelistic labours. It has had an immense circulation in Europe, having been translated into many languages; and English editions have been published both in Canada and the United States. Nearly a quarter of a million have been printed, all told.

But the faithful pastor, the loving husband and father, the earnest worker, has been called home.

The particulars of his death are as follows: Having built himself a little villa at Oban, he spent his holiday there, if such his absence from home might be called, for he preached as often as the general run of ministers care to do when they are in full work, and he filled up the intervals between the services with divers employments. Tourists made their way to Oban for the Sunday "to hear Mackay preach," and the Free Church was always crowded when he was there, late comers being unable to find a seat even it they gained admission. From Oban, Dr. Mackay went for a trip to Thurso. The steamer called at Portree, and with some of the passengers he went on the pier. While returning, the night being dark and the lights defective, he missed his footing, and fell into the water, striking his head against the belting of the steamer. When he was rescued he was quite unconscious, but on being taken to the hotel he rallied.

A beautiful trait of character was displayed in his request, made immediately after regaining consciousness that his family should not be informed of the accident. The following night congestion of the lungs set in, when a message to Mrs. Mackay was sent, and she arrived the next morning, only to learn that he was dead.

He seemed slightly to wander during his last moments, but his thoughts refused to leave the green pastures and the quiet waters with which they were so familiar; and though these retreats may have seemed to his vision shrouded, as when the light grows dim, two precious landmarks were recognized and clung to. The first of these was, "God is love;" and the other, "God is light." He repeated these over with great assurance shortly before his death, and made feeble efforts seemingly to gather other words around these; but he was now to deal with *realities* instead of with mere names. Instead of the mere vision of the light and love of God, by means of weak earthly faith and hope, he was to feast his eyes on that light and love as he stood where they see face to face.

One of the latest articles written by Dr. Mackay for the *British Evangelist*[16] (of which he was editor) was entitled, "Change your Money." In it he urged upon Christians to make a proper use of the talent of wealth, and he closed with these words: "It is not an occasional or periodic earnestness that God desires, but a calm, constant, life-long work. A man moving about this world with the Holy Ghost within him, prepared for anything, at every step, by every look and word, testifying for his Lord, conscious of no effort, but living in calm peace with his Saviour God, in the unhindered power of an inner life, in the patient hope of a glory soon to dawn, is the type of God's true servant. His service does not depend on his rank, his circumstances, his position; these are all subservient to what the man is. He may be the wealthiest in the world, or have

---

[16] We have just received a letter from Mrs. Mackay informing us that this valuable paper, published monthly at one penny, will hereafter be edited by herself. She also adds that among the contents for the coming year will be the Expositions of John's Gospel by the late Dr. Mackay. Leading thoughts on the International Lessons for the help of teachers. Gospel articles by the Rev. Dr. Fraser, London, and others. Persons sending address and one dollar to Mrs. Mackay, So. Morningside Drive, Edinburgh, will receive four copies monthly.

to sweep a street, but his joy in the service is the same. Such will have a natural entrance into the courts above, where the servants serve their Lord day and night.

"Dear fellow-servant, get so accustomed to serve your LORD JESUS CHRIST, and Him alone, that your entrance into glory will not be unnatural, and thus an abundant entrance will be yours."

In no better words could we picture his own life. His was no "periodic earnestness, but a calm, constant, life-long work." He had become so accustomed to serve his Lord that his entrance into glory was not unnatural, but was an "abundant entrance into the everlasting Kingdom."

His funeral was the occasion of the expression of the loving esteem in which he was held, as well as of regret that he had passed away. Business was suspended, shops were closed, and the streets were lined with spectators as he was borne to his grave. From out of silence of the great grief which had fallen upon the hearts of all, ears attent might still catch the lingering echoes of one of his latest utterance as he lay a-dying—"For Thine own glory." In this language of confidence and hope there dwells a sacred solace for the friends he has left behind, which may well cheer them "till the day break, and the shadows flee away."

CONTENTS

PREFATORY NOTE, BY DR. BROOKES	iii.
MEMORABILIA, BY MISS ANNIE MACPHERSON	v.
BIOGRAPHICAL SKETCH	ix.
THE GRACE OF GOD	1
GRACE AND TRUTH	13
WHAT MUST I DO? WHAT SHALL I DO FIRST?	22
CHRIST A PERSONAL SAVIOUR	31
NAAMAN THE LEPER	41
DEATH AND LIFE	53
THE ACCEPTABLE SACRIFICE	60
THE ACCEPTABLE WILL OF GOD	73
WALKING WITH GOD	84
CHRISTIAN WARFARE	94
THE CHRISTIAN LIVING ON EARTH	100
THE CHRISTIAN WORKING ON THE EARTH	107
OUR CONSECRATION AS PRIESTS UNTO GOD	113
PRIEST AFTER THE ORDER OF MELCHISEDEC	122
THE POWER OF GOD IN THE CHURCH	134
THE FULNESS OF BLESSING	142
THE PRACTICAL ASPECTS OF THE HOPE	148
MISCELLANEOUS	157

THE GRACE OF GOD.

"For the grace of God that bringeth salvation hath appeared to all men, teaching us that denying ungodliness and worldly lusts, we should live soberly, righteously, and godly, in this present world looking for that blessed hope, and the glorious appearing of the great God and our Saviour Jesus Christ."—TITUS ii. 11-13.

THROUGHOUT these six millenniums of years God has been unfolding man's need of His grace. He has been unfolding His method of grace, and He is now unfolding His scheme of grace, and gathering the individual subjects of His grace, and will continue to do so until the great white throne is set, when sufficient specimens of His grace shall be gathered from the east, and from the west, and from the north, and from the south, to sit down with Him in the glory yonder, "that in the ages to come He might show the exceeding riches of His grace." I have ofttimes thought that this is a precious idea connected with the grace of God, that God has saved us, not so much out of pity and compassion to us, but that He might manifest Himself and show forth His own glory.

In visiting the British Museum, those of you that have gone through it will remember how rich the collections are in various departments of Natural History, Zoology, Palaeontology, and all other departments where specimens are required to complete families, or orders, or species, or genera. What expense the British nation puts itself to in order to complete these species, or genera, in order to show completed specimens of all classes contained in a certain genus; what money they will spend on what ordinary on-lookers think contemptible, such as little reptiles, which may be very worthless in themselves, but by their very collection they show the richness of the nation in gathering them together for the instruction of the people. If the British nation might send away to South America to get some interesting individual of some small insect to complete an order of family, look at what God is doing in these days:—He is gathering specimens of His grace from all quarters of the world, so that in the ages to come there will be a number that no man can number who will show forth the exceeding riches of His grace towards us through Christ Jesus our Lord. Poor devil-chained sinner, will you not let God gather you in to be a specimen of His grace? He wants you, to place you in the glory yonder to show what He can do, and how—

"His blood can make the foulest clean:
His blood avails for thee."

He needs you, devil-bound sinner, for the great museum of His grace; and I will tell you what, there will be no duplicates there. I have met some people who said, "Ah, there is nobody that understands me; I am like nobody else." I am glad to hear it, because there are no duplicates in heaven; there are only special sinners up there, who needed a special Saviour, and, therefore, are wanted in the big museum of grace in the glory yonder.

We read in Scripture of the prayers of two men. One of them was the prayer of a Publican; the other, that of a Pharisee. The Pharisee was thanking God—what for? For what he was *not*. The poor Publican could not even lift his eyes up to heaven, but he smote upon his breast, crying, "God be merciful to me *a* sinner." No, that is very near it, but not what he said. In our translation there is a precious word left out and slightly altered. "God be merciful to me *a* sinner" is not in the Bible, but it reads, "God be merciful to me *the* sinner." It should be the definite article. The man was definite: he tells God what he *is*; while the Pharisee thanked God for what he was *not*. And that is the whole difference between a genuine prayer and a false one. The Publican feels as though there was not another sinner in all creation. He gathers, as it were, in a focus the whole law of God, and says, "I have broken it." When we stand before God as *the* sinner, we need a plentiful use of the definite article to define ourselves right down before God. It is this indefinite business, this impersonal salvation, that I have no patience with.

Firstly:—We have in this passage. The salvation which grace brings. "The grace of God which bringeth salvation hath appeared unto all men."

Secondly:—The lessons which grace teaches. The grace of God teaches us that we are to deny ungodliness and worldly lusts, and that we are to *live*, not to *die*.

When I was a young boy, I thought that the good boys died and went to heaven, and so I thought, as I wanted to live, there was no use of my being good. It does not say the grace of God teaches us to die; it teaches us to live—soberly and righteously and godly in this present world.

Thirdly:—It not only brings salvation to us, and teaches us lessons, but it also causes us to look for "that blessed hope and the appearing of the glory of the great God and our Saviour Jesus Christ." We have this salvation to begin with,—a life to live,—and a hope to look forward to; and all brought down to us by the grace of God. "Now the grace of God that bringeth salvation hath appeared unto all men," &c.

It would be utterly hopeless on my part to suppose that I shall be able to do justice to these three subjects. I would rather direct your attention to the connection between the first and the second, and to the truths connected therewith. Sometimes we are apt to transpose the 11th verse and the 12th verse, and sometimes we are tempted to separate them. We must take care nether to transpose, nor to separate them. We must not put the salvation that grace brings subsequently to the lessons that grace teaches: we must get the salvation that grace brings before we are entitled to learn the lessons that it teaches.

This is of great importance, that we must first be enrolled in the army of God before we can be taught the warfare of God. God will not teach His enemies—they would fight against Him. We must become His children before we are taught the rules of His house. We must be the saved of the Lord before we can learn the lessons of the Lord. We must receive the salvation of grace before we are taught the lessons of grace. Do not transpose them; if you do you dim the entire lustre of God's grace. You must keep the grace saving before the grace teaching. But you must not omit the 12th verse after you have read the 11th. You must not begin to talk about the salvation of grace without following it up with the lessons of grace: you must not merely say,

"My happy soul is free, for the Lord hath pardoned me."

That is not the whole of it, my friends, that is only the beginning of it.

There are soldiers, those who have just got the Queen's coin, they are enlisted, soldiers no doubt, and enrolled into the army of Queen Victoria, but you would never think of putting these raw recruits in the front of the battle where the veterans are face to face with death. No, they must know first all about the drill. I know it myself from hard experience; I had to go at it day after day when I was a volunteer for our noble Queen. It seemed very odd to us to go this way and that way at the command of another, but I assure you that all British victories have been gained by that splendid discipline.

I remember a friend of mine who was in attendance at one of the classes in the University; he was one of the very few that came out scatheless from the "Charge of the Light Brigade" at Balacalva; he was one of the six-hundred that "rode into the jaws of death, though they knew some one had blundered." I asked him, "What did you think when the charge was sounded?" He replied, "I thought nothing about it; I knew we had to go, and there was the end of it." That is what we want among the soldiers of Christ who have been enrolled under the banner of the great Captain; they need to learn the drill, the discipline which will enable them to contend successfully against principalities and powers and spiritual wickedness in high places.

So you see the grace of God saves us in order that it may teach us; it does not save us that we may live as we list, and do just as we please; but that we may, day by day, and hour by hour, become indoctrinated into the lessons of His grace, so that we may live *soberly* and *righteously* and *godly* in this present world. With these cautions let me now consider the first division of our subject.

"For the grace of God that bringeth salvation." I love that word, "*bringeth*." You lady visitors sometimes find out the joy of this, don't you? There is a poor consumptive patient lying down, unable to move about; you have been visiting that poor man day after day; when you want that patient to have a little fruit, don't you think it much nicer to take it yourself than to send your servant with it? In the one case it is *bringing*, and in the other it is *sending*. I like the *bringing* better. God did not *send* His salvation, He *brought* it. He did not entrust it to the highest angel, nor to the highest of all the everlasting host who love to do His will. The grace of God *brought* salvation. It was God Himself who, in the strength of His own pity, passed seraphim, passed angels, passed cherubim, passed principalities and powers, passed all those stars of night from the height of His eternal throne down, *down*, DOWN, to become one of us; down to our sorrows, our circumstances, and our sins, until last of all He became our Substitute on the cross, crying out, "Eloi, Eloi, Lama Sabacthani: my God, my God, why hast Thou forsaken Me?" "He was wounded for our transgressions, bruised for our iniquities," "made sin for us who knew so sin." Ah! it was only when He was alongside of us that He said, "Come to me," He did not stand up in heaven and say, "Come up here." It was when the Son of Man came to seek and to save that which was lost that He said, "Come unto me." You remember that poor Jew who was lying in the ditch, left there by the thieves; you know the parties that passed by on the other side—Priests and Levites—their work had been done already, they passed on the other side, nothing more to get. But a certain Samaritan as he journeyed (although there were no dealings between the Jews and the Samaritans) came to where he was—*came to where he was*, what a beautiful expression! Ah! so it is with God manifested in the flesh. He came to us dead—dead in sins as we were. He became dead for sin, and the dead for sin came alongside of the dead in sin and brought salvation. Remember, our only plea is, that we are lost, our only plea is, that we are ruined; but He is come to seek and to save that which was lost. It is only when the sinner gives up all efforts to save himself, and feels himself undone, wretched, and good for nothing, it is only then that God finds him. God has to bring him down to be without strength. "When we were yet without strength, in due time Christ died for—" whom? "The *ungodly*." No man on earth dare have invented that sentence. That one sentence is enough to prove to me that the Bible is true. "For the *ungodly*." What angel in heaven dare have written such a word? What devil from hell dare have coined such a word? What sinner on earth dare have conceived such an idea? He died not for merely sinners or transgressors, but for the *ungodly*—for those who were against God, who hated God, and, let me add, who would kill God if they could. That is the height of man's lawlessness. And yet Christ died for the *ungodly*. Oh, chief of sinners, dare you be lost? *dare you be lost*? If so, these words will ring in your ears throughout eternity; for you heard that He died for the ungodly, and yet you would not have Him.

"The grace of God bringeth salvation." *Salvation*; oh, the precious sound! But is has no meaning, but as we have its counterpart *lost*; for "they that are whole need not a physician."

Look at Naaman, he had made up a beautiful programme of how he was to be healed; but imagine his disappointment when the prophet sent him word that he was to go and wash in the river Jordan. He thought that he would have come out and called upon the name of his God, and struck his hand over the place—perhaps made some mesmeric passes, and that he would be healed. He had driven up with a magnificent retinue, and a splendid fee in his possession, and he thought he would have created quite a sensation before this poor prophet. The great man's programme was knocked on the head: he must "go and wash."

Do you see that Naaman was not going as a patient, willing to accept the prescription that was given him; but he was going to prescribe for himself. The great beauty of our salvation is this, that faith uses what grace prescribes. The devil makes out sometimes that I am not a believer at all; he begins to argue with me and talk to me about my coldness, my indifference, etc. But I find there is a good way to stop all argument; viz., always to let my opponent have the talk to himself. I don't contradict him, and then he stops arguing. Ah, friends, there is no use arguing with the great enemy of souls, he is far more experienced than a poor sinner like myself; we have not any chance with him. Eve in the garden, Noah when he became drunken, David when he sinned, Peter when he denied his Lord—all found that arguing with the devil only resulted in failure. Best let him have his own way, and have done with him altogether. I am suspicious of him. When he tells me I am not a believer, I do not turn round and tell him I was converted at such an hour. When he shuts the believer's door, I run in at the sinner's door.

Mark you, friends, I do not depend upon my faith to save me; I do not depend upon the fact that I was converted to save me; I depend on the person of the Lord Jesus Christ to save me here and now; it is a present salvation. So when Satan would raise doubts in my heart that I am not a believer, and that I am a sinner, I tell him, "By your own showing I am a sinner, but by the infallible word of God I find that Christ died, not to save believers, but to save *sinners*." Glory be to God in the highest! I come as a sinner every day to the blood which cleanseth, and I cry "I the chief of sinners *was*"—no, no, the Apostle Paul uses the present tense, "*am*." "This is a faithful saying, and worthy of all acceptation, that Christ Jesus came into the world to save sinners; of whom I *am* chief." "I the chief of sinners am," so sang dear John Wesley (they were among his last words), "but Jesus died for me." Ah, it is our loss that makes that salvation so precious; it is "nothing but Christ."

Many people are trying to work their way up out of the horrible pit that the Psalmist speaks about. We don't work *for* our salvation from the pit; it is on the rock that we work *out* our salvation. We are saved before we begin to work. In the days of Christ there were two classes of people spoken of, the Jews and the Greeks—the Jews requiring a sign and the Greeks seeking after wisdom. And these two have their representatives in modern times. There is Mr. Rationalist; he thinks that man is an intellectual being, and has to be educated and elevated. He says the three "R's" are indispensable, and then he begins to teach him the higher branches, to tell him about conic-sections, spherical trigonometry, Latin, Greek, German, and French, until he becomes quite an educated sinner; but he is still down in the horrible pit and miry clay, and he is no further up than ever. Then, again, there is Mr. Ritualism depending upon his ceremonies. He thinks that this being down in the pit is a devotional being, and that he must be devotionalized, and so he gets the dim religious light, the music, the millinery, machinery, and gymnastics, and things of that sort; and now the poor fellow begins to be devotional and to kneel as solemn sounds come across his ears. He is a devotional sinner, but still a sinner in the pit after all; and with all his devotionalism, unsaved.

Now, friends, our argument is this, that man is not merely an intellectual being to be educated, nor a devotional being to be devotionalized; but a *lost* sinner that must be saved or damned to all eternity. And here we find the grace of God coming in and bringing salvation to men, reaching down to him in that horrible pit the Gospel rope-ladder by which he can escape.

People waste their time in mud-measuring. One says, "My foot is only covered with the mud, but look at that fellow, he is ankle-deep in it;" the one who is ankle-deep in mud says, "Look at that man, he is up to his knees in mud;" while he, in his turn, says, "I am not so bad as that man, he is up to the neck in mud." It is of no use to talk like that, here is a rope-ladder to help you all up from the pit. "Oh," says one, "I am as good as my neighbor, and better than many." Very true, perhaps, but that is only the difference between being up to the knees in mud or up to the neck; if you are in the pit, you need a rope-ladder that you may get out and get your feet on a rock, "for there is no difference." One man with decent boots on, and only one foot a little muddy, says, "I do not believe there is 'no difference.' Do you mean to say I am no better than that fellow there up to his neck in mud?" No, my friend; and very likely the man up to his neck will get hold of the ladder first, for he is so shocked at the mud that he is glad to get out of it; while the respectable man spends his time in arguing about the depth of mud he is in. It is not mud-measuring but salvation we have to do with, for "there is no difference, for all have sinned and come short of the glory of God."

I remember once swimming with some friends in Scotland; I had not measured the current, and they had got across; and I found my strength was giving way. My two friends saw the condition which I was in, and at once sprang in from the bank to my rescue. When they reached me where I was—just in time, for my strength was exhausted—they each put a hand under me. I at once stopped all my efforts to save myself, and I was carried to shore in that position. I was saved *from under*. That is just where Christ saves from, beneath; He saved from *under*. You must let go the last rag, the last tatter, the last hope, and let yourselves be saved from *under*; "for *underneath* are the everlasting arms" of salvation.

BUT WE HAVE *LESSONS* AFTER THE SALVATION.

Very briefly let me say, that the lessons which grace teaches are similar in completeness to the salvation which grace brings. It teaches us to *deny ungodliness* to begin with, and *worldly lusts*. If a conqueror enters the enemy's country and has plenty of forces at his command with which to reduce it into subjection, and he is determined not to go back; in the first place he gives orders to burn the ships and blow up the bridges, so that there shall be no way back. And so when you come to Christ, Christian friend, I advise you to burn the ships and to blow up all the bridges and make no provision to go back again; you are done with ungodliness and worldly lusts.

Ah, my friends, Christianity is something that has to be lived every day; it is not something that can be put on and off at pleasure. Some people, you know, put on their religion when Sunday comes, taking care on the Sunday night to fold it away in their religious drawers. No, my friends, that is not the way; Christianity is something that has to be lived all through the week. The grace of God teaches us to *live*. What we need to do is to *live*, and *fight*, and *work*, and *witness* for our blessed Master. The grace of God teaches us the lessons for three kingdoms. We have a kingdom that is *within* us; we have a kingdom that is *around* us; and we have a kingdom that is *above* us. The kingdom that is within us is represented by the word "*soberly*;" the kingdom around us, that is our neighbours, is represented by the word "*righteously*'" and the kingdom above is represented by the word "*godly*." So we are to live soberly, righteously, and godly in the present world.

Soberly. We are enjoined to govern our own hearts, our own spirits. "Better is he who ruleth his spirit than he that taketh a city;" and so the exhortation is to live soberly. I think it is a great disgrace to our morality that this all-comprehensive word has come now to be limited to a mere phase in a man's life; the word *sober* has got profaned down to the level of a mere abstinence from the intoxicating cup. When you say that a man is sober—it is rather suspicious to say it. My friends, we must not pull down God's word to our own use of language. This word as used in the Bible has the widest significance. There is a word to us that are young men, we are exhorted to be *sober-minded*. We are, some of us, apt to be so self-sufficient, and think we are up to a thing or two, and to think of ourselves more highly than we ought to think. We might apply this word to young women as well, and exhort them to be soberly dressed. I believe that the grace of God comes down to a young man's mind, and to a young woman's dress, or it is nothing. I believe in bringing down these high matters to every-day life—to your eating and drinking, and dressing and clothing. I am not one of those who believe in uniformity of dress for Christians; but if we were just to take that one word *sober* it would cover everything beautifully—sober dress, sober living, sober-minded.

I believe that God in the creation gave us a principle that we still have, though in our ruins, and that was this: He made what was in the garden of Eden "good for food and pleasant to the eyes;" for God gives us good food; and what is pleasant, yet still sober. I do not believe in Christians making guys of themselves. This exhortation also applies to old men and old women. To those who have made money, be sober with your gold, and if this is practiced the bank notes will not come away, as they do in many cases, as if they were stuck all over with glue. It is to be remembered that we are only stewards of the manifold blessings of God; we are also to make to ourselves friends of the mammon of unrighteousness. Old and young, whoever and whatever we may be, we must never forget that the grace of God teaches us to live soberly, and that this word covers all the kingdom that is within us.

Righteously. This word has reference to the kingdom that is around us, when we go down to the shop, or mingle up with the world. It is a grand old rule, "Do to another as you would another should do to you." If you are a merchant, everybody knows that you have to get your profit; you have to live; but do it in a fair way, *righteously*; let the word *righteous* govern all your dealings; it is not twenty-one shillings to the pound, or nineteen shillings to the pound, but it is twenty shillings to the pound straight down and square all over—that is righteousness. We are to carry the principles of grace right down to the domain of the world. But there is with some people a misconception as to this. A Christian has no right to demand help from another Christian, if he happens to be in a difficulty of any kind, on the plea that Christians are enjoined to bear one another's burdens. He must remember that the Scripture says that "every man shall bear his own burden," and this principle applies to the domain of the world.

Godly. This has reference to the kingdom that is above. I am to be God's witness, God's representative, to manifest God in the world. My life is to be like the sun shining in its fulness; I am to carry salvation to the dying, hope to the miserable, and help to the needy. I am to be God's exponent of liberality in the world. Christ said, "It is more blessed to give than to receive;" but this was never intended to be applied to business. You dare not go to your shop, and write over the door, "It is more blessed to give than to receive." If you did, your stock would soon be gone, your coffers empty, and all you would get would be the blessing. These words refer to the voluntary outgoings of love in the heart when renewed by God's grace, and it would never do to traverse this principle across a domain where such principles do not apply. I believe there is no more powerful lever in connection with our personal sanctification than the giving of material wealth to the cause of Christ.

I believe the lowest ideal of existence is that which neither gets nor gives—a diabolic existence. A higher, but still a very low ideal of existence is that which gets all and gives none—the existence of unsaved men. But higher in the scale of existence is the man that gets all, and gives some, and is anxious to give more, and wants to give all—that represents the Christian here below, who gets all, is giving some, and is anxious to give all, as he will do by-and-by. And lastly, the highest ideal of existence is He who gives all and gets none—*God Himself*. Oh my friends, let us strive to imitate God in the luxury of giving. He gives as the sun gives, as the rivers give. From Him shall flow rivers of living water. Look at our Church schemes—why the money that is spent on tobacco in twelve months would go far toward evangelizing the world. And I believe that if ladies were to send the money that they use upon superfluous dress, it would do the same thing. I believe that the money spent on superfluities would do far more than all the money of our missionary enterprises is doing. It is a standing disgrace upon us who profess to live godly. I want to reach your pocket; I want your pockets converted. I am not pleading for any special object, so that I can plead on the merits of the question all the better. Let us live like God in this present evil world. The only representative of God here is the Christian. Are we manifesting Him in our deeds and in our lives? A cup of cold water He will never forget. Look at the widow who put in her two mites. She is always spoken of as putting in her mite; but she had two mites, which made a farthing. It was the widow's farthing, and not the widow's mite, that she put in. The Holy Spirit is never tautological. He might easily have said that the woman had a farthing. No; but it said "that she threw in two mites, which make a farthing." She might have kept one and given the other. But no; she gave the two—all that she had. I believe that the divided state of her purse showed the undivided state of her heart; for she gave all that she had. I will guarantee that that poor woman's gift has brought more real coin into the treasury than all the gifts that any man ever put in; it was a heart giving out of its fulness. Brethren, let us rise up to the manifestation of this divine unselfishness. Selfishness is sin, and sin is selfishness; unselfishness is God-likeness. Let us strive to have more of the grace of God in our hearts "which bringeth salvation, teaching us to deny ungodliness and worldly lusts, and to live soberly, righteously, and godly in this present world."

Lastly, we should be looking forward to our only certain future and our happy home, "looking for that blessed hope, the appearing of the glory of the great God and our Saviour Jesus Christ; who gave Himself for us, that He might redeem us from all iniquity, and purify unto Himself a peculiar people, zealous of good works."

GRACE AND TRUTH.

"The law was given by Moses; Grace and Truth came by Jesus Christ."—JOHN i. 17.

THE law was given by Moses; Grace and Truth came by Jesus Christ"—or rather, *were* by Jesus—the *came* is not in the original. Grace and Truth found embodiment in the Lord Jesus Christ. Do you want to see perfect Grace and perfect Truth in one? Then we find them in the person of the Lord Jesus and in Him alone. The law was given to prove men. Grace and Truth are here up in contrast to the law. The law was given by Moses. It does not say it came by Moses. It was given as a test to try what man was. Now we find that Grace and Truth have descended to this earth, and have been fully manifested in the person of the Lord Jesus. If you don't see this distinction, you will get into constant confusion about the use and place of the law of God. The law of God was not given to save men, it was given to damn men; the law was not given to bless men, but to curse; the law was not given with God's thought that we would keep it; no, but "that every mouth may be stopped, and all the world may become guilty before God."

I remember one day when I was crossing from Dublin to England, between Kingston and Holyhead, in one of the steamers there, I was admiring the beautiful scenery as we were leaving Kingston Harbor, when a gentleman came up to me and entered into conversation. He said, "You are admiring the beauties of this bay." I said "Yes." I found he was an intelligent man, and we commenced to talk about natural history. I had been that season busily engaged in pursuing my medical studies at the University of Edinburgh. I brought my friend on from one topic to another. I presumed that he was a minister of the Gospel, which I found afterwards to be the case. We talked about birds and fishes, &c. We did not begin about theology all at once. Then we got on the subject of natural laws, the Darwinian theory. I was telling him that I had been studying this, that, and the other, and we got on the consistency of God in all kinds of law. He then said something about the moral law. He said, "How is it that when God has made all these physical laws men will not believe His moral laws?" I let him take the lead; I wanted to see where we were. He spoke about the obligation man was under to obey that moral law. "Where do you find that?" I asked. "In the Bible," he said. "The Bible, what book is that?" I said. He said, "It was a book from God." This was just what I had wished to bring him to—God's righteous demands in law. When thus he began a talk about our moral obligations that men were under to keep the law, and about God commanding obedience to its requirements, I turned round to him and said, "Honour bright, have you kept it all from the beginning to end?" He replied, "Indeed, I have not." "Very well, then," I said, "it is all up with you, you are done for if the Bible is true; for what was the Apostle Paul's statement, 'When the commandment came sin revived, and I died;' it was all up with the apostle then. It is no use of you going on and asking God to help you to keep it, you have broken it once; if you were to keep it all now to the end of time it would be of no use, as you have broken it already." He then asked me, "Have you kept it?" "Oh, not I," I said. "I never professed to have kept it." He then wanted to know what I was going to do. "What you are going to do? you have done it already, that's enough; the junction between heaven and earth is broken; you have broken the connection between you and God; that's enough. If I were a stonemason, and wanted to build a house, the size of the stones would be a matter of great importance and consequence to me; but suppose I was a scientific man, and not a stonemason; suppose I had to show, not what stone had to do with building a house, but the nature and quality of stone; if I want to determine its specific gravity, I would not need to take a stone a ton weight into the middle of the ocean; I would take a small pebble and drop it into a glass-full of water and show the specific heaviness of stone. The smallest stone would demonstrate the quality of stone equally with the largest mass of a ton's weight. So with sin; it is not the *quantity* of sin, but the *quality* of sin that God considers; 'he that offends in one point is guilty of all,' there is the divine statement, and it stands to reason." So I explained to my friend that it was of no use, as far as obtaining pardon was concerned, of us trying to keep the rest of the law, for we had broken at least part of it, and we were therefore done for; if we had broken it in only one point we were done for. While I was speaking I was looking quietly over the bulwarks. He was getting rather excited. He said, "What then do you think should be done?" "That is a different question," I replied. "I will tell you—it does not matter what you and I think; the fact is that the law of God is a sword hanging over both you and me, suspended by a thread, and it will be upon us before we know where we are." He wanted to know what was to be done. I told him that the law of God comes as an executioner, and the sooner the offender is executed the better. It is said, "I through the law am a dead man to the law." "Why," I said, "I was hung with Christ on the cross eighteen hundred years ago, that was the end of me, and the law came and did its worst." "What is all this about?" he asked. "It is this," I said, "the sooner you know that the better—that it is all up with you as to law-keeping, and if the sword falls into you personally as you are, you are damned to all eternity." I told him the law came demanding a life, and that life must be given either in the person of the offender or in the person of a substitute—and that our only salvation rested in accepting Christ as our Substitute—it was our privilege to accept what He has done and suffered for us on Calvary; all that He has done in His grace and truth; all that is true of Him is true of me; it is on the cross of Calvary where the demands of the law were satisfied. I was crucified with Christ and buried with Him. He was crucified for me and His death is mine—His burial is mine. What the law says to the rebel is, "Thou shalt die." It is no use saying, "I will repent and do better." "Thou must die, die in Christ, or to all eternity in your sins; to die is your doom."

I left him for a while, and went with some friends of mine to the stern of the vessel. A few minutes after he caught sight of me, and came and took hold of me by the arm. "Come here," he said; "I want you to speak to those friends about what you have been telling me—about dying." So I went and spoke to them, and said that I was just upon the A. B. C. of the subject, that God comes demanding my life, and I must give it up either in the person of Christ or in myself to all eternity. The man all at once said, "Glory be to God, I see the gospel now as I never saw it before, I am a saved man." When we landed he was so happy that we could scarcely get him ashore; he was almost leaping and dancing; he was praising God that the law had done its work, that it had demanded his life, and he had given it in the person of his Substitute—Christ. He asked me if I could sing, and he kept me singing until I was perfectly hoarse. He kept saying, "I was dead through the law that I might live unto God, I have been crucified with Christ."

The law was given to test man, to show man that he could not keep it; but we find that Christ not only kept the law, but magnified the law. Let me here say, my dear friends, that I believe grace was before law; the law came in by the way, as it were, parenthetically; but the first idea of God was grace. I do not believe that grace and redemption were any afterthought with God, but that they were the thought upon which the whole creation was moulded; that they were in the long eternity of God, before man loved man, or before angel loved angel, but that it was only during these six millenniums that the wondrous plan has been worked out; grace was not known in heaven before. Angels knew the meaning of justice; they knew the meaning of righteousness—these words so full of awe, when those angels who kept not their first estate were cast out from heaven. Ah! they then knew what rebellion against the Eternal meant. Well might they weep when they saw our first parents drawn captive by Satan. Is this, they might have wondered, to be another holocaust; another manifestation of righteousness merely? No; God is to show what grace means.

I have often witnessed illuminations expressive of the loyalty of the people. At one of these, on the occasion of the marriage of the Prince of Wales, Sir Walter Scott's monument in Edinburgh was covered with gas jets from top to bottom, and all Edinburgh was bright as day. But what a day that will be when, in the ages to come, there will be an illumination from one end of heaven to the other, when God will show forth the exceeding riches of His *grace*. Angels will gaze with wonder at the scene. And who will be the little jets sparkling with the manifold grace of God? You and I, my dear friends, and millions of redeemed sinners, the Manassehs, and the Bunyans, and the Luthers, and a great number that no man can number; they are to be all filled with the very light of God; illumined with His grace. Angels will wonder; seraphs will adore; cherubs will again rise up in adoration, and the hosts of heaven will strike their harps anew to the glory of the infinite God, and the top stone shall be brought forth with shoutings of *grace, grace* unto it. The great word seen in that heavenly illumination will be—GRACE.

It is *grace* that we have been learning something about these six millenniums. And in our evangelistic efforts, my dear friends, we are trying to gather little jets to show forth the riches of His grace. "But God who is rich in mercy." He is not spoken of as rich in *gold*; that is only used as pavement in heaven, it is of no use for anything else up there. You had better make good use of it *here*; as up *there* it will only be trampled underneath your feet. Send it on then, my friends, to the glory yonder, "Make to yourself friends of the mammon of unrighteousness, that when ye fail they may receive you into everlasting habitations."

People talk about the Eastern question, and the Egyptian difficulties, and all the rest of it. Well, perhaps it is just as well that the world should look after those matters, but we too must look after ours, and this is what we are looking to. What is the rise and downfall of great kingdoms to the grace and truth in Jesus Christ, who came as the great revealer of the deep, deep bosom secret of Almighty God? "Grace and truth came by Jesus Christ."

And here let me say just one word, with all respect to our scientific friends. I love science and profess to be a devoted scholar in the school of science; wherever science can teach me, I love to learn. I love to ponder on the blue depths of the heavens with the telescope, or to study the minutest creation of God with my microscope. I believe in studying all that my Father has made, with all the aid that science can give me. I profess to be a devoted and reverent scholar in the school of science. I believe in science, and I believe in scientific men. I am not one of those who say science is dangerous; no science is dangerous, except science falsely so called. For instance, I believe in geology, and love to study it. But the facts of geology are one thing, and the inferences of so-called geologists are another thing altogether. The facts of geology I love as I love my Bible; because the one is my Father's building, and the other is my Father's writing. But do you think that I am going deliberately to accept the assumptions of men who perhaps between two editions of their book will be 500,000 years out in their calculations. No, thank you; I do not believe in such flickering will-o'-the-wisps, but in the Sun to guide me. I believe in the facts of geology, and the facts of geology are not very difficult to find out. They try to make you believe that their inferences are very perfect and very deep, when they are only *muddy*; they would have you think that it is very difficult to find out the facts of geology. Indeed, there are very few facts. Their argument in effect is that as a cook takes a certain time in laying one layer of pastry after another, so God must have taken ages to build the different strata of the earth's crust. Scientists talk about the theory of development, and in some respects what they say seems very feasible, but while Darwin & Company are very good philosophers, they are very clumsy as creators. While they keep to their own department we will listen to them, but let them not enter into the domain of *creating*. Five minutes with the Creator Himself will tell me better than all their books. I would rather go to Him, if you please, because it is more scientific to go to the Being who was the only one there, than to go to a lot of guessers who have come afterwards. Theorists indeed, when they attempt to philosophize about creation. In order to help the Creator they bring creation down to the dot of a small microscopic object, or protoplasm, as it is called, the minim of creation. But it must be remembered that it is just as difficult to create this minim as it would be an elephant. We say to science, we believe in what you can teach us, but when we come to our dealings with our Creator, then we come into a domain that you know nothing of. I do not plead either for the reconciliation with revelation, nor do I defend their seeming opposition. I neither try to say that science and revelation coincide, nor shall I be careful whether I say that science fights against revelation. In the domain we are now studying the science of man can have no place whatever. I say to science, God gives a revelation that you can either accept or reject, but regarding which you cannot use the methods of science.

The foundation truth that I have to plead for in the manifestation of grace and truth is this, that *God became man*; that grace and truth thus came by Jesus Christ. Where did ever science hear of that? It is outside your court, sir; it is beyond the range of your telescope; it is beyond your measuring line; I cannot listen to thee, O science, when thou dost leave thy department. *God became man.* You have no measuring rod to measure that; you can only accept it or reject it as a revelation.

The second truth is like unto it, *that Christ is risen from the dead.* These are our two foundation truths.

1. That God was manifested as man.
2. That man was raised from the dead.

And these two truths are referred to in the tenth chapter of Romans, where it says, "Say not in thine heart, Who shall ascend into heaven, that is, to bring Christ down from above; or, who shall descend into the deep, that is, to bring up Christ again from the dead." "That if thou shalt confess with thy mouth the Lord Jesus, and shalt believe in thine heart that God hath raised Him from the dead, thou shalt be saved."

These are the works that have to be done before any one soul can be saved. Oh, science, whom I love in thine own domain, didst thou ever hear of the resurrection? Of a man taken from the cross and placed at the throne of God? Didst thou ever hear of a sin-burdened man sitting down at the right hand of the Majesty in heaven? When we enter this temple, adieu,—stand aside as long as we are in this holy place. When, again, we meet in our botany, in our natural history, or wherever thou canst measure and examine, we will be friends again. But in the meantime we are in the domain of the incarnation and resurrection. The incarnation manifesting grace and truth to us; the resurrection giving us the right to enter into, and the title to appropriate all that grace and all that truth. It is a revelation from the Most High, the deepest, the brightest, and the best that ever came down out of the silence above.

I have sat in my little observatory, on a starlight night, watching with wonder and admiration some of the phenomena of the heavens, as, for instance, the nebula of Orion with its unnumbered worlds, which appear even through a large telescope like a film; and sitting there, when all is hushed and no sound of man's voice, no sound of man's tread is heard, I have sometimes felt the silence to be overwhelming. The poets used to sing of the music of the spheres, but it was only a poetical idea, for no sound or utterance comes down. I have then gone to my knees and thanked my blessed God that He has broken the silence, and that "God, who at sundry times and in divers manners, spake unto us by the prophets, hath in these last days spoken unto us by His Son," the manifestation of the Father, "full of grace and truth."

The creation that is above me I cannot fathom it. I feel like a little child tossed upon a boundless sea; the heights and depths are far above me. I have to exclaim, "How can man by searching find out God? and who can find out the Almighty to perfection?" If I look at His blessed law, I find that all the thunderbolts of His justice are against me. I have deserved them all; I have deserved his wrath—eternal punishment; I have deserved "weeping and wailing and gnashing of teeth;" for His own holy law is against me. But when I hear whispers of love, and whispers of grace and truth—a truth that comes to reveal me as I am, and a grace to reveal Him as He is—I stand under the shadows of His love. I feel that I can do nothing but wonder and worship; and the more I wonder, the more I worship; and the more I worship, the more I wonder at the height and the length and the breadth and the depth of the love of Christ that passeth all knowledge. When Adam had sold his God deliberately; when he had wandered from God and chosen Satan, God might have left him to himself. But no. God says, "If you can do without me, I cannot do without you. Adam, where art thou?" What a loving heart is shown in those words, "I want you; I do not want you to go to Satan. There was an exhibition of grace and truth before even the first gospel was preached. The activities of this God of love were the activities of grace and truth. And does it not remind you of the New Testament statements, "that the Son of Man is come to seek and to save"—what He seeks—"that which was lost"; and so He tells Adam what he is and what God is. Adam was afraid, and went and hid himself; and the grace of God followed him until the seeking God found the fleeing sinner. I do not wish to prescribe for other brethren in the way of dealing with anxious souls, but you will pardon me if I give my own experience with anxious souls. For many years now I have never told an anxious soul to seek the Lord. Don't go away with the wrong impression; I will explain it to you just now. It is certainly the bounden duty of every man, anxious or not, to seek the Lord, just as it is the bounden duty of every man to keep the law of God; but still, while we find the Old Testament telling us to "seek the Lord while He may be found," what do we find the result as detailed in the third chapter of Romans? "There is none that seeketh after God." In fact the whole germ of the law is contained in the expression, "Seek the Lord," and the whole result of the law is found in the third chapter of Romans, "There is none that seeketh after God." But when we turn to the gospel and study its grace and truth, the position is reversed. We read, "The Son of man is come to seek and to save that which is lost," which shows that it is the Lord who is the great seeker now, and who has come down in the strength of His own pity and the activities of His own love. And "the Son of man is come to seek and to save," and I will guarantee that He will find all that He seeks. But the moral responsibility rests upon you and me what to do; viz., to take the lost sinner's place; for it is only the lost sinner that lies in the pathway of the seeking Saviour, and thus can be saved. That is what I have to do; I have to accept the grace and the truth that came by Jesus Christ—the truth that puts me down guilty, condemned, lost, ruined, without a plea, without an excuse, without a palliation. He will do the rest. He saves; for He is seeking to save. The Son of Man is come—the fulness of the Father—"full of GRACE AND TRUTH."

WHAT MUST I DO?

WHAT SHALL I DO FIRST?

"What must I do to be saved."—ACTS xvi. 30.

"Seek ye first the kingdom of God, and His righteousness; and all these things shall be added unto you."—MATT. vi. 33.

HOW often in your own history have you asked this question? Did you ever meet a man who has not asked it? If you could get into the inner secrets of all you meet in the street, you would find that the great majority are asking this question—What must I do? High and low, grave and gay, lazy and idle, good and bad, ask this question—*What must I do?*

The boy at school, anxious to get to the top of his class and obtain the prize, often asks it; and when he leaves school to push his way, this is his great question.

The ship captain in the lashing storm, with the waves threatening to engulph him, and his canvas flying in tatters, has this question often before his mind.

The doctor, baffled by the disease in his patient, puts his hand on the pulse, gathers up all possible information, and having completed his diagnosis, resolutely, says, *What must I do?*

The lawyer, anxious to bring his client successfully through, is often pondering the best arguments, obtaining fresh facts and witnesses, in answer to this question.

The merchant has his bills to meet, and you see him going hither and thither with hurried step the day before, and the question he asks of his confidant is— *What must I do?*

WHAT MUST I DO?

The engineer has been commissioned to lay a telegraph wire through the ocean, to send a canal through the desert, to bore a tunnel through the mountain, and day by day, night after night, he asks himself the question —*What must I do*?

The beggar, not knowing where to get his next meal; the queen on the throne; the poorest peasant; the prime minister, all in their spheres, are day after day asking the same question.

Shall we look to the drunkard, after he has pawned the clothes off his wife and children, ruined his body and damned his soul, without a copper, and turned out by the drink-seller? He is revolving this question—*What must I do*?

So with the licentious man, the greedy man, the covetous man, with his lust or his gain—*What must I* do to have more?

Look at that young lady, cursed with what many people think the highest point of blessing—"plenty of money and nothing to do." She dresses, goes to parties, undresses, dresses, and so on. As she stands miserable at the looking-glass, there is one question in her mind, and perhaps only one, and it is—*What must I do*?

In the village of Gravelotte, I sat in a peasant's house, in a chair in the corner of a window. The peasant's wife informed me that in that same chair and place, the Emperor Napoleon sat the day after he left Metz, on his way to Chalons, after he had heard that the German forces were rather nearer than he expected. For a whole afternoon he sat there and spoke not a word, but smoked his cigars and drank the black coffee which the peasant's wife could give him, and I know the question that was uppermost in his mind, and that was—*What must I do*?

Opposite this, in another small house, I entered the apartment in which King William, Bismarck Von Moltke, and others sat, some days after and planned that awful day's work at the quarries of Gravelotte, and the question in the king's mind was—*What must I do*?

Vanquished and victor, emperor and beggar, ruler and serf—all mankind—ask the question. Is it not a question peculiar to man? Does it not hint that he is dissatisfied with present attainment, and is pushing onward to something in the future? No animal improves by failure except man. The swallow's nest in Noah's ark was just as good as the one in the eaves of your house. Man's longing after something better in the future finds expression in this question—*What must I do*?

We are most taken up with what most concerns ourselves. It is not, what must my friends do, my brothers do, my neighbours do? but, What must *I* do?

This question increases in intensity in direct proportion to the amount of work to be done, and to the anxiety of the doers that it should be rightly done. Let us now look specifically at the greatest of all works, and ask. What ought I to do in order that I, a sinner, may get to heaven?

Sin has to be put away. What a statement! And we are sinners who love sin, and cannot, by nature, help loving it, and we have to do with a holy God.

Sins have to be pardoned, and we have committed them. We are the offending and not the offended party, and we have to do with a righteous God.

Peace has to be made, and we have no power nor place in the making of it. We have to do with an all-powerful, all-truthful God.

A way has to be made into God's presence, righteously hid from sinful man by the sword of His justice, by the veil that shrouds His glory.

God's majesty has to be manifested, God's righteousness has to be vindicated, God's holiness conserved, God's truth maintained, God's law magnified, and we are unrighteous, unholy, untruthful transgressors.

Not only has every barrier to be broken down, a way made, and a robe prepared, but an entirely new nature has to be provided for the sinner—a nature that loves what the sinner used to hate, and hates what the sinner used to love; a nature native to heaven—"ye *must* be born again."

Self has to be set aside, denied, and mortified—and we by nature know nothing but self.

The world has to be overcome; and we were born in it, are part of it, and love it and its ways.

Satan has to be vanquished, and we are his servants, willing slaves, powerless beneath his allurements, weak against his wiles.

How can we, in sight of such work, ask the question, *What must I do*? God's authority all the while is demanding that all this has to be done; and if the callous conscience for a time forgets it, the demand is none the less imperative, the duty is none the less binding. All this has to be done; and I am a sinner who does not love God; an enemy, who cannot suggest the terms of peace; guilty, and therefore deserving wrath, and condemned already; lost, and unable to find my way; without strength, and incapable of righting myself; *dead*—the climax of all—spiritually dead in trespasses and sins. Let us now ask, What could I do? Could I not pray? Then the prayers of the wicked are an abomination to God. Could I not try to do better, or repent? What does this mean from a dead man's lips?

But I am doing the best I can; the works of righteousness I try to perform in my own feeble, failing, faltering way. But God says, "All our righteousnesses are as filthy rags;" and this does not mean bad deeds, but our good ones. All the righteous things I ever did, when looked at in the light of the work to be done, are filthy rags. Can I not hope? If you are unsaved, you are without God; and if without God, you are without hope in this world. You may think you have hope, but it is a poor will-o'-the-wisp spectre and death-sparkle, alluring you to the lake of fire—not the pole-star of God, set for the guidance of his own tempest-tossed children.

Let us now look at the glorious good news. Carefully look over all that has to be done; leave out no jot of it; for God says it must be done, and there is no getting past it. Look over our utter inability to do anything. Take, for example, but one of the *must-be's*. "Ye must be born again." Confess your entire helplessness, and then you are ready to hear God's own glorious news concerning this work—"It is finished." (John xix. 30.)

Yes, God began it, and God ended it, and you and I have nothing to do but to accept it—enter into the enjoyment of the fruits of what He has procured. Look at these wonderful words.

God says, "Ye *must* be born again."

The sinner says, "What *must* I do to be saved?"

God says, "The Son of Man *must* be lifted up, that whosoever believeth in Him should not perish, but have eternal life."

If we are to sum up shortly the immeasurable work to be done, we find that there are two pillars on which the whole rests.

Our sins are to be pardoned; our sin has to be put away. This, as it were, settles all that stands against us.

A new nature has to be given us, as our first nature is utterly unfit to enter heaven.

God laid our sins on Jesus (See Isa. liii. 6.) He bore our sins in His own body on the tree. He was delivered for our offences. He gave Himself for our sins. God made Him to be sin for us. Does all this not satisfy you?

He has been raised again. We are invited to Him. We are made partakers of the divine nature. We receive a new creation by the power of the Holy Ghost. Is this not sufficient? Praise the Lord, it is.

God laid the whole case on Christ.

Christ bore it all, and settled every question.

The Holy Ghost now proclaims it to every creature, and urges all to accept it. Will you cease from your thought of, "What must I do?" and ask, What has God done? Must I not believe? Yes; and with many this seems to be the hardest of all works—a sort of toll that God demands to test our sincerity!

A friend one day asked me to take a drive and spend the day with him. I accepted his invitation. He paid for everything. As we neared the town, we had to pay a toll. Another friend sitting beside me, thinking I was to pay the toll, said:

"Mr.———will pay."

"I should think so," I replied. "After having paid for everything, I didn't think I would insult him by paying the 4½d. of toll.

God has done all the word; but the striving, anxious inquirer thinks if he could only get up a tender heart, or a good feeling, or a little faith, that he would then be doing his part—paying the toll and accepting the drive. But God is the noblest of all givers. Let us be the simplest of all acceptors. Accept it for nothing. Do not come as a believer—one with good feelings—but come as a sinner, and listen to one of God's answers to "What must I do to be saved?" as found in Romans iv. 5:—"To him that *worketh not*, but believeth on Him that justifieth the ungodly, his faith is counted for righteousness."

WHAT SHALL I DO FIRST?

We find in the word of God that human nature is not subject to the will of God. The history of the world shows us a strange thing existing in it—a something that we cannot understand. That there should exist in this universe of God something called sin, and beings called sinners, is inexplicable to man, and has not been explained by God; the fact, however, stands that we are sinners. The apostle Paul calls himself "the chief of sinners." And we shall have to add "sinner" as part of our name; but, blessed be God, we can add too, "saved by grace." The child of God starts with this as his first principle, that there are no contradictions in the Bible. We clear God at the expense of our own understanding. Listen to what God says in these verses, "Take no thought for the morrow; for the morrow will take thought for the things of itself." Is this not a capital text for a lazy man, who sits down and thinks God will send him loaves of bread showered out of heaven? This is to turn the truth of God to licentiousness. "Be careful for nothing." "Ah, well," says one, "I'll be careless of everything." Very well, friend, go on and do as you like. Write it on your table, and enjoy it for your dinner if you please. Faith sees another text, "If any would not work, neither should he eat." It is infidelity and man's evil heart that makes God's Bible read wrong. "Seek ye first the kingdom of God." And here we get a double meaning of this word "first." We must seek it *first* as relating to time, and seek it first as the most excellent at morn, noon, and night; we have to seek the kingdom of God, and thus God gets His claim first met. What are you living for? For God. Does that not ennoble the meanest toil? "Seek ye first the kingdom of God."

I. What is this kingdom of God? It is very little spoken about in Matthew. It certainly is mentioned several times, but it is not characteristic of the gospel. The great thing Matthew speaks of, is the "kingdom of heaven." In Luke we find it is always the "kingdom of God." When we speak of the "kingdom of God," one thing is meant, and by the "kingdom of heaven" another. As we usually speak, we see no difference; but God does not write for the poetry of the sentence, but for the truth. When we talk of the kingdom of heaven, we mean the rule of the heavens, and thus get an idea of earth as contrasted with heaven, as we find it in the whole of the 13th of Matthew; but the "kingdom of God" links in the whole character of God, not contracted by heaven and earth, or the Jew and Gentile dispensations, but it is the bowing of the creature to the Creator.

It is defined in Scripture (Romans xiv. 17) to be, "not meat and drink; but righteousness, and peace, and joy in the Holy ghost." Therefore, "Seek ye first the kingdom of God, and His righteousness." This kingdom you see is *not* meat and drink. What, then, do you live for? What is the meaning of your existence? Are you laboring with those hands, toiling in the sweat of your brow? What is to be the Saturday night of your existence? Are you merely to work to get money; get money for food and eat that you may get muscle to work again? What an animal existence! Nay, dear working man, God would have you take a far higher aim than food and drink, higher even than the princes of the earth. The kingdom of God is *not* meat and drink, therefore the poorest man may have the noblest aim. Seek it first; seek it everywhere—in business, in trade, in repose, in prosperity, in adversity. What a high position you thus have! No man can work like a Christian, for it is not for meat and drink he works, but for righteousness, and peace, and joy in the Holy Ghost"—that is his aim.

The first thing that has to be settled since sin came into our world is the question of RIGHTEOUSNESS.

How can God be *just* and yet pardon the sinner? You can easily see how He can be merciful; but how can He be *just*? Many people trust to the *mercy* of God; don't lie down on that; there is not mercy at God's judgment-seat. What is to be done then? Look at those bleeding hands on Calvary—those bleeding feet and brow, and at that pierced side. Look at the debt paid there! Who hangs there? The spotless, sinless Son of God, manifest in the flesh. Ask the meaning of that sun clad in darkness, of the rocks riven and of the veil rent by God's own hands right from the top to the bottom. What is the meaning of that awful agonizing cry, "My God, my God, why hast thou forsaken me?" It means that "*we* might be made the righteousness of God in Him." Ah! we have got the keynote now—not merely mercy and pardon, but *righteousness*. We are asked to seek "His righteousness"—God's righteousness is *first* to be established. That burden upon the Son of God tells me the debt is paid, therefore God can in perfect justice save the greatest sinner.

God is righteous in doing it, that "He might be just and the justifier of him who believeth in Jesus." Righteousness is one of the brightest jewels in the diadem of glory—that gem of untarnished justice—and the Christ of God "is made unto us wisdom, *righteousness*, sanctification, and redemption." Thus shall every saved soul show the exceeding riches of His grace, and the perfection of His righteousness.

The second part we consider, connected with the kingdom of God is—PEACE.

Peace with God, the peace of God, a peace made, a peace manifested in a person, a peace proclaimed as already made—

> A mind at "perfect peace" with God,
> Oh, what a word is this!
> A sinner reconciled through blood—
> This, *this* indeed is peace!

We have peace with God through our Lord Jesus Christ—not within our own breasts. We have no peace with what is not subject to the law of God. Peace with a heart at enmity to God—never! Did you ever feel the conflict that goes on in a man's heart? Before we had the righteousness of God in Christ, the fight was not with ourselves, but *with* God.

Now, too, we have the peace of God fortifying our souls. Many persons, looking at the heathen all around, and at the evil on every side that seems to be getting so bad, say "they don't know what is to be done." But "when these things begin to come to pass, then look up, and lift up your heads, for your redemption draweth nigh." It is consistent with the hope of the Christian that "wicked men and seducers are waxing worse and worse." Seek that peace that God alone can give.

Lastly, there is JOY in the Holy Ghost. Jesus does not want us to go hanging our heads like bulrushes. A Christian ought to be the happiest man in the world. God says, "Rejoice in the Lord always;" but this is not the joy of false fire, of the theatre, of the concert, or the ball-room; the flesh never heard of the "joy in the Holy Ghost." You wish to be merry! Well, "if any one is merry, let him sing psalms." It is the joy that is found in the kingdom of God, founded on righteousness, and manifested to the glory of God. Thus the pillars of the throne of the kingdom are acknowledged. Righteousness is the foundation, peace is the state, and joy in the Holy Ghost is the manifestation of the state of the subject.

II. We are told to *seek* it. Jesus the King has come to seek subjects. Where can I find the kingdom? Not within us, not around us, not at the throne above us, but in the person of Jesus, who could truly say of Himself, when on earth, that the kingdom was among them. In Him righteousness and peace have met, and seeking the kingdom amounts to looking to Christ. And since the incarnate Word has gone, I must find Him, and it is in the written Word, thus believing the record that God gave of His Son.

III. All things will be added. Men have turned this round. Seek the things of earth and eternity on a death-bed. The father tells his son—religion is very good, but see and get on in the world first, and sometimes not at all scrupulous as to the first elements of the kingdom, even righteousness. The *last* thing men generally seek is the kingdom of God. "Let all things be done decently and in order," and take God's order. Therefore, till a man has got the kingdom of God, he is in disorder. All his life is out of order. Earth, time, money, fame, honour, fill up man's thoughts, and hence the disappointment, misery, and eternal ruin. Deliberately, willfully, they put last what God has put first. To the one who has entered the kingdom God promises all things. By-and-by the saints shall reign over the earth; and meantime all things are ours, for we are Christ's, and Christ is God's. Meantime, having such title-deeds in our hands, we can well afford to wait and accept food and raiment with contentment, while we manifest the life of God in a world that rejects Him. In the discharge of our duty, in the labour to God, in obeying the principles and commandments of the kingdom, no good thing will He withhold from us. Reader, have you sought this kingdom *first*? If not, your whole life is a mistake. Seek it now.

CHRIST A PERSONAL SAVIOUR.

"If a man love me, he will keep my words: and my Father will love him, and we will come unto him, and make our abode with him." —JOHN xiv. 23.

"Lo, I am with you alway."—MATTHEW xxviii. 20.

CHRIST *is* a personal Saviour. It is not a *proposition* that saves our soul, but a *person*. It is not in some abstract way that Christ becomes a Saviour to us, but we as persons must have to do with this person—so there is the personality of the *saving* one, and the personality of the *saved* one. We find that in the Apostolic days the apostles never went anywhere, in the exercise of their function of preaching the Word, and preached mere doctrines; they did not preach the atonement, or the extent of the atonement, or the nature of the atonement; they did not tell people even to believe in the atonement, or to believe in something *about* Christ, or to believe in what Christ had done for them; but they went everywhere preaching Christ—Christ a personal Saviour, not a propositional Saviour, not a logical Saviour, but a *personal* one. They did not go in the acute exercise of their powers preaching syllogisms to people, and putting before them premises and conclusions, and saying if such and such is the case, if such and such is the major premise, and such and such the minor premise, and if you put these two premises together, you will reach a syllogistic conclusion, and therefore you have salvation. This might satisfy the schools and the schoolmen; but it does not do when appeals have to be made to the consciences of men. A sinner cannot be brought before his God except individually as a sinner, and through his conscience; nothing of the man is reached until the conscience is reached. I remember well, when I was passing through college, and at my being set apart for the ministry, a dear old man, whose name I forget, in his charge to us students, told us that, as preachers of the Gospel, we should not be content to reach the intellects of men, but that it should be our aim to reach their consciences. But before we reach the conscience, we must first of all see to it that we reach the *tympanum* of the external ear. We can always reach this, if we preach loud enough. Some people don't consider this of much importance, and that mumbling will do. If we have a message from the king to deliver to any person, the first thing we do is to knock at the outer gate or street door. This fitly represents the tympanum of the ear, and we have to get through this first before we can reach the man himself. We find that there are two roads from the outer gate up to the man. The first is, the road by the intellect; and the other road is by his emotions. Sometimes I may take the one, and sometimes the other. If I think a man has a good deal of intellect, I will try that road, and aim at convincing his intellect, and so walk up by this avenue to the man—I try to impress the intellect with the truth of my propositions. If, on the other hand, I find his nature principally emotional, I tell him touching stories full of pathos that bring tears to his eyes; or it may be that I may convince the man by first appealing to the risible faculties. But we must remember that after you have reached the outer gate of the ear, and have walked up the avenue of the intellect, or of the emotions, then, it is only then, you have reached the front door of the man's heart. The conscience has now to be dealt with. The conscience, you know, is the man. The conscience tells him very humiliating truths; it does not puff him up a bit; it does not tell you that you are of importance. When quickened before God, it tells you your duty; not only that you have not done it, but that you cannot. It tells you what is right and what it wrong; it tells you that you have no power to do right; it humbles you before God. It is only when the conscience is thus awakened that we have reached the personal sinner, and then we can present to him a personal Saviour; and then what do we do? We retire, because we are not priests, but ministers. There is a great difference here, friends. We have a great function. Some people think that the age of pastors and teachers and evangelists is gone. Their presence and statements are the greatest proof that it is not. I say this with the greatest amount of confidence. If any man comes to me and says that he does not need a teacher, I say, "My friend, your statement just now is the greatest proof that you do."

I will tell you another kind of twaddle I don't believe in, it is this: when a man comes to me and says that he can get all the instruction he needs from the Bible, and that he doesn't want any teacher to instruct him, I don't believe in that at all; it is not true. The chances are, that instead of reading the Bible, you will find him busily perusing some monthly periodical. I think that when a man believes he is so clever that he gets everything from the Bible, it is the very germ of Godless independence. We are all dependent the one upon the other; just as every bone and muscle, and every part of our body, are inter-dependent the one upon the other. Think of an independent finger, for instance, trying to move on its own responsibility. We are not a lot of independent balls in a basket, we are not a lot of electrified hairs at the end of a broom. There are three names given to Eve. The first name given to her was Isha, which means, "woman from the man." The next, I believe, was the manifestation of Adam's faith. For I believe that Adam is in heaven, and I think we have it in the Old Testament. I believe that he repented, and that is all that ever we have done. I believe that Adam repented, and believed the Gospel. He hadn't a big Bible; we have 66 books; he had only one verse, and he believed it all, and he knew it all. He believed all his Bible; it was a very little Bible, but he believed it all. I do not know mine yet. Adam said, "The woman whom thou gavest to be with me, she gave me of the fruit, and I did eat;" and the Lord said that the seed of the woman was to bruise the head of the serpent, and that life was to spring from her. We find that Adam repents, and believes because of that, and accordingly calls her Hava (or Eve), the mother of all living. It stands recorded in our old Bible that she was no longer to be called Isha, but Hava (living), the mother of all living. Adam's faith is implied in the change of name that he gave to Eve. But there is another name that Eve had; it is this, "Male and female created He them, and blessed them, and called their name *Adam*." She was part of the man Adam; she was called Adam with him and in him, *Adam*. "So as the body is one, and has many members;" it does not say, "So also is Christ's body," but, "So also is *the Christ*;" so that the body and the head all form together one great eternal unity, that through all eternity will show the meaning of God's grace, and God's righteousness, and God's wisdom, and God's power, with Christ the head and we the members. Brethren, let us shun that spirit of independence, and let us cultivate that disposition to minister unto, and to be ministered to by all, and rejoice if we can by any means communicate a blessing to, or received a blessing from, others. We are *ministers* of the Gospel of God; we entirely disown all priestly interventions; we have nothing priestly in out ministry; no priesthood now but the common priesthood of all believers, and Christ, the High Priest, and we ministers of the Gospel believe that we are at one here. Our work is this: when we get a personal sinner, stripped bare of all his pretences, we have reached his front door—his conscience—and there knocked, sometimes knocked very loud; we cannot knock too loud. Then we bring him down before the Holy One revealed in all His perfection, the sinner revealed as he is, stripped of all his pretences, and when now we have brought them together, we retire; we have no more to do; we do not go with the sinner in this hand and God in that, and thus untie them. No, my friends, we have no priestly connection between God and the sinner, glory be to God! As soon as we bring the sinner and God together we retire, and say that the work must be done by you two, and we are nowhere; we retire from the scene. There is one thing I would like to say, and that is, that the sinner must be stripped bare of all his pretences, and brought before God as he is, and this is the only successful preaching if you want souls saved; you may lose your character as a preacher; it is the best thing never to have one. But we are in for work, business, business. I know a friend of mine; he is a smart business man. I can scarcely see the man during the day on church work. When I come into his office, I find his whole faculties alert in attending to business; he has no time to waste in talking, it is business, business, with him. We ministers, I think, should go in for business; not to make nice sermons, but to save perishing souls.

    I have had considerable experience, when after meetings were not at all so popular as they are now. Sometimes we found, when a person was thoroughly in earnest and required some difficulties to be removed, that a private conversation did him good. I very much shocked a friend of mine by saying that I had not held many after meetings lately. I think we may get into canals and forget the rivers. Many people seem to be dissatisfied with the ordinary means, with the simple preaching of the Word, and are not content until they arrange for what they call *after meetings*, in which, in my opinion, there seems to me ofttimes too much of man's interference; too much seeming additional work to Gospel preaching. Let me not be misunderstood; I do not object to after meetings, but to their abuse. In their proper place they do good, but they must not be regarded as essential, but rather *as incidental*. In my own experience, I have found the best standing cases to be those who have been converted just where they were and who have had to do with God alone, and whom I have perhaps never seen privately until they have come to profess their faith in Christ, and asked to be admitted to church fellowship. I have found another class of individuals, who through their darkness and sinfulness have come to a personal God without even a minister coming to help them, and I have found them afterwards calmly, quietly persevering in well-doing, when others chronically required to be flipped up with chronic flips of religious excitement, and pushed on their way by any amount of religious perambulators to carry them up on their way to heaven.

Christ, my dear friends, is a personal Saviour all the way through. Salvation is a many-sided word; it is a blessed word. It is often confounded merely with justification; but it must be remembered that salvation never ends until glorification. There are three aspects in which we may consider it. Why I almost think that in every truth peculiarly divine, there are three aspects to it, and why? Because there is a three-one God. It is a remarkable thing that our discourses often run into three divisions, whether we will or no, and without having any reference to this; of course we all know that it is very convenient, and easily remembered, and so on. We often say that truth has a two-fold aspect; but I am not sure but what it has three. I know salvation has, as distinctly as it can be, a three-fold aspect at least; I do not of course exclude any other methods of looking at it. We read of a salvation in the New Testament that is complete to start with, "Receiving the end of your faith, even the salvation of your souls." Faith and the salvation of our souls are here linked together. So the apostle writes, "Unto you who are saved;" he does not say, Unto you who are *going* to be saved. There is a salvation to begin with, which is spoken of as complete. There is another salvation that we read of, where it says, "Work out your own salvation with fear and trembling"—work it *out*. Some people misconceive the meaning of this passage; but they forget that before they can work it *out*, God must have wrought it *in*. Paul here, in effect, says to the Philippians, "You have always been consulting me as your spiritual father; you have acted well in my presence; what I wish is, that you should be just as good when I leave you. I am going to leave you, I cannot always be at Philippi; but God is not going to leave you. Paul is going to leave you, but God is going to stay with you, and He can carry on His work without Paul. It is God, my friends, that worketh in you; you cannot have me to consult, but you have God to work in you both to will and to do of His good pleasure." Now as to the "fear and trembling," let me explain. A man may take large blocks of granite, and he need not be careful in working at them; but with the diamond polishers it is a very different thing; they put on their glasses, and take out their instruments, and with fear and trembling they set about their delicate work. Now, friends, you are working with diamonds, not with granite blocks—with diamonds that are going to shine in the diadem of Christ for ever and ever. We cannot, therefore, be too careful, friends; we cannot have too much fear, not too much trembling—not fear and trembling that I am going to be lost, but lest the diamond should not come out nicely edged; lest the gem should not have all the clearness of the glory of God; lest the nice face should not have the exact angle. "Work out your own salvation with fear and trembling;" for it is a precious work you have to do; "it is God that worketh in you both to will and to do of His good pleasure."

We are all delighted with that blessed thought that we are not left without a friend—a paraclete now. In the second chapter of 1 John, first verse, it reads, "And if any man sin, we have a *paraclete* (it is translated, advocate) with the Father." When Christ was going away He said, "I will send you another paraclete" (in our translation, comforter). The reason why the word paraclete is rendered in so many different ways, appears to me to be because our translators considered the words that they used expressive of the different functions of the paraclete intended to be conveyed. The meaning of the word *paraclete* is *going alongside of*. So, my friends, He is one alongside of you to look after your interests—all that you need, whether comfort or instruction. Sometimes we may require chastisement; well, He can do that. Remember that God is a chastising Father; He does not send us back to the devil to chastise us; He has a chastising room of His own. The Paraclete is always with us, to look after our waywardness, and wonderings, and weaknesses. Christ is a personal Saviour.

There is also an aspect of salvation which is future, entirely future. "Now is our salvation nearer than when we believed." And here let me say that we often fall into a confusion of terms, and confusion of thought, by mingling up things that differ. Thus there is a salvation completed, a salvation going on, and a salvation future; if I mingle all these up together, what a piece of mixed mosaic shall I have. If I do not put things exactly as they are in Scripture, I shall get into confusion. The Old Testament saints looked forward a good deal to these two salvations being together. They discerned very little difference between them; it is only since the Gospel light has come that we have been able by that light to distinguish between the two aspects of salvation. These Old Testament saints saw the cross and the crown on the same hilltop; we know that there is a valley between, and that we are treading that valley; that the cross is behind us, and the crown before us. They looked forward to the sufferings of Christ and the glory that should be revealed, as if they were together, and the salvation they spoke of appeared to them as a unit.

The work of salvation was a gradual and progressive work, although, in one aspect of it, it was instantaneous and complete. The implanting of the seed is an instantaneous act, but the growth of the plant is progressive. We are not to be disheartened because we do not see every step of this progress. God is looking after the bearing of the fruit; God is seeing that we are growing in grace, and in the knowledge of God our Saviour; and the more we grow in grace the more will we be conscious of our own self-insufficiency, of our own *nothingness*. Young Christians, you know, in their fresh experience, feel like mounting up as with the wings of eagles. I often see them soaring away to the sun, flying up as on wings of eagles, and looking down upon us older ones as perhaps somewhat cold and dead. Well, I don't like to clip their wings; let them have their time of it, they will be back soon enough. Let them have their fly; they are mounting up as on wings of eagles; I do not like to discourage them; I do not like to take a flying shot and damage their wings; let them have it out, I say. Just wait a little while; they are flying now, they will soon want to come back here and *run*. "They shall run, and not be weary;" this is how our strength is to be renewed, according to Isaiah. "They shall *run*, and not be weary;" and some of us know the meaning of that. Many have run and run a long while, but weary we have got after all, you know; but grace will teach us to run and not be weary. They are running, but wait a little; their pace will shorten by-and-by, and then they will come to the walking. "They shall run, and not be weary; and they shall *walk*, and not faint;" that is how the saints renew their strength. Progress in the divine life is to get lower down; ambition prompts us to get higher up. Brethren, we need to get lower down, lower down. After mounting up as on eagles' wings, running and not being weary, walking and not fainting, having done all in the evil day, we are to *stand*. Stand and meet the foe face to face. It is then time to learn the sword exercise; it is time to know how to point and parry; time to know how to take the enemy at his weak points; time to know when to strike him. There is no use attempting to prove the Bible to an infidel, but the best thing to prove that it is a sword is by running him through with it; that will soon teach him that it is a good genuine steel from God's armoury, then slash away at him, and give him no quarter. There is not fear, my friends, of the work of the Lod, it is always getting on well. Sometimes, you know, He is sowing, and sometimes reaping; sometimes saving, and sometimes teaching young souls how to use their swords. When there is a little calm, it is time to practice the sword exercise. Some people do not know what end of the Bible to take; they use the sword by the wrong end. Then, my friends, having learned your sword exercise, when the evil day comes you will not be able to fly, nor to run, nor even to walk, but, having done all, to *stand*. There you have the different spiritual exercises, from the highest flights down to standing face to face, and foot to foot, with the

CHRIST A PERSONAL SAVIOUR.

devil, the world, and the flesh. And then, after I have done all I can do, what does the Lord do with me? After I have stood in the fierce conflict upheld by the power of His Word, what then? Oh! my friends, there is something higher than the active gymnastics. Listen, "He maketh me to lie down in green pastures." Friends, that is the way we are to renew our strength. "To lie down"—mark the position, expressive of our weakness, our passivity, our nothingness. What is a cipher? Some school-boy will tell me that its value is nothing, and a million of them raised to the millionth power will only be nothing. Stop, stop a bit; I have a use for nothings. Put the cipher (0) on the corner of a sheet of paper; now put one (1) before it, and what have you? Why, ten (10). And so when I came to Christ I found I was nothing (0); no mistake about it; but I found that Christ was ten (10) times more valuable to me than ever I had heard Him spoken of, and that He was ten (10) times more precious than I ever could have thought Him. Years rolled on, and I found I was still nothing, and that I had another nothing (0) to add to the sum; but then I found that Christ was 100 times more valuable. Now don't you see the use of nothings when you have one (1) before them all—the great "One," the Lord Jesus Christ, before all our nothingness? Another year rolled on, and I found I was still nothing, so that I had to add still another cipher; but then I found that Christ was a thousand (1000) times more valuable than ever He was before. Now, brethren, we must exalt His name, and sink ourselves in the very dust. As I stand here and think of my own unworthiness and of my utter nothingness, I find I have to add still another cipher; but I can praise His holy name that I can put the glorious ONE before them all, and sing, "He is the chiefest among ten thousand (10,000), and the altogether lovely." Let us add on the nothings, my friends, and we shall find that Christ will become more and more precious, and we will sing in the hope of a future salvation, "Our salvation is nearer than when we believed." "To them that look for Him shall He appear the second time without sin unto salvation." I believe that every Christian is looking for Him; whatever his theological notions of the future may be, he is waiting for Christ, the heart is waiting. There may be a difference of thought as to the manner of His coming. I must emphatically denounce the thought that any

Christian is not looking for Christ. I am very strong in my thoughts as to the future, but then I don't press them on my brother. In this matter it is the heart and not the head; it is the bride waiting for the bridegroom; and to such will He appear "the second time without sin unto salvation." Then shall we receive the redemption of the purchased possession, and then shall our bodies be redeemed. The apostle Paul was waiting for that on earth, and he is waiting for the same thing in heaven, and he has not got it yet.

We have salvation perfect to start with; we have salvation working out, that we have not yet completed; and we have salvation that we are waiting for, when this body of humiliation will be fashioned like unto Christ's body of glory. "I shall be satisfied when I awake in His likeness," and not until then. "Beloved, now are we the sons of God; and it doth not yet appear what we shall be; but we know that when He shall appear we shall be like Him; for we shall see Him as He is; and every man that hath this hope in Him purifieth himself, even as He is pure."

Now, brethren, is not Christ a personal Saviour? I do not speak of Him as our Saviour, but as my Saviour, and I do not believe that ever a man who went to his closet burdened with sin, and knowing himself, and knelt down on his knees before a holy God and said these two words in reality to Christ, was ever lost—"My Saviour." But it must be to God, you remember, and it must be genuine, it must be the utterance of faith. When alone there is little tendency to say it to any other but God. If any dear anxious soul reads these lines, let me urge you to go to Jesus Christ yourself; do not let anybody know; go yourself, and say, "My Saviour"—"*My* Saviour." Friends, Christ is a personal Saviour, past, present, and to come.

NAAMAN THE LEPER.

"Now Naaman, captain of the host of the king of Syria, was a great man with his master, and honourable, because by him the Lord had given deliverance unto Syria: he was also a mighty man in valour: but he was a leper."—2 KINGS v. 1.

I would call your attention to the fifth chapter of second Kings—the story of Naaman the leper.

"Now Naaman, captain of the host of the king of Syria, was a great man with his master, and honourable, because by him the Lord had given deliverance unto Syria; he was also a mighty man in valour." He was worthy to be entrusted, bringing glory to the arms of Syria; his career might have been envied by others, if it were not for one damaging word that had to come alongside of the description of his otherwise great position and high character and name; a word that carried with it everything that was repulsive and disgusting, especially to the Jew—that was, a *"leper."* The original has it, "He was also a mighty man of valour, a *leper."* It dashed the whole cup of greatness from his lips, and he stands before a Jew disgusting and repelling. This exactly describes the state of the greatest man on the earth away from God, apart from Christ; it matters not, whether he has got $1,000,000 or $5,000,000, and a great estate, and a splendid house and magnificent equipages; there is one little word that mars it all in the eyes of the eternal God—a *sinner.* It matters not what his position, high or low, rich or poor, this word stands against him.

When Nicodemus spoke about being born twice into this world, that would not have helped the matter any; for "that which is born of the flesh is flesh;" it might be rich flesh, but still it would be flesh after all. High or low, rich or poor, the same word is true of all, whatever the adjective may be—a *sinner*. This poor rich man; this small great man; this decrepit captain who now stands before us, was in the eye of a Jew repulsive and disgusting. Here was a man that had every kind of circumstance in his favour; but what he was, was against him. Sometimes our circumstances may be all that are desirable, but we carry about with us a band and a curse that makes all our life a gloom and a shadow. His circumstances were all that could be desired from a worldly point of view; but what good did that do him, he was a *leper*. But mark the entire contrast. "The Syrians had gone out by companies, and had brought away captive out of the land of Israel a little maid; and she waited on Naaman's wife. And she said unto her mistress, Would God my lord were with the prophet that is in Samaria; for he would recover him of his leprosy."

Look at this little girl, a grand preacher of the gospel; she had not to leave her place to do it; she could preach while in the kitchen where she was; she did not require to go on a platform to do it— no, she could do it in the kitchen. We require more kitchen preaching, as well as more dining-room preaching. Look at the little maid; what a contrast she is to Naaman! She had all circumstances against her; but she carried about in her bosom the secret of healing. All *around* her was against her; but all *in* her was for her. The rich captain had all in his favour around him, but the leprous blood was beating in his heart. The little maid had left her father's home, and her mother's love, and her happy childhood friends, and she was among strangers there; she had become a slave of an alien. But when she sees her master in trouble she forgets all about herself, and remembers that there is living in Samaria a holy prophet of God, who was the representative of God, and had the power of God to heal that which was otherwise incurable, and which in all ages has been incurable. So she says to her mistress, "Would God my lord were with the prophet that is in Samaria; for he would recover him of his leprosy.

There is one striking thought in connection with this story, and that is, how many people God used before that man got cleansed. Why there was first the little maid who set the stone rolling; if it had not been for this private preacher, there would have been no healing at all; she set the whole thing going. A little child can start an avalanche. Then there was the mistress, to whom she spoke on the subject; and then there was one of the servants that had come in while they were talking and had overheard the conversation, who carried it to the King of Syria; and then there was the King of Syria who sent a letter to the King of Israel, and so on all through. There is a great lesson for us here, and it is this. I believe, in my experience as an evangelist, I have found the same to be the case. I cannot point to one individual instance, that I know of, of any one being brought to Christ through my instrumentality alone, where I was the means altogether from beginning to end—not a single instance; and I believe that to be the experience of other evangelists; and the reason seems to be this, that no one should glory but God alone; and if any of us think that we are to be used exclusively, it would be well for us to read the story of the little maid, and to strive to know the work which God wishes us to do, and then to do it; to know our place, and then to fill it; to do our work and stick by it, and not encroach on another's work. I believe in individuality of labour—there should be no imitation; there is nothing more painful than to see one person imitate another in the work of the Lord. We should be willing to be all taught of God, and to do the one work that God would have us do, and then if we work faithfully, we shall have enough to do.

"And one went in, and told his lord, saying, Thus and thus said the maid that is of the land of Israel. And the King of Syria said, Go to, go, and I will send a letter unto the King of Israel." There he was wrong; this little maid talked about the *prophet* in Israel, not the *King* of Israel. But he thought the King must know all about it; so instead of writing what the girl had said, he wrote down what he thought the girl should have said. And so I find when I have been preaching the word to sinners, people would say afterwards, "Do you know what Dr. Mackay said?" and then they would put in what Dr. Mackay should have said.

There is not a more consistent type of sin in the flesh, as corruption, than leprosy, in all the word of God. Medicine in all its departments has advanced very much since that day, but at this moment physicians are as far from finding a cure for leprosy as they were then; it is as incurable to-day as it was then. In Norway, there is a large hospital containing as many as two thousand lepers. Some years ago I had a conversation with the professor who superintended this establishment, and in describing, among other things, the treatment they had there, he gave me some interesting facts concerning this disease. One fact in particular which he mentioned was this, that the disease of leprosy sometimes apparently attacks the very optic nerve of many of the patients, so that they look at everything with a leprous eye. He showed me some portraits of hideous lepers afflicted with what is called the tubercular kind of leprosy. There were large tubercules upon the face of the men, making them hideous to look upon. He said that if you were to ask some of the lepers in the hospital who were the best-looking people in Norway among their acquaintances, they would actually point to some leper more hideous than themselves. The leprosy seems to have taken such hold of their taste for the beautiful that they actually believe that leprosy is beautiful. We may well shudder at such a horrible and hideous thought. And yet young men look upon that fellow who struts about and smokes and drinks and knows all about fast life as a jolly good fellow, and the finest-looking fellow in the world. "Oh," they say, "if I could only be like that fellow!" What is he? A poor bloated tubercular leper in the sight of the living God, covered with sin and uncleanness "from the crown of the head to the sole of the foot, full of wounds, and bruises, and putrefying sores."

"And he departed, and took with him ten talents of silver, and six thousand pieces of gold, and ten changes of raiment." Yes, he took a good fee with him as if it had been to pay a practicing physician.

"And he brought the letter to the King of Israel, saying, Now when this letter is come unto thee, behold, I have therewith sent Naaman my servant to thee, that thou mayest recover him of his leprosy." That was a mistake; nobody ever said that the King could do it. The prophet could do it; but the King of Syria could never think of that, and therefore he sent to the King of Israel.

"And it came to pass, when the King of Israel had read the letter, that he rent his clothes, and said." He did not know about Elisha. The little maid knew a secret that kings did not know. So it is not with the great and learned that the secret of salvation has ever been.

This story shows that God does not use the great, the mighty, and the noble of this world to do His work, but the poor and despised, "that no flesh should glory in His presence." The little maiden knew more than the King of Israel.

He said, "Am I God, to kill and to make alive, that this man doth send unto me to recover a man of his leprosy? wherefore consider, I pray you, and see how he seeketh a quarrel against me. And it was so, when Elisha the man of God"—Ah, there was the power, God was there; He was working through the man. "*The man of God*;" not the king of Israel. If some of you were to take a good concordance, and look up those places where the phrase "*man of God*" is used, you would have a good Bible reading. Every Christian is not called a man of God; he may be considered so in the widest sense, but not specifically so. "And it was so, when Elisha the man of God had heard that the king of Israel had rent his clothes, that he sent to the king, saying, Wherefore hast thou rent thy clothes? let him come now to me, and he shall know that there is a prophet in Israel. So Naaman came with his horses and with his chariot, and stood at the door of the house of Elisha." He came up in full driving order right away, to show that he had a good team, to show that he was not any poor patient that required to be sent to the dispensary. The prophet, he thought, would come straight out to him; but no, we read, "And Elisha sent a messenger unto him." The prophet, I expect, was somewhere; perhaps in a back-room that had very little furniture; there was not much furniture in those days. This poor man was perhaps reading the law of God, or perhaps was praying; at any rate, he did not think it worth while even to go out himself to see this great captain. I imagine the servant coming in, and saying, "Elisha, there is a grand man at the door; he has a capital pair of horses and a splendid chariot; he appears to have lots of gold and silver, and changes of raiment; he don't look like a leper." Ah, but Elisha sent a messenger unto him, saying, Go and wash in Jordan seven times, and thy flesh shall come again to thee, and thou shalt be clean."

There are many people who think of the *messenger*, but they forget the *message*; many people can judge the messenger, but they forget that all the time the message is judging them. I believe if an archangel came here, many of those who had been hearing would be critics in about five minutes after they had got into the street. I know that it is an easier thing to criticise than to preach. I have found some good critics, but the best way to silence them is to tell them to try the pulpit themselves for a Sunday. We don't profess to be perfect; and if you find anything crooked in us, the best way is to pray to God, and He will put it right. Don't mind the *messenger*; it is the *message* that you must look at. When the children of Israel were bitten with serpents in the wilderness, and Moses set up a serpent of brass, so that whosoever looked upon that brazen serpent would live and not die, it would have availed them nothing to have *talked* about it; it was absolutely necessary that they should *look* at it in order to live. It would have done them no good if they had even looked at the *pole* upon which the serpent was raised, to have considered whether it was an oak pole, or maple pole, or a straight pole, or a crooked pole; no, they must look at the *serpent*.

If you come here and ask one another, "Did you like that man, or the other man?" you will go away without receiving benefit. My friends, lose sight of every one of us; we are only *poles* and if you have not seen the *Serpent*, we will go away in self-reproach, crying, "O Lord, I took these people's minds away from the *Serpent*; they are looking at the character of the pole." My friends, do not look at the pole to see whether it is of Presbyterian, Methodist, Congregational, or Baptist grain—never mind all that—what we want you to do is to look at the serpent on the pole. We want you to see "no man save Jesus only." If you do so, we shall go away happy, singing, Hallelujah! all the way to the glory, till we meet you in the glory. Remember that when the sun rises all the lesser stars are eclipsed. It is the *message*, not the *messenger*.

"But Naaman was wroth." I like that. I do not like people to be pleased with my preaching all around; there is something wrong when that is the case. I have been preaching the Gospel now for over twenty years, but I am not at all satisfied that I have reached the point of successful preaching, nor do I know of any person that has. The Gospel is the power of God to salvation. The Holy Ghost has given us the Gospel, and that is the instrument in our hands; but it is the Holy Ghost who must drive it home to the sinner's heart. I tell my boy, "You hold that chisel straight over that piece of wood, and I will come down upon it with this heavy hammer." It is I who supply the power to cleave the wood; all my boy has to do is to hold the chisel straight. And that is what I have to do: I have to hold the chisel straight; sometimes I see it held to one side, and the result is that the preaching is unsuccessful; it is the straight chisel that is wanted to go deep down into the sinner's heart through the power of the Holy Ghost. What I wish is, that my preaching may be so real that, in such an audience as this, there should be some scene like this—that (eschewing all attempts at eloquence, but by the straightforward statement of facts burning into me, and through me into you, by the Holy Ghost: incarnation facts, crucifixion facts, resurrection facts, ascension facts; not doctrines even, not pathos, not rhetoric, not logic, but facts of God, the Holy Spirit would so use me as an empty vessel, that after I had finished,) there would only be two classes in this audience: one class crying, "Hallelujah! Christ is mine, and I am His; and the other, gnashing their teeth with rage, and thrusting their fists into by face, crying, "Away with him, it is all lies." This, I believe, would be the plain result of that kind of preaching.

"But Naaman was wroth, and went away." If I degrade you (you may be a respectable man in your own esteem) to the level of a *sinner*, you don't like it, but it is no use getting angry at me. Suppose a lad came to you with a telegraph message that contained very unpleasant news: it would be foolish of you to get into a rage with the boy, he is only the bearer of the message and is only waiting to take the answer back. That is the best telegraph operator that does not alter the message. So, my friends, I am only an operator; I do not make up the Gospel, and it is great folly to get angry at me. The Gospel levels us all down: we have all to take our places in the pit. Here is a respectable man, who says, "I am a regular subscriber to the cause of Christ, and sit in the church every Sunday; I am honest; I pay my debts; I don't profess so much as that other man, but I would not like to be seen in his company: he is a great hypocrite, if you only knew him as well as I do, you would not believe all his religion." My friends, do you know in England we are sometimes bothered with counterfeit sovereigns; but I don't refuse real sovereigns simply because there are counterfeits. You are comparing yourself with another; "measuring yourselves with yourselves, and comparing yourselves among yourselves." And what does the apostle say of such? "Ye are not wise." What is the use of doing it? You are down in the horrible pit. You are a respectable sinner, perhaps, and you see a poor fellow trying to get out, and only falling deeper into the mud; but it's no use going about with a two-foot measure measuring the depth of the mud. You are not wise to compare yourselves with yourselves. You know Nicodemus, one of the most respectable of men, and teacher in Israel, had to be born again, just the same as the very worst and greatest sinner. And so it is that God's blessed gospel levels down all distinctions and all pretences to self-righteousness.

Some people think they must do something. Like the young man in the Gospel, who came to Jesus saying, "What shall I do to inherit eternal life?" He wanted something to do; so Jesus replied, "Go and keep the commandments." Why did He not say to him, as He says elsewhere, "Come to me, and I will give you rest"? He did not want rest; he was wanting to *do* something. The young man told Jesus that he had kept all the commandments from his youth. But the great Teacher just put His finger upon the weak spot—*he was very rich*—"Go and sell that thou hast, and give to the poor." By telling him this, Christ showed him that he had not kept the law, for the law enjoined in effect that he should love his neighbour as himself. He did not go over the detailed statement, but showed in the result that he had not kept the law. I have never yet seen a man that loved his neighbour as well as himself. If a neighbour's house was burnt down, perhaps he might start a subscription right off, and not rest satisfied until he could replace the furniture; but after coming home from the fire, you would probably hear him say, "Well, I'm thankful it wasn't our house." The Lord Jesus gave the result, "See all that thou hast, and give to the poor." To put this in an algebraic form, let A equal your neighbour and B yourself. If B has $100, on the principle of loving his neighbour as himself he would give A $50 if he has none, and retain $50; and if this principle is still acted upon with other needy neighbours, the result will be that he gives away all that he has, the very result which is indicated in the injunction of the Lord to the young man, and that would be the result of trying to do the best we can to meet the Divine requirements.

NAAMAN THE LEPER.   49

"But Naaman was wroth, and went away, and said, Behold, I thought" —what business had he to *think*? If that man is going to get his disease cured by the only man in the world who can cure it, what right has he to *think* anything? He has no right to put in his thoughts at all. So in regard to divine revelation, you have no right to put in your thoughts: "I will hear what God the Lord will speak"—that is it. A medical friend of mine in Edinburgh had a patient once who wrote him a long letter, in which he gave a very elaborate account of his ailments, and made an appointment to meet him. When he came to his house, he went over the whole story again, and then said, "Doctor, don't you think such and such medicine would do?" "Oh, very well," said the doctor, "There it is, that is what you want." He went away, but he did not get any better. At last he wrote another letter, in which he said, "The last time I wrote to you I told you all about myself, and the medicine I *thought* I should have; but I am no better, so the next time I come I want you to tell me what *you* think, and give me the medicine *you* think I ought to have." That was the proper thing to do. When you go to a doctor it is not for you to prescribe for yourself, you must let him find out the disease and apply the remedy.

Poor Naaman said, "*I thought*." He had a nice programme made out, but the prophet's cure had no part in it. He thought, "He will surely come out;" but he sent a messenger instead. He thought that he would come and call upon the name of the Lord his God, and strike his hand over the place, and recover him of his leprosy. So, my friends, put away all your *thinkings* and hear what God will speak. Come unto God—not to His angels or ministers, but to God Himself. "Are not Abana and Pharpar, rivers of Damascus, butter than all the waters of Israel? May I not wash in them, and be clean?" Have I to come all the way from Syria to plunge into that little brook, Jordan? "So he turned and went away in a rage." There are many of his descendants that do likewise; they turn and go away in a rage, because they are told "there is life for a look at the Crucified One;" they cannot come down to the lost sinner's place, and therefore they never can claim the lost sinner's Saviour. If all the preachers on any platform were asked one after another to give their ideas of the Gospel, I guarantee that I could gather all up in one single sentence, and every minister would say amen to it, however we might differ in doctrine, or in ecclesiastical polity; and it is this, that there is a CHRIST FOR EVERY SINNER OUT OF HELL, AND A HELL FOR EVERY SINNER OUT OF CHRIST. This is the Gospel, state it as you please. Mark you, I said nothing about the atonement; nothing about its nature, extent, or application. It is Christ, a living Christ for every man, woman, and child out of Hell; a Christ ready to save.

"And his servants came near, and spake unto him, and said, My father, if the prophet had bid thee do some great thing, wouldest thou not have done it? How much rather then, when he saith to thee, Wash, and be clean?" That is commonsense, my friends. And in like manner you are not required to do some great thing, or to take a long journey, in order to be saved. God won't give you credit even to the extent of turning of an eye-lash, or lifting a straw, to save your souls. It is, "Go and wash, and thou shalt be clean."

> "There is a fountain filled with blood,
>   Drawn from Immanuel's veins;
> And sinners plunged beneath that flood
>   Lose all their guilty stains.
> The dying thief rejoiced to see
>   That fountain in his day,
> And there have I, though vile as he,
>   Washed all my sins away."

Try it, friends. You do not get the cleansing before you go, or *after* you go; it is *when* you go. You are not saved before believing, or after believing, but in believing. The cure is lying in the water; the cure is lying in the blood. "Wash and be clean." There is life and peace in believing. "Believe on the Lord Jesus Christ, and thou shalt be saved."

A friend of mine, many years ago, was told that there was salvation for any sinner, within the boards of the Bible. It was said in a rather strange way, that led him to believe that he had only to search and he would find it. He said, "Well, then, I will have it if it is there." So he began at Genesis, and read all through the first chapter, and he could not see how he could be saved. He then read the second chapter, and the third, and on and on. However, he could

NAAMAN THE LEPER. 51

not find it. He read through the whole of Genesis, and he was just as far from it as ever. He then read Exodus, all about the burnt-offerings, and the sin-offerings, &c. All through Leviticus and Numbers (including the hard names), and in the same way with Deuteronomy. He read all through the Pentateuch, and the subsequent books, until at last he came to Isaiah; and when he was reading the fifty-third chapter, he came across these words, "By His stripes we are healed;" and then he shut the book and said, "I have had enough." It does not say, "by His stripes we may be healed," but, "*by His stripes we are healed.*" This man from that day on became a Christian, and ever since reading those words he has always taken a special interest in circulating printed Christian literature as a great means of spreading God's gospel.

One word more, and I have done. Some years ago I had the privilege of addressing about sixteen thousand people in the Agricultural Hall, in North London, England, after my beloved brother Moody had finished there. At the after meeting, held in the body of the hall, we had about six to seven thousand people. I had preached so much that I was so tired that I left the after meeting to the other helpers there. As I came down the steps into the street, I saw a young man coming from the crowd. I saw him just at the side of the door. As I went out I accompanied a friend on the way to my lodgings. Turning the street, I saw the same young man again, coming after us. "That young man is following us out of the anxious room," I said to my friend. "We will soon find out," I said; "he won't miss us if he is really anxious." So we went on until we came opposite the "*Angel*," A large brilliantly lighted public house. As I was passing round there, the traffic was so great that the young man, I suppose, was afraid of missing me, so he pressed out of the crowd and came and tapped me on the shoulder. He asked, "Were you the man who was preaching in the Agricultural Hall?" "Yes," I replied. "I want to speak to you." "What have you got to say?" I asked. He looked somewhat confused, and at last said, "I really don't know." "Well," I said, "that is rather hard on me. It reminds me of Daniel and Nebuchadnezzar, he didn't even get the dream; you won't give me wither dream or the interpretation. But I think I know where to fetch you. Isn't it this? You would like to know whether you are saved or not?" "Ah! that is it," he said. "That is not very difficult to manage," I said, "if you are really wanting to know." "I am indeed anxious to know," he said. I then directed him to read the sixth verse of the fifty-third chapter of Isaiah. I repeated the words to him: "*All we like sheep have gone astray.*" "Isn't that you, friend?" "Well, that's just me," he said. "Thank God, the battle's half fought and won; '*We have turned every one to his own way.*' That's you." "Yes," he said. "Now do you know the last part of that passage?" "I do not know it." "*And the Lord hath laid on Him the iniquity of us all.*" God does not wait till we lay them. "Now," I said, "go to your room, get on your knees, and open your Bible before you at this passage, with your finger upon it, and repeat every word, every syllable, before God, and now good-night." I had to go home to my own people the next day, and the following morning, after I had answered my letters, my servant came in and said that a man wanted to see me. I went into the drawing room, and who was it but my friend of Islington, all the way from London to Hull, and he said, "Excuse me, but since you told me to write to you, I thought you would not be offended if I called upon you. I came here to see if my soul is rightly saved. There is one thing I want to know in the first place, will that text hold?" I smiled in his face. "Well," I said, "it has held some pretty big sinners for about twenty centuries, and I do not think you look such a very big weight; I think it will stand your weight." Then we sat down, and had a Bible reading between two. We read the Bible from eleven until four in the afternoon, he was so anxious to learn. He said he never saw such a text in all his life. Then I told him before he left to go into Moody's anxious meetings, that there was nothing like talking to the anxious. I got letter after letter from him: "I am so enjoying the work among the anxious;" and, "There is no text like Isaiah liii. 6, 'All we like sheep have gone astray.'"

Ah, my friends, this text is open yet, will you take it as you are, and where you are? If you do, you will never regret it to all eternity. Ah, if you knew the sinner who is speaking to you! If there ever was a sinner deserved hell, it is I, the chief of sinners; but Jesus dies for me. We come to plead with you to accept this Christ as your Saviour, "for the Lord hath laid on Him the iniquity of us all."

DEATH AND LIFE.

"For I through the law am dead to the law, that I might live unto God. I am crucified with Christ: nevertheless I live; yet not I, but Christ liveth in me: and the life which I now live in the flesh I live by the faith of the Son of God, who loved me, and gave Himself for me."—GALATIANS ii. 19, 20.

OUR subject you will find in the epistle of Paul to the Galatians, ii. chapter, 19th verse, "For I through the law am dead to the law, that I might live unto God." What is the chief end of man? "Man's chief end is to glorify God, and enjoy Him for ever." Here it is more shortly—to live to God. That is the ultimate, the highest thought of man's existence—living to God. What men actually live for since the fall is self—this is the centre, the natural centre of all men born from Adam. It may be sometimes a very vulgar and sensual self, or it may be a very polished and religious self, but it is not so very much the quality of the circumstances that are around that self, as the selfish centre that these circles go around. Man's centre is self. And the true light of God shining upon this world is to show that the highest living and aim of man I s to live to God; and that in order to live to God, there must something happen in that man, whatever we may call it—faith, repentance, conversion, new-birth. In fact the Bible has many illustrations, and looks at it from many points; it is, in short, a change of centre. Man's centre being self, God comes down to every man, and asks him to change his centre. It is a remarkable thing that when man was under trial, god is spoken of sometimes as repenting. Man was tried from the day of Eden's innocence to the cross of Calvary, for man was not shown in all his iniquity until Calvary; that which showed the greatest love of God also showed the greatest hate of man, for man's history was the history of the gradual development of what was evil in him. We hear a great deal about the development of man. When we go into very suspicious company with some of the would-be developers, they talk about development in an upward way; they talk about development, I suppose, from oysters up to apes and men; but if we read the history of man, we certainly read of development, but it is all in an opposite direction—it is a development of evil, and not a development of good. It is a degeneration from innocence to evil, and not a growth from savage culture. This is God's teaching concerning the development of man. We find that in Eden, where he was innocent, and not knowing any evil, and away from sin, he was so weak and unable to stand, that he sold his God for a bit of fruit. We find that when he had conscience telling him what was right and wrong, that he did what was wrong in the face of what he knew to be right, and after sixteen hundred and fifty-six years of melancholy history we find that God pronounces that "every imagination of the thought of his heart is only evil continually," and He had to sweep away the whole of creation, Noah's family excepted, in that flood of judgment.

The say, leave a man to his conscience and it will be all right. Will it be all right? My friend, you are about four millenniums too late. God has tried man with his conscience long ago. Men had no Bible from Adam to Moses, but conscience could not tell Noah's sons the theology of the fifth commandment; and conscience could not tell Joseph the theology of the seventh.

God then tried man in the flesh under His law, and it brought out only that man was a transgressor; that the law that he had he broke, so that if our friend the Rationalist is four millenniums too late, our friend the Ritualist is three millenniums late. God has thus tried man in the flesh, not that God might know—He knew the end from the beginning—but to prove it to men. So when Christ, a person, came, it is no longer merely conscience, and no longer merely law, but it is a person now; and in man's rebellion not only was the mind of the flesh weak in innocence, the mind of the flesh against what was good in conscience, and a transgressor under law, but the mind of the flesh is enmity against God, hates a Person, and hates a Person of God's likeness in the flesh; and the cross of Christ, while showing out all the love of God to the chief of sinners, has shown out all the hate of man against the best God, the glorious God, the God and Father of our Lord Jesus Christ. They have murdered Him. Oh, brethren, we must not always look at the mere atonement side of the cross, we have also the other side of the cross which has brought out man's greatest hate and enmity against God.

Now, up to this you may read of God repenting, but from the moment that man was proved to be good for nothing and enmity against God, you never hear of God repenting. God calls upon men everywhere to repent. The repenting is now put upon man. There is no thought of God changing His method of thought, or seeming to do so now, for man is proved at his worst, and man's self is sin—self-seeking carnal self, and he would make all in heaven and earth revolve around himself to serve his own selfish ends. The old astronomers had a strange theory of the motion of the heavenly bodies. They thought that this little earth was so big and mighty that all the heavens revolved around it; that this little speck of creation that we now know to be so little, was so vast and of such great importance that the sun went around it, and the planets went around it, and the starts and all went around our little globe. The erratic motions of planets rather put them out a little. They could not make out for one or two wanderers that they saw there, still they had to discount these discrepancies, and make out that really the whole heaven went around the earth. They never thought that we were one little point revolving around a sun, and that those fixed stars were other suns, possibly with planets revolving around them. We have now reached the true and exact science of modern astronomy by a change of centre.

Now, unsaved man, you have to get into the God of the bible, you have not to think that you are the centre, that heaven and earth and men have got to revolve around you, but you have got to find that God is the centre, and that revolving around Him you will get your true place, and you will live to God and not to self. This was the apostle's thought, "That I might live to God." His great aim was, that God might be his centre. Now how did the apostle Paul reach that? By the words of the text, "I through the law am dead to the law, that I might live unto God," You see it is not quickly done; you must see one or two things before you change the centre.

Before you plan how to govern Canada, you have to be elected governor; you have to get your seat first, and you have to do several things. A man says, "I am bound to live for God; I am going to live for God." Not quite so quick, my friend. We have something to look into that the apostle Paul looked into when he said, "I through the law am dead to the law, that I might live unto God." You have to be a dead man unto the law in order that, being dead through the law to the law, you might live unto God. Very shortly, I would just fix your thought and mind upon this great subject by three words; first, our condemnation; secondly, our justification; and thirdly, our sanctification.

Firstly, condemnation—"I through the law am a dead man;" secondly, justification—"I am a dead man to the law;" thirdly, sanctification—"that I might live unto God."

"I through the law am dead"—that is first. You must take the dead sinner's place, you must know that you have been in the ditch, before the Samaritan is of any use to you. "They that are whole need not a physician, but they that are sick." Go to any decent man anywhere that attends church or chapel, and say, "Friend, are you lost?" "Oh, no," he will say, "not I. I hope I never shall be. I am a respectable man; I have a pew, two of them perhaps, and I pay my part in connection with all church doings; I always have my subscription paid." "Do you mean to say that you have never found out that you are lost?" "Oh, no, not I." "Well, I am sorry for you, you have to find it out very shortly; for Christ came not to call the righteous, but sinners to repentance. My friend, you have yet to find out that you are lost. You have to find out that the law of God is demanding your death, saying, 'Die, die.' Do you feel that you are condemned?" "Oh, no, that is a different question." I think there is rather a confusion in terms. I will ask him if he feels guilty, and if he says yes, it is all right. The condemnation is the sentence of the Judge; it is yours to accept the condemnation. Do you accept this character that God has given you? It is not a matter of our feelings at all, it is of God's righteous judgment. Now, friend, are you prepared to subscribe your name to these lists of sinners, and say that is the stuff of which you are made? I do not ask you if you feel guilty of all the sins of the first chapter of Romans, I am sure you are not inclined to murder any one. The question is this, Will you go by yourself, or occupy the character as given you? Or, in other words, God has weighed you in the balance, I give you your weight as God has weighed you, will you accept it, or go by your own notions? It is more God-glorifying to accept the character there given, though you be as spotless and blameless as could be. It is more than for the debased drunkard to accept it. You accept it because God says it; he accepts it because he has experienced it; you therefore submit to the righteousness of God, but they, "being ignorant of God's righteousness," have gone about "to establish their own righteousness, and would not submit themselves to the righteousness of God." Now, here we come to another point, How can God be just, and justify such a man? Guilty—I have accepted the doom. Condemned—I believe it.

How can God be just, and how can I be just with God? That was the question that rose from the smoke of ten thousand altars; that was the question that flowed in the blood of thousands of victims, all raising the question, How can man be just with God? It is not the question of God's love there, it is the question of God's justice. How can He be just, and yet let guilty sinners into His presence? Ah! this was the great question of the Old Testament, answered in the New, How may God be just, and justify all men who believe in Jesus?

A gentleman came to me at one of my meetings in England where I was speaking, and said, "I cannot believe in that gospel you preach; it is a shocking thing, a shocking gospel. Do you mean to say that an innocent man dying for a guilty man is just, or fair, or honest? An innocent man dying for a guilty man, is it just to the innocent man?" I looked him straight in the face, and said, "No." "Is it just to the guilty man?" "No." "Then why do you preach it?" I said, "You may have heard that from someone else, but it is not my gospel." "What do you preach, sir?" "Listen," I said; "be very careful what I tell you: my first position is this, that God became man; now, sir, where is your logic? In what system or syllogism do you find that statement, that God became man? Where is your measuring-rod that can measure that thought? Hast thou scaled the highest heights of heaven? Hast hour measured the deepest depths of hell? Dost thou know the comprehension of God? then tell me the meaning of God's becoming man? You may reject it or accept it; but this you cannot do, you cannot measure it; you cannot argue upon it; you can only accept or reject it as a revelation from God. And my second is like unto my first; the gospel that I preach is this, that God became man, and put away sin by the sacrifice of Himself. Can you tell me the meaning of 'putting away sin by the sacrifice of Himself'? I cannot, cannot comprehend that."

Blessed by God, the simplest child in this meeting can apprehend it. It is one thing to comprehend a thing, and another ting to apprehend it; and if the well is deep, yea, bottomless and fathomless, that well of His gospel is full and running over, and the child's little tumbler can be filled, as the well is full to the brim. God became man, and put away sin by the sacrifice of Himself; that is God's gospel, that is the gospel in the New Testament, that is the gospel of Revelation, that is the gospel to the glory of God.

Darius loved Daniel; the advisers of Darius were jealous of Daniel; they entrapped Darius into making a rash decree in order that they might entrap Daniel; Darius could not fall back from his word; Daniel had to go away to the lions' den. Darius might have gone all day long endeavouring to get Daniel off; but his love could not do it, his mercy could not do it, and his pity could not get Daniel off. He might have gone to the council, but they would have said, "The law cannot be broken." The law came in at every point. He could not let him off. He might scheme from the rising of the sun to the going down thereof; but the grace and the love, and the mercy, and the pity were of no avail because there was the law— the law, righteous or unrighteous, the fixed law of the Medes and Persians, standing dead between Darius and Daniel, and he must away to the den of lions, and I have often thought that when Daniel sat that night with the lions' mouths graciously stopped, he could look up to the mouth of the den and say, "Well, you have done your worst now, what more can you do? I, through the law, am dead; but I am more not, I am dead to your law; you cannot put me in again." And then, next morning, when Darius came to him and said, "Daniel, Daniel, has God delivered you?" "Yes, I am here," and he could then live as the brightest specimen of the righteousness of Darius in all the kingdom of the Medes and Persians. I, through God's law, in my substitute, am a dead man to the law, that I might live unto God. I have death and doom behind me, and nothing before me but the blessed hope of the return of my Lord. "I through the law am dead to the law, that I might live to God. I have been crucified with Christ, nevertheless I live no longer, but Christ liveth in me."

If you take the lost sinner's place, what does God say to you, my friends? "I can do nothing but save you." Let Him save you. You will forget your unworthiness when you are in the embrace of your heavenly Father, as did the prodigal son.

THE ACCEPTABLE SACRIFICE.

"I beseech you therefore, brethren, by the mercies of God, that ye present your bodies a living sacrifice, holy, acceptable unto God, which is your reasonable service."—ROMANS xii. I.

THE special aspect of truth before us is, "Our bodies are to be presented as a living sacrifice, holy, acceptable unto God, which is our reasonable service." God is wanting service from us, and sacrifice. The sacrifice is characterized as being living. It is not a dead animal put upon an altar. It is a living man—living to God. It is a living sacrifice. It is wholly separated by God Himself—by His own sanctifying act—unto the Lord. It is acceptable to the Lord, who is seeking workers, worshippers, witnesses; and in the person of the redeemed sinner, sanctified and consecrated unto Him, we have a holy worshipper, a true worker, and a consecrated witness—a priest, a Levite, a Nazarite. And it is our "reasonable service," not the irrationalism of mere externalism and attitude and action of the body, but that which proceeds from that internal mind that God has given, a reasonable service—reasonable as being holy, and in being acceptable unto God, and reasonable as being sent up to God by the whole man. Our body is presented to God as a casket which contains the priceless gems. We find the Lord Jesus spoken of as tabernacling here in the flesh. So we have this tabernacle—the body—which contains in it the holy place and the most holy, which are to be given up entirely to God for His work for His worship, and for His witness.

This is all founded, you will see, with the greatest, because the divine caution, that this is no legal sanctification, no legal consecration, no act or profession of holy service as Israel gave on the mount, when they did not know their own weakness, when the

Lord came down to prove them, and they said, with the confidence of the flesh, "All things that are written, we will do." They had the intention to do it, no doubt, at the time, but they had not the power; and this is why fallen humanity, sprung from Adam, must always be a liar. "Let God be true, and every man a liar," springs from the necessities of the case of fallen humanity, because fallen humanity will strongly promise to do what it has not the power to do, as revealed in God's word, without strength, but still with the presumption of promise.

It is not then the offering of legalism, in the strength of the flesh, that we are asked to present our bodies, living, holy, acceptable sacrifices unto God; but as those who have known and experienced the mercies of God, for it is by them we are besought. "I beseech you, therefore, by the mercies of God"—the mercies of God as revealed fully in the whole sweep of doctrine taught in the epistle to the Romans up to this point. In the divine settling of every question, that has arisen, or may arise, concerning the standing, the state, the position, the guilt, the innate corruption of every sinner born from Adam—when every question has been raised—in the wisdom of God every question has been met by the grace of God, according to the righteousness of God; and His grace and His righteousness have thus both been untied by His eternal wisdom. His infinite grace and infinite righteousness seem to be in opposition, so far as we poor, guilty, weak sinners were concerned; but infinite wisdom came welding these together, so that grace reigns now through righteousness, and God can be just and the justifier of him that believeth on Jesus, when His love is thus seen flowing down free and full as a river, bringing pardon and peace and joy, giving us those grand hallelujah choruses—songs of God, as seen in chapters five to eight of this glorious epistle—giving us peace with God through our Lord Jesus Christ; giving us access into that grace wherein we stand; giving us to rejoice in the hope of the coming glory; and if the glory should be a little distant, even to give us to "glory in tribulation also: knowing that tribulation worketh patience; and patience, experience; and experience, hope." Also the very love of God is shed abroad in our hearts. And our final salvation depending on His life in resurrection, we thus can make our boast in God Himself.

These are some of the mercies, as far as the question of our sins in concerned, that are at the foundation of all our consecration; and when we come to the question of our sin—of what we are, as contrasted with what we have done—we find all full of mercies—no condemnation to them that are in Christ, and God Himself dwelling in us, and God Himself standing for us. "And if God be for us, who can be against us?" Now with all the mercies of God thus poured out upon us, chief of sinners among the Gentiles, or among the Jews, with a revelation from God, or without a revelation from God, wandering far from Him the worst and the vilest of men, provided for according to the righteous requirements of God, everything is settled in the past, everything settled in the present, everything settled for the future, what more befitting than to come in now: "I beseech you, brethren, by those mercies, that ye present your bodies a living sacrifice, holy and acceptable unto God."

I think it will be profitable to look, in the first place, at the God-ward side of this truth, because if there was no God-ward aspect of this consecration there could be no man-ward. God is the beginning, and God brings in the beginning; and on the foundation of what God is, and what God has done, and how God has done it, we are called upon to present our bodies to Him. And these two lines of truth you will find in the grand old picture-book Bible; namely, the Old Testament.

Little children—and this we are taught to be in simplicity in learning our Father's will—are often taught by pictures. Just as little boys are much more interested in pictures than merely dry doctrinal teaching, so the Lord has graciously given us a picture-book.

You remember, when Nicodemus could not understand the new birth, the Lord Jesus took him away to the picture-book of the Bible, and showed him a serpent lifted up, and said, "These is where eternal life is to be secured." As! Friends, we are safe when we use our Old Testament as Christ used it. The enemy is trying, on all sides, to take away our Old Testament from us—our grand Old Bible, with Moses, and the Prophets, and the Psalms; but we are all safe when we keep by Christ's use of them, and he used them reverently and fulfilled them to the letter, and used them

THE ACCEPTABLE SACRIFICE. 63

defensively against all the temptations of Satan. It is very remarkable to note the use that Christ made of the Old Testament in the in His conquering of Satan, fulfilling the word of prophecy— "By the words of thy lips I have kept my from the paths of the destroyer;" and that these words were taken from the book of Deuteronomy, the very book that the enemy now most savagely assails, and that the Lord Jesus Himself used this book in the act of defence against the fiery darts of the enemy.

We go back to the picture-book, and there you find two pictures—one in Leviticus and the other in Numbers. In Leviticus viii. you have the divine consecration of the priest and Levite. in Numbers vi. You have the self-consecration of the Nazarite, and all this must be taken into account in connection with the truth of this subject, else we shall not have an all-sided view of the method of divine consecration. All through there is a rotundity about truth. We are so apt to look upon truth from one point of view, and to be carried away by that; but we are told to walk about Zion, and go round the high towers thereof, to consider her palaces and mark her bulwarks well. We are to go round Zion. We are to go round all the revelation that God has given. So if God consecrates the priest and Levite on the one side, the Nazarite consecrates himself to God on the other; and in the priest we have the worshipper consecrated to God, in the Levite we have the worker, and in the Nazarite we have the witness. The separated witness, the active worker, the holy worshipper, are the three thoughts that we have in the picture-book that God has given us in connection with the history of Israel.

Let us then look at the first, as contained in the first twelve verses of the eighth chapter of the book of Leviticus. When we get Aaron in the priesthood, he stands before us as the great type of Christ. Aaron alone represents Christ alone. Aaron and his sons represent Christ and the Church. When we get Aaron and Moses we have priest and prophet. Moses, Aaron, and the elders, as seen in Leviticus ix., point to Christ as Prophet, Priest, and King on the eighth day (the millennial scene).

We have the same questions raised as are raised in Romans iii. and v., and met by the figure here, and by types and illustrations, as we have them met doctrinally in the epistle to the Romans.

We have the ram of consecration, we have the basket of consecration, and we have the days of consecration now brought before us in Leviticus viii. And these are to be before us as the priests and Levites of the Lord. Verse 12 shows us Aaron getting the oil poured on him without any blood. Christ required no sin-offering before the Holy Ghost fell on Him without measure. But when we come to the sons of Aaron, there is no consecration until sin-offering and burnt-offering have been presented.

In verses 12 to 21, we see not only is the sin-bearer identified with all the guilt of the sinner; but the sinner is identified with all the worth of the victim. All the worth of the preciousness of Christ is ours, as all the guilt that we had was His. It was a burnt sacrifice of a sweet savour, and the offering made by fire unto the Lord, as the Lord commanded Moses. Here we have the sin-offering and the burnt-offering presented, before there is a word of the consecration of the sons of Aaron. Then after the whole question of sin and acceptance were met in the sin-offering and burnt-offering that were presented, we read: "Aaron and his sons laid their hands upon the head of the bullock for the sin-offering." This was the Eastern method of identification, in which the sinner came confessing his sins; and the sin-offering was identified with all the sin of the offerer, the offerer identified with all the value of the burnt-offering.

"And he slew it; and Moses took of the blood of it, and put it upon the tip of Aaron's right ear, and upon the thumb of his right hand, and upon the great toe of his right foot." (Lev. viii. 23.) Here is the blood before the oil, and in the blood we have the life taken. The blood in Scripture is never spoken of as coursing through the arteries of the living victim. It is not the life in the victim, but it is the shedding of blood: "Without shedding of blood there is no remission." The perfect and co-equal with God, comes in the strength of His own love, and the power of His own holiness; and we can be anointed with the Spirit of the living God, for the service which he is to undertake. And when the anointing oil is poured upon Aaron's head, God separated him for the work. He sanctified him. We shall never get into the full idea of consecration until we see it in the aspect of separation—separation from, and separation to. Its use is very wide in the Old Testament—separation from and to all things concerned.

The Spirit of the Lord could be given to Christ without measure, for He was holy, and harmless, and undefiled, and separate from sinners. The perfect moral glory of the Lord Jesus, His entire separation from all that was of this world of sin, is thus shown forth. He stood there and hear the voice of God, and received the anointing of the Holy Ghost. When He stood there, and the voice was heard, and the dove rested upon Him—"This is My beloved Son, in whom I am well pleased"—no sacrifice did He require for Himself. Hence He is the uncreated One—the all-creating One; because if any creature had laid down his life at the command of God, he had nothing to spare to transfer to another, because God had given him his life, and could, in justice, at any time demand it. Christ is separated with His own as brethren, just as Aaron and his sons together were consecrated with blood. In verses 22 and 23 we have the whole body a living sacrifice consecrated by the act of God through His prophet—by the act of God, to the Lord. And this is the fundamental truth of it all, and what makes the other a natural sequent. When I realize I am not my own, but am bought with a price, and the blood of consecration is upon my ear, and the blood of consecration is upon my hand and the blood of consecration is upon my foot, and the whole man, from head to foot, his whole spirit, his whole soul, his whole body—all that the man is—his mind, his will, his affections, everything that the body contains, as the tabernacle containing all the preciousness of the gold and glory—all by the act of God, by the blood of consecration separated to God, —what manner of persons ought we to be? This truth, in connection with the Christian's walk, should have the greatest power upon everyone of us—what the Lord has done—not so much what I am to do—that follows, but what the Lord has done. If the *blood* of consecration is upon that hand by a Divine act, dare that hand do anything that is against or inconsistent with that precious One whose blood was shed? Would that not carry a consecrated hand into all business? I have sometimes been asked by some Christians about this secular call, and the other secular call. "My friend," I say, "if a consecrated hand is put to anything, that call becomes immediately consecrated." It is a sacred hand, and the carpenter with his saw, or plane, or chisel, imitating the carpenter of Nazareth, is going forth as a royal priest with a consecrated hand to provide things that are honest in the sight of all men, and laboring and working with his hands the thing that is good, that he may have to give to him that needeth. And thus the consecrated priest, let him be preacher, or carpenter, or mechanic, wherever he may go, he carries a consecrated hand right in to every part of his work. Then shall we find the exhortation of Paul, concerning consecration, to be consistent with servants obeying their masters, whether converted or unconverted. "Not with eye-service as men-pleasers, for ye serve the Lord Christ." It is with a consecrated hand, by the blood of the consecrated ram, that thus we go forward to the business of the world. This is very practical; this goes down to the business, to the counter, to the shop, to the office. If these were known and practised, such a hand could lift no pen to write a name, but what would be for the glory of that blood shed. We should find more practical testimony for the Lord among those who profess his name. We should hear of no Christian being involved in suspicious things in the world's business, if he carried the consecrated hand into the city, and into all his business; and if there was a doubt about any line of conduct, he would say, "But that hand is consecrated with the blood of consecration; I am holy to the Lord." And only holy communications would be received by the ear; because it is holy to the Lord. If we realized more that we had consecrated ears, the revelation of God would come into us much more simply than it does. We should find fewer difficulties among Christians about interpretations of the Word of God, if we all realized that we approach that Book with the blood of sprinkling, and come to listen, as holy priests, to the voice and communication of the living God, with the blood of consecration marked upon us. Then my foot—shall it tread in paths that would not become a consecrated foot? Do you ask me to go here or there? I go at once if the blood-touched foot can go. We go at once if we can carry our Christ as slain, and rejected, and murdered by this world. Then we can go, knowing that the blood of consecration is upon the foot, and ear, and hand—the living man thus consecrated to the Lord. This blood that we have here is the measure of our consecration. "Ye have not resisted unto blood." How much must I seek to do for the Lord?

THE ACCEPTABLE SACRIFICE. 67

Love my neighbor as myself? A little further—what? to love one another as Christ loved us. And how far? To lay down our lives for the brethren, for we are consecrated by blood, and until we have gone on to the full measure of it, we are short of what the consecrated One has done.

If in the service of the Lord my ear has to be taken from me, and my right hand taken off, and I have to lose my right foot, I am doing nothing more than I have been consecrated for. We have been consecrated by the blood mark upon us, and as Queen Victoria's troops know how to charge at the word of command, but never to reason why, though they go into the valley of death, so the soldiers of the Lord Jesus, consecrated with blood, go forward, calmly but resolutely, to fight, with the oath of consecration of the ear, on the foot, and on the hand, crying, life, life is the measure of my consecration to the Lord, consecrated by the blood." Well might he say, "Who is sufficient for these things?" It is enough to dishearten a poor struggling one down here when we see such a great ideal before us; but God will never bring down the ideal to our level. He will raise our level up to His ideal. We are predestinated to be conformed to the image of His Son, and He will never be satisfied till we are so, and we shall never be satisfied till we wake in His likeness. God puts the consecration of Christ unto the death as the point at which we are to aim. He does not tell me to follow Paul, or Abraham, or any other saint. Ah! we are always aiming at lower models and saying, "I wish I were like Mr. So-and-so." My friends, all the mirrors on earth have cracks across them, and the cracks are reflected when we take the reflected light from them; and just as often as reflection goes from mirror to mirror upon earth, we imitate, it may be, even the flaws, while we forget the beauties. Let us go straight to the Lord Himself, and see the measure of His consecration. But if we have the measure of it in the blood, we have also the power of it in the oil of consecration. Moses took of the anointing oil, and of the blood which is upon the altar, and sprinkled it upon Aaron and upon his garments. If I am told to clear away a mountain, I have not the power to do it, and it is to me an impossible thing; but if I get sufficient engines and men, it then can be done. If I am told I am to be consecrated unto the death, I may say, "Who is sufficient for these things?" But God has provided his

Spirit, that will not rest within us, but feed us by the truth of God, until we are in the likeness of Jesus. "When He shall appear, we shall be like Him; for we shall see Him as He is. And everyone that hath this hope in HIM purifieth himself, even as He is pure." And as the blood tells us of the measure of our consecration as the priests of God, so the oil tells us of the power that God has given to enable us to rise up to this ideal. And it is by the indwelling Spirit of God, ungrieved and unhindered, and the activities of His work within us, that we go onward, calmly and surely imitating the Lord, and going forward in the path that He has trod, raising within us those holy aspirations and those holy determinations now to live wholly and unreservedly for Him. It is by the oil of the Spirit of God giving the power within, that now we live in the path of priests.

I need not explain that every child of God is a priest of God. All children of the living God now are as the sons of Aaron, for "He hath made us unto our God kings and priests." Meantime we exercise our functions as priests in interceding for others around us. By-and-by, in the glory to come, there will be the manifesting of the royal priesthood, of the glory of the Lord; but if you turn to Peter, you will find two things spoken of as to our priesthood—we are a *holy* and a *royal* priesthood. We manifest what Christ is, within as before God, and without us in the world at large. As the first of these, "Ye are also a *holy* priesthood to offer up spiritual sacrifices acceptable to God by Jesus Christ;" And at verse 9, as to the second, "But ye are a chosen generation, a *royal* priesthood, an holy nation, a peculiar people; that ye should show forth the praises of Him who hath called you out of darkness unto His marvelous light." The two aspects of our priesthood, as they are within the veil, and outside in the world, are these: *holy* to offer sacrifices, *royal* to spread out here in a royal way, to the world at large, the praises of Him.

Are we acting as a royal priesthood? Do we act as the great ambassadors from God? Have we spread the testimony of the Lord Jesus as a royal priesthood to the ends of the earth? Have we satisfied our consciences, and gone like kings with the embassy of God? An ambassador carries with him the honour of his country. Have we come down from the height of our glory, and sounded the proclamation over "vale and hill"? I am glad to see that one phase

THE ACCEPTABLE SACRIFICE. 69

of Christian word is getting popular—the missionary aspect; but we are truly guilty in this matter. We talk about consecration, and about being the Lord's but what are we doing? "Ye shall be witnesses unto be moth in Jerusalem, and in all Judea, and in Samaria, and unto the uttermost parts of the earth;" and millions of people have never heard there is a Christ for them, or that there is a salvation from God. We have all fallen from the height of our royal priesthood by not going outward to these lost brethren. The history of Missions in the present day is only about one hundred years old. Seventeen centuries have elapsed, and Christian thought their fellow-Christian mad when they tried to rise up to the height of their obedience, and of their responsibility in this matter. If Queen Victoria desired a proclamation sounded through all the world, how long would it be before that proclamation would be known, with the machinery—the Army, the Navy, the Exchequer—that would be set in motion to issue it? Would it take eighteen centuries? Rather let me say it would take eighteen months. The proclamation, as the little hymn says, would be "sounded over vale and hill." What is the command, and what are our resources? All the power of the British Navy, the British Army, and the British Exchequer? No. "All power is given to Me in heaven and on earth." What for? "Go ye therefor into all the world, and preach the gospel to every creature." And then? "Lo, I am with you. "I think that gives us a good hint; this has been the mistake of the dispensation. Christians have been trying to get universal conversion instead of universal evangelization. That is the mistake, that is at the root of it all. Instead of obeying the Lord's command, and giving the whole world a chance, we have been high-farming little corners, and setting workers down so closely as to interfere with each other's work, and the poor heathen lying in their heathenism and godlessness. Let our hearts be burdened to begin with, and our prayers rise up, and our money stream forth, and our young men be told that the great crown for the worker is the foreign field, and that the great call of the day is to stand up in obedience to the Lord, and to go forth in His name to tell the gospel of peace through the nations of the earth. For it is not written: "Lo, you will be successful; lo, you will get the whole world laid at your feet; lo, everyone will receive you; lo, every nation will turn to you." No, no; but, "Lo, you will find that it is hard work gathering out the new from the ea." It is not the abundance of the sea, yet it is the netful out of it, and you will find that you will need to go to Him very often; for it will be hard work. "Lo, men will all believe you." No, no; but, "Lo, I am with you always, even to the end of then age.: And this is the practical outcome of our consecration to Him, the obedience that would depend upon that promise. It is lying there for faith to act upon it. All power in heaven and earth has been lying there for eighteen centuries. Shall we not rise up and take hold of it, and get our should burdened, and see wherein we are guilty each in this matter.

But we must pass on. There is the *basket* of consecration. Some do not attend much to this: "And there eat it with the bread that is in the basket of consecration." We see this perfectly in the Lord Jesus. When His disciples went to buy bread, He said, "I have meat to eat that ye know not of." And what was His meat? Doing His Father's will. And here it is in the basket of consecration. It is finding the will of God, and knowing it, and doing it, that we are thus fed day by day. The morning's blessing will not do for the evening, and the manna of yesterday will not do for to-day; but the bread of the basket of consecration bust be partaken of day by day. Thus we have to say, "Give us this day our daily bread."

And last of all, "Ye shall not go out of the door of the tabernacle of the congregation in seven days, until the days of your consecration be at an end…Therefore shall ye abide at the door of the tabernacle, and keep the charge of the Lord, as He hath commanded." Here is our attitude now as those who are waiting for God's Son from heaven. We are to abide all the days of our consecration; that is, until the Lord comes, and takes us into His own presence. And what are we doing? Keeping the charge of the Lord—the charge that He hath given us—turned to serve and wait. And we are waiting here in obedience to His command as the waiting and working ones—waiting for Him to return. And to see the glory that we have mirrored forth in the ninth chapter, going forward in the power of His glorious truth, and in the energy of His mighty Spirit, keeping that charge, doing His will. Thus we shall be in that frame that the Nazarite was in, which I refer you to at your leisure in Numbers vi.; consecrating himself, laying himself down, all that he has and is, for the Lord. So now we are not living as men who shut themselves out from the world, and separate themselves from its midst, but living as men to bear the testimony of the Lord, to fight the battles of the Lord. Thus separated by God Himself, acceptable to Him as workers, worshippers, and witnesses, the only thing that as rational men we can do is to present ourselves to the Lord, with no reserves. What else do we live for but this? We are fools if we live for anything else. We are throwing away the very existence that God has given us. And when I look upon the mass of men, the great majority of whom, I believe, are professing that blessed name that is being trampled upon by the world; when I behold that open infidelity, and that certain kind of Christianity that professes the name, but has not the reality, I think of the potential energy there is with us, if we could only rise up to the dignity of our sonship, and be holy and acceptable and consecrated to the Lord—not a part of our being, not a little part of our time, but entirely. Realizing what the Lord has made me, I fall into His way, and I say, "Yes, Lord, this goes with my whole soul and mind.' "What shall we then say to these things?" It is a beautiful thought, putting our hand into Christ's; and it reminds me also of these warlike customs in the days of old Rome, when the *sacramentum*, or oath, was given to the soldiers. The leader of the detachment that was to be sworn to live and die for the Senate and the people of Rome read over at large the *sacramentum*, and then the right-hand man held up his right hand, and repeated the Latin words, "*Idem in me*" ("The same for me"). And down it went, till the last left-hand man held up his right hand in what he thought the most holy attitude, and swore the same oath. And the apostle says, "What shall we say to these things?" Are we ready to hold up our right hand to him, each individual of us, and cry, "*Idem in me*" ("The same for me"), and to pass along the lines the shout of praise and glory, to sing as we go on like a mighty host unto the Lord, filled with His Spirit, and sublimated, sanctified, and purified, made more and more like to Him, transformed into His image, joying in His mercies, humbled with our failures, glorying in His grace, glorying in what He is, not even in what Christ has made us. Let us not glory even in that our names are high up in heaven's list yonder, and that we are strong before the Lord; but rather glory in the grace that has put us there, and in the God of grace that has made us what we are in Christ; for we make our boast in God.

THE ACCEPTABLE WILL OF GOD.

"I beseech you therefore, brethren, by the mercies of God, that ye present your bodies a living sacrifice, holy, acceptable unto God, which is your reasonable service. And be not conformed to this world; but be ye transformed by the renewing of your mind, that ye may prove what is that good, and acceptable, and perfect, will of God."—ROMANS xii. 1, 2.

I beseech you therefore by the mercies of God." The mercies of God have been explained in the epistle already, but I draw your attention to this "therefore." "I beseech you *therefore*." Sometimes, as you know, the division into chapters breaks the continuity of the teaching; and we shall go back, therefore, a verse of two, to link on the former teaching in the end of the eleventh chapter of Romans, with the teaching now before us. "O the depth of the riches both of the wisdom and knowledge of God! How unsearchable are His judgments, and His ways past finding out!" And if poor, ignorant man would take a lesson from this, he would not try to measure the infinite by the finite; "for who hath known the mind of the Lord? or who hath been His counsellor? Or who hath first given to Him, and it shall be recompensed unto him again? For *of* Him, and *through* Him, and *to* Him are all things: to whom be glory for ever." There is the *highest ideal* of God in the creature—"Of Him, and through Him, and to Him are all things: to whom be glory." From Him, through Him, and back to Him, and glory to Him. "I beseech you *therefore*" immediately coming after this wonderfully comprehensive statement, "Of Him, through Him, and to Him are all things; to whom be glory for ever." "I beseech you therefore, brethren, by the mercies of God, that ye present your bodies a living sacrifice, holy, acceptable unto God, which is your reasonable service." Since the highest ideal that we, intelligent, fallen, and now saved beings, have of being entirely in the mind of God is, "Of Him, and through Him, and to Him are all things," and glory in all—from eternity, through time, to eternity again; from His counsels, through the manifestations of the activities of His grace, on to the final triumphs in glory yonder—we receive the exhortation with all its force, "I beseech you therefore"—and this is the way we should aim at reaching the highest ideal—"that ye present your bodies a living sacrifice, holy, acceptable unto God, which is your reasonable service. And be not conformed to this world: but be ye transformed by the renewing of your mind, that ye may prove what is that good, and acceptable, and perfect, will of God. For I say, through the grace given unto me, to every man that is among you, not to think of himself more highly than he ought to think; but to think soberly, according as God that dealt to every man the measure of faith." There, in what comes after the exhortation, we have what is to be cultivated, in order that that ideal, being before us, may be produced in us and by us in our education down here, as being educated for the eternity that is to stretch on before us. Here we get as essentials for rising up to this thought, "Oh Him, to Him, and through Him are all thing; unto Him be glory."

We have, in the first place, devotedness, *thorough devotedness* of the whole man, and no reservation, nothing kept, the whole burnt-offering upon the altar, the living sacrifice; then obedience, *unquestioning obedience*; and with this unquestioning obedience the deepest spirit of *humility* and dependence; for if we have the devotedness and the obedience, we have an indication of proof of the will of God, essentially good and perfect, leaving nothing out. We have reached the terminus of it, and it is "well pleasing" (the same word used as that about the sacrifice). For devotedness, thorough devotedness, and unquestioning obedience precede this proving, and we find that it is obtained in the spirit that follow: "Through the grace given unto me; to every man that is among you, not to think of himself *more highly* than he ought to think; but to think soberly, according as God hath dealt to every man the *measure of faith*." *Humility* as to the place that he has, and the walk to which he is called, and *dependence* upon the Sovereign God, who gives as He wills.

Do not let us boast of the place that grace has given us, but let us boast of the grace that has given us the place; not taken up with being even seated in the heavenly places in Christ, but worshiping Him on the throne, whose grace has set us there—every eye thus turned to the God of grace that set us upon the throne. Ah! let us not think more highly than we ought to think, but, in utter humility and daily dependence, live the life that God has been calling men to during these six millenniums—the manifestation of creatures thoroughly depending on Him for every breath, and so lost in His will, that they have no wills of their own; not in innocence, and not in ignorance, but in righteousness and truth. Man has fallen from innocence, and God, making the wrath of man to praise Him, has raised him to a higher level in righteousness, holiness, and truth. Not in ignorance, as the stars of night, and the creation around us, which obey the will of God. When we say, "Thy will be done," we may look abroad to the stars of night, and we see the planets circling round the centre of light and heat, and they are all dong the will of God; even the erratic comets, stretching out their wide paths, are fulfilling His will, the stars of the universe are doing His will, and the blades of grass that spring up in our path are doing His will, and the flowers that burst open on a spring day, and the summer fruits of nature, and the rushing river, and the rolling ocean, and the thunder-storm, and the lightning, are all His messengers in nature, are all doing His will. He could, when He was here on earth, speak to those waves of the Sea of Galilee, and thy would listen to His voice, and do His will, as has been beautifully said—

> "Calmly He rose, with sovereign will,
> And hushed the waves to rest;
> 'Ye waves,' He whispered, 'Peace! be still!'
> And the calmed like a pardoned breast."

It is not as ignorant nature, but as men made in the image of God, the highest thought of existence, that has been formed by Him, and by His re-creating Spirit, and according to the blood shed, that we are now to be trained to prove what is His perfect, and good, and acceptable will.

We have, in studying this subject in the connection in which it is thus given, to look at three thoughts especially—*the measure* of His will, *the rule* to guide us in following that will, and the *power* given for proving that will.

Let me draw attention to this, that it is not to prove the good, and perfect, and acceptable *work* of God; it is His *will*, not His *work*. It is not merely active service, such as evangelizing, or preaching the gospel, or teaching, or in any way being ministers or evangelists, and so on. This is for the whole body of believers at every place where they may be. The lowest servant in the godless man's household, doing the most menial work, may have a high, a holy, and heavenly calm, and rest, and joy, and satisfaction in doing his daily work, and doing tit as to the Lord, feeling that he was proving that good, and holy, and acceptable will of God, and that in the place that God had put him, and with the work that God had given him. He ought not to rush away, and perhaps get into work whereto he was not sent, but calmly—not only at an occasional time, as on Sunday, when he could do a little tract-distributing, or something else, but moment by moment, on Monday and Tuesday, every day, and every hour of every day—calmly be doing everything, with the consciousness within him that he and the Lord were in the same school—the Lord as the Master and he as the willing scholar, being taught "the good, the perfect, and the acceptable will of God."

Nothing short of this is God's ideal for us. "Lo, I come (in the volume of the book it is written on Me,) to do thy will, O God." And when He came here, Satan's first temptation was to make Him go out of that path; for he said, "If thou be the Son of God." From the moment Christ came to do His Father's will, He had no will of His own. He went about doing many mighty deeds, because God was with Him. He took the place of a perfect man—a man in subjection to the will of another—and thus showed His Godhead. Those who deny the Godhead of Christ point to Christ's own words—"My Father is greater than I." Why, it is the very proof of His equality.

Take a human illustration. If two partners, equal in business, had a great number of servants, and they found that they were not obeyed, and one of the partners said, "Now we must teach them a lesson in obedience, and in not having their own wills. And so I will go and do your will." He asks no questions when the command is given, for whatever it may be given. If the other partner comes in and says, "You go and do such a menial work," the partner goes away, to the astonishment of the servants, and they say, "Why, you are equal in partnership; why go and do this menial work?" "I am a servant in the meantime," he replies, "and the master is greater than the servant."

Thus Christ took the servant's place so thoroughly, that at every moment He acted from this motive, "Lo, I come t do thy will," and will do so, until the kingdom being delivered to God the Father, God is *all* in *all*. He is not now doing His own will; He is set down on His Father's throne. He took the cup from His Father's hand, and will take the crown also. It is not given the Son of man to know the times, but God Himself will give the crown to Him, and He will wait the Lord's time.

If we take this thought in reading the gospel, that there was a perfect servant doing the acceptable will of God, many of these texts will explain themselves. He will wait the time that the Father takes to give Him His own throne; for "He must reign until He hath put down all authority, and then shall the Son deliver up the kingdom to God the Father, that God may be all in all "—in that eternal day that is to dawn.

The measure, then, is the perfection of Christ. It is not mere law; it is not "thou shalt" or "thou shalt not"—which brought out the inability of man, as sprung from Adam, to rise up to the level of human righteousness—but it is the grace of God in all He was, in all He said, in all He did; this is the measure that we are called upon to follow.

We find His will revealed in the written Word, as we find His example in the incarnate Word. We have in the written Word, the will of the Lord revealed to us so far as concerns our path here—that will which, by-and-by, will perfect us by making us subject to it; that blessed will that, as it were, turns back the whole of a man's being, and gives it back to God again in the perfection that God Himself has provided—not merely the imputed righteousness or justifying of a man, but a man made morally like God, morally like the Christ of God, and moulded and fashioned to manifest to the angels, and the principalities, and the powers, through the ages to come, the wonders that God has wrought, the exceeding riches of His grace, the wonders of His righteousness, the manifestation of infinite holiness and infinite grace, and the bond that unites them—His infinite wisdom. This is the purpose for which we have been called of God, justified by God, are being sanctified, and soon will be glorified and made perfect with Him. What a glorious destiny!

What a fearful thing, then, self-will is—that will of Adam that "brought death into the world, with all its woe!" Self-will and sin are just interchangeable terms. What is sin? Self-will. And what is self-will? Sin. Self is man's centre. Round him must revolve all in heaven and earth, it matters not how tiny or minute the little self. Even the less the self, the mightier the thoughts of the importance of all falling down before it. Self is man's centre. By faith we have changed our centre; we have got into the true astronomy of the heavens. We have found Christ, the centre; for everything in heaven and earth, and, I may say, under the earth, in hell (for all is linked and related to Him) revolve round Him. We have taken our stand upon Him, and rejoice in Him; and as we study our Bibles, from Christ the centre, and as we live our lives from Christ the centre, and as we mould our conduct from Christ the centre, so shall all our study, and all our thoughts, all our ways, and all our words, manifest the true harmony of the heavens of God, and send up in all our actions a constant psalm of praise. By Him we shall be offering "the sacrifice of praise continually—that is the fruit of our lips giving thanks to His name." The old philosophers dreamed of the stars singing round the throne of God, but here will be true worship in the moulding of our hearts to Him, proving the good, the perfect, and the acceptable will of God.

The power is given to take that Word, and not merely have it in our heads, and know the doctrines clearly and exactly. It is not the mere pages of the Word that are of value to us; it is not the mere printing, or the doctrine contained in it. It is as that written Word forms the incarnate Word within us, and the incarnate Word goes out in activity in doing the will of God. that the Spirit takes of the things of Christ, and makes us drink into the river of His own good pleasure. Thus we get the Holy Spirit sent to indwell within us, to prove the good, and holy, and acceptable will of God, going onward in the path of Him who said, "Take my yoke upon you and learn of Me: for I am meek and lowly in heart, and ye shall find rest to your souls."

It is not merely, "Come unto Me, and I will give you rest." That is to the unsaved sinner. There is nothing between the unsaved sinner and the seeking Saviour but the man's unbelief. When sinners are brought to God, there is salvation; but there is a yoke put on after the coming to Christ—"Take my yoke upon you." This is for those who have accepted the gospel. What was the yoke of Christ? If you remember, in the eleventh chapter of Matthew, it says that He had been doing most of His mighty deeds in certain cities of the land of Canaan, and the cities wherein He had done most of His mighty deeds would not have Him; and then He pronounced His woes upon them in judgment—"Woe unto thee, Chorazin! woe unto thee, Bethsaida!" There was the yoke—doing good and being cast out. We ourselves do not like to do good and to be cast out. Doing good, and being ill-used for doing it; doing good to all men, having a heart of love to every man, to the poorest and most wretched upon earth; to do good to those, and to be cast out, is a yoke hard to bear. Well, in those cities Christ did most of His mighty deeds; and as they cast Him out, He had to pronounce His woe upon them, and that we His yoke. It is human nature for us to wish people to like what we way and teach, and to be patted on the back for it, and to be "appreciated," as it is called; that is not the yoke. You find it in Peter. "To do good, and suffer for it, and take it patiently;" that is grace. This is the more exact translation of it: "To do good, and suffer for it, and take it patiently"—a very hard thing to do, and nothing but the grace of God will enable us to do it. To do evil, and suffer for it, and take it patiently, is only what we ought to do; but to do good, and suffer for it, and take it patiently, that is grace in the sight of God.

"Take my yoke upon you, and learn of Me, and ye shall find rest." Where did He find His rest? The moment He denounced Chroazin and Bethsaida, He turned to His Father, and raised His eyes to heaven; but He does not say, "Lo, this world has rejected Me. I will go back to thy bosom, and be in the unspeakable calm as thy eternal Son." No, but He turns His eyes to heaven, and says, "I thank Thee, O Father!"—thanksgiving in the midst of abuse, thanksgiving with eyes turned up to an open heaven, and these revilers, and abusers, and Pharisees, and Scribes, all about Him, like the bulls of Bashan, ready to devour Him. "I thank Thee, O Father, Lord of heaven and earth." It says in Luke that "He rejoiced in spirit." "I thank Thee, O Father, that Thou hast hid these things from the wise and prudent, and hast revealed them unto babes; even so, Father, for so it seemed good in thy sight."

"Learn of Me; for I am Meek"—how unlike what we are!—"and lowly," going down under everything. Is that like us? "Stand up for your rights!" Ah! that is old Adam, and we, that have been taken from old Adam into the new, know something better than speaking about our rights. We know perfectly well, when we are on this ground, that if it is standing up for our rights, we mean that we should have been all in the lake of fire for ever. Nothing short of that. That is our due.

And now we are to be meek and lowly, not merely in the external appearance (that can be put on); but meek and lowly in heart. Are we prepared to follow Him? Are we prepared to learn of Him? Are we prepared to go in the paths of Him who said, "I come to do thy will"? Count the cost. It is hard self-denial, the breaking of the human will, and the moulding of that will into the will of God. All the principles of the old Adam are entirely swept away, and "Learn of Me" can stand in the midst of the fire of the artillery of man's wrath as calm as the God of heaven's calmness can make it.

What a calm man a Spirit-filled man should be—calm amidst the wreck of worlds, the ruin of empires, and the great crash of the world's catastrophe at last; still calm you "shall find rest," and the more yoke-bearing, the more rest-finding. That is, the more that we learn of Him, the more we are merged into His will, and prove it. "If any man will serve Me, let him follow Me." I think we sometimes read it the other way—"If any man will follow Me, he must serve Me." That is not how it reads in the 12th of John: "If any man will serve Me, let him follow Me." There is no such Christless service. All that we are to do for Him, let it be with a single eye; and while we ask, "Is this *what* He would have me do? *how* He would have me do it? and *when* He would have me to do it? and the *spirit in which* He would have me to do it, if He had been here?"—let us remember His words, "If any man will serve Me, let him follow Me."

And we have all the provision given us by the blessed Spirit. The Spirit has given us to know our need in order that we may take up the yoke, and go and find rest, and prove His will here. We shall have it in perfection by-and-by.

The Lord Himself, knowing our weakness, and knowing the condition of His disciples, taught them to pray in those their circumstances, that inimitable prayer that we all know so well, but that we ofttimes think so little about. In that prayer, commonly called "the Lord's prayer," but more correctly the disciples' prayer (the Lord's prayer being John xvii.), we have every provision in every condition, from the highest, and always descending to the lowest, in doing His will. We have to pray, "Thy will be done on earth as it is in heaven." And we have before this, "Our Father, which art in heaven." There is the highest relationship of all, the *sons of the Father*; and, as children, being far from home, in fact, but made nigh by faith, we can draw near unto Him. Next we come down a little, "Hallowed be thy name." We are now *worshippers in the temple*, reverently hallowing the name of the Lord; sons and worshippers. "Thy kingdom come." We are also *kings waiting for a kingdom*. Angels are worshippers, but they are not kings waiting for a kingdom; and we say, "Thy kingdom come," in which we are to reign with Him, as we suffer with Him now. But as sons, and worshippers, and kings, we are also *servants aiming at perfect obedience*; and we say, "Thy will be done on earth as it is in heaven." But if we are sons and worshippers, and kings, and servants, we are also *needy dependents*; and we say, "Give us this day our daily bread," all our needs always anticipated, and always met with the most perfect wisdom. But we are lower than needy dependents; we are *sinner requiring forgiveness*. "Forgive us our debts, as we forgive our debtors." Grace saves us for ever, but His government regulates out lives here according to His laws. But more than that, we are not only sinners, but *sinners ready to be led astray*. "Lead us not into temptation." And further than that, to the very lowest depths of all, we have a great enemy going about seeking whim he may devour; his net roundabout us trying to entrap us—the wicked one. Hence, "But deliver us from the wicked one;" for such is the full force of the word used. It is not merely indefinite evil, but a person—"Deliver us from the wicked one"—whose existence is being so sadly denied in these days, and thus his own tactics are being carried out. God preserve us from this! From sons of the Father, down to those that have to meet the wiles of the devil in performing the will of God, all is anticipated by the blessed Spirit of God, and all has been met in the provision of His grace, as sons, worshippers, kings, servants, dependents, sinners, tempted ones, besieged ones. We know that path, wherein we prove the good, and acceptable, and perfect will of God—the path which no fowl knoweth, and which the vulture's eye has never seen, and the lion's whelps have not trodden it, nor the fierce lion passed by it. And may it be to us day by day as in the language of the beautiful hymn—

> "I bow me to Thy will, O God,
>   And all Thy paths adore;
> And every day I live I'll seek
>   To serve Thee more and more.
>
> "When obstacles and trials seem
>   Like prison-walls to be;
> I do the little I can do,
>   And leave the rest to Thee.
>
> "And when it seems no chance or change
>   From grief can set me free,
> Hope finds its strength in helplessness,
>   And patient, waits on Thee.
>
> "Man's weakness, waiting upon God,
>   Its end can never miss;
> For men on earth no work can do
>   More angel-like than this.
>
> "Lead on, lead on triumphantly,
>   O blessed Lord, lead on!
> Faith's pilgrim sons behind Thee seek

THE ACCEPTABLE WILL OF GOD.

The path that Thou hast gone.

"He always wins who sides with God,
    To him no chance is lost;
God's will is sweetest to him when
    It triumphs at his cost."

WALKING WITH GOD.

"And Enoch walked with God: and he was not; for God took him."—GENESIS v. 24.

"Noah was a just man,*** and walked with God."—GENESIS vi. 9.

PETER walked with God, and he was enabled to walk in a very wonderful place, because he walked upon the word of God. "If it be thou, Lord, bid me come to thee." And Jesus said, "Come;" and on that word Peter walked upon the sea; for the word of God is much stronger than the law of gravitation, or any other law. When God speaks, the sea is His, and it obeys Him. Then Peter began to sink, and he found that the sea was not so solid after all. And why? Because he looked upon the boisterous waves; and, in fact, the boisterous waves had nothing to do with the matter, because it was as easy to walk over the boisterous waves as over a smooth sea. But, you see, unbelief is always foolish; faith is always wise. But faith does not contradict reason; it transcends it, it rises above it. I can reason that I am specifically heavier than water; but when God tells me to come over the water, specific laws, and specific gravity, and everything else, have to obey the Lawgiver; and thus I quite object to the controversy that there is between true science and revelation. I love science. We all love true science, when science can teach us; but science cannot tell me how to walk with God.

Then there are other saints that have been in strange places walking with God. There were three dear ones away in the olden time that, instead of walking on water, were walking through fire. And why? Because God was with them, and "one like unto the Son of God: was there, and there was no burning. They did not know but that they might be burnt; for they said, "Our God is able to deliver us from the burning fiery furnace, but if not"—oh, I love the faith which is in that "if not"! I think there is more faith often in the "if not" than in saying, "We can be protected." Any man could go in and say, "I may be protected;" but they said, "But is not, we will not worship your image. We will be faithful to God in spite of fire or anything else." But they went into the fire, and nothing was burnt, as we all well know. They were thrown in bound, but they were seen walking with God.

Another wondrous march with God, another wonderful walk; one of the most wonderful walks I know of in all history. "It came to pass after these things that God did tempt Abraham, and said unto him, Abraham," and the ear was open. It was no itching ear. It was an open ear, and he said, "Here am I." The itching ear listens to man. Some people buy the new Revised Testament, and they think that they have got a new Bible. They say that it is something easier than our old-fashioned evangelistic Bible. Thank God, everything stands as it was as far as all the essentials are concerned. They want something new. But Abraham was wont to listen to his God, and he said, "Here am I." And God said, "Take now thy son." Oh, what a trial! "The son of thy old age"—the son of faith, the son of resurrection-power. "Take not thy son." And God dilates upon it, as if to intensify it. "Thine only son." Not only so, but He names him, "Isaac"—not Ishmael. "Thine only son Isaac"—He adds to it still—"whom thou lovest." What intensity of trial! "That the trial of your faith might be as gold that is tried in the fire." "Take now thy son, thine only son Isaac, whom thou lovest, and get thee into the land of Moriah; and offer him there for a burnt-offering upon one of the mountains that I will tell thee of." What is the result? "Abraham rose up early in the morning." He might have been permitted to sleep on till mid-day with such a journey before him; but the prompt is his obedience. "Early I the morning"—as if anxious to obey, even to cut his own heart-strings—"early in the morning, and saddled his ass, and took two of his young men with him, and Isaac his son, and clave the wood for the burnt-offering, and rose up, and went unto the place of which God had told him." Then "on the third day"—think of that, three days' walk with God—three days to think over it—three days to get to Mount Moriah. It seems to me much harder than Peter's attempt and failure—much harder than the three Hebrew children's attempt and cusses—this protracted thinking and revolving, with his loved son at his side, walking onward, and onward only, upon the word of the everlasting God, day succeeding night, and night succeeding day, and his own heart breaking, and his heart going up to God. And he said, "Did I hear God? Do I know God? Have I His word under me?" Take thy son, thine only son Isaac, whom thou lovest, and offer him."

At the end of a very spiritual and delightful meeting, when our hearts are filled with love to our Master and His truth, if an enemy should come and seize us, and say, "Now we must take your life, or you must bow down and worship an image, "I believe that a great number of us in the heat and warmth of our spiritual life would be prepared to say, "Take my life then, and have done with it." That would be in the heat of the moment. We could do lots of thing in the heat of the moment, when we are warmed up, which we could not do in what is called could blood. But there was no heat of the moment here in this walking with God, but persistent, steady, strong faith, and there was everything against him. If you had gone to Abraham then, and said, "Abraham, how do you feel as a father? What is your paternal affection like?" He would have said, "Do not speak to me;" and he would wipe the tear from his eye. "What do you think of a man going to kill a fellow-man?" "Do not speak to me." Abraham believed God, that was all. "And how do you feel to God, Abraham? That is the son that the promise is given to, and the coming seed is to spring from him. God's name will be dishonoured, and God's cause and God's purposes will be foiled." "God can look after His own purposes; I have only to obey." What a sight! Oh, if we had but the power of some great painter to picture that wondrous scene under that eastern sky! The faith of Isaac too must have been strong. Remember that he was not a young lad. He was a strong, stalwart young man, in his prime, and to allow himself to be bound and laid upon the altar to be an offering to God was a part of his faith got from his father's teaching; and there, as the young man lay, every bit of Abraham's heart goes against the act which he has to do. In Abraham's heart his parental love, his human feelings, and his regard for God's purposes, are all against it. There is a calm, silent sky above him, and the mountain beside him and beneath him, and he lifts up the dagger with that hand; and he has nothing to support him but the word of God. There is nothing between him and God, but God's word, "The mouth of the Lord has spoken it;" and the knife comes down, and it falls upon the arm of Jehovah. God is never too late. The angel said, "There is a ram." The angel comes and says, "Stay thy hand." He lifted up his eyes to look, and beheld the substitute. Oh, friends, it may be on the water, it may be through the fire, it may be through the bitterest trial, but it is the God that is in it that makes the walk glorious.

My heart has been thinking to-day of the God that we have to walk with—not so much the walk, but the *God* that we have to walk with. We have a glorious aspect of the truth in walking, as showing companionship. It does; but it also shows identification. I should not like every man to come and take me by the arm, and walk with me down the streets. Not likely! I am identified with his character to that extent. The man whose arm I take and I, are quite content to change characters one with the other, to a certain extent, as far as it can be done. But here we are the representatives of God upon this earth, to let the world know about God; and our walking with God is to show the people what God is like. Alas! alas! how the Church has failed!

I remember a statement that I heard not many years ago from one who has the best right of any man living to give an opinion upon it, and that was Lord Shaftesbury. As he stood at a meeting, and as I sat by his side, he said these awful words—true and awful, because true—"That he had been identified with a great number of humanizing influences and activities during the last half-century, and he had seen humanity improved, and classes being drawn together; but the more that he saw them getting improved in that way, the further they were getting from God." I would not have dared to make that statement myself, because I have not the practical information; but from lips such as those of that honoured man of God, and that honoured philanthropist, I think they are most weighty words for us to ponder, and which should make us ask ourselves why it is that God is being shown out of His world, and why we are not waling to manifest Him.

God is the great fact that the world needs—a living God for a dead world. The speaking from the divine into the human—from heaven to earth, from the eternal into time—is the whole history of these six millenniums, the whole history of the bible, from Genesis to Revelation. From the creation of the world to the great while throne, and beyond it, God is the idea. What does a man that does not want God see upon opening the Bible? "In the beginning God created—" The fourth word is "God," and the first chapter has five and thirty mentions of the one solemn word "God"—God the Creator and the Ruler, making all, forming all, none to help Him, none to hinder Him. Go down to the last point in history, beyond the new heavens and the new earth, in Rev. xxi., and further on in the eternal day, you will find again the word comes up. Six times there we read the word "God," when Christ has delivered up the kingdom to His Father, that God may be all in all. And we are men of God, and men walking with God, and men working for God; and this is our position, and the reason of our existence here—that men may know of God.

And, above all, the typical man that we have, whose history has been before us, is the grand old preacher, the first of all preachers that we read of—Enoch. We have his walk in Genesis. We have the foundation of that walk in Hebrews. We have the outcome of that walk in Jude. And we have a threefold history of the great man—walking with God in the midst of times very like our own; for if you look at his testimony, you will find in Jude that "Enoch, the seventh from Adam, prophesied of these things to those round about him, saying, Behold, the Lord cometh with the myriads of His saints, to execute judgement upon all, and to convince all that are ungodly among them, of all their ungodly deeds which thy have ungodly committed, and of all their hard speeches which ungodly sinner have spoken against Him." Four times the word "ungodly" is in the one chapter, and four times does this man of God, who walked by faith with God, on God's word, throw it in the teeth of these men that there is a God, and that there is a judgment, and that God is coming in judgment, and the thing that will be judge is their ungodliness and their want of knowing God—"the ungodly deeds which they have committed, and all their hard speeches which ungodly sinners have spoken against Him." It is not that we care for ourselves. It is what they have said against God, "enduring such contradiction of sinners against Himself." And it is a remarkable thing, that when we have come in Hebrews to find how it was that Enock walked with God, we find that by faith Enoch was translated, that he should not see death. By faith he walked, and by faith he was translated; and it is added in Hebrews, that he was not found. And why? He believed that God was the Rewarder of them that diligently seek Him. He diligently sought God, and therefore found God; and when he found God, the world could not find him. And so it is, we shall be sure to be utterly unable to be made out by the world if we have found God. They cannot make us out if we walk with God. The walk with God is of such a character that the world knows nothing about it. They cannot find us. Translated or not translated, we are utterly unfindable by them.

There is a similar statement in the second chapter of the book of Kings, of another mysterious disappearing one. When Elijah was caught up similarly to Enoch, we find that Elisha came and told it; but they said to him, "Behold, now there by with thy servant fifty strong men, the sons of the prophets: (fifty theological students). "Let them go, we pray thee, and seek the master." There was rationalism, you see, in colleges then' they will not believe a word that Elisha says about God having taken Elijah, and so they appointed a rationalistic committee. "Let them go, we pray thee, and seek thy master, lest peradventure"—here is the reason, they could not believe that he was gone, that they had walked with God, and that he was caught up with God to walk with Him for ever— "lest peradventure"—man is always coming in with his 'lest peradventure"—"lest peradventure the Spirit of the Lord hath taken him up, and cast him upon some mountain"—thrown him back again—"cast him upon some mountain or into some valley," as if the Holy Ghost made such mistakes that He could not end the journey if He had begun it. They believed not in Him. "He cannot begin it, He cannot uphold us, He cannot preserve, He cannot keep us when He has got us." That was the rationalistic reasoning of this committee of theological students. "And he said, Ye shall not send." Well, done, Professor Elisha! That was well don for the teachers; he said, "Ye shall not send." He stood upon the word of God. But they urged him till he was ashamed—"a little leaven leaveneth the whole lump"—and he said, "Send." He came down after all.

When we see Elisha coming down and being influenced thus, the Lord reserve us all from that which is so truly sad, and which is sapping the very morality and the very life of the Church of God. When we see what is being taught in high quarters, we may all well tremble, and l9ook out for our sons of the prophets, and look out for our Elishas, and go to the living God, and walk with Him in truth. We will neither have the Romanism on the one side, which tells us of a cross without a Christ; nor the Rationalism on the other side, which tells us of a Christ without a cross. We are "determined to know nothing among men save Jesus Christ and Him crucified." When God was about to walk here below, what was said of Him: "He shall be called Emmanuel"—"God with us." He came. He does not say, "I come simply as God to be your ex ample, or your friend, or to lead you, or to be your teacher." "She shall bring forth a Son, and they shall call His name Jesus; for He shall save His people from their sins." "And all this was done that it might be fulfilled which was written, Behold, a virgin shall bring forth a Son, and they shall call His name Emmanuel." People might say, "He is not called Emmanuel. Friend, you are not taking the New Testament commentary, written by the Holy Ghost, on the Old Testament truth. The Old Testament truth was "Emmanuel." God is to be with us. But look at the tremendous truth involved in that—God cannot visit this world as a friend, as a teacher, as a leader, as a rationalistic great one. If He is to come at all, He must come as Jesus, the Saviour, to save His people from their sins; and if a Saviour is to be provided for sinners, nothing but "Emmanuel" can be the Saviour, nothing but "God with us." If all the angels and seraphs and cherubs and created intelligences that ever were created by God had been executed in man's behalf, not a single sinner could have got to glory; for after they had given back their lives, they had only received their lives from God, and they were bound to give Him all that He had given before. It was only the uncreated One that was for ever in the bosom of the Father, "God manifest in the flesh," that could become our "Jesus to save His people from their sins."

I must close with the testimony that Enoch, this great teacher from God, gave us. He walked with God. It is one of the most difficult lessons which I have to learn, to go into my closet and shut the door, and there talk with God, realizing first that God is; and

WALKING WITH GOD.

secondly, that He is a rewarder of them that diligently seek Him. Enoch came to Him. He walked with Him; he pleased Him. And mark how pleasing is put in connection with walking, as in Col. i. 10: "That ye might walk worthy of the Lord unto all pleasing." And Enoch before his translation received the testimony that he "Pleased God." He was taken to Him, he was translated by Him; he is with Him; and he will return again with Him, when the rest of us come back as the Master comes to fulfil in all its fulness that great prophecy which Enoch, the seventh from Adam, was privileged to give. Enoch, one who walked with God, walking on His word, walking by His word, walking through His word, and God filling all—God filling my theology, God filling my family, God filling my life, God filling my testimony. Some who will not go to the extreme length of Rationalism have tried to get as little of God in the Bible as they can. We want as much of God as we can get hold of in all Scripture—a Scripture full of God from its beginning to its end, out testimony full of God, our life full of God: "For to me to live is Christ"—To "WALK WITH GOD."

Now, friend, let us be practical as we close this subject. Jest let us take a slip of paper, and do not write that text which I have begun to quote, but let us be upright before God. There is the walking which the psalmist speaks of—"No good thing will He withhold from them that walk uprightly." We need a great deal of practical uprightness, uprightness of soul with God; not playing with religion; not trafficking with truth; but straight up and down with God—honour bright before Him, and honour bright with our fellow-men, walking uprightly there. Let us be conscientious and not slip it over, veneering it before God. It is to live we want. The word in Hebrew which says that "Enoch walked with God," means that Enoch walked *habitually* with God. It was the habit, the tendency, the bend of the whole man. Let us go away, preachers and hearers, and say, "For to me to live is _____," then fill in the blank for yourself. I cannot fill it for you. By grace I try to fill it in for myself. I am speaking of Christians, remember. We know that Paul said: "For to me to live is"—pleasure? enjoyment? meetings? religious service? visiting the sick? Sometimes the more holy the things are, the worse they may become. "For to me to live _____." I know some genuine Christians whom I have met, and I fear that there are many more, who invert the text, and they think that Christ is a nice pillow to lie upon on a death-bed, and then when they get to glory it will be so happy to see Him; and their work seems to be this: "For me to live is gain, and to die will be Christ." If we had a little less of that, you would not have to be pleading for moneys to carry on Missions. This would not be so if gain were less before the minds even of Christian people, and they knew that it sanctified gain to give it to Him who has given all for us; for, though we may speak ofttimes very happily about it, it cost Him everything. He loved us and gave Himself for us, and if we can fill it in with the apostle in some degree, "For to me to live is Christ,": it may seem a rough way, and it may seem a thorny way, but—

> "There is but that path in the waste
>   Which His footsteps have marked as His own,
> And I follow in diligent haste
>   To the seats where He's put on His crown."

It *is* thorny. We do not believe in the broad way, we do not believe in the delightful way; but we believe in the true way—the true, and the new, and the living way, and the path that may seem rough; for we believe that—

> "'Tis first the true, and then the beautiful,
>   Not first the beautiful, and then the true;
> First the wild moor, with rock and reed, and pool,
>   Then the gay garden, rich in scent and hue.
>
> 'Tis first the good, and then the beautiful,
>   Not first the beautiful, and then the good;
> First the rough seed, sown in the rougher soil,
>   Then the flower-blossom, on the branching wood.
>
> "Not first the glad, and then the sorrowful,
>   But first the sorrowful, and then the glad;
> Tears for a day, for earth of tears is full,
>   Then we forget that we were ever sad.

"Not first the bright, and after that the dark,
　　But first the dark, and after that the bright;
First the thick cloud, and then the rainbow's arc,
　　First the dark grave, then resurrection light.

"'Tis first the night—stern night of storm and war—
　　Long night of heavy clouds and veiled skies;
Then the fair sparkle of the Morning Star,
　　That bids the saints awake, and dawn arise."

CHRISTIAN WARFARE.

"Wherefore take unto you the whole armour of God, that ye may be able to withstand I the evil day, and having done all, to stand. Stand therefore, having your loins girt about with truth, and having on the breastplate of righteousness; and your feet shod with the preparation of the gospel of peace; above all, taking the shield of faith, wherewith ye shall be able to quench all the fiery darts of the wicked. And take the helmet of salvation, and the sword of the Spirit, which is the word of God."—EPHESIANS vi. 13-17.

AN ADDRESS TO YOUNG MEN.

OUR strength is in a knowledge and confession of weakness, and the realization of an unseen, but real God. Before we can hope to fight successfully, we must become supplicants and dependents. Prayer is not offered with a view to change God's plans, but to show that we are dependent and confident. It is part of the *design* of God that we, worms of the dust, should hang upon and trust in Him. It was not the worm Jacob that was to thresh the mountains, but he prevailed with the angel when his thigh was out of joint—in his weakness. As long as we have energy in the flesh to wrestle, we have not the dependence of the worm to hang, trust, and cling to the feet of the Angel of the Covenant, saying, "I will not let thee go unless thou bless me."

QUALIFICATION.

In 1 John ii., middle of the 14th verse, we read, "I have written unto you, young men, because ye are strong." The speciality of young men is, that they are strong, and they glory in their strength. That strength, to be used to bring about the end for which it is intended, requires to have, in the first place, *a living man* to *wield* it, and we must have the constitution that can fight. We "must be born again," for we have not a single power within us by nature. God does not find us soldiers, sons, nor heirs, but makes us such. And now that He has begotten us into His family, are we not a kingdom of priests to Him? Are we not His soldiers now, to use His strength and armour, and to exercise our arm in the use of His sword, "the sword of the Spirit, which is the word of God."

CONDITIONS OF SERVICE.

Having thus seen wherein our strength consists, there is the Word, "If any man will come after me, let him deny himself." Not merely abstain from luxuries or comforts. We have a deeper thought in the sentence. The first thing is to deny *myself*—my existence altogether as a man. Paul challenged some that they lived as men. We are not to live *as mere* men, but as sons of God. What do I confess? Christ alone. I live, *walk*, speak Christ. "For to me to live *is* Christ," not self. I deny my own power to save myself, to live to God, or to move a finger. The next thought we take up—"I have written unto you, young men...the word of God abideth in you." There is the secret of strength.

There is no man strong *from* the divine standpoint, but the man in whom His Word abides. You may have all the intelligence of past ages gathered up into one brain, and may be a very Plato, Socrates, or Shakespeare, but if you have not the word of God in you, He does not allow the word "strong" to be applied to you.

This is the great characteristic of the Lord's warriors, of that class of soldiers that come to the front; and John evidently puts them in the forefront of the battle as the young men of valour, strength, and activity. I believe, dear friends, that aas we go onward towards the latter days, more and more will this word of God be the rallying-point for the Lord's own. We get tired of sectional fightings in the Church of God; we get sick of men reasoning about their "isms." We respect every man's ecclesiastical convictions, and ignore no man's; to his own, Master he stands or falls; but there is a higher level than each man looking out for his corner of the garden, where he thinks, perhaps, the truth of *God* may be bewst seen. I would like to have the blessing of Joseph. He was a fruitful bough, and his branches ran over the wall. Rejoice to be able to run over the walls of all the denominations.

THE PRESENT WARFARE.

The battle at the *present* day is about the word of God. Ignorant and learned alike are attacking it. It is the key to the position, as a certain farm was at Waterloo. The enemy are trying to turn our flank; for you find but few advocates of the coarse atheism of former days. Perhaps some vulgar, fluent speakers may try to catch people by speaking strongly about no God; but there is not great thinking unbeliever of the present day who has the madness to deny God's existence. They acknowledge Him under various names; and in the recent work of that sadly-wonderful man, John Stuart Mill, he takes the position that if any man succeeds in believing that there is a God—wonderful experiment, you know!—we can never prove the proposition to be untrue. That is a great admission from a professed unbeliever. In fact it is only a *fool* who can say there is no God. Unphilosophical, unscientific, irrational—"The fool hath said in his heart, There is no God."

THE ENEMY'S POSITION.

A man may say he has lived here, and never saw any marks of God. Well, if you spent a summer in the moon, you might find that there is One who would overcome even your skepticism. Man must search every corner of the universe before he can say there is no God. And not only so; he must be in every star at the same time, for if he left one for another, he might be a moment too late. If I have to say there is no arsenic in this glass of water, how many tests must I not employ? At my examination in chemistry, the question, "What is pure water?" nearly overthrew me. The unbeliever asks you to believe that he himself is God.

Can God speak? If you say no, you reach the absurdity that He who made the mouth cannot speak. The third question *is*, Has He spoken? If you say no, you land yourself in the dilemma of having an immoral God, one who could let you know what He required, and would not. We must answer, He has spoken. What has He said? "I have written to you, young men, because the word of God abideth in you." How do I know it? I will tell you the best test. "Come, see a man that told me all that ever I did." Come, see a Book that tells me all that ever I did, and alone satisfies my conscience with a righteous God, and yet a God of love. I s not that the divine Book? You may know it, as you know the sun shines, by opening your eyes.

If a man came a told me to strike a match in order to see the new light he had invented, I should say, "Well, if the light cannot show itself, there is none." But the reason people have doubts about the Book is because *they* do not get it in the right line. They try to get it through the head instead of the conscience. The revelation *must* come through that which puts the man before God in his true moral light.

GOD'S GREAT ONES.

The greatest revelations ever made to mankind were not to great philosophers, reasoners, and thinkers; none such *clustered* round Christ. "I that speak unto thee am He," was addressed to a poor self-confessed sinner. To whom did He make the revelation, "I ascend to my Father and your Father"? To the two great theologians, Peter and John? No; they ran away too soon. But to a poor weeping woman, whose conscience was thoroughly at one with her God, and whose heart was longing for her Lord. This poor woman heard the accents, "Mary," and knew her Lord. Ah! the microscopic revelations of those tears. I have never been able to convince any by argument of the truth of anything got from the Bible. It is like David putting on Saul's armour.

OUR WEAPON.

If you run a sword through a man's body you have not to prove it is a sword. So use the Word. Some tell me the Bible is not the word of God; but let us prove it by a simple illustration. If I have a book enabling me to put all the parts of a sewing-machine together, I know the writer is a maker of that machine. We are as poor machines out of order, but by looking into the Word our spirits are corrected. Pilate, like an owl shutting its eyes, asks, "What is truth?" Did not Christ say, "I am the Truth"? The youngest man who has accepted God's revelation may say, "I know the Truth." I am wanting to know more of truth; but I am not ignorant as to where to find it.

What a glorious *thing* to have a firm tread, and not like man with his wisdom, trying to find the stars among the sands of the seashore, or to build a tower up to heaven. We know the incarnate Word, Jesus, who has given us this written Word. We have certainty; our responsibility is not to let it abide—live with us. The Word made you a child of God. "By His own will begat He us, by the word of truth." "Faith cometh by hearing, and hearing by the word of God." I used to pray, cry, and open my mouth wide for faith; but it is now, I will *hear* what God the Lord will speak." "Hear, and your souls shall live." God speaks: I will listen.

But Christian life is a continual warfare. It is easy enough to think lightly of sin; but the more light in a house the better we see. I see the evil of my heart now, more than when I came to Christ at first. We have to fight all the *way* along, for we find we are prone to sin.

Now, by what means "shall a young man cleanse his way? By taking heed thereto according to Thy Word." What a beautiful figure is the "water" of the Word. (See Ephesians v. 26, and John iii.) Look at the *action* of water in cleansing; your ideas and mine are as foul mud, and the first thing you need is to be washed out of all your thoughts by the Word.

It is still a hard fight which the Christian carries on throughout his course; if you are full of God's thoughts you will *have* no room for the devil's. The "Word is a lamp to our feet," and we only know it as the darkness comes around us. Here is a man who takes, to light him on a windy night, a lucifer match; but out it goes. See the man with the strong, steady light of God's Word. When Satan comes to you, do not try him with your experience, as is often done, but give him a text. You do not become swordsmen in a day, remember. Some come to me and say, "Does it not say so and so somewhere in the Bible?" My friend, you have hold of the sword by the wrong end. We want young men in whom the Word abides to treasure the Word in our breast. Wield the sword of the Spirit, and you will have constant victory.

THE CHRISTIAN LIVING ON EARTH.

"Now the just shall live by faith."—HEBREWS x. 38.

"For to me to live is Christ, and to die is gain."—PHILIPIANS i. 21.

OUR subject is:—"The Christian living on earth." Not the mere moralist, but the Christian. The Christian, not in heaven, but the Christian living on earth. The subject before us is not a fancy, is not a feeling, is not a doctrine. It is what it is stated to be—a Christian living.

The Christian is "to live;" not merely to be saved, and to praise Christ's name together in happy joy; for to acknowledge Him in all His perfections as a man, but to manifest His life upon the earth.

I wish now to briefly draw your attention to this fact: that no fancy, however high; no feeling, however deep; and no doctrine, however sound, can make up Christian living. Christian living must be originated in heaven, in the life of God Himself; Christian living must come down from heaven to earth, in the presence of Him who said to us, "I am the Way, the Truth, and the Life;" and Christian living must be communicated by Him who has been sent from the Father and the Son—the Third Person of the glorious Trinity, to beget that great reality within us, and to make us sons and daughters of the Lord God Almighty—begotten of God.

In the first place, I draw your attention to a passage in God's Word that shows us the common tenure of this life in the saints of all ages. For I believe that no sinner was saved or shall be saved, from the days of Abel down to the days of the great white throne, but by being cleansed in the blood of Christ, and regenerated by the Holy Ghost. I take you to an Old Testament prophet, perhaps little read in these days, Habakkuk. The third chapter speaks of

Habakkuk resigning himself to the words of God, and falling under His rod in submission, if not in joy. He finishes by telling us that even "though the fig-tree shall not blossom, neither shall fruit be in the vines; the labour of the olive shall fail, and the fields shall yield no meat; the flock shall be cut off from the fold, and there shall be no herd in the stalls; yet I will rejoice in the Lord, I will joy in the God of my salvation. The Lord God is my strength, and He will make my feet like hinds' feet, and He will make me walk upon mine high places."

How is this consummation to be reached? In the first chapter of Habakkuk, where we find his burden, in the thirteenth verse, when he speaks to God, he says: "Thou canst not look on iniquity; wherefore lookest Thou upon them that deal treacherously, and holdest Thy tongue when the wicked devoureth the man that is more righteous than he, and makest men as the fishes of the sea, as the creeping things, that have no ruler over them?" Are we not in a similar condition to-day? In the present day we see these things happening, and God silent amidst it all. Falsehood and deceit, and murder and theft, and all that dishonours God, are seen all around, and He sits silent upon His throne of glory. But "God shall come," says the Psalmist, "and shall not keep silence." Habakkuk was waiting to be relieved of the burden that had pressed upon his soul, and ground him down; he was waiting for the great and glorious emancipation that was to make him rise up to the throne of God, and be like Him, and with Him for ever. This holy man waited for the revelation of God. "Write it and make it plain upon tables of stone, that a man who reads it may run." Sometimes it is thought that the letters were to be so large and legible, that even a runner could read them; but it really is that the reading of them may impart power to his running. And thus we find in the Old Testament, the prophet Habakkuk receiving a special revelation from God, in the second chapter—"The just shall live by faith." This beautiful text has been transfigured in glory by the apostle Paul, and three times we find in his writings this text used on various occasions: first, in the Epistle to the Romans; second, in the Epistle to the Galatians; and third, in the Epistle to the Hebrews.

This is Christian living; Christian living in its Alpha, Christian living in its Omega, and Christian living all the way between.

Christian living to start with, Christian living to end with. They first shall come into spiritual existence, into the living of Christ, into that love and fellowship with Christ by faith, shall grow therein and be perfected therein.

I have had to do with many anxious inquirers, and I find the greatest stumbling-block of all is this—they wish to be able to feel faith. Even the telephone cannot let us *see* a sound; it can let us *hear* a sound. You might as well speak of hearing a sight as feeling faith. "Faith is the substance of things hoped for, the evidence of things not seen." If feeling were justification, or were the means of applying justification, then this would be the consciousness of what was going on within. It is not faith in what is felt.

The just shall come into this relation of justified sons with God, by faith (Rom. i. 17)—

"There is life in a look at the Crucified One."

All God's ways are unnatural, because we approach them by sense of feeling. All God's ways are against man's ideas. Moses, by divine command, had an extraordinary way of healing snake bites. "You don't mean to tell me," any doctor would have said, "looking at this little bit of brass will stop that hemorrhage? Do you mean to say we have only to look to that brass?" It is not a question of what you have or feel. It was a revelation that came from a great God who had sent those serpents upon them. You must accept His thoughts, and reject your own. He has revealed Himself. Sometimes men come to the Bible and think they can judge it. You can never judge a revelation of God. You can accept or reject it, but you cannot judge it. God's light shines upon every man in the world. It brings light, and life, and joy; but a man that does not wish or require God, and does not wish for a revelation, must be left to find out that he does require those things. If our great theologians had to write that Bible of ours, it would have been a proper course to have begun by an introduction concerning the *à priori* or *à posteriori* argument for the existence of a God. But God makes no such preface. He says, "In the beginning God created." People are trying to make out the beginning of creation without a Creator; they have been fighting all the days of thinking man about it. The wise have discussed various theories as to whether God makes a white and a black man from the same original parents, or develops him from the lower animals.

The last thing any man will give up is his utter and total incompetency to do anything for his own salvation. There is nothing live answering a fool according to his folly. If a man comes and asks me how he is to carry five tons of coal on his back, I would not argue with him, I would give him half-an-hour to try it, and let that answer his own question.

The last thing we give up, is the thought that we can do something. Now, the first step is to accept God's record of us, not our opinion of ourselves. We have got to have faith in God's record of what man is, and faith in God's record of what He is, and it is said "the just shall live by faith." He has weighted us in the balance. We may think ourselves of some importance. Paul, when his eyes were opened, instead of climbing up the mighty elevation of self-confidence, went down into the deepest valley of humiliation, not singing the self-sufficient solo at the top of the mountain, but he is down in the depth. It is a bass solo, O Paul, you are singing, and not at all highly strung. What have you now? I have a revelation. "This is a faithful saying, and worthy of all acceptation, that Christ Jesus came into the world to save sinners." That is a saying, and a beautiful saying too. It is sayings we go by, not feelings.

A photographer told me once that he had an order for six dozen photographs, by touching up the negatives that was refused by a young man, who thought the original not nice enough. But an ugly truth is much better than a pretty falsehood. The truth, although it is ugly, is still truth in the end. Falsehood, though beautiful, is false in the end. Let us have the truth, whatever comes of it. God always like to have a man confess his sins; he likes to have truth in the inward parts.

People must come down from the mountain of self-conceit, and take God's opinion of themselves. God's photograph of you is full size from the crown of your head to the sole of your foot. We are "full of wounds, and bruises, and putrefying sores." How would you like that in your album, and write under it, "That's me"? You don't know how the glory of God shines upon you, and diagnoses you. You know nothing about self. You know nothing about

Christ's love, because you have never accepted the saying of the revelation of the truth of God. "And the just shall live by faith." I know I address some who say, "I have, by the grace of God, found out, by God's word, and bitter experience, that I am undone." Praise God, that is the right step to take. Lie down and say, I need a Saviour. It is not, "Who shall ascend into heaven? That is to bring Christ down from above; nor, Who shall descend into the deep? that is, to bring Christ up." One night I was trying to reach along the coast of England in a yacht. We could not weather the point, and our good captain said we should have to go under the lee, and cast anchor; and having let out a long length of chain—we had to do that because there was such a storm blowing—our men got ready, and when they were cleared thy said, "Let go the anchor." I did not see any one open the hatches and lower the anchor into the hold. That is what your "feeling" people attempt to do—they lower it into the hold. They won't let it go outside. "If I could feel some sensation coming over me and telling me I am saved," they say, "I would be satisfied." My anchor is Christ. My anchor cannot fail until His power and my Bible fail. I shall anchor fast to the eternal Rock of Ages, and stand the storm, and live by faith. "The just shall live by faith." (Gal. iii. 11.)

There is nothing like making a good start. Start well and start fair; that is, take the place that God has given you, in the ditch, and there you will find a good Samaritan having come all the way to you.

The Epistle to the Romans is justification by faith. The Epistle to the Galatians is justification by faith alone. This faith is characterized by three things in the living—dependence, obedience, and (it leads to) experience. Dependence, trusting upon God day after day. Obedience, "If ye love Me, keep my commandments." This life is essentially a life of obedience, dependence, and experience. Our life goes on from day to day in a condition of dependence.

Remember, the bread of yesterday will not do for to-day. We must gather the manna fresh day after day, and the water the same way.

We sometimes hear of such and such an evangelist living by faith; such and such a philanthropist. It may be in greater or less measure we live by faith. But all believers live by faith. For instance, here is a man that sends three thousand pounds, we will suppose, for some charitable purpose. His giving is by faith. The gifts of faith are as real as its receipts. We must live by faith in the highest sense of the word. Day after day we have to grow in this life. We are told that we are to "renew our strength," if we wait upon the Lord, depending, and confiding, and trusting in Him. How is this accomplished? First, "we mount up on wings as eagles." Now and then we see people who have received this sudden inspiration at conversion, start up and think they are in the seventh heaven. Don't clip their wings sooner than you can help it, let them speed toward the sky. They will know what it is to come back to earth and run by faith the "race that is set before them." Christian living, not talking, but Christian waiting and living;' running the Christian race, and even *walking* and not fainting.

It is not every one who will go to the cave of Adullam with rejected David. Let us stand by him in adversity. "Yes, having done all, to stand." It sometimes takes all our strength and time to stand. It is all right in the revival times, in large meetings; but let us go away to our little fields, our small corners, with every one against us, and everything against us; then, having done all, to stand has something very grand in it. The grace that will make you full will make you stand. "My grace is sufficient for thee;" and after this the Master will come to you and say, "You have been going about getting experience; you have come here; you have been failing, and you have been running, and you have been walking, and you have been standing; and I will make you to lie down." "He makes me to lie down," but it is among the green pastures and the still waters. A shepherd once said to me, "Did you ever see a sheep that was hungry lying down in green pastures? Not a bit of it; it is only the satisfied sheep that lies down in green pastures."

Finally, we must turn to the last passage, and we shall come to the words, "The just shall live by faith," in the 10th chapter of Hebrews. There is a future, as well as the past and present; and He that keeps me calm and patient, also keeps me looking to the right place for the reward. Emotionalism and sensationalism will not last. We must do our own little, calm work here, and look forward for a reward hereafter. We look forward, not to borrow to-morrow's troubles. If you wish to know the meaning of Christianity, don't borrow to-morrow's troubles. There will always be a way out of it. We know not the path, but we know the guide; and

> "The guide who led me hitherto
> Will guide me to the end."

We have been too long looking at the working side of life, instead of the outcome of life. Were you ever in a manufactory where pianofortes are made? Of all places in the word, don't go there for good music. I have been there, and of all the places of discord—tuning, tuning, tuning, and thump, thump, thumping, you ever heard—it is dreadful. But if you want music, go to the band an orchestra in its force. Down here is the place for tuning, and making the instruments. By-and-by we shall have such a concert to the glory of our God; every one of us, small and big instruments, sounding to His praise and glory.

"The just shall live *by faith*," *to the glory of God.*

THE CHRISTIAN WORKING ON THE EARTH.

"And he said unto them, It is not for you to know the times or the seasons, which the Father hath put in His own power. But ye shall receive power, after that the Holy Ghost is come upon you; and ye shall be witnesses unto me both in Jerusalem, and in all Judea, and in Samaria, and unto the uttermost part of the earth."–
–ACTS i. 7, 8.

WE read in the first chapter of the Acts of the Apostles, just before our Lord left this world to go to glory, "It is not for you to know the times or the seasons, which the Father hath put in His own power. But ye shall receive power, after that the Holy Ghost has come upon you: and ye shall be witnesses unto me both in Jerusalem, and in all Judea, and in Samaria, and to the uttermost part of the earth. And...He was taken up; and a cloud received Him out of their sight." Three parties are spoken of—the Holy Spirit, God, and Christ. These are the three persons most interested in carrying out God's work on earth. They are at the foundation, and the laying on of the top stone in Christian work.

"God sent forth His Son, born of a woman, born under the law, to redeem those who were under the law." Christ was sent from glory to perform the work of redemption—to fulfil the law of God, and put away sin, and to redeem us. He was God's witness on this earth, displaying the majesty of His law, and the fulness of His grace. Who are the witnesses of God now? "Ye shall be witnesses unto Me in Jerusalem, and in all Judæa, and in Samaria, and to the uttermost part of the earth." We are the witnesses, commissioned from the throne of the eternal God. That word "sent" has much in it. It implies, in the first place distance; in the second place it implies activity or energy; in the third place it implies purpose, intention, design. We are as sheep far from home, out on the mountain; but the Shepherd was sent into the world from such distance to save us. All the distance from heaven to earth has been covered by the "sent" one. God, in the strength of His own strong pity, in the energy of His holy love, sent His Son to do the work which was to be done. The sinner did not ask God to send His Son; but God sent His Son unasked for, and in wondrous grace, and He is now bringing many sons to glory; not only the Son in whom He was so well pleased, but the sons for whom He was offered up for the remission of sins, and offered on the cross as the first-fruits. His purpose is, *we* shall be members on one body.

We take up now in our Christian work this peculiar mission. I am trying to get at the reason of our existence as Christian workers here, that which the world knows nothing about. The world knows something about philanthropy and morality, but our subject is not that to-day; our subject is Christian work. It is something heavenly and divine, not human; something eternal, and not of time. We come now to talk about Christian work, and that which separates it from all work, and that which is peculiar to it as *Christian* work. "Ye shall be witnesses unto Me." We know of nothing that so ennobles men as Jesus Christ and Him crucified. I don't say anything against philanthropy, nor against morality; for there is not any real or deep morality, in fact, except that which springs from Christianity. But morality does not go far enough. I don't think all our Christianity is absorbed where mere morality is preached. How often the philanthropists of the world speak slightingly of the position assumed by Christianity in regard to philanthropic work. But are they right, when in Christian lands alone are to be seen the noble institutions for the relief of the sick, the outgrowth of the teaching of Christianity, and supported by Christian men? But there is something higher than mere philanthropy in Christianity. What is it? "Ye shall be witnesses unto Me."

Look at the Christian's work. First, the object for this work. We have a great work to do, but we have also a great power to perform our work with. If I send my little boy to blow up five tons of solid rock, and give him a small chisel and a tack-hammer, it would be a long time before that rock was blown to pieces; but if you get a hole drilled, and put in dynamite or some other explosive agency, the

THE CHRISTIAN WORKING ON THE EARTH. 109

rock soon gives way before that explosive agents. The Lord gives you and me a great work to do, but with that work He has given us a great power to go forward with. "Ye shall be witnesses unto Me, when ye shall receive power from the Holy Ghost." We have received the Spirit of God, not to keep it to ourselves, but that from us rivers of living water might flow. Before all things, we are to be men of God. The world knows nothing about this, and in the unrest, and weary work, and rushing hither and thither, and striving to outdo one another, they know little about the great Spirit who is carrying out His purposes now. You read early history, and there you find the ride and fall of nation after nation. You find the Jew giving place to the Babylonian, the Babylonian giving place to the Persian, the Persian giving place to the Greek, and the Greek giving place to the Roman, and dynasty after dynasty treading after the other, and wars and blood shed and all thoughts of evil passing across this world; but faith rises above all these little points, and stands firm from eternity to eternity, and takes its stand with God, and says, "As for me, I wish to manifest God upon this earth."

Very soon you grow to look upon things according to your own standpoint. On the top of the high hill things look very insignificant. God says we must look at His work from His own point of view. If every one were endued with a sense of his own littleness, he would see that the great things of the world are but as a speck in the eye of God. Our determination then should be, that our work should be done, not by spasmodic efforts, and fits and starts, but to put it thus: "For to me to live is Christ."

Above all things we desire to be practical. Perhaps you may forget all else, but there is one thing I want you to try and remember. When alone in your own closet, before God, you may take a sheet of paper and put upon it, "For to me to live is _____." What? Go on your knees for five minutes and see what it is. Some people's religion seems to be like a beautiful rose, to be put on the coat and worn on special occasions. That is not the life-work, and that is not the working-life of Christianity. Let your Christian life be more than mere profession and sentiment. It was the *false* prophet that said, "Let me die the death of the righteous, and let my latter end be like his."

Go to a working man who has to work with his hands. You see him get up early on Monday morning, and he says he is going to work. You ask him why he is working. He looks at you suspiciously, and says, "I must work in order to get money." Your work is indeed changed into money. What is the use of money? "Money, sir? I must get money to get my good." Good/ What is the use of food? "Why, it is to get strength." What is the use of strength? "Why, that we may be able to work." Oh, you are back at the first corner again! This is your round—work, money, food, strength. Work, money, food, strength, all over the world. The rich man's condition is far worse. Instead of the work he has got laziness, and money, and indigestion; and I don't think his condition is any better. The Christian must take his place in his work and say, "I have set the Lord always before me." "For to me to live is Christ."

What is it that peculiarly distinguishes the Christian's work from other work? The Christian's work is the work of faith. His life is the life of faith, and so is his work a work of faith. It is not the work of the philanthropist, or the work of the mere moralist, abut it is the work of faith. The two works of faith mentioned in the word of God are most beautiful and wonderful works—most peculiar works, I might say. In the Epistle of James, we find that Abraham wrought a work of faith and was justified. Rahab wrought a work of faith, and was also justified. Abraham's work was his intention to slay his son Isaac, the son of promise. What was Rahab's work? To betray her country. Now infidelity comes and throws these things in our face, and says, "What is the use of this kind of work?" We stick to the word of truth, and know how to use the sword that will not only be able to capture the gun from the enemy, but be able to turn it against him, and let him have the full force of it as he runs from the field. Never spike the enemy's gun, but take it from him. Before all things we need the Bible. You can't command people's consciences by order You can't feed people upon fig leaves, you must give them strong meat that they may grow thereon.

The works of faith mentioned in the Bible were works for God, only so far as they had faith in them. Strip them of faith, and they were not only immoral and unfeeling, but they would have been sinful. The thing that characterizes the works of God is faith in them. Abraham had faith in order to have slain his son Isaac. If you asked Abraham if he had any feelings when he was asked to slay his son, he would have said: "I have feelings, but I have also faith. Every feeling of my heart goes against it, but I am to do a work of faith, and perform what God tells me to do, and therefore all my feelings and sentiments must give way to the great Lawgiver, for whom alone I work, and to whom alone I listen." We must remember our own work, and must not think of another man's work. Every man has his own work to do. No other Christian can do your work. I have my work to do, and no other being in all heaven and earth can do it for me. You are the same. Christian, you have a work to do that none other can do, for God keeps no duplicates. No two beings are alike, and no two works in the great work of God are alike.

We regard the small stones in the temple as well as the large ones. A small stone can go where a large one would have to be cut down to fit. Some Christian people are often wishing to do something heroic, and to be seen. There are two classes of believers—those in the Christian work, that are building what seems to be great in quantity, but precious little worth in quality. It is what we do, and how we do it, that makes it acceptable to God. There is some of this work that is called gold, and some of it hay, and some of it stubble. I would rather have the gold than any amount of hay, and especially of there should be a fire; for the fire is to try all men's work. And if that is so, I would rather go in for the gold and silver and precious stones. We are to build the temples of God that will rise up to His glory in the endless ages, where all the wood and hay and stubble will be burned up in one great conflagration. Let our work be that which will survive the conflagration.

Build the greatest monuments of earth, and have the greatest number of jewels that you please, it is only to be added to the great conflagration at the end. "The earth shall be dissolved, and the elements shall melt with fervent heat." Get something that will not be burned. The beauty of real Christianity is this: none will sing a louder hallelujah than the believers themselves over the hay and stubble, and reserve the gold and silver to the glory of God. The best way for us all to do our work is for us to do it ourselves. If each man does his work thoroughly, and each one sticks to his own place—has found out his place and sticks to it—and finds out his work and does it, then the great Christian work will go on.

In the coral reefs in the southern seas you see the corals working. They don't ask if the other is doing its work; they don't appoint committees to see if they are all working. They each work along, and build up those great barriers and reefs. They are unconscious, but not unworthy, instruments by which a hand invisible rears magnificent structures in the mysterious deep. Look at wrestling Jacob. I believe Jacob's wrestling was his weakness. God in His grace would make him His witness. A man wrestled with him, and he had to put his thigh out of joint before he could get him to his senses.

Just one word more. One great hindrance, if not the greatest hindrance that I know of, is this. I draw your attention to a passage in the Gospel according to Luke, the ninth chapter, Christ called His twelve disciples, "and gave them power and authority over all devils, and to cure diseases. And He sent them to preach the kingdom and heal the sick," and so on. They got authority over all devils and diseases without exception. The next thing you hear of them is, a poor man brought his son to have a devil cast out of him. They had all authority, and it was not a question of divine power. They had authority given to them. Why had they not power to do it? They had no faith. But why did they not have faith. Read on, and you will find where the secret of it lies. "Then there arose a reasoning among them, which of them should be greatest." That is the point. Is it the case with us? The Lord help us to examine our work, and see if "for us to live is Christ" or self.

OUR CONSECRATION AS PRIESTS UNTO GOD.

"Ye also, as lively stones, are built up a spiritual house, an holy priesthood, to offer up spiritual sacrifices, acceptable to God by Jesus Christ.
But ye are a chosen generation, a royal priesthood, an holy nation, a peculiar people; that ye should shew forth the praises of Him who hath called you out of darkness into His marvelous light."—1 PETER ii. 5, 9.

SOMETIMES we can understand a building better if we see the plans. In a large building with many rooms, corridors, and recesses we are apt to get confused, and it is very convenient to get the plans and study them, when we can see out way about the house itself better than before. Now, that is just why we go back to the book of Leviticus, in order that we may get the plans of the New Testament, and see the plans upon which its doctrines are reared.

Hence the absurdity of those who go back to copy the Old Testament ritual. It is just as if you have engaged a contractor to build a house for you, and when the day comes for him to give you the keys, he presents you with a nice bundle of plans, and says, "There's the house." That is absurd! Well, so it is with those who go back to the old ritual. Now we have the house, and although we look at the plans it is simply that we may understand the house better, and not that we may copy them. Thus it is that in the details of the New Testament teachings we get many precious lessons from Leviticus.

The subject under consideration is, "priests unto God;" but I dare not attempt to enter upon this vast subject; I can scarcely deal even with on department of it; but I will try to call your attention to a few thoughts upon the consecration of priests, as shown in the types of the eighth chapter of Leviticus.

We all know well that Christ is the great High Priest of the Bible. He is spoken of as such, specially in the book of Hebrews—that book of which we are not told who was the writer. Theologians are divided as to who wrote it—some say Paul and some Apollos, but we have not key to the human hand that was used to write it. It begins as no other Epistle does—"God, who at sundry time," &c. It is from Himself; and the child of God who reads it is led in the third chapter to consider Jesus Christ as his Apostle and High Priest. Only in the Epistle to the Hebrews is He called the Apostle. The Apostle, not only coming from God to man, but also now appearing in the presence of God for man.

Now, it is generally allowed that we are Christ's representatives on earth; we appear before men as witnesses for God. The converse of this is also true, and we, as priests, appear before God for man. We are priests unto God, and through the grace of Jesus Christ we have the power of intercession. We stand as ministers and officiating priests before Him, offering sacrifices daily unto His name. Sacrifices have never ceased. We are offering them day by day before the throne of grace. And it is just because we have life this great truth out of sight that spurious sacrifices are so continually offered. We ought to be offering the sacrifice of praise continually.

He hath made us kings and priests unto God; we are made nigh by the blood, brought into the holy of holies, the veil rent, and therefore *no veil between*. Thus we are in the brightest Shekinah of the glory of God; and this, remember, is not the privilege of a few Christians, but of all who are in Christ. It is our normal place.

We are not merely out of Egypt by faith in Christ; not merely through the desert by faith in Him; not merely into Canaan by faith; not merely entered into the holy place by faith; but into the holy place without a veil between. That is the place of *all* who are in Christ; through Him who has entered by His own blood into the heavens, there to appear in the presence of God for us.

Thus, when we read of Aaron, we have a type of Christ as the great High Priest; when we read of Moses, we have a type of Christ as the Great Prophet; and when together with these we have the elders spoken of, we have a type of Christ as our King. So, in Leviticus, we have Christ shown forth as Prophet, Priest, and King. And thus, in the eighth chapter, we have the manifestation of Christ Himself, and of the provision He has made for us.

I cannot go into this wonderful chapter in detail, but to you who study your Bibles I will give a few hints, that you may find out these precious truths for yourselves.

First, then, we have here Aaron as representing the great High Priest. In the first thirteen verses of the chapter we have this consecration spoken of; but when we come to the fourteenth verse, we find there is a sin-offering. This refers to our priesthood. Before there can be consecration we have two most important sacrifices to be offered. First, the sin-offering, and then the burnt-offering for a sweet savour. That is a lesson to anyone who may be wishing to do anything for the Lord, to consecrate his time, is talents, his money, or his service to the Lord. Till he come to the cross there can be no consecration. Whatever he may do, it is but dead works. He may even give his body to the flames, in the hope that there will arise to God the incense of a sweet saviour. But, no, no! till there be a sin-offering, there can be *no* consecration.

The place of the sin-offering. And remember the place of sin-offering is far away—outside the camp. A man may come offering his money; but no, it cannot be accepted until he has taken his place as a poor sinner—outside the camp. "What," he says," must I go away beyond the tribe of Dan?" Yes, you must go past their camp; they are nearest the place of sin-offering. The publicans and sinners are nearest it, and it is easiest for them to take their proper place. It is hard for the self-righteous to go there; bur until they have been there their service cannot be acceptable to Him. We must be clear about this.

Have we gone in the consciousness of our own guilt outside the camp, and there seen our guilt sinners, are saved through His blood? If you have not been there, then the sooner you go the better, "Behold, now is the accepted time; behold, now is the day of salvation." Cain tried to leap through all these barriers, and to be a worshipper at once. He came with the beautiful fruits of the earth ere he brought the blood; but to his offering God had not respect.

So with you if you have not been to the sin-offering your sacrifice is in vain.

But now, after the sin-offering, where the victim is identified with the sin of the offerer, we have the burnt-offering for a sweet-smelling savour. And thus we find Christ offered Himself for our sins, and also for a sweet-smelling savour—an offering without spot or blemish. And we have all the virtue of the glorious fulness of Christ. All that He is, I am. All His goodness is put to my account. Just as I am identified with Him in death, so in resurrection; and thus I am not only absolved from guilt, but also accepted in the Beloved. Not only are out sins put away, but we are in the risen One—standing in Him.

And thus God can smile upon us without compromising His glory. He cannot put the consecrating oil upon an unclean or unworthy sinner; but in Christ I am worthy—worthy in Him alone. All His work is mine, and thud standing in Him, I am of the blood-royal of heaven—"accepted in the Beloved, complete in Him." And now, after all this, God comes down with the consecrating oil and blood.

Now then we can pass on, the sin and burnt-offering being past, to the consecration of priests. From the twenty-second verse to the close of the chapter, as also the few closing verses of the following chapter, will be found profitable reading on this subject.

We have three thoughts about consecration here. First, we have the blood (the blood first), and the oil of consecration; second, the basket of consecration; and third, the place of consecration.

We sometimes hear about Christian *consecrating themselves* to the Lord. Well, this is right enough in a modified sense. But I believe in scriptural expressions, such as, "Yield yourselves unto God, as those that are alive from the dead, and your members as instruments of righteousness unto God."

In these Old and New Testament words, the great work of consecration is kept in the Lord's hand. He alone can consecrate us, if the consecration is to be valid. In His consecration I find power and strength. It is not the meeting of few friends and others, who say, "I will consecrate myself to the Lord," where true consecration is to be found; but it is when the Lord, by His Spirit, comes and shines into my soul, and says, "You are consecrated already—the blood is upon you, the oil is upon you; ye are not your own, ye are bought with a price." Then we are consecrated. God has made us kings and priests to Him, and has consecrated us to Himself. It is that alone which makes us rise to the full dignity of our priesthood, and dare to bear testimony for God before our fellow-men. It would be no use for me to say that I can take upon me the duties of the Home Minister, and to go to the Home Office, and say I will put everything right. Why, stop till you are put into the Home Office, and then try to do your best. It is when a man is put into a certain office that he rises up, or ought to rise up, saying, "I will do the duties of that office properly."

And so here. It is not I who consecrate myself to the Lord, but it is He who has taken me from the miry clay, and set my feet upon a rock, and established my goings." And not only so—He has made me His witness upon earth. "I am not my own, I am bought with a price."

There is just now too much of we, we! We do this or that; we consecrate ourselves. Let us get rid of this doing, and remember that it is not *we*, but it is the Lord. Through Christ "we are accepted in the Beloved," and the oil and the blood has been put upon me by God Himself.

This consecration is not to be confounded with moral progressive sanctification, which is so necessary to us all. That goes on day by day, and week by week, in calm steady continuance in well-doing. But this consecration is done by Himself once for all. Of His own will He has consecrated us, once for all, to Himself. From the very day of our separation to Him, on the day when we first came to Him and had our sins put away, and were made priests unto Him, we have been consecrated to the Lord.

Oh, how many of us have been groping about when that thought should have raised us from the earth! We have been living as earth-born, instead of heaven-born men. It is even as if we had been in heaven, and sent back to earth to be witnesses for Him. The cross of Christ has taken us out of the world, and by His resurrection we have been sent back to the earth to testify for Him.

It is then for you, fellow-priests unto God—for all God's children are priests—it is for you to forget the things that are behind, to let them pass with old years, and now to start as heaven-born priests. Let us rise and take our position and standing as priests unto God; to see the blood upon my ear, and therefore I listen to no communication that is not in accordance with the Word; to see the blood upon my hand, and therefore I touch nothing that is not for the glory of God; to see the blood upon my feet and therefore I will go nowhere, and mix with no society, where I cannot testify for Him. Thus have we the "beauty of holiness."

We might well tremble if we found that consecration was only by the blood. For while blood stands for atonement, it has also a deeper meaning. What does it stand for here? It signifies that we are wholly His, that we are bought. It is the measure of our consecration. One man may be much exercised as to how much he shall give to the Lord. Shall it be tenth, even as the godly Jew gave a tenth to the Lord? Or shall it be nine-tenths, or this or that amount? Oh, friends, this settles all, "Ye are not your own." And though we have not yet resisted unto blood, nor are we called upon at the present day, yet we are wholly His—life, treasure, all I have and all I am, belong to Him and not a part only. The whole of our being, right on to death—spirit, soul, and body—right to the end of life, belong to God.

That is what we are called to as priests unto God. And this is the reason the oil is put upon us. The oil signifies the Spirit which is given us, that we may follow Christ in His utter abandonment of self, and His full devotion of service for life and for death. Consecrated with the oil, the whole of our life must be utter and entire unselfishness—continually imitating Christ, not only simply doing our duty, but following Him who gave Himself for us.

The second thought here is, that this consecration by blood and oil is fed and nourished at "the basket of consecration." What was the food that our blessed Master fed upon? For we must always look to Him as the great model. He said to His disciples, when they returned from buying bread, and pressed Him to eat, "I have meat to eat that ye know not of." What was that meat? "To do the will of Him that sent Me, and to finish His work." Now this is what we are to feast upon continually. One feast will not do. The basket was to provide food for all the days of consecration. And as we need out daily bread for the support of the temporal body, so we need the divine good for the support of our consecrated nature; and that food is nothing more than doing His will. Just as we are following Him, and are content to give up our own will, whatever it may cost, so shall we be nourished and strengthened.

And remember, this is not one act, but a continual going on, imn serving and following Him. We must seek to know His will, not our own. Remember that we have much to contend with in this world. Why? Because there is not a Christian man or woman who has not in them something older than their spiritual life. In other words, the old nature is older than the new. Some of you were twenty years old when you started the new life; by that time a young man has all his plans for his future laid. These plans were laid before his consecration, and it is natural that with the new life should come an entire change. Yet, many of us are continuing in our daily life to follow out our old purposes. Thus, perhaps, some of you are working or business men, who should be missionaries or preachers.

Let us be feeding upon the will of the Lord, and resigning ourselves entirely to His will. Let us seek to know His will. "Lord, what wouldest thou have me to do?" Month by month, and year by year, let us seek to know His will, and His alone. This is feeding from the "basket on consecration."

Lastly, we are to abide at the door of the tabernacle, and keep the charge of the Lord. We are here as His witnesses, keeping His charge. He Himself said, "For their sakes I sanctify myself, that they also might be sanctified through the truth." Christ was separated from all His glory and possessions while on earth in order that He might have us waiting for Him *when He comes*.

These then are our days of consecration. We are passing along surely to the end. We know not the hour, but we know that we are a year nearer the glory than a year ago.

Eighteen centuries ago He said, "Behold, I come quickly!" and yet here we are waiting still. What have we to do whilst waiting? What is our place? Keeping the charge of the Lord. "What I say unto you, I say unto all, Watch." Why? Because we "know not the hour when the Son of man cometh." Let us keep His command, abiding His will, waiting for His presence. It is thus that we shall fulfil the days of consecration.

What have we been doing? Alas! alas! none of us have risen to this glorious privilege. He has told us to keep His commands. His last command was, "Go ye therefore, and teach all nations, baptizing them in the name of the Father, and of the Son, and of the Hoy Ghost: teaching them to observe all things whatsoever I have commanded you: and, lo, I am with you always, even unto the end of the world"

That was His last command, and yet a hundred years have scarcely elapsed since Christians began to think that the heathen should be looked after at all, or told the story of the cross. And at this moment more than half the glove has never heard of His name. Yet we, who are priests unto God, and pledge to do His will, and keep the charge of the Lord, stay at home at ease, and keep our money in our pockets when demands are made for the help of those who have gone. Is this carrying out His will, which is beautifully expressed in the hymn—

> "Send the blessed tidings all the world around!
> Spread the joyful news wherever mean if found:
> Whosoever will may come."

Shall we not then rise up at once as those who are waiting for the full manifestation of His glory? Let us be waiting at His door, looking for the time when all shall fall on their faces before Him. Brethren, the days are few. Soon shall He come whose right it is to reign; and then, amid brighter glories than ever man in his wildest dreams thought of, we shall see Him in the glory, and shall be hailed with, "Well done, good and faithful servant." Not for the success we have met with, but that we have been keeping His charge.

Many are at home in quiet corners, who ought to be out to every place under the sun, spreading His name. Oh, brethren, we are priests! We, who have come to Christ as the sin-offering, who have known Him as the burnt-offering of a sweet-smelling savour, who have had the blood and the oil put upon us, the charge of the Lord is upon us to keep His commands, and the provision for our need is there. Oh, let us be steadfast, immovable, always abounding in every good work abiding at the door of the tabernacle; "for he that shall come will come, and will not tarry." And remember that in the day of the full blaze of the manifested glory of the Lord, if a regret were possible amidst that glory, it will be that we have done so little to "keep the charge of the Lord."

PRIEST AFTER THE ORDER OF MELCHISEDEC.

"For he testifieth, Thou are a priest for ever after the order of Melchisedec."—HEBREWS vii. 17.

"For this Melchisedec, king of Salem, priest of the most high God, who met Abraham returning from the slaughter of the kings, and blessed him' to whom also Abraham gave a tenth part of all; first being by interpretation King of righteousness, and after that also King of Salem, which is, King of peace; without father, without mother, without descent, having neither beginning of days, nor end of life; but made like unto the Son of God; abideth a priest continually."— HEBREWS vii. 1-3.

WE are now to speak of the Melchisedec priesthood of the Lord Jesus Christ, and to that end let us read the Word of God upon it, in Hebrews vii., "For this Melchisedec, king of Salem, priest of the most high God, who met Abraham returning from the slaughter of the kinds, and blessed him; to whom also Abraham gave a tenth part of all; first being by interpretation King of righteousness, and after that also King of Salem, which is, King of peace; without father, without mother, without descent, having neither beginning of days, nor end of life; but made like unto the Son of God; abideth a priest continually." "Now"—and mark the Divine exhortation—"consider how great this man was, unto whom even the patriarch Abraham gave the tenth of the spoils. And verily they that are of the sons of Levi, who receive the office of the priesthood, have a commandment to take tithes of the people according to the law, that if, of their brethren, thought they come out of the loins of Abraham: but he whose descent is not counted from them received tithes of Abraham." This is the true explanation of that—"Without father or mother." It is, that his descent is not counted. His descent is not reckoned as from the ordinary line of the priesthood. He received tithes from Abraham, "and blessed him that had the promise"—two wonderful marks of superiority—got tithes from Abraham, and blessed Abraham, "and without all contradiction, the less is blessed of the better." Now, the position that we take in considering how great this man was, is this, that all that we have heard of the Aaronic priesthood, and of the mediatorial kingship, merely goes by a process of *à fortiori* reasoning in the consideration of the greatness of Christ in the Melchisedec function. That He, the King and the Priest united in one man, absorbs all that was seen, and much greater than all that is seen, either in the Divine or the mediatorial reign, so-called, or in the Aaronic priesthood. Christ is the order of Medchisedec, and not of Aaron. He performs all the functions now of the Aaronic priesthood; but, sin being in the way, and sin being in the question, requires sacrifices from man to God, and, if we turn back to the original account of Melchisedec, we find there was no sacrifice mentioned in connection with Melchisedec's blessing Abraham. There was no incense. There is no hope from any sacrifice to God there. And if we look at the priesthood in the various ways in which God is manifested to man, we shall learn very much of the blessed teaching of the Lord Himself. Perhaps it may not seem to be what people call "practical." People are always talking about what is "practical." "Let us have," they say, "what is practical." I often ask the question, "Whether do you mean, practical from God's point of view, or practical from your own point of view?" When Abraham was taken into the confidence of God about Lot, he never uttered a word about himself. It was all interceding for Lot. "And shall I hide from my friend Abraham what is going to come upon his nephew Lot, in Sodom?"

My friends, we must be—if we are in God's mind, we shall be—interested in God's truth because it is God's We may rise up to it if we say, "Give us this day our daily bread," but we shall be eating the old corn of the land, instead of the finest of the wheat. God is not for Himself and in Himself. What God in His majesty, in His might, in His history in the past, in the present, and to come, in a past eternity, in a present dispensation of time, in the glory, and in the coming glory—all is from the Godward point of view, and we shall all find it practical to the glory of Him whose name is put above every name. If we look at the patriarchal time, we see this first, and the first shall be last. That which was first found in the seed-plot of Genesis will be the development of the glory that is the last of the dispensations. The Melchisedec priesthood and kingship that came first representing the last before the roll of time is wrapped up. We there find when the servant was coming from the wars, as in the book of Exodus, the first scene recorded in all history, whether sacred or profane, long before the *Iliad* of Homer was sung, we find it was so when they were delivered from the Egyptian slavery. God for them destroyed their foes, and on the wilderness shore of the Red Sea they sang, as the first song of history, the song of redemption—and the first shall be last. And the first battle as recorded in history is the type of the last. The first shall be last again; and the battle, the first that is recorded in profane or sacred history, is the battle at the close of which Melchisedec met Abraham. Melchisedec appears to him on his return, and does two things—the two proper things in connection with king and priest. As priesthood represents headship for man in things pertaining to God, and kinghood represents representation in rule of God over man Melchisedec came thus with the provision, the nourishment, the refreshment, and joy of the king, and he did two things—he blessed Abraham from the Most High God, and he blessed the Most High God from Abraham. He had blessings rising up, and blessing flowing down; and we know when Jesus came in the first and second chapters of John, before He shows how love is communicated to us on the earth, He gives us a glimpse of all His glories. In the first of John you will get all the personal and official glories of our Lord essentially portrayed, and in the second chapter you get two wonderful acts symbolic of the Head, of His glory when there He purges the Temple; and of His power when He begins His series of miracles at Cana, where He turned that which is required to cleanse, into the wine of the kingdom, for the first shall be the last, and the water shall be the wine, and all shall rejoice when David is king, and the day of feasting is come.

The Lord in patriarchal days (and Melchisedec shows the great thought) was God in heaven, and the worshippers and sacrificers were upon the earth, and the great thought is the glory of God in heaven, ministering to men—He as the Judge and the Ruler—here upon the earth with rebellious man. Or is, as it is said sometimes, as if to take the royal attributes from our blessed Lord, that God is love, and would make such a sentiment a mockery of the great and holy God, as would make it appear that He had no authority, and no power, and no righteousness, and no holiness *to damn*—the is His own word—to kindle wrath, we have to ask another question and a prior question—What is God? We have to ask who it is that is love? Who is it? It is not the sentiment of man. It is the God that cannot live in the presence of sin without punishing sin. It is the God that cannot bear sin because He is love. It is the God of Calvary, whose own Son, when lying under it, had to say, "My God, my God, why hast thou forsaken me?" It is the God who will have a solid peace—a blessed peace. Let it be war as it may be, for while we may wish to take the easy texts of Scripture that may read of the time when men should beat their swords into ploughshares, and their spears into pruning-hooks, I ask of you also to study God on another side, when He tells them to "Proclaim ye this among the Gentiles; prepare war; wake up the mighty men; let all the mighty men of war draw nigh; let them come up beat your *ploughshares* into swords, and your *pruning-hooks* into spears."

God does not bless when sin has been here, but through the judgment of sin; that is, individually or nationally. So the world wide; *He cleanses always by judgment*. So, when His returning warrior, Abraham, who had beaten his ploughshare into a sword, went away, leaving his nomadic practices to betake himself to the new trade of warrior, the Most High God puts Himself near him, like some wondrous strange flash never before seen, and never again to be seen, after He has fulfilled the function of His type; and there he blesses as the high priest, not of Jehovah and of a nation, but of the Most High God, the possessor of heaven and earth. Our Lord is called "King Jesus." Our Lord is called "King of kings." Our Lord is called "King of nations." Our Lord is called "King of glory." It is now conceded that the passage in Revelation "King of saints," is *Ethnol*, not *Hagnel*. It has to do with nations; and His true, royal rights in connection with this earth are not seen until Israel is seen as the centre, and the nations of the earth blessed in Him, calling Him blessed. Such is His true scriptural kingship—

first seen as God in the heavens, and man upon the earth a worshipper with His sacrifice to the living God.

When we come now to Exodus, or to Jewish times, we find that the way is to be seen, and God is found upon the earth and the worshippers and the sacrifice upon the earth also; that He makes, or gets man to make for Him, a dwelling-place upon the earth, a tabernacle, and worshippers and sacrificers are there to show the way of approach to Him. Then when we come to our dispensation, we find that God is in heaven, but worshippers and sacrifice are there too. We are seated in the heavenly places, not *with* Christ yet, but *in* Christ, and there is our standing in heaven, with boldness to draw near without a veil between. And in the glory that is to come, when Christ takes His Kingship, then we shall find that the heavens and the earth are united, and God is in both heaven and earth, and as His witnesses, and worshippers in the heavens and in the earth, in the Church of God with His heavenly ones, and with the Jew and the nations of the earth, and all the earth filled the knowledge of the Lord. Then we have the characteristics of God's kingship and priesthood as represented in Melchisedec. It is a remarkable thing when we study this book of Hebrews, which tells us of the way into the holiest—not the blessings of the Melchisedec, but the blessings of Aaronic priesthood—we never hear anything about a temple. The word temple, or that temple, is *never* found in Hebrews. Just as when we come to the study of the book of Revelation, the thought of our being the children of the father is *never* in all Revelation found. He is never "our Father" in the Revelation. His is the Lord God Almighty, and the Lamb. But the New Testament Fatherhood is not taken up in the Revelation. So in Hebrews. There is not the temple, but the tabernacle, because it was the pattern of things in the heavenlies that was given in the book of Hebrews, and the temple refers to an established state of thing in the land. For in the book of Exodus we have the priesthood in connection with the tabernacle, with all its furniture, symbolism, and the like. Now, if you look at Exodus, Leviticus, and Deuteronomy, we have the tabernacle in Exodus, and where? Where God was to be met. In Leviticus, the priest's service book; in Numbers we get the kingdom, but as a lamp in the wilderness; not a settled and

PRIEST AFTER THE ORDER OF MELCHISEDEC. 127

established and fixed thing in the land. Then we have the condition in which they were to be in the land, in the book of Deuteronomy.

And so when we get to heavenly things themselves, in the bbook of Hebrews, it is all according to that which we have in the wilderness making way. Now when Christ has come and finished the work; when it is that He has done the work that will put away sin and bring in everlasting righteousness, why does He not at once step on to Melchisedec's throne? Why is it that now He does not exercise the functions of the king and of the priest evidently before the world?

Ah! there comes in the wondrous silence, this wondrous pause, this wondrous drag upon the wheels of time, when God might have come down with one fell swoop on all the rejectors of His Son. Nay, He makes the wrath of man to praise Him, and He postpones Melchisedec's glory, that He may reveal from His own heart's love a more wondrous mystery that was hid in God from the foundation of the world; not blessing to a nation, or to a nation through a nation, but the model wall of partition broken down, the new body , the bride of the Lamb gathered out of every nation, kindred, and tongue, to the glory of His blessed name, and receiving the royal glory there: "And He has not sat down on His throne," as He tells us. "To him that overcometh will I give to sit on my throne."

His father said, "If the world won't give you the throne as the Son of man, and if the Jew won't give you the throne of David, I will set you at my right hand, I will give you a higher throne, and a better throne, a more wonderful throne than all;" and that is why He is to convince the world of righteousness, because "I go to my Father." If the world is so unrighteous that they can't see any beauty in Him, and give Him nails instead of a sceptre, and thorns instead of glory, and mocking instead of worship; oh, He has a righteous Father, and the Father will reward Him for the travail of His soul even now, and the Father will show what a righteous, and perfect man, and God-glorifying man, He was here upon earth. And he says, "Sit at my right hand, until I make my enemies thy footstool."

And so in this wonderful time that He spanned right over, and said that He was coming back quickly (He does not say very *soon*, it is quickly), it is the heart of love; it is not the date of time, because you know that to a man on a dark night the nearest point if the lighthouse. He does not see hills, and valleys, and rivers, but the lighthouse. Keep looking forward to the lighthouse. It is the nearest point to us in the darkness of night; and His heart runs over all this pause when He is showing that wondrous thing—resurrection life. Risen men were not merely a number of people testifying on the earth of Jew and Gentile, but risen men—men identified with Him, standing at the heaven-side of Jesus, at the resurrection side of the tomb—identified with the heavenly one, holy, heavenly men, living upon the earth. Such is our true character, if we would rise up to it.

That would soon strip the jewels off you—not that we are going to heaven all at once. It is not that we are earthly men, wishing to go to heaven; we are heavenly men sent back to earth, the witnesses for Him; for, mark you, before I can get into a place I must be out of it. "As thou hast sent Me into the world;" this is the root of all our worldliness. Some people say they don't like doctrine. I believe there is no practice without doctrine for its basis. A man's practice will never rise above his doctrine, and his doctrine just is to make everything as comfortable as he can, and get to heaven by the easiest practicable road. And so like a musty parchment, they shut up their title-deeds to heaven in a safe, fire-proof, judgment-proof, and hell-proof, and hope to get into heaven I the long run. Is that the resurrection life? Is that "risen with Christ?" Is that a "sent man"—as the Father sent Me into the world—the meaning being a "sent man." The cross of Christ takes us out of the world, and the resurrection of Christ sends us back a firebrand, with motives, principles, aims, ambitions, hopes, and joys that they cannot understand, or comprehend where we got them from.

So thus in this little pause He has identified Himself with us in resurrection life. In the Melchisedec idea the full truth of him in blessing was seen. In the Jewish priesthood the full idea of the way was seen. In the Christian dispensation the full idea of the life is seen. And you see all put together with Melchisedec, and Aaron, and Jesus. Now we have the way, the truth, and the life. Time fails us, but the glory won't. They that are Christ's at His coming will continue this subject in the Melchisedec glory that is then to be revealed; but we have the benefits of it now.

So, just looking at the different methods in which our blessed Lord left us, we see that in John, where we have the manifestation of Him in all His perfection here upon the earth for us, it is never said that He went into heaven at all. There is no ascension in John. It says, as His parting words, "Follow Me;" to heaven you see is naturally implied. He is not to be separated from us. We are heavenly men by the admonition of John. His last words to Peter, John, and the rest were, "Follow Me;" not a word about the cloud receiving Him.

In Mark, the beautiful little gospel that tells us of this service, He shows that they would have miraculous power over evil, and adds, "So then after the Lord had spoken unto them, He was received up into heaven, and sat on the right hand of God."

In Matthew He gives His grand marching order. What a sensation *The Times* would cause if some morning it could say that in some of the low parts of London had been found the true heir of the House of Brunswick. You never heard such a commotion as that would cause, if it could be shown that by indisputable rights our blessed Queen should be deposed, and that the true King was found. We read Matthew as if it were a mere human prediction of names; but it is to prove His royal rights to the throne of His father David, and do you think God will let them off when He has had the trouble to prove them? Do you think that we can spiritualize it into His spiritual throne, when He has taken great care to make it a genealogical throne? He has shown that He must reign as the successor to David, and He will do it; and at the end of that He gives us the great marching order: "Go ye into all the world, and preach the gospel to every creature;" which, if we do not do, we shall not get the privilege to do before the return of the Jews, for the Jews will do it in spite of us. That is what will happen. If we do not rise to the dignity of our call, it will be done by them. "This gospel of the kingdom shall be preached in all nations for a testimony;" but it may not be the privilege of the Church of God. Those godly Jews who have come through great tribulation may get the privilege.

"From Greenland's icy mountains,
From India's coral strand,

> Where Africa's sunny fountains
> Roll down their golden sand;
>
> From many an ancient river,
> From many a balmy plain,
> They call us to deliver
> Their land from error's chain.
>
> "Shall we, whose souls are lighted
> With wisdom from on high,
> Shall we, to men benighted,
> The lamp of life deny?

And so He gives us this commission in Matthew at His departure; but when, as the Son of man and true Melchisedec, He is taken away, at the end of Luke's gospel, what do we find it said of Him? Similar to what is said in Matthew: "And He led them out as far as Bethany, aand He lifted up His hands, and blessed them. And it came to pass while He blessed them, He was parted from them, and carried up into heaven." The last look that the believing eye saw was the uplifted hand, and the blessing left by their Friend; gaze upon Him, for He goes that way. The true Melchisedec—blessed be Abraham. The uplifted hands, the blessing, is for us. I think that we shall be very much humbled when He tells us, "Lo, I am with you always," to do the work. He has never altered the attitude of blessing. But, oh, how disobedient have we been in the line of service!

"I am with you!" My friend, *there* is the royal presence. You talk about mimicking and aping Rome, with all its tomfoolery and its flummery, and music and machinery, and gymnastics. You talk to them, and they will make it appear to you they have some royal presence. My friend, off to China with you, off to Japan with you, with the living God alone at your back, and then you will realize the royal presence—"Lo, I am with you always, to the end of the age." And you will see Him in China, and in Japan, with uplifted hands, just as here; for it is the Son of man of Luke, it is the Melchisedec story—that He uplifted His hands, and as He was blessing them, He was caught up into heaven.

Brethren, there is a great danger in even being taught the truth of God under some circumstances. It is this, and it is a very subtle danger, that we are taken up more with blessings that we get, than with the blessed Lord Himself; more with the little cup that is so cracked that it cannot hold the stream that is poured into it, than with the great fountain from whence the stream flows. Mr. Moody used to say, "The only way to keep a broken vessel full is to keep it always under the tap." Now that is it. You need to tap to-morrow. You can't live upon to-day's food to-morrow. It breeds worms in the wilderness. There is no food kept over for to-morrow, but the Giver is there. We are taken up more with what grace has done for us, than the grace that has done it. This is the subtle error, and a very subtle error, especially to those who are Christians, and who have studied the Word of God. We are taken up with the idea of our seat in the heavenlies, out comfort and joy, and singing and everything else, but not with Himself. We must draw attention to error as well as to the knowledge of the truth. It must be with us a it was with the disciples on the Mount of Transfiguration—"They saw no man save Jesus only." What would be more appropriate than to read 1 Chron. xii., where we read that glorious lesson to men in such a state as we are now, when David had not his throne, just as where our Christ is now when He has not His throne—in a parenthesis; there is the similarity between the anointing and the crowning at Hebron and the coronation at Jerusalem. So we are in the little interval while he yet keeps himself close. He was not the manifestation of the Son of God; but 'While He yet kept Himself close because of Saul," then we find the brave men gathered to him in the wilderness, many men of war from among the Gadites fit for the battle. We need that. We need the Gadites. We need the men of war. Romanism, Ritualism, and Spiritualism are coming in like flood; and besides, we scarcely know the amount of open infidelity that is about us. We need therefore the men of war able to "contend earnestly for the faith once delivered to the saints." Then we require the Benjamites, "famous throughout the house of their fathers." And there is another kind that we require—the children of Issachar, "who have understanding of the times." There is so much misunderstanding of the times, that we are all adrift. We have been trying to convert Britain, instead of to evangelize the world. These things should be done, but the others not left undone; and they would not be if we had "an understanding of the times." "They had an understanding of the times, to know what Israel ought to do; and all they their brethren were at their commandment." They studied the times, and we should study the times by the light of God's Book. Al these were men of war, and there was one noticeable thing about them—they kept rank. "They came with a perfect heart to make David king." And that is what we want—to make Christ King, that He may receive His royal tights as the Don of David, the Son of man, the Son of God, over the universe.

And they could all keep rank. I fear that we are bad soldiers in keeping rank. When I was a volunteer, we had to be out at six o'clock in the morning practising to keep rank. Hour after hour we went at it, and the young recruits were always falling out of rank. I remember our sergeant used to go with his naked sword along the line to see that we "dressed up," as he called it. Dress up, Christians; let us keep rank. Do you know the way we did it? We took our line from the left-hand or right-hand man, whoever might be in front. Take your line, Christians, from the Captain. Keep your eye upon Him, and dress up to His level. Do not rush in front, or lag behind. Dress up! Keep rank! Have you any extra power as a believer? Then go and help the weak one to keep rank. Don't try to patronize a fellow-Christian, but try to dress him up and keep him in rank. And do so with singleness of heart. We may differ on many points. We do differ on many points, but we are one in Christ. We could throw a bombshell into the middle of a meeting in a moment, but the love of Christ constraineth us to avoid this. We wish every heart to be filled with one thought, absorbed with one feeling, which finds its expression in—

> "Worthy the Lamb that died, they cry,
> To be exalted thus;
> Worthy the Lamb, our lips reply,
> For He was slain for us."

We are all of a single heart, beloved. With all our failure, ignorance, and aim, we have a single heart; and thought we do not all dress up as we ought to do, we have the single heart to proclaim our David King. Yes, we are waiting for Him not that we may get away from the strife and the toil. We are not all tired of the battle. We have with Paul the desire to depart and to be with Him, which is far better p; but not that we may get comfortable away into nice easy-chairs, to sing the songs of bliss, to wear the crowns of gold, and to have all tears wiped away from our eyes, that is not what we are waiting for—David to be king; for Him, my friends. It is that the prince of darkness may be cast out; it is that the right may triumph over the wrong it is that righteousness may run through our land and through the world like a river, and not the ungodliness of sin that is now polluting this fair earth. It is that antichrist may be cast down, Babylon destroyed, and truth triumph above all error. It is that all that was lost by our first Adam may be gathered up in the hands of the Son of man; that all that was lost in the covenant with Noah may be gathered up in the hands of Him who is the Judge of all the earth. It is that all that was lost in David and in Solomon's reigns may be gathered up in Him who will gather up and restore Ephraim and Judah; and they shall sing of the same brotherly love in the temple of their God, "Behold, how good a thing it is for brethren to dwell together in unity."

THE POWER OF GOD IN THE CHURCH.

"That the righteousness of the law might be fulfilled in us, who walk not after the flesh, but after the Spirit. For they that are after the flesh do mind the things of the flesh; but they that are after the Spirit the things of the Spirit. For to be carnally minded is death; but to be spiritually minded is life and peace. Because the carnal mind is enmity against God: for it is not subject to the law of God, neither indeed can be." ROMANS viii. 4-7.

THOSE to whom the Lord Jesus Christ gave power and authority were not privileged to be the instruments, by the Holy Ghost, of explaining that power to us. It was that apostle who was saved by the risen Christ from the glory, the apostle Paul, who has been privileged to put before us the source, the manifestation, and the outflow of the power that is in Christ for His people. Such, I take it, is the meaning of the subject before us; it is power in the individual saints, and not so much power in the church collective. We know very well that it is the apostate church that claims to be endowed with power as a church. So in our subject it is, I believe, power in the individual saints of God that is meant—power in those who are united to the Lord Jesus Christ in the glory.

Now I wish to draw your attention to the teaching of the apostle Paul concerning this power, and to his prayer concerning this power that is in Christ, for us who believe.

The first of these—his teachings as to the power—is given in Romans vii, while his prayer is presented in Ephesians i. and iii. His teachings you find in the middle of the three parts of Romans viii. That chapter is very readily divided into three parts. The first closes at the tenth verse, the second at the thirtieth verse, and the third goes on to that end of the chapter. In the first we find what we are before God in Christ—"There is therefore now no condemnation to them that are in Christ Jesus." Our standing before God is given in contrast to what our standing was, as shown in Romans v. As we were in Adam, so are we now in Christ. The second part gives us our present subject; not so much what we are in Christ, as what the Spirit of God is in us. And the last part gives us what God is for us.

Now I intend to confine myself to a few thoughts from the Word, so that you may study them, with the aid of the Holy Spirit, for yourselves, and thus be taught of God.

In the first part of the chapter we have a new nature communicated to us, with new faculties. In the second part we have the Spirit of God with power, the Holy Ghost, the third Person of the blessed Trinity, given unto us. Not here is meant the new creation, which is sometimes called the spirit, but it is the Holy Ghost, the third Person of the Trinity, who is dwelling in us. In the last part we have God as our protector—"If God be with us, who can be against us?"

Notice that the mere possession of the new nature does not of itself imply that we have the power in us. Saved though we be, we are still dependent upon the Holy Ghost every moment for power, and it is not sufficient that we should be born again; we must have the power. There must be the living presence of the living person to energize the new man and the new creation. We are as dependent on the Spirit of God, moment by moment, for power, as we were when we first turned our dying eyes on the crucified Christ for salvation. This is God's great cure for Antinomianism—this inward power of the Holy Ghost. Not an *ab extra* power merely, but an *ab intro* power controlled and guided by the power of God within us.

Now I will give you only a few watchwords from the eleventh verse onwards: "But if the Spirit of Him that raised up Jesus from the dead dwell in you, He that raised up Jesus from the dead shall also quicken your mortal bodies by His Spirit that dwelleth in you." The Holy Ghost is spoken of in this chapter under four names. He is called the "Spirit of God;" He is called the "Spirit of Christ;" His called the "Spirit of Him that raised up Jesus from the dead;" and He is called the "Spirit that raised up Christ form the dead." In the ninth verse we have "the Spirit of God" as contrasted with the flesh:

"Ye are not in the flesh, but in the Spirit, if so be that the Spirit of God dwell in you." Then as to our practical state we have, "If any man have not the Spirit of Christ, he is none of His." Then he comes to the indwelling of the Spirit, he takes us from the humiliation of Jesus to the exaltation of Christ.

Now the first thing we learn is that He will quicken these mortal bodies of ours, which attach us to the earth, and to the sins of this earth. Thus the Spirit is given us as a guarantee that our mortal bodies shall be quickened, and thus we know that by-and-by we shall reach the *terminus ad quem* when we reach the glory. Then our bodies shall be fashioned like unto His glorious body, not by any external force, but by His power dwelling in us. We shall not be dragged as felons before the bar of judgment; but, by the power of the Holy Ghost dwelling in us, we shall be quickened whenever the Lord Himself shall come. It is worthy of remark, that this indwelling of the Holy Spirit is passed over until the grand finale is introduced. It is the guarantee of the glory that is coming to Him, and to us. The guarantee that "when He shall appear, we shall be like Him; for we shall see Him as He is. And every man that hath this hope in Him purifieth himself, even as He is pure."

But till that glory is reached what is the power in us? The apostle goes on very consistently, "Therefore, brethren, we are debtors, not to the flesh, to live after the flesh. For if ye live after the flesh, ye shall die: but if ye through the Spirit do mortify the deeds of the body, ye shall live." The first thing then is resurrection, the next is mortification. Legalism would put mortification first, and then resurrection . But no, it is resurrection first, "If ye then be risen with Christ...mortifiy therefore your members which are upon the earth."

So the second thought in connection with the indwelling of the Holy Spirit is this: that we are to mortify the deeds of the body, and those who are thus indwelt will still go forward; for it does not stop there—they will be led of the Spirit. "For as many as are led of the Spirit of God, they are the sons of God." We are not merely actually mortifying that which is evil, but actively pursuing that which is good, and that led by the Spirit of God. Thus mortification precedes leading. We are not, as some would have it, led and then mortified, but we are to mortify, and then be led. "For ye have not received the Spirit of bondage again to fear; bur ye have received the Spirit of Son-standing, whereby we cry, Abba, Father." "The Spirit of *Son-standing*," not merely children by adoption. Not simply as we might adopt a child, and then put him away when he comes of age and fit to shift for himself, but sons by birth. There is a vague idea of that sort, but it is not found in Scripture. There we are shown to be sons by the new birth; we are born children of God, born again with the risen Christ. And thus we have the Son-standing by the Spirit dwelling in us; not the spirit of Sinai, not the spirit of the bond-woman, but the spirit of the free; and we cry, "Abba, Father." Thus we reach the climax. Risen with Christ, mortifying the deeds of the flesh, led by the Spirit, by that heavenly, unnatural, unearthly, supernatural power we are guided and led through whatever maze this world may present. Then by this indwelling of the Holy Spirit we realize our Son-standing, and cry, "Abba, Father."

But further, "The Spirit Himself beareth witness with our spirit, that we are the children of God." The Spirit dwelling in us is a witness, not to our salvation, as is often said by mistake, but to our sonship. It is remarkable that there is no mention made of the Holy Spirit in the Epistle to the Romans (which is God's grand book for anxious inquirers), until the man is taught to say that he is justified by faith, and has peace with God through our Lord Jesus Christ. Before that even the name of the Holy spirit is never mentioned, as if He would not abstract the thoughts of the anxious inquirers from the grand point. But when the child is brought into the family, he learns the family secrets, and the family truths. He learns that he is no longer under the spirit of legalism, and that he is not expected to force himself to love God through fear; but rather he is to serve God through love, and that by the power of the Spirit dwelling within him, which shall lead him to rise instinctively to that higher motive of the new creation. He cries "Abba, Father," from no outward force compelling, cut by an interior power witnessing with his spirit that he is the child of God.

But now we pass on to the next aspect of this indwelling of the Holy Spirit. We have seen the power of resurrection, the power for mortification, the power of guidance, the power of sonship, the power of hope, but now we have the power of sympathy. "Not only they, but ourselves also, which have the firstfruits of the Spirit, even we ourselves groan within ourselves waiting for the adoption, to wit, the redemption of our body." Thus we have groanings in sympathy with the whole creation, and these groanings are produced by the Spirit of God. "For we are saved by hope: but hope that is seen is not hope: for what a man seeth, why doth he yet hope for?" And then in the twenty-sixth verse: "Likewise the Spirit also helpeth our infirmities: for we know not what we should pray for as we ought: but the Spirit itself maketh intercession for us with groanings which cannot be uttered." We know not what we ought to pray for, but one thing we do know. And here I make a little variation in our translation. Verse 28: "*But*" (it should read *but*, not *and*) "we know that all things work together for good to them that love God." The contrast is here made with our ignorance; what we do not know is contrasted with what we do know. We do not even know how to pray aright, and what to pray for; and we do not know how to speak, and we put the Word awkwardly before the people. But one thing we do know; and that is, that it will be well in the morning. Yes, "we know that all things work together for good to them that love God." So then from the hope, the anticipation of the resurrection of the body, we have every gradation of His power till we reach the groaning in sympathy with the whole creation around us, and in sympathy with every part of our being—mental, moral, and physical groanings. So while the material creation groans, the spiritual creation groans for the full manifestation of the sons of God. It groans, and is not yet satisfied; and rightly so, because it is the Holy Spirit that produces these groanings. Thus we have not merely the power of communion, the power of mortification, the power of guidance, the power of sonship, the power of witness, and the power of sympathy, but also the power of groaning within ourselves, for all that is abnormal in ourselves, and in the world around us, for all the evils and wars and woes and miseries produced by sin; we sigh and groan for the time when we shall solve these mysteries. We do not want to be wise above what is written, but we find ourselves sighing and groaning in sympathy with the Holy Ghost, and by His power indwelling in us.

Then, last of all, in the teaching of the apostle, we find that by the power of the Spirit dwelling in us we arrive at the grand confidence amid all mutations and change. "If God be for us, who can be against us?"

Now we must pass on to the prayer of the apostle Paul, in the epistle to the Ephesians: "Blessed be the God and Father of our Lord Jesus Christ, who hath blessed us with all spiritual blessings in heavenly places in Christ." In Christ—all our well-springs are in Him, and all God's blessings for us are in Him. "According as He hath chosen us in Him before the foundation of the world, that we should be holy and without blame before Him in love." No one, even of the great angelic host, can stand before God without being holy, without blame and in love. So we too, if we are to be before God, must be holy, must be without blame, and must be in love—holy in character, without blame in all our ways, and loving in our nature. When we find ourselves on earth—the very opposite of all this, by nature unholy, full of blame, and loving ourselves and nothing else—well may we rejoice that in Him we have all we need, and in Him alone we are made presentable before God. In Christ we are made holy, in Him we are blameless, and in Him we learn to love.

Then, in connection with all this, the Apostle prays, in the fifteenth and following verses, "Wherefore I also, after I heard of your faith in the Lord Jesus, and love unto the saints, cease not to give thanks for you, making mention of you in my prayers, that the God of our Lord Jesus Christ"—he does not bring in the title, "Father of our Lord Jesus Christ" here; that is in the third chapter, and opens up a wonderful domain of thought which we cannot now enter upon—"that the God of our Lord Jesus Christ, the Father of glory, may give unto you the spirit of wisdom and revelation, that the eyes of your understanding being enlightened"—this is the Apostle's prayer for the saints; and we also pray that the eyes of our understanding may be enlightened, our eyes opened; so that we "may know what is the hope of His calling, and what the riches of the glory of His inheritance in the saints, and what is the exceeding greatness of His power to usward who believe." The Apostle prays that we may thus rise to the hill-top, and that the mists and fogs may be taken from our eyes, so that we may see somethings of the wondrous extent of the inheritance gained for us. Here we have, as in other passages, word piled upon word, to enrich the teaching.

We have here three distinct words in the Greek for *power*, each expressing a different shade of thought, and showing the power within us from our resurrection positions. "The exceeding greatness of His power" (*dunamis*). "The working of His mighty power" (*kratos*). "Which He wrought in Christ when He raised Him from the dead, and set Him at His own right hand in the heavenly places, far above all principalities and power" (*exousia*). And you hath He quickened who were dead in trespasses and sins." For we must go on with that second chapter, for it follows from the resurrection power. May we go on to know more of His power, as those waiting for the manifestation of Christ. Then, remember, we have to tell the world these things, and we have a wonderful message for any unconverted man here. We have to tell the good news, the glad tidings. The Gospel of God, which is the power of God unto salvation to every one that believeth.

One word more I must say ere close. In the first chapter of Ephesians the Apostle prayed that we may know what we have got; but if we study the prayer of the third chapter we shall find there is something higher still. When you read it you find that there is something better than the knowledge of the glory, better than to know the possession we have got, and it is to "know the love of Christ which passeth knowledge," that love which was before the glory, that love which planned the glory; for the love that planned is higher and deeper than even the glory, so the Apostle bows his knee to the Father of our Lord Jesus Christ, that we may know that wondrous love.

One more solemn thought comes to me as we speak of this love, of this glory, of this eternity, and it is this: What is to be thy eternity, my friend? Men try to get quit of that thought of eternity, and try to blot out these two words, *eternity* and *punishment*; but put them out for a moment from Matt. xxv., and read the chapter without them. Is it not a solemn thought even yet? "These shall go away"—stop there if you will. Away—*away*—where? The sweetest word uttered by Christ to poor man is, *Come*! To the weary soul He says, "Come unto Me"; and to those on His right hand, "Come, ye blessed." But away, away!—may those awful words never be heard by any here. God grant it may not be. "These shall go away." Away from Christ, away from God, away from life, away from love; away from His tears, His cross, His power, His glory, and His Spirit. Away, away! Is the word for you to be *away*, or *come*? Now He has opened your way to the glory and pleads with you to come!

THE FULNESS OF BLESSING.

"Blessed be the God and Father of our Lord Jesus Christ, who hath blessed us with all spiritual blessings in heavenly places in Christ."—EPHESIANS I. 3.

THE first chapter of the Epistle of Paul to the Ephesians, 3d verse, says, "Blessed be the God and Father of our Lord Jesus Christ, who hath blessed us with all spiritual blessings in heavenly places in Christ." This seems to be the fulness of blessing, and to tell us in whom it is provided. "Blessed be the God and Father of our Lord Jesus Christ, who hath blessed us with all spiritual blessings in heavenly places in Christ." It seems also to draw before our eyes a contrast with former blessing that the great Creator, Jehovah, had given to Israel in the days of Israel's glory. The basket and the store being full, we have evidences of righteousness and righteous living. That they should dwell in the land, and have food, was the great promise given to Israel. They were blessed with all temporal blessings in earthly places—in Canaan. Their blessings were earthly and temporal, and their sphere was Canaan. But now, since the Christian dispensation has dawned, and since in Christ Jesus there is neither male nor female, Jew nor Gentile, barbarian, Scythian, bond nor free, our sphere is changed, our position is changed; we are blessed with all spiritual blessings—the heavenly places; and He, in whom is found blessing, is Christ. "Hath blessed us." It doesn't say "shall bless us, "or "is about to bless us." It is "hath blessed us." There is not a single Christian, a single believer in the Lord Jesus Christ, but has all blessing. There has always been a tendency in all ages, among all men, among all minds, to make distinctions between genuine Christians. Laity and clergy have no foundation in the Word of God. There is no such thing. We have pastors, teachers, evangelists. There is no inner circle—a chosen lot that comes nearer to God. He has blessed us with all spiritual blessings. The church of Rome has introduced all these things, making it appear that one Christian has more favour in the Church of God than another. There is no such thing as mediatorial priesthood, one Christian for another. We are all priests unto God. "He hath made us unto our God kings and priests." We have all an equal right of drawing near. There is no selection of some people as having got the blessing. There is no blessing that we can have, but God has already given us in Christ; though, alas! there are many blessings we have received that we never think of. There is no blessing—let is be called the fulness of blessing, let is be called any sphere of blessing—there is no blessing that you require, or your heart can think of, that we have not already in Christ.

Fellow-believer in the Lord Jesus Christ, there are many blessings in Christ that we never think of, and we don't know of. And it is on this account, among others, that we try and stir one another up to know what blessing is—to know of whom to be got, to know how it is to be appropriated, to know how it is to be communicated. The youngest child of God, the youngest convert to the Lord Jesus, has a whole Christ, and nothing else; and the most aged saint, having the greatest experience, has a whole Christ, and nothing more. We need the experience of the blessing as granted by the God and Father of our Lord Jesus Christ in the gifts, or the gift of His Gift of Gifts—all other gifts in one—Christ. I might illustrate this subject, by saying that the gift He gives us is like a large casket full of choice jewels. He gives us a casket, and it is all the jewels. At first we only find the necessary provision for our daily use. The first thing that we rejoice in is in the anthem— we read of it in the 5th chapter to the Romans—"Being justified by faith, we have peace with God through our Lord Jesus Christ." We are too prone to look at what we have done ourselves, the sins we have actually committed; but the first thing we find is peace. The young convert comes to find that not only does he need peace, not only was he guilty of what he had done, but that he produced sin. Not only had he something against him, but something within him. He looks into the casket. He needs no new casket. He has only to unfold what he has already received. After a time he finds that he requires more, so he goes on to the 8th of Romans, and sees he is standing in a new man. His sins are blotted away, and the righteousness of God's law fulfilled. Now he sees some of the preciousness of the casket, and he sings the anthem of the 8th chapter of Romans—"There is therefore now no condemnation." Not only, "I am not condemned, but there is no condemnation for me."

Thus we have the second stage in the examination of the ripe, full blessing we have received. We have got past the initial stages—got past the idea of condemnation, and have found out that by the righteousness and blessing of God, there is no condemnation. But we require to learn more. We are taken away to the desert of loneliness, we are taken away to adversity, to sadness and sorrow, to the toils of every-day life. We don't need to apply for a new casket of blessing. We have only to come to the old one that we already have. We have all in Him—in Christ. We don't go to receive a new Christ. Do I get weary and retire to a corner of the desert? I find in Him my food still. Do I get to some bleak, barren desert, and find that I am thirsty? I find that He is the water of refreshment. Do I get into some benighted part, and see no opening out? He is a pillar to guide me by night, and a cloud to shelter me by day. And thus I find another layer of blessed gems of glorious perfection, and the more experience I get, the more I know of these jewels. Thank God for experience!

Young Christians know little about Christ. It may be, as often as not, that they use their strength pretty freely. There is progress in all Christian life, and in all Christian knowledge, and it is a remarkable thing that the progress in the experience is quite different from what we should expect. We all renew our strength; but how do we renew it? The first thing we do in renewing our strength is to mount up on wings like eagles. They fly. You would think that that was a fair development of strength, whereas it is only the first manifestation of it. You will generally find young converts practicing this. Let them. We have all to sink soon enough. Why, I have seen scores of young converts who thought that they would never tread the earth again, never see a bit of mud all the rest of their life, never do anything wrong. Let them have it, dear fellow-believer. Let us all have wings if we can. We may be all the better for a little Christian gymnastics. We don't fly long. We soon come back to the earth. The next stage in advancement is to run and not be weary. It is a long race, and a hard race, and a difficult race, and we have to lay aside every weight. What do you know about running? There is a day coming when you will have to walk—to walk and not to faint, in that narrow path, in the footsteps of that One in whom I am blessed.

There are days of fainting as well as flying. There are days when fainting fits come on. But we have not only to walk, we have to stand—a different experience from flying. The evidence of blessing we had in the flying will not do for the standing. We must go back to the casket—to the store-house; but still God hath blessed us with all spiritual blessings. "And having done all, to stand." As Martin Luther, the grand reformer, said, when told that all the world was against him, "Well, I'm against all the world." He knew the grace that could be found in the fulness of blessing. Anything more? Oh, yes. We have another stage yet. After we have done all, and got the blessings to know what to do in standing—"He maketh me to lie down in green pastures," but it is the perfect repose of his own provision.

In whom is it provided? It is in the God and Father of our Lord Jesus Christ. I have given you some specimens in one line of action. Israel got their blessings from the Creator and Jehovah; our peculiar blessings are from the God and Father of our Lord Jesus Christ. This is why the blessings are spiritual, the blessings are in heavenly places, and the blessings are in Christ. The next two verses, the fourth and fifth, throw some light on these two relations. In the fourth verse it is in connection with Him as God, in the fifth verse as Father; in the fourth verse, he sees the necessity of God's nature, that we "be holy and without blame before Him;" in the fifth verse the purposes of His love, "Children to Himself."

Any being to live before Him must be "without blame, holy, and in love." How can we ever have such blessing in which to stand "before Him"? He chose us "in Him before the foundation of the world," and therefore nothing can alter this, because it was before time, before man was created.

The prayer in the first chapter is to the *God* of our Lord Jesus Christ, that He may give us the spirit of wisdom and revelation that we may know what we have. In the third chapter there is quite a different prayer, to the *Father* of our Lord Jesus Christ, that we may know the love of Christ, which passeth knowledge.

In the present day there is much sentimental talk about the Fatherhood of God; I should like to hear a great deal more about the Godhood of God. "The world's universal Father!" There is no such thing in all Scripture. He may be talked of in the way of Father, as He is our Maker, and we are His offspring. A carpenter could be called the father of a chair. Read from the 15th verse of this 1st chapter of Ephesians, and you have there the most remarkable prayer in the whole Bible. Mark you, there is not a single word about love, or kindness, or peace, or mercy. The holy God must have holy creatures before Him. All who stand before Him must have this characteristic—angels, principalities, and powers. The necessity of His nature requires it. But how can we stand before Him blameless, and in love? I know that I am blameworthy, and I know I have that within my heart which is not love. But He chose us in Him before the foundation of the world. The question has been settled. The arrangement was before time and man, and cannot be altered by time. Some men talk about the gifts, the atonement, justification, as just little somethings which God has given. Some have a limited atonement, and some a universal. We come to Christ, and get the atonement in Him. You would think that there were only scattered bits of atonement flying about for a few people to appropriate. There is Christ. I come to Him—to the holiness, to the blamelessness, to the love God has seen in Him, and the Father has ordained in Him, before the foundation of the world; and there I get life. In Him I get all the righteousness of God, and the holiness of God. That is the meaning of standing before Him in holiness, and blamelessness, and in love. He must be God; He may be Father. In all circumstances the necessities of His nature must be met. It is quite a mistake to sing, "I wish I were an angel." We have a far better and higher blessing than an angel. You are made priests to God. God was never manifested in the nature of angels. He took not upon Him the form of principalities. He became Man. And this Man holds the scepter of the universe in His hands. Oh, brethren, let us rise up to the dignity of our sonship, and dare to be like Him, dare to live up to

Him. He has the fulness of blessing. He wanted some "to Himself"—not merely to stand before Him; He has angels who serve Him day and night. But He has given us Christ, who is the fulness of blessing. Let us get to the top of this Ben Nevis of blessing. Look above you, look up the empyrean. He has given you gifts and blessings. The blessings are there for us to appropriate as we need them. We have a full Christ; in Him we see our God, in Him we see our Father. Open your eyes to see what you have; it is all your own, given by the God of glory. But remember there is something before the gifts. Remember the Blesser. I fear there is a danger in being taken up with the blessings instead of the Blesser. Let us rejoice in the blessings that Christ has given us, and let us also rejoice in the grace that has given us the blessing.

THE PRACTICAL ASPECTS OF THE HOPE.

"Beloved, now are we the sons of God; and it doth not yet appear what we shall be: but we know that, when He shall appear, we shall be like Him; for we shall see Him as He is. And every man that hath this hope in Him purifieth himself, even as He is pure."— 1 JOHN III. 2, 3.

THE study of prophecy is not the hope of the Church. It is exceedingly interesting, full of interest at every point, every chapter, every verse, every word, but the study of prophecy is not the hope of the Church, and my subject is, "The practical aspects of this Hope." The hope of the Church is something more tangible, and more sweet. It is a living Person, and His return. It is the return of our blessed Lord, and not the details of prophetical truth, either enunciated in the Old or New Testament, or fulfilled in detail, but the return of a person, so that while some might think, "I have not the knowledge, I have not the Hebrew, I have not the Greek, and I lack many other qualifications to follow all these distinctions," my friends, all I want to ask of you is this, Have you a heart for the return of our blessed Lord? It is the heart for Him that is the great hope of the Church of the living God. And my text has been largely painted for me for this occasion. I do not ask you to look at your Bibles, because the painter has been very kind, and painted it in full blaze before you. My text you will find in the words, "SURELY I COME QUICKLY." This is from the heart of the Bridegroom. "Surely I come quickly,"—and a couple of millenniums is quickly in His mind. "I come quickly"—for the desire to return, oversteps all millenniums—"Behold, I come quickly." Then we have the response in the next place, the response of the Bride, which echoes back and says, "Amen, even so come, Lord Jesus." We are not to be behindhand in the response of love,

THE PRACTICAL ASPECTS OF THE HOPE. 149

because it is the same Spirit that energizes us in measure, that fills Him without measure; and so the challenge of love, "Surely I come quickly," is met with the response of love, "Amen, even so come, Lord Jesus." It limits all those hundreds of years, and seals, and vials, and everything else, because the nearest point to a benighted traveller on a dark night is a light-house. He sees nothing between. "Amen, even so come Lord Jesus." Then the practical application of the hope, "Let your loins be girded about, and your lamps burning." I am thankful my text is so patent that we have not to look down, but we have all to look up; and I trust we shall all be looking up, and in that attitude be knowing the aspects of the blessed truth. "Let your loins be girded about, and your lights burning." It concludes all—fitly chosen and well put. It includes all that we ought to be, and all that we ought to do. We ought to be as men, whose loins are girded, not in confusion and disorder, but tucked up for the fight, and ready for anything, ready as men of war, not as men going to sleep, but as men who are putting on the armour of good soldiers and not sleepers, with loins girt about with truth, and then what we ought to be doing, just letting our light shine, because in the midnight darkness we are waiting for God's Son from heaven. I remember the time—and you will pardon personal reminiscences—when I am sure, though I was a Christian, I did not realize the least about girding up the loins and tucking them about with the girdle of truth. All the garments were in the mud. When one tried to run, one tripped, because of the long flowing Eastern robe. You cannot run unless you are made snug and ready for a race, or a battle. I know myself that while I merely stood on the grand, glorious central truth of salvation from sin, it was as though the battle had not been completely won. In my own experience I tried to think that when you get one foot down on the cross, you are there secure, but that did not feel so strong, till I got the other on the crown, and there a man can stand, and having done all to stand, in the evil day, with cross and crown as the grand groundwork on which He stands.

"Let your loins be girded about, and let your light shine in this world." "Ye are the salt of the earth: ye are the light of the world." It is, "Let your light shine." It is not by any forced sort of artificial method by which we pump up oil, or make great spurts, or make large fireworks on great occasions. There are some firework Christians. They seem by some incidental accident to blaze up occasionally, and then they relapse into a quiescent state, waiting for some other blazing time, when they can make some further wonderful demonstration, and do something great. That is not the testimony of our blessed Lord. I believe that we all have need of patience—a patient continuance in well-doing; and if you look at the Lord's coming, you will find it often mixed up and connected with patience. "Be patient, for the day of the Lord is at hand." Sometimes district-visitors, in a little corner of God's vineyard, get paralyzed in their action, and they think, "If I could only preach to twenty or more old women, I should do very well; but I have not the gift of utterance;" and instead of going the round of their little beat, bearing a glorious testimony, and with their light shining to His dear people, they get disheartened. "Let patience have her perfect work." Ye have need for patience. It is by patient continuance in well-doing that we are to reap the glory of immortality. I was asked if it was not a great thing to be able to preach to a lot of people. I said, "Whether it is or not, the Lord tells us that true religion does not consist in that at all. He tells us that true religion consists in visiting the fatherless and widows, and we can all do that." It is not some great work, some spasmodic effort, some great throwing off of scintillas of light on occasional opportunities, but it is by that constant living in communion with an absent one, filled with His oil, and showing forth His light, that we fulfil the text, "Let your lights be burning." If you look through the Word of God, you will find that there is scarcely a subject—scarcely a practical subject connected with Christianity—but is linked with the coming of the Lord. Holiness—that deepest of all subjects to us: "Beloved, now are we the sons of God, and it doth not yet appear what we shall be; but we know that, when He shall appear, we shall be like Him; for we shall see Him as He is. And every man that hath this hope in Him purifieth himself, even as He is pure." Every one that hath the hope—this hope of being with Him, and being like Him, His own being with Him, and His own being like Him—"purifieth himself, even as He is pure." His own heart goes out towards us, and says, "What I say to you, I say unto all, Watch." It takes us into the line of watchfulness. I know well,

THE PRACTICAL ASPECTS OF THE HOPE. 151

when I am a few days away from home, the longer I am away, the more my little boys are watching for my return. I say to them, I will be back such and such a time, and there is not a cab that comes to our door but what they say, "This is father now" and why? Because they have got all the little things that I would like, put out for me. If they have been into my study scattering things, all the papers are put right and tidy, because they know I am coming quickly and soon. They are watching. They have perhaps got a little flowerpot, with a flower in it, stuck on my study table, and they want to make it nice, and beautiful, and happy against my return. They know that their father is coming. They are watching for him, and waiting.

Talking about prophetical questions, and knowing about these most interesting things which we sometimes would have a great delight to go into (I do not say always to agree upon), is very interesting; and I think we have a considerable amount to say in a difference. However, all is apart from the blessed hope of watching for a glorious Person Himself, to come at any moment, and nothing between Himself and me—waiting for Him to return to-night. A friend said to me the other day, "Was not Paul waiting for Him?" "Certainly; and that is why I am, because I find Paul was so anxiously waiting." "Then," he said, "is not Paul disappointed?" "Disappointed!" I said. "How can Paul be disappointed? Is it a disappointment to go up and be waiting in the beautiful drawing-room, rather than in the dark, dingy apartment, where we are waiting for Him now? I should think he is a little more comfortable where he is; but he is waiting for the same thing now as he was upon the earth. First of all, it is much nicer in the drawing-room than down in the dungeon. 'I have a desire to depart, and to be with Christ, which is far better.' But show me that by departing and being with Christ, he is not waiting for the same blessed hope as you and I are waiting for here, and 'the appearing of His glory.' It is not so much the glorious appearing; it is the appearing of the glory of our great God and Saviour Jesus Christ. Not only you and I are panting and saying, 'Lord Jesus, come;' and not only the apostle Paul and all the sainted ones, I believe, from Abel downwards, are saying, 'Lord Jesus, come;' but I believe that, better than you waiting, and better than Paul waiting, is this, that the Lord Jesus Christ Himself is waiting for the blessed day. The saints in the disembodied state, and the saints upon the earth, are waiting; but, brighter and brighter than all, the Saviour in the glory is waiting patiently till His enemies are put under His feet to stand upon, when He shall take to Himself His great power and reign.

Are we asked to sit down in fellowship, and show the Lord's death? What is it that our eyes are lifted up to? "To show the Lord's death till He come." It is the one visible link between the two advents of our Lord, that blessed supper that he originated. The one visible link is the breaking of the bread and the tasting of the wine, between the death of Christ on Calvary, and the crowning glory that is to fill the whole world. Are we in sorrow? Have we lost loving ones? "The Lord Himself shall descend from heaven with a shout, with the voice of the archangel, and with the trump of God: and the dead in Christ shall rise first. Then we which are alive and remain shall be caught up together with them in the clouds, to meet the Lord in the air: and so shall we ever be with the Lord. Wherefore comfort one another with these words." It is not "now they have died, they have gone from us, and they will not return to us." That is not our hope; but "we wish you quickly back for us for the Lord shall descend with you for us." You have to comfort one another with *these words*, that the dead in Christ shall rise first, and we who are alive and remain shall be caught up.

Then as for Israel, poor, broken, defeated, scattered, rebellious, unbelieving Israel, driven to the winds of heaven, has the Lord no eye for thee? Ah, yes; we know it, and we know that He is looking for them in all parts of the earth; and Israel will be gathered again, and will be united, and will stand together in the house of the Lord. And then will come the day when Ephraim shall no longer envy Judah, nor Judah vex Ephraim. They will stand tighter, and sing the grand fraternal Psalm, "Behold how good a thing it is for brethren to dwell together in unity?"

Whatever we look at around us, or within us, we have the solution to all our difficulties in that glorious fact that our Lord is to return, and that right is to take the place of wrong, and that the Prince of Peace is to take the throne usurped by him who is the prince of the power of the air.

THE PRACTICAL ASPECTS OF THE HOPE. 153

I must confess my words on a subject that eternity will unfold must be weak; but every kind of Christian, whatever he may be, is cheered up, and is comforted, and is stimulated, by this blessed hope. And as for its being practical, tell me one truth more practical. Certainly we have one truth more precious, we must say; for the cross can never cease to be the most precious truth, as on it depends our peace for time and eternity. The cross! oh, let us never forget it! The cross! the most mighty centre that ever the universe of God, or the eternity of God heard of or saw, where God has been glorified, and His law magnified, and His name honoured, and His righteousness vindicated, and His holiness seen, when He could by no means clear His own Son when sin was upon Him; and where the poor sinner can see the hatefulness of his sin, and the love of his Saviour-God. Oh, it is the cross!

> "The cross, the cross! The Christian's only glory;
>   I see the standard rise!
> Sing on, sing on, the cross of Christ before thee!
>   That cross all hell defies!"

But when we have rejoiced our spirits with the life that is in the look—

"There is life in a look at the crucified One"—

then what, as Christian, are we to get? Why, the very next truth, with nothing between, which is the crown of our blessed Lord. It is the sufferings of Christ, and the glory of Christ, that shall be revealed. There is no gulf between, in His mind; and if He in His own love and wondrous wisdom has made a pause between the two, that He might show the wonders of His grace, in gathering together one new man, out of Jew and Gentile, and to show the power of a resurrection life, and a resurrection bride, shall I not enter into His view, into His idea, into His glorious hope, of the return of my Master, and the appearance of His crown upon the earth?

If I am a sufferer, if I am a soldier, or if I am a student, this blessed Book is altogether, and at all times, and only, practical in its bearing from God to me. If I am a sufferer, the aching head shall soon be decked with the crown of gold; the weary feet shall soon walk in the streets of the golden city. Sufferer, lift up thy head! Weary one, thy Lord is coming! Thou mayest not have to face death at all. There is no certainty. A Christian that says, "I shall not die," is very foolish; a Christian that says, "I must die," is very ignorant; so between the two we take whatever the Lord sends first. We have no voice in the matter; we take what He sends. And so the suffering one sees the Lord coming for Him to reveal all the glory of His name.

Fighting one! soldier! servant! stand fast; "Hold fast that thou hast; let no man take thy crown." Our salvation is nearer than when we believed. Do not be wishing to do some great thing, like Naaman, but go ye and do your little things faithfully. You do not know what it is to be in the true "King's" college. This is the "King's" college, where we are all being trained for kings. When a captain of a vessel has some important thing to do, he does not send the youngest apprentice to do it. If it is to hold a rope, the letting go or holding fast of which may entail the safety or capsizing of the vessel, he sends the old grim veteran that can stand, and knows nothing but to obey. "Now," he says, "hold fast the rope;" and there the old weather-beaten tar will hold. Suppose some friend comes, and says, "Tom, what are you holding on to that rope for—it goes through a hole, and we can't see where it is going, or know what it is doing?" "Get out of my way; let me hold on here!" "But you should see what you are doing, and see the results." "Go away, and mind your business," would reply the weather-beaten tar, if, indeed he deigned to reply at all. Or perhaps he would be asked, "Why are you holding on there?" "Because captain told me; that is enough for me." And the captain knows well who will stand by him, and who he can put to the execution of a difficult enterprise. It is to the man who will obey without asking any questions. And so in the glory that is to come, I believe our Lord will know who He can depend upon, and who knows how to obey without asking any questions, and what is meant by "Well done, good and faithful servant!"

Are you a student of God's blessed word? Are you desirous to know His mind? Then look at the Lord's coming back again as the solution of all your difficulties. Do you say, the love of many is waxing cold? My friend, is not that the fulfilment of the Master's word? Do you find the whole of Christendom being leavened? Is not that the Master's word? Would it not have been very strange if it had not come true? Is it not the solution of all your difficulties? Instead of sitting at home and wondering how God could permit such things, rise up in the dignity of intelligence, in His own mind, and go forth to do His work; daring to do for Him, knowing He has the whole of the responsibility in His hand. This is the practical aspect.

I was told, but it was many years ago, that such a blessed hope would stultify missionary effort. I deny it; emphatically I deny it. It is the very opposite. I believe that this hope, that this one mainspring of thought, ought to lead us to evangelize the world. I believe that the great, grand, criminal mistake of our dispensation has been (and especially of our land at this moment), that we have been trying with a false idea to convert patches, instead of to evangelize the world. "Go ye into all the world" is the command, and what do we find? You keep thirty thousand men, as it were, on the point of your finger, and all the rest is dark. Thirty thousand ministers and preachers in Great Britain, and four hundred millions in China who never heard the gospel, because we have been trying to convert Great Britain, and not to evangelize China and Japan. It is because we have been disobedient that we have met with so little success. Suppose every minister of every church and denomination in this land were swept away to China and Japan to the glory of God, and that twenty-five or twenty-eight peripatetic evangelists were left at home to go through England and Scotland, and give an occasional day's preaching in London, Liverpool, Hull, and Edinburgh, then you would about equalize what heathenism is just now. It is disobedience, and I confess to my belief that part of the penalty for it is, that we have not been seeing what this dispensation exists for—to gather out a people for His name who shall be unto Himself, gathered out of every kingdom, and nation, and tongue. If the state of the church is thus made plainly seen, and the responsibilities of the saints made sure and fast by that blessed hope, what about the world that we are in? Just the same. Congresses may meet, and God grant that peace may follow; but thought statesmen may seem bewildered, and the greatest in the earth may stand appalled, the Christian, with that blessed hope, stands calm; whatever the notions about the seven seals may be, whatever his idea of progressive, or historical, or futurist notions may be, he stands calm. "He that believeth shall not make haste." We pray for peace, and, blessed by God, He has told us to do so. We pray that we may have peace in our times; but whatever comes amid the overturning of nations, and wreck of kingdoms, the Christian is calm—calm amid war, or famine, or pestilence, or sword, or destruction, or nakedness, knowing that in all these things we "are more than conquerors." As patiently waiting for God's Son from heaven, who, instead of the congresses that men can gather, and the scheming of worldly politicians, will return to put down all rule and all authority, and to break principalities and power, and let the peers of glory see what government is upon this world; when He shall come down to make all wrongs right, to chain the prince of darkness, and to reign before His ancients gloriously.

MISCELLANEOUS

"PEACE ON EARTH."

Luke ii. 14.

THE Crimean War, the Franco-Germanic War, the Turko-Russian War, are all fresh in the memories of this generation. Has there ever been universal peace in this world since the days of Christ? Professor Tyndall wishes to explain the anthem of the angels, when they sing of "Peace on earth," as being merely the dramatic representation of the devout wishes of men; because, he thinks, that if it were a real anthem struck by superhuman beings as the key-note of the result of the visit of the Prince of Peace, history has proved that it was a mistake. Scientific men are to be carefully listened to when they are in their own department; but they make sad havoc when they enter into another room of God's great universe. On bones, muscles, nerves, cerebellum and brain, the information they give is most exact, and, therefore, interesting; but when with scalpel, microscopes, and mere scientific method they enter the domain of revelation, theology, or exegesis, they are as miserably adrift as a blacksmith with his tools would be entering a watchmaker's workshop; the anatomy of the human body is perfect; the anthem of the angelic host is perfect; but anatomy does not explain anthem, as anthem does not disturb anatomy.

Nothing could be more perfect, comprehensive, and extensive than that beautiful *Gloria in Excelsis*.

1. "Glory to God in the highest." The whole universe must re-echo this note. Not a sun, nor planet, nor comet, nor system, but sounds back this strain. Mountain, rock, river, and ocean, peal forth its music. Forest and field, and everything that hath breath adds, Amen. And first above and beyond all things, for which Christ came, was to show glory to God in the highest, infinitely beyond

man's interests, or thoughts, hopes, or fears. But we descend from the generic song of all the universe to the specific note for earth.

2. "Peace on earth." We know the desolation of war, the absurdity of war, the unreasonableness of war, the inhumanity of war, the ungodliness of war. We have yet to learn the supreme, God-like blessings of peace on earth. Professor Tyndall finds difficulty here; we can see none. Professor Tyndall proposes to deliver a lecture. Let us suppose that on arriving at the place announced he was arrested and put into prison on a charge of treason. Does Professor Tyndall not see that his lecture must be postponed? The path of the Prince of Peace was correctly notified by the angelic anthem. But men by wicked hands took Him, imprisoned Him, and murdered Him, finding no fault in Him. A sense of the most common justice would tell us that "Peace on earth" must be postponed till the murder of the Just One be investigated and avenged, and He shall return in His glory to establish His kingdom in peace. So He taught us: "When ye shall hear of wars and commotions, be not terrified, for these things must first come to pass. And when these things begin to come to pass, *then look up, and lift up your head; for your redemption draweth nigh.*" "Our God shall come, and shall not keep silence." Men have to beat their "ploughshares into swords" (Joel iii. 10), before they beat their "swords into ploughshares" (Isa. ii. 4). Science can tell us much of human steps rising up to heaven; it can tell us nothing of that ladder let down from heaven to earth, on which angels ascend and descend. Nothing but "a sword" can be for the earth, till the Prince of Peace is accepted as Lord—

"When the crowns that are now
Round the false one's brow,
Shall be worn by earth's rightful Lord."

Not only have we the widest circle, "the highest," giving glory to God by the mission of Christ, and the more limited one, "earth," gaining peace, but we have the condition of the individuals on earth detailed.

3. "Good pleasure in men." For this we believe is by far the most correct and satisfactory explanation of the original. "Good will to men" is in every way unsatisfactory, weak, and untenable. The Douay, and several Protestant editions, take this as a part of

the second clause, making it, "Peace on earth among men of God's good pleasure" (reading the genitive, and not the nominative); the Douay explaining it, that there is peace on earth among the Roman Catholics (which there is not), and the Protestants, that there is peace on earth among God's elect (which there is not). We believe "God's good pleasure in men" solves all the difficulties. The universe, the earth, and men, are thus thought of in three parts of this "*Gloria.*" It is the same thought as, "This is my Beloved Son, in whom I am *well pleased.*" (See *eudokia*, in Matt. xi. 26; Luke x. 21; Rom x. i; Eph. i. 5-9; Phil. i. 15, ii. 13; 2 Thess. i. 2, besides the frequent use of the verb). God was now for the first time well pleased with a man; saw his good pleasure in a man; and the divinely-given guarantee that, not only in this man, but on the many men to be saved by, identified with, and sanctified through this man, His good pleasure should rest with complacency. His delight shall be in the sons of men; in individuals now, but in the whole earth as such by-and-by, when men shall be blessed in Him, and call Him blessed; when none shall say to his neighbor, "Know the Lord, because all shall know Him." And universal peace shall be on the earth, and this little planet shall choir forth without discord, among the other orbs of God, its true note of praise, blending with all others in "Glory to God in the highest."

"WHO DELIVERED US, AND DOTH DELIVER, AND WILL DELIVER."

2 COR. i. 9, 10.

GOD'S works may be near us, around us, but His person unknowable. At Sinai we hear a holy God speaking to His creatures, and there we find a God of inflexible justice. In this text we listen to God, not as a mystery, nor a destroyer, but a deliverer. Here we find Him, not as one whose work is to garnish the heavens, or deck the earth, but a God who has come Himself to deliver us. Man has tried to conquer death, but he is as far from it as ever. Money may go far and do much, but death is the end of all. Your fame may extend far, but death is the limit of fame. But the apostle speaks here of more than the mere separation of soul and body, when he says "so great a death," namely, that of the separation of man from God. God's way is not to shirk the question of death, but to interpose as a deliverer from it.

When the Israelites were bitten by the fiery serpents, God did not remove them, but He comes and says, "Here is my way." The serpent of brass must be put on a pole, and *whosoever*, however severely bitten looked on it, was healed. Some might have tried their own ways of deliverance, by attempting to kill the serpents near to them, by endeavouring to staunch their bleeding wounds, by using remedies of their own devising. But God's way is above and beyond all man's plans, and when man takes God at His word, then God is honoured. All the bitten Israelites had the sentence of death in themselves, but if any would look right away from self, and take God's method, it mattered not how many, nor how virulent, his bites might be, he was healed. When the question of man's deliverance from eternal death comes in, we want nothing between the sinner and the Saviour. Many want to come to God's ministers and get a certificate from them that they are saved; but the question is, Have you found yourself in God's word? God's Word comes as to a rational being, and the question is, "What does He say?" A minister can only say to the anxious one, "There is the truth of God; that is what God sys." He cannot interfere between God and the sinner; his work is done when he has brought the sinner face to face with what God says. The apostle Paul took the sentence of death in himself; then he accepted God's way of deliverance.

We find deliverance here in three aspects,—
1. Delivered.
2. Doth deliver.
3. Will deliver.

Deliverance in the past, leading up to the present, and going on continuously into the future. We get deliverance in the past, as justification, in the present, as sanctification and cleansing. There is great misconception oftentimes concerning the cleansing blood. It is not only true that it *has cleansed*, but it *is cleansing*; once applied it is of continual efficacy. The holiest saint needs the blood continually, at every moment.

Take the life-boat as a picture of this deliverance, for it is not help that the shipwrecked mariner needs, but deliverance. Therefore the life-boat carries no luggage, no boards, or anything wherewith to patch up the wreck; but the shipwrecked ones must leave all, and simply drop into the lifeboat. Some try to save people by making them religious. This will never do. Self must be left. A man is willing, it may be, to leave his sins, but not his good deeds; but all must be relinquished. In the lifeboat we are delivered form the great wreck, but not yet ashore. There is a present as well as a past deliverance needed, and the same who delivered us from so great a death, is delivering still between the wreck and the shore; and as we look at the lights in the harbor, we say, "In whom we trust that He will yet deliver us."

The important point is the first step. Faith consists in letting go, as well as laying hold. As the life-boat comes under the wreck, and the crew drop into it, so must we let go of all other hope, and cling only to Christ. Let us not trust in our faith, nor repentance, nor conversion; the devil may argue us out of these, as he argued Adam and Eve out of Paradise. Put yourself into the middle of a text, as, "All we like sheep have gone astray; we have turned every one to his own way." Is that true of you? Well, then, having walked in at one end of it, walk out the other: "And the Lord hath laid on Him the iniquity of us all." Resist the devil with a text. He can soon make out that you are not a believer; but get in at the sinner door. He will never prove you are not a sinner, and "Christ Jesus came into the world to save sinners."

Anchor to a text that is something worth gripping. Many look to their feelings, to something within, to see if they are saved. What would you think of a man who should drop the anchor into the hold of a ship, and say, "We must keep it on board; we must not lose sight of it." Let go; cast the anchor outside; then, fixed on rock outside, the anchor is fulfilling its function. Faith goes outward, not inward; Christward, not selfward; has to do with the Word of God, not feelings.

"HE CAME WHERE HE WAS."
LUKE x. 30-35.

BY chance a certain priest *came that way*." "And a Levite, when he was *at the place*, came and *looked*." "But a certain Samaritan, as he journeyed, CAME WHERE HE WAS." So the Lord Jesus Christ did not stand away up in heaven, and say, "Come to Me." He did not come halfway; He did not come and say, "I will give you help." No. There are some people who speak about stepping-stones to the gospel. What an absurdity, when Christ has done all the work! Where stands the cross? Between two malefactors. Did they need stepping-stones? Stepping-stones, indeed, to Him who says, "Him that cometh unto Me I will in no wise cast out." There is only one illustration of stepping-stones spoken of in the Bible, and that was the altar of burnt-offering. The Bible itself says, "There shall be no steps to my altar." God would not allow a step to be put up: the altar had to be set on the sand within the reach of the lowest sinner. You do not need a pair of religious steps to help Christ to do His work.

I. "HE CAME WHERE HE WAS."

That is the gospel of God. He became one of us that He might become one with us under our sin, that we might be saved, and become one with Him. The blessed Christ of God came to where we were. That is the most beautiful word to my soul in all the tenth chapter of Luke. He came not to the palace, or to the house, but to the side of the devil-forsaken ditch. Remember, the devil had left, the thieves had left; they had nothing more to get out of the poor Jew. And so with the poor drunkard; when the landlord has taken his last penny and left him, Christ was waiting to be his friend.

He "*came where he was*." Beautiful sentence! I have seen a poor drunkard going to the public-house where he had spent his last penny, asking bread, and met by the landlord, who had got his money, with, "Go away, or I will get a policeman to you." He has been stripped by the thieves. The Samaritan comes right down to the ditch where the Jew had been left, but does not say, "You are too bad company for me." Yes, to those that the devil had cast out, He came to where they were. "Thank God," say some, "that I am not like other men!" But there is no distinction with God. You are not a whit better than the worst drunkard in creation. God has weighed you all in the scales, and He says there is not a bit of difference between you. In God's sight there is no difference. We would like to think there are degrees of guilt and of forgiveness; but God says there is not a bit of difference. Certainly, there are what men call greater sinners and lesser sinners. Just like a man, for instance, wanting to get into the Life Guards. You may think yourself the biggest man in the village. The recruiting-sergeant does not care whether you are the biggest or smallest. He puts up his six foot measure. The man five feet six inches in height has no chance. And in a man five feet eleven and a half inches there is, of course, a difference as to size; but in his case it is just the same as regards his exclusion from the Life Guards. So God says there is no difference between any of those who have sinned, and come short of the glory of God. It is not that you are a big sinner, or a little sinner; but you have come short. You may be five feet six inches, or five feet eleven and a half inches, or even more; it does not matter. This is the way we are leveled down. Take the opinion that God has of you. He puts you on a level with every sinner.

2. "HAD COMPASSION ON HIM."

"He came where he was: and when he saw him, he had compassion on him, and went to him, and bound up his wounds, pouring in oil and wine." He did not leave him. It was not the theology of Christ to take him up to-day and leave him to-morrow. He takes care of him, sets him on his own beast, takes him to an inn, and provides for him there. It is Christ's salvation. Christ has sent His Spirit to lead us through the journey, to support, to strengthen and guide us all the way through. He brought us to an inn. He takes His people to this pastor, or teacher, and He says to them, "There is a soul I have got saved. Keep him, house him, feed him well, and there is enough for you to keep a-going just now; and if you spend any more, when I come back I will repay you." I do

not believe in these quarrelings and wranglings about churches, which are now so common, instead of looking to the poor wounded Jew lying beside them.

3. ALL DONE—ALL PAID.

What did the poor relieved Jew do now? He would ask, "What have I to pay?" "Oh! it is all for nothing. The Samaritan paid it all." We could suppose the man sitting looking out at the window, turned from his enmity to the Samaritans, waiting to thank his deliverer—as it says in Thessalonians, "turned to God from idols to serve the living and true God, and to wait for His Son from heaven." So the Jew was waiting for the Samaritan. Why is it we hear of little of the return of the good Samaritan? It would be awkward for many people if He did return just now. The next time Christ comes He will not be despised and rejected. "Behold, He cometh with clouds; and every eye shall see Him, and they also which pierced Him: and all kindreds of the earth shall wail because of Him." The unfaithful servant said, "My Lord delayeth Him coming," and began to smite his fellow-servants, and to eat and drink with the drunken. But "the Lord of that servant shall come in a day when he looketh not for him, and in an hour that he is not aware." The man that is not quite square with his books, does not like his master to come in unawares upon him, and look at them. But there are even genuine Christians, and behold they all slumber and sleep. Does not Satan manage it well? "But He that shall come will come, and will not tarry." "And when I come," He says, "I will repay thee for what thou didst unto Me."

THE WHOLE ARMOUR.
Ephesians vi. 11-18.

THE Master says it is our weakness He requires in order to show His strength. I bring you St. Paul's words: "Finally, my brethren, be strong in the Lord, put on the whole armour of God." Let me remind you that we have a great Trinity in our favour—Father, Son, and Holy Ghost; the Father loving us from all eternity, the Son sending us the Holy Spirit, the Holy Spirit keeping us, by throwing us back on Christ, who again throws us back on the Father. "Holy Father, keep through Thine own name those whom Thou hast given Me." But we have a trinity against us—the world, the flesh, the devil. Satan aims primarily, not at us, but through us, at the Prince of Peace. The power to meet the flesh is the Spirit, the power to meet the world is the Father, the power to overcome the devil is Christ. It is our intrinsic *red-hotness* that must make us intolerable to the world. There is still war in the world; there will be war to the end. The Christian's attitude is war—righteousness against sin. "Put on the whole armour of God;" mark, this is not to cover us in the sight of God. God has put on us Christians His righteousness; it is not the *robe*, but the *armour*, we are bidden to put on. Soldiers, not invalids, strong men, not babes, are wanted to fight the battles of the Lord.

"Loins girt about with truth," not truth in the Word, but subjective truth; a man must be true to himself; God must have a true witness; falseness of any kind entangles him. This Epistle, which gives us the highest thoughts about our standing, comes down to the plain truth, such as "speak truth." Then comes the "breastplate of righteousness," not the righteousness which fits me for Heaven, but righteousness between man and man. The apostle's injunction is, "Owe no man anything but love." Then you can face the devil. How can you face him if you have done injustice to your fellow-man? "Feet shod with the preparation of the Gospel of peace." I have nothing to bear to the world but the Gospel of peace. If peace is the Gospel from me, the world are to know only my footfall as I bring the Gospel of peace. Next, the "shield of faith." This is the faith that shields me, not the faith that saves me. "Helmet of salvation." If a man goes without the assurance of salvation, he goes into battle with his head uncovered, exposed to danger at every blow. As an old divine says, salvation is a helmet, not a nightcap; for battle, not for idleness. "Sword of the Spirit." No weapon formed on earth is like the word of God; we believe in its temper and its steel. In modern warfare, shield and breastplate are not used, but the sword has to take their place; so more and more we have to use the Word of God for every purpose of defence and attack. I was puzzled for a time at the inveteracy with which Deuteronomy has been attacked, till I remembered that it was the armoury from which our Lord drew His weapons with which to foil the tempter. No marvel Satan hates the remembrance of his defeat, and the texts that quelled him. We might also find in these texts a motto for each day of our life. The source of strength—"Man shall not live by bread alone, but by every word of God." The danger of losing it—"Thou shalt not tempt the Lord thy God." The power for maintaining it—"Thou shalt worship the Lord thy God, and Him only shalt thou serve." "Stand fast in the Lord." You may have the finest sword, and yet lack power to wield it. What will nerve your arm? "Praying always with all prayer and supplication in the Spirit." All prayer is all power, no prayer is no power. God give us to put on all this armour!

WITNESSING FOR GOD.
ACTS i. 8.

IN our peculiar work, as preachers, we must be REAL, if others are to be benefited by our ministry. And if we desire that others shall be sealed through our labours, we must be sealed ourselves. No man can expect a blessing, unless he goes into the work with the power of the Holy Ghost. The Holy Ghost is essential to the dispensation of the gospel. Believers sometimes make a mistake with regard to the Holy Spirit, especially in reference to His office in the salvation of sinners. There is a door which God has opened into the holy of holies, and there is no other way to get near God but by that door. Jesus is the door—the only door—by which we can enter; but it is in vain to expect that men will receive the Son, and enter by the door, until they have been inclined to receive Him, and have been drawn by the Holy Spirit.

It is vain to expect that men will be saved, or even led to seek salvation, by listening to elaborate and beautiful discourses upon the wondrous works of creation, or the beauties of God in His providence.

You can never lead a man to God, by simply telling him about God. It is a hard truth, but it is, however, a correct one. "No man cometh unto the Father, but by Me." Again, "No man can come to Me, except the Father which hath sent Me draw him." These two truths cover the whole circle. You cannot bring any man to God save by the Spirit, and you cannot have the Spirit without Jesus. Through the Spirit we can approach the Infinite, by Him who hath condescended to make Himself finite for us. We are to rejoice in the Holy Ghost, of whom I have been speaking, as the instrument of our salvation. If we would see fruit, we should teach Him, preach Him. He is ever present with His people. Let us seek that His pervading and energizing Spirit should be operating upon our hearts; and that He will take of the things of Christ, and reveal them plainly unto us.

You, my brethren, are the instruments raised by God to do His work in an important part of the vineyard. Oh, let us pray that we ourselves may know the truth, and be filled with the Spirit—the earnest of our inheritance.

APPENDIX I

What follows is the history of Mackay's salvation. This all unfolds when he, as an adult, was a physician and after a life of debauchery. This account is written up in many places. While the story line is the same, some of the details are somewhat different.

The Tract Magazine and Christian Miscellany, 1864, p. 71. The Hospital Patient.

Before I came to this place, I was assistant-surgeon in a hospital; and in a variety of forms I there saw a vast amount of human misery. But it was not *all* misery. There were patience, and resignation, and hope, as well as pain, weariness, and despair. I had known something of the power of religion—that is, I had seen it in others. In my home, far away, I had seen its power to sanctify sorrow, to invigorate the mind, and to bless. My mother was a Christian; and she had prayed for my eternal wellbeing, striven for it; hoped, perhaps against hope, that I should some day be brought under the influence of the gospel, be savingly converted to God, —become His child by surer and more lasting ties than I was her own. Against hope, I say; for I was wild and reckless, even in my boyhood.

I left home, unchanged; passed through the earlier stages of my professional career unchanged, only for the worse. I cared nothing for my mother's God: I forgot Him: that is, as far as I could I banished Him from my mind. In the subsequent stages of my professional history, I removed still further away from my home, and further, if possible, from God: far, far from him, by wicked works. Professionally, I "walked the hospitals," passed examinations, and was said to be a promising man. Morally, I was degraded. My companions were among the most dissipated of medical students; and from this cause principally, I became so seriously involved in pecuniary embarrassments that I occasionally had to sell or pawn all my available personal property to "carry on the game," as I said.

One day a poor fellow was brought in, badly injured by a fall. He was a bricklayer's labourer; the round of a ladder had broken under his weight while he was ascending with a hod of mortar, and he was, in consequence, precipitated from a considerable height to the ground, with fearful violence. There was no hope for him. All that could be done was to alleviate pain, and in this we were tolerable successful. The man knew that he should die, for his mind was clear; and he asked me, on one occasion, how much longer he had to live. There was no reason for reserve, and I told him what I thought.

"So long!" said he, when I told him; "I thought it would have been sooner; but He knows best."

"Yes, perhaps I do, my friend," I said, soothingly. "I believe you will last as long as that."

"Yes, sir; but I meant something else," said the poor fellow, faintly smiling.

"Have you any friends for whom you would like to send?" I asked.

The man shook his head: he was alone in the world, he said; but his lodgings were not so far off, and if I would not mind, he would like the people he had lodged with to be told of his accident; and perhaps the woman would come to see him, as owed her a trifle of money, which he wished to pay her. There was enough in his pocket, he said, to do this, or was when he had his fall.

His request was complied with: the woman was sent for, and came to see her poor dying lodger two or three times, as I understood, though I never saw her, and knew nothing of the nature of any communications that passed.

My predictions were verified. The man lingered about a week, and then died. Of course I saw him daily, and oftener, all the while he lasted, but very few words escaped his lips. I noted only a peculiar expression of calmness, and quiet happiness, almost, on his countenance, as which I rather wondered; for his pain at times must have been excruciating. Well, the man died, and of course certain formalities were immediately necessary, at which I was present.

"What shall we do with this, doctor? The nurse asked, holding up a book.

"What is it?"

"The poor fellow's Bible, sir; the woman brought it to him the second time she came to see him, because he had asked her to do it. And up to the last, he was reading it as often as he could get a little ease; and when he could not read, he kept it under his bolster."

Could I believe my own eyes? It was the Bible which had once been my own. The Bible which my mother had put into my hands when I was a youth, first leaving home, and which afterwards I had sold—yes, sold to supply some trifling need in the day of my profligacy, when, as I have said, almost all my personal property went in the same way for the same purpose. Yes, there was my own Bible, or what had once been mine; my name written there by my mother's own hand, still unerased, with the passage of Scriptures she had written underneath, yet legible. I had sufficient control over my self not to betray the emotions of my mind; and I even found words to say to the nurse in a tone of assumed indifference. "It is of no consequence; I'll take care of the book."

I took the Bible home with me. As to money value it was worth nothing, for it was dirty, torn in places, with many leaves loose. It had evidently been long and well used. Long comparatively, I mean, for not very many years had passed since it left my own hands. Possibly it had had no other possessor besides myself and the poor hospital patient; but this of course, I never knew. But I knew one thing, that a better use of it had been made after it passed away from me than ever before. Almost every page, as I turned it over, bore testimony to the care and diligence with which it had been perused, in pencil and pen marginal marks, or interlineations. And I could repeat, now, passage after passage thus indicated, which had doubtless been the solace of the Bible's poor possessor in times of doubt or trial or difficulty, and had smoothed his passage to the grave, and lighted it with heavenly glory. No wonder that he was so calm and happy! Its POOR possessor, I said. Well he was poor in this world, and friendless, and unknown: yet, as I firmly believe, "rich in faith, and an heir of the kingdom that God hath promised to them that love Him."

Shall I write more? Shall I say that that strange event was the turning-point in my history? That the accusations of an awakened conscience drove me almost to despair, until I was enabled to embrace the faithful saying, worthy of all acceptation, that Christ Jesus came into the world to save sinners, even the chief; and that my new recovered Bible is dearer to me than all the books in my library, because the gospel it contains has been made to me, through faith in Christ, the poser of God unto salvation?

APPENDIX 2

REVIVE US AGAIN

Words by William P. MacKay
Music by J. J. Husband

APPENDIX 3
MORE HYMNS BY W. P. MACKAY

- ACCEPTED IN CHRIST, WHO HAS STOOD IN OUR PLACE

- BE STRONG IN JEHOVAH, THOUGH HARD BE THE FIGHT

- LOOK UNTO ME, AND BE YE SAVED! LOOK MEN OF NATIONS ALL

- NO WORKS OF LAW HAVE WE TO BOAST

- NOTHING LORD I BRING BEFORE

- PRAISE THE LORD WITH HEARTS AND VOICES, GATHERED IN HIS HOLY NAME

- REJOICE AND BE GLAD, THE REDEEMER HAS COME

- THE GREAT PHYSICIAN NOW IS HERE

- THE LORD IS RISEN, AND DEATH'S DARK JUDGMENT

- THE LORD IS RISEN, THE RED SEA'S JUDGMENT FLOOD

- WE PRAISE THEE, OH GOD! FOR THE DAYS OF OUR YOUTH

- WE PRAISE THEE, OH GOD! FOR THE SON OF THY LOVE

- WE PRAISE THEE, OH GOD! FOR JESUS WHO DIED

- WHEN WE REACH OUR FATHER'S DWELLING

- WHEN WE REACH OUR PEACEFUL DWELLING

- WORTHY, WORTHY IS THE LAMB, WORTHY, WORTHY IS THE LAMB

www.ingramcontent.com/pod-product-compliance
Lightning Source LLC
Chambersburg PA
CBHW031417150426
43191CB00006B/309